Pro WordPress Theme Development

Adam Onishi

Apress®

Pro WordPress Theme Development

ISBN-13 (pbk): 978-1-4302-5914-5

ISBN-13 (electronic): 978-1-4302-5915-2

President and Publisher: Paul Manning
Lead Editor: Louise Corrigan
Technical Reviewer: Chris Mitchell
Editorial Board: Steve Anglin, Mark Beckner, Ewan Buckingham, Gary Cornell, Louise Corrigan, Jonathan Gennick, Jonathan Hassell, Robert Hutchinson, Michelle Lowman, James Markham, Matthew Moodie, Jeff Olson, Jeffrey Pepper, Douglas Pundick, Ben Renow-Clarke, Dominic Shakeshaft, Gwenan Spearing, Matt Wade, Steve Weiss, Tom Welsh, James T. DeWolf
Coordinating Editor: Christine Ricketts
Copy Editor: Nancy Sixsmith
Compositor: SPi Global
Indexer: SPi Global
Artist: SPi Global
Cover Designer: Anna Ishchenko

Distributed to the book trade worldwide by Springer Science+Business Media New York, 233 Spring Street, 6th Floor, New York, NY 10013. Phone 1-800-SPRINGER, fax (201) 348-4505, e-mail orders-ny@springer-sbm.com, or visit www.springeronline.com. Apress Media, LLC is a California LLC and the sole member (owner) is Springer Science + Business Media Finance Inc (SSBM Finance Inc). SSBM Finance Inc is a Delaware corporation.

For information on translations, please e-mail rights@apress.com, or visit www.apress.com.

Apress and friends of ED books may be purchased in bulk for academic, corporate, or promotional use. eBook versions and licenses are also available for most titles. For more information, reference our Special Bulk Sales–eBook Licensing web page at www.apress.com/bulk-sales.

Any source code or other supplementary materials referenced by the author in this text is available to readers at www.apress.com. For detailed information about how to locate your book's source code, go to www.apress.com/source-code/.

For my family, I hope this comes in handy.

Contents at a Glance

Contents

About the Author

Adam Onishi is a web developer working at the Architect digital agency in London, England. Starting as a developer at a small design agency in Oxford, Adam began developing custom WordPress themes for a variety of clients. He has produced hundreds of themes to varying degrees of client requirement, and over the years has learned how to get the best from the open source content management system that powers millions of web sites across the world.

Adam's previous experience has included working with clients from all areas, including brand names such as Tyrrells Crisps, Yeo Valley, Sting, and Unilever. Adam also plays an active role in the web community, running events and helping out with education initiatives such as 12 Devs and Code Club, and helping to promote education in technology and on the Web.

About the Technical Reviewer

Christopher Mitchell has spent the last 13 years working around the world in print design and web design and development. He loves all things to do with WordPress, developing custom themes and bespoke web sites for his clients. Christopher now lives and works from his office in Ledbury in Herefordshire, where he lives with his wife.

Acknowledgments

This book has been made possible by a number of amazing people. The team at Apress has been fantastic from start to finish. My editor, Louise Corrigan, has had endless patience and faith in me from the very start, supporting everything from the initial proposal all the way through to the end. I cannot thank you enough. Thanks to the technical reviewer, Christopher Mitchell, whose support and reviews have kept the book up to scratch and kept me going throughout. And thanks to my coordinating editor, Christine Ricketts, who has the utmost patience and has given me plenty of encouragement.

Huge thanks are also owed to my family and friends who have at times not seen me for months on end, but have always been understanding and supportive throughout. Thank you Mum, Dad, Nan, Grandad, Grandma, and Steve; as well as Ricky, Louise, Graham, Ness, Dave, Andy, Zanny, Sarah, Chris, and Vikkie. And sorry to Ben: I've missed seeing you grow up over your very first year among us; I hope I can change that from now on.

I owe my colleagues a huge amount of thanks for how patient they've been with me, especially over the last couple of months of writing. It's not easy starting a new job, and doing so while also writing a book has been a struggle. You have all been fantastic and made it a pleasure joining your team. So thank you Tom, Hannah, Jon, Thomas, Stef, Kerry, Claire, Ant, Sam, and everyone else on the team for your constant encouragement and for putting up with me!

This book would not have been possible without the fantastic WordPress community, from all the work that is done creating and maintaining WordPress through to the detailed documentation that helps us all understand what's going on. The community around WordPress is probably the best thing about the platform, with so many people willing to share their knowledge and help others; it's a great group to be a part of.

Finally, thanks to all my friends in the web community. Your support has been excellent. I really hope that for those of you who will be reading this book that it's been worth the amount I go on about it.

Introduction

Welcome to *Pro WordPress Theme Development* and thank you for shelling out your hard-earned pennies to buy this book. From here on, you'll delve deep into the world of WordPress, looking at everything there is to know about WordPress theme development.

I'll cover every topic you can think of (and probably even a few you haven't), covering all aspects of WordPress theming. You'll learn the basic functionality of the core template files, how custom post types and taxonomies work, how to allow users to customize your theme, and even how to build your own plugins. This book really is your comprehensive guide to WordPress theme development.

I'll be covering everything in great depth so you can not only create this or that cool bit of functionality but also understand how the core concepts work inside of WordPress. With that level of knowledge, you should be well equipped to really be able to manipulate WordPress to create seriously advanced functionality and to know when something might be better served being built with a different system.

With WordPress, you're joining a huge community, which I'll be discussing throughout the book. Because WordPress is open source, the community is responsible for almost everything that goes along with it: from the development of the core code through the documentation in the WordPress Codex (http://codex.wordpress.org/), and including the plethora of available themes and plugins. If you really want to be involved in shaping the future of WordPress, joining this community allows you to do so. Whether you want to be part of the continued development of the core, to help out by reporting bugs, or by creating plugins for others to use with their system, it's all part of shaping the way we use WordPress today.

Besides the huge community, there is also a huge user base for WordPress that is always on the lookout for new themes and plugins. I'll show you how you can capitalize on that as well. Developing a business as a theme developer still has potential today; many people have made it a successful career.

Who This Book Is For

The *Pro* in the title refers more to the depth with which you will be learning WordPress, not the skill level required for the contents to be accessible. If you are a capable web developer and have used at least a couple of content management systems in the past, you should be able to keep up with the subjects discussed.

You should have at least a working knowledge of PHP. The code examples within will be explained in full, enabling you to get up to speed easily enough. If you don't know any PHP, I recommend that you begin by taking a few lessons on the server-side language before you delve deep into WordPress.

Working with WordPress means that you will be writing a lot of PHP. Unlike some content management systems that create their own tags for you to use, WordPress sticks with standard PHP functions, so understanding the core concepts is necessary. To get you started, there are plenty of resources online, as well as a couple of books I thoroughly recommend:

- *PHP Academy* (https://phpacademy.org/)

- *Codecademy PHP* (http://www.codecademy.com/tracks/php)

- *Treehouse PHP* (http://teamtreehouse.com/library/topic:php)

- *Beginning PHP and MySQL* (http://www.apress.com/web-development/php/9781430231141)

- *Essential PHP Fast* (http://www.springer.com/computer/database+management+%26+information+retrieval/book/978-1-85233-578-6)

WordPress Versions

This book has been predominately written using WordPress version 3.6 (and version 3.7 in some parts). Although most of the code contained within should be compatible with most future versions of WordPress, be careful when using the examples. If you are working with a more-advanced version of WordPress, make sure to check the Codex regularly for updates.

WordPress is constantly being updated with new features and bug fixes; it's important that you stay up to date, as you'll learn later on in the book. Updates will now be even more regular. Over the course of writing the book, WordPress has gone from version 3.5 to 3.7, with a major update in version 3.8 due by the end of 2013.

What You Will Need

Before you begin, you need a few things to work with and have set up on your computer:

- Your favorite text editor (Sublime Text 2 is my choice)

- A local server set up to run PHP and MySQL on your own machine (WAMP, MAMP, XAMPP, or other MySQL, and PHP solution)

- A working WordPress install

Installing WordPress

Once you have your server set up with one of the "AMPs" (or the built-in Apache server on a Mac), you have to install WordPress. Fortunately, this is pretty easy thanks to the "Famous 5-Minute Install" (`http://codex.wordpress.org/ Installing_WordPress#Famous_5-Minute_Install`).

Although you could follow this link, because you've gone to all the trouble of buying this book in the first place, I'll tell you how I install WordPress quickly whenever I work with the system.

Go to `http://wordpress.org/download/` to get the latest version of WordPress; you can also find the direct download of the latest version at (`http://wordpress.org/latest.zip`). Set up a folder for your site in your local development environment and extract the contents of the ZIP file inside.

Set up a database for WordPress to use on your local environment. You can do this through PHPMyAdmin if you have it set up or through a database program if you have one. Make sure that the database user has all the privileges to read and write to the database.

With your database set up, visit the address for your development folder. You'll receive a message letting you know that there is currently no configuration created and that you need to create one to set up WordPress. Select Create a Configuration File and follow the steps to install WordPress with the database details and the information for your new site.

You should be all set up and ready to start learning how to become a pro WordPress Theme developer.

CHAPTER 1

■ ■ ■

Getting Started

WordPress was born out of a desire for an elegant, well-architectured personal publishing system.

http://wp-themes-book.com/01001

An Introduction to WordPress

WordPress was created in 2003 by Matt Mullenweg and Mark Little as a fork of the previous system: b2/cafelog. Since then, the open source system has evolved from a simple blogging platform into what is today: the most popular content management system (CMS) on the Web. More than 60% of web sites using CMSs on the Web use WordPress, and a whopping 15% of all web sites on the Web have WordPress at their core.

The release of version 3.0 (Thelonious) in 2010 saw the introduction of custom post types, easier taxonomy management, and custom menus, which increased the use of WordPress as an out-and-out CMS. The 2012 WordPress survey results backed this up, showing that the most dominant use case for WordPress sites is now as a CMS.

WordPress may not be a typical system build on a Model-View-Controller (MVC) framework, and many people lament the "WordPressy" way of doing things, but it's a process that over the years has worked well for its users and developers. I'm not about to question it.

Community

WordPress is also a very community-driven project. Because it is open source, anyone can contribute, so the development of the system is global with hundreds of contributors. Anything created around WordPress—from the core to themes, plug-ins, and the documentation—all come from the community for the community.

If you want to get involved with WordPress development long term, a good way is to get involved with the community, whether that is through the mailing lists or on Internet Relay Chat (IRC). After a while, you might even answer questions on the support forums instead of asking them.

The Codex

Unlike other platforms, even the documentation for WordPress is created by the community, which is one of its greatest assets. The WordPress Codex (available at http://wp-themes-book.com/01002 and shown in Figure 1-1) is where you can find valuable information on everything and anything related to WordPress. From full-blown "lessons" to a reference for almost every function available for use in templates, it's a great resource that should be known by all WordPress users.

The main page (shown in Figure 1-1) contains links to the main areas of the Codex, the main content links to the basics of coming to grips with WordPress—for example, how to download the CMS, use key aspects, and access the WordPress lessons directory. Because this is Pro WordPress theme development, you will probably find most use from areas linked to in the sidebar on the far right, such as the Developer Docs (http://wp-themes-book.com/01003) and Advanced Topics (http://wp-themes-book.com/01004) sections.

1

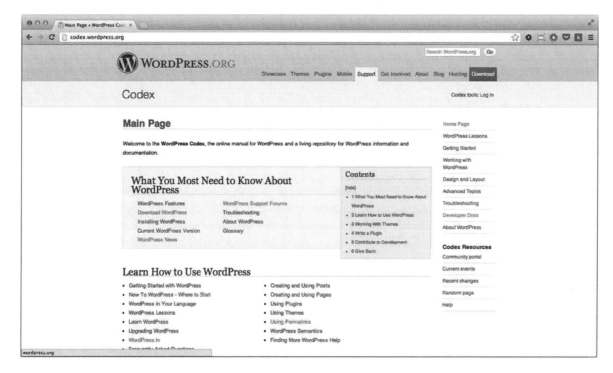

Figure 1-1. *Get used to using the codex as much as possible*

I regularly explore one of the main areas of the Developer Docs in the Codex: the Functions reference (http://wp-themes-book.com/01005). It holds a list of almost every function available in WordPress and how to use it, so by the time you finish this book you'll likely be pretty *au fait* with it as well.

WordPress Themes

Themes are what bring your content to life through the power of the WordPress core and database. Using a combination of PHP template files and Cascading Style Sheets (CSS), as well as optional JavaScript files and images, themes manage all the structure and style of your web site. Here's how WordPress describes the theme system:

> *"Fundamentally, the WordPress Theme system is a way to "skin" your weblog. Yet, it is more than just a "skin." Skinning your site implies that only the design is changed. WordPress Themes can provide much more control over the look and presentation of the material on your website."*

http://wp-themes-book.com/01010

Themes in WordPress weren't always there from the start; they appeared in version 1.5 (Strayhorn). Before then, the job of structuring blogs was down to a simple templating system using PHP, usually created as just one template file with any others being handled by PHP include() tags.

The introduction of themes was the beginning of a whole new world for WordPress users. They could now "switch between themes with a single click" or build their own custom themes using a variety of template files at their disposal (more on this later).

Default Themes

This introduction of theming WordPress also came with one of most iconic themes WordPress has seen throughout its years: Kubrick. Named after the designer Michael Heilemann's favorite movie director, Stanley Kubrick, the theme showed off several of the new powerful features of WordPress 1.5, including the capability to break your site up into separate sections with template files. It also showed off the new template functions. You can see Kubrick in action in Figure 1-2.

Figure 1-2. *The iconic Kubrick theme by Michael Heilemann*

This default theme for WordPress lasted half a decade and was replaced only when version 3.0 (Thelonius) was released. Even today, the theme is still used by more than 4 million WordPress users and is the 37th most popular theme in the WordPress.com themes database.

The Twenty-somethings

Since the release of version 3.0, WordPress has released a new default theme each year named Twenty-something, with the aim of showcasing the latest new features of the CMS. The first of the Twenty-somethings, Twenty Ten, is still the most downloaded theme in the WordPress themes repository, with more than half a million downloads. It is much improved from Kubrick (see Figure 1-3).

Figure 1-3. *Twenty Ten: Still the most popular theme with 500,000+ downloads*

Why this popularity? Probably because it was the first of the Twenty-something themes, which for the first time in years gave users a brand new style of WordPress. Twenty Ten introduced all the major new functionality introduced in WordPress 3.0 and brought a simple clean design with great typography that was also user-customizable, allowing people to mold their own versions of this incredibly popular theme and design.

WordPress version 3.2 (Reinhardt) heralded the release of the Twenty Eleven theme, which was the first theme to allow users to choose custom page layouts and offered theme options in the form of choosing colors and custom backgrounds.

The next default theme was of course Twenty Twelve, released along with WordPress version 3.5 (Elvin). It showed off plenty of the new goodies at the time, including the Theme customizer and a new, clean, mobile first responsive design. Twenty Twelve is also the theme that brought with it a custom home page template and widgets, which at the time, seemed to be a nod to the shift of WordPress to a CMS as opposed to a conventional blogging platform.

Twenty Thirteen

Twenty Thirteen is the latest of the Twenty-somethings (see Figure 1-5) a dramatic contrast to past years' themes. The focus has shifted massively back to blogging with extreme use of the new post formats introduced in version 3.1 and with the latest version, 3.6, there has been even more focus on the post formats interface and coding (Figure 1-4).

Figure 1-4. The new Post Formats selector in version 3.6

Figure 1-5. A preview of Twenty Thirteen

The theme, released earlier this year with version 3.6, is extremely bright and colorful with strong serif headings (Bitter) and a neat flowing sans-serif body copy (Source Sans). There's now unique styling for each post format, putting an emphasis on the new functionality like that of the updated post formats and new media player.

As much as I can't see the new version of WordPress making another dramatic shift away from acting as an out-and-out CMS, I can see it as a move from the people at Automattic to turn the default theme's focus back to its primary job as a blogging theme for use more with `WordPress.com` than with the self-hosted solutions you see today.

There is a lot to be learned from the way themes are built in terms of new functionality from the updated CMS. But you can also see how WordPress has evolved into what it is today and ultimately what you're getting yourself into as a WordPress theme developer. Throughout this book, I hope to give you the skills to not only understand how a theme works but also to build your theme from scratch and be a true "Theme Wrangler" (Automattic's words, not mine!).

WordPress in the near future

At the time of writing WordPress is on version 3.6.1 a recent update that I'll talk about more throughout the book, but by the time of release the next major update 3.7 will probably have already launched. Scheduled for mid-October version 3.7 is a major update but focuses more on the infrastructure of the system. From reading the Make WordPress Core blog it seems like automatic updates (for minor versions only) will be a big feature coming to version 3.7, along with updates to search and a lot more system and development updates, like inline documentation and a new structure for the Subversion repository.

The next and possibly more interesting major update is also being worked on in parallel with the version 3.7 update. Version 3.8 looks at the moment as if it will include a major update to the WordPress admin interface, it's something that `WordPress.com` users have had for a while now but will be coming to WordPress core in a few months (or less). The new admin shown in Figure 1-6 is a shift to a much cleaner design removing a lot of gradients and multiple colors.

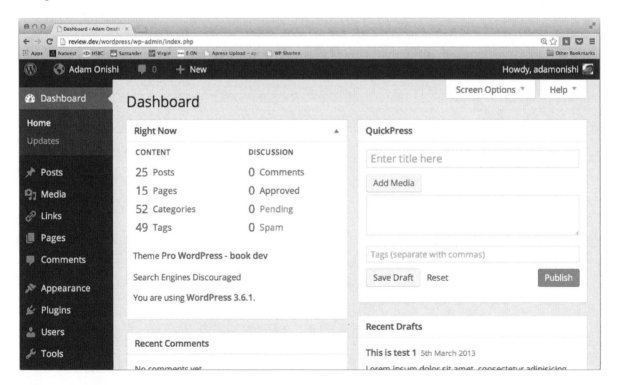

Figure 1-6. The new WordPress admin design

At the moment it's possible to see the new admin design thanks to a plugin (MP6 - `http://wp-themes-book.com/01006`), which is forming part of the active development of the new feature. This is part of a system the WordPress core team is calling "Features as Plugins."

Features as Plugins

The new system for feature development at WordPress is taking the route of writing new features as plugins instead of into a development branch of the core. This has a whole host of benefits to the core development process, as Sam Sidler mentions in the WordPress core blog:

> *The features-as-plugins model makes it easy to wait for a feature to be ready before including it in a release. It also allows for a lot of experimentation.*
>
> Sam Sidler (`http://wp-themes-book.com/01007`)

Another major benefit is that if these new features developed as plugins don't eventually make it into the WordPress core, they can still live on and benefit the community and not feel like the developers time has been wasted. New features have always come with the suggestion to be developed this way before eventually the core team, along with the feature team add it to core, however this is now become a formalized process.

Looking at the core blog currently there's a whole host of new features being developed as plugins:

- MP6 – the new WordPress admin interface
- Omnisearch – the new search system for the WordPress admin
- DASH – a new dashboard design
- THX38 – looking at improving the themes part of the admin
- Featured Content – a way to allow users to highlight content

The next default theme Twenty Fourteen

Another update due to be released with potentially version 3.8 is of course a new default theme. The preview of next year's planned Twenty Fourteen theme has also appeared on the make WordPress core blog (Figure 1-7). Similar to Twenty Thirteen this is another radical move away from past default themes, including a lot of differences from it's soon to be predecessor.

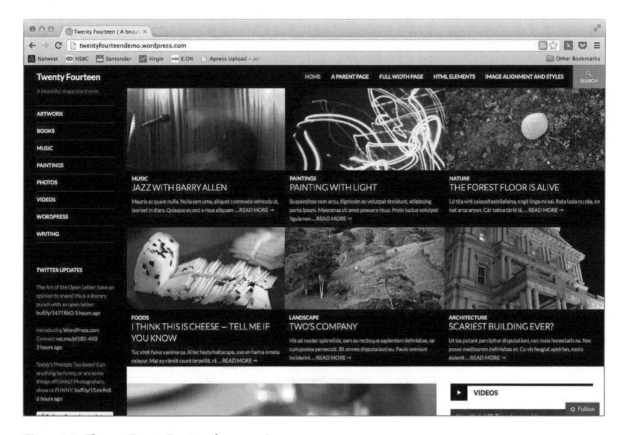

Figure 1-7. *The new Twenty Fourteen theme preview*

I think this goes to show how Automattic are looking at using the default themes nowadays, as more experimental and innovative themes, looking to show off the latest features in the WordPress core releases. With Twenty Thirteen came a focus on blogging and post formats, something that was worked on for release of WordPress at that time. Twenty Fourteen is set for release with version 3.8, scheduled for early December 2013, the main focus of this release seems to be the admin UI at the moment. The Twenty Fourteen theme design is likely to therefore cover aspects of WordPress as a whole and show off more general aspects than specifics tailored to the release.

Themes from Scratch versus Premade

Frameworks, templates, boilerplates and resets make for a very speedy production of prototypes and can help create complex and cross-compatible layouts requiring minimal prior knowledge.

—Laura Kalbag

The last few years have seen a massive surge in development frameworks, and the popularity of the Twitter Bootstrap and the 960 Grid System, to name but two, have seen a rise in the battle of writing from scratch versus building on top of a ready-made solution. The quote from Laura Kalbag covers some of the great aspects of these solutions.

In the article from which the quote is drawn (http://wp-themes-book.com/01008), Laura makes a good argument against frameworks being such great solutions. From a lack of good markup and semantics, to being a quick fix that ultimately could lead to an absolute headache in maintenance further down the line, frameworks should be left to prototyping and not to production code because it sullies a craft that many work so hard for.

You know which side I'm on. The argument mentioned previously applies directly to theme development: if you don't take the time to build your themes from scratch (or from a base you develop yourself—more on that later), you might be dealing with poor code that can lead to more hassle than it's worth.

There are certainly some positives of taking a premade theme and hacking it yourself until you have what you are aiming for. It's a quick process, you might think; most of the work is already done for you. It's great if you're not very familiar with PHP, HTML, JavaScript, or CSS.

Taking something that another developer has written and trying to modify the way it works isn't always as easy as it seems, however. Most developers have their own nuances, so decoding the theme might take a lot longer than you think.

There might also be licensing to consider. If you're planning to buy a premium theme and modify it, you might find that it's actually prohibited by the terms of the sale. Although WordPress is an open source platform, private designers/developers may want to protect their work and not release it under an editable license. For me, these are more than enough reasons for building your themes from scratch. Good thing you're reading a Pro themes development book!

PHP in WordPress

Now it's time to take a look at some code. But before you dig into WordPress theming fully, I want you to take a quick look at PHP and how it's utilized within WordPress. Please take a few minutes to read on for the rest of the chapter because I'll cover some of the nuances of WordPress and how it uses PHP, which may come in handy later in the book.

I think this is the main reason why I have those strange tingly feelings about WordPress; it's the way it treats PHP that makes me enjoy using it so much. When it comes to building your templates and creating your themes, there's one thing you see in WordPress that you don't often see in many other CMSs: it is straightforward PHP. A lot of other systems create their own template tags using special syntax and different ways of passing in information, but WordPress uses this well-known language. I think that's why WordPress is one of the easier systems to come to grips with; although there are still functions to get to know and logic to understand, most of it boils down to getting your hands dirty with straightforward PHP.

■ **Note** Throughout the book, I assume that you have at least a working knowledge of PHP in general; for a list of handy resources to get you up to speed, refer to the introduction before this chapter.

Functions

Most things you deal with in WordPress are functions, whether template tags such as the_title() or the_content(), or theme-related functions such as get_header() or wp_head(). Functions in WordPress can work in several ways: they can return data to a variable or output something directly to the template. In the following example, two functions act on similar content: the get_the_title() function returns the title string, and the the_title function echoes it straight out to the HTML:

```
// get_the_title() returns the title to a variable for use in the PHP code
$title = get_the_title();
// Do stuff with $title variable
echo "<h2>$title</h2>";
```

```
// whereas the_title() prints the title out straight from the function ?>
<h1><?php the_title(); ?></h2>
```

Some functions can also take parameters, so you can choose how the data is returned. In WordPress, there are a variety of ways in which functions can receive parameters. The usual way is the following:

```
do_something_cool('dance', true);
```

You can also pass in an array as the only parameter (this is one of the WordPress favorites):

```
$params = Array (
                'arg1' => 'dance',
                'arg2' => true
        )
do_something_cool($params);
```

Finally, there is the query-string style of parameter passing:

```
do_something_cool('arg1=dance&arg2=true')
```

If you want to keep the code a little tidier, you can separate out the parameters inside the string by adding spaces around the ampersands, like so:

```
do_something_cool('arg1=dance & arg2=true');
```

This final method is nothing new to PHP; it is used in WordPress quite often, but not in all functions. It is mostly found in the functions beginning with wp_ or in the WordPress query functions (discussed a bit later). The reason for using these types of parameter passing is for functions with a lot of defined parameters. One example is wp_list_categories(), which has a total of 24 parameters. Instead of writing out a long list of comma-separated options in the function call, you can use an array-style or query-string-style function call and set only the ones you want to change. WordPress uses the defaults for all the other parameters.

Objects and Classes

You'll mostly find objects and classes behind the scenes in WordPress, but every now and then they appear in the theming system and can come in very handy. The main example is when you're creating a custom query in one of your templates. (I won't go into detail about it too much here because it will be covered in Chapter 3.)

Objects can be thought of as representations of things that have properties and methods. In WordPress, an object is an individual post, for example. The post's properties include its title or content; and its methods are functions such as save, edit, and so on. A class can be thought of as the blueprint or plan for that object, so in WordPress WP_Query is a class that can be used to create instances of query objects.

When you're theming WordPress, you don't have to worry too much about creating classes until you're building plug-ins (you'll learn more in Chapter 8). For now, take a look at how to create and work with objects in PHP. I'll use the WP_Query object as an example.

To create a new object, you use the new keyword and the name of the class:

```
$new_query = new WP_Query();
```

Now the variable $new_query becomes the object. To access the methods or properties of the object, you need to use the object operator -> followed by the name of the property/method:

```php
$new_query->the_post();
```

You'll learn more about the WP_Query object in Chapter 3 when you look at ways to get content for templates. The important thing to note here is how you access the methods of an object, because you'll be using them a lot, later in the book.

Alternate Syntax for Control Structures

Control structures are blocks of code that affect the flow of the code. They usually come in the form of conditional statements (if, switch, and so on) and loops (for, while, foreach, and so on). In PHP, there are two different ways of expressing these control structures. The first is the usual way in PHP, which uses curly braces:

```php
if( condition ) {
        // do something
}
```

The alternate syntax that replaces the opening curly brace with a colon (:) and the closing curly brace with a closing statement depending on the control being used: endif;, endfor;, endwhile, and so on, as shown here:

```php
if( condition ):
        // do something
endif;
```

This alternate syntax also applies to the else: and elseif: statements, which look like this:

```php
if( condition ):
        // do something
elseif( condition ):
        // do something different
else:
        // if all else fails do this
endif;
```

In WordPress theme development, you see this style of syntax an awful lot because alternate syntax is the main way of using control structures in the theme templates. For example, take a look at the loop in the index.php template from the default theme, Twenty Twelve:

```php
<?php if ( have_posts() ) : ?>
                <?php /* Start the Loop */ ?>
                <?php while ( have_posts() ) : the_post(); ?>
                        <?php get_template_part( 'content', get_post_format() ); ?>
                <?php endwhile; ?>
                <?php twentytwelve_content_nav( 'nav-below' ); ?>
        <?php else : ?>
                <h1 class="entry-title"><?php _e( 'Nothing Found', 'twentyeleven' ); ?></h1>
        <?php endif; endwhile; ?>
```

The major advantage of using this alternate syntax is readability. It makes the template files much more understandable, and when you look through them, you can easily see which control structure you are inside based on the more obvious endpoints.

There are a couple of things to consider when using this syntax. If you are nesting control structures (of similar or different types), you must continue to use the same syntax at each level, and the alternate syntax should be used predominantly in the display template files in the theme. When writing code inside the functions file or any template that doesn't necessarily deal with HTML output, you should use the standard syntax with the curly braces (you'll take a look at that and more in the following "Coding Standards" section).

Coding Standards

With WordPress being such a large and distributed project among the core and thousands of plug-ins and themes available, it makes sense that it should have a set of standards. WordPress uses these standards as a way of ensuring that the code stays as accessible as possible, allowing anyone who develops on the platform to work on code created by anyone else. This is extremely important given the nature of WordPress as open source software.

Keeping to the coding standards ensures that the code is easier to maintain and debug. If code is well-formatted instead of a scattered mess, it is easier to see where the bug is on line *n*. Standardization also enables people to easily learn from the code you've written, meaning that others can start coding based on something you've done. It is always a good idea to give back to the community in this way.

Let's have a look at some of the standards WordPress wants you to adhere to when writing your code.

■ **Note**　The full details of the WordPress code standards can be found in the codex at `http://wp-themes-book.com/01009`.

No Shorthand PHP Tags

When writing PHP code in WordPress, you should always use full PHP tags:

```
<?php // some code ?>
```

Never use shorthand tags:

```
<? // some code ?>
<?=$title ?>
```

While this appears in the coding standards to ensure WordPress code is kept consistent throughout, it's also a good idea to stick to the full PHP tags regardsless due to the frailty of support on servers. Prior to version 5.4 of PHP, shorthand tags needed a flag to be set in the PHP.ini file to function. As you cannot always guarantee this will be set correctly it's best to stick to the full tags for you PHP files. Further to this, there is talk that in version 6 of PHP shorthand tags will be deprecated entirely, so best to be safe than sorry.

Indentation, Spacing, and Tabs

All code throughout the themes and plug-ins should reflect a natural indentation flow, including cases of following the correct HTML flow when mixing PHP and HTML in templates. For example, the flow here is correct:

```
<div id="primary" class="site-content">
        <div id="content" role="main">
```

```
<?php while ( have_posts() ) : the_post(); ?>
        <?php get_template_part( 'content', 'page' ); ?>
        <?php comments_template( '', true ); ?>
<?php endwhile; // end of the loop. ?>

        </div><!-- #content -->
</div><!-- #primary -->
```

All indentations should be made with tabs and not spaces, except for mid-line indenting in which spaces should be used to line up values in lists of variable assignments and associative arrays:

```
$var      = "These";
$var2     = "are";
$var_long = "variables";

$var_array = Array (
                'arg1'  = 'this',
                'arg2'  = 'is',
                'arg_4' = 'array',
                'arg_3' = 'an',
        );
```

It's also in the coding standards (and is good practice) to keep a comma after the last item in the array. This makes for easier switching of the order in the array and is perfectly valid in PHP.

Use spaces in control structures to ensure better readability for the conditions and statements, as well as in function calls when passing parameters. When accessing arrays, use spaces around the index only if it is a variable, not when it's a string.

```
if( condition ) {
        // do stuff
}

for( $i=0; $i<10; $i++ ) {
        // do stuff 10 times
}

do_stuff( $arg1, $arg2 );

echo $array[ $idx ];

echo $array['index'];
```

Quotes and Braces

WordPress coding standards are fairly lenient concerning using quotes in PHP. You can use whichever ones are best suited for the job. If you're evaluating a variable in the string like so, it's best to use double quotes to avoid having to escape the string to evaluate the variables:

```
echo "<h2>$title</h2>";
```

Usually I prefer to use single quotes because I use double quotes in my HTML. Again, I don't have to escape any strings when writing the following line:

```
echo '<a href="/about">About us</a>';
```

In control structures, braces should be used to define blocks unless you are in a template file for which the alternate syntax applies. Although the WordPress codex says that braces can be omitted for one-line statements, I prefer to always use them for better readability. The layout of braces should follow this structure:

```
if( condition ) {
        // do stuff
} elseif( condition ) {
        // do something else
} else {
        // do this if all else fails
}
```

Yoda Condition

A great convention to stick to, the Yoda condition requires you to keep the comparison variable on the right side of the conditional statement. This means that a missed equals sign results in a parse error instead of returning true; it takes time to debug a hard-to-spot mistake.

```
if ( true == $the_force ) {
        $victorious = you_will( $be );
}
```

Naming Conventions

In WordPress, you should stick to strict naming conventions. All words should be separated by underscores at all times and the following rules should be followed:

- Functions and variables should be lowercase.

- Class names should always use capitalized words.

- All constants should be uppercase.

- CamelCase should never be used.

- File names should be lowercase with words separated by hyphens.

HTML

In order for the HTML for the code to be accepted by WordPress, it needs to pass validation using the W3C validator. All tags should be properly closed; even though WordPress is still based on the XHTML 1.0 standard, code should still be in line with XML serialization, which is part of the HTML5 standard, so "XHTML5" (essentially HTML with self-closing tags and strict lowercase elements) is fine here.

WordPress keeps these coding standards to ensure that the code is easily readable and accessible. To write good code, always put these ideals ahead of brevity or cleverness of code.

Debugging WordPress

Finally, I want show you how to debug code as you develop your theme in WordPress. WordPress is actually set up really well for handling debugging; it comes with its own built-in system to help you through the development process. The debugging system enables WordPress to not only help its developers but also standardize the code within the plug-ins, themes, and core.

Ensuring that your theme is well tested is part of the requirements to gain any promotion from any official WordPress tools such as the themes or plug-ins repositories. Using the WordPress debugging system is not mandatory, but comes highly recommended and is a great resource so is worth taking advantage of.

To enable debugging in WordPress you simply have to set the 'WP_DEBUG' PHP constant to true, which is usually best done through the wp-config.php file as standard. 'WP_DEBUG' is meant for use only during development, so it should not be left in for a live site. By the time your web site/theme goes live, you should be thoroughly tested and not be relying on 'WP_DEBUG' to catch anything.

```
define('WP_DEBUG', true);
```

An alternative way to do this, used by Joost de Valk at Yoast, is to put the constant declaration inside a conditional so it can be used if you encounter any issues during development:

```
if ( isset($_GET['debug']) && $_GET['debug'] === 'debug') {
        define('WP_DEBUG', true);
}
```

This is a nice idea, but I still recommend keeping this code only in your WordPress setup for development, not in live sites, mainly because any code you put out in the world should be heavily tested and free from error. If an error were to occur on the live site, the one thing you most certainly don't want to be doing is debugging on your live server. So to remove that temptation, I recommend keeping any handy tricks like this safely in your development code.

By enabling 'WP_DEBUG', you get access to a whole host of information. It enables all PHP errors, warnings, and notices; and although some of these notices/warnings might relate to code that is working fine, fixing it is usually quick and easy and is worthwhile doing to prevent future issues. Using 'WP_DEBUG' also notifies you if you are using any deprecated WordPress functions and gives you direction about which newer function you should be using.

There are a few other options that come with the WordPress debugging system that enable you to deal with the debugging information the way you want:

- **'WP_DEBUG_LOG'**: When set to true, this option stores all errors, warnings, and notifications in a debug.log file in the wp-content/ folder.

- **'WP_DEBUG_DISPLAY'**: Set to true by default, this option inserts all debug information as and when it happens. If setting to false, ensure that you use 'WP_DEBUG_LOG' to store the information somewhere.

- **'SCRIPT_DEBUG'**: This option can make the WordPress admin use the development styles and scripts in case you are editing anything in the WordPress admin area (see Chapter 11 for more information).

- **'SAVEQUERIES'**: When set to true, this option saves all queries made to the database as well, as where they were called from in an array, so you can get more detail about how the pages are constructed. It can cause some performance issues, however, so turn this feature on only when actively debugging your theme.

On top of all the great built-in information that you can access from WordPress, there are many plug-ins out there to help you with debugging and testing your theme. I'll cover some of them in Chapter 7 when I discuss when and why to use plug-ins.

Summary

This chapter introduced you to WordPress and, more specifically, WordPress theme development. You took a brief look at how it all got started and some of the history behind the more iconic of the WordPress default themes that have helped shape WordPress theme development as we know it today.

I also gave you a quick guide to PHP and how it relates to WordPress. This knowledge will help make the coding you do throughout this book seem relatively straightforward, allowing you to concentrate on the nuances of WordPress theme development.

In the next chapter, you start to build a WordPress theme when you take a look at the anatomy of a WordPress theme and how to use the template hierarchy to your advantage to target specific pages for unique functionality.

CHAPTER 2

■ ■ ■

Theme Anatomy and Template Hierarchy

This chapter looks at the anatomy of a WordPress theme, starting with the absolute bare minimum files needed for creating a theme, to creating templates, and to fully customize every aspect of your theme.

All WordPress themes can be found in the /wp-content/themes/ directory, with each theme located in its own folder (see Figure 2-1). In the latest install of WordPress version 3.7, you already have two themes available for use: Twenty Twelve and the latest version Twenty Thirteen.

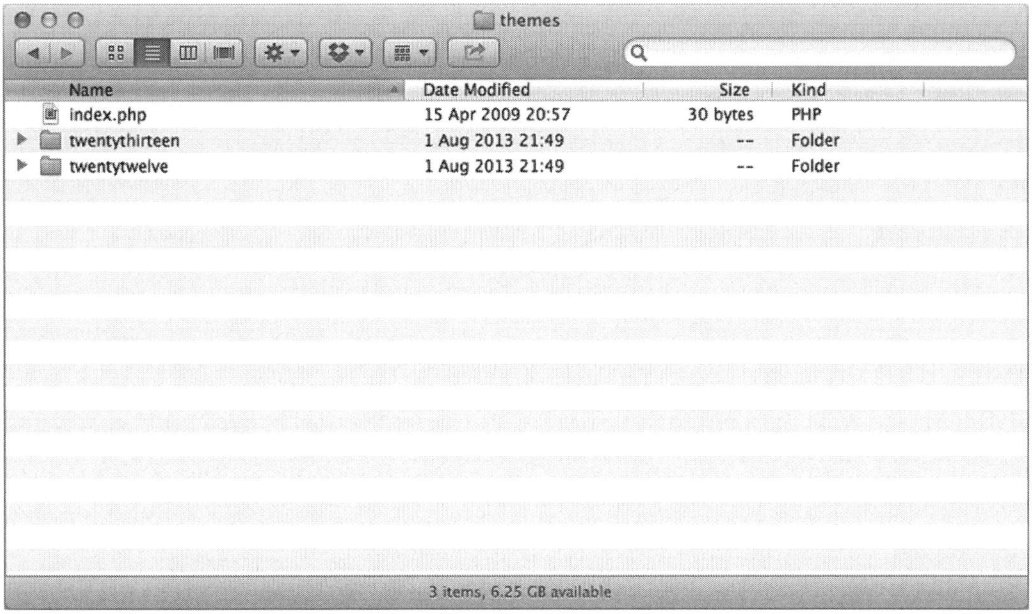

Figure 2-1. *The default themes directory*

Note the strict naming convention for WordPress themes: theme names must never include any numbers; otherwise, the WordPress theme manager won't display them (see Figure 2-2). You'll learn more shortly about how to customize the information displayed for your theme in the themes manager.

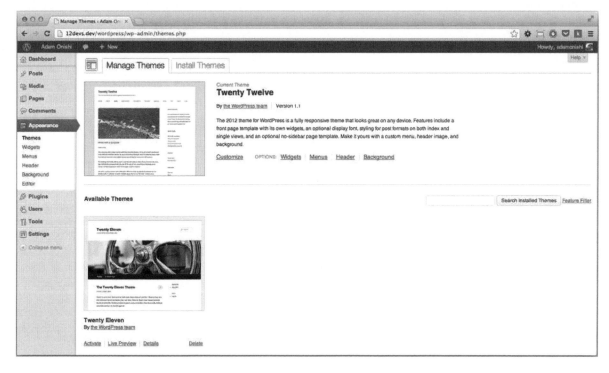

Figure 2-2. *WordPress theme manager*

The Bare Minimum

Let's start with the absolute basics of a WordPress theme. It must contain two files:

- `style.css`
- `index.php`

Every theme created must have at least these two files, as well as any others that the developer chooses to include. Even though you can use other templates (discussed shortly) to display all your content, you have to have the index file because it is the final fallback for anything that gets displayed in your theme. If one of these files from your theme is missing, it simply won't appear in the theme manager for you to activate it.

The index.php File

WordPress uses the `index.php` file as the default file for rendering a web site. If there aren't any other files in the theme, WordPress will use this template for everything; and if there is no file for the type of content being asked for, WordPress will fall back to `index.php`. You could create your theme with an `index.php` file and a `style.css` file; but as you'll see through the course of this chapter, there are plenty of ways to customize the output of your web site using the templates in WordPress.

The style.css File

The `style.css` file should be the main Cascading Style Sheets (CSS) file in a WordPress theme. It is perfectly fine to create more style sheets for more maintainable code, but the main style.css file should always exist.

The most important feature of the `style.css` file is that it holds all the metadata for your theme, which is displayed in the theme manager. They are set through the style sheet header in comments using specific attribute names, which WordPress finds and outputs in the theme manager. Here are the comments from the Twenty Twelve style.css header:

```
/*
Theme Name: Twenty Twelve
Theme URI: http://wordpress.org/extend/themes/twentytwelve
Author: the WordPress team
Author URI: http://wordpress.org/
Description: The 2012 theme for WordPress is a fully responsive theme that looks great on any
device. Features include a front page template with its own widgets, an optional display font,
styling for post formats on both index and single views, and an optional no-sidebar page template.
Make it yours with a custom menu, header image, and background.
Version: 1.1
License: GNU General Public License v2 or later
License URI: http://www.gnu.org/licenses/gpl-2.0.html
Tags: light, gray, white, one-column, two-columns, right-sidebar, flexible-width, custom-background,
custom-header, custom-menu, editor-style, featured-images, flexible-header, full-width-template,
microformats, post-formats, rtl-language-support, sticky-post, theme-options, translation-ready
Text Domain: twentytwelve


This theme, like WordPress, is licensed under the GPL.
Use it to make something cool, have fun, and share what you've learned with others.
*/
```

This is a very comprehensive style sheet header that includes everything from the author of the theme to any additional details that are found at the bottom of the comments.

Here's a quick guide to the information you can set in the style sheet header:

- **Theme Name:** The full title of the theme, including spaces; it can be capitalized.

- **Theme URI:** The location in which you find the theme to download.

- **Author:** The theme creator's name. Although WordPress suggests the username the author uses to log in to wordpress.org, it's left up to the author.

- **Author URI:** The author's web site.

- **Description:** A brief description of the theme's features and design.

- **Version:** The version of the theme as you work on it. As you update your theme and upload it to the WordPress themes directory, the version number is used to trigger notifications for theme updates for anyone using your theme.

- **License:** The license the theme uses.

- **License URI:** The web address in which you can find more information on the license.

- **Tags:** A list of appropriate tags that can be used to help users find the theme in the WordPress repository. The full list of acceptable tags can be found at http://wp-themes-book.com/02001.

- **Text Domain:** A unique identifier for use in localization in WordPress. This is often a lowercase (with no spaces) version of your theme name (refer to the previous Twenty Twelve example).

Any further comments about the theme can be added to the bottom of the style sheet header comments.

Not all the preceding meta information is required for the theme; WordPress picks up the information that is there and ignores anything else.

■ **Note**   In addition to the information in the style sheet header, an image with the name screenshot.png can be used for the theme manager. The image is usually a screenshot of how the theme looks, so the user can have a brief preview before activating the theme. The image is recommended to be sized at 600 x 450px and should be located in the root of your themes folder.

Basic Template Files

The anatomy in Figure 2-3 should be fairly familiar if you have developed a WordPress theme before. It shows a simple example of the makeup of a page using the basic template files available in WordPress.

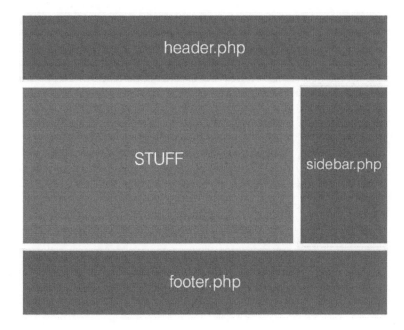

Figure 2-3. *A typical WordPress theme anatomy*

All pages in a WordPress theme can be constructed using a series of basic template files, including the following:

- `header.php`

- `footer.php`

- `sidebar.php`

- `comments.php`

- `searchform.php`

This section takes a more detailed look at each of these files (what they can and should be used for) and some important WordPress functions that have to be included in these base sections.

header.php

The `header.php` file is used for any common markup to show at the top of the HTML page. It usually includes the following:

- DOCTYPE declaration

- Opening `<html>` tag

- Entire `<head>` of your HTML document

- Opening `<body>` tag

It can also contain any markup to be used consistently across all site pages, for example, the main logo and navigation, which won't change throughout your site. The `header.php` file can include as much or as little content as you want to be used consistently across your theme. Here's an example of a simple `header.php` file:

```php
<?php
/**
 * The Header for our theme.
 *
 */
?><!DOCTYPE html>
<html <?php language_attributes(); ?>>
        <head>
                <meta charset="<?php bloginfo( 'charset' ); ?>" />
                <meta name="viewport" content="width=device-width" />

                <title><?php wp_title( '|', true, 'right' ); ?></title>

                <!-- HTML5 SHIV for IE --><!-- If using Modernizr you can remove this script! -->
                <!--[if lt IE 9]>
                        <script src="//html5shiv.googlecode.com/svn/trunk/html5.js"></script>
                <![endif]-->

                <?php wp_head(); ?>
        </head>
```

```
<body <?php body_class(); ?>>

        <header class="site-header">
            <h1>
                    <a href="<?php echo home_url(); ?>">
                            <img src="<?php bloginfo('template_directory'); ?>/images/
                            logo.jpg" alt=" ">
                    </a>
            </h1>
        </header>
```

This is a pretty straightforward example of a header file that you can use throughout the development of the theme; it includes the usual HTML5 DOCTYPE, opening `<html>` tag, the full `<head>` of the site, and an initial `<header>` block to display the site's logo.

In the `<head>` section, no style sheet is declared because WordPress has a great way of dealing with the style sheet (and JavaScript) includes, which are handled by the `wp_head()` function.

The wp_head() Function

This function is a mandatory inclusion inside the `<head>` section of all pages in a theme and should always be located before the closing `</head>` tag. This WordPress function is used to include style sheets and scripts from the theme and any plug-ins that might be used. If you don't include it, you might end up inadvertently breaking your site. Here is the HTML generated from the preceding `wp_head()` function call:

```
<meta name='robots' content='noindex,nofollow' />

<link rel='stylesheet' id='twelvedevs-style-css'  href='http://12devs.dev/wordpress/wp-content/
themes/12devs/style.css?ver=3.5.1' type='text/css' media='all' />

<!--[if lte IE 7]>
<link rel='stylesheet' id='twelvedevs-ie-css'  href='http://12devs.dev/wordpress/wp-content/
themes/12devs/ie-old.css?ver=3.5.1' type='text/css' media='all' />
<![endif]-->

<script type='text/javascript' src='http://ajax.googleapis.com/ajax/libs/jquery/1/jquery.min.
js?ver=3.5.1'></script>

<link rel='canonical' href='http://12devs.dev/events/12-devs-at-easter/' />
```

As you can see, there are two style sheet includes and a script include for jQuery as well as a canonical link tag and a robots meta tag. This output can be controlled using functions in WordPress; you'll take a look at how to include style sheets and scripts a bit later in this chapter.

The wp_title() Function

Another function that you might have noticed in the `header.php` example is the `wp_title()` function. This function is used to create a title for the browser based on the current page being viewed. The function can take three parameters: a separator string, whether to display the title or return it as a PHP string, and the location for the separator. By default, this function outputs only the name of the page you're on, but later in the book you'll learn ways to customize it, turning it into something a lot more useful and more (ahem) search engine optimization (SEO)—friendly.

■ **Note** This function can also be used throughout the WordPress theme, just not inside the loop; the `<title>` tag is the most common place to find the function.

footer.php

The `footer.php` template is similar to the `header.php` file, but it contains the end of the HTML document. It's the place where you'll most likely find the `</body></html>` pairing, but it could also be used for common markup that is located at the bottom of every page in your theme. Once more, there is the need for a special WordPress function, `wp_footer()`, to be included.

The wp_footer() Function

As with the `wp_head()` function, `wp_footer()` is a mandatory function required in all themes, located just before the closing `</body>` tag. This function is used mostly to output script files at the end of the document or analytics code. If you don't include it, you risk some of the features of your theme or included plug-ins not working. It is where WordPress includes the markup for the admin bar that appears when a user is logged in to WordPress. You'll soon learn to always remember the `wp_footer()` function if (like me) you spend ages wondering why there's suddenly a 30px space at the top of your site.

sidebar.php

The sidebar is another of the basic templates that can be used to make up a file. It is usually used for content that appears on multiple pages, but is not directly linked to the main content of the page. The sidebar file is often used to display widgets, which exist in WordPress natively, or can be created by plug-ins or in the themes functions (you'll get more information in Chapter 6).

comments.php

As the name suggests, `comments.php` is used to generate the markup for the comments on a particular post. Until recently, WordPress had a default template for displaying the comments that could be overwritten using a `comments.php` file in your theme. This functionality is being deprecated, however, so in newer versions you will be required to have a `comments.php` file in your theme if you want to render comments. (You'll take a deeper look at comments in Chapter 13.)

searchform.php

The `searchform.php` file does pretty much exactly what it says on the tin. WordPress has kept a default version of this file for use in your theme, however, so if one isn't declared, WordPress falls back to its own default:

```
<form role="search" method="get" id="searchform" action="<?php echo home_url( '/' ); ?>">
    <div><label class="screen-reader-text" for="s">Search for:</label>
        <input type="text" value="" name="s" id="s" />
        <input type="submit" id="searchsubmit" value="Search" />
    </div>
</form>
```

Keep in mind that when creating a custom search form, to render it correctly in WordPress you should be using a GET method directed at the home page of your site. (More on search is covered later in the chapter.)

Including Basic Template Files

Learning about all these template files is all well and good, but now you need to actually include them in your main template files. Each of the previous files could be included with a regular PHP include() call, but WordPress goes one better and furnishes some template functions to use specifically for each of the base files:

- get_header()
- get_footer()
- get_sidebar()
- get_search_form()
- comments_template()

Each of these functions includes the correct default file in the location in which it has been called. Here's what a standard template file looks like with all the inclusions:

```php
<?php get_header(); ?>

    <div class="container">
        <div class="search">
            <?php get_search_form(); ?>
        </div>

        <div class="main">
            <?php // do stuff ?>

            <?php comments_template(); ?>
        </div>

        <?php get_sidebar(); ?>
    </div>

<?php get_footer(); ?>
```

Another trick with these include() functions is that get_header(), get_footer(), and get_sidebar() can each be passed a string as a parameter. By doing this, WordPress searches for a different file from the default to include in the template. For example, you could have multiple sidebars to use in different places in your theme to allow for better structure or just easier maintainability. To create a second sidebar, create a template file named sidebar-secondary.php; to include it in your template files, simply call the get_sidebar() function with 'secondary' as a string parameter:

```php
get_sidebar('secondary');
```

The same can be done with the header and footer files. It might seem a bit odd to have multiple headers for your site, but I had an experience in which a client wanted two main sections to their website. They were linked together but displayed differently, with a separate brand and main navigation. It was achieved using two header files and two footer files, one for each of the main site sections. It allowed me to build the site on one install of WordPress, which meant better management for the client and only a few more template files built into the theme.

The `comments_template()` is the other function that can have parameters passed to it. By default, the function simply outputs the contents of the `comments.php` file, but you can pass it two parameters. First is a template name; in this case, it has to be the whole template name and path relative to the template directory (for example, `'/custom-comments.php'`). The second parameter is a Boolean that determines whether to have the comments separated by type; this is set to `false` by default.

Functions File

In a sense, the functions file of a WordPress theme (`functions.php` in the root of your theme) acts as your own little plugin. It gets loaded automatically by WordPress when a page is initialized in both the front end and admin of your site. It can be used for a variety of functions:

- To set up WordPress functionality such as post-thumbnails or custom post types
- To define functions that can be used throughout your theme templates
- To change the WordPress admin or add in options pages

This is an example of a small `functions.php` file:

```php
<?php
/**
 * Pro WordPress functions and definitions
 *
 * @package prowordpress
 */

        add_theme_support( 'automatic-feed-links' );
        add_theme_support( 'post-thumbnails' );
```

All this code does is set up a couple of theme support features: the feed links feature to enhance the RSS feeds generated by the site and the post-thumbnails feature, which is always handy on any WordPress site. It enables you to attach an image to any post or page that can be included specifically in your templates.

■ **Note** Because a `functions.php` file acts much like a plugin, there might be a point when you need to consider actually writing a plugin instead. (Creating plugins is discussed in Chapter 7).

Template Hierarchy

Now that the basic template files have been introduced, you can start to look at ways to customize the output of your theme with more specific template files. All the files discussed in this section work in a similar way to the `index.php` file and normally have some or all of the basic template files included inside them. If you take a look at the template hierarchy (see Figure 2-4), you see a plethora of options when creating custom templates for almost any part of your content. The diagram has actually become so big that to fit it in the book I included a partial section. (For a full view of the hierarchy, see `http://wp-themes-book.com/02002.`)

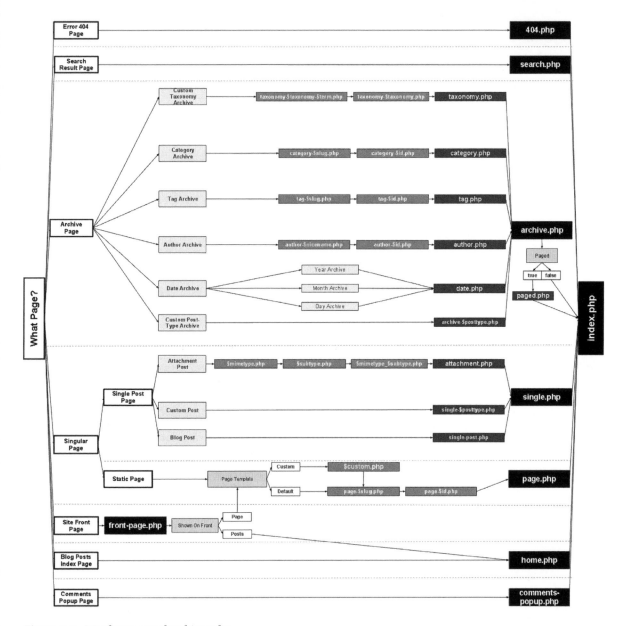

Figure 2-4. *WordPress template hierarchy*

Take a look at some of the base files that appear on the right of the hierarchy:

- `page.php`
- `single.php`
  - `attachment.php`

- archive.php
    - taxonomy.php
    - category.php
    - date.php
    - tag.php
    - author.php

Here are some of the special template files used for more specific purposes:

- front-page.php
- home.php
- search.php
- 404.php
- comments-popup.php

The main thing to remember about the hierarchy is that the farther right the template appears, the more general it is. Any template file format to the left of the one on the same row is more specific to a certain page or type, and is given priority.

page.php

As its name suggests, this template is used to generate and display the pages in your WordPress site. If you need to create a custom template for a specific page, you can do it easily by using the page's slug, which is usually a lowercase, hyphenated version of the page title. In WordPress, the page slug is located beneath the main title in the editor.

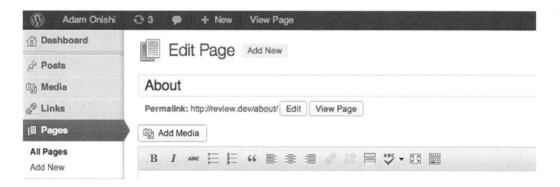

Figure 2-5. *The permalink below the title shows the page slug after the site address*

You can also use the page ID in place of the slug, but I don't recommend it because it's not very easy to see which template is for which page. I can't think of a situation in which you would often change the location of a page but keep the same format.

The two templates you need to remember when using pages are page.php for general use and page-{slug}.php for targeting specific pages for custom layout (where {slug} is the page slug of the targeted page).

single.php

The single.php template is used to display all individual posts. It is also used when custom post types have been created, and you want to display an individual post of that type. To target a specific post type, you need to use the name of that post type as you use the page slug to target a specific page. To create a template to display all standard posts in WordPress, use single-post.php, but remember that all individual posts fall back to single.php if single-post.php does not exist. My usual approach is to use single-posttype.php for all custom posts and single.php for the native post type in WordPress.

The single.php template is used to display all post attachments if you allow them to be linked to in WordPress. To create a more basic page for attachments, use the attachment.php template file.

attachment.php

The attachment.php file is used to display any attachments that can be directly linked to from the WordPress front end. When you upload images/videos/documents to WordPress, it creates the file's path where it is stored in the WordPress file system (usually /wp-content/uploads), and then an attachment URL, that can be linked to directly to show the attachment within the front end of your WordPress site.

You can also create more specific template files for certain attachment types by using the MIME type as the template name:

- image.php
- video.php
- text.php

archive.php

The archive template is used whenever a group of posts or information is being accessed through the query. It can be used for anything from a date-specific archive, to posts by a certain author, or to posts that are in a certain category. The main archive.php template displays everything, but as shown in the template hierarchy shown in Figure 2-6, there are many template files that can be used to overwrite the archive.php.

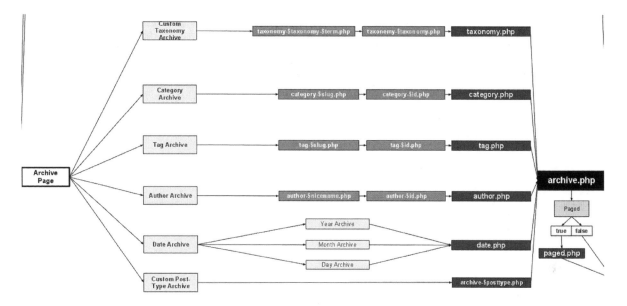

Figure 2-6. *The archive section of the template hierarchy*

The archive types include the following:

- category
- tag
- author
- date
- taxonomy

■ **Note**   Custom post–type specific archives are covered in more detail in Chapter 4.

You can also target specific categories, tags, and authors by using the specific category, tag, or author name (author *nicename* as used in WordPress). The date template file catches any archives relating to a specific date period including year, month, and day; but you cannot target other types of date information.

The taxonomy template can be used to target custom taxonomies you create in WordPress as well as specific terms in that template. To target a custom taxonomy, append the taxonomy name to the template name (for example, taxonomy-taxonomyname.php). To access a specific term of a specific taxonomy, append the term name to it (for example, taxonomy-taxonomyname-termname.php).

Now that I've covered some of the more general templates available in the template hierarchy, look at some of the templates that have more specific functionality in WordPress.

front-page.php

The `front-page` template is used when a static front page has been selected from the WordPress admin options in Settings ➤ Reading (see Figure 2-7). When this option is set, the page template is overwritten with `front-page.php` ahead of any others, enabling you to create a custom home page for your site based on a specific template file and making that template file a lot easier to spot among your template files.

Figure 2-7. *Set up a static page at the top of the reading settings*

home.php

The home template is used in two circumstances: as the main template for the home page for your web site or as the main listing page template of your site when you have set up a static front page using the reading settings, as shown in Figure 2-7.

search.php

The search page template displays the results of any search performed on the web site. To get this template to load a search, you need to submit a GET request to the home page of the site. For example, `mysite.com?s=about` would search `mysite.com` for the term "about", and the search template would be used to display those results.

In this template, to display the search that was performed, you can use the `the_search_query()` function:

```
<p>You searched for " <?php the_search_query() ?> ". Here are the results:</p>
```

It is also possible, although it requires a bit of trickery, to change the default location of the search while retaining the correct page template, thanks to this code snippet from Paul Davis:

```
function search_url_rewrite(){
    if(is_search() && !empty($_GET['s'])){
            wp_redirect(home_url("/search/"). urlencode(get_query_var('s')));
            exit();
    }
}
add_action('template_redirect', 'search_url_rewrite');
```

This function adds on to the `'template_redirect'` hook, which determines the page template WordPress needs to load. When a search is detected, it redirects the URL to /search/searchterm, which creates better URL structures and means you are no longer required to use a GET to perform a search.

404.php

The 404 template is displayed by WordPress when it cannot find a result for the query for a specific page or post. General queries for an archive page that turn up no results still load the correct archive template with errors for that handled in the template file using the Loop (more on that in the next chapter).

A custom 404 page helps users who may have been redirected to the wrong page or have mistyped a URL by giving them a way back into the site and allowing them to find what they were looking for. Have a bit of fun, as with the GitHub 404 page in Figure 2-8. A fun 404 page is good design because it can help reduce any user frustration from not finding something on your site.

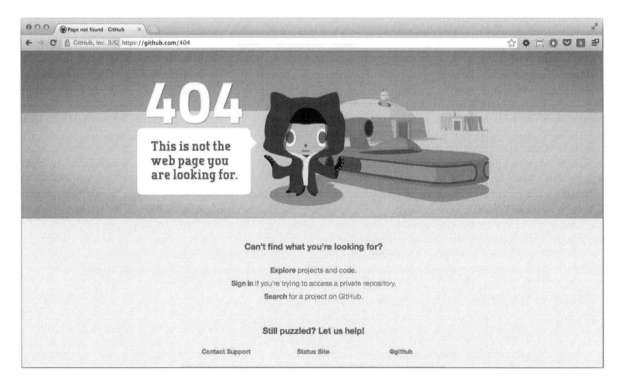

Figure 2-8. *GitHub 404 page*

Custom Template Files

So if all the options for different page templates discussed here aren't enough, there's even a way to create custom page templates in WordPress to give you even more opportunity for customization.

You might need a custom template file when you want to offer an alternative layout or piece of functionality as an option for any page on the site.

■ **Note**   Custom page templates are available only for pages in WordPress, not for posts or custom post types.

To create a custom page template, you need to create a new file in your theme directory and ensure that it doesn't conflict with any of the reserved template names already in the WordPress template hierarchy. (A full list of names can be found at http://wp-themes-book.com/02003.)

Begin the file with a PHP comment similar to that in the style.css file:

```php
<?php
/**
 * Template Name: Custom page type 1
**/
?>
```

After you set up your custom template file, it activates a new option in the Page Attributes box on the right side of the editor page (see Figure 2-9).

Figure 2-9. *Custom template selector in the WordPress page editor*

Post Formats

Post formats are relatively new to WordPress; they were introduced in version 3.1 (Gershwin). They allow users to add specific metadata to a post to enable more specific formatting and styling in the theme.

WordPress has a list of standardized post formats that are specifically controlled to be supported across a wide range of themes and have the potential to allow external tools to access the feature in a consistent manner. Themes don't have to support the full list or even support formats at all, but the addition of some simple metadata is a great way to add some easy customization to a theme.

This is such a big addition to WordPress that in the new default theme Twenty Thirteen there is a major focus on showing off the capability of the post formats to create beautiful and dynamic themes. In fact one of the major focuses of the version 3.6 update was to improve the UI of the post formats, giving them more focus in the post admin.

This full list of available post formats can be found at `http://wp-themes-book.com/02004`, but a small selection includes these:

- `gallery`
- `image`
- `video`
- `status`
- `quote`

The formats are labeled to give the post they're attached to more context and to enable better layout or styling based on the format. For example, the `image` format should be used for a post that contains a single image as the main focus, and the `video` format should be used for a post that contains a video. Formats such as these allow the image or video to be styled differently and perhaps as the focus of the post, instead of a generic post display that might render a smaller image and not draw any extra attention.

By adding a format to a post, WordPress doesn't change the way it stores or renders the post; it is left up to the theme to control, either by querying the post format or accessing it through the post class.

To enable post formats, you need to use the `add_theme_support()` function shown here:

```
add_theme_support( 'post-formats', array( 'image', 'gallery', 'video' ) );
```

The `add_theme_support()` function usually takes only one parameter: the feature name that you want to add to the theme. To enable post formats, however, you need to pass a second parameter in the form of an array of the formats you want to include. If you don't pass an array of formats, WordPress doesn't display any options; only the option box displays. After you include the previous code, you will see an option box appear on the right side of the editor page (see Figure 2-10).

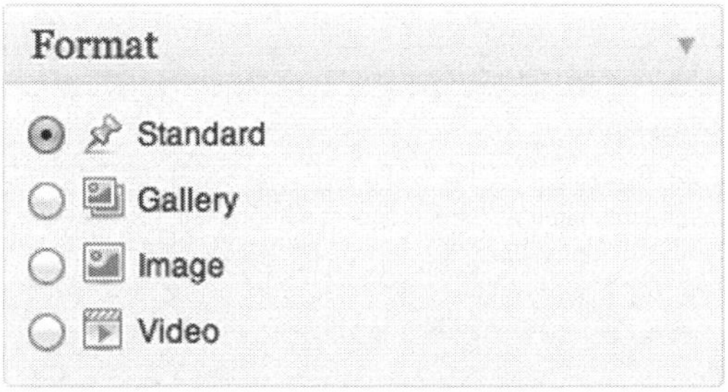

Figure 2-10. *Post formats option box*

By default, post formats can be used for posts and custom post types if specified when you create them, but not by pages. To add post formats to pages, you need to call the add_post_type_support() function like this:

```
// add post-formats to post_type 'page'
add_post_type_support( 'page', 'post-formats' );
```

There are many ways to access the post format in your theme; for example, you can use a conditional tag to check in the template file whether the post has a certain format:

```
if( has_post_format('video') ):
        // do something
endif;
```

You can get the post format as a PHP string:

```
$format = get_post_format($post_id);
```

You could then use this information any way you want in your template to display the post differently. If this function is called inside the loop, you don't need to pass in the $post_id value. The most common use of this method of getting the post format is to call in a special template part, as shown in this code used in the Twenty Twelve theme:

```
<?php get_template_part( 'content', get_post_format() ); ?>
```

In this code, the theme is using the post format as a parameter in the get_template_part() function to include a separate template file to use specifically with posts with a certain format.

Template Parts

You can think of the basic template files header.php and footer.php as template parts as well; the only difference is that they are common files that have been used in WordPress for many years and come with their own functions for inclusion. In version 3.0, WordPress introduced the get_template_part() function that allows you to include partial template files for use in the theme with a native function in WordPress. Before this function was introduced, you would have had to use a standard PHP include.

You can create template parts with any naming convention you want as long as you avoid the reserved template names discussed earlier. The get_template_part() function works with two parameters: a *slug* and a specific *name* for the template file. It assumes that the names are made up: slug-name.php. So if you assume the post format will be video for the previous code snippet, the function will include the content-video.php file from the main theme directory, if it exists. If the theme file doesn't exist, the function tries to find a template file using just the slug parameter passed (content.php); if it still can't find a file matching that name, instead of throwing an error like a PHP include would, it simply won't include anything.

If you want to store your template parts in a subfolder inside your theme to help keep your theme neat and tidy, you can pass the file structure of the slug as part of the first parameter like so:

```
<?php get_template_part( 'parts/content', get_post_format() ); ?>
```

More Theme Setup

There are some conventions and best practices to follow when setting up your theme. They include how to structure the file system of your theme and how to load in your style sheets and JavaScript files. I'll show you a couple of tips regarding the anatomy of your theme to make things a little easier for you when you develop it.

Theme Folder Structure

You already know that themes reside in the `wp-content/themes/` directory. But within your themes you often have a range of template files, style sheets, JavaScript files, and images. To keep the theme tidy and manageable, the following is a basic folder structure based on past default themes and my own experience of theme development:

- **/**: The root theme directory is where all main template files and the `style.css` file are stored. Any template file you find in the template hierarchy should be stored here to ensure that WordPress can load the template when required.

- **/images/**: The main folder for all images used in the theme. These images are ones usually used for presentation and styling of the theme, which are different from images uploaded to WordPress as content, which are stored in the uploads folder in `wp-content/`.

- **/js/**: All JavaScript files should be stored in their own folder (could also be named javascript, depending on your personal preference).

- **/languages/**: If your theme is multilingual, all languages files should be stored in a languages directory (a best practice, not a WordPress requirement).

- **/css/**: Any additional CSS files should be stored in and loaded from a `css/` directory.

- **/inc/**: Can be used for additional PHP files that may be needed for functionality in the theme. As an example, you can group common functions inside their own file inside the inc folder before loading them into the `functions.php` file. This is also a common practice among other themes.

- **/scss/** or **/less/**: If I use a CSS preprocessor, I like to keep the files located within the theme and use a compiler such as Codekit or specific settings in the configuration of Compass to compile them into `style.css` in the root of the theme.

That's about it for folder structure. You may have seen some themes using other folders such as page-templates or partials to group template parts together to keep them organized, but this is up to you and is not a requirement.

Loading Styles and Scripts

As you saw earlier, no style sheets or scripts were loaded in HTML in the main <head> of your document because you can now use a function in WordPress to add style sheets and script files dynamically. This has a few advantages in that all scripts and style sheets can be added to the theme in one place and distributed to the correct places in the <head> and end of your documents. You can also add things like version numbers programmatically.

Both of these file types has two separate functions that can be used to insert style sheets and scripts into the pages:

- `wp_register_style()`

- `wp_register_script()`

- `wp_enqueue_style()`

- `wp_enqueue_script()`

The register functions are used to tell WordPress there is a style sheet or script available to be used and give it a handle. The enqueue functions are used to add the style sheet or script to a generated WordPress page through either `wp_head()` or `wp_footer()`.

Adding Styles

First, here's how to register and add the main style sheet for the theme:

```
// Get the current theme object
$theme = wp_get_theme();
wp_register_style( 'prowordpress-style', get_stylesheet_uri(), false, $theme->Version, 'screen');
wp_enqueue_style('prowordpress-style');
```

Using the preceding functions, you call wp_register_style() with the following:

- A handle for the style sheet (to be used later in the wp_enqueue_style function)

- The location of the file—in this case using the WordPress function get_stylesheet_uri()

- Any dependencies for this style sheet (false if none)

- The theme version using the theme object you queried for previously

- The media type, in this case screen.

Then, using the handle you set in the previous function, you add the style with the wp_enqueue_style() function.

In most sites I develop now, I use a separate style sheet for older versions of a certain browser. From here, it's hard to see how that would be done because it is where HTML conditional comments would be used. Fortunately, WordPress has a function for that, too. Here's the code I use to include a style sheet specifically for a certain troublesome browser:

```
global $wp_styles;

wp_register_style( 'prowordpress-ie', get_template_directory_uri() . '/ie-old.css',
array( 'prowordpress-style' ));
$wp_styles->add_data( 'prowordpress-ie', 'conditional', 'lte IE 7' );
wp_enqueue_style('prowordpress-ie');
```

In this bit of code, you get a reference to the $wp_styles WordPress global in which all registered styles are stored. You can register your style as normal, but with the addition of your main style sheet as a dependency, it will get added to the templates after the main style sheet. After you register the style, use the add_data() function of the $wp_styles global to add a conditional around the style with the condition 'lte IE 7'.

Adding JavaScript

Adding JavaScript to a theme is almost the same as adding a style sheet. The only difference is that you replace the parameter for setting a media type for the style sheet with a Boolean parameter showing whether the script should be loaded into the footer or header (true for footer, false for header; the default is false).

Here's an example of how to include a JavaScript file into your theme:

```
$theme = wp_get_theme();
wp_register_script( 'core', get_template_directory_uri() . "/javascript/core.js", array( 'jquery' ),
$theme->Version, true);
```

In this example, you use jQuery as the handle for a dependency on the script you're loading. WordPress does have a version of jQuery loaded as a default, but depending on how recent the version of WordPress is and whether you've kept WordPress up to date (I hope so), you may not always have the latest version of jQuery to use in your theme. To ensure this is not the case, you can load jQuery using a short snippet of code:

```
if (!is_admin()) {
        wp_deregister_script('jquery');
        wp_register_script('jquery', ("http://ajax.googleapis.com/ajax/libs/jquery/1/jquery.min.js"), false);
        wp_enqueue_script('jquery');
}
```

This bit of code checks whether WordPress is trying to load an admin page; if it is, you don't want to overwrite the latest version of the framework just in case the WordPress admin area is using code that is dependent on the version of jQuery bundle with the content management system (CMS). Remove the registered jQuery version with `wp_deregister_script()` and then include your own using the Google API–hosted version of the code.

■ **Note**   You can download your own version of jQuery to bundle with your theme, but the Google API version is so widely used now, a lot of people already have it cached and ready for use, which improves the performance of your site as a whole. You also won't have to worry about keeping the jQuery version up to date because Google takes care of it.

Where should you include these styles and scripts? I normally do this inside the `functions.php` file because it keeps everything in one place, allowing for more manageable and cleaner template files.

Conditional Tags

The conditional tags in WordPress are related closely to the template hierarchy, with most types of template file available being covered by a conditional tag (for example, `is_front_page()`).

Each function simply returns `true` or `false`, and can be used inside or outside the loop without you having to pass a post ID to the function. Some conditional tags do accept parameters, however, which are used in addition to the conditional tag's main function to narrow down the condition. An example is the `is_single()` conditional tag that accepts parameters in a series of formats:

- `is_single()` if a single post is displayed.

- `is_single( 7 )` if a single post with the ID 7 is displayed.

- `is_single( 'Hello World' )` if a single post with the title 'Hello World' is displayed.

- `is_single( 'hello-word' )` if a single post with the slug 'hello-world' is displayed.

- `is_single( array(7, 'hello-world', 'Bob has new shoes') )` if any of the conditions passed through in the array is `true`. An array can be passed in with any of the preceding values, in whichever order or format. If the post being displayed matches any of them, it returns `true`.

The best example of the use of WordPress conditional tags is in the `archive.php` template of any of the default WordPress themes, which uses them to display a different title based on the type of archive being displayed:

```
<h1 class="archive-title"><?php
        if ( is_day() ) :
                printf( __( 'Daily Archives: %s', 'twentytwelve' ), '<span>' . get_the_date() . '</span>' );
        elseif ( is_month() ) :
                printf( __( 'Monthly Archives: %s', 'twentytwelve' ), '<span>' . get_the_date( _x( 'F Y',
                'monthly archives date format', 'twentytwelve' ) ) . '</span>' );
        elseif ( is_year() ) :
                printf( __( 'Yearly Archives: %s', 'twentytwelve' ), '<span>' . get_the_date( _x( 'Y',
                'yearly archives date format', 'twentytwelve' ) ) . '</span>' );
        else :
                _e( 'Archives', 'twentytwelve' );
        endif;
?></h1>
```

A full list and examples of the conditional tags in WordPress can be found at `http://wp-themes-book.com/02005`.

Find Out Which Template Is Being Used

Before you start creating your own theme, I want to share a code snippet I like to use that functions in a similar way to the WordPress conditional functions, but allows me to check which template file is used on a certain page. It can also be used to return the current template name so I can view which template is being used for debugging purposes:

```
function prowordpress_is_template( $name = false ) {
        global $post;

        $template_file = get_post_meta($post->ID,'_wp_page_template',TRUE);

        // check for a template type
        if( $name ):
                if ( $name === $template_file ):
                        return true;
                else:
                        return false;
                endif;
        else:
                return $template_file;
        endif;
}
```

The function takes in a parameter of the template name you are checking against, and by using the `_wp_page_template` metadata attached to the current post or page being displayed, it returns `true` or `false` if they match. It can be used if you want to include only certain functionality in the functions file when certain templates are being used. For example, a custom script or style sheet file that relates only to a specific template could be queued using this conditional function:

```
if ( prowordpress_is_template('custom-template-1.php') ) {
        wp_enqueue_style('custom-template-style');
}
```

Building Your Theme, Part 1

Now it's time to put into practice what you've learned throughout this chapter. You will do this in most of the chapters throughout the book to build up a theme, putting into practice everything you learn through each chapter. In this part, you will set up your folder structure and main template files. At this stage, none of the template files you'll be creating displays any content, so it won't make for the best viewing of the web site (but you have to start somewhere).

Folder Structure

Earlier in the chapter, you took a look in detail at how you should structure your folders and templates, so they aren't covered in any more detail here. For now, you just need folders for JavaScript; images; and, for this theme, your CSS partials.

Base Template Files

Now you need to get some templates into your theme. As you know, the most important theme files needed for any theme are the `index.php` and `style.css` files. You will also set up some other base files to use here: `header.php`, `footer.php`, and `functions.php`.

Now your theme folder should look something like Figure 2-11.

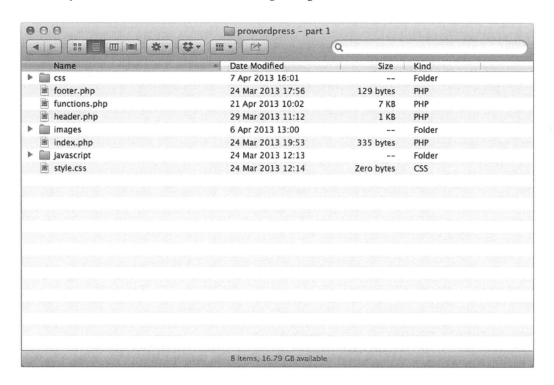

Figure 2-11. *Basic theme files and folders*

Now that your files and folders are created, you can start to add some code. First, add your theme information into the `style.css` file to make sure your theme can be picked up by WordPress.

Style.css

You can use whatever information you prefer here; just remember to substitute anything you customize yourself when you work through the rest of the examples so things work correctly. I suggest that you always have a few attributes as an absolute bare minimum. Here's an example of the style sheet header you'll use for your theme:

```
/**
 * Theme Name: Pro WordPress
 * Author: Adam Onishi
 * Author URI: http://adamonishi.com
 * Description: An example theme for the Pro WordPress theme development book
 * Version: 0
 * Text Domain: prowordpress
 */
```

Next, you can start adding some markup to your theme. Start with the header and footer, which create the base of the generated HTML pages.

header.php and footer.php

You will use a very similar version of the code you've already looked at in the `header.php` example, but with a few modifications just to keep the header a bit cleaner and more compact.

```php
<?php
/**
 * Pro WordPres header file
 *
 */
?><!DOCTYPE html>
<html class="no-js" <?php language_attributes(); ?>>
    <head>
        <meta charset="<?php bloginfo( 'charset' ); ?>" />

        <meta name="viewport" content="width=device-width" />

        <title><?php wp_title( '|', true, 'right' ); ?></title>

        <!-- HTML5 SHIV for IE --><!-- If using Modernizr you can remove this script! -->
        <!--[if lt IE 9]>
            <script src="//html5shiv.googlecode.com/svn/trunk/html5.js"></script>
        <![endif]-->

        <?php wp_head(); ?>
    </head>
```

```
<body <?php body_class(); ?>>

        <header class="site-header">
                <h1>
                        <a href="<?php echo home_url(); ?>">
                                Pro WordPress Theme Development
                        </a>
                </h1>
        </header>
```

Again, this is just a very simple header template with a few PHP functions to output some useful bits that are set up or accessible via WordPress. I also included the HTML5 shiv for IE because the rest of the theme uses HTML5 markup.

Next is the `footer.php` file; for now all you do is close the main tags like so:

```
        <!-- END OF THEME -->
        </body>
</html>
```

Now you have really simple header and footer files for your theme; you're doing just enough to get the basic information about your site output on every page at the top of your document. Your final basic template to set up is the functions file.

functions.php

The last of the basic files is the theme functions file. You will set up a couple of functions to enable you to use certain features in your theme. Here is where you'll include your style sheet and where you can add your JavaScript files later on.

When you write things into your theme functions file, you don't always want the code to be run as soon as the theme is being set up because it might not be necessary. So in the following examples, I use some WordPress hook functions to make the code you add run only for certain actions. (Don't worry too much about the details; you'll learn about actions and hooks in much more detail in Chapter 6).

```
<?php
/**
 * Pro WordPress functions and definitions
 *
 * @package prowordpress
 */

if ( ! function_exists( 'prowordpress_setup' ) ) :

        function prowordpress_setup() {

                /**
                 * Add default posts and comments RSS feed links to head
                 */
                add_theme_support( 'automatic-feed-links' );
```

```
                    /**
                     * Enable support for Post Thumbnails
                     */
                    add_theme_support( 'post-thumbnails' );


            }

endif; // prowordpress_setup
add_action( 'after_setup_theme', 'prowordpress_setup' );
```

This example sits at the top of your theme and is the main theme setup function you'll use throughout your theme development. You'll keep adding to it as you go along. The function is wrapped in a conditional to see whether the function already exists, which prevents any issues when using child themes. Inside the function are two simple setup functions that you saw earlier in the chapter, and the hook function is in the last line. It tells WordPress that when the after_theme_setup action is performed, it should run the function that's in the second argument.

The only other bit of setup you'll do in the functions file is to include your style sheet. Instead of including the style sheet directly in the header.php file, you can do it programmatically using the wp_enqueue_style() function:

```
/**
 * Enqueue scripts and styles
 */
function prowordpress_scripts_and_styles() {
        wp_enqueue_style( 'style', get_stylesheet_uri() );
}
add_action( 'wp_enqueue_scripts', 'prowordpress_scripts_and_styles' );
```

The function is named scripts_and_styles because it is also where you include any JavaScript files. Next, you can start creating some page templates to use in the theme.

Starter Templates

Finally, you'll set up some templates that you'll likely use throughout your theme. For now, you'll just create them all with the same code snippet, so you just need to create one of the templates to copy from. The code you'll use is just to include the header and footer of your theme, so they'll all just look like this for now:

```
<?php get_header(); ?>

        <!-- Stuff will go here -->

<?php get_footer(); ?>
```

Using this as your code for each template, go ahead and create the following list of primary template files:

- index.php
- front-page.php
- home.php
- single.php
- page.php
- archive.php

Now your theme directory should look something like Figure 2-12 with all the main templates you've just created and your main folder structure.

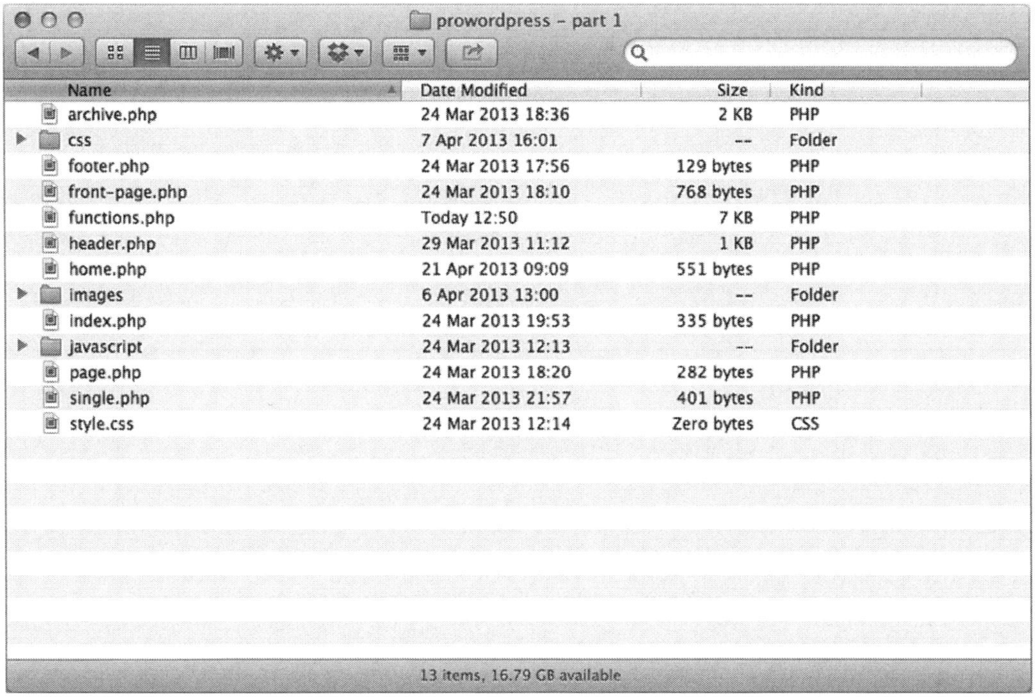

Name	Date Modified	Size	Kind
archive.php	24 Mar 2013 18:36	2 KB	PHP
▶ css	7 Apr 2013 16:01	--	Folder
footer.php	24 Mar 2013 17:56	129 bytes	PHP
front-page.php	24 Mar 2013 18:10	768 bytes	PHP
functions.php	Today 12:50	7 KB	PHP
header.php	29 Mar 2013 11:12	1 KB	PHP
home.php	21 Apr 2013 09:09	551 bytes	PHP
▶ images	6 Apr 2013 13:00	--	Folder
index.php	24 Mar 2013 19:53	335 bytes	PHP
▶ javascript	24 Mar 2013 12:13	---	Folder
page.php	24 Mar 2013 18:20	282 bytes	PHP
single.php	24 Mar 2013 21:57	401 bytes	PHP
style.css	24 Mar 2013 12:14	Zero bytes	CSS

13 items, 16.79 GB available

Figure 2-12. *The initial set of files for your theme*

The theme structure and templates just created can work out to be the base of many themes and is often my main starting point for any theme I develop. You'll build on this throughout the course of the book and develop an outstanding theme with plenty of advanced features that will give you a chance to work on the skills you learn along the way.

Summary

This chapter took a detailed look at how to structure a WordPress theme. You should now have a good understanding of how the basic template files work and how to manipulate them to create more custom and complex web sites.

You navigated the template hierarchy and learned a bit more about how the templates are loaded based on what content is being queried for. I covered in detail the new post formats that will allow you to customize the content of your posts in more detail and how to use custom template parts to do this in a tidier fashion to keep your theme maintainable.

You also looked at ways of managing your theme, how to include style sheets and JavaScript files, and use some best practices for structuring your theme folder. Finally, you put all this information to good use by starting to develop your custom theme, creating the starting point of what you'll develop throughout the book.

The next chapter digs into displaying content using the Loop and different ways of querying for content to create a dynamic web site.

CHAPTER 3

■ ■ ■

Content Options and the Loop

The Loop is what makes WordPress go. It's how all of the WordPress magic happens. It's the most important thing. Everything else is secondary.

—Justin Tadlock

This chapter explores the variety of ways of getting content into your WordPress themes. You'll take an in-depth look at querying for content in WordPress and how to output that content to your pages using The Loop and WordPress template tags (more functions). You'll also look at how to use the different functions available in WordPress to give you plenty of information about the current content to give classes and IDs to use in Cascading Style Sheets (CSS) and JavaScript for styling and giving interactivity to your site.

WP_Query

At the heart of WordPress is the query, or more accurately, WP_Query: the PHP class that holds the functionality you will use a lot in this chapter. The query can be created in a variety of ways, whether from the initial load when WordPress is generating a page or from a customize query being put together inside a template or plug-in. The WP_Query class handles all this information and more, giving you a lot of control over the content being returned, as well as holding information about how that content was requested in the first place, which is great for debugging, among other things.

The WP_Query class also handles a lot of things for you, such as security with MySQL requests, so you don't have to worry about it in your code. The WP_Query class doesn't make database requests; it acts as the main gateway through which you pass the parameters for your queries. Doing this means that WordPress can take care of the requests and give you a nice easy access point to query for content in the database.

The WP_Query class also makes creating queries a lot easier through modularity. It allows you to pass information through to the class in easy-to-read associative arrays, which means creating even the most complex queries becomes a lot more understandable. You'll have a look in more detail later in the chapter at how to create custom queries using the WP_Query class.

Before you start looking at how your content is generated, though, I want you to take a brief look at how WordPress initializes everything before you even output a single bit of HTML.

Constructing the Page

Before WordPress gets to any of the template pages you created in the second chapter, it has to go through a series of initializations to make sure it returns the correct page and content. If you've ever looked at the files WordPress contains, you'll notice that there are a lot! Just counting the PHP and JavaScript (JS) files in the main WordPress folder and wp-includes folders only (not the admin or content folders, which go into displaying content); there are well over 200 files that go into creating the WordPress content management system (CMS).

45

It all begins with one file, though; every request made to a WordPress web site goes through the index.php file. And here it is:

```php
<?php
/**
 * Front to the WordPress application. This file doesn't do anything, but loads
 * wp-blog-header.php which does and tells WordPress to load the theme.
 *
 * @package WordPress
 */

/**
 * Tells WordPress to load the WordPress theme and output it.
 *
 * @var bool
 */
define('WP_USE_THEMES', true);

/** Loads the WordPress Environment and Template */
```

require('./wp-blog-header.php');As the comments state this file mainly does nothing, but there are two lines that start you off, setting up the WP_USE_THEMES constant and then including another PHP file, the wp-blog-header.php file. Which can be seen here:

```php
<?php
/**
 * Loads the WordPress environment and template.
 *
 * @package WordPress
 */

if ( !isset($wp_did_header) ) {

        $wp_did_header = true;

        require_once( dirname( __FILE__ ) . '/wp-load.php' );

        wp();

        require_once( ABSPATH . WPINC . '/template-loader.php' );

}
```

This is where it gets a bit more interesting. The inclusion of wp-load.php here basically sets up WordPress. The wp-load file sets up the database connection and a whole load of other things (such as the settings for the theme) and includes most of the other files that are necessary for WordPress to work. (Don't worry; I'm not going to show you every PHP file in WordPress—just these two for now.) After wp-load has done its work, the wp() function is called, which sets up the main query by adding the current query parameters to the main WP_Query instance in use.

Get Query Parameters

The query parameters are based on two main things: the settings in WordPress and the page GET/PATHINFO data. The page GET/PATHINFO data is the information passed in via the URL navigated to. The first thing most people do when they set up WordPress is to change the permalinks to 'pretty permalinks', which means that instead of this:

example.com?p=hello-world

you get this:

example.com/hello-world

But if you take a quick look at the default permalinks in WordPress, what you'll see is the GET parameters that you are passing into your queries. (You'll learn more later in the chapter, when I discuss editing The Loop with queries.)

Decide on Template File

After the query parameters have been set and passed through to the main WP_Query object, the template-loader.php file can then use the conditional tags that were covered in the last chapter to work out what template file to use. The decision is based on what type of query will be run and what the available templates are in the current theme. As covered in Chapter 2, this is where the template hierarchy comes into play, with WordPress using it to decide which template in the theme it should be loading.

Following is the function that retrieves the correct template to display a page. If you remember the discussion of how you can specify templates for a certain page in Chapter 2, you should be able to see how the template is loaded based on the order they are looked for and the available files in the theme:

```php
/**
 * Retrieve path of page template in current or parent template.
 *
 * Will first look for the specifically assigned page template
 * The will search for 'page-{slug}.php' followed by 'page-id.php'
 * and finally 'page.php'
 *
 * @since 1.5.0
 *
 * @return string
 */
function get_page_template() {
        $id = get_queried_object_id();
        $template = get_page_template_slug();
        $pagename = get_query_var('pagename');

        if ( ! $pagename && $id ) {
                // If a static page is set as the front page, $pagename will not be set. Retrieve it
                from the queried object
                $post = get_queried_object();
                $pagename = $post->post_name;
        }
```

```php
    $templates = array();
    if ( $template && 0 === validate_file( $template ) )
            $templates[] = $template;
    if ( $pagename )
            $templates[] = "page-$pagename.php";
    if ( $id )
            $templates[] = "page-$id.php";
    $templates[] = 'page.php';

    return get_query_template( 'page', $templates );
}
```

So now that the page template loaded, you can actually display the content, which is where you finally get to tackle the WordPress Loop.

The Loop

As shown by the quote at the start of the chapter, the Loop in WordPress is a pretty crucial area. There is a lot more to the Loop than just these few lines of code:

```php
<?php
if( have_posts() ): while( have_posts() ): the_post();
        // Stuff...
endwhile; endif;
?>
```

So to take a proper look at the Loop, I will focus on the main two parts of it—its two functions:

- have_posts()
- the_post()

The remainder of the Loop is an if and a while loop using the alternative control structure in PHP, as discussed in the opening chapter. I've already spoken a bit about the WP_Query class in this chapter, but here's a first actual look at functions from the class. The have_posts() and the_post() functions are actually just functional wrappers around the WP_Query object. If used as they are here, the functions simply call the method on the main WP_Query object currently in use.

have_posts

The have_posts() function is the first of the two functions in the Loop; notice that it comes up twice as well. The function of have_posts() is actually pretty self-explanatory: it checks a Loop counter to see whether there are posts available to output; if so, it returns true and if not, it returns false. Simple. This is why it is used twice in the main Loop code you often see. If the function returns false the first time (in the if statement), it means there are no posts to display. It is where you'll often see an else with an error message as well:

```php
<?php else : ?>

        <p>Apologies, but no results were found for the requested archive.</p>

<?php endif; ?>
```

In the `while` loop, it will allow you to continue running the code inside the Loop until the function returns `false`. It also has one last little function. When it finds that there are no more posts to display, it will return `false` but also call `rewind_posts()` so that WordPress is ready to set up another loop should it need to. You'll look more at resetting the query later in the chapter.

the_post()

This is the function that does all the hard work; when you call `the_post` it goes through the current posts array and sets up the post data that gets used in the template tags so you can start crafting your templates. It also sets up the `global $post` variable and advances the loop counter ready to access the next post when `the_post` is called again (in the next iteration of the `while` loop).

Do You Need to "Loop" Every Time?

This is a question I've asked a few times: do I always need to have an `if` statement and `while` loop when accessing the post data? The simple answer is no, to be honest. If you're accessing a page that you know will always return only one "post" and not a series of posts, it's perfectly fine to call `the_post()` only at the beginning of your template so that you have access to the post data and template tags.

However, be careful with this use because it is not a convention in WordPress, and if you plan to sell your themes or market them in the themes directory, my advice is to stick with the conventional Loop format. Conventions happen for a reason because they help others pick up code more easily, which aids collaboration. So sticking to a convention such as this would be far easier and more helpful to the overall WordPress community. Who knows—there might come a time when you need help from other WordPress developers, and that tiny difference in your code could ensure they find it a lot easier to help.

Custom and Dynamic Content with Queries

Now you know how the Loop works and how the data is collected, let's have a look at the different ways of running custom queries to create pages with the data you want. The ability to manipulate the query such as this is one of the more powerful parts of WordPress. You can even run multiple queries and loops on the same page to create pages made up of a variety of different types of content.

This section discusses the various ways you can create custom content for your sites. First, I'll introduce you to the main four methods of manipulating the WordPress query. Then you'll take a look at some examples of when you might want to use them and for what circumstances. Finally, you'll look at some advanced examples of custom queries so you really can see the power you have in WordPress.

Methods of Querying in WordPress

WordPress gives you three functions to use when you want to customize the query in your templates:

- `query_posts()`
- `get_posts()`
- creating a new `WP_Query` instance

You'll look at each function in turn; in the rest of the section, you'll look at when these functions can or should be used.

query_posts()

If you take a look at what the WordPress Codex has to say about `query_posts()`, it's mostly made up of warnings about when and when not to use the `query_posts()` function. I'll discuss this in more detail later, but for now let's look at how to use the function itself. The `query_posts()` function takes an argument made up of query parameters. It can do it in two ways. The first is with an array of arguments like this:

```
$args = array(
        'cat' => 5,
        'posts_per_page' => 2,
        'order' => 'ASC'
);
query_posts($args);
```

The second way is in a string of parameters (discussed in Chapter 1):

```
$args = "cat=5&posts_per_page=2&order=ASC";
query_posts($args);
```

This code will modify the main query and allow you to use the WordPress Loop normally without any modifications. Here's a look at it in action:

```
query_posts("cat=5" );

if( have_posts() ): while( have_posts() ): the_post();

        // Do stuff

endwhile; endif;
```

As you can see, I made no edits to the regular WordPress Loop; I just added the `query_posts()` function above it. The parameters passed will simply run a query returning all posts that are in the category with the ID of 5.

get_posts()

Another way of querying in WordPress is by using `get_posts()`. The difference here is that `get_posts()` returns an array of post objects as the result for you to manipulate. To go through the data this time, you need to loop through the result in a slightly different way from the other options:

```
$new_posts = get_posts( $args );

foreach ( $new_posts as $post ):

        setup_postdata($post);

        // Do stuff - using normal template tags

endforeach;

wp_reset_postdata();
```

In the preceding example, I used a standard foreach loop in PHP to go through the array. The important part is to use $post as the value argument in the foreach loop. By doing this, it allows you to use the setup_postdata() function to give you the template tags to use as normal. However, when this method is used, the main post data from the default query is overwritten. When you do this, you need to reset the data so that functions you may want to use later on that relate to the main query don't get caught up with the leftover data from your modified query. That's where the wp_reset_postdata() function comes in. (You'll be taking a more detailed look at resetting things in WordPress later on in the chapter.)

If you don't use the setup_postdata() function to make the template tags available, you need to use the raw data returned by the get_posts() function as follows:

```
$new_posts = get_posts( $args );

foreach ( $new_posts as $post ):

        echo '<h1>'.$post->post_title.'</h1>';

        echo $post->post_content; // raw
        echo apply_filters('the_content', $post->post_content); // formatted

endforeach;
```

The preceding code shows how to access the raw data through the post variable you get from the get_posts() query. I also included two ways of outputting the content data. The first gets the raw data as you've written it into the content editor, so if you leave some of the formatting to WordPress (such as p tags), you'll need to use the apply_filters() function to process the content data the same way WordPress does when it sets up the post data as normal.

One more thing to note about get_posts() is that although it does take many of the same arguments as the previous two query types, there are a few subtle differences. For instance, to change the number of posts queried for, use numberposts instead of posts_per_page. (For a full list of parameters, take a look at http://wp-themes-book.com/03001.)

WP_Query

To loop with a WP_Query object, you use query parameters as arguments when creating a new instance of the WP_Query class. It's similar to the way in which you use query_posts()—both functions accept the same parameters—but you use the new constructor and pass the result into a variable that looks like this:

```
$new_query = new WP_Query( $args );

if( $new_query->have_posts() ): while( $new_query->have_posts() ):  $new_query->the_post();

        // Do stuff - with normal template tags

endwhile; endif;
```

The $new_query variable now becomes an instance of the WP_Query class. To set up your loop instead of calling have_posts() and the_post() functions as usual, you need to call them as methods of the new instance of the class you created $new_query->have_posts. This then gives you use of the same template and conditional tags used before in a regular loop.

Modifying the Default Query

Now you'll look at customizing the queries you create using the methods just discussed. The first way of customizing content is to modify the default query, the one that I talked about that gets created based on the settings and page URL.

But if the query is being created automatically, how can you modify it? The query parameters are also stored in a variable in WordPress that you can access in your template files: the $query_string global. This is one of those variables created by the WP_Query class early on in the setup of the initial page load (I told you it would come in handy):

```
// access the global variable which stores the default query string
global $query_string;

query_posts( $query_string . "&cat=-5" );

if( have_posts() ): while( have_posts() ): the_post();

        // Do stuff

endwhile; endif;
```

The preceding code takes the $query_string variable and uses query_posts()—more on that in a second. You can do this because the $query_string quite literally does exactly what it says on the tin: it's a string containing the current query that will be run on the database. You create the new query by simply concatenating more query parameters to the end of the default string and then pass it as the argument to the query_posts() function.

■ **Note** Remember to start your additional parameters with an ampersand (&) as you add to the current query parameters; think of it as 'query_string' & 'new parameters'.

I already mentioned that there lots of caveats to be aware of when using the query_posts() function. It is not the most preferred or efficient method of setting up a new query in WordPress. It is, however, the best method of modifying a default query when you're already in the page template. If you want to intercept the query before you get to the template, however, you can use the pre_get_posts hook, which is called after the query variable is built, but before the query is actually run by WordPress. This method does come with a few caveats. Because the query has yet to be run, there are a lot of functions that aren't available (namely, the is_front_page() conditional function), but is_home() is available, so you can use it for tasks such as modifying what appears on the post listing page.

Here's an example of using the hook to remove a category from display in the main posts list:

```
function exclude_category( $query ) {
    if ( $query->is_home() && $query->is_main_query() ) {
        $query->set( 'cat', '-5' );
    }
}

add_action( 'pre_get_posts', 'exclude_category' );
```

The $query object is the main instance of the WP_Query; the object variable is passed in by reference here, so the function doesn't need to return the variable after you've modified it—you're working with the $query object itself. Also notice that you're using more methods of the WP_Query object to check the conditional functions and to add an extra parameter using the set method (it just takes the parameter you want to set and the value to set it to as two arguments of the function).

Multiple Loops

When you build a web site, there will be times when you want to display multiple types of content on the same page. As you can imagine, the easiest way of doing this is to use multiple queries on the same page.

The codex seems a little confusing on this subject; it says that it is perfectly okay to use the query_posts() function to create a new query. I say that this should absolutely not be the case, however. Because query_posts() overwrites the main query, you lose all the information for the current query, information that might be useful if you need to do things after the second loop has been used. The better way is to create a new instance of the WP_Query class and run the second loop with that object. The bonus of creating a brand-new WP_Query is that you get all the useful information along with it as well.

Now let's get to an example of creating a secondary loop in the template with the WP_Query class:

```
if( have_posts() ): while( have_posts() ): the_post();
        // Do stuff
endwhile; endif;

$secondary_query = new WP_Query( $args );

if( $ secondary_query->have_posts() ): while( $ secondary_query->have_posts() ): $ secondary_query->the_post();
        // Do stuff - with normal template tags
endwhile; endif;

wp_reset_postdata();
```

It doesn't have to stop at just a secondary loop; by using the new WP_Query instance you can create as many queries as you like on a page. Be cautious, however, because for each new query created you are making an extra MySQL request on the database, and this can hamper performance.

Remember that when you're creating multiple loops you should always ensure that you reset the postdata or the query as soon as your new query has finished in order to put back the default query.

Resetting the Loop

Even with the WP_Query method of creating new loops, you still need to reset the postdata back to the default query. In fact, any time you change what will be output by the template tags away from that default query, you need to reset it. In the previous multiple loops example, I used the wp_reset_postdata() function after the secondary loop to ensure that the template tags and $post variable go back to reflect the default query.

There are three functions you can use to reset the query and postdata:

- wp_reset_postdata()
- wp_reset_query()
- rewind_posts()

wp_reset_postdata()

First up is the wp_reset_postdata() function (discussed earlier). This function is simple and easy to use; it just needs to be called after the end of any additional or custom loops you create and requires no parameters.

wp_reset_query()

Used in exactly the same way as the wp_reset_postdata() function, this should be called straight after a custom loop and with no passed parameters. It is a function created specifically for use when modifying the query with the query_posts() function. As you already know, query_posts() modifies the main query, so this function is used specifically to counter that action and get you back to the main query you started with when WordPress was initialized.

If you take a look at the latest core files and find these functions in includes/query.php, you'll find that wp_reset_query() actually calls the wp_reset_postdata() function. The important thing to note is that the wp_reset_query() function additionally resets the global query variable to the initial default query by overwriting it with the main query global. As shown in the following comments, this function was created purely to fix bugs when the query_posts() function gets used (which is why I strongly advise against its use unless you want to modify the main query).

```
/**
 * Destroy the previous query and set up a new query.
 *
 * This should be used after {@link query_posts()} and before another {@link
 * query_posts()}. This will remove obscure bugs that occur when the previous
 * wp_query object is not destroyed properly before another is set up.
 *
 * @since 2.3.0
 * @uses $wp_query
 */
function wp_reset_query() {
        $GLOBALS['wp_query'] = $GLOBALS['wp_the_query'];
        wp_reset_postdata();
}

/**
 * After looping through a separate query, this function restores
 * the $post global to the current post in the main query
 *
 * @since 3.0.0
 * @uses $wp_query
 */
function wp_reset_postdata() {
        global $wp_query;
        if ( !empty($wp_query->post) ) {
                $GLOBALS['post'] = $wp_query->post;
                setup_postdata($wp_query->post);
        }
}
```

rewind_posts()

This function is less about resetting the query as it is about resetting the Loop so you can run it again somewhere else in the page. For instance, if you were to create an FAQ page with a listing at the top of the page of each post title with links to the content of the post farther down the page, you could call the loop once and then run rewind_posts() after your first loop before starting again farther down the page. Here's an example:

```php
<?php if( have_posts() ): while( have_posts() ): the_post(); ?>
        <h2><a href="#faq-<?php the_ID(); ?>"><?php the_title(); ?></a></h2>
<?php endwhile; endif; ?>


<?php rewind_posts(); ?>


<?php if( have_posts() ): while( have_posts() ): the_post(); ?>
        <article id="faq-<?php the_ID(); ?>">
                <h3><?php the_title(); ?></h3>
                <?php the_content(); ?>
        </article>
<?php endwhile; endif; ?>
```

Multiple Loops with get_posts()

You can also use get_posts() to create a secondary loop of content. The usual use for get_posts() is when you require the data to be used in PHP, possibly for creating some new functionality through the functions file or in a plug-in, for instance. When creating a secondary loop to get secondary content for a page, I usually go with the WP_Query option, but if I'm getting only a small amount of data, such as listing the post titles of some related posts, get_posts() can be a good option.

The following example is a loop using get_posts() at the base of a single post page, showing posts from the current posts category:

```php
<?php if( have_posts() ): while( have_posts() ): the_post(); ?>
                <div <?php post_class(); ?>>
                        <h2><?php the_title(); ?></h2>
                        <p><?php the_content(); ?></p>
                </div>
        <?php endwhile; ?>
        <p>Sorry that post could not be found</p>

<?php endif; ?>

<div class="related-posts">
        <h2>Related Posts</h2>

        <?php
        // globalise the post
        global $post;
        // get the categories the post is in
        $cats = get_the_category( $post->ID );
        $cat_ids = array(); // empty array to put the IDs into
```

```
        // Loop through the categories and store the IDs in an array
        foreach( $cats as $cat ):
                $cat_ids[] = $cat->term_id;
        endforeach;
        // Set up the arguments for the query
        $args = array(
                                        'post_type' => 'post',
                                        'category__in'          => $cat_ids,
                        );
        // Run the query
        $related_posts = get_posts($args); ?>

        <ul id="related-posts">
                <?php foreach( $related_posts as $related ): ?>
                        <li><a href="<?php echo get_permalink( $related->ID ); ?>"><?php echo
                        $related->post_title; ?></a></li>
                <?php endforeach; ?>
        </ul>

</div>
```

The preceding code could be created using a WP_Query just as easily, but this way you don't overwrite the current global post or the function of the template tags because the result of the additional query is stored in the $related_posts variable only.

Advanced Queries

Now that you know how to create queries in themes correctly and how and when to run certain types of queries, let's take a look at some of the more advanced queries you can create with the power of the WordPress query. The amount of control you have over the posts you can query for in WordPress is getting pretty impressive, so here is an advanced look at some of the complex queries you can create to get use extremely specific information from the database.

There are two ways to pass arguments into a new query: with an array or as a query string. To create more complex queries, the best method of doing this is with arrays because many more detailed options can be passed and in multiple levels with associative arrays.

■ **Note**   Most of the queries you'll look at in this section can be created with either a new WP_Query object or with the query_posts() function. However I'll be opting for the much more robust WP_Query object option.

First take a look at a standard custom query using the WP_Query class:

```
$args = array (
                'post_type' => 'post',
                'cat'       => '5',
                'orderby'   => 'title',
                'order'     => 'desc',
        );
$new_query = new WP_Query($args);
```

That's the first simple query using an associative array with only one level of parameters. Next, you'll see how you can handle a multiple category query using an array of IDs passed as one of the parameters:

```
// Get posts which are in categories 2 and 6
$args = array (
                'post_type'      => 'post',
                'orderby'        => 'title',
                'order'          => 'desc',
                'category__and' => array( 2, 6 ),
        );
$new_query = new WP_Query($args);
```

Okay, still not that advanced and not that impressive, but it does get better, I promise.

Taxonomy Queries

The next chapter covers how to create and manage custom post types and taxonomies, but in this chapter I'll briefly discuss how to query for them using more advanced taxonomy queries.

With the tax_query parameter in the query, you can start to query based on a range of different possibilities. The new tax_query parameter was introduced in version 3.1 and takes as its arguments an array of arrays (I told you it was going to get more complex). But it wasn't done to create added complexity; it actually means that you can query multiple taxonomies and compare them with each other.

For instance, if you had a movie review web site and wanted to look for a review about a sci-fi movie with a certain actor, you could use the following query:

```
// Get review posts which are in the category sci-fi and actors included Matt LeBlanc and Heather Graham
$args = array (
                'post_type' => 'review',
                'tax_query' => array(
                        'relation' => 'AND',
                        array (
                                'taxonomy' => 'genre',
                                'field'    => 'slug',
                                'terms'    => 'sci-fi',
                        ),
                        array (
                                'taxonomy' => 'actor',
                                'field'    => 'slug',
                                'terms'    => array('matt-leblanc','heather-graham'),
                                'operator' => 'IN',
                        ),
                ),
        );
$new_query = new WP_Query($args);
```

It may have sounded complex to start with, but just look at how simple that code makes it look. Inside the tax_query parameter you have a couple of arrays to look for each of the taxonomies you're after. You also have the relation parameter, which goes at the first level of the tax_query and states how to compare the included taxonomies. In this case, you used AND because you want all posts that come under both categories (the other option, OR, returns the posts that are in either taxonomy).

Metadata Queries

In the next chapter, you'll learn to create custom fields for posts; here you'll look at how to query for them. WordPress has a built-in capability to add custom metadata to a post, so even before you get to the next chapter you can start applying this code to what you already created in WordPress.

Similar to the tax_query parameter, the meta_query parameter was added to the query parameters in version 3.1. This powerful query parameter allows you to do a multitude of comparisons on the metadata of your posts to return posts with extreme precision.

Although meta queries have been around in WordPress for a while, the new meta_query parameter adds a lot more complexity, but in a very easy-to-see-and-understand manner like the tax_query. Here's a regular meta query you might have seen in earlier WordPress versions:

```
$args = array (
            'post_type'  => 'any',
            'meta_key'   => 'title',
            'meta_value' => 'desc',
       );
$new_query = new WP_Query($args);
```

That query simply returns any posts with the meta x set to y. But with the new meta query, you can get a lot more complex. You can start to query multiple metadata and compare it with each other and use conditional operators, as you did with the taxonomy queries:

```
$args = array (
            'post_type'  => 'any',
            'meta_query' => array(
                 array (
                         'key'     => 'publisher',
                         'value'   => 'Marvel',
                         'compare' => '=',
                 ),
                 array (
                         'key'     => 'price',
                         'value'   => array( 50, 100 ),
                         'type'    => 'numeric',
                         'compare' => 'BETWEEN',
                 ),
            ),
       );
$new_query = new WP_Query($args);
```

For a full list of the comparison operators available and how to use them in the meta_query, take a look at the WordPress codex, which has a full list and more detail on how to use them:
http://wp-themes-book.com/03002

The possibilities that this type of querying, along with the previous taxonomy queries, give you is fantastic. These queries allow you to give great control to your users through filtering the content on the site or advanced searching options, for instance.

Pagination with Custom Queries

Unfortunately, one thing you do lose when you're creating a custom query for a page is the ability to do pagination automatically. If you are modifying the current query on the page, you should be all right, but if you're manipulating the query entirely, you need to take care of the pagination yourself.

Fortunately, pagination is really simple to do. As WordPress does with the $query_string variable it uses to store the current default query string for the page, it also sets up a global variable for the current page number trying to be accessed: the $paged variable. Here's how to use the $paged global variable to add back pagination to your page with a custom query:

```
global $paged; // globalize the paged variable.

query_posts('post_type=review&posts_per_page=4&paged='.$paged);

if( have_posts() ):
        while( have_posts() ): the_post();
                // Do stuff...
        endwhile;

        next_posts_link();
        previous_posts_link();
endif;
```

■ **Note** The previous_posts_link and next_posts_link page navigation links still work normally and return a link only if there are next or previous posts to display.

Properties and Global Variables

Along with WP_Query, you get a lot of handy properties from the WP_Query class and global variables that you can use in your theme for various development and debugging purposes. These properties and globals should never be altered inside your template files, but they are extremely useful during development and debugging.

WP_Query Properties

You used the WP_Query a lot in this chapter; after all, it does power most of the WordPress content in your themes. It is also good to use because of the amount of information it gives you access to for help throughout development. The WP_Query contains a lot of properties with information about the current query and posts it has returned. To interact with these properties, you use a series of methods of the WP_Query class, a few of which you've seen already. Methods such as have_posts, the_post, and rewind_posts are all methods of the WP_Query class and can be used from any object of the class you create.

Here are some of the more useful properties that can come in handy when building themes:

- **$query**: The query string passed to the query object.

- **$query_vars**: An associative array of the full list of query vars and values, such as the array of arguments you can pass to your query constructors.

- **$posts**: Holds the requested posts from your current query. It is rarely needed because it is the data used in loop(s).

- **$post_count**: Holds the number of posts being displayed. It can come in handy on a paginated page to see whether you have a full page worth of posts or the number of the last few posts.

- **$found_posts**: Total number of posts found from the query ignoring any pagination limits (posts_per_page and numberposts).

- **$max_num_pages**: Number of pages based on the number of found posts and the pagination limit.

Globals

You have seen a variety of global variables get used in one form or another in this chapter. You just used the $paged global which stores the current page number you're on, and earlier you used the $query_string global to get the current query in a template file. Apart from these global variables there are a lot of other globals set by WordPress.

To access a global variable in WordPress, you must first globalize the variable using the global keyword, which allows access to the global data from inside the template. If you don't globalize the variable, you create a new variable entirely that could lead to issues further along the line.

```
global $paged;
```

A full list and explanation can be found at http://wp-themes-book.com/03003, but here are a few globals that might come in handy throughout theme development:

- **$post**: The current $post object, it stores all the information about the current post and is used by the various template tags to output the information neatly. This variable is handy if odd data show up and you want to check a full list of the entire post data.

- **$authordata**: All the available data about the author of the current post.

- **$wp_query**: All the data referring to the default query; it gets overwritten by query_posts, but other functions should leave it alone.

- **$wp**: Holds all the data relating to the initialization of the WordPress instance.

- **$wpdb**: The global object for accessing the database, this global becomes much more useful in plug-in territory (discussed later in the book).

- **$wp_rewrite**: Holds all the current information on what rewrite rules apply to the site; used primarily for the pretty permalinks you see in WordPress. It is possible to add to them when creating new post types (you'll find out about that in the next chapter).

- **$query_string**: Holds the current query for the page.

- **$paged**: Holds the current page number; if on the first page. $paged is set to 0.

Although these globals come in handy throughout theme development, they should never be modified. The information stored in the globals can be used for debugging and access purposes only; to use and modify data stored in the globals, use the functions provided in WordPress.

Template Tags

Now you can start to look at the content of your themes. The WordPress template tags are a simple way to access all the content you store in WordPress and get it into your themes. Again the template tags; although they have the name "tags," they are still just functions. They are built into the WordPress core and process, and return or output the content stored in the database. Here's how the WordPress codex describes the template tags:

> [W]hen you view your WordPress [theme], it doesn't say "My Blog Name" in the template file. In fact, it has a bunch of strange arrows and parentheses and words that don't make much sense.

This is an example of a template tag: `http://wp-themes-book.com/03004`. I'm sure by now you can recognize a template tag and understand what it allows you to do. The next section takes an in-depth look into how the template tags work, how to modify their output, and where you can use them in your templates.

Template Tag Varieties

There are hundreds of template tags available for you to use in your themes. They can be used to get data about the current post, get comment information, list categories and tags, show a limitless number of settings, and even sometimes provide functionality not related to content.

Here I'll discuss some of the main groups of template tags and show some examples of the useful functions in these groups—ones that help you create really dynamic themes based on every detail you can set in the WordPress admin. For a full list of template tags, go to `http://wp-themes-book.com/03005` to view more information and get the full list of tags that belong to each of these groups. To see more functions available to you in WordPress, take a look at `http://wp-themes-book.com/03006` for a nicely organized list of every available function.

General Tags, Including Site Information and Settings

The tags I'm denoting as "general" are those that don't really have anything to do with the content, so to speak, of your site. Instead, they deal with things like settings or information about the site that often won't change. Tags such as these can come in very handy for programmatically getting at information about the current site without hard-coding it into the templates, which is extremely important when you have separate dev/live sites (which you should have by the way; it's 2013, after all).

Here I'll discuss one tag in particular: the `bloginfo()` tag. I've used this tag countless times throughout multiple templates in all my themes. It's extremely useful because, as the name suggests, it returns information about the site, based on the parameter you pass it. For instance, you can get the name of your blog, which you set in the Settings ➤ General page in the admin.

```
bloginfo('name');
```

The function then outputs the value directly to the HTML; no need for the "echo" PHP command. I use it all the time to get the current template directory for the site, so I can output assets such as JS files or images; for example, here's how I access a logo image from the `template` directory:

```
<img src="<?php bloginfo('template_directory'); ?>/images/logo.png" alt="Site logo" />
```

For a full list of the information that just this one function can output, take a look at the function reference page here: `http://wp-themes-book.com/03007`. Other functions that come under the "general" group would-be template include `get_header()`, `get_footer()`, and `get_sidebar()`; as well as functions such as `wp_title()` that you can use to generate a title in the head of your blog (refer to Chapter 2).

Post Tags

The post tags are probably the most used functions in WordPress templates (no surprise) because they are the means for getting your content out into the world. Tags such as the_title(), the_content(), and the_excerpt() are just a few examples of the ones you'll most likely see in every WordPress theme.

A tag you might not see very often is the_title_attribute(), which is a function used to return the title of the post, but with HTML tags stripped and characters encoded properly for use in HTML attributes. Here's an example:

```
<h2><a href="<?php the_permalink(); ?>" title="<?php the_title_attribute(); ?>"><?php the_title(); ?></a></h2>
```

Comment Tags

If you've ever built a blog before (or a web site with a commenting functionality), you most likely know a bit about the comment tags in WordPress. Similar to the post tags, the comment tags let you get at almost every bit of information attached to a comment. The main function you'll be seeing in your themes is wp_list_comments(). This is the main template tag for displaying all the comments attached to a post. It also allows you to pass in a set of arguments (in an array) to customize how the comments will be listed:

```
<?php $args = array(
            'style'       => 'ul',
            'per_page'    => 10,
            'avatar_size' => 50,
        );

wp_list_comments($args); ?>
```

Category Tags

There are two types of category tags in WordPress: those that return categories in relation to the current post and those that return information on categories in general. A function such as the_category() is used inside the loop to output categories that the current post belongs to, and functions such as wp_list_categories() is used to list all categories in the site. Note that when referring to categories here, I am explicitly talking about the post categories taxonomy, not taxonomies in general. There are functions to deal with taxonomies, including the post categories (discussed in more detail in Chapter 4).

For now, take a look at the wp_list_categories() function, which can give you a list of all the categories in WordPress and can be heavily customized again by passing in a few arguments:

```
<?php $args = array(
        'orderby'       => 'count',
        'order'         => 'ASC',
        'style'         => 'list',
        'show_count'    => 1,
        'hide_empty'    => 0,
        'title_li'      => '',
        'number'        => 10,
        'depth'         => -1,
);

wp_list_categories( $args );
?>
```

This list of arguments means that the category list is displayed in a series of <li> tags (you have to provide the wrapper <ul> or <ol>), is ordered by the number of posts in each category, and shows the number of posts in each category while not hiding any empty categories. You also set title_li to be a blank string so it doesn't give you an extra <li> tag with a title for the list in, and you limit the number of categories to display to ten. The depth argument lets you determine how many levels down the hierarchy of categories you want to go. You can set it to a positive number to explicitly set a number of levels, or pass it -1 to tell the function to list all categories and show them all as a flat list without worrying what categories are children or parents.

Author Tags

The author tags can be used to output information on the author of a current post or get information on authors on the web site. Note that the author functions don't relate to the WordPress role "author"; they are aimed at any WordPress user that has been attached to a post or piece of content as the "author".

The most obvious author function is to list the name as part of what could be called a *byline* (taken from newspaper terminology). You want to show the name of the author alongside the articles published date; here's an example:

```
<header>
        <h1><?php the_title(); ?></h1>
        <p class="byline">by <?php the_author(); ?> | <?php echo get_the_date(); ?></p>
</header>
```

Or you may want to give site visitors a link to view more posts by the author of the current post they're reading.

```
<p class="more-posts">More posts by <?php the_author_posts_link(); ?></p>
```

Link Tags

A link tag can be classed as any tag that interacts with a link in some form or another. If it returns a URL or an HTML link tag, it can go into this group. That means that the permalink functions get_permalink() and the_permalink() could be grouped here. Because these functions are familiar to many, let's discuss a few different ones.

There are functions to return links for pagination purposes, such as next_posts_link() and previous_posts_link(); or functions that go to the next and previous post, such as next_post_link() and previous_post_link(). A function I use quite often when I create a home page link via the site logo or when I'm linking to the home page from another part of the template is the home_url() function. I know you could use a simple slash (/) to link back to the relative home page on the site, but what if that sometimes doesn't cut it? The home_url() function is great for that, and it means all links in my sites are maintained programmatically, not manually. It saves a lot of changes if something messes up and has to be changed in a number of places.

Here's an example of the function being used in a code snippet similar to the one used earlier:

```
<h1><a href="<?php home_url('/'); ?>"><img src="<?php bloginfo('template_directory'); ?>/images/logo.png"
alt="Site logo" /></a></h1>
```

Menu Tags

Menu tags can be used to output a custom menu for your WordPress theme. In WordPress 3.0, custom menus were introduced so you could create a menu for your site to include links to any content on the site and even add custom links.

To output a custom menu in your theme, you can use the template tag wp_nav_menu() that, like many other tags, takes a series of arguments. The most important argument is theme_location, which requires it to be defined in your theme for the menu to be attached to. There are fallbacks in place to output a custom menu if you do not create a theme_location, but it could result in the easy overriding of a nav menu where you don't want it. So the best option is to register a navigation menu location to be used. Here's how you can do it:

```php
// Register the menu location in your functions.php file
register_nav_menus( array(
        'primary' => __( 'Primary Menu', 'prowordpress' ),
) );

<?php
// To be able to access the menu in your templates through the wp_nav_menu function
wp_nav_menu( array('theme_location' => 'primary', 'container' => '' ));
?>
```

I also used another argument in the wp_nav_menu() function called 'container' and passed it an empty string because normally the function will output the menu inside a <div> tag. If you want to control that yourself or not have the menu wrapped at all, however, the easy way to do so is by passing an empty string to the argument.

Template Tags and the Loop

Now you can look at where certain tags can be used. When I talk about location in the template, I mean which tags must be used inside of the Loop and which ones can be used outside.

The basic rule is that any template tag relating to post-specific content must be used inside the Loop, and tags that hold information about the web site itself can be used anywhere in the templates where they're needed.

Other location-specific tags include the comment information tags that need to be included inside the loop for returning comments and the get_search_query() tag that, for obvious reasons, is only really worthwhile when used on a search page.

■ **Note**   There are some exceptions to the rule that has to do with post–specific template tags because some tags accept a post ID parameter, which means they can return information based on the ID passed.

Display, Return, or Both

The plethora of template tags used in WordPress all operate in one of two ways: they echo out the information or return in PHP. And, as the heading title suggests, some functions can do both.

The majority of tags that will output the information straight to HTML are ones that begin with the. Here's an example:

- the_title()
- the_content()
- the_permalink()

All these functions echo out HTML directly to the page. You'll often find them used in the templates looking something like this:

```php
<h1><a href="<?php the_permalink(); ?>"><?php the_title(); ?></a></h1>

<?php the_content(); ?>
```

Notice that two functions are put inside of HTML, and one of them is left out of any HTML tags entirely. The reason is that the the_content() function uses a content filter on the data entered in to the CMS to add <p> tags and other formatting that the user can add through the edit screen.

I chose those three template tags because they also have alternative tags that instead return the data as PHP. These tags can usually be identified by the get keyword at the beginning of the function. Alternatives to the three functions are these:

- get_the_title()

- get_the_content()

- get_permalink()

Each of these functions returns the information to PHP so they must be echoed out using one of the PHP print functions (echo, print, and so on). Two of these are also unique functions in that they can be used inside or outside the loop; the get_the_title() and get_permalink() functions take an optional parameter of the post ID that you want to get the information from. The parameter is optional because when the tag is used within the Loop, the post ID will be assumed from the current post being accessed.

Finally, there are a few template tags that allow you to choose whether the data returned is either output directly to the HTML or returned as PHP. One of these is the the_date() function that takes a Boolean parameter (among its other parameters) that asks whether or not to echo or return the data from the tag.

Passing Tag Parameters

As discussed in Chapter 1, there are a variety of ways to pass parameters to functions in WordPress, and the template tags are no different. Some template tags don't require any parameters, many have optional parameters that are used to modify or add to the content being output, and some require mandatory parameters to return specific data.

Remember that certain template tags must be used in accordance with certain parameter formats and cannot be interchanged with other formats, such as query string parameters. This is a slightly confusing standard set by WordPress, but it's fairly easy to see how each template tag should be used by checking with the codex. Most functions are listed with the parameters they take and the format in which they must be passed (http://wp-themes-book.com/03008). One rule of thumb is that functions with a smaller number of parameters usually require them to be passed with PHP function–style parameters, and ones with a larger number of parameters can use the array- or query string–style parameters.

Many template tags with parameters often have defaults set, so they don't need to be passed to the function. When using tags with PHP function–style parameters, if you want to set one parameter and keep some of the defaults, you must always keep parameters in the correct order.

Using body_class() and post_class()

The body_class() and post_class() functions always come in extremely handy when creating WordPress themes. As their names suggest, they output classes that you can use on HTML elements in your templates. To use them in your templates, simply add them before the closing arrow bracket of the HTML tag you want them to be used in:

```
<body <?php body_class(); ?>>
```

This code outputs something along these lines:

```
<body class="page page-id-744 page-template-default">
```

The body_class() and post_class() functions output the full class attribute and a series of classes that can be used to identify the page being generated. Here's an example of how detailed the classes can be:

```
<body class="paged page page-id-744 page-template-default logged-in admin-bar no-customize-support
paged-11 page-paged-11 custom-font-enabled debug-bar-maximized">
```

As you can see, there are many classes that you could potentially hook into with the CSS. Some might not be all that helpful, but some (such as paged, for instance) could be used to style the page slightly differently now that you know you're traversing through a list of posts. If you look a little farther through the list, you'll notice a paged-11 class that can also let you know the exact page number you're on.

Here's another example, this time using post_class(), which can be used on any HTML page, but usually the one that wraps around the main content of the page (in this case, an article tag):

```
<article <?php post_class(); ?>>
```

It outputs the following:

```
<article class="post-675 page type-page status-publish hentry">
```

Here are a couple of examples that could be useful in styling as well: the type-page class would allow you to style content based on the post type (a post would have type-post in the class list) and a status class.

These two functions can be passed a string value as a parameter that will get output in the class list as well. This can come in really handy if you create a custom page template for some specific function and want to use a specific class to also use for custom styling. Here's a quick example:

```
<article <?php post_class("custom-page unique-styles"); ?>>
// Outputs
<article class="post-675 page type-page status-publish hentry custom-page unique-styles">
```

Notice that to pass multiple classes, you just need to use a space between the two classes because they will just be entered directly into the class tag as they were passed in.

More Useful Classes with Hooks

A great function of WordPress is the fact you can hook into pretty much any function and play with the intended output to your advantage. You'll learn more about hooks later in the book when plug-ins are covered in Chapters 7 and 8, but for now you'll look at an example of some code:

```
/**
 * Include category IDs in body_class and post_class
 */
function add_category_classes($classes) {
        global $post;

        foreach((get_the_category($post->ID)) as $category) {
                $classes [] = 'cat-' . $category->slug;
        }

        return $classes;
}

add_filter('post_class', 'add_category_classes');
```

In the functions file, you can add this snippet of code, which will add some extra classes based on the categories the post is in. First, you can create a function that takes in a $classes parameter that contains the classes that would normally be output using the post_class() function. The $classes variable is actually an array at this stage, so to add extra classes to it you just add them on to the end of the array. The function gets the current post being accessed, and using the get_the_categories() function gets the categories the post is in and then loops through them, adding the category slug (the lowercase hyphenated version of the category name) prefixed with cat- (so you know it's a category class). After you set up the function, using the add_filter() WordPress function you "hook" your function into the post_class() function, meaning it will be called when the post_class function() is executed.

Adding this function to the post_class() tag will result in a class list like this one:

```
<article id="post-168" class="post-168 post type-post status-publish format-standard hentry
cat-championship cat-winners">
```

Toward the end of the class list are two extra classes, cat-championship and cat-winners, which are added through the function. This is just one example but using a similar function essentially you could add any classes that would be useful through a function like this.

Styling Sticky Posts

As you've seen, the post_class and body_class functions generate classes for you to use in the CSS to help style aspects of your sites. A great example can be seen when used in conjunction with the WordPress sticky posts functionality. *Sticky posts* are blog posts that can be set to "stick" to the front page of your blog list page (imagine an important announcement that you want to be constantly visible on your site).

To set up a sticky post, you need to select the Stick This Post To The Front Page check box in the Visibility options of the Publish box in the post editor window (see Figure 3-1).

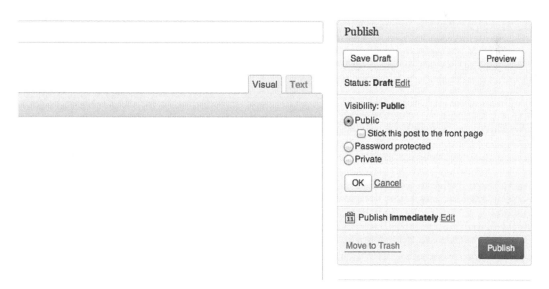

Figure 3-1. *The Publish box showing the sticky post check box*

With this check box selected, the post will always be retrieved on the posts listing page and any pages that query for a list of the posts, even a custom query. So with a post that is stuck as the first one appearing on any page listing your posts, it might be worth giving it a different look from the rest so people understand that it's different or there for a reason. It is extremely simple to do, thanks to the post_class() function. By using it on the containing element of the post, you have the class sticky to use in your CSS (see Figure 3-2). Here's an example:

```
.sticky {
        background-color:lightblue;
        color:darkblue;
}
```

This gives a clearly different style to the rest of your posts.

Figure 3-2. *A sticky post at the top of a blog page*

A Note on HTML IDs

Something you see quite often in WordPress themes, and even in WordPress default themes, is the use of the post ID in the ID attribute of elements. Here's an example from the Twenty Twelve theme:

```
<article id="post-<?php the_ID(); ?>" <?php post_class(); ?>>
```

This code would give an ID of "post-23" for you to use in your CSS (or, more likely nowadays, to use as a hook in your JS). This seems like a great idea; it will always be a unique identifier for the post or page you're displaying, so you can be confident it can be used as a JS or CSS hook.

More and more often, developers work with separate development and live versions, so with WordPress being a database-driven CMS it's unlikely that your development and live databases will be the same. This means if you're transferring code from your development to a live environment, you'll lose the accuracy of your post IDs. It's unlikely that you'll add content in exactly the same order, so you need another option for your CSS and JS hooks.

To have a more accurate hook, you need to look for something that's likely to stay the same on both the development and live environments. The best option I've come up with so far is the post slug that acts as the URL of the post (with pretty permalinks). With WordPress, the slug does not come with its own function to retrieve it easily, unlike a lot of the post data. You can access it through the global post data but that requires more code and access to the global $post variable, for example:

```php
<?php
global $post;
$slug = $post->post_slug;
?>
<article id="post-<?php echo $slug; ?>" <?php post_class(); ?>>
```

It would be much nicer if there were a function to make this a lot cleaner to access in your templates. So how about this one?

```php
function get_the_post_slug($id) {
        $post_data = get_post($id, ARRAY_A);
        $slug = $post_data['post_name'];
        return $slug;
}
```

Then in the template file, you can access it like this:

```
<article id="<?php echo get_the_post_slug(get_the_ID()); ?>" <?php post_class(); ?>>
```

This code keeps your template files a lot cleaner and promotes reusable code, which is always good.

Building Your Theme, Part 2

Now you can take what you've learned about the WordPress Loop and content options and apply it to the theme you started creating in the last chapter. At the moment, all you have are template files set up ready to display the different content you add to your site. In this section, you'll add loops and template tags to make your templates actually display some content.

Content First

Before you get started though, you need to have some content in WordPress. To save a lot of hassle, throughout the book and construction of the theme I've created a series of content files that can be imported into your WordPress installs.

If you have migrated content to WordPress, you already know about the WordPress import function; if not, first you'll need to download the WordPress importer plug-in. You can get this either through the WordPress plug-in installer page (Plugins ➤ Add New) or download it from the web site: `http://wp-themes-book.com/03009`. Then go to Tools ➤ Import and select WordPress. It gives you the page shown in Figure 3-3, in which you can select the `Chapter_3_content.xml` file to upload. Make sure when importing that you choose to add the new authors as well as the content.

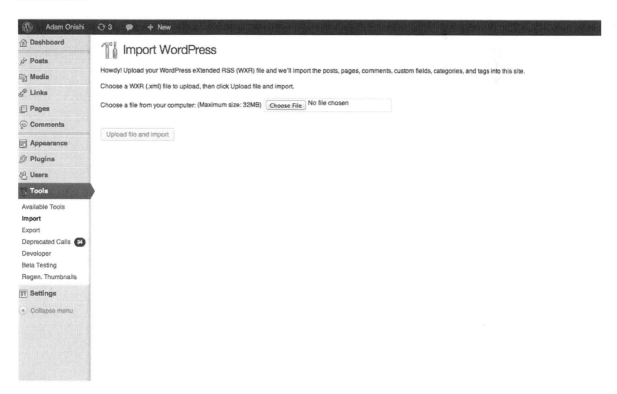

Figure 3-3. *WordPress import page*

Have a look around the WordPress admin; you should now have a few posts and pages to play around with, as well as a few new authors and categories. This data should be enough to allow you to go ahead and build out some of the templates in your theme to get the content displayed.

Adding Code to Your Templates

At the end of Chapter 2, the only template files you'd really added content to were the header.php, footer.php, and functions.php files. Here you'll add the code needed to display the content of your site in the form of a series of loops. Using some of the template tags discussed in the chapter so far, you'll also see a couple of new tags (their functionality should be fairly straightforward).

Let's start with the home page; you'll use a static page as the home page for your theme and make use of the front-page.php template. First, you need to tell WordPress to do this through the settings. Go to Settings ➤ Reading and make sure the Front Page Displays options is set to A Static Page; then choose the page named Home as your front page from the drop-down menu. You also want to set a posts page here; in this site, your posts will represent news about the company, so select News as the posts page.

Coding the front-page.php Template

The idea behind the front page of your web site is to give some introductory information about the company and show a brief summary of the latest news as well. This means you get your first example of multiple loops in action in your theme:

```php
<?php get_header(); ?>
<?php the_post(); ?>

        <article class="page-content">
                <?php the_content(); ?>
        </article>

        <aside class="latest-news">
                <h2>Latest News</h2>

                <?php
                // New Query for news articles
                $args = array(
                                'post_type'       => 'post',
                                'orderby'         => 'date',
                                'order'           => 'ASC',
                                'posts_per_page' => 2,
                        );

                $latest_news = WP_Query( $args );

                if( $latest_news->have_posts() ): while( $latest_news->have_posts() ):
$latest_news->the_post();
                ?>
```

```
            <article <?php post_class(); ?>>
                    <h3><?php the_title(); ?></h3>

                    <?php the_excerpt(); ?>

                    <a href="<?php the_permalink(); ?>">Read more &raquo;</a>
            </article>
        <?php endwhile; endif; ?>

        <?php wp_reset_query(); ?>
    </aside>

<?php get_footer(); ?>
```

Notice the lack of a loop for the first section of your page; it is because you know you will list only the one page, and if it's already made it to the front page template, you're sure that you'll have one single page in your query to work with. Therefore, at the top of the previous template I just used the the_post() function to set up the $post global and the template tags.

Next is the second loop in the template, which is for the latest news list. The new query here is created using the new WP_Query instance option and is passed the arguments through an array variable. The arguments ask for only two posts from the post type posts and in the most recent date order. The following loop lists out the returned posts with the excerpt and a link to go read the full article. Finally, after you close the secondary loop, run the wp_reset_query() function to make sure you go back to the original query while WordPress finishes rendering the page. With that page done, you can move on to your home template, which will display the list of posts (the news section in this case).

Coding the home.php Template

The home template will be a pretty straightforward posts listing page based from the default query. Don't forget that you'll have to paginate this page as well if you reach the posts-per-page limit that you set in the WordPress admin under Settings ➤ Reading. Because this is a news section of the site, you can make your default something like 5 and then paginate the rest, but this can vary depending on how regularly people might want to update the site with news. If it is more frequently, they might want to show a lot more on each page.

Let's have a look at the code and see whether there's anything else you can do to make this page more dynamic:

```
<?php get_header(); ?>

    <h1>Latest news</h1>

    <?php if( have_posts() ): ?>

        <?php while( have_posts() ): the_post(); ?>

            <?php get_template_part( 'content', get_post_format() ); ?>

        <?php endwhile; ?>

    <?php else: ?>

        <article class="error">
            <h2>Sorry there were no news articles found</h2>
        </article>

    <?php endif; ?>
```

```
        <p class="post-page-navigation">
                <?php previous_posts_link( "&laquo; More recent news"); ?>
                <?php next_posts_link( "Past news &raquo;"); ?>
        </p>

        <?php get_sidebar( 'news' ); ?>

<?php get_footer(); ?>
```

The content for this page will be fairly simple and not require anything too amazing. The previous and next post page links at the bottom have been included with the template tags, but I passed a parameter to the function to give the link a different label. Usually these functions would just say "Next posts »" and "« Previous posts", but because you're on a news page the language could be misread as "Next posts." This link is actually a link to older posts, so the ability to add a label to the links through the functions comes in very handy.

In Chapter 2, you set up separate sidebar for the news pages, which is included by passing the string 'news' into the function. Let's look at the code you're will have in this template file.

Coding the sidebar-news.php Template

The sidebar for the news section will allow users to navigate to some archives and categorized news stories. You've already seen the wp_list_categories() function earlier; and here I'm just using a couple of arguments to get a list of categories sorted by popularity. The other function is wp_get_archives(), which is used to show links to monthly archives of posts by default. You want that here; this function is quite powerful and can be used with a variety of different options to give you really custom archive displays. I suggest checking out the codex for more details about the tag.

```
<aside class="sidebar news">

        <h2>Archives</h2>
        <ul class="news-navigation">
                <?php wp_get_archives(); ?>
        </ul>

        <h2>Popular categories</h2>
        <ul class="news-navigation">
                <?php
                $args = array(
                                'title_li' => '',
                                'orderby' => 'count',
                        );

                wp_list_categories( $args ); ?>
        </ul>

</aside>
```

The links created from these tags direct to pages handled by the archive template.

Coding the Archive Template

This template is another fairly straightforward list page similar to the home.php template. Because the posts listed on this page can come in a variety of formats, however, you'll use the conditional functions to display different title and error messages depending on what you're displaying.

```php
<?php get_header(); ?>

        <?php if (have_posts()) : the_post(); ?>

        <?php if (is_category()) : ?>
            <h1>Archive for category: <?php single_cat_title(); ?></h1>
        <?php elseif( is_tag() ) : ?>
            <h1>Posts Tagged: <?php single_tag_title(); ?></h1>
        <?php elseif (is_day()) : ?>
            <h1>Archive for <?php the_time('F jS, Y'); ?></h1>
        <?php elseif (is_month()) : ?>
            <h1>Archive for <?php the_time('F, Y'); ?></h1>
        <?php elseif (is_year()) : ?>
            <h1>Archive for <?php the_time('Y'); ?></h1>
        <?php elseif (is_author()) : ?>
            <h1>Author Archive</h1>
        <?php elseif (isset($_GET['paged']) && !empty($_GET['paged'])) : ?>
            <h1>Archives</h1>
        <?php endif; ?>

        <?php rewind_posts(); ?>

        <?php while (have_posts()) : the_post(); ?>
            <?php get_template_part( 'content', get_post_format() ); ?>
        <?php endwhile; ?>

    <?php else : ?>

        <?php if (is_category()) :  ?>
            <h1>Sorry, but there aren't any posts in the <?php single_cat_title(); ?> category
yet.</h1>
        <?php elseif (is_date()) : ?>
            <h1>Sorry, but there aren't any posts with this date.</h1>
        <?php elseif (is_author()) : ?>
            <?php get_userdatabylogin(get_query_var('author_name')); ?>
            <h1>Sorry, but there aren't any posts by <?php echo $userdata->display_name; ?> yet.</h1>
        <?php else : ?>
            <h1>No posts found.</h1>
        <?php endif; ?>

    <?php endif; ?>

<?php get_footer(); ?>
```

You may have noticed a different format of your loop this time. Here you call the_post() before you start the while loop.

```php
<?php if( have_posts() ): the_post(); ?>
```

Doing this allows you to use conditional tags and tags such as single_cat_title to create the title of your page before you list the posts below it. Because calling the_post() advances the post counter only by one, by the time you get the while loop and call the_post() again, you'll be setting up the template tags for the second post in your query. You can get back to the beginning of your list of posts before you start the while loop, however, by calling rewind_posts(), which you'll see at the start of the while loop:

```php
<?php rewind_posts(); ?>
```

```php
<?php while (have_posts()) : the_post(); ?>
```

Coding the Page and Single Templates

You can display a single page or post in your site with the page.php and single.php templates. They are fairly similar, so the following code is only from the page.php template. The only difference is that the single template has the get_sidebar() function called after the content instead of before and with the name parameter "news" on the single template.

```php
<?php get_header(); ?>

        <?php get_sidebar(); ?>

        <?php if( have_posts() ): while( have_posts() ): the_post(); ?>

            <article <?php post_class(); ?>>
                    <h1><?php the_title(); ?></h1>

                    <?php the_content(); ?>
            </article>

        <?php endwhile; endif; ?>

<?php get_footer(); ?>
```

This is a really simple template; it just creates an article containing the title and content of the page. For now that's all you need, but there is a nice bit of functionality in the sidebar for you to look at.

Coding the Sidebar Template

This sidebar is used for any page on the site; for now, it lists a simple subnavigation. To do this, you can use the wp_list_pages() function and pass it the ID of the current page so you can see the child pages in the sidebar. You also need to be able to list the menu when you're on one of those child pages. You do that using the get_post_ancestors() function (you get all the higher-level pages of the current page); with the PHP function end you get the last element in the array. The array of ancestors will always be sorted with the highest ancestor at the end of the array, and for subnavigation you generally want the highest-level parent page. After you have the top-level page information, you can use it to get the title of the subnavigation and pass the ID into the child_of parameter of the wp_list_pages() function to get the subpage navigation.

```
<aside class="sidebar page-navigation">
        <?php
                global $post;
                $ancestors = get_post_ancestors( $post );
                $top = get_post(end($ancestors), "OBJECT");
        ?>
        <h2><?php echo $top->post_title; ?></h2>
        <ul class="sub-nav">
                <?php wp_list_pages('title_li=&child_of='.$top->ID); ?>
        </ul>
</aside>
```

Last Bits

Now you'll look at some additional bits added to the template files that you already added code to in the previous chapter: the header, footer, and functions files.

In the header, you have a logo included with the use of the bloginfo tag to get the theme directory and the main menu for the site being included with the wp_nav_menu() function.

```
<header>
        <h1><a href="<?php home_url('/'); ?>"><img src="<?php bloginfo('template_directory'); ?>/
images/logo.png" alt="Pro WordPress Theme Development"></a></h1>
</header>

<nav class="main-navigation">
        <?php wp_nav_menu( array( 'theme_location' => 'primary', 'container' => false )); ?>
</nav>
```

The menu 'primary' has been set up in the functions file to allow you to add this to your WordPress admin, and these few functions setting up the site have been moved into a theme setup function, which is common to a lot of WordPress themes.

```
if ( ! function_exists( 'prowordpress_setup' ) ) :

        function prowordpress_setup() {

                /**
                 * Add default posts and comments RSS feed links to head
                 */
                add_theme_support( 'automatic-feed-links' );

                /**
                 * Enable support for Post Thumbnails
                 */
                add_theme_support( 'post-thumbnails' );

                /**
                 * This theme uses wp_nav_menu() in one location.
                 */
                register_nav_menus( array(
                        'primary' => __( 'Primary Menu', 'ao_starter' ),
                ) );
```

```
            /**
             * Enable support for Post Formats
             */
            add_theme_support( 'post-formats', array( 'aside', 'image', 'video', 'quote', 'link' ) );
        }

endif; // ao_starter_setup
add_action( 'after_setup_theme', 'prowordpress_setup' );
```

You can check to see whether the function hasn't already been set up before using the line:

```
if( ! function_exists( 'prowordpress_setup' ) ):
```

Just in case you're using a child theme and the function is called somewhere else. In the footer I added a footer tag with a small function I created a while back to add a simple dynamic copyright to the site. This function has been declared in the functions file as well, so it can be used in the theme. It is something that you might consider creating as a plug-in as it's not going to be unique to this theme, but because it's so small, it's not worth the effort.

```
function simple_copyright () {
        echo "&copy; " . get_bloginfo('name') ." ". date("Y");
}
```

The last addition to your functions file is a function to include the scripts and styles in the web site. I put this in the functions file so it is all in one place, but some people include these functions in the header of the theme, which is fine (I just don't like the clutter).

```
/**
 * Enqueue scripts and styles
 */
function prowordpress_scripts_and_styles() {
        wp_enqueue_style( 'style', get_stylesheet_uri() );

        /**
         * Better jQuery inclusion
         */
        if (!is_admin()) {
                wp_deregister_script('jquery');
                wp_register_script('jquery',
("http://ajax.googleapis.com/ajax/libs/jquery/1/jquery.min.js"), false);
                wp_enqueue_script('jquery');
        }
}
add_action( 'wp_enqueue_scripts', 'prowordpress_scripts_and_styles' );
```

Summary

Wow, that was an absolutely epic chapter. Apologies for the length, but the Loop and content methods in WordPress are the absolute core of WordPress theme development.

The chapter went into real depth with the WordPress querying method, and I showed you in detail how the `WP_Query` class operates as well as how to edit and customize the query to get custom content into your templates. With these query methods, you can create extremely powerful queries to display almost any combination of content on your site.

I also covered in great detail how the template tags work in WordPress, covering the main groups and how the template tags work in a variety of ways to output the content the way you want it for your site. As well, I showed you how the `body_class` and `post_class` functions can be used to add useful classes to HTML to help create custom designs for content through clean CSS.

Finally, a lot of code was added to your templates to generate the content output for your theme. You should now have the beginnings of a WordPress theme displaying dynamic pages of content from WordPress.

The next chapter looks at how to extend the functionality of WordPress to give you more contextual content through the use of custom post types, custom taxonomies, and custom fields.

CHAPTER 4

Using Custom Post Types

You could say that the catalyst for the evolution of WordPress as a fully-fledged content management system (CMS) came about through the introduction of the custom post type. For me, that was when the agency I first worked for moved toward using WordPress as the back end for the sites we built. This major functionality gave WordPress the capability to easily move away from what had been its key functionality, a blogging system, and toward a more dynamic system for storing content. This chapter shows you how to take advantage of custom post types in WordPress, how to create them, how to display them, and how to add advanced functionality to your post type to make it extremely easy to work with as a content author.

Everything Is a Post

When I say, "Everything is a post," I mean that all the main content types in WordPress are stored as a post. This goes back to the very first version of WordPress, in which the only content type available was posts. It wasn't until WordPress version 1.5 (Strayhorn), in which the field post_type was introduced to the posts table (see Figures 4-1 and 4-2) in the database, that you started to see custom post types, the first being the static page type that still forms one of the main parts of WordPress today.

| Browse | Structure | SQL | Search | Insert | Export | Import | Operations | Triggers |

#	Name	Type	Collation	Attributes	Null	Default	Extra	Action
1	ID	bigint(20)		UNSIGNED	No	None	AUTO_INCREMENT	Change Drop Browse distinct values Primary Unique More
2	post_author	bigint(20)		UNSIGNED	No	0		Change Drop Browse distinct values Primary Unique More
3	post_date	datetime			No	0000-00-00 00:00:00		Change Drop Browse distinct values Primary Unique More
4	post_date_gmt	datetime			No	0000-00-00 00:00:00		Change Drop Browse distinct values Primary Unique More
5	post_content	longtext	utf8_general_ci		No	None		Change Drop Browse distinct values Primary Unique More
6	post_title	text	utf8_general_ci		No	None		Change Drop Browse distinct values Primary Unique More
7	post_excerpt	text	utf8_general_ci		No	None		Change Drop Browse distinct values Primary Unique More
8	post_status	varchar(20)	utf8_general_ci		No	publish		Change Drop Browse distinct values Primary Unique More
9	comment_status	varchar(20)	utf8_general_ci		No	open		Change Drop Browse distinct values Primary Unique More
10	ping_status	varchar(20)	utf8_general_ci		No	open		Change Drop Browse distinct values Primary Unique More
11	post_password	varchar(20)	utf8_general_ci		No			Change Drop Browse distinct values Primary Unique More
12	post_name	varchar(200)	utf8_general_ci		No			Change Drop Browse distinct values Primary Unique More
13	to_ping	text	utf8_general_ci		No	None		Change Drop Browse distinct values Primary Unique More
14	pinged	text	utf8_general_ci		No	None		Change Drop Browse distinct values Primary Unique More
15	post_modified	datetime			No	0000-00-00 00:00:00		Change Drop Browse distinct values Primary Unique More
16	post_modified_gmt	datetime			No	0000-00-00 00:00:00		Change Drop Browse distinct values Primary Unique More
17	post_content_filtered	longtext	utf8_general_ci		No	None		Change Drop Browse distinct values Primary Unique More
18	post_parent	bigint(20)		UNSIGNED	No	0		Change Drop Browse distinct values Primary Unique More
19	guid	varchar(255)	utf8_general_ci		No			Change Drop Browse distinct values Primary Unique More
20	menu_order	int(11)			No	0		Change Drop Browse distinct values Primary Unique More
21	post_type	varchar(20)	utf8_general_ci		No	post		Change Drop Browse distinct values Primary Unique More
22	post_mime_type	varchar(100)	utf8_general_ci		No			Change Drop Browse distinct values Primary Unique More
23	comment_count	bigint(20)			No	0		Change Drop Browse distinct values Primary Unique More

Figure 4-1. *The structure of the posts database table*

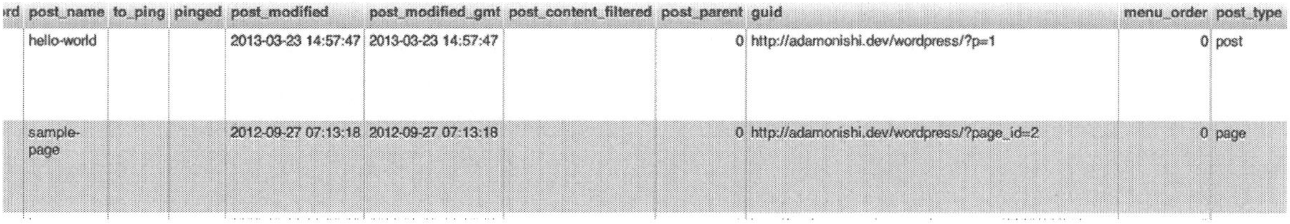

rd	post_name	to_ping	pinged	post_modified	post_modified_gmt	post_content_filtered	post_parent	guid	menu_order	post_type
	hello-world			2013-03-23 14:57:47	2013-03-23 14:57:47		0	http://adamonishi.dev/wordpress/?p=1	0	post
	sample-page			2012-09-27 07:13:18	2012-09-27 07:13:18		0	http://adamonishi.dev/wordpress/?page_id=2	0	page

Figure 4-2. *Database records showing the post_type in action*

Although the ability to create custom post types has been around for quite some time now (by passing a post_type parameter to the wp_insert_post function), it didn't get "officially" included until the major release version 3.0 (Thelonious). Version 3.0 is what heralded most of the new functionality such as custom menus and custom post types, and came with the introduction of the first of the Twenty-somethings' default themes Twenty Ten. However, if you look into the WordPress release notes it mentions "improved custom post types and custom taxonomies" because really the functionality was added in version 2.9 when the register_post_type function was originally included.

Before I tell you why custom post types are so great and how they can improve your WordPress themes, let's take a quick look at when and why they should be used.

When Do I Need a Custom Post Type?

I find myself asking this question more and more as I work on larger sites. There are times when a custom post type is definitely necessary, but at other times the hierarchical nature of the page post type can be used to display content that you might at first have thought required a custom post type. For example, I've used child pages for an instance in which the content would be displayed only on the parent page, not as a single page themselves, but where I needed more functionality than a standard custom field could offer. Initially in that example I would have used a custom post type. However, because of the size of the site and the limitation of how the data would display, I went with the child pages solution instead to keep the WordPress admin a bit smaller.

Although it could be considered a controversial approach, based on the requirements at the time, not using a custom post type was the correct method. It's best to approach each situation as unique and take into account the circumstances around which you're building your admin. If the site in the example was to be maintained by a client, for instance, it might be better stored in a custom post type.

What Is a Custom Post Type Used for?

A custom post type should be used when you have a series of content to be grouped in one way or another. All content that goes into this post type should conform to the same format and page structure, or revolve around the same theme. The usual examples of custom post types are these:

- Products
- Movies
- Books
- Events
- Testimonials
- Staff/team listings

You can probably see a certain commonality among the types in the list. They are all likely to be accessed in a similar way on the site—displayed in a list with a possible drill-down to a single display. They all need to be managed separately from the rest of the content on the site. The posts contained within them all have a similar structure and content. The main thing is that none of those examples identifies easily with the characteristics of a page or post.

Creating Custom Post Types

Now that you know why you may need a custom post type, you can start looking at how to add your own to the WordPress admin. When you create a custom post type in WordPress, you create an entire new section of the WordPress admin, which means for the post type to be fully integrated into WordPress there's a lot of extra options you can and should be looking to set up for the new post type. In this section, you'll look at all these options and more so that your custom post types are not only set up correctly but also give users of the admin area as much information to make the best use of these new types as possible. You'll look at the following:

- Naming conventions
- Using a plugin or the theme functions file
- Setting up a basic new post type
- Full set up and advanced options for custom post types
- Custom interaction messages
- Custom contextual help
- Custom help tab content

Naming Conventions

First up, let's look briefly at how you should be naming your post types. Apart from post type identifiers being all in lowercase, the WordPress Codex suggests that you use a prefix (or namespace) when creating your post types. This book uses the namespace ptd (for Pro Theme Development), so using the earlier examples of post types, they use these identifiers:

- `ptd_product`
- `ptd_movie`
- `ptd_book`
- `ptd_event`
- `ptd_testimonial`
- `ptd_staff`

This method is used to help prevent conflicts with any other themes or plugins you may use in the future. It's also incredibly important if you consider creating premium themes or plugins because you lose control over what will be used in conjunction with your theme. So adding a namespace to your post types saves a lot of support requests in the future.

Also notice that the examples I list here use a singular word to describe the post type—"product" over "products", for instance. This conforms to the convention set in the WordPress for default post type names: "post", "page", "revision", "attachment", and "nav_menu_item" as well as keeping the reference from post type to post correct because you will create instances of the post type in the singular. It's not until you group them on the web site that they become "products", so to speak.

Note that your custom post type identifiers must not exceed 20 characters in length, possibly for the cause of brevity but also simply because the database field for post_type is set to accept a maximum of 20 characters.

Using a Plugin or the Theme Functions File

When looking through tutorials on how to set up a custom post type, you will invariably see a lot of suggestions for putting all the code for creating a custom post type in a custom plugin. To me, this all depends on the circumstances of creating the custom post type. If the post type will be unique to the theme with custom templates created specifically for that post type, adding it to a plugin just adds one more thing for the user to download and install to get your theme working. In this case, it's much more sensible to add your custom post type declarations to the themes functions file, which (as discussed in Chapter 1) acts as the theme's own little plugin file. This way, the code is kept related directly to the theme.

However, if your custom post types will be used across multiple themes and set up the same way each time, I definitely recommend the use of a plugin. The functionality will stay the same for each site, and any updates that are required need the code base to be updated only once to get the improvements.

This section looks primarily at building your custom post types into the theme itself, so you'll use the theme functions file for now. Later, when you add to your theme, I'll also show you a method for separating your custom post type code from the rest of the functions file so you can keep it neatly away from the rest of your custom functions because (as you'll see later in the chapter, the code for custom post types can get quite big).

Setting a Basic Custom Post Type

To set up a basic custom post type you'll be using the register_post_type function. This function comes with a whole array of options that cover everything you could possibly imagine that's related to a post type in WordPress and a few things you probably didn't. Let's take a look at a quick example of how to set up a post type of 'Movies', which is using possibly the most basic options you will need to use in the register_post_type function:

```
register_post_type( 'ptd_movie',
            array(
                    'labels' => array(
                            'name' => __( 'Movies', 'prowordpress' ),
                            'singular_name' => __( 'Movie', 'prowordpress' )
                    ),
            'public' => true,
            'has_archive' => true,
            )
    );
```

The previous function call contains all you need to get a custom post type set up in WordPress and displaying in the WordPress admin menu (see Figure 4-3). The preceding options give the post type two different name labels: a singular name and a plural name—using the 'name' label setting becomes the main label used throughout the admin (again shown in Figure 4-3).

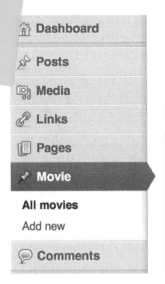

Figure 4-3. *The Movie post type displaying in the admin menu*

Other options shown previously mean the function will be visible to users (the `'public'` option) and allow the post type to have its own archive page: the `'has_archive'` option. This means you can view a list of the posts in this post type at a specific URL; in this case, because an alternative is not set, it uses the post identifier `"ptd_movie"` using the URL `http://website.com/ptd_movie`.

You may have also noticed the post type names are wrapped in a function themselves, the `__()` function. This is to allow them to be localized for a particular language. The `__()` function takes two parameters, the text to be translated and the text domain of your theme/plugin. For now that's all you need to know, however you will be covering internationalization and localization in a lot more detail in Chapter 12.

This function should be run as soon as possible; when WordPress is constructing pages, the theme functions file is loaded automatically when any page is set up by WordPress, front-end or admin pages. However, the `register_post_type` function needs to be called at a certain time before other functionality in WordPress has been set up so the new post types can be taken into account. The best way to do this is to hook the `register_post_type` function to the WordPress `init` action by putting all the calls to `register_post_type` inside a containing function and use the `add_action` function to add this on `init`:

```
add_action('init', 'new_post_types');

function new_post_types() {
        register_post_type( 'ptd_movie',
                    array(
                            'labels' => array(
                                    'name' => __( 'Movies', 'prowordpress' ),
                                    'singular_name' => __( 'Movie', 'prowordpress' )
                            ),
                    'public' => true,
                    'has_archive' => true,
                    )
            );
}
```

This is the first example of creating a custom post type. Next, you'll take a deeper look into the `register_post_type` function and all the options you have available to highly customize how your post type will work, what content it can store, and how it can be accessed.

Full Setup and Advanced Options for Custom Post Types

Now that you've seen a basic custom post type and how it can be set up, you can have a look at the full set of options available when creating custom post types:

```
$labels = array(
        'name'                  => 'Movies',
        'singular_name'         => 'Movie',
        'add_new'               => 'Add New',
        'add_new_item'          => 'Add New Movie',
        'edit_item'             => 'Edit Movie',
        'new_item'              => 'New Movie',
        'all_items'             => 'All Movies',
        'view_item'             => 'View Movies',
        'search_items'          => 'Search Movies',
        'not_found'             => 'No movies found',
        'not_found_in_trash'    => 'No movies found in Trash',
        'parent_item_colon'     => '',
        'menu_name'             => 'Movies'
    );

$args = array(
        'labels'                => $labels,
        'description'           => "",
        'exclude_from_search'   => false,
        'public'                => true,
        'publicly_queryable'    => true,
        'show_ui'               => true,
        'show_in_nav_menus'     => true,
        'show_in_menu'          => true,
        'show_in_admin_bar'     => true,
        'query_var'             => true,
        'rewrite'               => array( 'slug' => 'movie' ),
        'capability_type'       => 'post',
        'menu_icon'             => bloginfo('template_directory'). '/images/movie-menu-icon.png',
        'has_archive'           => true,
        'hierarchical'          => false,
        'menu_position'         => 20,
        'supports'              => array('title', 'editor', 'author', 'thumbnail', 'excerpt', 'comments'),
        'can_export'            => true,
    );

register_post_type( 'ptd_movie', $args );
```

As you can see from this code, there is a plethora of options available to you when setting up a custom post type. You'll take a look at what they all do over the course of this section, starting with possibly the most obvious option, the labels.

Labels

Probably the most self explanatory of all the options, the labels allow you to set a number of different bits of text that make up the WordPress admin for the custom post type. Although the basic example sets up only the name and singular_name labels, by setting a lot more labels, as shown previously, you can create a much more informative admin area. You can see the comparison in Figure 4-4.

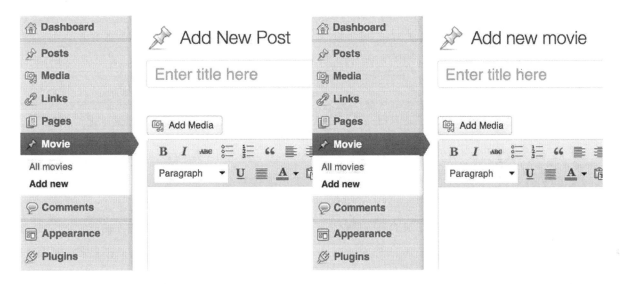

Figure 4-4. *A comparison showing the use of standard custom labels (left) vs. advanced custom labels (right)*

All the label titles are pretty easy to follow, the format of all the labels are set out to be similar to the regular WordPress admin, with the new post type name replacing what would normally be "post" or "page".

For the example code I have intentionally left off the internationalization functions to make the text easier to see, however in your themes you should always be internationalizing any content that a user will be seeing.

Although this may not look like a major difference in the admin area, these options allow you to make the admin feel more complete; even little touches like these can lead to a much more improved user experience in your theme.

Display Options

What I'm going to call the "display options" are any options passed into the functions that control how and where the new post type is displayed in the admin area. They include the following:

- public
- publicly_queryable
- exclude_from_search
- show_ui
- show_in_menu
- show_in_nav_menu
- show_in_admin_bar
- menu_position

You saw the `public` option before in the basic post type setup. This is the option that sets whether the post type appears in the admin user interface (UI) and is displayed in the front end as well. This is also the main option for most of the display options listed previously in that the rest of the options (all apart from `menu_position`) inherit their setting from the `public` setting. However, they do not all rely on this setting and will take whatever setting is passed through with the function.

The `publicly_queryable` setting determines whether you can query for the post type from your theme. It should be set to true for most post types; if it's set to false, you can't view any custom posts from this post type. Although this may seem to be an irregular option, suppose that you are creating a shopping system that needs to store the orders in the database for administrators to monitor. You could easily do this using a custom post type and by setting `publicly_queryable` to false. No one from the front end would then have access to view the orders placed in the database.

The setting `exclude_from_search` is fairly self-explanatory: if set to true, searching the site via `website.com/?s=searchterm` would return no results. This could be useful, but be aware that if set to true you cannot use taxonomy-based filters to display the custom post type because that functionality requires the post type to be searchable, so this option is likely to be set to false most of the time.

The `show_ui` option tells WordPress whether to generate an admin interface for the post type. It's unlikely that you will need to change this setting if you have set `public` to true because I can't imagine many situations in which you would want a post type to be usable but not have an admin interface.

The options `show_in_nav_menus` and `show_in_admin_bar` should also be self-explanatory. Both are true or false settings; the first is whether this post type should be usable in custom menus, and the second is whether this post type shows in the admin bar from the Add New drop-down menu (see Figure 4-5).

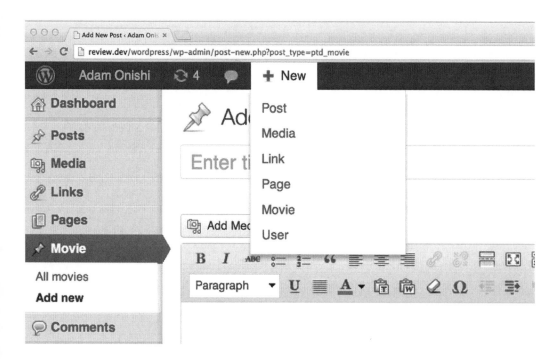

***Figure 4-5.** The Add New drop-down menu showing the Movie post type in the list*

The `show_in_menu` option can act as a simple Boolean option, setting whether the post type should be displayed in the admin menu. The other function that the `show_in_menu` option can be used for is set up by passing a string to the option. This string is used to tell WordPress which admin menu the post type should appear under. For instance, if you wanted your item to appear in the Page drop-down menu, you can pass the string `"edit.php?post_type=page"`, the result of which you can see in Figure 4-6. This functionality can be seen a lot in different WordPress plugins and frameworks, which add post types to the Tools submenu (using the string `"tools.php"`) or add multiple post types under the same main admin menu.

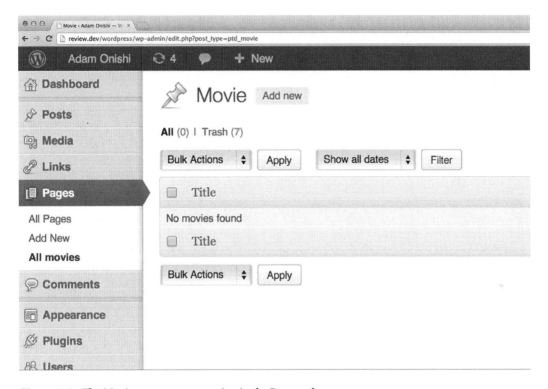

Figure 4-6. *The Movies post type appearing in the Pages submenu*

The final setting of the display options is `menu_position`. This takes an integer value, which decides where in the admin menu the new post type will appear. The default is to appear after the comments menu item, but here is a full list of the stop points you can use to position your post type anywhere in the admin menu:

- 5: below Posts
- 10: below Media
- 15: below Links
- 20: below Pages
- 25: below comments
- 60: below first separator
- 65: below Plugins

- 70: below Users

- 75: below Tools

- 80: below Settings

- 100: below second separator

Supports and Capabilities

The supports option is probably one of the more important options for creating a post type. This option takes an array argument containing all the different post features that you want to be able to use in the post type being set up. The defaults are `title` and `editor`, which give you the main title field and the main content editor for the post type. But there are many more options available to theme developers than this basic pair of features; almost any feature that can be used in a WordPress post or page type can be added to a custom post type:

- `title`: default post title field

- `editor`: main post content

- `author`: set an author of the post

- `thumbnail`: add post thumbnail support

- `excerpt`: add an excerpt field

- `trackbacks`: recognize trackbacks

- `custom-fields`: have the WordPress built-in custom fields added to it

- `comments`: enable the post type to have comments

- `revisions`: enable the post type to track and store revisions

- `page-attributes`: give the post type page attributes such as post order and page template

- `post-formats`: add post format selectors to the post type

To add any or all of these, you need to add each one to the array passed to the `'supports'` option:

```
'supports' => array('title', 'editor', 'thumbnail', 'page-attributes', 'author'),
```

Besides what the post type supports in terms of features, you can also set the capabilities of the post type with the argument `'capability_type'`. When talking about capabilities, I'm referring to the read, edit, and delete capabilities that the user has over the post type. The default setting for `'capability_type'` is post, which means that access to the custom post type will be granted to users in the same way it's granted to the `'post'` post type. For instance, using the post `capability` type, users of the author role can create and edit their own posts in the custom post type, but if the capability type were set to page, you would need to be an editor to be able to do this. I'll go into more detail on WordPress roles and capabilities in Chapter 8.

There is also a `'capabilities'` option for this function that allows you to construct a custom set of capabilities for the post type. Suffice it to say, this is an extremely large subject that will be covered in more detail in Chapter 8.

Custom Rewrite Rules

The next set of options cover how to set custom rewrite rules for the post type. Rewrite rules relate to how you access the post type through the front end from specific URLs, one of the many great parts to WordPress as a CMS. This only applies however when you've set up "pretty permalinks" in the WordPress settings.

The rewrite option in the `register_post_type` function takes an array of arguments that control how WordPress handles the permalinks for the post type. It can also just take the argument `'true'`, which will set the permalink structure for the post type to the post type name passed in at the beginning of the function. However, because of the way I'm setting up the post type name with a prefix—`"ptd_movie"`—the permalink structure would actually be quite untidy: `http://website.com/ptd_movie/clerks`. That's where the extra options of this function come in handy; in the code example, the rewrite argument looks like this:

```
'rewrite' => array( 'slug' => 'movie' ),
```

You see a nice clean URL in the form of `http://website.com/movie/clerks` instead. Much better.

The other options in the array help customize the permalink structure further and allow you to set whether WordPress should process other permalink structures based around this post type:

- `with_front` (defaults to true): If set to true, the permalink structure will use the front base set in the permalink settings; if false, it will ignore the base and use the slug only.

- `feeds` (defaults to `has_archive` setting): If set to true, WordPress will generate a feed permalink structure for the post type.

- `pages` (defaults to true): If set to true, WordPress will accommodate the pagination permalink structure for the post type (e.g., `/movie/page/2`).

- `ep_mask` (default not set): This option takes in an endpoint mask to be used for the post type.

Most of these defaults are taken care of automatically or based on other settings passed to the function, meaning that if the main post type settings are taken care of, you need to worry only about setting a slug parameter for this option.

Flush Rewrite Rules

When creating custom post types and setting custom rewrite structures, you need to tell WordPress that you've made these changes. This applies to when you're activating your new post types, which can occur when you're activating the plugin or theme that contains them as well as when you first set them up. To do this, simply use a function provided by WordPress that tells the CMS to check and reset all the rewrite rules for the current active install, which is called `flush_rewrite_rules()`.

This function should be used *only* when setting up the custom post types because it is quite operation-heavy and will slow down your site if used every time you load a page. To make sure to run the function only when necessary, you can call it only when the plugin or theme is loaded.

```
add_action( 'after_switch_theme', 'prowordpress_flush_rewrite_rules' );

function prowordpress_flush_rewrite_rules() {
        flush_rewrite_rules();
}
```

This code simply wraps the `flush_rewrite_rules()` function in your own function so you can call it on the `after_switch_theme` action using the action hook. This way, whenever the theme is changed and your theme is activated, the `flush_rewrite_rules()` function will do its magic.

It's a similar process if you create custom post types in a plugin, except that you need to call the function when the plugin is activated and deactivated:

```
add_action( 'init', 'my_cpt_init' );
function my_cpt_init() {
        // register our post types
}
```

```
function my_rewrite_flush() {
        my_cpt_init();

        flush_rewrite_rules();
}

register_activation_hook( __FILE__, 'my_rewrite_flush' );

function myplugin_deactivate() {
        flush_rewrite_rules();
}
register_deactivation_hook( __FILE__, 'myplugin_deactivate' );
```

This code gives you a rough idea of how loading custom post types in a plugin should work. First, the function at the top in which you create post types and then two functions that are hooked on to the activation and deactivation hooks of the plugin containing the flush_rewrite_rules() function.

Menu icons

To add even more customization to the new post type, you can add a custom menu icon, which will be used in the WordPress admin menu. The easy way of doing this is to take a standard 16-pixel-square icon and add the location of it to the menu_icon option in the function call, as in the earlier example code:

```
'menu_icon' => bloginfo('template_directory').'/images/movie-menu-icon.png',
```

The icon then is included in the admin menu tab for the new post type, which you can see in Figure 4-7.

Figure 4-7. *Custom post type menu item with a color icon*

Unfortunately, it's likely that your new color icon, will stick out like a sore thumb among the rest of the default WordPress icons. There is a way to get past this—you'll look at that in the next section on customizing the admin interfaces.

Miscellaneous Settings

The last few options should be fairly easy to figure out, but I'll mention them nonetheless.

- `'description'`: Contains a short summary of the post type.

- `'can_export'`: If set to true or false, allows the post type to have its content exported via the WordPress export function.

- `'hierarchical'`: Another true or false option that sets whether the posts in the type can have children, meaning that they act in a similar way to pages; if set to false, they are more like posts.

- `'query_var'`: Sets the string which can be used to query for the post type using the format `?{query_var}={single_post_slug}`. For instance, if this were set to `"movie"` for the movie post type, you would be able to return a post with the URL `http://website.com/?movie=clerks`. This setting does not interfere with the custom rewrite settings, but it's not very useful because it's preferable to use a custom URL rewrite such as `http://website.com/movie/clerks`.

So there are a lot of settings available to truly customize post types, enabling you to create really dynamic content types using WordPress. I also touched on some options in the form of menu icons and custom labels, which help set up the admin interface so the post types actually feel like a truly integrated part of the WordPress admin.

Next, you'll look into more detail at how you can make the WordPress admin custom post types even more user-friendly with custom interaction and helper copy.

Customizing the Admin Interfaces

When creating a custom post type, you create all this new functionality for the user, but by default (apart from editing all the labels associated with the post type) you're left with an admin interface that still talks about posts. This would be a lot more user-friendly if it referred to the post type you'd created instead, and maybe have more specific instructions about how to use and edit the custom post type.

Luckily, WordPress has this functionality; although it's a bit of a mess of code, there is a way of updating all the interaction messages, contextual help, and even the Help tab that appears with your post type. As I said, the code in the following examples may look a bit untidy and cumbersome, but in the long run it's really worth it to make sure your users are getting the complete experience and most user-friendly interface for managing their content.

Interaction Messages

Interaction messages are little bits of microcopy shown by WordPress based on user actions around the interface. If a person updates, publishes, or searches within a post screen, they trigger one of the interaction messages.

To create custom messages for the post types, you can use the `post_updated_messages` hook and manually edit the messages output for the post type. Let's have a look at the code:

```
function prowordpress_updated_messages( $messages ) {
        global $post, $post_ID;
        $messages['ptd_movie'] = array(
                0 => '',
                1 => sprintf( __('Movie updated. <a href="%s">View movie</a>', 'prowordpress'),
                        esc_url( get_permalink($post_ID) ) ),
                2 => __('Custom field updated.', 'prowordpress'),
                3 => __('Custom field deleted.', 'prowordpress'),
                4 => __('movie updated.', 'prowordpress'),
                5 => isset($_GET['revision']) ? sprintf( __('Movie restored to revision from %s',
                        'prowordpress'), wp_post_revision_title( (int) $_GET['revision'], false ) ) : false,
                6 => sprintf( __('Movie published. <a href="%s">View Movie</a>', 'prowordpress'),
                        esc_url( get_permalink($post_ID) ) ),
                7 => __('Movie saved.', 'prowordpress'),
                8 => sprintf( __('Movie submitted. <a target="_blank" href="%s">Preview movie</a>',
                        'prowordpress'), esc_url( add_query_arg( 'preview', 'true',
                        get_permalink($post_ID) ) ) ),
                9 => sprintf( __('Movie scheduled for: <strong>%1$s</strong>. <a target="_blank"
                        href="%2$s">Preview movie</a>', 'prowordpress'), date_i18n( __( 'M j, Y @ G:i' ),
                        strtotime( $post->post_date ) ), esc_url( get_permalink($post_ID) ) ),
                10 => sprintf( __('Movie draft updated. <a target="_blank" href="%s">Preview movie</a>',
                        'prowordpress'), esc_url( add_query_arg( 'preview', 'true',
                        get_permalink($post_ID) ) ) ),
        );
        return $messages;
}
add_filter( 'post_updated_messages', 'prowordpress_updated_messages' );
```

This function doesn't look too friendly, I'll grant you, but unfortunately it's the only way to update the messages in WordPress at the moment. (With WordPress being updated so regularly, it may make some changes to this soon). In the function, you first need to grab the current post global variable and the `$post_ID` variable, which you'll use in the messages when outputting links and various other bits for your messages. The `$messages` variable in the function is passed in by reference from the hook and is what stores all the messages for all custom post types, so if you want to update multiple post types here, you can do so in this one function.

The messages for the post type are stored in the messages array using the post identifier as the key and then each message is simply contained in that array. The improvement in the future could be that the messages get stored in an associative array so you know what each message is referring to, but for now you have to go from the current messages that exist. The messages are simply using the example from the WordPress codex with all references to `'post'` replaced with `'movie'`. The code in and around the messages are WordPress internationalization functions and string building functions that you can leave alone because they do the job superbly.

Adding Contextual Help

Along with interaction messages, there is also contextual help you can add to your post types to give the user more information on how to use the custom post type or what to add. All this is done via the Help drop-down list in the top corner of the page (see Figure 4-8). It is visible on most of the pages throughout WordPress, although it does not appear on your custom post types unless you set up some information to go in it, which is what you will do here.

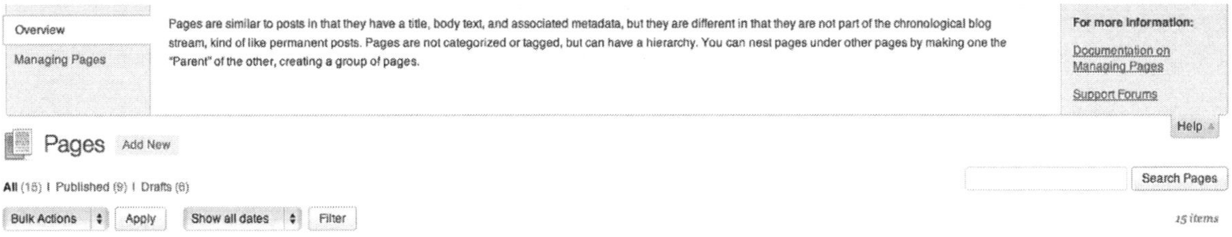

Overview	Pages are similar to posts in that they have a title, body text, and associated metadata, but they are different in that they are not part of the chronological blog stream, kind of like permanent posts. Pages are not categorized or tagged, but can have a hierarchy. You can nest pages under other pages by making one the "Parent" of the other, creating a group of pages.	For more information:
Managing Pages		Documentation on Managing Pages
		Support Forums

Help ▲

Pages   Add New

All (15) | Published (9) | Drafts (6)   Search Pages

Bulk Actions ⬍   Apply   Show all dates ⬍   Filter   15 items

Figure 4-8. *The Help tab content dropped down for you to see*

To add to the Help tab, you need to write a function that hooks into the display of the editor pages of WordPress. For this, you have the contextual_help hook. You can also write different help text based on the screen you're viewing, which is where the contextual part comes in. Each screen has its own ID, so you can use it to figure out what content to display.

```
function prowordpress_add_help_text( $contextual_help, $screen_id, $screen ) {
    if ( 'ptd_movie' == $screen->id ) {
        $contextual_help =
            '<p>' . __('Things to remember when adding or editing a movie:',
                'prowordpress') . '</p>'.
            '<ul>' .
            '<li>' . __('Add the synopsis to the main content editor.', 'prowordpress'). '</li>'.
            '<li>' . __('You can also add a custom excerpt of the synopsis to display on the
                listing page in the excerpt box', 'prowordpress') . '</li>' .
            '</ul>' .
            '<p>' . __('If you want to schedule the book review to be published in the
                future:', 'prowordpress') . '</p>' .
            '<ul>' .
            '<li>' . __('Under the Publish module, click on the Edit link next to Publish.',
                'prowordpress') . '</li>' .
            '</ul>' .
            '<p><strong>' . __('For more information:', 'prowordpress') . '</strong></p>' .
            '<p>' . __('<a href="http://codex.wordpress.org/Posts_Edit_SubPanel" target="_
                blank">Edit Posts Documentation</a>', 'prowordpress') . '</p>' .
            '<p>' . __('<a href="http://wordpress.org/support/" target="_blank">Support
                Forums</a>', 'prowordpress') . '</p>' ;
    } elseif ( 'edit-ptd_movie' == $screen->id ) {
        $contextual_help .=
            '<p>' . __('Pick a movie to edit from the list or add a new movie from this screen',
                'prowordpress') . '</p>' ;
    }
    return $contextual_help;
}
add_action( 'contextual_help', 'prowordpress_add_help_text', 10, 3 );
```

Here you're adding content for two different screens for the post type: the first has the screen ID of the post type identifier and relates to the editing page of the post type; the second is the post type list page that has the screen ID of the post type identifier but is prefixed by *edit-*. All the function then does is add content to the $contextual_help variable, which is passed in by reference. You return it at the end of the function and you get a Help tab with the content shown in Figure 4-9.

Figure 4-9. *The contextual help content added to the drop-down list*

Custom Help Tabs

In WordPress 3.3 (Sonny), tabs were added to the Help drop-down lists to be able to provide better help to the user when working with WordPress. This allowed for more detailed help content and for it to be displayed in a much nicer way. In the previous example, you added the help content to the drop-down list, but it created only one tab: an overview tab (refer to Figure 4-9). If you want to emulate the WordPress experience, though, and create more useful help content, you can create your own custom tabs:

```
function prowordpress_custom_help_tab() {
        global $post_ID;
        $screen = get_current_screen();

        if( isset($_GET['post_type']) ) $post_type = $_GET['post_type'];
        else $post_type = get_post_type( $post_ID );

        if( $post_type == 'ptd_movies' ) {

                $screen->add_help_tab( array(
                        'id' => 'movie_help_genre', //unique id for the tab
                        'title' => 'Genres', //unique visible title for the tab
                        'content' => '<h3>Choosing genres</h3><p>For help with selecting the correct
                                    genre for your movie you could check out the information on
                                    <a href="http://www.imdb.com/">imdb.com</a>.</p>',
                ));
        }
}

add_action('admin_head', 'prowordpress_custom_help_tab');
```

This code is called on the admin_head hook; if you were to use it on the contextual_help hook as you did in the previous example, it would overwrite the help you set up first. However, if you will use tabs in your contextual help, I suggest taking this approach and leaving out the contextual help method. For instance, you could combine the two functions shown in these examples and set up tabs for each screen using the conditional tags from the previous example.

Advanced Custom Menu Icons

If you look back at the example in Figure 4-7, you can clearly see the difference between the new custom post type menu icon and the rest of the icons. When inactive, the menu icon, despite having its opacity lowered, still shows up in color, whereas the rest of the default icons appear in grayscale. The reason is that when you set an icon up through the `register_post_type` function, WordPress adds the icon that you've set as an `img` tag into the menu structure, whereas all the default icons are controlled with CSS using a sprite.

To add an icon to the custom post type that acts in a similar way to the WordPress defaults, you have to veer slightly off the path suggested by the WordPress Codex. To get the custom menu icon working as default WordPress icons do, you need to create some custom icons and add some CSS to the admin area of the theme.

To fully customize the post type icons, you need to create more than just the color and grayscale icons for the admin menu; you also want to create a large grayscale icon, 32x32 pixels in size, to go at the top of the main screens of the post type. (You can see an example of one at the top of the Page editor screen in Figure 4-7.) With WordPress being kept up to date with modern technology, you'll need to have versions of the icons at 2x the size for high-dpi screens, too. On top of that, WordPress also has a blue admin theme (not that I know anyone who uses it) that uses icons with a blue tint, whereas the normal theme uses grayscale icons. This means that in total you can be creating up to 10 icons per post type to make the menu icons fully compatible with all aspects of the WordPress admin. For this example, though, I look only at the standard WordPress admin; for the blue tint admin, you can use similar CSS but note that the body class to look for is `'.admin-color-classic'`.

First, you need to create the graphics. The method I use is having the icons all in one sprite graphic, but you can do this in whatever way you prefer; just substitute the images where necessary in the CSS.

To add these icons to the admin, you need to do it via CSS, not via the post type function, so if you use this method, you can remove the `'menu_icon'` option from the function, and instead allow the default icon to be used, which you'll overwrite in the CSS. To add CSS to the admin pages, some people pass a function with CSS written into a `<style>` tag to the `'admin_head'` function; it simply places the styles into the page `<head>` tag. However, I prefer to use a separate style sheet for any extra admin styles I want to use, and it is really simple to do with another hook and the `wp_enqueue_style` function you used in Chapter 2.

```
add_action('admin_enqueue_scripts', 'my_admin_theme_style');

function my_admin_theme_style() {
    wp_enqueue_style('ptd-admin-theme', get_bloginfo('template_directory') . '/css/admin-style.css'
);
}
```

If you add the previous few lines of code to the functions file in your theme, you have a style sheet included in the WordPress admin pages. In the style sheet, you can add the following CSS to change the menu icon for the new post type:

```
/* Admin Menu - normal */
#menu-posts-ptd_movie .wp-menu-image {
    background: url(../images/icon-movie-sprite.png) no-repeat 0 0;
}
/* Admin Menu - hover/active */
#menu-posts-ptd_movie:hover .wp-menu-image,
#menu-posts-ptd_movie.wp-has-current-submenu .wp-menu-image {
    background-position: 6px -26px;
}
/* Post Screen */
.icon32-posts-ptd_movie {
    background: url(../images/icon-movie-sprite.png) no-repeat 0 0;
}
```

```css
@media
only screen and (-webkit-min-device-pixel-ratio: 1.5),
only screen and (   min--moz-device-pixel-ratio: 1.5),
only screen and (     -o-min-device-pixel-ratio: 3/2),
only screen and (         min-device-pixel-ratio: 1.5),
only screen and (               min-resolution: 1.5dppx) {

        /* Admin Menu */
        #menu-posts-ptd_movie .wp-menu-image {
                background-image: url('../images/icon-movie-sprite_2x.png');
                -webkit-background-size: 16px 48px;
                -moz-background-size: 16px 48px;
                background-size: 16px 48px;
        }
        /* Post Screen */
        .icon32-posts-ptd_movie {
                background-image: url('../images/icon-movie-sprite_2x.png');
                -webkit-background-size: 32px 32px;
                -moz-background-size: 32px 32px;
                background-size: 32px 32px;
        }
}
```

This CSS makes use of only the WordPress-added IDs that include the post type name given to the new post type. All you would have to do to add icons for the blue theme is to add the same selectors again but with the body class '.admin-color-classic' prepended to the selectors.

Plugins and Code Generators

As you've seen so far, setting up a custom post type can be one heck of a task: there are a lot of options and a load of information to go with the post types you create to make the admin interfaces as user-friendly as the rest of WordPress for your new post types. Because of all this complexity and because WordPress is so easily extendible, there are a lot of plugins available to make setting up and managing custom post types easier. You might think that I will have a bit of a moan at people using plugins to manage things that are easily solved with code, but this is one of the times when it's not entirely the case.

If you're building and maintaining a site and theme yourself, a custom post type plugin might be a good idea. It helps by saving you a lot of time and gives you a better way of managing your post types without having to write a lot of code. However, there are none I have seen so far that deal with the custom functionality of customizing the admin interfaces and help messages.

If you're creating a theme that will be distributed and managed by others, asking them to download a plugin and add specific custom post types to work with your theme is a complete no go. If you are distributing a theme for others or creating a premium theme, you can't expect to list a series of dependencies for your users or customers to be able to use your theme. In this case, you should be writing the code in with the theme so everything will be set up ready for users to get going as soon as they install your theme.

For this reason, I like the idea of code generators. For WordPress and for custom post types there are quite a few of these available; the best I've found so far is at http://generatewp.com/post-type/ (see Figure 4-10). Here you can create the bulk of your code very quickly by inputting the main naming details into the site, and it will generate the code for the post type for you. Then you're free to edit it and add to your theme yourself. It will save you a lot of time and you will have complete control over the code you're putting into your theme.

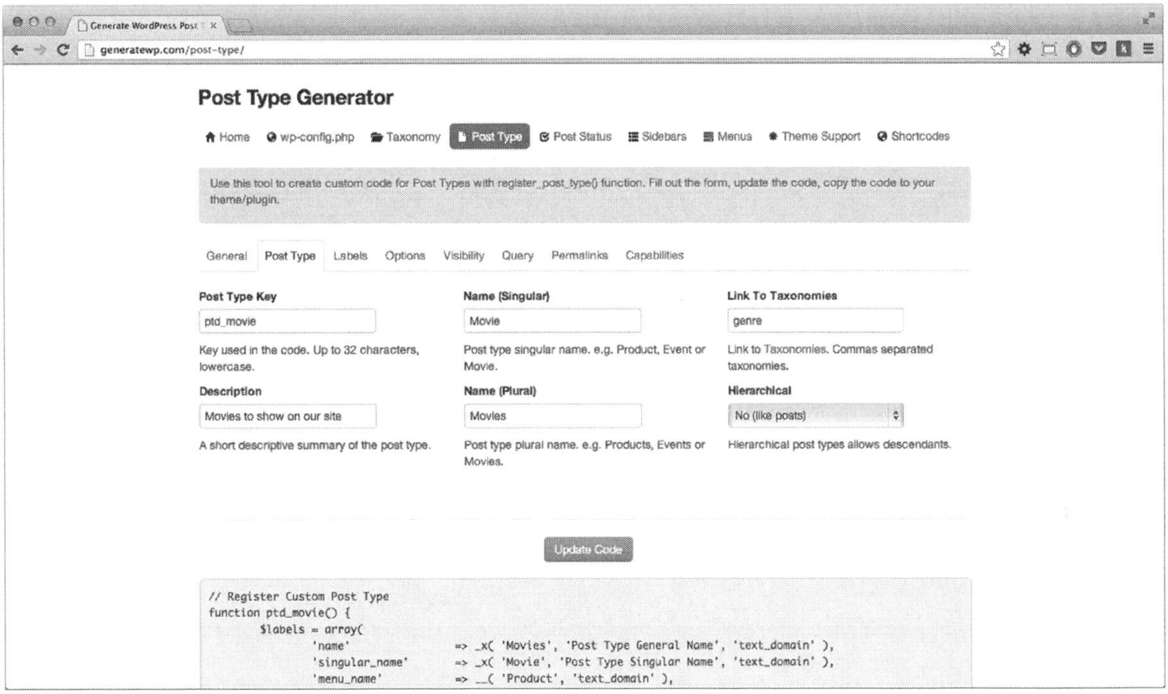

Figure 4-10. *The GenerateWP post type generator*

Displaying Custom Post Types

Once you set up the custom post types in WordPress, you'll need a way to display the content in your themes. As I talked about at the beginning of the chapter, custom post types are stored in a similar way to the rest of the main content of posts and pages in WordPress. Because of this, it means that accessing them in your theme uses very similar techniques. You can do it through the WordPress query, which you learned about in the last chapter; or through custom page templates, as discussed in Chapter 2.

Querying with Custom Post Types

The first method you'll look at is using the custom query. You've already seen this in action a lot in the previous chapter, so you should be familiar with the main code you'll be using. To get the custom post type to appear in the query, you simply use the custom post identifier you created the post with as the value of the post_type option in the query arguments. Using the example of the ptd_movie post type you created earlier, the query would look a lot like this:

```
$args = array(
            'post_type'      => 'ptd_movie',
            'posts_per_page' => 10,
            'orderby'        => 'title',
            'order'          => 'ASC'
            );
$movies = new WP_Query( $args );
```

```
if( $movies->have_posts() ) : while( $movies->have_posts() ) : $movies->the_post(); ?>

        <article <?php post_class(); ?>>
                <h2><?php the_title(); ?></h2>

                <?php the_content(); ?>
        </article>

<?php endwhile; endif; ?>
```

You just created a new instance of the WP_Query with the arguments querying for the posts in the ptd_movie post type and then run a loop normally, including all the usual template tags.

You can also add your custom post type to the default query so it will be intermixed with the normal posts and displayed on your home and standard archive pages. To do this, you need to add the custom post type to the query before it has run, which is easy to do using the pre_get_posts hook:

```
add_action( 'pre_get_posts', 'prowordpress_custom_post_types_in_main_query' );

function prowordpress_custom_post_types_in_main_query( $query ) {
        if ( is_home() && $query->is_main_query() ) {
                $query->set( 'post_type', array( 'post', 'ptd_movie' ) );
        }

        return $query;
}
```

This is a simple function that modifies the main query if on the homepage via the WP_Query set method. The set method is another way of editing the options in the WP_Query object, which should be used when modifying an already built query. This function changes the current value of the post_type option and sets it to an array containing the standard post type and the custom post type ptd_movie. Using this method, the home page of latest posts could now be used to show a series of latest updates, which can include any new movies that have been posted as well as most recent blog posts.

Custom Post Type Templates

The next method of displaying custom post types in your WordPress theme is with the page templates in your theme. When you set up the post type earlier, you set some URL rewrite options, which means that the ptd_movie post type can be accessed through URLs on your site at these locations, for example:

- http://website.com/movie: For a page listing posts in the ptd_movie post type

- http://website.com/movie/clerks: To access a specific ptd_movie post: *Clerks* in this case

The pages these URLs go to are generated through different page templates, usually when working with the standard post type and the archive.php and single.php templates, respectively. Since version 3.1, you can now create specific templates to be used to display the custom post types by adding the post type identifier to the template file name as with the page slug to create bespoke page templates. The template files look like these:

- archive-ptd_movie.php

- single-ptd_movie.php

They now work the same way as standard WordPress page templates and will output the custom post type information from the default query passed into the template.

■ **Note**   Sometimes WordPress doesn't recognize a new template file for custom post types right away. To remedy this, you need to edit the permalink settings in Settings ➤ Permalinks, change them to something different, save the change, and then reset to your desired settings. This procedure forces WordPress to flush the rewrite rules, so you don't have to run the function in your theme when you're creating new post types.

Extending Post Types

Now that you know how to create and display custom post types in WordPress, you can take a look at how to extend the functionality of the post types to allow you to do all sorts of things. This extended functionality can also apply to the standard post types, meaning that you can customize the WordPress admin area to be as useful to you as possible.

Post Type Supports

You saw earlier the `'supports'` option, which is used when setting up the custom post type:

```
'supports' => array( 'title', 'editor', 'author', 'thumbnail', 'excerpt' ),
```

This option sets up what functionality the post type can have; each option has its own specific keyword (e.g., editor, for the main WordPress editor box that gets stored as the post content).

WordPress also has functions that can be used on already created post types to add support for any desired features that weren't set up within the register post type function. Although it may seem unnecessary, if you're using a plugin that creates a post type, you can add support for a certain feature to that post type without modifying the plugin code. Likewise, you can add different feature support to the WordPress default post types: post, page, attachment, and so on.

There are three main functions for dealing with post type supports:

- `add_post_type_support()`,
- `remove_post_type_support()`, and
- `post_type_supports()`

The first two functions simply take two arguments: the post type identifier (post, ptd_movie) and the support feature you want to add or remove. For example, adding support for an excerpt on the page post type looks like this:

```
add_action('init', 'prowordpress_add_excerpt_support');

function prowordpress_add_excerpt_support() {
        add_post_type_support( 'page', 'excerpt' );
}
```

As with setting up custom post types, you should be running these functions on the init hook to make sure the setting is implemented before the rest of the WordPress setup is run.

The final function checks whether a post type supports a certain feature. This is useful when you develop themes and plugins because it ensures that the content you look for is actually there for the custom post type. Here's an example:

```php
<?php if( post_type_supports( 'ptd_movie', 'excerpt' ) ) : ?>

        <div class="movie-synopsis">
                <?php the_excerpt(); ?>
        </div>

<?php endif; ?>
```

The code makes sure that the movie post type has an excerpt before displaying it. Of course, you know the outcome of this statement because you created the post type, but if you're using a custom post type, created by a plugin for instance, it might be worth checking.

Customizing the Post Type Overview Screen

Since WordPress 3.1, it's now extremely simple to add custom columns and information to the post's overview screen for a post type, allowing for a much more user-friendly interface for your WordPress admin. To do this, you can use two functions attached to two different hooks through WordPress. The first adds the columns to the overview page; the second populates that content on a post-by-post basis. The two hooks you'll be using are constructed using the post type identifier to make sure they get called on the correct post type; an example is manage_{post-type-identifier}_posts_columns. So for the ptd_movie post type, the hooks look like these:

- manage_ptd_movie_posts_columns
- manage_ptd_movie_posts_custom_column

First, you'll set up the custom columns:

```php
function prowordpress_custom_columns( $cols ) {
        $cols = array(
                'cb'        => '<input type="checkbox" />',
                'title'     => __( 'Title', 'prowordpress' ),
                'director' => __( 'Director', 'prowordpress' ),
                'year'      => __( 'Year', 'prowordpress' ),
        );
        return $cols;
}
add_filter( "manage_ptd_movie_posts_columns", "prowordpress_custom_columns" );
```

This function receives a parameter containing the current columns for the overview display. The following is the default content of the $cols array, so you can see what the settings are for the default columns:

```php
Array (
        ['cb']     => '<input type="checkbox" />',
        ['title'] => 'Title',
        ['date']   => 'Date',
)
```

If you wanted to continue using one of the default options, you would need to replicate the entry in the array for the default columns in the new array, or you could append the new columns to the array if you want only to add to what's already there. In the example function, I simply copied in the title entry to ensure that you get the title in the overview page as normal.

The 'cb' entry in the array is required for the select all check box, which appears in the first column by default; this is the only required field. As you can tell by the <input> tag in the value for the 'cb' entry, the values of the array store what will be output to the header of the columns so the column titles in plain English format are needed there, including any spaces.

To populate the columns, you need to use another function attached to the second hook I mentioned:

```
function prowordpress_custom_column_content( $column, $post_id ) {

        switch ( $column ) {
                case "director":
                        echo get_post_meta( $post_id, 'director', true);
                        break;
                case "year":
                        echo get_post_meta( $post_id, 'year_released', true);
                        break;
        }
}
add_action( "manage_ptd_movie_posts_custom_column", "prowordpress_custom_column_content", 10, 2 );
```

This function, which is called every time a column is populated, takes two parameters: the name of the column and the id of the current post. So you can get the correct data for the post, but you need to make sure to output the function into the correct column. You solve this by using a switch statement to decide which column you're populating based on the column parameter passed to the function; it is set to the same key you used when you created the columns. You need to get the content only for the new custom columns you created because any default columns are populated automatically.

The result of these functions is a nice and informative overview page that you can see in Figure 4-11.

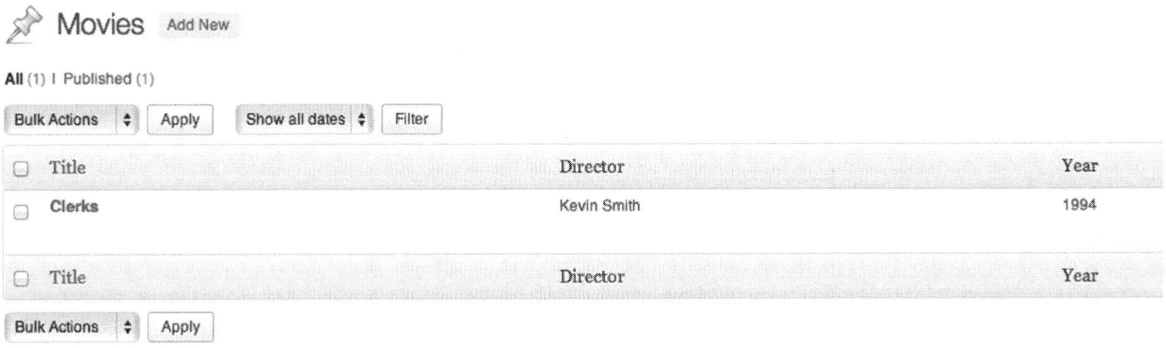

Figure 4-11. *Custom post type with custom columns on the overview page*

There is one last trick you can do with the custom columns: make them sortable by each column. If you look at the title header in Figure 4-11, it appears as a link compared with the Director and Year titles that are just static text. This means the Title column can be used to sort the posts by the content of that column. You can do this for the new columns very easily in one last function, which uses the manage_edit-{post-type-identifier}_sortable_columns hook or the manage_edit-ptd_movie_sortable_columns hook:

```
function prowordpress_sortable_custom_columns() {
        return array(
                'title'    => 'title',
                'director' => 'director',
                'year'     => 'year'
        );
}



add_filter( "manage_edit-ptd_movie_sortable_columns", "prowordpress_sortable_custom_columns");
```

For this function, all you need to do is return an array of the keys for the columns that you want to be sortable. Unlike the previous function for setting up the content of the column, you do need to include all columns that should be sortable, so any default columns must be included as well.

Add Post Types to Feed

By default, when WordPress generates an RSS feed for your site, it includes only the 'post' post type and no others. This does what a feed is meant to do, but it might be good for you to also be able to add custom post types to your feeds. Again this is done through a hook; in this case the 'request' hook, which fires when the query is generated but before it is executed on the database. With this hook, you can also find out where the request is coming from by using the argument's passed parameter:

```
function prowordpress_customise_feed($args) {

        if( isset($args['feed']) && !isset($args['post_type']) ) {
                $args['post_type'] = array('post', 'ptd_movie');
        }

        return $args;
}
add_filter('request', 'prowordpress_customise_feed');
```

This function first checks the arguments to make sure that the request being made is for a feed; it then checks whether the post_type argument has been set. If the post_type argument is set, the feed being requested is for a certain post type so you want to let that continue. If both criteria pass, you then simply add the post_type option to the arguments variable with an array containing the post types. The array must include all the post types you want to be in the theme, including the 'post' post type because you are setting the post_type option here, which will override all other options.

Building Your Theme, Part 3

Again it's time to put what you've learned in the chapter to some good use by continuing to build your custom theme. In the last chapter, you set up the theme to display the basic content for your site through the default WordPress back end with posts and pages. This time, you can start to really customize the site with what you've learned about custom post types by adding a couple to your theme.

You're creating a web site for a boutique restaurant, so the obvious post type is one for the items on the menu. Because it's a boutique restaurant you're building the site for, you'll also want to add a more personal feel to the site, which you can do by adding a staff member's post type as well.

Adding Custom Post Types

The first thing you need to do is register the post types in the `functions.php` file because the post types will be tied directly to the theme; you won't be creating a plugin. In the code example, I was a bit creative and used a loop to save you a lot of time when creating new post types. All you need to do is set up a new entry in the array, and the loop will take care of the rest. This saves you a lot of typing, especially when it comes to setting up all those custom labels.

```php
function prowordpress_post_types() {
    $types = array(
                'ptd_staff' => array(
                        'menu_title' => 'Staff',
                        'plural'     => 'People',
                        'singular'   => 'Person',
                        'supports'   => array('title', 'editor', 'excerpt', 'thumbnail',
                                            'author', 'page-attributes'),
                        'slug'       => 'staff'
                        ),
                'ptd_menu' => array(
                        'menu_title' => 'Menu',
                        'plural'     => 'Items',
                        'singular'   => 'Item',
                        'supports'   => array('title', 'editor', 'excerpt', 'thumbnail',
                                            'author', 'page-attributes'),
                        'slug'       => 'menu'
                        )
        );

    $counter = 0;
    foreach( $types as $type => $arg ) {

        $labels = array(
                    'name'          => $arg['menu_title'],
                    'singular_name' => $arg['singular'],
                    'add_new'       => 'Add new',
                    'add_new_item'  => 'Add new '.strtolower($arg['singular']),
                    'edit_item'     => 'Edit '.strtolower($arg['singular']),
                    'new_item'      => 'New '.strtolower($arg['singular']),
                    'all_items'     => 'All '.strtolower($arg['plural']),
                    'view_item'     => 'View '.strtolower($arg['plural']),
                    'search_items'  => 'Search '.strtolower($arg['plural']),
                    'not_found'     => 'No '.strtolower($arg['plural']).' found',
```

```
                              'not_found_in_trash' => 'No '.strtolower($arg['plural']).' found in Trash',
                              'parent_item_colon'  => '',
                              'menu_name'          => $arg['menu_title']
                );

                register_post_type( $type,
                        array(
                                  'labels'          => $labels,
                                  'public'          => true,
                                  'has_archive'     => true,
                                  'capability_type' => 'post',
                                  'supports'        => $arg['supports'],
                                  'rewrite'         => array( 'slug' => $arg['slug'] ),
                                  'menu_position'   => (20 + $counter),
                        )
                );

                $counter++;
        }
}
add_action('init', 'prowordpress_post_types');
```

I'm just setting up the post types with the most basic settings at the moment; both have a set of custom labels, a unique slug, and their own list of features they support. Although both post types are similar at the moment, this function allows you to change them pretty easily and add new ones without much hassle. If you need to make one of the post types more customizable, you can either add that option to the $types array and add that setting to the register_post_type function, or create a new one entirely.

Interaction Messages

The post types wouldn't be complete without setting up some custom interaction messages as well to make sure the admin area is more consistent and feels better to use. Again there is a quick win to be had here by using an array containing each post type and its unique title. You can again use a loop to set up the different messages you need. The reason you only need the singular title here is because all the interaction messages talk only about interactions with a single post, so the array you'll use is a lot more straightforward.

```
function prowordpress_updated_messages( $messages ) {
        global $post, $post_ID;

        $types = array(
                        'ptd_staff' => 'Person',
                        'ptd_menu' => 'Item',
                );

        foreach( $types as $type => $title) {
                $messages[$type] = array(
                        0 => '',
                        1 => sprintf( __('%s updated. <a href="%s">View %s</a>'),$title, esc_url(
                                get_permalink($post_ID) ),$title ),
                        2 => __('Custom field updated.'),
                        3 => __('Custom field deleted.'),
```

```
                4 => __(strtolower($title).' updated.'),
                5 => isset($_GET['revision']) ? sprintf( __('%s restored to revision from %s'),
                    $title, wp_post_revision_title( (int) $_GET['revision'], false ) ) : false,
                6 => sprintf( __('%s published. <a href="%s">View %s</a>'), $title, esc_url(
                    get_permalink($post_ID) ), strtolower($title) ),
                7 => __($title.' saved.'),
                8 => sprintf( __('%s submitted. <a target="_blank" href="%s">Preview %s</a>'),
                    $title, esc_url( add_query_arg( 'preview', 'true', get_permalink
                    ($post_ID) ) ), strtolower($title) ),
                9 => sprintf( __('%s scheduled for: <strong>%2$s</strong>. <a target="_blank"
                    href="%3$s">Preview %1$s</a>'), $title, date_i18n( __( 'M j, Y @ G:i' ),
                    strtotime( $post->post_date ) ), esc_url( get_permalink($post_ID) ) ),
                10 => sprintf( __('%s draft updated. <a target="_blank" href="%s">
                    Preview %s</a>'), $title, esc_url( add_query_arg( 'preview', 'true',
                    get_permalink($post_ID) ) ), strtolower($title) ),
            );
    }
    return $messages;
}
add_filter( 'post_updated_messages', 'prowordpress_updated_messages' );
```

At the start of the function, include a small associative array with the post type identifier with the title as the value. This means when you do the foreach loop you can use the two values as their own variables in the message settings.

The code does seem fairly complicated to look at because there are many string-formatting functions (sprintf), but you should be fine as long as the options are in the correct order.

Custom Columns

The last bit of setup for custom post types is to give them their own custom columns in the overview screen. Unfortunately, unlike the previous two examples, there isn't a quick way to do this because to set up columns for each post type you need to use a hook specific to each post type. However, because each post type for the moment has similar columns (this will change in the next chapter), you can cheat a little by calling the same function to set up the columns and column content from the two different hooks:

```
function prowordpress_custom_columns( $cols ) {
        $cols = array(
                'cb'     => '<input type="checkbox" />',
                'title'  => __( 'Title', 'prowordpress' ),
                'photo'  => __( 'Thumbnail', 'prowordpress' ),
                'date'   => __( 'Date', 'prowordpress' ),
        );
        return $cols;
}
add_filter( "manage_ptd_staff_posts_columns", "prowordpress_custom_columns" );
add_filter( "manage_ptd_menu_posts_columns", "prowordpress_custom_columns" );
```

```
function prowordpress_custom_column_content( $column, $post_id ) {

        switch ( $column ) {
                case "photo":
                        if( has_post_thumbnail( $post_id ) ) {
                                echo get_the_post_thumbnail( $post_id, array(50,50));
                        }
                        break;
        }
}
add_action( "manage_ptd_staff_posts_custom_column", "prowordpress_custom_column_content", 10, 2 );
add_action( "manage_ptd_menu_posts_custom_column", "prowordpress_custom_column_content", 10, 2 );
```

There are only two functions here: one to set up the columns and one to add the content. But because you want the columns to be the same for each post type, you just call the same functions in the add_action argument for each of the post types. You will need to change this in the future when you develop the post types further, but for now this is a good example of how the actions work. You don't need to create a unique function for each action; you can simply pass the same one to multiple if they're doing a similar job. You'll see actions, filters, and hooks described in much more detail in Chapter 6.

flush_rewrite Function

The last thing to do in the functions.php file is to add in a function to flush the WordPress rewrite rules when your theme is activated:

```
function my_rewrite_flush() {
        flush_rewrite_rules();
}

add_action( 'after_switch_theme', 'prowordpress_flush_rewrite_rules' );
```

This function and action simply make sure that the flush_rewrite_rules function is called whenever anyone activates your theme. There is no need to add in the call to activate the custom post types because it is done through their own actions on the WordPress init hook.

Post Type Templates

Now that you set up the post types, you need to set up some templates for displaying your content. For the moment, you have only the post types listed on their own pages with a click-through to the individual post content. So you need to add only four files:

- archive-ptd_staff.php
- single-ptd_staff.php
- archive-ptd_menu.php
- single-ptd_menu.php

These templates are used here just to output the basic content of the post types, so they don't look too different from the ones you've created so far. As an example, here are the menu archive page and menu single page templates:

```php
<?php
/**
 *          Template menu archive
 */
?>
<?php get_header(); ?>

        <h1>Our menu</h1>

        <?php if( have_posts() ): ?>

                <?php while( have_posts() ): the_post(); ?>

                        <?php get_template_part( 'content', 'menu' ); ?>

                <?php endwhile; ?>

        <?php else: ?>

                <article class="error">
                        <h1>Sorry there were no news articles found</h1>
                </article>

        <?php endif; ?>

<?php get_footer(); ?>

<?php
/**
 *          Template menu single
 */
?>
<?php get_header(); ?>

        <?php if( have_posts() ): while( have_posts() ): the_post(); ?>

                <article <?php post_class(); ?>>
                        <h1><?php the_title(); ?></h1>

                        <?php if( has_post_thumbnail() ): ?>
                                <?php the_post_thumbnail(); ?>
                        <?php endif; ?>

                        <?php the_content(); ?>
                </article>

        <?php endwhile; endif; ?>

<?php get_footer(); ?>
```

In the code for the first template, a template part of `content-menu.php` is also called in, which just contains the basic code to display the menu on the archive page:

```
<article <?php post_class(); ?>>
        <header>
                <h1><a href="<?php the_permalink(); ?>"><?php the_title(); ?></a></h1>
                <?php if( has_post_thumbnail() ): ?>
                        <?php the_post_thumbnail(); ?>
                <?php endif; ?>
        </header>

        <?php the_excerpt(); ?>

        <p><a href="<?php the_permalink(); ?>">Read more &raquo;</a></p>
</article>
```

The templates for the staff page for now are exactly the same, but with a different page title on the archive page because you currently have only basic functionality from the post types. In the next chapter, you'll learn how to customize post types further to develop the page templates more there.

Content

Finally, there's another content file for you to upload to your web site that adds some content into the custom post types. Just make sure that the post type identifiers are the same as the ones shown previously and the import should work perfectly. Now you'll be able to navigate to `http://website.com/menu/` to see a full list of all the menu items for the site, and see `http://website.com/staff` for a list of staff members. If it doesn't work, try editing your permalink settings, which were mentioned earlier in the chapter when you set up the new post types and page templates.

Summary

This chapter took a really detailed look at creating custom post types for WordPress, which is a core functionality that has led WordPress to become better positioned as a fully-fledged CMS.

Along with how to set up and display custom post types, you learned how to make them an integral part of the CMS admin. You saw how to avoid them looking like a stuck-on extra at the end, which makes a much better user experience for site admins. By using the extensibility of WordPress custom post types, you can add unique touches such as custom columns to the post types, making the interface more dynamic than WordPress by default.

In the next chapter, you'll look at extending custom post types even further with custom taxonomies and custom metadata. This functionality enables all sorts of dynamic filtering of content, which makes your site even more customizable and easier to use.

■ ■ ■

CHAPTER 5

Creating Custom Taxonomies and Fields

The last chapter looked at one of the main game-changing features of WordPress as a fully fledged content management system (CMS). Another couple of aspects that have contributed just as much are allowing users to customize taxonomies and add custom fields to their content. This gave users the ability to control the organizational structure of their content and add extra information any way they like. This chapter looks at how to get the most from custom taxonomies and custom fields, how to add them to post types, even specific posts, and then at the myriad of ways you can display your content based on this data. First, you'll take a look at WordPress taxonomies; later in the chapter, you'll delve into custom fields. Finally, the two are combined to give users the power to find specific content on their sites.

Introducing Taxonomies

Taxonomies in WordPress are a way of grouping your content and are used in a variety of ways throughout the CMS. In WordPress, there are now five default taxonomies:

- Categories
- Tags
- Link categories
- Navigation menus
- Post formats

Even though you're unlikely to see the last two used in a way you're used to seeing taxonomies, they are still stored and accessed in much the same ways as typical taxonomies such as categories and tags. However, to describe taxonomies in more detail, I'll stick with the two well-known forms of taxonomy: categories and tags.

In a post for *Smashing Magazine*, Kevin Leary classes these two taxonomies as hierarchical and multifaceted. Categories in WordPress are an example of a *hierarchical* taxonomy; the terms (an individual classification defined within the taxonomy) can be related to each other and are usually used for a more broad and general grouping of the post. *Tags* are classed as multifaceted; a tag can be descriptive of just one small aspect of the current post, and a post can be tagged with multiple terms. The way I classify the two is by thinking this: a post is *in* a category and a post *has* one or more tags.

Before custom post types were fully introduced to WordPress in version 3, custom taxonomies were already around for a little while. But as with custom post types in version 3, they were introduced as a core feature, and later on in version 3.1, there was a whole bunch of new features and functions to make custom taxonomies even more useful. In the following section of this chapter, you'll look at how to create custom taxonomies and the range of ways you can use these new taxonomies to display content.

When Do I Need a Custom Taxonomy?

But first, as with the previous chapter on custom post types, let's take a quick look at reasons for using custom taxonomies. You can create taxonomies not only for a custom post type you created but also for use with the default post types in WordPress. As you'll see, you can create custom taxonomies for almost anything.

Taxonomies are used to group content together, so the main reason for adding a custom taxonomy is to make your content more dynamic and easy to find/understand/display.

First, ask whether one of the built-in taxonomies will suit the purpose in the first place. Even for custom post types, you can still use the built-in taxonomies of categories and tags; the only issue being that when you attach built-in taxonomies to custom post types, the content for these post types becomes linked. If you use the taxonomy categories on both the posts and a custom post type, you must use the same terms, and both post types will be returned when looking to display that individual term. This applies unless you're querying for the term, in which case inside the query you can specify the post type along with the term and taxonomy.

Going back to creating a custom taxonomy and sticking with the examples in previous chapters, you'll again look to movies to help you out. If you build a site to display a bunch of films that have a lot of content, the best thing is to classify them in some way so users can get to the information they want more easily. Luckily, movies are easy to categorize:

- Genres
- Actors
- Directors
- Writers
- Film studio

I could go on and on—there are lot of taxonomies you could create. When creating them, think about the method you'll use to create the taxonomies if you create a hierarchical category such as taxonomy or a tag style multifaceted taxonomy. Let's look at those taxonomies again, but think about what sort of taxonomy they will be:

- Genres (hierarchical)
- Actors (multifaceted)
- Directors (hierarchical)
- Writers (multifaceted)
- Film studio (hierarchical)

You may wonder why I've given them such different classification. Why should a director be created differently from an actor? This for me is because of the way WordPress works with and displays taxonomies (see Figure 5-1).

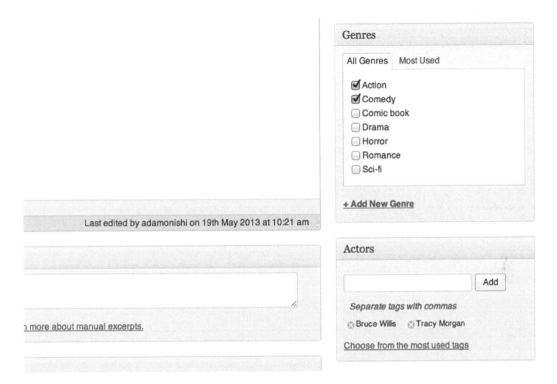

Figure 5-1. *The contrasting displays of hierarchical vs. multifaceted taxonomies*

Hierarchical taxonomies usually have their terms defined first; then posts are added and classified with a term when it's written. Whereas multifaceted taxonomies are usually created on the fly and generally hold a lot more terms than hierarchical ones. In this situation, films have many actors, with new actors coming into films more often than new directors, so the on-the-fly adding of a tag like taxonomy would suit actors well. Although not strictly using the "hierarchical" nature of the taxonomy with the director's taxonomy, it makes much more sense from a content management point of view to have them added earlier on in the process and a visible list in the post editor screen when adding a new movie.

Creating Custom Taxonomies

Now that I've covered the whys of creating custom taxonomies in quite a lot of detail, let's take a look at the how. Again, as with the previous chapter on custom post type creation, you'll look at creation in a few stages:

- Naming conventions
- Basic creation of a custom taxonomy
- Full setup with advanced options
- Custom help tab content

Naming Conventions

WordPress suggests certain naming conventions when creating custom taxonomies, which are very similar to those used when creating custom post types. All names should be in lowercase with no spaces and fewer than 32 characters long (because of the database field limit).

When naming your taxonomy, be careful not to conflict with any other taxonomies in use by WordPress or the themes/plugins and avoid clashing with any of the WordPress reserved terms. The full list can be found here: http://wp-themes-book.com/05001.

As with the custom post types, I recommend that any custom taxonomies you create are named with a prefix so you can reduce the chance of any possible conflicts with plugins or themes you may use alongside your own. Looking at the list you made before with the movie taxonomies, the names for these would look something like this:

- ptd_genres
- ptd_actors
- ptd_directors
- ptd_writers
- ptd_film_studio

Setting Up a Basic Custom Taxonomy

As you did in the previous chapter when setting up a custom post type, here you'll have a look at setting up a custom taxonomy with the bare minimum of options and then look in more detail later on in the chapter. This is so you can see just how little there is needed for you to get up and running right away while leaving WordPress to handle the rest.

To create a new taxonomy, you'll use the register_taxonomy function. In functions or plugin files, you also need to remember that it needs to be hooked onto the WordPress init action the same as the custom post type functions were before. With that in mind, let's have a look at the code to create the first custom taxonomy:

```
function prowordpress_taxonomies() {
        register_taxonomy( 'ptd_genre', 'ptd_movie',
                array(
                        'label'       => __( 'Genre', 'prowordpress' ),
                        'rewrite'     => array( 'slug' => 'genre' ),
                        'hierarchical' => true,
                )
        );
}
add_action('init', 'prowordpress_taxonomies');
```

This code is what I consider the absolute minimum for creating a custom hierarchical taxonomy. Of course, if you want to create a custom multifaceted taxonomy, you can remove the hierarchical argument from the array because that argument is false by default. The result of this code can be seen in Figure 5-2, which shows the location of the taxonomy under the Movies post type on the left and the edit screen for the Genres taxonomy.

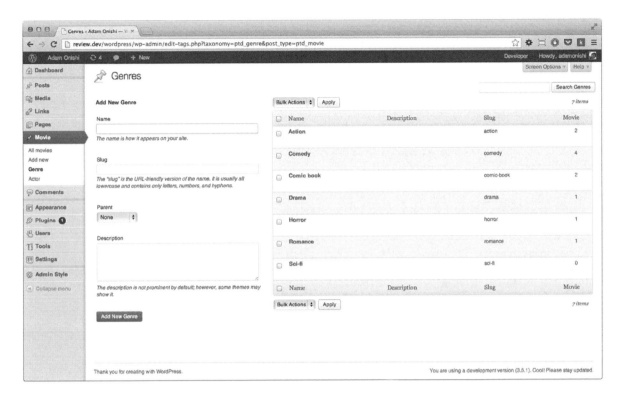

Figure 5-2. *Genres taxonomy edit screen*

The `register_taxonomy` function takes three parameters: the name of the taxonomy, the name of the post type the taxonomy should be attached to, and an array of options for the taxonomy. The final parameter of arguments is actually optional for this function because WordPress will get the main settings from the defaults and infer the labels from the taxonomy name parameter passed in. So realistically all you need to define a simple multifaceted taxonomy is the following code:

```
function prowordpress_taxonomies() {
        register_taxonomy( 'ptd_actors', 'ptd_movie' );
}
add_action('init', 'prowordpress_taxonomies');
```

This would technically work, but in using this approach you would end up with a taxonomy called "Tags" as WordPress would use the default label for a multifaceted taxonomy, and you would have to access tags through a URL with the prefixed `taxonomy` identifier instead of a nice clean rewrite URL.

The final thing to mention about the `register_taxonomy` function is that technically the second argument of post type could be set to null when the taxonomy is created. This seems a little odd, but it means that later on in the code you can use the `register_taxonomy_for_object_type` function to assign the taxonomy to a post type or use the taxonomies argument in the `register_post_type` function. What this could allow you to do is from within a plugin, set up a custom taxonomy that your plugin would use but allow it to be assigned to a custom post type by the user. In your user's code, they could take that setting and use the `register_taxonomy_for_object_type` function to assign your taxonomy to the user's plugin of choice.

■ **Note** When registering a taxonomy using a null post type argument and adding it instead to the `register_post_type` function, you must ensure that your taxonomies are declared before the custom post types.

Full Setup of a Custom Taxonomy

Now that you've seen the basics of the `register_taxonomy` function and how to get a custom taxonomy set up quickly and easily, let's have a look at the full options available for the function and see the full detail of the custom taxonomies you can create.

First, here's an example of a full function call making use of most arguments you need to customize your taxonomy:

```php
function prowordpress_taxonomies() {

    $labels = array(
        'name'              => _x( 'Genres', 'taxonomy general name', 'prowordpress' ),
        'singular_name'     => _x( 'Genre', 'taxonomy singular name', 'prowordpress' ),
        'search_items'      => __( 'Search Genres', 'prowordpress' ),
        'all_items'         => __( 'All Genres', 'prowordpress' ),
        'parent_item'       => __( 'Parent Genre', 'prowordpress' ),
        'parent_item_colon' => __( 'Parent Genre:', 'prowordpress' ),
        'edit_item'         => __( 'Edit Genre', 'prowordpress' ),
        'update_item'       => __( 'Update Genre', 'prowordpress' ),
        'add_new_item'      => __( 'Add New Genre', 'prowordpress' ),
        'new_item_name'     => __( 'New Genre Name', 'prowordpress' ),
        'menu_name'         => __( 'Genre', 'prowordpress' )
    );

    $args = array(
        'labels'            => $labels,
        'hierarchical'      => true,
        'public'            => true,
        'show_tagcloud'     => false,
        'show_admin_column' => true,
        'query_var'         => true,
        'rewrite'           => array( 'slug' => 'genre' ),
        'sort'              => true,
    );

    register_taxonomy( 'ptd_genre', 'ptd_movie', $args );
}
add_action('init', 'prowordpress_taxonomies');
```

This is probably the set of arguments that most make sense when setting up a custom hierarchical taxonomy. There are more options that can be used in this function, but I'll cover them separately later on.

Again you'll look at each option in detail as you did in the last chapter with custom post types; you've already looked at the first two parameters of the `register_taxonomy` function, so you'll concentrate on the `arguments` array and the options you can pass using that.

Labels

Again the labels are probably the easiest place to start, being extremely self-explanatory. However, this time you'll notice a couple of differences with the label definitions compared with the custom post type function you used before because here you're using some different internationalization functions.

There's a second example of the WordPress internationalization functions at use in the labels code: _x(). This function is used to translate words in which the context might change the meaning of the word; for example, post can be used as a verb ("click here to post your comment") or as a noun ("edit post"). For help with the translations in situations like this, the _x() function takes a second argument for the context of the word being used, so in the preceding case of the labels, you have two labels that need their context adding. The text in the second argument is set specifically from WordPress to help with the translations, so you can just copy the wording there into your functions. You'll read more about the use of the _x() function and the other internationalization functions in Chapter 12.

Taxonomy Display Options

As with the `register_post_type` function, there are a few different display options that can be used when setting up a custom taxonomy. They're pretty similar to the post type options, but with a few exceptions/additions:

- `public`
- `show_ui`
- `show_in_nav_menus`
- `show_tagcloud`
- `show_admin_column`

The first three should be fairly familiar, and they work in exactly the same way as the same options in the `register_post_type` function. The last two, however, are unique to taxonomies.

The `show_tagcloud` option is a Boolean setting that either allows or prevents the use of the tag cloud function on the chosen taxonomy. If you haven't seen a WordPress tag cloud before, see Figure 5-3. It's a collection of all the terms in the taxonomy, which are then formatted in size based on the popularity of each term. From the name, the tag cloud might suggest that the function is available only for taxonomies that resemble tags in function (i.e., multifaceted). That's not the case, however, and by using the `wp_tag_cloud` function you can display a tag cloud of any taxonomy on your site.

Popular Tags

Figure 5-3. Example of a tag cloud from the tags edit screen

The `show_admin_column` function is a new option that was added recently in version 3.5. Again, it's another Boolean option that when set to true sets up an admin column for the taxonomy on the associated post type; an example can be seen in Figure 5-4.

	Genres	Actors	Date
iishi	Comedy, Romance	Elizabeth Banks, Jason Mewes, Jeff Anderson, Seth Rogen	2013/05/19 Published
iishi	Action, Comedy	Bruce Willis, Tracy Morgan	2013/05/19 Published
iishi	Comedy	Ben Affleck, Brian O'Halloran, Jason Lee, Kevin Smith	2013/05/19 Published
iishi	Comedy	Ben Affleck, Jason Lee, Jason Mewes, Jeremy London, Kevin Smith, Shannen Doherty	2013/04/20 Published
iishi	Comedy	Brian O'Halloran, Jason Mewes, Jeff Anderson, Kevin Smith, Scott Mosier	2013/04/20 Published
	Genres	Actors	Date

Figure 5-4. Genres and Actors admin columns on the Movies post type

The query_var and rewrite Options

The query_var and rewrite options work in almost the same way here as they do when used for registering custom post types. Both settings relate to how you can query for the taxonomy by using the web site URL or using the WordPress custom queries which was talked about in Chapter 3.

When setting query_var to true, you have access to your taxonomies via URL queries; when set to false, this method is prevented from working. However, when set to false, the taxonomy can still be queried by using a query within WordPress (more on this later):

```
new WP_Query( array(
            'post_type' => 'custom_post_type_name',
            'tax_query' => array (
                        'taxonomy' => 'taxonomy_name',
                        'field'    => 'slug',
                        'terms'    => 'taxonomy_name'
                ),
            )
    );
```

You can also use a string for the argument of the query_var parameter to set a custom query_var for the taxonomy.

Capabilities

I'll discuss custom capabilities in more detail in Chapter 8, but just a quick mention here that there are four capabilities that can be assigned by using an array as the argument: assign_terms, edit_terms, manage_terms, and delete_terms.

Sort

The sort argument allows you to set whether the taxonomy remembers in which order the terms were added to a specific post.

Hierarchical

The last main option to discuss is a pretty straightforward one, as discussed at length in this chapter. This Boolean option is the difference between a hierarchical taxonomy and a multifaceted one.

The very last argument to discuss is the update_count_callback option, which acts like a hook and takes a function name as the parameter, much like the add_action function that's used a lot in the book already. The function passed to the argument is called when the count of the associated post type is updated. It has one useful function that is related to when you create a multifaceted taxonomy with hierarchical set to false. For your taxonomy to behave like the WordPress default tags taxonomy in which the user can enter multiple tags at once, comma-separated, you need to pass the update_count_callback function the parameter _update_post_term_count. It is the function that WordPress has built-in to deal with separating tags and storing them correctly in the database. Otherwise, if you tried to add multiple comma-separated terms to a post without this function, you would end up with a single string as the term.

Contextual Help and Help Tabs

Again this is something I think is very important to the all-around user experience when you create a custom theme. The ability to add custom help messages throughout the user interfaces (UIs) you create will help improve the usability of your theme and allow your clients or customers to get the best from the themes you create.

Adding contextual help text and help tabs is just as simple for custom taxonomies as it was for custom post types, and you can even add them to the functions created before.

Here's a snippet of the code you used before, but with the addition of the contextual help for the new taxonomy:

```
function prowordpress_add_help_text( $contextual_help, $screen_id, $screen ) {
        if ( 'ptd_movie' == $screen->id ) {

                // Add contextual help to $contextual_help variable

        } elseif ( 'edit-ptd_movie' == $screen->id ) {

                // Add contextual help to $contextual_help variable

        } elseif ( 'edit-ptd_genre' == $screen->id ) {

            $contextual_help .=
                '<p>' . __('Add movie genres to the Genre taxonomy to help classify the movies added',
'prowordpress') . '</p>' ;
        }

        return $contextual_help;

}
add_action( 'contextual_help', 'prowordpress_add_help_text', 10, 3 );
```

The bit you want to focus on is the last elseif statement. Here you're checking the screen ID is edit-ptd_genre, the identifier of the taxonomy, and then adding the help text to the contextual help variable as before.

To add custom help tabs to the help section, you can again use the function you had before for the custom post type; then add in an extra bit of code to check whether you're viewing the newly created taxonomy:

```php
function prowordpress_custom_help_tab() {
        global $post_ID;
        $screen = get_current_screen();

        // Custom post type code here

        if ( is_taxonomy( 'ptd_genre' ) ) {
                $screen->add_help_tab( array(
                        'id' => 'movie_help_genre', //unique id for the tab
                        'title' => 'Genres', //unique visible title for the tab
                        'content' => '<h3>Choosing genres</h3><p>For help with selecting the correct
genre for your movie you could check out the information on <a href=
"http://www.imdb.com/">imdb.com</a>.</p>',
                ));
        }
}

add_action('admin_head', 'prowordpress_custom_help_tab');
```

And it really is as simple as that. If all you need is a few lines of code to add some help text to the admin interfaces, it seems silly not to add that little bit of extra effort for the benefit of clients and customers.

Displaying Posts by Custom Taxonomy

Now that you have set up taxonomies to group content, you can start to look at how to view the content based on these taxonomies. Again, as with custom post types, there are two main methods of displaying posts based on the related taxonomies, you can do it programmatically with the WordPress query or through custom URLs with custom page templates to catch and display the content uniquely.

The tax_query Parameter

You saw the tax_query parameter in Chapter 3 when you looked at the WordPress query. Here you'll look at it in more depth and go over the different options you have to query for posts using taxonomy information.

What I didn't mention in the earlier chapter is that since WordPress 3.1 and the introduction of the tax_query parameter, now every query argument relating to taxonomies is filtered through into a tax_query. For example, if you were to take a look at a simple tag query that used the tag__in parameter, it would look like this:

```php
'tag__and' => array( 37, 47 )
```

However, inside the core files you can see what happens to this query once it reaches the query.php file:

```php
if ( !empty($q['tag__and']) ) {
        $q['tag__and'] = array_map('absint', array_unique( (array) $q['tag__and'] ) );
        $tax_query[] = array(
                'taxonomy' => 'post_tag',
                'terms' => $q['tag__and'],
                'operator' => 'AND'
        );
}
```

Since WordPress 3.1, when the tax_query parameter was introduced, the previous method of querying taxonomies using just the taxonomy slug and terms slug has been deprecated (this doesn't apply to the built-in taxonomies, categories, and tags that still work as shown previously). Currently, it's still possible to use the old method, and it will return results; however, the deprecation of the method means that at some stage it will be removed from the core code and any remaining queries using that method will no longer work.

So with that in mind, make sure that you know exactly what you're doing with the tax_query parameter. A simple tax query for one term in a taxonomy would look like this:

```
'tax_query' => array(
            array(
                    'taxonomy' => 'ptd_genre',
                    'field' => 'slug',
                    'terms' => 'comedy'
                    )

        ),
```

The tax_query parameter takes its arguments in the form of an array of arrays, so a single taxonomy query requires one nested array with at least the three fields shown here. There are five parameters you can set in total:

- taxonomy: Taxonomy identifier

- field: What to search for; either the term ID or terms slug (defaults to ID)

- terms: A string or number for one term and an array if querying for multiple

- include_children: A Boolean for whether to look into the return; also the child terms of the term being queried (defaults to true)

- operator: Database comparison operator for which to compare the terms; can be IN, NOT IN, or AND (defaults to IN).

A full query for a single taxonomy could look something like this:

```
'tax_query' => array(
            array(
                    'taxonomy'          => 'ptd_genre',
                    'field'             => 'slug',
                    'terms'             => array('horror', 'thriller', 'drama'),
                    'operator'          => 'NOT IN',
                    'include_children' => false,
                    )

        )
```

This code returns movies that are not horror, thriller, or drama films, but would return posts in their children terms, so maybe a comedy horror might slip through.

The real power of tax_query, however, comes when querying for multiple taxonomies. To do this, you pass in multiple arrays constructed in the same manner as you've seen before, but with a multitaxonomy query, there's one more parameter that the tax_query uses: the relation parameter. This argument can take one of two options, which then dictates how the terms are queried for in the database: either OR or AND, with AND being the default. Therefore, if you were to add a query for the ptd_actor taxonomy to the tax_query, it might look something like this:

```
'tax_query' => array(
                'relation' => 'AND',
                array(
                        'taxonomy'          => 'ptd_genre',
                        'field'             => 'slug',
                        'terms'             => array('horror', 'thriller', 'drama'),
                        'operator'          => 'NOT IN',
                        'include_children' => false,
                        ),
                array(
                        'taxonomy'          => 'ptd_actor',
                        'field'             => 'slug',
                        'terms'             => array('simon-pegg', 'nick-frost' ),
                        'operator'          => 'AND',
                        )
        )
```

That now gives you the power to really narrow down the query using taxonomies. But besides narrowing down the query by using the AND operator for the relation parameter, you can also use the OR operator to broaden the query between several categories. Here you can query for movies that aren't a horror, thriller, or drama film; OR star Zooey Deschanel; OR are directed by Seth Rogen or Kevin Smith. Granted, that's a myriad of unrelated options, but it returns a bunch of movies that someone might want to watch:

```
'tax_query' => array(
                'relation' => 'OR',
                array(
                        'taxonomy' => 'ptd_genre',
                        'field'    => 'slug',
                        'terms'    => array('horror', 'thriller', 'drama'),
                        'operator' => 'NOT IN',
                        ),
                array(
                        'taxonomy' => 'ptd_actor',
                        'field'    => 'slug',
                        'terms'    => array( 'zooey-deschanel' ),
                        ),
                array(
                        'taxonomy' => 'ptd_writer',
                        'field'    => 'slug',
                        'terms'    => array( 'seth-rogen', 'kevin-smith' ),
                        ),
        )
```

That was a pretty detailed look at how to use the tax_query option in your WordPress queries; next you'll see what options you have when it comes to custom templates and displaying posts based on custom taxonomies.

Custom Taxonomy Templates

Because taxonomies are a method of grouping your posts, there's only one lineage of page templates that you can work with, which is part of the archive template route. However, there are many ways to create a template to show content for specific taxonomies down to specific taxonomy terms. The hierarchy for custom taxonomy templates looks like this:

- taxonomy-taxonomy_name-term_name.php; if not available, use

- taxonomy-taxonomy_name.php; if not available, use

- taxonomy.php; then finally use

- archive.php (followed by index.php if you want to be thorough)

To translate them into page templates using the genre taxonomy you've created, you would need to use the taxonomy identifier you used when you set up the taxonomy and the term slugs; they would look like these:

- taxonomy-ptd_genre-comedy.php

- taxonomy-ptd_genre.php

Besides the different custom templates you can use, custom taxonomy information will also be added to the body classes when using the body_class function. This would allow you to use classes in your CSS such as the following:

- tax-ptd_genre (the taxonomy identifier prefixed with tax)

- term-comedy (the term slug prefixed with term)

- term-3 (the term ID prefixed with term)

Now you've looked at ways of getting posts from WordPress using custom taxonomies, you'll now look at ways of displaying and using the custom taxonomy information in your templates.

Taxonomy and Term Conditionals

When using any of the preceding templates, you can also use the taxonomy conditional function that can help you decide what information to display. Much as you did in the archive page template to decide what title to show in previous examples, you can use the is_tax function to show a title suited to the listing of a taxonomy archive.

The excellent thing about the is_tax function is that it can be passed a series of different arguments that gives you a variety of choices about how you can query which taxonomy or term is being displayed:

- is_tax(): Alone, this returns true if any taxonomy archive page is displayed. Note that this works only for custom taxonomies, not for built-in taxonomies such as categories.

- is_tax('ptd_genre'): With the taxonomy identifier as the only parameter, this returns true when you're on any ptd_genre taxonomy archive page.

- is_tax('ptd_genre', 'comedy'): With a taxonomy and one of the terms passed as two parameters, the function returns true if you're on the specific term's archive page.

- is_tax('ptd_genre', array('comedy', 'comic-book')): When passed an array of term names in the second parameter, the function returns true if you're displaying either of the terms archive pages.

Besides the taxonomy conditionals for use on archive pages, there are also term conditionals that you can use when displaying a single post. The has_term function works in a similar way to the preceding taxonomy conditionals, except with the arguments the other way around:

- has_term('comedy', 'ptd_genre'): Returns true if the current post has the term comedy from the taxonomy ptd_genre.

- has_term(array('comedy', 'horror'), 'ptd_genre'): Returns true if the post has any of the terms in the array from the taxonomy ptd_genre.

Displaying Custom Taxonomy Information

Now that you have your content being displayed based on the taxonomies and terms being used, you can start to look at how to display these taxonomies in your themes to help users navigate and understand the content better. Here you'll look at ways to display content based around the taxonomy and based around the posts that use the taxonomies. Most of the functions you'll be looking at can be found in the Codex at http://wp-themes-book.com/05002, but I'll focus on a few of the main ones that will be most useful here.

Listing All Taxonomy Terms

The first method you'll look at is a way of showing all the terms in your custom taxonomy and allow users to navigate to the specific archive page of a term. You've already used this function in previous examples, so it should be fairly familiar: the wp_list_categories function.

What I didn't discuss in the earlier chapter is that the wp_list_categories function also has an argument for taxonomy. So to get a list of terms from your custom taxonomy similar to the categories list, you can use the following code:

```php
<?php $args = array(
        'taxonomy'      => 'ptd_genre',
        'orderby'       => 'name',
        'order'         => 'ASC',
        'style'         => 'list',
        'show_count'    => 0,
        'hide_empty'    => 0,
        'title_li'      => '',
        'depth'         => 1,
);
?>

<ul class="genre-terms">
        <?php wp_list_categories( $args ); ?>
</ul>
```

This code displays an alphabetical list of genres from the ptd_genre taxonomy that should look something like Figure 5-5.

Movie genres

- Action
- Comedy
- Comic book
- Drama
- Horror
- Romance
- Sci-fi

Figure 5-5. *List of genres from the ptd_genre taxonomy*

There is also a function that allows you to retrieve all the terms as an array of objects called get_terms. This function takes two arguments: either a string of a taxonomy name or an array of multiple taxonomies, and an array of arguments similar to the wp_list_categories arguments (but without the taxonomy argument). The function looks like this:

```php
<?php
$args = array(
        'orderby'        => 'name',
        'order'          => 'ASC',
        'style'          => 'list',
        'show_count'     => 0,
        'hide_empty'     => 0,
        'title_li'       => '',
        'depth'          => 1,
);

$genres = get_terms( 'ptd_genre', $args );
?>
```

It then returns the data for each term as an object that gives you information that looks like this:

```
[1] => stdClass Object
(
        [term_id] => 105
        [name] => Comedy
        [slug] => comedy
        [term_group] => 0
        [term_taxonomy_id] => 106
        [taxonomy] => ptd_genre
        [description] =>
        [parent] => 0
        [count] => 1
)
```

The information returned is everything WordPress stores about the terms for the taxonomy, which can come in very handy if you want to do something more programmatically with the term data.

Term Name and Descriptions

While there is a function that returns just the term description information exclusively: `term_description()`. It might be best to get an object of the entire terms details by using the `get_term()` function.

The most useful place I can think of using these is on the taxonomy archive page, in which you can display a title and header for the current term before you list the posts in the current term. To do this, you need access to the current term ID to get the title and description. Because there's no function to get the current term ID, you need to use the current query object to find the term ID. Using the following code, you can generate a header for the taxonomy archive pages:

```php
<?php
$term_id = get_queried_object()->term_id;
$current_term = get_term( $term_id, 'ptd_genre' );
?>
<header class="taxonomy-heading">
        <h2><?php echo $current_term->name; ?></h2>
        <p><?php echo $current_term->description; ?></p>
</header>
```

By using the get_queried_object function and returning the `term_id` property, you can now use the `get_term` function to get the information for the current term and display it as the header of the taxonomy archive pages.

Tag Clouds

You can also list all your taxonomy's terms by using the `tag_cloud` function; this is probably my least favorite way of displaying term information, but it's still worth a mention. Similar to the way to list a taxonomy's terms, generating a tag cloud uses the same function as the default tag cloud function, but with a `taxonomy` parameter for the chosen taxonomy. So to generate a tag cloud for the ptd_genre taxonomy, you can use the code:

```php
wp_tag_cloud( array ( 'taxonomy' => 'ptd_genre' ) );
```

This generates a tag cloud that looks a little like Figure 5-6. There are many ways you can customize the tag cloud, including setting the size limits of the smallest and largest tag and whether to display it as a straight string of HTML or put each term into a list element. You can see the full list of terms in the Codex at `http://wp-themes-book.com/05003`.

Terms by Post

Besides displaying taxonomy terms in general, you can also display terms relating to a specific post. To do this, you have a few options including functions similar to the way you can return terms in general.

To display the terms for the post you're in, you can use the the_terms function. Unlike the the_categories function that will return something with no parameters passed, the the_terms function requires you to pass in at least the ID of the post (even if you're inside the loop) and the name of the taxonomy. To get a list of the associated terms for the post from within the loop, you can do this:

```php
the_terms(get_the_id(), 'ptd_genre');
```

This code gives you a comma-separated list of links to the relevant terms. There are also three other parameters that can be used: `before`, `separator`, and `after`. These parameters allow you to customize the display of the list a little more, so the following code:

```
the_terms(get_the_id(), 'ptd_genre', 'Genres: ', ' / ');
```

outputs the following:

```
Genres: Comedy / Romance
```

There are two more functions that can be used to return the associated terms. The `get_the_term_list` function works exactly the same as the `the_terms` function with the same parameters, but it returns the information as a string in PHP if you want to be able to manipulate it.

Finally, the `get_the_terms` function takes the post ID and taxonomy name as its two parameters and returns an array of objects similar to the `get_terms` function before, but only for the associated terms for the post.

Introducing Custom Fields

Custom fields have been in WordPress since way back in version 1.2. The ability to add a custom bit of metadata to content was considered a core feature being added so early in the life of the CMS, at the same time as the plugin architecture was added to WordPress.

First, take a quick look at how custom fields work as standard before you start to implement a custom UI for your fields with the use of WordPress metaboxes. With the release of WordPress version 3.1 in 2011, core developers were aiming to tidy up the post editor screen to be able to see the standard interface for custom fields, drop down the screen options tab from the top right, and turn on the check box for Custom fields. This process adds the Custom Fields editor box to your editing page, as shown in Figure 5-6.

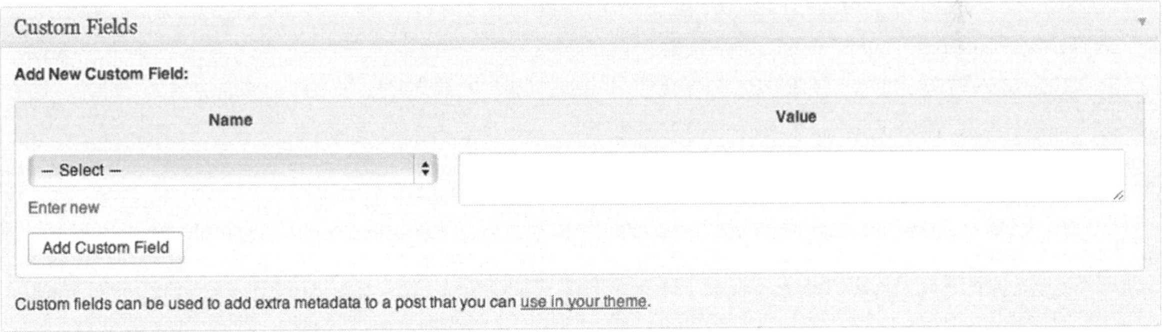

Figure 5-6. *Custom Fields editor*

Here you can select from a list of existing custom fields or create a new one, with the Enter New link below the drop-down menu. Custom fields are stored as key/value pairs: the key is how the metadata is referred to and accessed, and the value is the data that will be displayed. Keys can and should be used for multiple posts where the values for each field are unique for each post.

In the movies example you've used so far, a custom field could be used to store the classification rating of the movie, the release date, the running time of the film, and the review score (see Figure 5-7). They could then be displayed on the posts page.

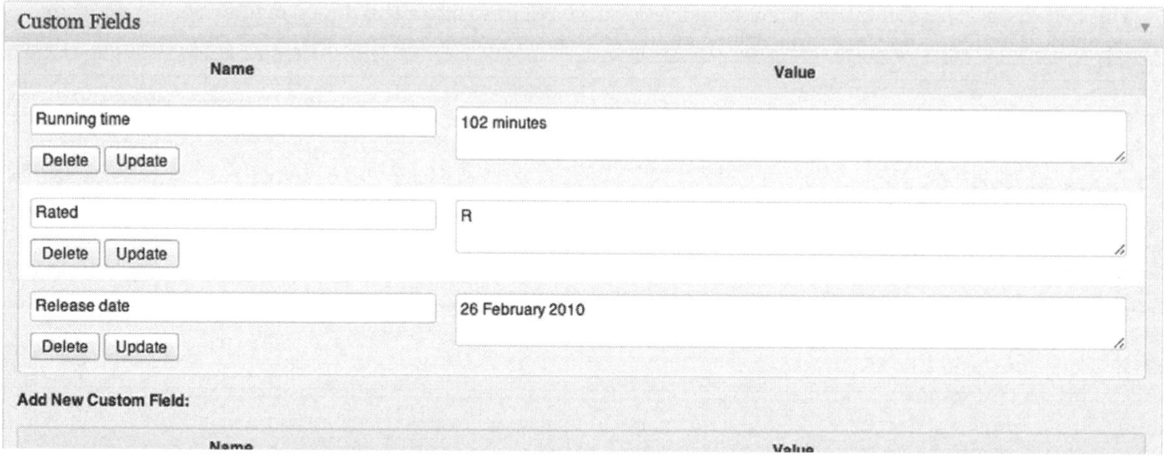

Figure 5-7. *Adding custom fields to the movie*

Once you add custom fields to your posts, you can use a few WordPress functions to output them to your posts page. Here I'll discuss one simple function that displays all custom fields for the current post: the the_meta function; later in the chapter, you'll look at more advanced ways of accessing the custom metadata.

Here's an example of the the_meta function used as part of the <header> area to one of the movie posts. The function takes no parameters and simply outputs the data in the form of an unordered list:

```
<header>
        <h1><?php the_title(); ?></h1>
        <p><?php echo get_the_term_list(get_the_id(), 'ptd_genre', 'Genres: ', ' / '); ?></p>
        <?php the_meta(); ?>
</header>
```

The meta function outputs the following HTML:

```
<ul class='post-meta'>
        <li><span class='post-meta-key'>Rated:</span> R</li>
        <li><span class='post-meta-key'>Running time:</span> 92 minutes</li>
        <li><span class='post-meta-key'>Release date:</span> 19 October 1994</li>
        <li><span class='post-meta-key'>Review rating:</span> 9/10</li>
</ul>
```

The function adds a couple of useful classes to help you style the metadata. Making use of them, you could add the following styles just to make the metadata list a bit more readable:

```
.post-meta {
        list-style:none;
        padding:0;
}
.post-meta .post-meta-key {
        font-weight:bold;
}
```

This code gives you a nicely formatted list of information to display inside the `<header>` area of the movie post (see Figure 5-8).

Running time: 102 minutes
Rated: R
Release date: 26 February 2010
Review rating: 5.6/10

Figure 5-8. *The metadata displayed using the the_meta function*

Custom Field Functions

Besides the simple custom field interface provided by WordPress, there is also an application programming interface (API) for working with the metadata in your themes. This API consists of four main functions:

- `add_post_meta`
- `update_post_meta`
- `get_post_meta`
- `delete_post_meta`

To understand the how these functions work, it's best to look at how the database stores the posts metadata. The database table for metadata is stored in (`wp_postmeta`) and has four fields: `meta_id`, `post_id`, `meta_key`, and `meta_value`. Ignoring `meta_id` for now because it's simply a database primary key, the other three fields get used most of the time in these four functions. Every time you store or access some custom metadata, you need to know the post ID under which the metadata is stored and the meta key being used.

The `meta_id` field is useful because this key is always unique; you can store multiple values for the same post *and* the same meta key in the database at the same time. This feature isn't often made use of, but you'll see how to deal with it when I discuss the functions in more detail.

add_post_meta

The `add_post_meta` function takes four parameters:

- `post_id`
- `meta_key`
- `meta_value`
- `unique` (Boolean)

The first three parameters should be fairly self-explanatory: the ID of the post for which you're adding the custom field, the key of the custom field, and the value you want to set. When adding or updating a custom field using these functions, you can submit an array of values to the `meta_value` parameter. When doing so, WordPress serializes the array into a string for storage in the database.

The last parameter, `unique`, is used to make sure that the post meta key is the only one being used. When set to true, the function returns false and has no effect on the database if there is already a post meta entry for the post ID and the meta key passed to the function. If false, the function simply updates the database with a new entry, regardless of whether a metadata with that key for the post currently exists.

Here are two examples:

```
// Add running time meta data
add_post_meta( $post_id, 'running_time', '92 minutes', true );

// Add classification meta data with array
$classifications = array(
                'usa' => 'R',
                'uk'  => '18'
        )
add_post_meta( $post_id, 'movie_classification', $classifications, true);
```

These two examples show adding metadata for the running_time post meta and the classifications metadata, which also uses a data array that will get serialized by WordPress when inserted into the database.

■ **Note**   When you create custom fields in this way, they all become visible in the custom fields drop-down menu on the default post edit page. To prevent this from happening, you can prefix your meta keys with an underscore to keep them private (i.e., _private_custom_field). This is how WordPress stores the custom fields for things like custom page templates, for which the meta key is _wp_page_template.

---

update_post_meta

Again there are four parameters for the update_post_meta function; the first three are the same as the previous function, but the last is the parameter for prev_value. This final parameter is again used when there might be more than one value added to the same meta key for the same post.

If the prev_value parameter is set, the post metadata is updated only for a record in which prev_value matches the value currently stored in the database. If there is no match, the function returns false and doesn't update anything. If the value is omitted entirely, any and all records with the meta key passed to the function for the post ID are updated to the new value.

Here are two examples:

```
// Using update meta data if there is already a post meta in the database
if( ! add_post_meta( $post_id, 'running_time', '108 minutes', true) ) {
        update_post_meta( $post_id, 'running_time', '108 minutes' );
}

// update post meta for a value already in the database
update_post_meta( $post_id, 'running_time', '108 minutes', '92 minutes' );
```

The first example shows how you can use update_post_meta to update a metadata record when the meta key for the current post is already stored in the database. The second shows updating a record in the database when you already know the data you want to update.

delete_post_meta

Only three parameters this time to delete a post meta record: the first two are the post id and meta key for the field; the last parameter, meta_value, works similarly to the prev_value parameter of the update function.

If the meta_value parameter is present, the function will delete records that match the value parameter passed; if there are no matches, no records are deleted. If the parameter is omitted, any records with the meta key passed for the post ID are deleted.

Here's an example:

```
// delete metadata for running_time
delete_post_meta( $post_id, 'running_time' );
```

This is the straightforward way of deleting a post meta entry; with only one entry that you care about in the database, you can safely omit the meta_value parameter and delete the data for the key entirely.

get_post_meta

The final function, get_post_meta, is used to return the meta_value from the database. Again this function takes the usual two parameters to start with: the post_id and meta_key parameters. The last parameter is a Boolean called single. When set to true, it returns one result from the database as a string regardless of how many post meta entries with the same key are stored. When false, the function returns an array of all the entries.

This gets complicated only when dealing with serialized arrays that have been added as metadata to a single record. In this case, single should be true to return only the one record, and when returning the entry, WordPress returns an unserialized array. If set to false, the docs say that a serialized array is returned as a string as part of the returned array. However, as you can see from the following examples, the array is returned intact, even with the single parameter omitted.

Here are some examples:

```
// get the classification meta unserialized
get_post_meta( $post_id, 'movie_classification', true );

// Returns:
// Array
// (
//     [usa] => R
//     [uk] => 18
// )

// get the classification meta serialized
get_post_meta( $post_id, 'movie_classification' );

// Returns:
// Array (
//     [0] => Array (
//             [usa] => R
//             [uk] => 18
//             )
//     )
```

Although in practice it seems that the returned metadata does get unserialized, it's worth ensuring that you use the single variable just in case the old behavior still occurs in older versions of WordPress.

Custom Metaboxes

Now that you understand these functions, how will you use them to get the best from the custom fields in your themes? Where these functions come in handy is when you create custom metaboxes.

In version 2.5, the add_meta_box function was introduced to the WordPress core. This function allowed users to create draggable boxes for use in the post editor screen, much like you're already used to with the taxonomy input boxes you have seen. Combined with some advanced custom field functions that I'll discuss shortly, they made adding additional data to posts a lot more convenient and easier to do than simply using the previous custom fields interface.

Adding a custom metabox can be quite daunting task for some, and there have been many tutorials and even frameworks created that complicate the task even more. I've been adding custom metaboxes to web sites for as long as I've worked with WordPress, and to be honest it's not as complicated as people say. There seems to be a lot of code to do it, but when you break it down, it's actually quite straightforward.

There are three main functions that are used to add custom metaboxes to your posts, and two hooks. The three functions consist of the following:

- Initializing the metabox

- Displaying the contents of the metabox

- Saving the data

The two hooks are used to call two of the functions on the add_meta_boxes hook and the save_post hook; the third function is called from the add_meta_box function.

add_meta_box

Before you look at the three functions you'll create to set up your custom metabox, let's take a quick look at the add_meta_box function. This is the function that adds the box to a post edit screen, but doesn't create any of the fields you'll be setting up. It can take up to seven parameters, all of which need to be passed in order, not as an array of arguments, unfortunately.

- $id: The identifier of the metabox. This is a custom ID you create that will be used as the HTML ID for the metabox on the page.

- $title: A title for the edit screen. For best practices, it should be added using the WordPress internationalization functions.

- $callback: The name of the function you'll use to display the contents of the metabox passed in without the parentheses.

- $post_type: The post type on which the metabox should be displayed. It can be only one post type identifier passed as a string; to add the metabox to multiple post types, you need to call the function multiple times.

- $context: Where on the edit page the box should appear. Settings can be normal, advanced, or side; the default is set to advanced.

- $priority: The priority of the box compared with others within the context set. Settings can be high, low, default, or core; defaults to default.

- $callback_args: Here you can add arguments to be passed to the callback; the $post object is sent by default, but you can add custom arguments as an array.

All parameters up to and including the $post_type parameter are required for the function to work; the last three can be omitted if you don't need to change them from their defaults.

Now that you've had a look at the function, it's time to put it to some use and set up a post metabox of your own to work with.

Initializing the Metabox

The first function of the three you'll look at initializes the post metabox. Here you need to create a function to be run on the first hook I mentioned (add_meta_boxes), which runs the add_meta_box function.

The code you'll use will look something like this:

```
function prowordpress_movies_meta_box () {
        add_meta_box (
                        'ptd_movies_meta',
                        __('Movie details', 'prowordpress'),
                        'prowordpress_movie_meta_fields',
                        'ptd_movie',
                        'side',
                        'core'
                );
}

add_action ('add_meta_boxes', 'prowordpress_movies_meta_box');
```

As I mentioned, it's really simple to just call the add_meta_function with your chosen settings. All the functions here are prefixed with the theme namespace and the metabox ID is prefixed with ptd_ to stay consistent with the rest of your theme. Also note that the metabox title has been added with the __() internationalization function with the text domain of the theme.

Directly after the metabox initialization function is the add_action call, which attaches the function to the add_meta_boxes hook. For now, all this does is add an empty box with the "Movie details" header to the movies editor pages. Next you need to populate the boxes with some content.

Adding Content to the Metabox

The next function to create is the callback function that was previously defined in the add_meta_box function. This function deals with what's displayed in the custom metabox (when you're creating one to house custom fields, it is mostly made up of form elements).

You'll take a look at the code first, and then I'll explain what's going on because there's quite a bit to go through.

```
function prowordpress_movie_meta_fields ( $post ) {
        // Use nonce for verification
        wp_nonce_field( plugin_basename( __FILE__ ), 'ptd_movie_meta_noncename' );

        $rating = get_post_meta( $post->ID, 'ptd_movie_rating', true );
        $running = get_post_meta( $post->ID, 'ptd_movie_running_time', true );
        $release = get_post_meta( $post->ID, 'ptd_movie_release_date', true );
        $review = get_post_meta( $post->ID, 'ptd_movie_review_rating', true );
?>
```

```
        <p>
                <label for="ptd_movie_rating">Movie classification</label><br />
                <select name="ptd_movie_rating" id="ptd_movie_rating">
                        <option value="">Select a classification</option>
                        <option value="G" <?php if( 'G' === $rating ) echo 'selected'; ?>>G</option>
                        <option value="PG" <?php if( 'PG' === $rating ) echo 'selected'; ?>>PG</
option>
                        <option value="PG-13" <?php if( 'PG-13' === $rating ) echo 'selected';
?>>PG-13</option>
                        <option value="R" <?php if( 'R' === $rating ) echo 'selected'; ?>>R</option>
                        <option value="NC-17" <?php if( 'NC-17' === $rating ) echo 'selected';
?>>NC-17</option>
                </select><br />
                <span class="description">Select the US rating classification from the dropdown</span>
        </p>

        <p>
                <label for="ptd_movie_running_time">Running time</label><br />
                <input type="text" class="all-options" name="ptd_movie_running_time" id="ptd_movie_
running_time" value="<?php echo esc_attr( $running ); ?>" />
                <span class="description">Enter the running time in minutes</span>
        </p>

        <p>
                <label for="ptd_movie_release_date">Release date</label><br />
                <input type="text" class="all-options" name="ptd_movie_release_date" id="ptd_movie_
release_date" value="<?php echo esc_attr( $release ); ?>" />
                <span class="description">Enter the release date or year of the movie</span>
        </p>

        <p>
                <label>Review rating</label><br />
                <label for="review_rating_1"><input type="radio" value="1" id="review_rating_1"
name="ptd_movie_review_rating" <?php if( '1' === $review ) echo 'checked'; ?> /> <span>1 star</
span></label><br />
                <label for="review_rating_2"><input type="radio" value="2" id="review_rating_2"
name="ptd_movie_review_rating" <?php if( '2' === $review ) echo 'checked'; ?> /> <span>2 star</
span></label><br />
                <label for="review_rating_3"><input type="radio" value="3" id="review_rating_3"
name="ptd_movie_review_rating" <?php if( '3' === $review ) echo 'checked'; ?> /> <span>3 star</
span></label><br />
                <label for="review_rating_4"><input type="radio" value="4" id="review_rating_4"
name="ptd_movie_review_rating" <?php if( '4' === $review ) echo 'checked'; ?> /> <span>4 star</
span></label><br />
                <label for="review_rating_5"><input type="radio" value="5" id="review_rating_5"
name="ptd_movie_review_rating" <?php if( '5' === $review ) echo 'checked'; ?> /> <span>5 star</
span></label><br />
                <span class="description">Select the movie review rating</span>
        </p>
<?php
}
```

Now there's a heck of a lot of code, the result of which gives you something that should resemble what you can see in Figure 5-9: a metabox full of four different fields with three varieties of input.

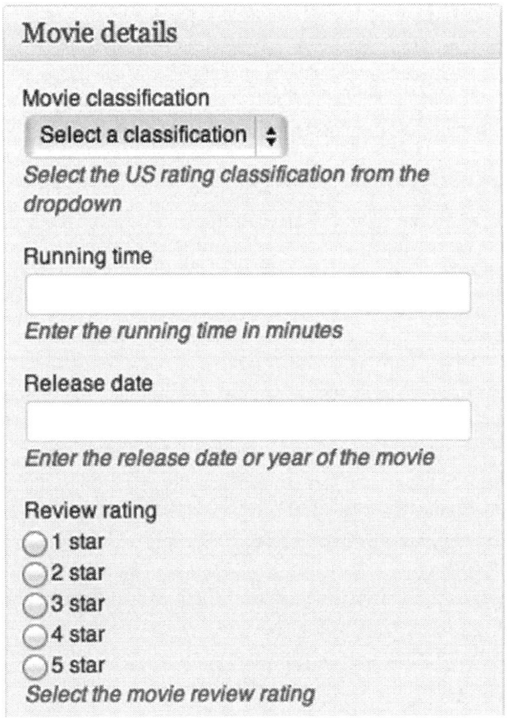

Figure 5-9. *The full Movie metabox with fields*

Although it looks like quite a scary amount of code, when you break it down you'll see that there are really only a few things going on. First let's look at the function declaration:

```
function prowordpress_movie_meta_fields ( $post )
```

This line is a normal function declaration with a $post parameter. Remember when discussing the callback arguments parameter of the add_meta_box function, I mentioned that the post object is sent by default? In the function now, the $post variable is set to the current post object you're viewing:

```
// Use nonce for verification
wp_nonce_field( plugin_basename( __FILE__ ), 'ptd_movie_meta_noncename' );
```

The next line may sound a little strange, but bear with me; it is what you use to validate that the sent form request came from the correct site. Using a nonce field is suggested by WordPress—although not mandatory, it's just good practice to do so. The function simply states where the nonce has come from, and you give it a unique identifier for the metabox you're creating:

```
$rating = get_post_meta( $post->ID, 'ptd_movie_rating', true );
$running = get_post_meta( $post->ID, 'ptd_movie_running_time', true );
$release = get_post_meta( $post->ID, 'ptd_movie_release_date', true );
$review = get_post_meta( $post->ID, 'ptd_movie_review_rating', true );
```

The next four lines are used to get the current metadata for your fields from the database. Doing this allows you to populate the form inputs you set out in the next section so that stored data is made visible to the user. You don't want to have a blank form on view every time users visit the page; otherwise, they'll think that the data hasn't been saved.

The remaining code is your form elements. Most of it is self-explanatory, but here's one to go through a few little bits that come in useful when you're creating your own.

```
<p>
        <label for="ptd_movie_release_date">Release date</label><br />
        <input type="text" class="all-options" name="ptd_movie_release_date" id="ptd_movie_release_
date" value="<?php echo esc_attr( $release ); ?>" />
        <span class="description">Enter the release date or year of the movie</span>
</p>
```

First of all, each form input is set up inside a paragraph tag, which is for layout purposes so everything is set out nicely in rows. Next is a standard label with a for attribute to enable a click on the label to select the input element.

Next is the form input. When creating a metadata input, I tend to use the same name as my metadata key for the input name; the naming is consistent at all times and allows me to easily see what input is for what metadata.

There are also a couple of little things to look out for here, too. First is the class attribute. WordPress has a lot of built-in classes for admin UI elements so it's worth using them so the styling stays consistent throughout the admin pages. Second, when you output the current value of the metadata, you use the esc_attr function to do so. This function encodes characters into HTML entities for use specifically when printing out variables into HTML. Last is the description class used on the span element containing a brief instruction on what to put in the input. The description class is there again to keep styling consistent across the WordPress admin.

Now you've been through the display function for your metabox, it doesn't seem so scary after all. Most of the code consists of fairly straightforward form elements used to input the metadata. Now that you have your shiny new metabox, you should probably look at storing the data that's input when the post is updated.

Saving Metabox Data

The final function in the set is used to update the metadata in the database. This function also uses the second of the hooks I mentioned, the save_post hook, because you want to call this function every time a post is saved to make sure you save any metadata that's been submitted. Again, this is quite a large amount of code, but nothing too complex. You'll see it in its entirety first; then I'll step through each bit separately to explain what's going on.

```
function prowordpress_movie_meta_save ( $post_id ) {
        // verify if this is an auto save routine.
        // If it is the post has not been updated, so we don't want to do anything
        if ( defined( 'DOING_AUTOSAVE' ) && DOING_AUTOSAVE ) {
                return $post_id;
        }

        // verify this came from the screen and with proper authorization,
        // because save_post can be triggered at other times
        if ( !isset( $_POST['ptd_movie_meta_noncename'] ) || !wp_verify_nonce( $_POST['ptd_movie_
meta_noncename'], basename( __FILE__ ) ) ) {
                return $post_id;
        }

        // Get the post type object.
        global $post;
        $post_type = get_post_type_object( $post->post_type );
```

```
        // Check if the current user has permission to edit the post.
        if ( ! current_user_can( $post_type->cap->edit_post, $post_id ) ) {
                return $post_id;
        }

        // Get the posted data and pass it into an associative array for ease of entry
        $metadata['ptd_movie_rating'] = ( isset( $_POST['ptd_movie_rating'] ) ? $_POST['ptd_movie_
rating'] : '' );
        $metadata['ptd_movie_running_time'] = ( isset( $_POST['ptd_movie_running_time'] ) ? $_
POST['ptd_movie_running_time'] : '' );
        $metadata['ptd_movie_release_date'] = ( isset( $_POST['ptd_movie_release_date'] ) ? $_
POST['ptd_movie_release_date'] : '' );
        $metadata['ptd_movie_review_rating'] = ( isset( $_POST['ptd_movie_review_rating'] ) ? $_
POST['ptd_movie_review_rating'] : '' );

        // add/update record (both are taken care of by update_post_meta)
        foreach( $metadata as $key => $value ) {
                // get current meta value
                $current_value = get_post_meta( $post_id, $key, true);

                if ( $value && '' == $current_value ) {
                        add_post_meta( $post_id, $key, $value, true );
                } elseif ( $value && $value != $current_value ) {
                        update_post_meta( $post_id, $key, $value );
                } elseif ( '' == $value && $current_value ) {
                        delete_post_meta( $post_id, $key, $current_value );
                }
        }
}

add_action ('save_post', 'prowordpress_movie_meta_save');
```

Although it's a bit more involved than the display function, once you've stepped through it you'll start to see that there's really nothing too scary going on.

The first thing to notice (although I won't pick it out in the code this time) is that the function is passed a parameter for you to use within the function: the `$post_id` of the post that's been saved. This means you know which post to access data for.

Next are three series of conditional statements:

```
if ( defined( 'DOING_AUTOSAVE' ) && DOING_AUTOSAVE ) {
        return $post_id;
}
```

The first statement is there to check whether the current post is being autosaved; if it is, you don't want to update your post meta just yet because WordPress autosaves brief amounts of content regularly when editing a post. The function you use to update the post meta run database queries so you don't want to be doing that quite so regularly. The return inside the if statement could just be left as a blank return, but it seems to be a convention to return the parameter passed in back as the function hasn't failed; you just chose to quit out early.

```
if ( !isset( $_POST['ptd_movie_meta_noncename'] ) || !wp_verify_nonce( $_POST['ptd_movie_meta_
noncename'], basename( __FILE__ ) ) ) {
        return $post_id;
}
```

The next if statement is where the nonce appears again. This time you're checking whether the nonce exists and verifying it with the wp_verify_nonce function before moving on. If the nonce isn't there or can't be verified, you'll quit out of the function. The nonce is used to ensure that you're getting data from a source that has your metabox in it; otherwise, the function could just be getting called as part of another save_post action.

```
// Get the post type object.
global $post;
$post_type = get_post_type_object( $post->post_type );

// Check if the current user has permission to edit the post.
if ( ! current_user_can( $post_type->cap->edit_post, $post_id ) ) {
        return $post_id;
}
```

The last conditional requires that you first get the current post via the global $post object and then use it to get the current post type. With the post type information, you can use it to check whether the current user has the capabilities to edit the current post. If not, you can exit out of the function early.

Next, you can actually start updating the metadata for your post. Let's look at the example of getting one field from the $_POST object:

```
$metadata['ptd_movie_rating'] = ( isset( $_POST['ptd_movie_rating'] ) ?
$_POST['ptd_movie_rating'] : '' );
```

Here you'll get each post metadata and store it in an associative array so you can easily enter it with a little less code. Because you're setting up a few custom fields here, it seems the logical way to go about it. In this assignment, you're using a shorthand if statement for brevity (the ternary operator), checking that the data from the $_POST object has been sent with the PHP isset function. If so, set your variable to it; otherwise, set the variable to nothing.

Once you have your array of metadata, you can run through it with the foreach loop and update the data in the database:

```
// add/update record (both are taken care of by update_post_meta)
foreach( $metadata as $key => $value ) {
        // get current meta value
        $current_value = get_post_meta( $post_id, $key, true);

        if ( $value && '' == $current_value ) {
                add_post_meta( $post_id, $key, $value, true );
        } elseif ( $value && $value != $current_value ) {
                update_post_meta( $post_id, $key, $value );
        } elseif ( '' == $value && $current_value ) {
                delete_post_meta( $post_id, $key, $current_value );
        }
}
```

Because each of the functions you'll use runs a database query to update the records in the database, you want to ensure that you really have to use them (the conditional block in the preceding code is used for just that reason). You want to use the add_post_meta function only if there isn't currently any data in the database for this post and key combination. So check to see whether you have a current value and whether there is a value to enter into the database. The second condition is whether there is a value for this post and key in the database; if so, use the update_post_meta function, but only if the new value is different from the current value. Finally, if data is already stored, but the value you've been sent is empty, you can delete the post meta record from the database. This is good practice because if you're storing a lot of data and lots of metadata for different posts, it's good to keep the database records tidy instead of having empty records everywhere.

Conditional Display of Custom Metaboxes

The last thing you'll learn in this section is how to display a custom metabox only under certain circumstances. For instance you might want certain custom fields to be used only when a page is being displayed with a certain page template, or when a post is in a certain category, you may want to allow for entering some additional details.

You can do this by editing your first function: the add_meta_box function. To decide whether the post metabox should be set up, you can use a simple conditional to check the circumstances of the page you're on. To get most information, you need the post object for the current post, which can be done by adding the global $post object declaration at the top of the function:

```
function prowordpress_movies_meta_box () {
        global $post;
```

Next, you need to do something with it. To check the custom page template for the current page (note that this is a setting only for the page post type), you can check a WordPress custom field called _wp_page_template. In this custom field, WordPress stores the file name for the custom template, so to test it, you can do the following:

```
if( 'template-page-custom.php' === get_post_meta( $post->ID, '_wp_page_template', true) ) {
        add_meta_box (
                        'ptd_page_meta',
                        __('Custom page fields', 'prowordpress'),
                        'prowordpress_page_meta_fields',
                        'page'
                );
}
```

If the current page is using the template-page-custom.php template, call the add_meta_box function and have a custom metabox on that page. If not, the metaboxes don't display.

Just as easily you can also check whether the current post has a certain term from any given taxonomy. This example may seem odd, but it's here just to demonstrate the ease with which you can test for situations in which you might want to show only certain custom fields for certain posts.

```
if ( has_term( 'comedy', 'ptd_genre', $post) ) {
        add_meta_box (
                        'ptd_movies_meta',
                        __('Movie details', 'prowordpress'),
                        'prowordpress_movie_meta_fields',
                        'ptd_movie',
                        'side',
                        'core'
                );
}
```

Here you're checking whether the current movie is in the comedy genre, and if it is, to display the movie some extra custom fields.

Now I've covered almost everything you need to create a custom metabox for your posts. You can even decide which specific pages or posts can use your custom fields. These can come in really handy if you have metadata you'll be using regularly in your posts and want a nicer interface than the standard custom fields section on the post edit screen.

Next, you'll look at how you can use these fields to generate custom queries on the database.

Building Queries with Custom Fields

As with custom taxonomies, you can also create custom queries for posts based around custom fields. With custom fields, however, the custom queries can be a lot more advanced. You took a look at custom field queries in Chapter 3, and already looked at the tax_query option earlier in the chapter. So here we'll just take a look at the differences between the two.

The first thing to note is that when the meta_query was introduced in version 3.1, it didn't lead to the previous methods of querying by metadata being deprecated. So you can still use the following options in your queries:

- meta_key

- meta_value

- meta_value_num

- meta_compare

So far, I haven't discussed the meta_compare option, which allows you to not only search for a specific meta_value but also compare the meta value of the post against the queried-for meta value to see whether it should be returned. The comparison operators available are '!=', '>', '>=', '<', or '<=', with the default being '='. These comparison operators enable you to query your movie posts, for instance, for movies that were released after the year 2000 (this would require the meta key to be stored in a comparable format) with a query similar to this one:

```
WP_Query( array(
        'meta_key'     => 'ptd_release_year',
        'meta_value'   => 2000,
        'meta_compare' => '>='
        )
);
```

The meta_query option gives you far more control, and like the tax_query option, you can compare multiple meta key/value pairs simultaneously. When comparing multiple custom fields, the relation option is the same as with tax_query and can be set to either 'AND' or 'OR'. The difference with the custom fields queries is with the meta_query arguments.

There are four options available to use in the custom field meta_query argument:

- key: The meta key to be queried

- value: The meta value to be queried, which can be either a string of one value or an array of many.

- compare: The comparison to use between the value and the post value you're querying for. It can be set to any of the aforementioned comparison operators or 'LIKE', 'NOT LIKE', 'IN', 'NOT IN', 'BETWEEN', 'NOT BETWEEN', 'EXISTS', or 'NOT EXISTS'. Again with the default is '='.

- type: The type of the value you're querying with. It can be set to 'NUMERIC', 'BINARY', 'CHAR', 'DATE', 'DATETIME', 'DECIMAL', 'SIGNED', 'TIME', or 'UNSIGNED', with the default value being 'CHAR'.

As you can see from the choice of comparisons and operators, you have a huge amount of power when querying with custom fields. There are two things to note. When an array of values is used, the only operators that can be used are limited to 'IN', 'NOT IN', 'BETWEEN', and 'NOT BETWEEN'; and when the date type is being used for comparisons, you can use the 'BETWEEN' value, but only with the date format set to *YYYYMMDD* in all cases.

Now that you know what tools you have, let's look at a brief example. Suppose that you want to take your release year query a bit further and look for films from the first decade of the 21st century that run for less than two hours. You could use this query:

```
WP_Query( array(
        'post_type'             => 'ptd_movie',
        'meta_query'            => array(
                    'relation'     => 'AND',
                    array(
                            'key'     => 'ptd_release_year',
                            'value'   => array(2000,2010),
                            'compare' => 'BETWEEN'
                    ),
                    array(
                            'key'     => 'ptd_running_time',
                            'value'   => 120,
                            'compare' => '<'
                    )
            )
        )
);
```

This is one very small example of how you can use custom fields in your queries, but you can now start experimenting with your own advanced meta queries.

Adding Custom Fields to the Feed

The last thing to look at for custom fields is how to add them to your RSS feeds. By default, the information provided in the RSS feed is fairly limited to mostly just the content or the excerpt, depending on the options the user has set. But there may be occasions when you create a custom field that would be very usefully displayed in your RSS feed.

It takes only a fairly simple function and a couple of hooks to do this. The hooks you need are the_excerpt_rss and the_content. (There used to be the the_content_rss function to hook on to, but it was deprecated in version 2.9; now feeds just use the regular the_content function). With these hooks, you can create one function that will be called when either hook is activated; then you can add your custom fields content. An example of the full function code follows; I'll discuss the important bits in more detail after.

```
function prowordpress_add_review_to_rss( $content ) {
        global $wp_query;
        $post_id = $wp_query->post->ID;

        $review = get_post_meta($post_id, 'ptd_movie_review_rating', true);

        if ( is_feed() && '' !== $review ) {
                $content = '<h2>Movie review score: ' . $review . ' stars</h2>' . $content;
        }
        return $content;
}
add_filter('the_excerpt_rss', 'prowordpress_add_review_to_rss');
add_filter('the_content', 'prowordpress_add_review_to_rss');
```

Note that the function has a passed parameter of $content. This is the content that will eventually get output by the function and the variable that you will be manipulating.

Next, you need to get the ID of the current post. You can do that with the $wp_query global variable and return the current post ID.

```
global $wp_query;
$post_id = $wp_query->post->ID;
```

When you have the ID, you can get the custom field data in the usual way with the get_post_meta function. When you have the data, you then use the if statement to check whether you're accessing a feed with the is_feed conditional function and whether there is some data in the review custom field.

```
if ( is_feed() && '' !== $review ) {
```

If both conditions return true, you can then add your custom field to your $content variable. Remember to concatenate in the current $content variable as well because you don't want to overwrite the content and just have your feed display the custom field.

```
$content = '<h2>Movie review score: ' . $review . ' stars</h2>' . $content;
```

Also remember to return the $content variable from the function no matter what the result, so that this function stays outside of any conditionals. You always need to return the content, regardless of whether you edited it or not.

```
return $content;
```

This is a relatively straightforward function that adds extra content to your RSS feeds. You can use it for any type of content; you can also add the data from the movie's genre taxonomy to the feed content.

Creating an Advanced Search Form with Custom Taxonomies and Custom Fields

This last section takes the two new pieces of WordPress content you've learned to create and makes use of them together to create a powerful search functionality for your themes. With the classification of taxonomies and the extra data of a custom field, you can open them up to users to give them an advanced way of searching your content. As an example, you'll use the movie post type with its taxonomies and custom fields to build your custom search form.

You'll go through the functionality in two stages: building your search form using the taxonomy data and custom form inputs, followed by receiving the data and creating your custom WordPress queries.

Taxonomy Drop-Down Input

First you'll look at how to create an input for a taxonomy; in this case, it is a select field with a drop-down list of all the terms in your taxonomy that can be searched. To do this, get the taxonomies for the movie post type with the get_taxonomies function:

```
$movie_taxonomies = get_taxonomies( array( 'object_type' => array('ptd_movie') ), 'objects' );
```

You want to get the taxonomies via this method so you have a result that gives you a taxonomy name and a label to use in the first select field. Once you have this data, you can create a function to build your drop-down list. This function takes two arguments: the taxonomy id and name for the label. It then uses the get_terms function to get every term in the taxonomy. Finally, it loops through each term to create the select field and returns it at the end of the function:

```php
// Create a select drop down from the given taxonomy
function prowordpress_build_tax_select( $tax, $label ) {
        // Get all terms - no arguments for the get_terms function means the
        // function will return only the terms which have been assigned to posts
        $terms = get_terms($tax);

        // Start the select field
        $select = '<select name="'. $tax .'">';
        // Our first option is the instruction field with a blank value
        $select .= '<option value="">Select '. $label .'</option>';
        // Loop through all the terms to create the dropdown list
        foreach ($terms as $term) {
            $select .= '<option value="' . $term->slug . '">' . $term->name . '</option>';
        }
        // close the select field
        $select .= '</select>';

        // Return the select field
        return $select;
}
```

If you look through the comments in the function, you'll see where each step is taking place. Note that in the get_terms function, you just pass the taxonomy name because the default arguments are good enough to return a list of only the terms that have posts assigned to them. It would be useless to add empty terms to your drop-down list here because they are guaranteed to return no results in your search.

Building the Search Form

Now that you can easily create a select field for your taxonomies, you can start building the full search form for the movie post type. The only thing you need to do here is set up an HTML form with some input fields for the rest of the fields you want to allow users to search through. In this case, I chose the classification and running time custom fields, as well as adding in a free text search field.

The form is shown in full here; I'll pick out some things to note after you've had a quick lookthrough:

```php
<h2>Search movies</h2>
<form action="/movie-search" method="post">

        <p>
                <label for="search_text">Search:</label>
                <input type="text" name="ptd_movie_search_text" id="search_text">
        </p>

        <?php foreach( $movie_taxonomies as $tax ): ?>
                <p>
                    <label>Movie <?php echo $tax->name; ?>:</label>
                    <?php echo prowordpress_build_tax_select($tax->name, $tax->label); ?>
                </p>
        <?php endforeach; ?>
```

```
        <p>
                <label for="movie_rating">Movie certificate:</label>
                <select name="ptd_movie_rating" id="movie_rating">
                        <option>Select rating</option>
                        <option value="G">G</option>
                        <option value="PG">PG</option>
                        <option value="PG-13">PG-13</option>
                        <option value="R">R</option>
                        <option value="NC-17">NC-17</option>
                </select>
        </p>

        <p>
                <label for="running_time">Running time (less than):</label>
                <input type="text" name="ptd_movie_running_time" id="running_time">
        </p>

        <p><input type="submit" value="Search"></p>

</form>
```

Note the form action, which goes to a custom page in which you can catch the form submissions and build the query (more on that shortly). Next is the free text field for searching (I made sure to use a name that doesn't clash with any WordPress reserved terms because it can cause the submitted form data to be confused with any WordPress functions that go on before the page is built and might redirect the result to the wrong page).

After the free text search input, you have three inputs for the custom taxonomy and custom fields. The first makes use of the function you looked at before, and the second is a simple drop-down list of the possible settings of the custom field you set up in the custom field and a free text input for the running time custom field (see Figure 5-10).

Search movies

Search: [   ]

Movie ptd_genre: [Select Genres ‡]

Movie ptd_actor: [Select Actors ‡]

Movie certificate: [Select rating ‡]

Running time (less than): [   ]

[Search]

Figure 5-10. *The full custom search form you created*

Now that the search form is built (refer to Figure 5-10), you can set up the page to catch the form submission and create the query for the search.

Setting Up the Search Query

The form action redirects users to the "/movie-search/" page, so you need to set up a page and page template to deal with the results. Once that's done, you can look at retrieving the form submission and building the search query.

All your data will come through as part of the $_POST variable, so you need to go through this variable, pull out the data in the correct order, and add it to your query. Because you're using three very different fields for the search query, there's no easy way to create it without checking which field is which before adding it to the query. However, you can use a nice foreach loop to make working with the $_POST variable a little easier to look at. To start, create this foreach loop:

```
foreach ( $_POST as $key => $value ) { }
```

Now you can start working with your custom search arguments. Do one quick check to see whether you need to add the current post argument to the query at all by checking whether the value has any contents, like so:

```
if( '' !== $value ) {
```

If the value does have something in it, you can start to check what needs to be added to the search query. The search text field needs to be added it to the 's' argument of the query (WordPress' generic search field):

```
if( 'ptd_movie_search_text' === $key ) {
        $args['s'] = htmlentities($value);
}
```

The code checks that the key of the field is the search text field you're looking for and then simply adds it to the arguments array. You use the htmlspecialchars function to encode any special characters into HTML entities. The function also takes care of single and double quotes, so you don't need to worry about them breaking your queries.

Next is to build the taxonomy part of the query:

```
elseif( 'ptd_genre' === $key ) {
        $genre['taxonomy'] = htmlspecialchars($key);
        $genre['terms'] = htmlspecialchars($value);
        $genre['field'] = 'slug';
        $args['tax_query'] = $genre;
}
```

Check the key to make sure it's the correct one; then set up an array with the tax_query arguments (discussed earlier in the chapter). The new array gets added to the tax_query argument of the $args array.

Add each of the custom fields to the argument. This one is a little tricky because you need to have two $meta_query arrays in the argument, and both queries use different comparison operators:

```
elseif( 'ptd_movie_rating' === $key || 'ptd_movie_running_time' === $key ) {
        $meta['key'] = htmlspecialchars($key);
        $meta['value'] = htmlspecialchars($value);
```

```
        if( 'ptd_movie_running_time' === $key ) {
                $meta['compare'] = '<';
                $meta['type'] = 'NUMERIC';
        } else {
                $meta['compare'] = '=';
        }

        $meta_query[] = $meta;
}
```

Because you're creating a $meta_query array for both fields, you can use similar code for both. In the condition, use the '||' (or) operator to catch both custom field keys. Add the key and the value as normal to an array and then perform another test to see which of the two fields you're looking at, so you can set the compare value. If the value is for the running time field, you're also going to set the meta type option to numeric so you can do a math comparison with the '<' operator. When you finish, you can add the array to another array that will eventually store both fields.

You can finish building the query inside the main $args array as so far they've only been built in the $meta_query array.

```
if( isset( $meta_query ) ) {
        $args['meta_query'] = array_merge( array('relation' => 'AND'), $meta_query );
}
```

The code first checks whether the $meta_query array was created in the loop because if there were no input for the two fields, you wouldn't have anything to add to your $meta_query.

Next you need to add the relation argument for the meta_query, which you can do with array_merge. This function takes two arrays and outputs a merged array into the variable, which is the $args['meta_query'] variable in this case. This is one example of how to do this; you could add the $meta_query array directly to the meta_query argument of the $args array because 'AND' is the default setting for the relation parameter.

To finish the search query, add any more parameters that are necessary to narrow down the search. In this example, you'll just add the post_type argument, but you could also add pagination options and a posts_per_page limit, for example.

```
$args['post_type'] = 'ptd_movie';
```

This is what the query looks like when someone submits a search:

```
Array
(
    [tax_query] => Array
        (
            [taxonomy] => ptd_genre
            [terms] => comedy
            [field] => slug
        )

    [meta_query] => Array
        (
            [relation] => AND
            [0] => Array
                (
                    [key] => ptd_movie_rating
```

```
                        [value] => R
                        [compare] => =
                )

        [1] => Array
            (
                    [key] => ptd_movie_running_time
                    [value] => 100
                    [compare] => <
            )

    )

    [post_type] => ptd_movie
)
```

It's a perfectly constructed query that allows you to perform really detailed searches on the database.

The last bit of the search is to set up the query using a new WP_Query object with the $arg array and away you go. You can create the bespoke page to be laid out however you like.

Building Your Theme, Part 4

In part 4 of building the custom theme, you'll make better use of the custom post types you created in the previous chapter by giving them some custom taxonomies and custom fields. You'll use them to help categorize the menu to make it easier to browse and add things such as prices to the menu items.

With custom fields, you'll also set up a couple of methods to be able to highlight certain menu items and staff members to be featured on different pages of your site.

Adding Custom Taxonomies

Let's start by adding custom taxonomies. You'll add a custom taxonomy of item type to your menu items. For the staff post type, you'll add a taxonomy for the different job titles. Inspired by the function in the previous section to define custom post types in a really simple loop form, I did the same here for your new taxonomies:

```
function prowordpress_taxonomies() {

    $taxs = array(
                'ptd_menu_category' => array(
                        'menu_title'    => 'Menu Category',
                        'plural'        => 'Categories',
                        'singular'      => 'Category',
                        'hierarchical'  => true,
                        'slug'          => 'menu-category',
                        'post_type'     => 'ptd_menu'
                        ),
                'ptd_job_roles' => array(
                        'menu_title'    => 'Job Roles',
                        'plural'        => 'Roles',
                        'singular'      => 'Role',
                        'hierarchical'  => true,
```

145

```
                                'slug'          => 'job-role',
                                'post_type'     => 'ptd_staff'
                                )
                );

        foreach( $taxs as $tax => $args ) {

                $labels = array(
                        'name'                  => _x( 'Item '.$args['plural'], 'taxonomy general
name' ),
                        'singular_name'         => _x( 'Item '.$args['singular'], 'taxonomy singular
name' ),
                        'search_items'          => __( 'Search '.$args['plural'] ),
                        'all_items'             => __( 'All '.$args['plural'] ),
                        'parent_item'           => __( 'Parent '.$args['plural'] ),
                        'parent_item_colon'     => __( 'Parent '.$args['singular'].':' ),
                        'edit_item'             => __( 'Edit '.$args['singular'] ),
                        'update_item'           => __( 'Update '.$args['singular'] ),
                        'add_new_item'          => __( 'Add New '.$args['singular'] ),
                        'new_item_name'         => __( 'New '.$args['singular'].' Name' ),
                        'menu_name'             => __( $args['menu_title'] )
                );

                $tax_args = array(
                        'hierarchical'          => $args['hierarchical'],
                        'labels'                => $labels,
                        'public'                => true,
                        'rewrite'               => array( 'slug' => $args['slug'] ),
                );

                register_taxonomy( $tax, $args['post_type'], $tax_args );
        }

}
add_action('init', 'prowordpress_taxonomies');
```

The function first sets up an array with the custom taxonomy details similar to the one you made before. It then loops through each one, creating the arguments for the register_taxonomy function before calling it at the bottom of the loop. Easy.

Unfortunately, there's no export file for the taxonomy data, so if you're following along with the theme build, here are the terms you'll be adding to the custom taxonomies. For the menu category taxonomy, add the following:

- Starters

- Main courses

- Desserts

- Drinks

  - Soft drinks

  - Alcohol

  - Hot drinks

And for the staff job roles taxonomy, add the following:

- Manager

- Chef

- Kitchen staff

- Waiting staff

You can now move on to setting up your custom fields.

Adding Custom Metaboxes

You'll set up a couple of custom metaboxes to house some custom fields for both post types. The menu item post type will have two custom fields: the first to set the price, and the second as a check box to set whether the product is a featured item. The staff post type will have a similar check box field for whether the current person is the staff member of the month.

This code can get quite long and quite involved for creating a couple of custom metaboxes, so I picked out some of the code examples from the functions to show you:

```
add_meta_box ( 'ptd_menu_meta',
                    __('Menu item info', 'prowordpress'),
                    'prowordpress_menu_meta_fields', // callback
                    'ptd_menu', // post type
                    'side',
                    'core'
            );

add_meta_box ( 'ptd_staff_meta',
                    __('Staff extra info', 'prowordpress'),
                    'prowordpress_staff_meta_fields', // callback
                    'ptd_staff', // post type
                    'side',
                    'core'
            );
```

Inside the first function, which calls the add_meta_box functions, I'll add metaboxes at the same time. There's no need to do this separately because the hook is the same for each. Notice, however, that as well as being added to the different post types, they each have a different callback function to build up the metabox content. You could do this with a single function and then test which post type you're viewing, but it's a lot easier to just use a different function.

The field creation functions are pretty straightforward, so I'll ignore them for now because you can catch up in the code downloads. You can also try to create them and then check your work against the example. The only thing I mention here is the nonce:

```
wp_nonce_field( basename( __FILE__ ), 'ptd_custom_meta_noncename' );
```

Here's the line of code to generate the nonce field for *both* the field population functions. I use the same nonce because it makes it a lot easier when saving the metadata in the next function. As long as you use a nonce and check it in the save function, you'll be perfectly fine.

Finally, the save function is pretty similar to the one you created earlier in the chapter, but you're using the one function to save both sets of custom fields:

```
if( 'ptd_menu' === $post_type->name ) {
        $metadata['ptd_menu_item_price'] = ( isset( $_POST['ptd_menu_item_price'] )
? $_POST['ptd_menu_item_price'] : '' );
        $metadata['ptd_menu_item_featured'] = ( isset( $_POST['ptd_menu_item_featured'] ) ?
$_POST['ptd_menu_item_featured'] : '' );
    } else {
        $metadata['ptd_staff_of_the_month'] = ( isset( $_POST['ptd_staff_of_the_month'] ) ?
$_POST['ptd_staff_of_the_month'] : '' );
    }
```

The code uses the $post_type object (the one you made when checking whether the current user has edit permissions) and checking which post type the post is for. This allows you to set up array entries only for the fields you'll save data for because if the field is empty (which it is if you're saving data for a different post type), it gets deleted from the database.

As shown in Figure 5-11, you're now all set to go with the custom metaboxes. Next you'll put the new custom taxonomies and custom fields to good use.

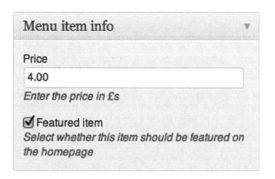

Figure 5-11. *Custom metabox for the menu items*

Setting Up the Menu Page

Now that the menu items are nicely split up into their different menu categories of starter, main, dessert, and so on, you can create a nice menu page based on this information. To do so, you need to create a custom page template to run a bespoke set of queries for, running through all the terms in the categories taxonomy and creating a custom query for each. Luckily, this is really easy to do in WordPress.

First create a page for "Our menu" and the custom page template "page-our-menu.php". Add the usual header and footer as you did before, but you'll create a bespoke function to run the series of loops and queries. Here's how the function will be structured:

1. Get all terms from the Menu categories taxonomy.

2. Loop through each term.

3. For each term inside the loop, create a custom query for posts within that term.

4. From the query, run the posts loop to output each menu item.

It probably sounds a lot more complex than it actually is, so take a look at the code you'll use to do it:

```php
function prowordpress_build_menu(){
        $menu_terms = get_terms( 'ptd_menu_category' );

        if( $menu_terms ){
                foreach( $menu_terms  as $term ){

                        $args = array(
                                'post_type' => 'ptd_menu',
                                "tax_query" => array(
                                                array(
                                                                'taxonomy' => 'ptd_menu_category',
                                                                'field'    => 'slug',
                                                                'terms'      => $term->slug

                                                )
                                        ),
                                'posts_per_page' => -1,
                );

                        $menu_items = new WP_Query( $args );
                        if( $menu_items->have_posts() ) {
?>
                                <h2 id="<?php echo $term->slug; ?>" class="tax_term-heading">
<?php echo $term->name; ?></h2>
<?php
                                while ($menu_items->have_posts()) : $menu_items->the_post();
                                        get_template_part('content', 'menu');
                                endwhile;

                        }
                        wp_reset_query();
                }
        }
}
```

You start the function by getting the terms using get_terms. Again, no need for any arguments because the default arguments give you a set of terms that you want to display on the page (i.e., the ones that have items). Check that you have some terms to loop through and then start the foreach loop.

For each of the terms, you build a simple set of arguments for the custom query, which includes the tax query argument to get only the posts for the current term. Run the query, followed by the usual if statement to see whether any posts have been returned. Before you run the while loop to output the posts, create a heading for the current term.

Before moving on to using the custom fields, I'll quickly mention the custom taxonomy you set up for the staff post type. This one is a pretty standard taxonomy; adding the attached term as a link next to the staff members' details so people can select the job role term and view a page listing all staff members with that job role. Simply list the person's job role with the the_term function:

```php
<?php the_terms( get_the_id(), 'ptd_job_roles', 'Position: ' ); ?>
```

You have the choice of using a new custom template such as taxonomy-ptd_job_role.php if you want some custom layout to a page for each of the single job roles, or the listing page will fall back and use the regular archive.php template. It doesn't use the archive-ptd_staff.php template that you created in the last chapter because here it looks specifically for the taxonomy display.

Displaying the Featured Menu Item

The last bit of code to add is for the new custom fields. Besides adding the price custom field to be displayed with each of the menu items with the get_post_meta function, you'll use the featured item custom fields to show a featured item on the home page.

I'll show the example code for only one of the two features because they both work in the same way, but display different content with a different title. The aim of these custom fields is display a featured item on the home page for the menu and the current team member of the month on one of the staff or about pages.

The code isn't that complex here; it creates a simple query using the meta_query argument to look for the featured custom field you created for the menu items:

```php
<aside class="featured-item">
        <h2>Featured item</h2>

        <?php
        // New query for featured menu item
        $args = array(
                        'post_type'         => 'ptd_menu',
                        'orderby'           => 'rand',
                        'posts_per_page'    => 1,
                        'meta_query'        => array(
                                array(
                                        'key'       => 'ptd_menu_item_featured',
                                        'value'     => 'on',
                                        'compare'   => '='
                                )
                        )
        );

        $featured = new WP_Query( $args );

        if( $featured->have_posts() ): while( $featured->have_posts() ): $featured->the_post();
        ?>
                <article <?php post_class(); ?>>
                        <h3><?php the_title(); ?></h3>

                        <?php the_post_thumbnail( 'small'); ?>

                        <a href="<?php the_permalink(); ?>">Find out more &raquo;</a>
                </article>
        <?php endwhile; endif; ?>

        <?php wp_reset_query(); ?>

</aside>
```

Most of the code is standard, but I'll go through the query arguments briefly. The code sets the post type to the menu type, uses the 'rand' orderby value, and sets the posts per page value to 1. The admin can set more than one item to be featured, but only one at a time is pulled out for the home page.

Last is the `meta_query`. When the value is stored from a check box, the `"checked"` setting is stored as `"on"`, so make sure to test for that in the query.

Now you can replicate this for the staff member of the month field or just check out the rest of the example code.

Summary

You're at the end of another pretty huge chapter, but I hope that covering two main topics didn't make it too overwhelming. With your newfound abilities in dealing with custom taxonomies and custom fields, you now have some great content organizational skills to add to your WordPress theme development toolkit.

The chapter covered everything you need to know about setting up custom taxonomies, including how to add some nice UI elements in the form of custom help text and help tabs. You looked at how to use these new taxonomies to great effect and give your users ways of filtering down your content.

You learned about custom fields, seeing where they come from and how to manage the fields as they are by default in WordPress. You saw how to create your own custom metaboxes to create a better admin interface when adding this extra metadata. You then looked at how these fields can be used for custom querying and how to display them both in your theme and in your feeds if necessary.

Before you added these new features to your custom theme, you learned how to combine both features to create a really detailed search form for your users.

The next chapter takes a look in detail at WordPress actions and hooks—how you've used them so far and what exactly you're doing every time you use the `add_action` function. Then you'll find out about shortcodes, what they're used for and how to create them to make it easy for your users to add dynamic content.

■ ■ ■

CHAPTER 6

Customize with Hooks, Shortcodes, and Widgets

Now that you have dealt with the main structural elements of setting up your WordPress theme, you can start to look at ways of adding customizable and dynamic content for your users to control. To do this, you'll look at three features in WordPress that have been added for these purposes: hooks, shortcodes, and widgets.

You've already used a lot of hooks in previous chapters, but here you'll look more deeply at what they're actually doing behind the scenes and how to get the best from them. You'll also take a look at shortcodes and how they allow users to add dynamic content through the WordPress content editor without having to use any code. Finally you'll take a look at the customizable options you have with sidebars (and sidebar widgets in particular), which allow you to create custom snippets of content that your users can choose to have in specified areas of your site.

Hooks

Hooks in WordPress were introduced as part of the plugin application programming interface (API) back in WordPress version 1.2. Hooks were the way of allowing plugin developers to "hook into" the functionality of WordPress and activate functions at certain times during the WordPress execution process. Hooks are the best way to add your custom functionality to WordPress and ensure that you're not hacking the core WordPress code. There are two types of hooks you should know about: actions, and filters.

Actions are points in the WordPress execution process where something happens; you can "hook" into an action and do something of your own. You saw actions in use in the last two chapters: you used add_action to call a function at a certain point when WordPress is constructing pages so that you could add your own functionality. So far, it has added custom post types, taxonomies, and custom fields to the WordPress admin.

Filters are hooks that manipulate data; they take an input based on the filter you're calling, modify it, and then output the modified data back into the execution process. So far, there's one example of a filter that you saw briefly earlier in the book: the the_content filter. This is a WordPress built-in filter that runs when the content is asked for from the database. Attached to this filter are several WordPress functions such as wptexturize and convert_smilies, which take the content, convert plain text into HTML entities, and convert text "smilies" to images, respectively.

The main difference between the two types of hooks is easy to remember: an action hook does something when something happens; a filter hook takes data and modifies it.

Why Actions Are Not Filters

Now I'm going to confuse you a little, but I promise there's a reason for it. Take a quick look at the add_action function from the WordPress core:

```
function add_action($tag, $function_to_add, $priority = 10, $accepted_args = 1) {
        return add_filter($tag, $function_to_add, $priority, $accepted_args);
}
```

Wow! It took me a little while to get my head around that one as well. Let me explain. Although WordPress handles the adding of actions and filters in the same way, the processing has one major difference. If you look at the two functions that call the actions and filters—do_action and apply_filters—you see a lot of similarities but one fundamental difference:

```
// From the apply_filters function
// Line 173 of the wp-includes/plugin.php file
$value = call_user_func_array($the_['function'], array_slice($args, 1, (int) $the_['accepted_args']));

// From the do_action function
// Line 406 of the wp-includes/plugin.php file
call_user_func_array($the_['function'], array_slice($args, 0, (int) $the_['accepted_args']));
```

The difference should be quite apparent: the function in the apply_filters function returns data to the $value variable, whereas the do_action function simply calls the function with nothing to return. Although it's already been mentioned that actions and filters are very different, it's important to understand why there is a difference and how that difference manifests itself in the WordPress core. Knowing this allows you to better understand how and where to use the functions in your theme (or plugin; more on that later).

When Do Actions and Filters Happen?

The simple answer is: *all the time!* But you're probably expecting me to go into a bit more detail.

There is always some action or filter happening; more than likely, many happening at the same time. For instance, publishing a post in the admin triggers the following:

- publish_post (action) or publish_page
- save_post (action)
- wp_insert_post (action)
- wp_insert_postdata (filter)
- category_save_pre (filter)
- content_save_pre (filter)
- excerpt_save_pre (filter)
- name_save_pre (filter)
- title_save_pre (filter)

There are quite a lot of things going on just for that one process. There are far too many actions and filters to list here, so I point you to the WordPress Codex, which has two long pages on actions and filters, and the actions are listed in the order they are executed.

- **Action reference:** http://wp-themes-book.com/06001

- **Filter reference:** http://wp-themes-book.com/06002

There is also a full list of all hooks that is kept up to date with every new WordPress release on Adam Brown's site at http://wp-themes-book.com/06003.

Actions in the WordPress Core Load

Back in Chapter 3, I spoke about the stages WordPress goes through to construct a page. Each time this happens, actions are fired as well, allowing theme and plugin developers to add to the WordPress core functionality. You saw a few of them in action already, but let's take a closer look at some of the actions triggered in a typical load of WordPress:

- `muplugins_loaded`: The very first action to be fired when "must-use" plugins have been loaded. It's a bit of a useless action because the theme hasn't been loaded. So none of your code can attach anything here. It is mainly for any must-use and network-wide plugins in multisite, but I'll talk more about them later.

- `plugins_loaded`: The next in the list of actions, which means that all plugins have been loaded and can start executing code if needed.

- `after_setup_theme`: The first real action you should care about. This action fires when the `functions.php` file for the active theme has been loaded. You can use this to set up certain theme functions and things you'll need from WordPress, it is the best time to use the `add_theme_support` function to add support for thumbnails and post formats (among others). You already used this action when constructing the custom theme by using it to call the `theme setup` function.

- `init`: Typically the first point at which plugins and themes start to add functionality to WordPress, this is where you previously added custom post types and taxonomies. At this point in the core load, the user has been authenticated, so you know what level of user you're dealing with to be able to add functionality.

- `parse_request`: The hook that exposes the current HTTP request and allows you to manipulate it if you need to.

- `pre_get_posts`: The point where the query parameters for the current page load are made available for you to edit. You looked at this briefly when the loop was discussed in Chapter 3. Using this hook is the best place to edit the current query and add things like custom post types to the default query.

- `template_redirect`: The hook called before WordPress allocates the template from the default request. It can be used to redirect users to a different page or load a new template to handle the current request. With plugins, it is typical to use this action to load a template from the plugin to create a bespoke page instead of allowing the default theme template to be loaded.

- `wp_enqueue_scripts`: Where you previously added the functions to enqueue the scripts and style sheets for the theme. It's used only for enqueuing styles and scripts for the front end of the WordPress theme, and even though it has "scripts" in the name, it's used for both scripts and styles.

155

That's a brief overview of the most-often-used action hooks when the WordPress core is loaded and before the theme is displayed. Each action has its own best uses to ensure that any custom functionality you want to add to WordPress happens at the correct time.

Actions in Your Theme Files

There are points in your theme files that you can use when writing functionality to add content/code to your themes in the shape of certain functions, but they need to be added to your theme files in order to ensure that they're available. You might recognize them because I've mentioned them already. And if you built a WordPress theme before, you will have almost certainly used them:

- wp_head: An action point that should always go in the <head> tag of your themes. This is primarily used for adding styles, scripts, and meta data but can be used by plugins to add anything else needed to go in the <head>.

- wp_footer: An action point at the end of the HTML <body>. Used for things such as scripts and any code that should be inserted last of all in your site. A popular use is by plugins to add Analytics tracking code or by WordPress to add the markup for the admin bar when a user is logged in.

- wp_meta: It might be new to you; it's usually seen in the sidebar of a theme under a "meta" section, which can be used by plugins to add advertisements or extra functionality for a sidebar. It's not very common, but when developing a theme for sale or that you will not be in control of administering, it should be added so any plugins the user might add can work correctly.

- comment_form: If the theme you're building has comments, you will definitely be using this function anyway. It also holds an action that plugins or theme developers can hook into.

These are the four actions that happen within your theme, but there are also plenty of filters going on at the same time that allow you to modify the content that will be output from your templates.

Filters Are Everywhere

Filters are used in almost every input or output action performed by WordPress. They sit between the admin and the database, and between the database and the templates, and can be used at any time to modify the data that's being passed between the various states.

Although WordPress has some of its own filters, which it uses to modify things coming out and going into the database, most of the available filters are largely unused unless a plugin or theme wants to use them. The best example is the content filter. WordPress uses it to run several functions to format the content for display on the site; you can also use this filter to add to the content before it gets output in your themes, say to add a generic sentence to the end of each post telling the reader about the author or where to find more information on the site.

Some filters happen before content or meta data is input into the database, and some instead work before outputting data to the theme. This is an important distinction to make, and you need to make sure you choose which to use carefully, based on the effect you want your filter to have on the content. For instance, if you use a filter to modify data before it goes into the database, the data you edit will get stored from then on and will be displayed in the edit screen (if you were modifying any post content, for instance).

Suppose you have a filter to detect swearing in an author's post. The filter you use to detect and modify the profanities depends on the effect you want to have on the content. If you filter the content before the content is added to the database, the author could see in the edit screen where the words have been modified. Whereas if you were to use this filter before the content was displayed on the front end, the content editor would stay the same, but the censoring would appear on the front end of the web site. How you want the user to perceive this profanity filter will determine the time at which you want to filter the content.

Now that you know what hooks are and when they happen, you can look at how they work and how you can add them to the theme.

Using Hooks

Although you previously used hooks throughout the book, here you'll take a closer look at what is actually going on and how to use them in detail. Hooks come in two forms, and you know that actions and filters are actually handled in the same way by almost the same function.

add_filter (and add_action)

Here you'll look at the add_filter function and remember that the same thing applies to the add_action function. To start off, look at the full function for add_filter, which takes four arguments:

```
add_filter( $tag, $function_to_add, $priority, $accepted_args );
```

- $tag: The tag name of the filter (or action) you want to hook your function to.

- $function_to_add: The name of the PHP function you're going to use to modify the data (or run on the action).

- $priority: Specifies an order in which the function should be called on that action. The lower the number, the sooner it gets called. The priority defaults to 10, and any functions that share a priority just get run in the order they are added.

- $accepted_args: The number of arguments the function can take when being called with apply_filters or do_action. This was added in version 1.5.1.

The common example for a function using a filter is the profanity filter already discussed. It's a fairly simple one, but bad as an example for the book because I can't write any actual swear words here. So let's move on with a better example. Let's filter the body_class and add your own classes to be output under certain circumstances:

```
function prowordpress_add_category_classes( $classes ) {
        global $post;

        // Adds classes for the current post categories
        if( is_single() ) {
                $categories = get_the_category( $post->ID );
                foreach ( $categories as $cat ) {
                        $classes[] = $cat->slug;
                }
        }

        return $classes;
}
add_filter( 'body_class', 'prowordpress_add_category_classes' );
```

In this example, you first check whether the current page being constructed is a single page. Then you get the categories for the current post and add the slug for each category to the $classes array. When you finish looping through them, you return the $classes array at the end of the function.

With this function set up, you can just as easily add the category classes to the post_class output by simply calling the add_filter function with the function you already created. Just switch out the body_class tag for the post_class:

```
add_filter( 'post_class', 'add_category_classes' );
```

> ■ **Note** Each filter handles content in a slightly different way. In the example, the $classes variable is an array of the classes being added. If, however, you use the the_content filter, the $content variable would be a string of text from the database because the filter you're adding is intercepting the flow of the WordPress core as it is, so the way the content is handled is exactly how WordPress is currently using that content.

The same concept applies to the add_action function: it's just a function wrapper to call the add_filter function. But you should always use the function, which applies specifically to the hook you want to use. This is just plain common sense; if you set up all your actions and filters using the add_filter function, it may still work and you may save yourself a function call. But you make your code unreadable because where people are expecting to find an action being created, they end up seeing add_filter, which just leads to confusion. So please ensure that you're using the correct function for the correct purpose.

You've seen many examples of the add_action function in use throughout the book so far, so I won't repeat myself by adding another one here. Action functions are called at a point during the WordPress core load or when something happens in the WordPress admin that allows you to execute your own code. For good examples, you can look back at the previous chapter, in which you used a couple of actions in the process of setting up the custom metaboxes for the posts.

Using Class Functions to Avoid Naming Collisions

Here you'll learn how to use PHP classes to help avoid naming collisions and also keep your hook functions self-contained nicely from the rest of your code. This mostly applies to plugins, which you will look at in more depth in the next chapter and later on in Chapter 13, but for now you'll take a brief look at how to use a class with the add_filter/add_action functions.

This comes in handy because when naming functions, it's entirely possible that another plugin could name a function the same as one of your functions and it could result in a conflict. PHP doesn't allow two functions of the same name, so this essentially breaks everything. It is not a gigantic problem when creating a theme because you'll likely be using a namespace on your function, which should reduce the possibility of a conflict. You could also do that in a plugin as well to help reduce the chances of a naming conflict. However, when writing a plugin it's likely that you're going to have a lot of functions and not want to be writing really long function names; it can be quite a pain to do so. This is where PHP classes come in.

A class can be namespaced easily, then within the class you can use more straightforward function names and have them protected from the global namespace based on their location within the class. In the following example of the class layout, you have a prefixed class name to make sure you have a unique class and then you have simply named functions within:

```php
class prowordpress_notifications {

    function email($post_ID) {

        $addresses = "someone@somewhere.com";
        $subject = "New post on Pro Wordpress: ".get_the_title( $post_ID );

        $content = "Hi x, \n\n Here's the latest from the Pro WordPress blog. \n\n";
        $content .= get_the_title( $post_ID ). "\n\n";
        $content .= 'Read it here: '.get_permalink( $post_ID);

        wp_mail($addresses, $subject, $content);
```

```
            return $post_ID;
        }
}

add_action('publish_post', array('prowordpress_notifications', 'email') );
```

This really simple class is used for notifications from the blog when something happens. In this case, it's when a post is published. I won't run through everything because the function is relatively straightforward, you're just building up an email and using the wp_mail function to send it. What you're looking at here is the add_action function on the last line. As normal it takes a tag for the action you're going to hook onto but the second argument is now in the form of an array:

```
array('prowordpress_notifications', 'email')
```

This is the way of passing a class function through to the action hook. You pass in the name of the class as the first entry in the array; the second entry in the array is the function name. This results in a static call of the function in the class from the action. If you were to do that with standard PHP, it would look like this:

```
prowordpress_notifications::email();
```

If, however, you had an instance of the class in your code already and you wanted to use that instance of the class (because other parameters/functions have already run on that class instance), you would simply pass the instance of the class as the first entry in the array parameter like so:

```
$wpd_notifications = new prowordpress_notifications();
add_action('publish_post', array($wpd_notifications, 'email') );
```

This is a really simple example at the moment; I'll develop this further when you look at building your own plugins in more depth in Chapter 13.

Creating Custom Action Hooks

Not content with the plethora of available action hooks already in WordPress, there is also a way of creating your own custom hooks to add functionality to. You might wonder why on earth you would need to create custom actions in addition to the multitude of actions you already have at your disposal. Most of the actions are related to theme setup, not from within the theme itself. By creating custom hooks, you can set up precise points from within the theme to attach functions specific to the theme.

To do this, it's fairly simple; you need to look to the do_action function. This is the function that tells WordPress an action is running and to run any associated functions to that action at that point in the execution. For instance, let's have a look at how the wp_head function is built in the WordPress core:

```
function wp_head() {
        do_action('wp_head');
}
```

Yep, it's that simple. The only thing that happens when you add wp_head to your header.php is that the do_action gets called with the argument 'wp_head'. The magic of the wp_head action doesn't happen until you connect functions to the action; take a look at what goes on in the WordPress core for example. Here's just a short example of what hooks are added to the wp_head action in the default-filters.php file:

```
add_action( 'wp_head',    'wp_enqueue_scripts',    1    );
add_action( 'wp_head',    'feed_links',            2    );
```

```
add_action( 'wp_head',   'feed_links_extra',                3    );
add_action( 'wp_head',   'rsd_link'                              );
add_action( 'wp_head',   'wlwmanifest_link'                      );
add_action( 'wp_head',   'adjacent_posts_rel_link_wp_head', 10, 0 );
add_action( 'wp_head',   'locale_stylesheet'                     );
```

There's a lot that goes on when the wp_head action gets executed. So for you to define your own custom action hook, all you need to do is create a function that does exactly the same thing as the wp_head() function:

```
function ptd_custom_hook() {
        do_action('ptd_custom_hook');
}
```

There it is; you now have your very own custom hook function to add to the theme at any point you like using the usual add_action function with the ptd_custom_hook as the tag name.

Action Hooks with Parameters

Now that you have a simple way of creating an action hook, have a look at how you can add extra parameters to that action to give you some better context of where you are in the theme or what you should be interacting with once you're performing your action.

If you look at the docs for the do_action function, it's possible to not only create an action with the necessary action tag but also with one or more arguments:

```
do_action( 'ptd_custom_hook', $arg1, $arg2, $etc );
```

This means that you can give the function you're running at the action a series of arguments to help with the functionality you're adding. The best example for this is to add the post ID as an argument so the function knows for what post the action is being called. You've seen this already when using the save_post action to update the metabox data in the last chapter, but here's how to put this functionality together.

As an example, you're going to add an action to the end of the loop on one of the single pages for the movie reviews, with the intent that it will be used to add an advertisement for the latest movie coming out related to the current movie being viewed. In this case, before the end of the loop you can add this do_action function:

```
        <?php do_action( 'ptd_movie_end_main_content', get_the_ID() ); ?>
<?php endwhile; endif; ?>
```

To set up the function to receive the post ID for the action, all you would then have to do is set up the function and add_action call like this:

```
function ptd_show_related_movie_trailer( $post_id ) {
        // Do stuff
}

add_action( 'ptd_movie_end_main_content', 'ptd_show_related_movie_trailer' );
```

You can use the defaults for the add_action function of priority and accepted arguments because you're passing in one argument: the post ID. However, if you were to add a second and third argument, for instance by getting the IDs of the genres the post is in and also passing the taxonomy name of the genres taxonomy to the action:

```
$genres = get_the_terms(get_the_id(), 'ptd_genre');
foreach( $genres as $gen ):
        $gen_ids[] = $gen->term_id;
endforeach;

do_action( 'ptd_movie_end_main_content', get_the_ID(), $gen_ids, 'ptd_genre' );
```

You would then need to set the function and add_action calls up like this:

```
function ptd_show_related_movie_trailer( $post_id, $term_ids, $taxonomy_slug ) {
        // Do stuff
}

add_action( 'ptd_movie_end_main_content', 'ptd_show_related_movie_trailer', 10, 3 );
```

Notice that the function takes three arguments ($post_id, $term_ids, and $taxonomy_slug—named generically so you could envision doing this for something other than just the related movie reviews) and that the add_action function now has the parameter '3' at the end to signify that there will be three arguments passed to the resulting function.

Creating Custom Filter Hooks

Now that you've seen how to create custom action hooks, you can take a quick look at creating a custom filter hook, which works very similarly to the custom action hook but with a couple of minor differences.

The first difference is the function used to create them. Where you used do_action to add an action point, you can now use apply_filters to add a custom filter. You used the apply_filters function before; what you were doing was adding another point in the code to set up the hook, and because you used the built in "the_content" filter, it just called all the functions attached to the hook already.

The second difference in creating a custom filter hook is the need for a second parameter, the $value parameter. This is the bit of data that will get modified by any filter functions you attach to the hook. Here's a simple example of a custom filter you'll add to the movie post type:

```
$title = apply_filters( 'ptd_movie_title', get_the_title() );
```

Here you're creating a filter point for the title of the post, which sets a custom hook tag of "ptd_movie_title" and passes through the title as the value you'll be modifying. The apply_filters function always returns some data—because filters are used to modify things—so you take the return value of the filter and put it in the $title variable.

The function and add_filter call would look something like this:

```
function ptd_edit_movie_title( $title ) {
        // Do stuff

        return $title;
}

add_filter( 'ptd_movie_title', 'ptd_edit_movie_title' );
```

Again the function is pretty straightforward except that by default you have the $title argument as part of the function. You have to make sure to return that value at the end of the function once you've made the modifications.

Similar to a custom action hook, a custom filter can also take more than one argument. but this means that you need to add the accepted_args argument to the add_filter call and pass in the necessary values to the apply_filters function as you did before with the do_action function.

Debugging Hooks

Finally, you need to know a little about debugging WordPress hooks and how they work internally so you can get the best out of them and resolve problems when things go awry.

All hooks, whether actions or filters, are stored in the same way: inside the $wp_filter array. This is a complex array containing every single filter and action added throughout the process of both the WordPress core execution and any other actions/filters added in theme and plugin files. To give you a better idea of how the hooks work, you can look at an example of how things are stored in the $wp_filter array. This is not a direct dump of the content of the array because that might be a couple of hundred lines long; it is a representative structure of the data:

```
Array (
        '[tag]' => Array (
                '[priority]' => Array (
                        '[idx]' => '[function_name]',
                        '[idx]' => '[function_name]',
                        '[idx]' => '[function_name]'
                ),
                '[priority]' => Array (
                        '[idx]' => '[function_name]',
                        '[idx]' => '[function_name]',
                        '[idx]' => '[function_name]'
                )
        )
        '[tag]' => Array (
                '[priority]' => Array (
                        '[idx]' => '[function_name]',
                        '[idx]' => '[function_name]'
                )
        )
)
```

The only part of that array structure that should be unfamiliar to you is the '[idx]' part; the rest is part of the add_filter function you've already seen. The 'idx' is a unique identifier created by WordPress when adding the function to the $wp_filter array to create a unique instance of the function for the tag. It ensures that the function is called only once for each tag it's added to.

Now that you know the structure of the $wp_filter array, it should be easier to dump the parts of the $wp_filter array you need to check. For example, if you need a closer look at the functions attached to the wp_head action, you can do this:

```
<pre>
        <?php
        global $wp_filter;
        var_dump($wp_filter['wp_head']);
        ?>
</pre>
```

Of course, this still gives you a massive list of data for each function attached to the wp_head action, so let's look at a more useful way of checking the hooks being used.

Debugging via the 'all' Hook

The 'all' hook fires every time apply_filters or do_action is called, and it gives you a nice way to track and trace the hooks being called in real time in your theme. To do this, there is a great set of functions written by Andrey Savchenko (aka Rarst) that looks at the $wp_filter variable and then, with the use of the 'all' hook, lists out hooks when they're being called in real time.

I haven't got room to list all his code here (it's included in the example code along with the book), but here is the example of the list_live_hooks function that shows which hooks are being fired when in your theme:

```
function list_live_hooks( $hook = false ) {
    if ( false === $hook )
                $hook = 'all';

    add_action( $hook, 'list_hook_details', -1 );
}
```

The function also takes a $hook parameter that allows the function to list the details of the functions called for whenever the passed hook is run.

Shortcodes

Introduced in WordPress version 2.5, shortcodes have provided a brilliant way for authors in WordPress to add dynamic content to their posts without having to know any code or go anywhere near theme files. Using shortcodes allows you to empower the content authors using your theme with the ability to easily add things like related posts or custom functionality to their content without the need to worry about how to do so.

Shortcodes in WordPress are added by including a tag inside square brackets in the content editor. For instance, the gallery shortcode in WordPress looks like this: [gallery]. When the post content is parsed, the shortcodes are then extracted and the functions related to them are run in their place, adding the dynamic content in the place where the shortcode appeared. At the heart of it, shortcodes are another type of filter in which the content is taken and then modified and added back to the original content.

Shortcodes can also be passed attributes in a similar way that you would with a HTML element, like so: [gallery id="custom-gallery"]. Or they can wrap around content to include the enclosed content in the shortcode function [related]Related posts[/related] (the last example is a custom shortcode created because the default WordPress gallery shortcode doesn't work as a wrap-around shortcode).

There is a series of shortcodes already built in to WordPress for authors to make use of, including the gallery shortcode, the embed shortcode, and the caption or wp_caption shortcodes. There's also a bunch of shortcodes that are in use on the WordPress.com installs of WordPress blogs (see http://wp-themes-book.com/06004), but the downloadable version of the content management system (CMS) comes only with the four main ones mentioned. This isn't necessarily a bad thing because you can easily create your own shortcodes to be added to your themes really easily.

Creating Custom Shortcodes

Now you know what shortcodes are and the concept behind how they work you can create your own examples and build some simple functions for authors to add to their posts.

Naming Conventions

As with anything in WordPress, you need to consider some naming conventions for your shortcodes. As always, the WordPress convention is to use only lowercase letters; for shortcodes specifically, try to stick to using a simple word or two. Because of their nature, I don't recommend using a prefixed or complex name for the shortcode tag because it would add more complexity for the authors who use your shortcodes. Instead, try to be aware of which other shortcodes might possibly be used by other plugins and name yours sensibly to not conflict.

The use of hyphens in shortcodes could be problematic, possibly due to a bug that exists in the functions that process shortcodes. And as yet there is no known fix. The best way to get around this bug is to avoid the use of hyphens in your shortcode names by either removing hyphens altogether or using underscores in their place to avoid issues.

WordPress allows only one hook for each shortcode, so if there are instances in which a shortcode is created with the same tag, the last one to be created will be the one that gets parsed. You could avoid this by using prefixes in your shortcodes, however, this is counterintuitive to the nature of creating shortcodes, as I've already mentioned. Another way to combat this is to make sure your theme shortcodes are set up after any plugins so that in a worst-case scenario in which a plugin does have a similarly named shortcode, your function will overwrite the one added by the plugin. You'll look at a method to do this in the next section.

Simple Shortcodes

Similar to the way you create actions and filters in WordPress, shortcodes require a function to create and output the information and a way of registering them with WordPress so it knows what shortcodes to look for.

First you'll create the function—note that the functions you create for the shortcodes don't output the content; they act much in the same way filters do in that they return the content from the function to be output when the shortcode is processed:

```
function prowordpress_related_posts_shortcode() {
        global $post;

        $tags = wp_get_post_tags( $post->ID, array( 'fields' => 'ids' ) );
        $output = false;
        if ($tags) {
                $args = array(
                        'tag__in'          => $tags,
                        'post__not_in'     => array($post->ID),
                        'posts_per_page'   => 5,
                );

                $related = new WP_Query($args);

                if( $related->have_posts() ) {
                        $output = '<h2>Recent posts</h2>';
                        $output .= '<ul class="related-posts">';

                        while ($related->have_posts()) {
                                $related->the_post();
                                $output .= '<li><a href="'.get_permalink().'">'.
get_the_title().'</a></li>';
                        }
```

```
            $output .= "</ul>";

        }

        return $output;
    }

    // if no related posts then show an error message
    return "<p>There are currently no related posts for this article</p>";
}
```

This function looks pretty big, but it's just an example of a way to get the tags for the current post and then use them in a query for posts that are tagged the same. Here you're using a variable ($output) to capture the intended output so you can return it at the end of the function.

You can now register this function with a shortcode tag so you can use it with your themes. To do this, add the add_shortcode function, which is as simple as they come. It takes only two arguments: the shortcode tag and the function that should be called. In this case, the function looks like this:

```
add_shortcode('related_posts', 'prowordpress_related_posts_shortcode');
```

As mentioned, it's best to ensure that your add_shortcode functions are called after plugins have been set up so that in case your shortcodes are named similarly to another plugin's shortcodes, you can try to avoid conflicts. Obviously, if the plugin uses the same technique, it will come down to the order in which they are created. If yours loses, you'll have to rename your shortcode or change the plugin that's generating the conflict. The easy way to add the add_shortcode functions after the plugins have been set up is by using an action hook on the init action:

```
function prowordpress_setup_shortcodes () {
        add_shortcode('related_posts', 'prowordpress_related_posts_shortcode');
}

add_action( 'init', 'prowordpress_setup_shortcodes' );
```

You've seen this type of action many times already; here you're adding the add_shortcode functions inside another function that gets called only after the init action is run.

Now you have the shortcode setup and ready to go, give it a whirl. You just need to add the shortcode [related_posts] to the content section of a post and see the results shown in Figure 6-1.

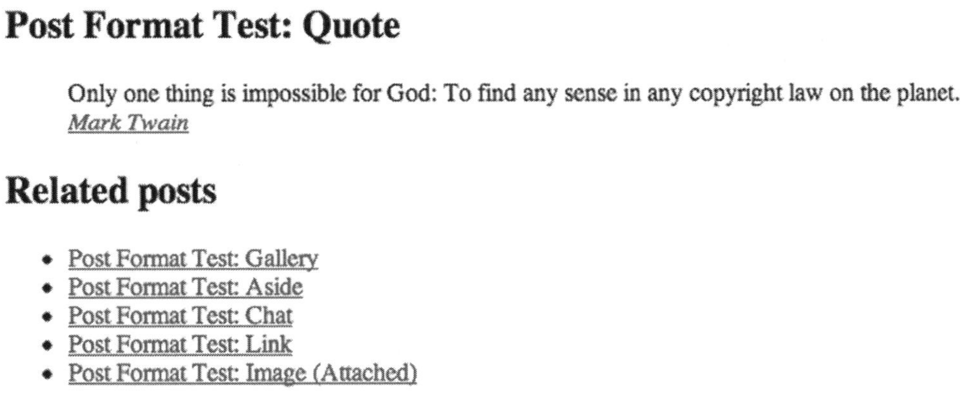

Post Format Test: Quote

Only one thing is impossible for God: To find any sense in any copyright law on the planet.
Mark Twain

Related posts

- Post Format Test: Gallery
- Post Format Test: Aside
- Post Format Test: Chat
- Post Format Test: Link
- Post Format Test: Image (Attached)

Figure 6-1. *The related posts shortcode in action*

Shortcodes with Parameters

Next you'll look at creating shortcodes, which take parameters, building on the previous example of a related posts shortcode. There are a couple of parameters you could add here to make the shortcode more dynamic and allow the user to have the content output that they want. Let's add a `limit` and a `category` parameter, so the shortcode looks like this:

```
[related_posts limit="3" category="review"]
```

To receive the attributes from the shortcode to the function, add an `$atts` parameter to the function, like so:

```
function prowordpress_related_posts_shortcode($atts) {
```

There's no need to add a default because WordPress handles it. The `$atts` variable is passed all parameters that are added to the shortcode, which means that even unknown attributes that an author adds will be passed, whether you can use them or not. The format the `$atts` variable takes is of an associative array with the keys as the names of the attributes. You could essentially use this array in the function and be done with it, calling `$atts['limit']` to get the value of the `limit` parameter passed through to the shortcode. However, there is a much better way of doing this: using a WordPress function, `shortcode_atts`. This function takes two parameters, the first is an associative array of the default arguments for the shortcode, and the second is the `$atts` array. It would look something like this:

```
$attributes = shortcode_atts( array(
            'limit'    => 5,
            'category' => ""
        ), $atts );
```

This function then returns an array of the parameters to the `$attributes` variable with only the two parameters from the default array, but with the values from the `$atts` array if they have also been passed. In this case from the earlier example, it would result in the `$attributes` array looking like this:

```
Array (
        'limit'    => 3,
        'category' => 'review'
)
```

It's pretty straightforward; the attributes have been set from the `$atts` array when you passed in the parameters from the shortcode. However, the power of this function comes in when there are no parameters set or the author has set up some parameters that you don't need for this shortcode. Suppose that someone used this shortcode in the post:

```
[related_posts limit="3" tag="action"]
```

You don't want a tag parameter for the function here, so by passing the incoming `$atts` array through the `shortcode_atts` function with the defaults as before, you end up with this array in `$attributes`:

```
Array (
        'limit'    => 3,
        'category' => ''
)
```

The tag parameter has been completely ignored, and you now have an array with two entries only and the category parameter set to its default. Pretty powerful stuff! The last thing to note about the shortcode_atts function is that when parsing the attributes, it converts all keys to lowercase but leaves the values alone, so a shortcode that looks like this:

```
[related_posts LIMIT="3" CATEGORY="review"]
```

You end up with an $attributes array that looks like the standard one you would expect.

```
Array (
        'limit'    => 3,
        'category' => 'review'
)
```

There is one more trick you can also use when setting up attributes for shortcodes: the extract() PHP function. The extract() function parses an array and sets up local variables for the attribute keys. Therefore, by using the following snippet of code to parse the attributes, you end up with the variables $limit and $category to use in the function, which is really very handy:

```
extract(shortcode_atts( array(
                'limit'    => 5,
                'category' => ""
        ), $atts ));
```

So let's put these attributes into action into the shortcode function:

```
function prowordpress_related_posts_shortcode($atts) {
        global $post;

        extract(shortcode_atts( array(
                        'limit'    => 5,
                        'category' => ""
                ), $atts ));

        $tags = wp_get_post_tags( $post->ID, array( 'fields' => 'ids' ) );
        $output = false;
        if ($tags) {
                $args = array(
                        'tag__in'          => $tags,
                        'post__not_in'     => array($post->ID),
                        // Using the extracted $limit attribute
                        'posts_per_page'   => $limit,
                        // Using the extracted $category attribute
                        'category_name'    => $category,
                );

                $related = new WP_Query($args);

                if( $related->have_posts() ) {
                        $output = '<h2>Recent posts</h2>';
                        $output .= '<ul class="related-posts">';
```

```
                            while ($related->have_posts()) {
                                    $related->the_post();
                                    $output .= '<li><a href="'.get_permalink().'">'
. get_the_title().'</a></li>';
                            }

                            $output .= "</ul>";

                }

                return $output;
        }

        // if no related posts just get recent posts
        return "<p>There are currently no related posts for this article</p>";
}
```

Now you have a more customizable shortcode that gives the user more control over the dynamic content that's being output using the shortcode.

Enclosing Shortcodes

So far, you looked at self-enclosing shortcode tags, but WordPress also has the power to use enclosing WordPress tags—those that wrap around content that will be output in some form along with the dynamic content generated by the shortcode. An example of such a shortcode would look like this:

```
[related_posts limit="3"]Some related posts[/related_posts]
```

This could come in useful for adding things such as headings to the dynamic content you produce, or adding intros or descriptions to go with the content you create. You could even pass full HTML into an enclosing shortcode and have that output as well; for instance, if you wanted a heading and intro paragraph, the shortcode could look like this:

```
[related_posts limit="3"]
<h2>Some related posts</h2>
<p>Take a look at some more posts that might be of interest</p>
[/related_posts]
```

To get this content into the shortcode you just need to add one more parameter to the function, the $content parameter, like so:

```
function prowordpress_related_posts_shortcode($atts, $content = null) {
```

Here you will use a default value in the parameter declaration as when no content is passed, the default allows you to check whether the shortcode is an enclosing or self-enclosing shortcode by using this quick test:

```
is_null($content)
```

If the default were false, you would know whether the content was empty, but not how the shortcode was used. Now look at the function again with the addition of the $content parameter to the code. There are only the two changes: one to include the $content parameter in the function setup and the other to add the content first to the output based on whether it exists:

```
function prowordpress_related_posts_shortcode($atts, $content = null) {
        global $post;

        $tags = wp_get_post_tags( $post->ID, array( 'fields' => 'ids' ) );
        $output = false;
        if ($tags) {
                $args = array(
                        'tag__in'           => $tags,
                        'post__not_in'      => array($post->ID),
                        'posts_per_page'    => 5,
                );

                $related = new WP_Query($args);

                if( $related->have_posts() ) {
                        if( ! is_null( $content ) ) {
                                $output = $content;
                        } else {
                                $output = '<h2>Related posts</h2>';
                        }

                        $output .= '<ul class="related-posts">';

                        while ($related->have_posts()) {
                                $related->the_post();
                                $output .= '<li><a href="'.get_permalink().'">'.
get_the_title().'</a></li>';
                        }

                        $output .= "</ul>";

                }

                return $output;
        }

        // if no related posts just get recent posts
        return "<p>There are currently no related posts for this article</p>";
}
```

Now you can see the shortcode in action in Figure 6-2, when you use it as an enclosing shortcode and pass through some intro text for the related posts.

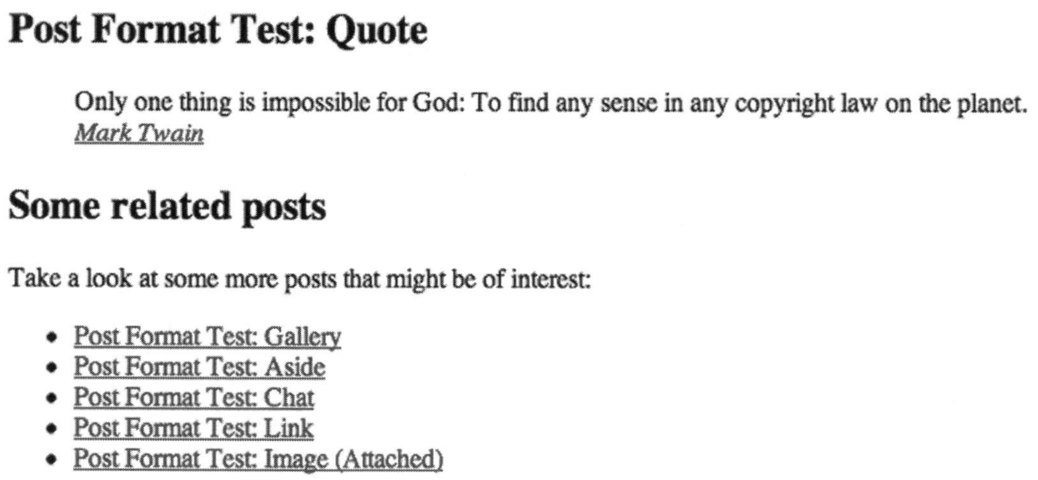

Post Format Test: Quote

> Only one thing is impossible for God: To find any sense in any copyright law on the planet.
> *Mark Twain*

Some related posts

Take a look at some more posts that might be of interest:

- Post Format Test: Gallery
- Post Format Test: Aside
- Post Format Test: Chat
- Post Format Test: Link
- Post Format Test: Image (Attached)

Figure 6-2. *Related posts shortcode output with added content*

Things to Watch Out for

When you create shortcodes, there are a few things you should be aware of that you may need to pass on to your authors, or exceptions you need to code for to make sure things work as expected.

Because the content is parsed only once by WordPress, you can't use a shortcode within another shortcode. If you wanted to do something like this, WordPress would ignore the [related_posts] shortcode within your [feature] shortcode and just output it as content:

```
[feature]Some related posts [related_posts][/feature]
```

There is a way to get around this problem: use the do_shortcode function on the content, inside of the function for your feature shortcode:

```
function prowordpress_feature_shortcode( $atts, $content = null ) {
        if( ! is_null($content) ) {
                return '<div class="feature">' . do_shortcode($content) . '</div>';
        } else {
                // return default filter
        }
}
```

The function first checks whether there is any content been passed through and then runs the do_shortcode function on the content you're returning. When doing this, you want to run the do_shortcode function in the place where the content for that shortcode should appear because, as with all shortcodes, the content will be returned in place.

You should also be aware that the WordPress parser can't make the distinction between enclosing and non-enclosing shortcodes at the same time. So using shortcodes in this manner:

```
[embed media="http://www.youtube.com/embed/LtE6kxgV3XE?rel=0"]
```

```
Now embed this too:
```

```
[embed media="http://www.youtube.com/embed/ng30C7t03v0?rel=0"]
```

```
Here's a caption
```

```
[/embed]
```

The parser just simply treats this as one shortcode and adds the start of the second shortcode as content of the first. Annoying, but you can see why this can happen.

Using Shortcodes in Other Parts of Your Theme

Shortcodes by default are only looked for in the main content section of your posts, which can be quite frustrating if you want to use them in other areas of your site. However, it is a simple and easy fix to enable shortcodes throughout other areas of your site. You saw the function you'll use to do this when you added a fix for adding shortcodes to enclosing shortcodes: the do_shortcode function.

Because the do_shortcode function is essentially just another WordPress filter, you can add it like any other filter to hooks for other parts of the WordPress content. For widgets, you can use the widget_text hook; for excerpts, you can use the the_excerpt hook:

```
add_filter('widget_text', 'do_shortcode');
add_filter('the_excerpt', 'do_shortcode');
```

Those two lines of code are enough to ensure that you can use the shortcodes throughout these areas of content as well as just the standard main content area.

Multiple Shortcodes with the Same Function

When creating shortcodes, you use the add_shortcode function to set the tag for the shortcode to be used and a function to handle that tag when the shortcode is parsed. However, nothing can stop you from using the same function for multiple shortcode tags, and actually there is a great use case for doing so. The best example is when setting up shortcodes to handle video embeds. There are a couple of ways you could do this. You could set up one function with an attribute to set the site you're embedding content from, like so:

```
[video site="youtube" id="FlYZnd7dEPw"]
```

In the function to handle this, you could then simply query the site attribute and return the embed code for a YouTube video:

```
function prowordpress_embed_shortcode($atts) {
        extract(shortcode_atts( array(
                        'site' => 'youtube',
                        'id'   => ''
                ), $atts ));
```

```
        switch( $site ) {
                case 'youtube':
                        return '<iframe width="853" height="480"
src="http://www.youtube.com/embed/'.$id.'" frameborder="0" allowfullscreen></iframe>'
                        break;
                case 'vimeo':
                        return "...";
                        break;
        }
}
```

Another method is to create a different shortcode for each site and have a series of functions to deal with each one in turn:

```
function prowordpress_youtube_embed_shortcode($atts) {
        extract(shortcode_atts( array(
                        'id'    => ''
                ), $atts ));

        return '<iframe width="853" height="480" src="http://www.youtube.com/embed/'.$id.'"
frameborder="0" allowfullscreen></iframe>';
}
function prowordpress_vimeo_embed_shortcode($atts) {
        extract(shortcode_atts( array(
                        'id'    => ''
                ), $atts ));

        return '<iframe src="http://player.vimeo.com/video/'..'" width="850" height="478"
frameborder="0" webkitAllowFullScreen mozallowfullscreen allowFullScreen></iframe>';
}

add_shortcode('youtube', 'prowordpress_youtube_embed_shortcode');
add_shortcode('vimeo', 'prowordpress_vimeo_embed_shortcode');
```

Both these methods are fine, but the first requires a more complex shortcode, and the second requires a load of code to do almost the same thing. So if you combine the two methods, creating multiple shortcodes and using one function to handle them all, you'll have a perfect combination.

If you do this though, how do you know which site to embed the video from? Fortunately for you, WordPress makes the tag name from which the function was called available to you in the form of a $tag parameter. The function and shortcodes can now look like this:

```
function prowordpress_embed_shortcode($atts, $content = NULL, $tag) {

        extract(shortcode_atts( array(
                        'id'    => ''
                ), $atts ));

        switch( $tag ) {
                case 'youtube':
                        return '<iframe width="853" height="480"
src="http://www.youtube.com/embed/'.$id.'" frameborder="0" allowfullscreen></iframe>';
                        break;
```

```
        case 'vimeo':
                return '<iframe src="http://player.vimeo.com/video/'.$id.'" width="850"
height="478" frameborder="0" webkitAllowFullScreen mozallowfullscreen allowFullScreen></iframe>';
                break;
        }
}

add_shortcode('youtube', 'prowordpress_embed_shortcode');
add_shortcode('vimeo', 'prowordpress_embed_shortcode');
```

The code reuse of a single handler function, combined with the ability to have a separate shortcode available for each, makes the code a lot more compact, avoids a lot of repetition, and makes the shortcodes more user-friendly.

Making Shortcodes More User-Friendly

As great as shortcodes are, there is still one small issue that can come up from time to time. Consider this snippet of code:

```
[related_posts limit="3" category="review"]
```

It may look simple enough to you, but remember that we are usually developers (although if you're not, kudos for getting this far along), so you're used to seeing code that looks like this. We developers generally can remember attributes and how to add them like this. However, for authors, it's more likely that they will never have seen code like this before, and remembering attributes and how to add them can be quite a foreign experience for someone generally just used to writing copy. Fortunately, there is a really easy way of adding a better method for the authors to insert shortcodes: the TinyMCE interface (see Figure 6-3).

Figure 6-3. *The TinyMCE editor interface is the range of buttons above the main editor window*

The TinyMCE editor has a range of controls for users to add things like headers or bold styling to their content, but there's also an API available for developers to be able to add their own buttons.

The first step is to create functions to register the button with the TinyMCE buttons and then include a JavaScript file that will handle the button processing:

```
function prowordpress_register_shortcode_button( $buttons ) {
        array_push( $buttons, "relatedposts" );
        return $buttons;
}

function prowordpress_add_shortcode_plugin( $plugin_array ) {
        $plugin_array['relatedposts'] = get_template_directory_uri() . '/javascript/shortcode.js';
        return $plugin_array;
}
```

The first function takes the $buttons parameter as an array of the TinyMCE buttons, and then adds the name of the button (relatedposts) to the end of the array. The second function is the one that handles the JavaScript file; here you have another array as the parameter that you then add another key with the name of the shortcode to, pointing to the JavaScript file you'll be using to control the functionality for the button.

Next you need to add a function to call the two other functions above to register the new button, of course this is done with actions but first you need to check whether the user is able to edit posts and whether you have the ability to use the rich editor (the TinyMCE editor).

```
function prowordpress_related_posts_button() {

        if ( ! current_user_can('edit_posts') && ! current_user_can('edit_pages') ) {
                return;
        }

        if ( get_user_option('rich_editing') == 'true' ) {
                add_filter( 'mce_external_plugins', 'prowordpress_add_shortcode_plugin' );
                add_filter( 'mce_buttons', 'prowordpress_register_shortcode_button' );
        }

}

add_action('init', 'prowordpress_related_posts_button');
```

This function is then added to the WordPress execution on the init hook, so you add the button before the page and editor are loaded.

Now you have the button being added via the PHP in the functions file, but you don't have any code to make it do anything; this is where the JavaScript file comes in. There seem to be a couple of methods out there to do this, but I've opted for a method similar to the one used by Konstantinos Kouratoras in his *Smashing Magazine* article. His code contains a couple more functions, but I've just included the main piece of code that's needed to give the button some functionality:

```
(function() {
        tinymce.create('tinymce.plugins.relatedposts', {
                init : function(ed, url) {
                        ed.addButton('relatedposts', {
                                title : 'Related posts',
                                image : url+'/shortcode-icon.png',
                                onclick : function() {
                                        var limit = prompt("Number of posts to display", "5");

                                        if (limit != null && limit != '') {
                                                ed.execCommand('mceInsertContent', false,
'[related_posts limit="'+limit+'"]');
                                        } else {
                                                ed.execCommand('mceInsertContent', false,
'[related_posts]');
                                        }
                                }
                        });
                }
        });

        tinymce.PluginManager.add('relatedposts', tinymce.plugins.relatedposts);
})();
```

This JavaScript function creates a new button based on the name you created in the PHP function `'relatedposts'`, and then you can add all necessary functionality within the `init` function.

The `init` function takes an object containing the title, image icon for the button, and what to do when the button is clicked. In the `onclick` function, you're using a simple prompt to ask the user how many posts the shortcode should show (with a default of 5). Once the prompt has returned you can check the result and construct the shortcode with the `mceInsertContent` function. The result determines how the shortcode is constructed. The shortcode button now appears nicely at the end of the top line of the TinyMCE editor (see Figure 6-4).

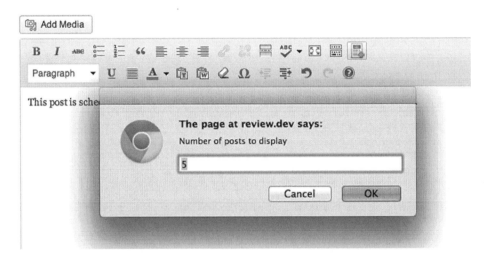

Figure 6-4. *Shortcode plugin button and the prompt to ask users for a number of posts*

This was just a very brief look at how to add a button for your shortcodes; there are many more in-depth articles on the subject by Konstantinos Kouratoras as mentioned in his *Smashing Magazine* article: `http://wp-themes-book.com/06005` and by Gary Cao on his blog: `http://wp-themes-book.com/06006`.

Widgets (and Dynamic Sidebars)

Widgets were introduced in WordPress in version 2.8 as another way to allow content editors to easily add and control dynamic content. Widgets can range from adding a search box, to listing categories, archives, and posts or pages. Widgets use a simple drag-and-drop interface (see Figure 6-5) to allow users to position content within the theme wherever a widget area has been allocated and can be customized from within the Widget control panel, adding titles and choosing options about what or how that content will be displayed (see Figure 6-6).

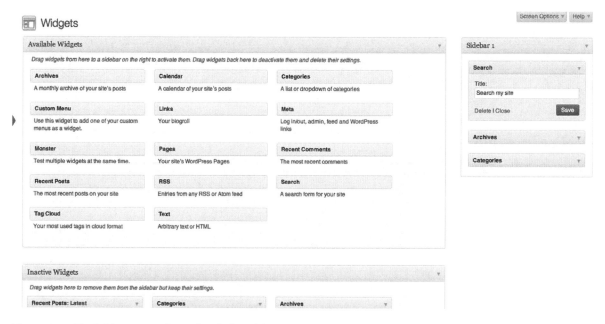

Figure 6-5. *The Widgets control panel with the sidebar containing displayed widgets on the right*

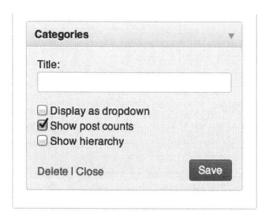

Figure 6-6. *Closeup of a Widget control panel, showing the customizable options available for users*

▓ **Note** Although I'm using the term *widget area*, the WordPress Codex and a lot of other documentation refer to them as *sidebars*, which is where the term *dynamic sidebars* comes from.

Dynamic Sidebars

When I use the term *dynamic sidebars* here, I'm not actually speaking about a sidebar.php template, although that is one of the more common locations for widgets to be added. A *sidebar* in this context is defined in your code using the register_sidebar function, which allows you to place a dynamic sidebar for the positioning of widgets in your theme. A good example of this is the WordPress default theme Twenty Twelve, which has a series of different widget areas defined for use throughout the theme (see Figure 6-7).

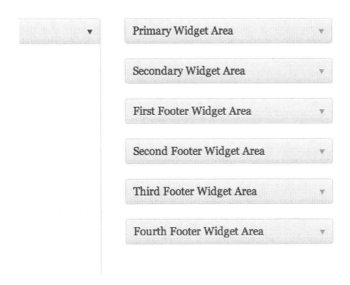

Figure 6-7. *The Twenty Twelve Widget control panel showing the number of available widget areas*

Adding Dynamic Sidebars to Your Theme

When adding dynamic sidebars, there are two steps you need to take. The first is to register a sidebar and set up any options for it using the register_sidebar function; the second is to set up an area of your theme to use the dynamic sidebar using the dynamic_sidebar function.

In the early days of WordPress, sidebars used to be set up as a series of list elements in an unordered list:

```
<ul id="sidebar">
        <li id="about">
                <h2>About</h2>
                <p>This is my blog.</p>
        </li>
        <li id="links">
                <h2>Links</h2>
                <ul>
                        <li><a href="http://example.com">Example</a></li>
                </ul>
        </li>
</ul>
```

The previous sidebar example is taken from the Codex page about widgetizing your theme (http://wp-themes-book.com/06007).

That markup is still perfectly fine today and you may find some people still using it. However, in the age of HTML5 and tags such as <aside>, you may see something a little more like this in your sidebar:

```
<aside class="sidebar news">
        <h2>Archives</h2>
        <ul class="news-navigation">
                <?php wp_get_archives(); ?>
        </ul>

        <h2>Popular categories</h2>
        <ul class="news-navigation">
                <?php
                $args = array(
                                'title_li' => '',
                                'number' => 10,
                                'orderby' => 'count',
                        );

                wp_list_categories( $args ); ?>
        </ul>
</aside>
```

You can still see the WordPress functions for sidebars and widgets tend to have defaults that relate more closely to the old method of marking up your pages. You need to overwrite a few of the defaults when registering the sidebars, so let's take a close look at the register_sidebar function now and see what's going on:

```
$args = array(
        'name'          => __( 'Sidebar {#}', 'theme_text_domain' ),
        'id'            => 'sidebar-{#}',
        'description'   => '',
        'class'         => '',
        'before_widget' => '<li id="%1$s" class="widget %2$s">',
        'after_widget'  => '</li>',
        'before_title'  => '<h2 class="widgettitle">',
        'after_title'   => '</h2>'
);
register_sidebar($args);
```

In the code are the defaults for the register_sidebar function arguments. The first thing to note is that in the 'name' and 'id' parameters, the "{#}" bit is in place of an auto incremented ID number. Your sidebar name will default to "Sidebar 1" and the ID to sidebar-1, and any subsequent calls of 'register_sidebar' will auto increment the numeric element of the name and ID. In the defaults, you can also see what I've been talking about when I mention the default setup of sidebars being in HTML lists. The before_widget and after_widget defaults contain <li> tags because that was normally the way widgets needed to be marked up in the sidebars. This process is somewhat outdated now, so you must remember to overwrite these settings each time you set up a sidebar.

■ **Note**   As with any good function that requires naming things in WordPress, there are a whole bunch of IDs you need to avoid when setting up the sidebars. Luckily, there is a handy list of all reserved IDs here: http://wp-themes-book.com/06008. The list is curated and kept up to date by John Landells,

---

Here's a look at a function call to set up a regular widgetized sidebar for your themes:

```php
function prowordpress_setup_sidebars() {
        $args = array(
                'name'          => __( 'Sidebar right', 'prowordress' ),
                'id'            => 'sidebar-right',
                'before_widget' => '<section class="widget">',
                'after_widget'  => '</section>',
                'before_title'  => '<h2 class="widget-title">',
                'after_title'   => '</h2>'
        );
        register_sidebar($args);
}
add_action( 'widgets_init', 'prowordpress_setup_sidebars' );
```

I enclosed the `register_sidebar` function in a function that will get called on the `widget_init` hook, which is set up specifically for use in setting up dynamic sidebars and widgets. Inside the function, I'm calling the sidebar "Sidebar right" (showing the user that the sidebar will appear in the right side of the theme) and then changed the before and after widget arguments to something that fits better with the more up-to-date markup.

Now that you've registered your sidebar, you can set up a place for it somewhere in your theme. You can do this with the `dynamic_sidebar` function, which is fairly simple to look at but actually does a whole bunch of functionality for you. The function takes one argument, which is the ID of the sidebar you want to use in that location, and then the function does the rest, looping through and outputting all widgets that have been added to that sidebar with the correct markup that you specified in your `register_sidebar` function.

Before you take a look at how to set this up in your theme, there's one quick thing to mention. Besides having your `dynamic_sidebar` function to run through the widgets available, you should also add content as a fallback in case there is nothing for the dynamic sidebar to display. You do this by enclosing the `dynamic_sidebar` function in an if statement and keeping your fallback content inside:

```php
<aside class="sidebar news">
        <?php if( ! dynamic_sidebar( 'sidebar-right' ) ): ?>
                <h2>Movie genres</h2>
                <ul class="genre-navigation">
                        <?php
                        $args = array(
                                        'taxonomy'      => 'ptd_genre',
                                        'orderby'       => 'name',
                                        'order'         => 'ASC',
                                        'style'         => 'list',
                                        'show_count'    => 0,
                                        'hide_empty'    => 0,
                                        'title_li'      => '',
                                        'depth'         => 1,
                                );

                        wp_list_categories( $args ); ?>
                </ul>
        <?php endif; ?>
</aside>
```

The if statement is using an ! operator to check whether the function returns false; if so, the Movie genres list will be shown, which is your fallback content. Otherwise, if the function returns something, it has run and will display the content of the widgets for that selected sidebar.

You now have a dynamic sidebar set up ready to display your widgets. I won't cover how to set up and customize default widgets because they are all pretty straightforward. If you need more information, you can always take a look at the Codex: http://wp-themes-book.com/06007. Instead, let's look at how to create your own widgets to add to your theme.

Creating Custom Widgets

Now that you know how to set up your dynamic sidebars to display widgets on your site, you can look at creating your own widgets to display in these areas. When widgets were released in version 2.8, it came with a complete developer API to enable developers to create their own widgets to go along with their themes and plugins.

Creating widgets involves using object-oriented PHP and setting up a class for your widget functions. This is made easier with WordPress creating the WP_Widget class that you can easily extend off of to make your own widgets. You'll look into how to set up the class for your custom widget in a moment; first you need to tell WordPress about your new widget with the register_widget function. Once again, this is loaded using the widgets_init hook you used when registering your sidebars:

```
function prowordpress_register_widgets() {
        register_widget( 'Genre_Widget' );
}

add_action( 'widgets_init', 'prowordpress_register_widgets' );
```

The register_widget function takes only one parameter—the name of the widget class that controls all the functionality for your widget. The name of the class is formatted similarly to that of all PHP classes with words separated by an underscore and each word in Title Case. This function can be used to add more than one widget by just calling the register_widget function multiple times.

■ **Note** So far in this chapter, all your code has been getting added to the functions.php file as in previous chapters. In the following section for your custom widget, you'll add a new widgets.php PHP file inside an inc folder in your theme directory. It can then be included at the same time as you set up your register widget function with require(get_template_directory() . '/inc/widgets.php'), placed above the register_widget function.

Setting Up the Widget Class

For this example, let's take the list of movie genres you already have in the sidebar of your theme and turn it into a widget with some options for the user. WordPress makes it easy to create your own widgets by giving you a class to extend from and build your functionality upon the existing code that all widgets in WordPress start with: the WP_Widget class. So your class function starts off like this:

```
class Genre_Widget extends WP_Widget {
        // Widget code here
}
```

Next you'll set up four functions in your class to take care of the different methods needed to control a widget:

- __construct: Sets up your widget with WordPress. You may sometimes see this function replaced by a function with the same name as the class; in this case, a Genre_Widget function. Before PHP 5, this was the method of creating a constructor function for the class. However, because we're now up to version 5.4 of PHP (supported by WordPress, but not the minimum requirement yet), you need to use the __construct method, because functions named with the same name as the class are treated as a regular method after PHP version 5.3.3.

- widget: Handles the front-end display of the widget.

- form: Handles the setup of the form to be used in the WordPress admin.

- update: Stores the form values when they are saved in the admin.

Next you'll go through these functions one by one. setting up each feature of the widget and seeing what goes into each function to make everything work.

__construct

```
public function __construct () {
        // Widget settings.
        $widget_ops = array( 'classname' => 'genre-list', 'description' => 'A widget that displays
the genres for our movies' );

        // Create the widget - calling the parent class construct method
        parent::__construct(
                'genre_widget', // Base ID
                'Genre Widget', // Name
                $widget_ops
        );
}
```

The first function is the __construct function. This is where you set up your function with any options you need and the ID and name that the widget will have when displayed in the widget admin area. The options are just an array with the settings you want to add; the main two you're using here are setting up a custom class and a description. Any other options are taken care of by the main WP_Widget class; you don't need to worry too much about them because they aren't used to display anything extra.

You then call the constructor function of the parent class WP_Widget. Here you're passing the ID of the widget, a name to display in the widgets admin, and the options array you just created. With that done, the widget is now set up and should appear in the widget admin page, albeit with no options and no method of displaying on the front end. So let's move on to the widget function.

widget

```
public function widget( $args, $instance ) {
        extract( $args );

        // Get the user-selected settings
        $title = apply_filters('widget_title', $instance['title'] );
        $order = $instance['sort_order'];
```

```php
$show_hidden = isset( $instance['show_hidden'] ) ? $instance['show_hidden'] : false;
$show_count = isset( $instance['show_post_count'] ) ? $instance['show_post_count'] : false;

// Before widget code (defined in the register sidebar function).
echo $before_widget;

// Title of widget - with fallback (before and after defined by register sidebar function)
echo $before_title;
if ( $title ) {
        echo $title;
} else {
        echo "Genres";
}
echo $after_title;

echo '<ul class="genre-list">';

$args = array(
                'taxonomy'      => 'ptd_genre',
                'orderby'       => $order,
                'order'         => 'ASC',
                'style'         => 'list',
                'show_count'    => $show_count,
                'hide_empty'    => $show_hidden,
                'title_li'      => '',
                'depth'         => 1,
        );

wp_list_categories( $args );

echo '</ul>';

// After widget code (defined in the register sidebar function).
echo $after_widget;
}
```

The bits you need to look out for are right at the start of the function. The function has two parameters: $args and $instance. $args are the argument from the register_sidebar function, and $instance is the settings for this widget instance. (I'll show you how they are created and stored in a second.)

Next, you use the extract PHP function to get the arguments in the $args array into their own local variables. This gives you the list of variables you can see being echoed throughout the plugin:

- $before_widget

- $before_title

- $after_title

- $after_widget

Next is the $instance parameter, which holds an array of your widget settings. In the next four lines of code, you simply check and store the values of the settings in local variables. The only one to note is that the title of your widget goes through a filter called widget_title before being stored in the variable.

The rest of the widget function is fairly straightforward; you display the title or a default title if none has been passed and then list the genres passing in the options you have for the arguments from your local variables.

Next you can move on to the admin part of the widget with the `form` function.

form

```php
public function form( $instance ) {

        /* Set up some default widget settings. */
        $defaults = array( 'title' => 'Genres', 'sort_order' => 'name', 'show_hidden' => false,
'show_post_count' => false );
        $instance = wp_parse_args( (array) $instance, $defaults );
?>
        <p>
                <label for="<?php echo $this->get_field_id( 'title' ); ?>">Title:</label>
                <input id="<?php echo $this->get_field_id( 'title' ); ?>" name="<?php echo
$this->get_field_name( 'title' ); ?>" value="<?php echo $instance['title']; ?>" style="width:95%" />
        </p>

        <p>
                <label for="<?php echo $this->get_field_id( 'sort_order' ); ?>">Sort order:</label>
                <select id="<?php echo $this->get_field_id( 'sort_order' ); ?>" name="<?php echo
$this->get_field_name( 'sort_order' ); ?>" class="widefat">
                        <option <?php selected( $instance['sort_order'], 'name' ) ?>>name</option>
                        <option <?php selected( $instance['sort_order'], 'slug' ) ?>>slug</option>
                        <option <?php selected( $instance['sort_order'], 'count' ) ?>>count</option>
                </select>
        </p>

        <p>
                <input class="checkbox" type="checkbox" <?php checked( $instance['show_hidden'],
'on' ); ?> id="<?php echo $this->get_field_id( 'show_hidden' ); ?>" name="<?php echo
$this->get_field_name( 'show_hidden' ); ?>" />
                <label for="<?php echo $this->get_field_id( 'show_hidden' ); ?>">Hide empty
genres?</label>
        </p>
        <p>
                <input class="checkbox" type="checkbox" <?php checked( $instance['show_post_count'],
'on' ); ?> id="<?php echo $this->get_field_id( 'show_post_count' ); ?>" name="<?php echo
$this->get_field_name( 'show_post_count' ); ?>" />
                <label for="<?php echo $this->get_field_id( 'show_post_count' ); ?>">Display post
count?</label>
        </p>
<?php

}
```

The widget form function has one parameter: the `$instance` array, again containing the current settings for the plugin. You then set up a `defaults` array with a set of default values for the form, which then gets combined with the current `$instance` array to create your set of current arguments using the `wp_parse_args` function. This works in exactly the same way as the `shortcode_atts` function you've seen already in the chapter.

After you have your current values or defaults, you can build your form. I won't go into too much detail about building the form (it's a fairly standard HTML form), but there are a couple of functions that I'll pick out.

```
$this->get_field_id( 'title' );
```

The get_field ID is a function found in the main widget class (hence the use of the $this operator), which builds a unique ID for the widget field. If you take a quick look at the function from the WordPress core, you can see what it's getting up to:

```
function get_field_id($field_name) {
        return 'widget-' . $this->id_base . '-' . $this->number . '-' . $field_name;
}
```

The function combines the name of the widget, the number of the widget (set by WordPress), and the name of the field, which creates something like this:

```
widget-genre_widget-2-title
```

The next functions are pretty similar, so you'll look at them together. These are handy form functions that make using check boxes and select inputs a breeze:

```
selected( $instance['sort_order'], 'name' );
checked( $instance['show_hidden'], 'on' );
```

Both functions work in a similar way: the first argument is the variable to check and the second is the value to compare it against. If the result is true, the functions output the selected and checked HTML attributes, respectively. This is a really useful function in WordPress, which saves you from writing long ugly code like this in every one of your select, checkbox, or radio button inputs:

```
if ( 'name' === $instance['sort_order] ) { echo 'selected="selected"'; }
```

Finally, you need to look at the update function, so the widgets options get saved when the user customizes the plugin.

update

```
public function update( $new_instance, $old_instance ) {
        $instance = $old_instance;

        /* Strip tags (if needed) and update the widget settings. */
        $instance['title'] = strip_tags( $new_instance['title'] );
        $instance['sort_order'] = $new_instance['sort_order'];
        $instance['show_hidden'] = $new_instance['show_hidden'];
        $instance['show_post_count'] = $new_instance['show_post_count'];

        return $instance;
}
```

The last function you need for your widget is almost the simplest of them all. The update function takes two parameters, the $new_instance array, which holds the latest values of the widget settings, and $old_instances, which holds the widget's previous settings. The function is a step in the process before the new variables are stored in the database, so you can do any data sanitizing you need. In your widget, the example is just to use the strip_tags on the title value because the rest are safe to add to the database as is. After you sanitize the values and add them to the $instance array you've created from the $old_instance array, you simply return the new array so WordPress can continue on and save the data.

That's all there is to creating your own widgets. Of course, they can be a lot more complex and do a multitude of things, but for now that's the basis of creating widgets to get you up and running and give your users the power to add extra dynamic functionality to their sidebars.

Building Your Theme, Part 5

In this section, you'll look at adding some dynamic content options for your users with what you've learned about hooks, shortcodes, and widgets. In the previous chapter, you set up a custom field in your metaboxes to set featured menu items and a staff member of the month. In this section, you'll set up a shortcode to display each of these as well as widgetizing your sidebar and adding a widget to do the same.

You have already seen a lot of code in this section, so I'll go over them only briefly to give you an idea of how to use the concepts to match the theme you're creating.

Adding shortcodes

You'll use a trick you learned earlier in the chapter when creating these shortcodes: using one function to handle both shortcodes for the featured menu item and staff member of the month. Let's dive straight in and look at the code for this:

```
function prowordpress_featured_shortcode($atts, $content = NULL, $tag) {
        // No attributes for this function

        // Set up an array for the arguments for our query
        $args = array(
                'posts_per_page'  => 1,
        );
        $class = $tag;

        switch( $tag ) {
                case 'featured_product':
                        $args['post_type'] = 'ptd_menu';
                        $args['orderby'] = 'rand';
                        $args['meta_query'] = array(
                                        array(
                                                'key'     => 'ptd_menu_item_featured',
                                                'value'   => 'on',
                                                'compare' => '='
                                        )
                        );

                        $title = "<h2>Featured item</h2>";

                        break;
```

```php
                case 'staff_of_the_month':
                        $args['post_type'] = 'ptd_staff';
                        $args['orderby'] = 'date';
                        $args['meta_query'] = array(
                                        array(
                                                        'key'     => 'ptd_staff_of_the_month',
                                                        'value'   => 'on',
                                                        'compare' => '='
                                        )
                        );
                        $title = "<h2>Staff member of the month</h2>";

                        break;
        }

        $featured = new WP_Query( $args );
        if( $featured->have_posts() ) {

                $output = '<div class="'.$class.'">';

                        if( ! is_null($content) ) {
                        $output .= '<h2>'.$content.'</h2>';
                } else {
                        $output .= $title;
                }

                while( $featured->have_posts() ) {
                        $featured->the_post();

                        $output .= '<h3>'.get_the_title().'</h3>';

                        $output .= get_the_post_thumbnail( get_the_id(), 'small');

                        $output .= '<a href="'.get_permalink().'">Find our more &raquo;</a>';

                }

                $output .='</div>';
        }

        return $output;
}

add_shortcode('staff_of_the_month', 'prowordpress_featured_shortcode');
add_shortcode('featured_product', 'prowordpress_featured_shortcode');
```

The code first sets up a couple of defaults that both shortcodes will need. Then the switch statement sets up the rest of the arguments specific to the type of query you'll be making. The last section of the function is the query itself, which also goes through storing everything in the $output variable ready to return at the end of the function, so the content you're creating stays in line with the shortcode's position in the content.

Leave it there for shortcodes in your theme for now, without adding a custom TinyMCE button for your new features. However, this is a great exercise for you to do if you want to try to build in this functionality on your own. The functionality was already covered in the chapter, so it would just be a case of adding it to your theme and making specific buttons for the featured items and staff of the month shortcodes.

Adding Widgets to Your Theme

Now take a look at how to create a widget similar to the functionality you just set up with shortcodes, but with a few customizable options so the user can choose what content to display where. However, first you need to set up a couple of widgetized areas in your theme. The first obvious one is in your sidebar for the news pages.

Creating Widget Areas

For your theme, you need three different widget areas for the user to customize. You can do this by using a similar function that you've used before, but this time looping through the arguments with an array of names and IDs for the different widget areas:

```
function prowordpress_setup_sidebars() {
        $widget_areas = array (
                        array(
                                'name' => __( 'News widget area', 'prowordress' ),
                                'id'   => 'news-widget-area'
                                ),
                        array(
                                'name' => __( 'Subnav widget area', 'prowordress' ),
                                'id'   => 'subnav-widget-area'
                                ),
                        array(
                                'name' => __( 'Homepage widget area', 'prowordress' ),
                                'id'   => 'homepage-widget-area'
                                )
                );

        foreach( $widget_areas as $area ) {
                $args = array(
                        'name'          => $area['name'],
                        'id'            => $area['id'],
                        'before_widget' => '<div class="widget">',
                        'after_widget'  => '</div>',
                        'before_title'  => '<h2 class="widget-title">',
                        'after_title'   => '</h2>'
                );
                register_sidebar($args);
        }
}
add_action( 'widgets_init', 'prowordpress_setup_sidebars' );
```

After you've added that bit of code to your `functions.php` file, you can add your `dynamic_sidebar` functions to the rest of your theme. In the `sidebar-news.php` and the `front-page.php` templates, you can wrap the `dynamic_sidebar` function inside a conditional statement around some of the content that's already there. For instance with the home page, you can wrap it around your latest news code so that if a user chooses a widget to be displayed there, the latest news content will be replaced by the widget.

```php
<?php if( ! dynamic_sidebar( 'homepage-widget-area' ) ): ?>
        <h2>Latest News</h2>

        <?php
        // Latest news code went in here...
        ?>
<?php endif; ?>
```

If you do this again for the `sidebar-news.php` template, you have the fallback of your two bits of content: the archives (which can be added back in with one of the built in WordPress widgets) and the popular categories. However, on the standard sidebar template you can just call the `dynamic_sidebar` function without the conditional wrapper statement because you don't need fallback content. If the user doesn't want to add a widget here, there's no need to display anything. So your function would look like this:

```php
<?php dynamic_sidebar( 'subnav-widget-area' ); ?>
```

Now that you have your widget areas set up, you can create your custom widget to display a featured item or the staff of the month.

Creating the Custom Widget

Creating the custom widget is quite similar to both the format of the widget created in this chapter and the shortcode you just created in this section. Very briefly, here's the code for the `widget` function for your widget. Then I'll show you what it looks like in the admin interface. You should then be able to create the rest (or you can copy the code from the example code that accompanies this book).

```php
public function widget( $args, $instance ) {
        extract( $args );

        // Get the user-selected settings
        $title = apply_filters('widget_title', $instance['title'] );
        $show_featured = isset( $instance['show_featured'] ) ? $instance['show_featured'] : false;
        $show_staff = isset( $instance['show_staff'] ) ? $instance['show_staff'] : false;

        // Before widget code (defined in the register sidebar function).
        echo $before_widget;

        if ( $title ) {
                echo $before_title.$title.$after_title;
        }

        if( $show_featured ) {

                $args = array(
                        'posts_per_page'  => 1,
                        'post_type'       => 'ptd_menu',
```

```php
                    'orderby'          => 'rand',
                    'meta_query'       => array(
                                    array(
                                            'key'     => 'ptd_menu_item_featured',
                                            'value'   => 'on',
                                            'compare' => '='
                                    )
                            )
            );

            $featured = new WP_Query( $args );
            if( $featured->have_posts() ) {

                    echo '<div class="featured-item">';
                    echo '<h3>Featured item</h3>';

                    while( $featured->have_posts() ) {
                            $featured->the_post();
?>
                            <h3><?php the_title(); ?></h3>

                            <?php the_post_thumbnail( 'small' ); ?>

                            <a href="<?php the_permalink(); ?>">Find our more &raquo;</a>
<?php
                    }
                    echo '</div>';

                    wp_reset_query();
            }
    }

    if( $show_staff ) {
            // As above with the arguments for the staff member of the month - see the shortcode
example before...
    }

    // After widget code (defined in the register sidebar function).
    echo $after_widget;
}
```

Because this is such a large function, you can see why I omitted the rest of the widget class and cut out the second section of the function. The widget function shown here gets the settings from the widget and then displays the featured item or staff member of the month, depending on which one the user has set to be displayed. You can see the result of the rest of the featured widget class in Figure 6-8, which shows you the widgets admin screen complete with the new widget and the open widget form contents.

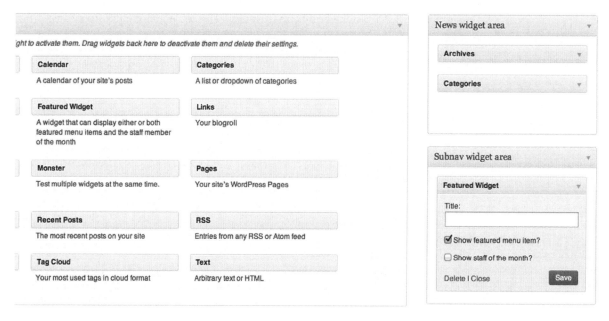

Figure 6-8. *The featured widget in the widget admin screen*

Spring Cleaning the functions File

One last task is a quick spring cleaning of your functions.php file because it's starting to overflow with a lot of code that can be split up into files to make finding and managing the code a lot easier.

First, move all the code relating to custom post types, custom taxonomies, and custom fields into a custom-types.php file in a directory called inc inside your theme folder. The widget class can be put into its own file called custom-widgets.php inside the inc folder. And finally top that off with any functions that add extra functions for use in your theme such as prowordpress_customise_feed and prowordpress_build_our_menu, which provide extra functionality to the theme but should be stored together neatly in their own section of the theme.

Once you set up these three files, you can include them in your functions files with the PHP require functions inside the theme setup function. At the bottom of the theme setup function, add these three functions:

```
/**
 * Include our custom types functions
 */
require( get_template_directory() . '/inc/custom-types.php' );

/**
 * Include custom theme functions
 */
require( get_template_directory() . '/inc/theme-functions.php' );
/**
 * Include the custom widgets file
 */
require( get_template_directory() . '/inc/custom-widgets.php' );
```

Now you have a nice and clean theme functions file and three organized files containing groups of similar functions. Because the theme setup function gets called on the after_theme_setup hook it means that all of your functions are there ready to go at the correct time.

Summary

Another slog of a chapter, but you got through it. The chapter covered a ton of great features in WordPress that allow you to customize WordPress and give your users access to some great dynamic content features. You used hooks throughout the book so far without much explanation, but back at the start of the chapter you took a deeper look at how hooks work in WordPress and why they're so important. Hooks have singlehandedly allowed WordPress theme and plugin developers to extend and modify the features in WordPress without having to touch the core code.

Next you looked at two options for giving the user the power to add dynamic content: shortcodes and widgets. Shortcodes give the power to authors to add dynamic generated content in line with the copy they're writing. However, even though they look like a nice simple addition for authors to use, the syntax and code might be confusing to a complete beginner. If that's the case, try adding in a button to the TinyMCE editor interface instead. Your users may thank you in the long run.

Finally you took a look at widgets and how to get them into your themes in the form of adding dynamic sidebars in various places throughout your theme. You learned about creating a basic widget of your own, allowing the user to customize the output with simple settings in the WordPress admin.

▨ ▨ ▨

CHAPTER 7

Theme Options and the Theme Customizer

Whether you're developing your themes for your clients or creating them to sell or distribute as standalone themes, adding theme options and customizations is worth considering. Adding customizable options to your themes can enable your users to make your theme feel like their own, adding their own unique touches to a theme that may be downloaded hundreds of times. And giving clients customization options allows them to make simple tweaks without having to come to you for support, saving you time and giving them a sense of ownership of their own site.

WordPress theme options have changed dramatically over the period of the last few updates. In version 3.4 (Green), launched in the middle of 2012, came a new addition to the WordPress core: the theme customizer (see Figure 7-1). This new addition sought to change up theme options dramatically, and in this chapter you'll see the newfound powers that the theme customizer gives to your WordPress themes.

Figure 7-1. *The theme customizer added in WordPress 3.4*

Before you get cracking with the new theme customizer, though, it's important to take a step back and look at where to start with adding customization options to your themes. You'll also look briefly at how options were added prior to version 3.4, what can be learned from past methods, and why others may be reluctant to move over to newer features. Toward the end of the chapter, you'll be diving back into building your theme once more by adding some options to allow your users to add their own little tweaks to your theme.

Why Provide Theme Options?

To some, this question may seem simple. However it's likely that you will be falling into one of two categories:

- Theme options are great; customize everything.

- Theme options are evil; I don't want my theme being altered.

On one side of the fence, people think that having customization options for everything in your theme is the best route to go, allowing your users the freedom to create the site they want from the base theme you've created. On the other side, people believe that if a theme is designed and built with care and consideration, giving users a chance to customize it will end up ruining it. They would much rather keep it as beautifully designed as they intended.

Like most things in life, I think there's something to be said for getting a comfy pillow and perching right in the middle of the fence instead. Too many options for customizations will lead to your theme being overly complex and your users left staring at a panel of options running off the screen, not knowing where to start or, in fact, what customizes what. On the other hand, few or no options may leave your users looking for another theme or regularly calling up for support when they need to change the tiniest thing:

> [A] large portion of [the Please Advise team's] support questions are customers who want help customizing their themes.

Andy Adams (http://wp-themes-book.com/07001)

For me, adding theme options is important where necessary. If you're creating your theme to sell or distribute via a themes directory (more on that in Chapter 11), you might want to consider adding some options for your users so they can make the theme feel a bit more unique. Conversely, if you're developing your theme for clients, there may be no need for them to have any theme options, so avoiding them is best because you need to have control over how the site is displayed. In my experience working for clients over the last 4 years, I've found it rare to have to add theme options for a client site. However, there have been times when adding them was worthwhile and cost effective for the amount of time I spent dealing with minor client requests for updates.

Choosing the Right Options

There's something to be said for choosing the right parts of a theme for users to customize. A header image, logo, and main background site color can be good options for a user to really see a major difference from a few small customizations.

However, also think about the way you offer the customizations. Allowing a user to change all the different colors on a web site—from body text, to links, to headers, and even the background—could result in a hideous combination of colors (not to mention a site that's completely inaccessible). You may say that it's completely up to the user if they want to make those choices, which is true. But what if the amount of choice you've given them is too much and they feel overwhelmed trying to choose something from a huge color picker?

What if you offered them a choice of several color palettes instead? How about offering color selections that you've worked on and designed to look the best with your theme design? Doing so not only helps ensure that your theme will look good but also gives the user a smaller set of options, removing complexity while still allowing them to customize the theme.

Remember to think about your user when you create theme options; consider what they might want to customize depending on the style of the theme, and remember to ensure that your options are also user friendly and complexity is kept to a minimum.

Simple Customizations with Theme Features

Before you start looking at the theme customizer and adding custom theme options, there are two WordPress features you should know that have allowed customization since version 2.1: custom backgrounds (version 3.0) and custom headers (version 2.1). In version 3.4, both functions got a slight makeover and were added as theme features. Although both theme features can ultimately be set through the theme customizer, each has distinct methods of adding them to your theme and creating a completely separate page to manage them outside of the theme customizer.

Both custom headers and custom backgrounds are added to your theme with the add_theme_supports() function, which you worked with in Chapter 2 when setting up some default features and post formats. These theme features work in a similar way to the post formats feature because they can be set up by just passing the name of the feature to the add_theme_supports() function. However both of these features can also take some optional arguments, in the form of an array, which you'll look at in the next sections.

Custom Backgrounds

The custom background feature is included with the following line of code:

```
add_theme_support( 'custom-background' );
```

This single line of code will set up the screen shown in Figure 7-2. It will instantly allow your users to add a custom image or select a custom color for the background. As mentioned before, there are options you can pass along with this feature to set up some defaults. The extended setup of the feature looks like this:

```
$defaults = array(
        'default-color'          => '',
        'default-image'          => '',
        'wp-head-callback'       => '_custom_background_cb',
        'admin-head-callback'    => '',
        'admin-preview-callback' => ''
);
add_theme_support( 'custom-background', $defaults );
```

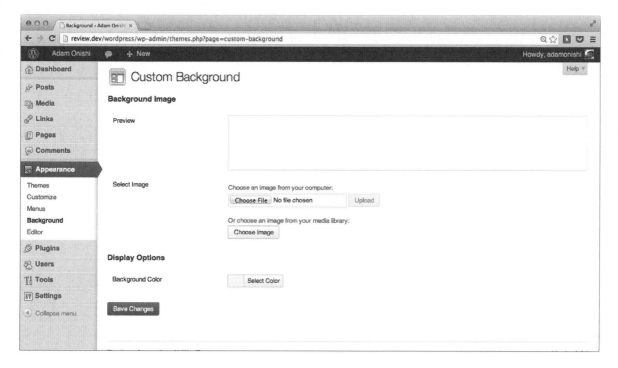

Figure 7-2. *The custom background setting page*

Looking at the full list of arguments, there are really only two parameters you'll ever need to customize: `'default-color'` and `'default-image'`. The remaining three are callback functions that apply to the setting of a custom background at various times. The only one you might customize is `'wp-head-callback'` because there's a quirk in the custom background settings. If you apply a default image in the arguments, it will be displayed, but if you set a default color, it won't get displayed until a user visits (and saves) the background customization page. I'll talk about this quirk in a bit more detail shortly, but for now it's worth looking at how the function makes changes to your theme.

■ **Note** When adding a custom background color, add it as a hex color value without the preceding #.

After the user has set a custom background (or when a default background image is set in your function), WordPress will output a custom inline style to the <head> of every page. The style is set up using the _custom_background_cb() function, taking all the settings the user has chosen (color, position, repeat, and scroll or fixed) and adding them to a custom background style declaration. The style is added to the body with a `'.custom-background'` class that gets added in the body_class() function when a custom background has been chosen.

```
<style type="text/css" id="custom-background-css">
body.custom-background { background:#000000 url(http://website.com/wp-content/uploads/2013/10/
matrix.jpg) 0 0 no-repeat scroll; }
</style>
```

This style will appear inline in the page and after any style sheet you have included with the `wp_enqueue_style()` function. I recommend that you avoid adding any styles to the `.custom-background` class in your default style sheet because it should be left to WordPress to customize with this feature.

Custom Background Color Quirk

The quirk with a default background color mentioned earlier happens for two reasons. First, the default callback function is set up to get a custom background color only if it's been set via the customization page. If you look in the `wp-includes/theme.php` file in the WordPress core and search for the `_custom_background_cb()` function, you will find these few lines of code:

```
// $color is the saved custom color.
// A default has to be specified in style.css. It will not be printed here.
$color = get_theme_mod( 'background_color' );
```

This code says that there must be a `'theme_mod'` for the `background_color` value for it to be displayed.

Second, if the user hasn't been to the background customization page and clicked Save, the `.custom-background` class will not be applied to the body. To get around both of these issues, Justin Tadlock wrote a replacement callback function that can be used to set up the default background color (you can find it here: `http://wp-themes-book.com/07002`). However I'm of the opinion that the WordPress core is actually correct: if you'll set up a default background color, it should be added to your theme style sheet in the first place. There's no need for the theme to add custom styles to the page if there's if the user hasn't selected a custom color, the default is there in case the user chooses to reset the setting after it's been customized.

Custom Headers

The custom header feature is set in a similar way, with the choice of passing some default options with the `add_theme_support()` function. However with the custom headers there are more options to choose from:

```
$defaults = array(
        'default-image'          => '',
        'random-default'         => false,
        'width'                  => 0,
        'height'                 => 0,
        'flex-height'            => false,
        'flex-width'             => false,
        'default-text-color'     => '',
        'header-text'            => true,
        'uploads'                => true,
        'wp-head-callback'       => '',
        'admin-head-callback'    => '',
        'admin-preview-callback' => '',
);
add_theme_support( 'custom-header', $defaults );
```

Because the custom header feature is aimed at the full header of your site, you get loads of options to customize how the header image will be displayed; whether to allow text inside the header; and defaults for height, size, and colors. The result is best seen in the Twenty Thirteen theme, which comes with a plethora of options for the user (see Figure 7-3).

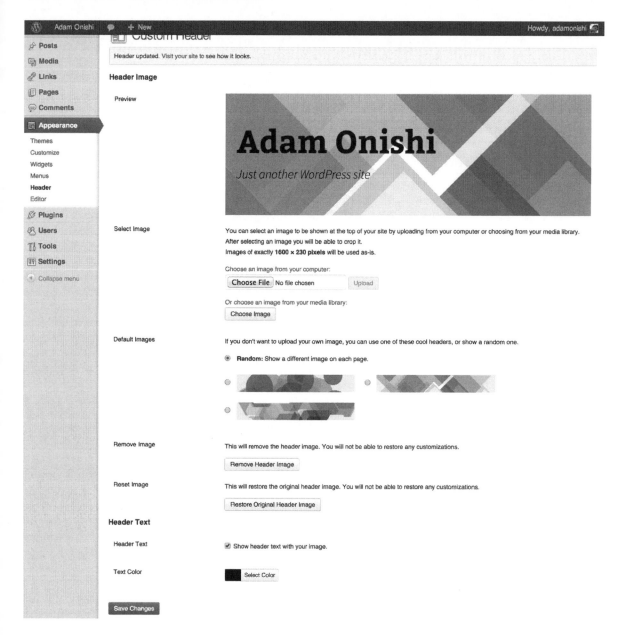

Figure 7-3. *Twenty Thirteen header customization page*

The size settings—`height`, `width`, `flex-height`, and `flex-width`—all relate to the cropping options given to users when they upload their image. With the `height` and `width` settings, they act as maximum sizes the user can crop their image to. If you set either of the flex settings to `true`, the user can change that specific size on the image crop. Whether either flex argument is set to `true`, when users upload an image, they are always met with a crop area the size you specified with the `height` and `width` settings. If you leave them at their defaults, the user can choose whether or not to crop the images.

The rest of the default options are relatively self-explanatory. The uploads and header-text arguments are true if you want to allow uploads and if you want to let the user add text to the header image. The random-default argument allows you to set the random display of headers to true by default.

To display the headers in your theme, WordPress provides a series of functions referencing different parts of the header:

- header_image() echoes out the URL of the header image.

- get_header_image() returns the URL.

- get_header_textcolor() returns the text color value (hex code without the preceding #).

- display_header_text() returns true or false depending on whether the user has selected to display the header text.

- get_custom_header() returns an object of the custom header, including url, thumbnail_url, width, height, and attachment_id.

The best example of these functions in action is again the Twenty Thirteen theme and the function it uses to output the header. There are also a lot of other great examples in the theme file inside inc/custom-header.php. The result of the output function is shown in Figure 7-4.

```
<div id="headimg" style="background: url(<?php header_image(); ?>) no-repeat scroll top; background-size: 1600px auto;">
        <?php $style = ' style="color:#' . get_header_textcolor() . ';"'; ?>
        <div class="home-link">
                <h1 class="displaying-header-text"><a id="name"<?php echo $style; ?> onclick="return false;" href="#"><?php bloginfo( 'name' ); ?></a></h1>
                <h2 id="desc" class="displaying-header-text"<?php echo $style; ?>><?php bloginfo( 'description' ); ?></h2>
        </div>
</div>
```

Figure 7-4. *Twenty Thirteen header*

In this code, the header_image() function is being used to output the header image URL inside a background-image inline style as well as the get_header_textcolor() function outputting the color of the text inline inside the links. The header text is provided by the bloginfo() function, and if the user has selected not to display the header text, the code also generates some inline style for the header of the page to hide the text.

Adding Default Images for Custom Headers

Look at the screenshot of the Twenty Thirteen custom header page in Figure 7-3 and notice that some default headers are already uploaded for the user to choose. WordPress allows you to do this with the `register_default_headers()` function. Again, you can see how the Twenty Thirteen theme is used to add the three default images you see in the screenshot:

```
register_default_headers( array(
        'circle' => array(
                'url'            => '%s/images/headers/circle.png',
                'thumbnail_url' => '%s/images/headers/circle-thumbnail.png',
                'description'    => _x( 'Circle', 'header image description', 'twentythirteen' )
        ),
        'diamond' => array(
                'url'            => '%s/images/headers/diamond.png',
                'thumbnail_url' => '%s/images/headers/diamond-thumbnail.png',
                'description'    => _x( 'Diamond', 'header image description', 'twentythirteen' )
        ),
        'star' => array(
                'url'            => '%s/images/headers/star.png',
                'thumbnail_url' => '%s/images/headers/star-thumbnail.png',
                'description'    => _x( 'Star', 'header image description', 'twentythirteen' )
        ),
) );
```

The `register_default_headers()` function takes an array as the only parameter containing one or more further arrays with the details for each image. The `%s` in the `url` setting will be replaced with the theme directory, and the description is used in the title tag for each image in the custom headers page.

With the allowance for you to create a set of custom headers for your theme, it means that if the `uploads` option is set to `false`, users can choose some carefully designed and selected header images. This again shows how you can offer better choices for your users. Giving them too much freedom could add unneeded complexity, whereas a choice of some carefully selected options allows for the ability to customize without the burden of too many choices. It's a subject you'll struggle with whenever you create options for your users: when are there not enough options and how many is too many? Throughout this chapter, I'll be coming back to this theme so you can learn to make well-thought-out decisions about how much customization you offer to your users.

Saying Goodbye to Theme Options Pages

Now that you've seen some of the simpler theme features offered for your WordPress themes, it's time to take a look at how you can add some serious customization features to your themes. Before I introduce the theme customizer in detail, however, I want to discuss how it came to be and what it has meant to previous systems such as theme options pages.

Before the theme customizer came along in version 3.4, the theme customizing landscape looked a whole lot different; themes developers created theme options pages to include all the customizations possible with their themes. Even default themes came with some theme options, as shown in Figure 7-5.

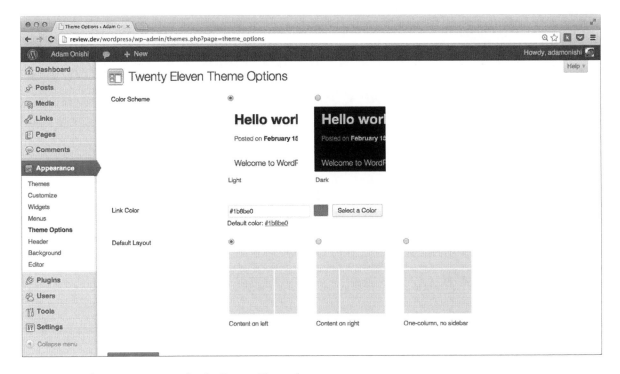

Figure 7-5. *Theme options page for the Twenty Eleven theme*

So when the theme customizer turned up in version 3.4, not all theme developers took much notice; the customizer was a new toy for WordPress, but nothing to take seriously. I can understand a lot of the reasoning for this; it was something brand new, and the default options did make it look like a bit like the next new shiny toy for theme users. However, when you look at the competition from the likes of Squarespace and Koken, to name just two, you see that interactive theme customization systems in those platforms were built in from the very start.

Some developers might feel reluctant to grab on to this new feature based purely on the amount of time they've already invested in creating the best way for to add options to their themes already. Theme option pages range from very simple implementations to extremely complex frameworks (see Figure 7-6), and once you have a system set up, it's hard to find the motivation to change something you're comfortable with.

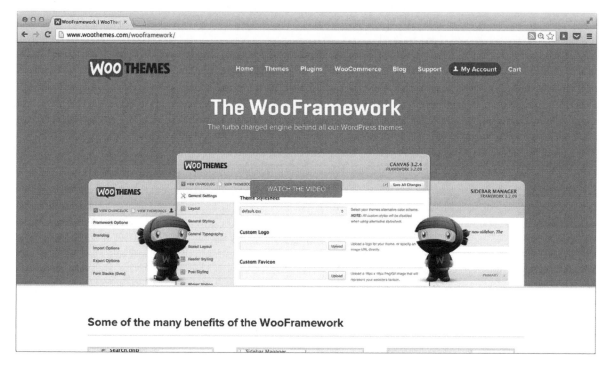

Figure 7-6. *WooThemes' own framework for theme options: the WooFramework*

On a more positive note, some theme development shops have really taken to the theme customizer by understanding the power it can give theme users. It's great to see quotes like the following, which was said back in June 2012 as the theme customizer was released:

> *We're planning on adding Theme Options for all themes to the customizer in future updates.*

> Andy Adams (`http://wp-themes-book.com/07003`)

So the old theme options page should now be a thing of the past, you'll start to see less and less of the old theme options pages and see people moving more toward the theme customizer—and for good reasons, too.

Introducing the Theme Customizer

Besides showing a quick screenshot, I haven't really mentioned much about the theme customizer except that it was introduced in version 3.4. It's now time to have a real look at what the theme customizer is, what it can do, and why it's so important to the future of WordPress theme development.

The theme customizer is essentially a WYSIWYG editor for WordPress themes; packed with certain customization options, users can edit options and see their updates in real time without having to update their site. Themes can now be customized from the WordPress admin without the hassle that came before with theme options. Users no longer need to save the option, refresh the front end, test that it looks okay, and if not rush back to change it before anyone else has seen it.

The customizer now lives in the Appearance menu, right below the Themes submenu. When first released in version 3.4, the customize option was available only from the themes page beneath the theme you had active. Now there's much more emphasis on the customizer; any installed theme can be opened in the customizer without activating it. This enables users to customize a new theme and preview any changes they make before putting the new theme live, which is certainly a significant improvement to the old system.

The customizer is also an important step for WordPress to take, as I mentioned in the last section. Other systems are starting to compete with WordPress on the ease-of-use and customizations front. Although there is still quite a stretch between the WordPress customizer and Squarespace's drag-and-drop layout interface, the move to a more user-friendly system for customizing themes definitely shows that WordPress intends to compete.

Although it will be a long time before WordPress loses its dominance in the blogging and content management system (CMS), it's telling that more offerings are starting to spring up that boast of more user-friendly interfaces. You can't deny that new systems such as Squarespace, and especially Ghost, intend to compete directly with WordPress on the blogging front and are taking aim at the "complexity" they feel WordPress still possesses.

Getting Started with the Theme Customizer

Having looked at the theory behind the customizer, it's time to get down to utilizing the customizer in your own themes. The customizer is built using fully object-oriented PHP (OOPHP), but fortunately you need only a very basic understanding to be able to use all the features of the customizer. When going through the system, I'll be explaining everything in plenty of detail as well, so you should be able to see how the object orientation helps make this system really easy to work with.

The theme customizer API is made up of four classes:

- `WP_Customize_Manager`
- `WP_Customize_Setting`
- `WP_Customize_Section`
- `WP_Customize_Control`

`WP_Customize_Manager` is the main class that looks after the entire customizer; the other three classes add the different parts found within the customizer. The `WP_Customize_Manager` class is accessed through the `$wp_customize` global object variable. To get access to the object, you need to hook into the `customize_register` action before adding your theme customizer options.

The remaining classes used in the customizer control the individual settings, sections, and controls, as their names suggest. The `setting` class controls what the customization is and how it's stored in WordPress, the `section` class defines where the option appears in the customizer, and the `control` class is the method of configuring a setting. All three must be used in conjunction to add a new setting to the customizer, although you can add controls to one of the default sections (but even then, the section has still been defined at one point).

This is just a basic overview of what each class does in relation to the customizer, now you'll see how they work together to enable you to create theme options.

Adding Options to the Customizer

Instead of adding everything to the `functions.php` file as usual, start by creating a new PHP file to keep all the code for the customizer separate. Because this section will produce a lot of code, it's worth keeping it in a file separate from the rest of your functions. I end up doing this a lot with my themes to ensure that everything is easy to find.

Create a new file called something like `theme-options.php` and include it inside your theme functions file (like you did in with the widget functions in Chapter 6). Because you'll run all the code through a hook in the file, you can just include this anywhere outside of a function in the `functions.php` file.

```
require( get_template_directory() . '/inc/theme-options.php' );
```

With your new file created, it's time to start working with the theme customizer. As I mentioned before, to access the WP_Customize_Manager class, you need to use the customize_register action. With this action, the $wp_customize object is passed in by reference for you to work with:

```
function prowordpress_customize_register( $wp_customize ) {
        // Settings, Sections, and Controls are defined here
}
add_action( 'customize_register', 'prowordpress_customize_register' );
```

Once the function is set up, you can begin to add settings, sections, and controls for your theme options.

Adding a Setting

Settings is the term used for each option for your theme. These settings are stored in the database and accessed by you in the theme to provide the customizations. To add a setting, use the add_setting() method of the $wp_customize object. The method comes with two parameters, the ID of the setting to be added and an array of arguments. The arguments are the following:

- default is the default value for the setting.

- type is the way the setting is stored, either as option or theme_mod. The differences and advantages/disadvantages of both will be discussed later in the chapter (the default is theme_mod).

- transport is the method with which the setting will be updated in theme preview, either refresh or postMessage. The differences will be covered later in the chapter (the default is refresh).

- capability is the capability required to use the setting (the default is edit_theme_options–more on this in Chapter 8 with users, roles and permissions).

- theme-supports tests whether the theme supports this setting (used with theme default settings such as custom headers).

- sanitize_callback is the data sanitization function to be used when data is saved.

- sanitize_js_callback is the sanitization function to be used when the data will be used in JavaScript.

The first three arguments are the ones you will be using most often: adding the default value of the setting, how it's stored, and how it's updated on the theme preview. To add a new setting for link colors on your theme, you could use the following:

```
$wp_customize->add_setting( 'link_color' , array(
        'default'               => 'FF00FF',
        'type'                  => 'theme_mod',
        'transport'             => 'refresh',
        'sanitize_callback'     => 'sanitize_hex_color_no_hash',
));
```

Here you are setting the default color, type, and transport methods; and adding a sanitization callback, one that is already included in WordPress (you'll look at how to create other sanitization functions later in the chapter).

Adding a Section

The next part of adding a new option to the theme customizer is to create a section in which your control will appear. A setting on its own actually adds nothing visible to the theme customizer; the setting is just for behind-the-scenes work in WordPress. A section is what appears in the left side of the customizer, as you can see in Figure 7-7. The sections shown are "Site Title & Tagline", and "Colors".

Figure 7-7. Sections in the theme customizer

To add a section, you need the add_section() method of the $wp_customize object. Again this method takes two parameters: the ID of the section and an array of arguments. This time the arguments include the following:

- title : The title of the section
- description: A description to display in the title attribute of the section
- priority: Where in the list of sections it should appear

Next is to add a section for your new setting. You could use something similar to the following (remember to always add text using the WordPress internationalization functions):

```
$wp_customize->add_section( 'prowordpress_content_customizations' , array(
        'title'       => __('Content customizations', 'prowordpress'),
        'description' => __('Customize the link colors in the theme', 'prowordpress'),
        'priority'    => 30,
));
```

With the section defined, you'll notice that it's not yet appearing in the customizer; this is because you still need to define a control to go in the section.

Adding a Control

With the setting and section defined, you're now all set to add your control. The control is the actual part the user is interacting with when it comes to customizing the setting, whether it is a text box or a color picker for instance. Although the control is set using the add_control() method of the $wp_customize object, there are two methods available for setting up a new control. You can either use the standard method of passing in an ID and array of arguments that define how the control will look and work, or you can pass an instance of a class that defines the control instead of passing the ID and arguments. Sounds complicated on the surface, but once you see an example, you should be able to see how it works in practice.

The standard method allows you to create a number of standard HTML form controls; the latter method using classes allows you to create more custom controls like the color picker or image upload controls. Let's look at both methods.

The arguments for the standard control give you quite a few options for the way your control will work:

- label: The label to appear along with the control.

- settings: The setting the control is for (if left blank, the control ID needs to be the same as the setting ID it will be controlling).

- section: The section in which the control will appear.

- type: The type of control—mostly standard HTML form elements with the exception of dropdown-pages, which will be a select list of all available pages on the site. The options are these:

  - text

  - checkbox

  - radio

  - select

  - dropdown-pages

- choices: If using either a radio or select type control, you need to pass in an array of the different selections.

- priority: The order in which the setting will appear in the section.

If you create a simple text entry control to set the custom link color, it might look like this:

```
$wp_customize->add_control( 'link_color_control', array(
        'label'      => __( 'Link Color', 'prowordpress' ),
        'section'    => 'prowordpress_content_customizations',
        'settings'   => 'link_color',
        'type'       => 'text',
));
```

However, as I mentioned, there is a method allowing you to add more-complex controls to the customizer. By default, five custom controls are available for you to use with the customizer. You can also create custom controls, which I'll cover later in the chapter. The default control classes are these:

- WP_Customize_Color_Control(): A color picker control

- WP_Customize_Upload_Control(): A media upload control

- WP_Customize_Image_Control(): An image upload control

- WP_Customize_Background_Image_Control(): A background image control that specifically displays the custom background options

- WP_Customize_Header_Image_Control(): A header image control specifically for the custom header options

To use one of these controls instead of a default HTML form controls, you need to create an instance of the class with the default arguments and pass it to the add_control() method. With PHP this isn't too complex; you can actually create the new instance of the class inside the method call itself. Each of the preceding classes is actually an extension of the initial class WP_Customize_Control, which is the class that is accessed whenever you create a control for the customizer. This means that when you create a new control using one of the classes, most of the standard arguments stay the same. Here's how your link color option control could be defined with the color picker control class:

```
$wp_customize->add_control( new WP_Customize_Color_Control( $wp_customize, 'link_color_control',
array(
        'label'      => __( 'Link Color', 'prowordpress' ),
        'section'    => 'prowordpress_content_customizations',
        'settings'   => 'link_color',
)));
```

With that control definition complete, you can add it to the rest of the theme customizer function to get a block of code that looks like the following code block (the result can be seen in Figure 7-8).

```
function prowordpress_customize_( $wp_customize ) {
        $wp_customize->add_setting( 'link_color' , array(
                'default'           => 'FF00FF',
                'type'              => 'theme_mod',
                'transport'         => 'refresh',
                'sanitize_callback' => 'sanitize_hex_color_no_hash',
        ));

        $wp_customize->add_section( 'prowordpress_content_customizations' , array(
                'title'       => __('Content customizations', 'prowordpress'),
                'description' => __('Customize the link colors in the theme', 'prowordpress'),
                'priority'    => 30,
        ));

        $wp_customize->add_control( new WP_Customize_Color_Control( $wp_customize,
'link_color_control', array(
                'label'      => __( 'Link Color', 'prowordpress' ),
                'section'    => 'prowordpress_content_customizations',
                'settings'   => 'link_color',
        )));
}
add_action( 'customize_register', 'prowordpress_customize_register' );
```

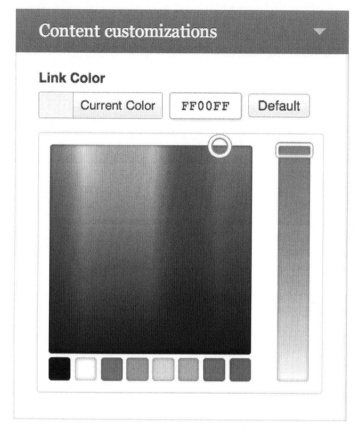

Figure 7-8. *The link color control*

Default Sections

There are a series of default sections in the customizer, so instead of always creating a new section for any control you want to add to the customizer, it's worth taking a look at these default settings to see whether your new control would fit in better in a section that already exists. For instance, the control you just created to customize the link color of the theme wouldn't be out of place in the default Colors section of the customizer.

To add to a default section, you simply use the ID of one of the sections instead of creating a new section entirely. Here's the full list of default section IDs:

- title_tagline: Site Title & Tagline

- colors: Colors

- header_image: Header Image

- background_image: Background Image

- nav: Navigation

- static_front_page: Static Front Page

By reusing the sections already available in the customizer, you can reduce complexity for the user by grouping your options more sensibly instead of creating a new section for every setting you create.

Using Settings in Your Theme

Once you have created your options for the theme customizer, you'll probably want to start using them in your theme. There are a few ways of doing this, depending on the type of result you're aiming for. Options in which a user can define styles (colors, background images, and so on) probably need to be output as inline style in the <head> of your pages, whereas text and content options need to be accessed in the templates directly.

Think back to when you were defining the theme customizer settings. You had the option of creating settings with a type setting of either theme_mod or option; this parameter defines how you will access the setting when you want to retrieve its value.

A theme_mod setting requires you to use the get_theme_mod() function, and a setting with the type option requires the get_option() function. In the next section, I will talk about the differences with the way data is stored, but for now all you need to know is how to access each one.

Both functions work in a similar way: they return the value as PHP, so you need to "echo" each result still or store it in a variable to use at a later stage. And both require the setting ID as the first parameter to know which setting to retrieve. The only difference is with the get_theme_mod() function, which can take an optional default value as the second parameter that will be returned if there is no value found for that setting ID.

As an example, if you access the link_color setting you created earlier, you have one of three options, depending on the type of the setting you created:

```
// type = theme_mod (with no default)
echo get_theme_mod('link_color');

// type = theme_mod (with a default parameter)
echo get_theme_mod('link_color', 'FF00FF');

// type = option
echo get_option('link_color');
```

All these can be accessed in your templates at any point, so if the example option were instead some introductory text meant for one of the pages, you could use either the get_theme_mod() or get_option() functions to output that text straight to the template.

Adding Inline Styles with Theme Options

The other method of adding customizations to your theme is to add them as inline styles to the head of your pages. This means that you can insert the styles after the main style sheet has been included so the inline styles will overwrite those set in the style sheet.

To do this, you'll need to hook into the wp_head action and output a style tag with your customizations inside. As long as your styles have been included with the wp_enqueue_scripts action, using the wp_head action means that they will be output in the correct order because the wp_enqueue_scripts action is fired toward the start of the wp_head action so the main style sheets are included early on in the <head>.

To include the inline styles for your earlier link setting, your function could look a little like the following code. Remember that when you output a color from the settings, it will be saved as a hex value without the #, so you need to add it manually:

```
function prowordpress_customize_css()
{
        ?>
                <style type="text/css">
                        a { color:#<?php echo get_theme_mod('link_color', 'FF00FF'); ?>; }
                </style>
```

```php
        <?php
}
add_action( 'wp_head', 'prowordpress_customize_css');
```

As your theme options grow, you need to add more and more styles to overwrite the default styles in your main style sheet. With this in mind, think about all the options you'll add and make sure to add the ones you think the user will benefit from most; don't be scared of limiting options in order to keep your theme maintainable and well structured. What you don't want is to set hundreds of styling options in the theme customizer and for the inline CSS to be as big as your default CSS because it is doing so many overrides.

How Theme Settings Are Stored

Having seen now how theme options are created and how you can add them to your theme, take a quick step back to look at how your options will be stored in the database. I already touched on this when I mentioned that each setting has a type parameter that defines how it's stored in the database, which then affects how you access it in your theme. Now I'll discuss the differences in the way these two methods store data and what the benefits and downsides are of each.

Theme Mods

Theme mods have been available in the WordPress core for quite some time now, originally being added to the core in version 2.1. Theme mods store data relating to a specific theme, so each theme has its own "mods" data that gets stored in the database.

Theme mods store every option in a single row in the database via a serialized array of key value pairs, so that when the theme is loaded, the theme mods are retrieved from the database ready to be available via the get_theme_mod() function by passing the key (the setting ID from which you initially created the setting). You can see what the data looks like when stored it in a theme_mod by looking at Figure 7-9.

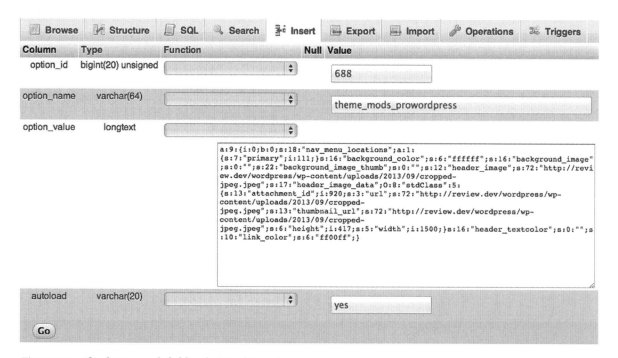

Figure 7-9. The theme_mods field in the WordPress database

Based on the active theme, the get_theme_mod() function will change which field in the database it will retrieve the settings from. With the prowordpress theme active, it will use the theme_mods_prowordpress field (as shown in the figure), but when the Twenty Thirteen theme is active, it will be accessing the theme_mods_twentythirteen field.

There are a few benefits of this method. All settings are stored in relation to a single theme, so there's no possibility that the options you create will leak into another theme. There's no need for complex naming conventions or even prefixes because the data is stored specifically under the theme name, which must be unique in the first place. And because the mods are stored in a single row in the database, using theme mods doesn't bloat the database.

However, some of these benefits might also be seen as downsides. Locking your options to a single theme means that if the user has a more general setting, it will be required to be controlled on a per-theme basis and result in users reconfiguring every time they switch themes. There are also some negatives to storing data as a serialized array in the database in that it negates searching and can have an impact on data portability. In that case, I would say that because of the way in which the serialized data is so heavily tied with WordPress, these issues shouldn't be too great a problem.

Options

The other method of storing your theme customizations is by using the 'option' type. Options are common in WordPress and are the usual method used by any theme authors when they were previously using theme options pages to add theme customizations. To use the options method is to use the Settings API in WordPress, which stores options in the database with some really simple functions. You'll find out more about the full Settings API in Chapter 13 when you look at plugin development toward the end of the book. For now, though, it's enough to know how the data is stored and the pros and cons when relating to the theme customizer.

As you can see in Figure 7-10, when using the option type in your customization setting, the setting gets stored as a single row in the database.

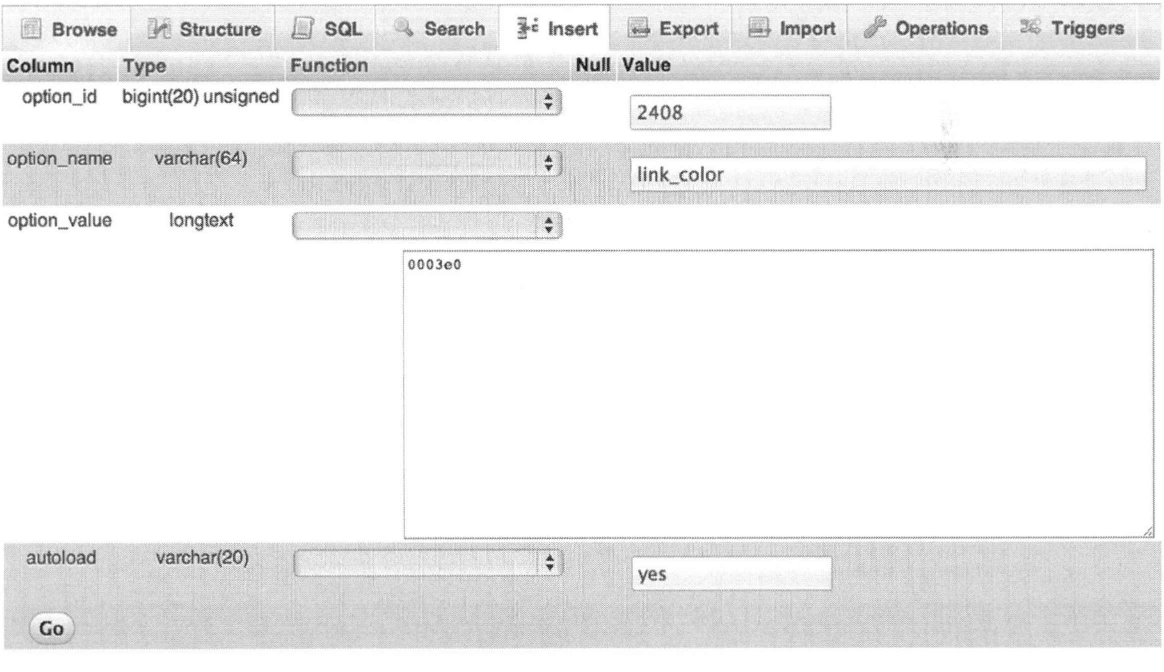

Figure 7-10. The link_color setting field in the database

The main advantage of this method is that the option will be stored in the database and persist across all themes, meaning that no matter which theme you currently have active, you can still access the setting with get_option('link_color'). This is good meaning that settings can now port across all themes and be used throughout the life of the site, no matter which theme is active.

However, I feel that there are far more downsides to this method. Although having theme options persist could be a good thing, it might potentially be useful only if the user is switching between themes by the same developer because it would require all options to be named the same and used in a consistent manner. This is probably a good thing for a theme development shop, but for an individual not so much. Also look at the way the setting is stored in the database; for your color setting, which will always just be stored as six characters, the field type is 'longtext'. The ability to not control the format of how the data is stored can be very costly to database performance and add bloat that could have been easily prevented.

Other disadvantages include requiring a naming convention to prevent data from being overwritten by other settings and plugins, and also that the more options you have, the more rows you'll add to the database, causing potentially unnecessary database bloat.

As you can probably tell, I have a distinct bias toward the best method to use here, but it does come down to a case-by-case basis, as always. If you are developing a series of themes and want to make a framework for adding common customizations to each one of your themes and market yourself with that consistency, the likelihood is that you will need to use the Settings API method for the main advantage it possesses. If you are going down this route, there is one more thing I suggest to make storing options in your theme a little easier on the database and negate a couple of the downsides I've mentioned so far: create an options array.

Creating an Options Array

Instead of setting up your options as a single option to be stored in the database, there's a method that many theme and plugin developers have been using for some time now: to store all related options together in one field in a serialized array. This works much like the theme mods method, but it removes the downside of the options being tied to one specific theme. With this method, the database will no longer be quite so bloated with all your options, and you no longer need to worry about naming conventions for each of your settings because you can set up one option name, and the rest will be fine as part of that option.

To enable this method to work in your settings, ensure that the type is set to 'option' and that your setting name is now something like this:

```
$wp_customize->add_setting( 'prowordpress_theme_options[link_color]' , array(
```

The ID is the option name, but as an index of the top-level option prowordpress_theme_options. You must also remember to set up the 'settings' option in your control to point to the full ID of the setting as well:

```
'settings'    => 'prowordpress_theme_options[link_color]',
```

By doing this, your option will now be stored in the database under the prowordpress_theme_options field name (shown in Figure 7-11) and be accessed across all themes, so you kind of get the benefits of both options.

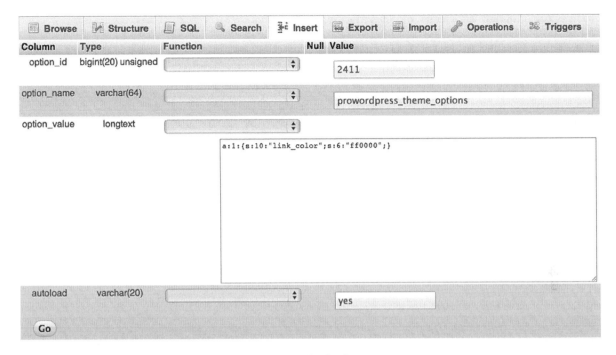

Figure 7-11. *The prowordpress_theme_options setting in the database*

Data Sanitization in Theme Options

In Chapter 10, I'll go into a lot more detail about data sanitization in WordPress in general and why it's extremely important that you are cautious around any data that interacts with your theme. For now, I'll just cover some techniques for data sanitization when using the theme customizer.

Earlier in the chapter when you set up your custom setting for the customizer, I talked about the two optional parameters of the add_setting() function: the sanitize_callback and sanitize_js_callback parameters. These parameters allow you to set functions to be run when the setting is saved so that you can perform some data sanitization on the data input by the user. In the earlier example, you passed the sanitize_hex_color_no_hash function, a WordPress built-in sanitization function, to the sanitize_callback parameter for your color setting.

The sanitize_hex_color_no_hash() function in the WordPress core is not very big and calls the sanitize_hex_color() function to perform the sanitization. You can see both functions here:

```
function sanitize_hex_color_no_hash( $color ) {
        $color = ltrim( $color, '#' );

        if ( '' === $color )
                return '';

        return sanitize_hex_color( '#' . $color ) ? $color : null;
}

function sanitize_hex_color( $color ) {
        if ( '' === $color )
                return '';
```

```
        // 3 or 6 hex digits, or the empty string.
        if ( preg_match('|^#([A-Fa-f0-9]{3}){1,2}$|', $color ) )
                return $color;

        return null;
}
```

The main function that performs the sanitization (`sanitize_hex_color`) just checks that the data passed to the function begins with a #. It is either three or six characters long and made up only of hexadecimal characters. If that's the case, it returns the data; otherwise, it returns `null`. This is just a really simple way of testing the data to ensure that it appears as you expect it to. There are also quite a few other WordPress functions for data sanitization that you can find by visiting the Codex at: `http://wp-themes-book.com/07004`.

Creating Your Own Sanitization Functions

In the theme customizer, besides adding a sanitization callback for color options, you might also need to add validation for other data types. For example, if you have a free text input box, you need to make sure that users don't input any malicious data, whether by design or by accident. If a user adds some HTML tags into a text input box, for example, you may want to allow it, but run a few checks to make sure it's safe (i.e., not containing any script tags) or just to ensure that all the HTML tags are closed correctly to stop the added HTML from breaking your theme when it's output.

WordPress provides two functions that you can utilize for these purposes: the `wp_kses_post()` function (known as KSES Strips Evil Scripts—a nice iterative acronym) and the `force_balance_tags()` function. With this combination, you can ensure that the HTML entered is safe and has removed any potentially malicious scripts, and that all the tags are balanced so that the HTML can't break your theme accidentally:

```
function prowordpress_sanitize_html( $input ) {
        return wp_kses_post( force_balance_tags( $input ) );
}
```

The `wp_kses_post()` function will format out disallowed HTML tags. The `wp_kses()` function requires an array of allowed tags to do this, but the `wp_kses_post()` function uses a default list of allowed tags based on the tags allowed in a post. The `force_balance_tags()` function is fairly self-explanatory; it just ensures that all tags included in the text are closed off correctly, which will help prevent some bad HTML from breaking your theme.

Another way to sanitize data is to make sure that if you expect a value from a certain range of known values (for example, from a check box or series of radio buttons), you ensure that the input value matches one of the values in your expected range of values. Data sanitization is about ensuring that if there's a known format the data should be in before being submitted, it's checked against it, and all other possibilities are removed.

Automatically Update the Theme Customizer

Another parameter that I didn't cover fully earlier in the chapter is the `'transport'` parameter. This parameter can have one of two settings: `refresh` or `postMessage`. The default is `refresh`, which means that when the option has been changed, the customizer needs to be refreshed before the change is shown in the customizer. The second option is `postMessage`, and this is where the customizer gets interesting. The `postMessage` option allows for the data to be sent via the HTML5 `postMessage` API, meaning that values can be updated in real time.

Having real-time updating of customizations is great for users to be able to see how each customization will look before they publish their changes. Also seeing things happen in real time makes your tweaks a lot easier to visualize, so overall this is a great addition to the user experience of the theme customizer.

■ **Note** To find out more about how `postMessage` works, you can visit the MDN article at:
http://wp-themes-book.com/07005.

To use the postMessage setting in your options, you need to set the 'transport' parameter of your setting to be postMessage and then create some JavaScript to handle the data sent by postMessage:

```
$wp_customize->add_setting( 'link_color' , array(
        'default'            => 'FF00FF',
        'transport'          => 'postMessage',
        'sanitize_callback' => 'sanitize_hex_color_no_hash',
));
```

The script will work alongside the theme customizer script in the WordPress core that gives you access to the wp object. With it, you can then access the customize object as well, which contains a few functions to allow you to access the controls in the customizer:

```
(function ($) {

        // Update  link color in real time
        wp.customize( 'link_color', function( value ) {
                value.bind( function( to ) {
                        $('a').css('color', to );
                } );
        } );

} )( jQuery );
```

The previous short function gets access to your setting via the setting ID 'link_color', and the callback function then adds a bind function to the value of your setting. By using a simple bit of jQuery, you can update the element with the new value of the setting every time it gets updated.

With the JavaScript file written, you just need to include it into the page when you're viewing the customizer. Fortunately, as with most things, WordPress has a hook to do just that:

```
function prowordpress_customizer_script()
{
        wp_enqueue_script( 'prowordpress-customizer-script',
                get_template_directory_uri().'/javascript/theme-options.js',
                array( 'jquery','customize-preview' ),
                '',
                true
        );
}
add_action( 'customize_preview_init', 'prowordpress_customizer_script' );
```

This function includes the script in the footer of the customizer page and ensures that the dependencies (jQuery and the customizer preview script) are loaded ahead of your custom script. With your JavaScript file in place and the script included in the page correctly, you can now test the script to ensure that it is working (see Figure 7-12).

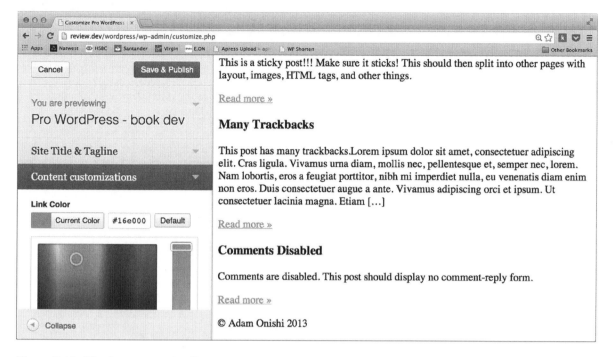

Figure 7-12. *The theme customizer live preview in action*

Adding Live Preview to Default Options

By default, all the standard WordPress options in the customizer use the transport 'refresh' option instead of postMessage, so to set this up you'll need to change the transport parameter and also add more to your script file to update the default options as well as your own custom options.

To change the transport setting in the default options, you need get the options with the customizer and then update them. Thanks to the way the theme customizer is built in WordPress, it is a lot easier with its object-oriented (OO) nature. To get the default settings, you use the get_setting() method of the customizer object and then change the property of the transport setting. This is all possible to do in one line of code because of the OO nature of the customizer. You also need to make sure that you perform this action from within the customize_register function you created earlier in the chapter.

```
$wp_customize->get_setting( 'blogname' )->transport = 'postMessage';
```

This is the equivalent of saving the blogname setting into its own object variable with the get_setting() method and then changing the property using the new object. But because of the way PHP works with objects, you can just chain the command (as shown previously). To update all the default options, run the same line of code with the other setting IDs:

```
$wp_customize->get_setting( 'blogname' )->transport = 'postMessage';
$wp_customize->get_setting( 'blogdescription' )->transport = 'postMessage';
$wp_customize->get_setting( 'header_textcolor' )->transport = 'postMessage';
$wp_customize->get_setting( 'background_color' )->transport = 'postMessage';
```

Once all the default options have had the `transport` function set to `postMessage`, you can add the JavaScript to handle their value changes to your theme customizer JavaScript file:

```
(function ($) {

        // Update site title in real time
        wp.customize( 'blogname', function( value ) {
                value.bind( function( to ) {
                        $( '#site-title a' ).html( to );
                } );
        } );

                // Update the site description in real time
        wp.customize( 'blogdescription', function( value ) {
                value.bind( function( to ) {
                        $( '.site-description' ).html( to );
                } );
        } );

        // Update site title color in real time
        wp.customize( 'header_textcolor', function( value ) {
                value.bind( function( to ) {
                        $('#site-title a').css('color', to );
                } );
        } );

        // Update site background color in real time
        wp.customize( 'background_color', function( value ) {
                value.bind( function( to ) {
                        $('body').css('background-color', to );
                } );
        } );

        // Update link color in real time
        wp.customize( 'link_color', function( value ) {
                value.bind( function( to ) {
                        $('a').css('color', to );
                } );
        } );

} )( jQuery );
```

With that JavaScript added, all the default options can now be updated, and the changes happen in real time as well as your custom options (see Figure 7-13).

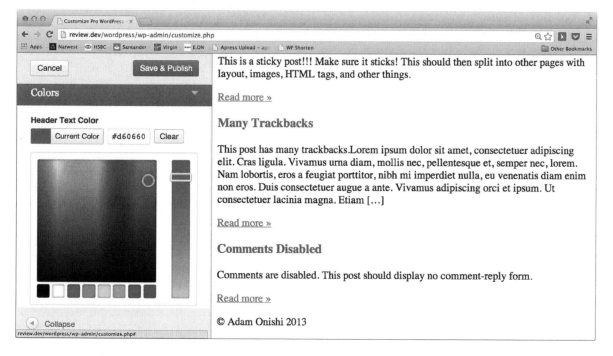

Figure 7-13. *Default theme options being updated in real time*

Adding Custom Controls

At the moment, WordPress has only a limited number of controls you can use for settings in the customizer. This situation is likely to change over time as WordPress updates, but what if you now want to add your own more bespoke controls to the customizer? Fortunately, because of the way the customizer has been built, this becomes quite a straightforward task, but it requires some knowledge of OOPHP. I will guide you through some examples that you should be able to follow even as a beginner with OOPHP.

It's worth looking at one of the controls that already exists in WordPress. The code is a little too large to include here, but if you go to your WordPre   ss install and look up the file class-wp-customize-control.php, you'll see all the code that goes into a customizer control. All the different controls are included in that file and all are created as classes (as you saw earlier in the chapter when you implemented the color picker control). If you take a look at line 318 of the class-wp-customize-control.php file, you'll see the WP_Customize_Color_Control class defined:

```
/**
 * Customize Color Control Class
 *
 * @package WordPress
 * @subpackage Customize
 * @since 3.4.0
 */
class WP_Customize_Color_Control extends WP_Customize_Control {
...
}
```

Here you can see that the `WP_Customize_Color_Control` is an extension of the main `WP_Customize_Control` class. This is where you start to see clues about how to create your own custom control. Every control that exists in WordPress for the customizer is an extension of the `WP_Customize_Control`; this holds a few properties and some methods:

- `enqueue()`: Used to enqueue control-related scripts/styles
- `value()`: Gets a setting's value
- `to_json()`: Refreshes the parameters passed to the JavaScript via JSON
- `check_capabilities()`: Checks if the theme supports the control and checks user capabilities—test if a user is allowed access to the control
- `maybe_render()`: Checks capabilities and renders the control
- `render()`: Renders the control wrapper and then calls the `render_content()` function
- `get_link()`: Gets the data link parameter for a setting
- `link()`: Renders the data link parameter
- `render_content()`: Renders the control's content

If you again look through the `class-wp-customize-control.php` file, you will see some control classes overriding these methods with their own and some not declaring them at all. In that case, as with all OOPHP classes, the extended class will inherit the functionality from the parent class' method.

When creating your own control class, you just need to do the same as the WordPress built-in controls have done. To start creating your own control, go back to the customizer file you created to add the settings before and create a new control class. This class will add a textarea control so the user can add a paragraph of text about the web site.

The first step is to create the class, which is done in the same way as the default controls have done in WordPress:

```
class PTD_Textarea_Control extends WP_Customize_Control {
    // Do stuff here
}
```

To make the function more resistant to errors in case someone attempts to use your theme on a WordPress install prior to version 3.4, you can add the class inside a conditional that checks for the existence of the default class:

```
if( class_exists('WP_Customize_Control') ) {

    class PTD_Textarea_Control extends WP_Customize_Control {
        // Do stuff here
    }
}
```

With your class set up, you can create the methods needed to override the ones from the parent class to output your new textarea control. The only real method you need to add for this control is the `render_content()` method to display the textarea itself. Make sure you are aware of how the customizer outputs the HTML for other controls, so you can be consistent when you do so for your custom controls. Take a quick look at the Site Title & Tagline section of the controls; if you view the HTML, you see this:

```
<label>
    <span class="customize-control-title">Site Title</span>
    <input type="text" value="Adam Onishi" data-customize-setting-link="blogname">
</label>
```

For consistency, it's best to stick to this format with the <label>, <span>, and <input> in the same structure.

Back to the controls render_content() function. To add a control with the textarea, you can create a function with the following code:

```php
public function render_content() {
        ?>
                <label>
                        <span class="customize-control-title"><?php echo esc_html( $this->label );
?></span>
                        <textarea class="large-text" cols="20" rows="5" <?php $this->link(); ?>>
                                <?php echo esc_textarea( $this->value() ); ?>
                        </textarea>
                </label>
        <?php
}
```

The function outputs the HTML, following the same structure as the default options. You also need to use some of the parent class methods to output the details for the input, such as the value, link (required for the input to be saved), and label, which is set by the user when they add the control.

Now the control is set up, so you can use the class to create a new control in the theme customizer in the standard way you've seen so far. Just add in the new control class where you previously had one of the defaults:

```php
$wp_customize->add_setting( 'site_intro' , array(
        'default'        => '',
        'transport'    => 'postMessage',
));

$wp_customize->add_section( 'prowordpress_site_info' , array(
        'title'          => __('Site information', 'prowordpress'),
        'description' => __('Custom site information for all pages', 'prowordpress'),
        'priority'      => 20,
));

$wp_customize->add_control( new PTD_Textarea_Control( $wp_customize, 'site_intro_control', array(
        'label'          => __( 'Website introduction', 'prowordpress' ),
        'section'        => 'prowordpress_site_info',
        'settings'       => 'site_intro',
)));
```

With this included in your theme, the textarea now appears in the theme customizer, as you can see in Figure 7-14.

Figure 7-14. *The textarea control in the customizer*

The simple textarea example I used is also part of a series of custom controls created by Paul Und. You can find some great examples of custom controls on his Github account (`http://wp-themes-book.com/07006`), including a lot of useful ways of selecting different post types and categories from the site through the customizer. Currently, the controls include the following:

- `Category Dropdown`: Creates a drop-down list of all categories on your WordPress theme
- `Date Picker`: Adds a date picker control to the theme customizer
- `Layout Picker`: Adds three images of layouts to the page for you to select a new style
- `Menu Dropdown`: Creates a drop-down list of all menus on your WordPress site
- `Post Dropdown`: Creates a drop-down list of all posts on your WordPress site
- `Tags Dropdown`: Creates a drop-down list of all tags on your WordPress site
- `Text Editor`: Creates a text box with the `TinyMCE` textarea
- `Textarea`: Creates a textarea input field
- `Taxonomy Dropdown`: Creates a drop-down list of taxonomies
- `User List Dropdown`: Creates a drop-down list of users for a role

Adding a Color Palette Selector

This is a feature I mentioned earlier in the chapter with regards to improving user experience when creating options for your themes. Instead of giving your users a whole list of different colors to customize in the theme (see Figure 7-15), why not curate a series of color schemes that work well for your theme and give the users a choice between only a few options? Doing so enables the user to make the theme a bit more unique and feel less overwhelmed by the number of choices. It is also a good way of keeping some design control over your theme.

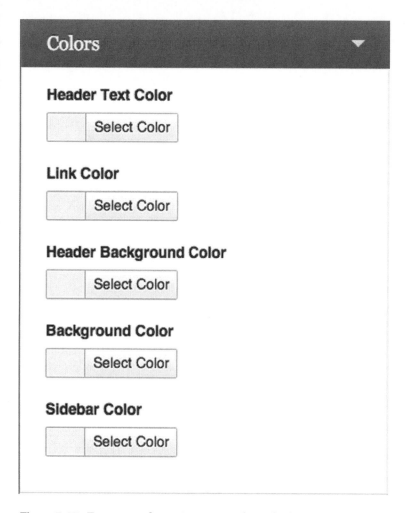

Figure 7-15. *Too many color options can result in a bad user experience in your theme*

This control could easily be created using a standard radio button selection, but it would have to show the color options for the user as well. When using the option in your theme, instead of outputting the setting via some inline CSS (as you've seen), it would be better to include a separate full style sheet containing the color scheme styles. I'll cover both of these methods here, starting with the control.

Building the Control

The control is a series of radio buttons with images that represent each different color palette. To use it, you can extend the basic control class and add something along the lines of the following code. Most of this is hard-coded to the control, but you could, in theory, set it up to enable users to add a custom location for the color palette files and pass in custom names for each of the color palettes. For now, however, this suits our purpose:

```
class PTD_Color_Scheme_Control extends WP_Customize_Control {

        public $type = 'color_palette';
```

```php
    public function render_content() {

            $name = '_customize-radio-' . $this->id;
            $values = array(
                            'palette-1' => 'Palette 1',
                            'palette-2' => 'Palette 2',
                            'palette-3' => 'Palette 3',
                    );

            ?>
            <span class="customize-control-title">Color palettes</span>
            <?php

            foreach( $values as $value => $label ):
            ?>
            <label class="color-palette-option">
                    <input type="radio" value="<?php echo esc_attr( $value ); ?>"
name="<?php echo esc_attr( $name ); ?>" <?php $this->link(); checked( $this->value(), $value ); ?> />
                    <img src="<?php echo get_template_directory_uri() .
'/images/color-palettes/' . $value . '.png'; ?>" alt="<?php echo $label; ?>">
            </label>
            <?php
            endforeach;
    }
}
```

This function creates a list of radio buttons in labels with images for each of the different color palettes available. As I mentioned, it is currently hard-coded, but if you're defining this in your theme, it should be no problem for you to edit the whereabouts of the images.

To go along with the new control, I also added another custom function to add a little styling to the radio buttons. When working with the WordPress admin, you usually add styles either inline or via enqueueing the styles with the wp_enqueue_style() function using the admin_head action hook. However, with the customizer open, this hook no longer fires, so you need to use the customize_controls_print_styles hook instead:

```php
function prowordpress_customizer_styles () {
        ?>
        <style>
                .customize-control-color_palette .color-palette-option { float:left; width:100%;
margin-bottom:10px; }
                .customize-control-color_palette .color-palette-option input { float:left;
margin:13px 10px 0 0; }
        </style>
        <?php
}

add_action( 'customize_controls_print_styles', 'prowordpress_customizer_styles', 30 );
```

This adds a couple of lines of style to the customizer to make the color palette look a bit more considered; you can see the results in Figure 7-16.

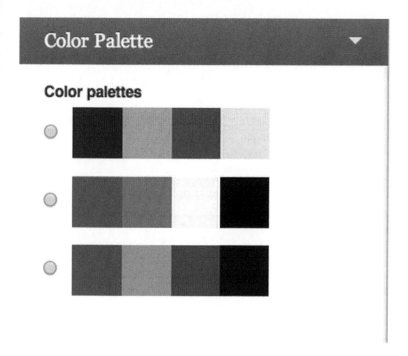

Figure 7-16. *The color palette customizer control*

Once the control is working, you can set up your theme to include the correct style sheet, depending on the color palette chosen.

Adding Color Palette Styles to Your Theme

There are two issues to consider when adding the new color palettes to your theme: the need to add the correct style sheet for the color palette to the theme and to display the color palette changes in the theme customizer. The first problem shouldn't be too hard; you can run a query in the function that includes your styles for the front end with the option set by the user using get_theme_mod(). However, the second is a little trickier.

To take care of the first method quickly, get the current setting from the database with the get_theme_mod() function and use it in the wp_enqueue_style() function (unless, of course, you used the type 'option', in which case you'll need the get_option() function):

```
$palette = get_theme_mod('color_palette', 'palette-1');
wp_enqueue_style( 'palette', get_template_directory_uri() . '/css/' . $palette . '.css' ,
array('style') );
```

That was quite straightforward; the color palette style sheet will be included in your theme after the main style sheet as the array of dependencies (the third parameter) contained the ID of the main style sheet.

Next is the tricky part: including your color palette as part of the theme customizer page. Instead of creating a style sheet for each color palette, you'll need a single style sheet for all of them or you'll need to create a second style sheet for each color palette to use specifically for the customizer. The reason is that to be able to update the preview, you need to be able to initiate the styles through JavaScript. Although you could add or update a single style sheet link in the preview, the quicker way to do this is through changing a class on the body of the preview that relates to each color palette.

To include the preview styles, you can add a line to the `prowordpress_customizer_script()` function you created earlier to add the live-updating functionality. I added a separate style sheet to preview all palettes in this example:

```
function prowordpress_customizer_script()
{
        wp_enqueue_script( 'prowordpress-customizer-script',
                get_template_directory_uri().'/javascript/theme-options.js',
                array( 'jquery','customize-preview' ),
                '1',
                true
        );

        wp_enqueue_style( 'palette', get_template_directory_uri() . '/css/palette-previews.css' );
}
add_action( 'customize_preview_init', 'prowordpress_customizer_script' );
```

For now, the style sheet being added is just an example that will change the background color based on the color palette selected:

```
.preview-palette-1 { background-color:rgb(10,44,85); }

.preview-palette-2 { background-color:rgb(207,31,40); }

.preview-palette-3 { background-color:rgb(13,121,58); }
```

With these in place, you can now add another function to the JavaScript file to update the body class of the page based on which color palette has been selected:

```
wp.customize( 'color_palette', function( value ) {
        value.bind( function( to ) {
                for(var i=1; i<4; i++ ) {
                        $('body').removeClass('preview-palette-' + i);
                }

                $('body').addClass('preview-' + to);
        } );
} );
```

The background color now changes every time you select a new color palette for the theme (see Figure 7-17). And when you save and go to the live site, the single color palette style sheet you created for each palette will be included based on the user selection.

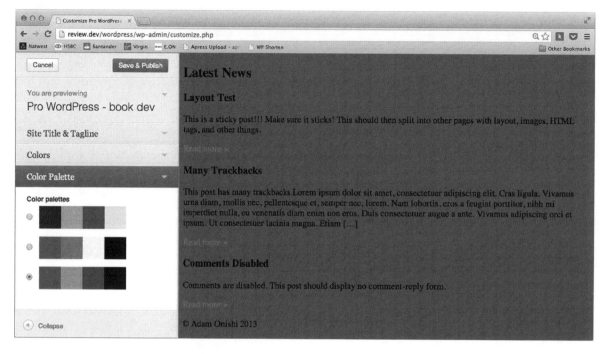

Figure 7-17. *The color palette live update in action*

Building Your Theme, Part 6

In the final part of the chapter, you'll extend your custom theme further with some theme options through the theme customizer based on what you've learned so far in the chapter. With the theme being aimed at restaurants to use and customize for their own locations, it's worth adding a few customization options for users to help make your theme more easily represent their restaurant.

In this section you'll look at creating four custom options for the customizer:

- Logo
- Contact details
- Featured product selector
- Color palette

I'll walk you through the the options, but you should be able to implement a couple of them based on what you learned so far in the chapter. Of the four options you'll create, two will use controls provided for you by WordPress as standard, and the other two will make use of custom controls that you can create yourself.

You should add the postMessage transport method in your custom theme to all the default options provided by WordPress. You've seen how to do that, so it shouldn't be too difficult.

Start by creating a new PHP file and include it in the functions file inside the main prowordpress_setup() function (similar to creating widgets for your theme). Remember to start your theme options file with the customize_register function and set up the postMessage transport value on the default WordPress options.

Adding a Logo Option

The first option is to enable the user to upload a custom logo, which needs to be positioned on the page in your theme and updated through the theme customizer preview screen. You can use the standard WordPress control class `WP_Customize_Image_Control`. It takes the same arguments as all the standard WordPress controls, so to set up a new image control in a new section of the customizer for your theme, your code could look something like this.

```php
$wp_customize->add_setting( 'site_logo' , array(
        'default'                => '',
        'transport'              => 'postMessage',
));

$wp_customize->add_section( 'prowordpress_logo_section' , array(
        'title'        => __('Custom logo', 'prowordpress'),
        'description'  => __('Add a custom logo for the site', 'prowordpress'),
        'priority'     => 30,
));

$wp_customize->add_control( new WP_Customize_Image_Control( $wp_customize, 'site_logo', array(
        'label'        => __( 'Site logo', 'prowordpress' ),
        'section'      => 'prowordpress_logo_section',
)));
```

With this code added to your `customize_register` function, you are ready to set up your template to add the logo to your theme as well as the JavaScript to add the logo to the theme preview page. Adding the image to the theme requires using the `get_theme_mod()` function to output the image to the template. With the image upload control, the data stored is the full URL of the image, so to output the image, echo the value returned from the `get_theme_mod()` function into the SRC attribute of an `<img>` tag.

```html
<h1>
        <a href="<?php home_url( '/' ); ?>">
                <img src="<?php echo get_theme_mod('site_logo'); ?>" alt="<?php
bloginfo( 'blogname' ); ?>" class="site-logo">
        </a>
</h1>
```

Next, add the JavaScript to update the header automatically in the theme customizer preview. This process is helped by adding a class, in this case `'site-logo'`, to the `<img>` tag. In the JavaScript file, you can now add a small amount of jQuery to update the SRC attribute of the image whenever the value is updated (similar to the way you updated CSS with other options in the chapter so far):

```javascript
wp.customize( 'site_logo', function( value ) {
        value.bind( function( to ) {
                $('img.site-logo').attr('src', to);
        } );
} );
```

With the first option complete, you can now add a text area option, similar to the one you created earlier in the chapter, to allow the user to add contact details to the site footer. I won't add the code to show you what to do because you should be able to write it yourself; it just requires you to re-create the text area custom control, as you did earlier in the chapter.

Adding a Featured Post Option

Two options down; just two more left to go before the end of the chapter. In Chapter 5, you created a custom field for the products to select whether a product should be displayed as a featured image on the home page. Although this is a great way to add the functionality to your theme, it would be good if users could see the featured product updated on the home page before they publish the change. This is something you can easily achieve with the theme customizer.

To add a featured product option to the customizer, you have to create another custom control based on the idea behind one of the controls in Paul Und's customizer controls on Github (http://wp-themes-book.com/07006). This control adds a drop-down list of the available products for the user to select from.

To begin, you need to create a new class, as you did before when creating a custom control. However, instead of just adding a single method, the render_content() method, you also need to add a new property to the class. This property will store the post type you want to list in the control:

```php
class Posts_Dropdown_Custom_Control extends WP_Customize_Control {

    /**
     * @access public
     * @var string
     */
    public $post_type = 'post';

    /**
     * Render the control's content
     */
    public function render_content() {
    }
}
```

The new property defined here adds a default value of 'post' so that if the post_type parameter isn't passed to the control, the control will just display the default 'post' post type. With the beginning of the new class setup, you can now create the rest of the render_content() function, which will set up a select input and add all the available posts to the options and also check whether one has been selected:

```php
public function render_content() {
?>
        <label>
                <span class="customize-post-dropdown"><?php echo esc_html( $this->label ); ?></span>
                <select id="<?php echo $this->id; ?>" <?php $this->link(); ?>>
                        <option value="">Please select</option>
                        <?php
                        $args = wp_parse_args( array(
                                    'post_type'    => $this->post_type,
                                    'numberposts' => '-1',
                                )
                        );
                        $posts = get_posts($args);

                        foreach ( $posts as $post ) {
                                echo '<option value="'.$post->ID.'" '.selected($this->value(),
$post->ID).'>'.$post->post_title.'</option>';
                        }
                        ?>
```

```
                        </select>
            </label>
<?php
}
```

That's all there is to the custom control: it will generate a drop-down option to allow the user to choose from any of the selected posts for the post_type you set the control up to display. Next is to add the control to the theme customizer:

```
$wp_customize->add_setting( 'featured_item' , array(
        'default'               => '',
        'transport'             => 'refresh',
));

$wp_customize->add_section( 'prowordpress_featured_item' , array(
        'title'         => __('Featured item', 'prowordpress'),
        'description'   => __('Add a featured item to the homepage', 'prowordpress'),
        'priority'      => 40,
));

$wp_customize->add_control( new Posts_Dropdown_Custom_Control( $wp_customize, 'featured_item',
array(
        'label'         => __( 'Featured item', 'prowordpress' ),
        'section'       => 'prowordpress_featured_item',
        'post_type'     => 'ptd_menu',
)));
```

Again, not much different from what you would expect because you've done this a few times now. One thing to point out, however, is that the transport parameter is set to 'refresh' for the setting. The reason is that instead of simply adding some content or changing a style whenever the control is updated, you will be changing the parameters of a query for the front page of the site. In JavaScript, this would involve doing some complicated Ajax request to some PHP to just return the data for the new content to appear. Instead of doing that, it's much easier to leave the page to refresh whenever the setting is updated so the new content can be generated with PHP instead.

Finally, you should add this option to your front-page template. You added the featured items to the page before, so you should remember this code that was used:

```
$args = array(
                'post_type'         => 'ptd_menu',
                'orderby'           => 'rand',
                'posts_per_page'    => 1,
                'meta_query'        => array(
                        array(
                                'key'       => 'ptd_menu_item_featured',
                                'value'     => 'on',
                                'compare'   => '='
                        )
                )
        );

$featured = new WP_Query( $args );
```

Create a meta_query to look for items with "featured" selected. This time, however, you can simplify the query slightly by querying only for a certain post ID because you can get it from the new theme customizer option:

```
$item_id = get_theme_mod( 'featured_item' );
$args = array(
                'post_type'       => 'ptd_menu',
                'posts_per_page'  => 1,
                'p'               => $item_id,
        );
```

Now the query to get the featured item has been hugely reduced and should save a bit of time executing because there's no longer a need to look up any metadata for the posts; the query can instead just pull out the post type directly from the ID.

Adding a Color Palette Option

This is another option I will let you create yourself. The final code is in the accompanying code examples, but based on what you've learned so far in the chapter, you should be able to create the color palette control yourself and add it to the theme.

With these four options complete, you should now have a fairly good set of theme customizations to launch your theme with. There are probably more options you could add to benefit the user, but these few give you a good starting point.

Summary

This chapter discussed why theme customization options are an important feature for your themes and how to go about adding them using the new theme customizer. Theme options are a great way to make your theme more appealing to users, enabling them to make your theme uniquely theirs.

I talked briefly about how theme options were handled prior to version 3.4 and the emergence of the theme customizer; it's likely you'll still see some theme options still appearing on some themes because people are still making the adjustment in their own practices. However, I say that it's important to embrace the new features of WordPress because they are there for a good reason, and it's safe to say that you should definitely make use of the theme customizer.

You also learned a lot about how to handle the theme customizer and how to add standard and custom controls to make your theme customizations more dynamic. Knowing the power of what can be done with both standard and custom controls will be a great benefit to your themes and give a lot more power to your users.

Finally you have once again added to the restaurant theme you've been building throughout the book, adding extra power with the theme customizer.

In the next chapter, you'll take a look in depth at how the user system works in WordPress, discovering the power of the Roles and Capabilities system and learning how to add some custom user features to your themes.

CHAPTER 8

■ ■ ■

Users, Roles, and Capabilities

So far, this book has covered a lot of ways to work with and customize the content of a WordPress site through theme development. This chapter will focus on who manages the content in the form of users. Users, in this sense, are people who can log in to your site through WordPress, as opposed to people who visit the front end of the site.

In this chapter, you'll look at the core system behind users in WordPress—how they get their privileges and how you can manipulate them. You'll also see how to create some user-oriented features for your WordPress sites, such as custom login and registration pages, as well as creating user-only sections of your web site.

User System

A WordPress site can use its users for any number of reasons, not always just for managing the site content. Thanks to the comprehensive WordPress user system, doing this is made very easy. Whether you have a site that has a lot of article authors, requires editors to manage the main site, or even has a set of users who can just maintain a profile and post comments, the WordPress user system makes doing so a breeze.

The user system in WordPress consists of two main concepts: Roles and Capabilities.

Roles

In WordPress, roles refer to a grouping of users; each user is assigned a role and that role is assigned a series of capabilities. In total, there are six default roles in WordPress, five of which you're probably familiar with, and the sixth you know only if you have used a multisite install. Following is a summary of the default roles and examples of their initial usage; later in the chapter, you'll find out more about how to modify/extend their default capabilities.

- **Subscribers**: Have access only to their own profile and can leave comments under their username.

- **Contributors**: Have access to write their own posts, but can't publish them.

- **Authors**: Have access to write and publish their own posts.

- **Editors**: Have access to manage all posts and pages on the site.

- **Administrators**: Have access to all administration features on a single site install; limited to the individual site administration features on a multisite install.

- **Super Admins**: Have access to all administration features across the network of sites in a multisite install.

When a site is created, during installation you always set up the initial administrator user, but from then on, the default new user type can be set in Settings ➤ General.

Another concept about user roles that some people find hard to grasp is that WordPress user roles are not hierarchical. Although it may seem to be because of the way default roles are set up, it is not the case. Editors are not superior to authors; they simply have more capabilities. I think Justin Tadlock puts it really well in his article on Roles and Capabilities:

> *[R]emember this — roles are defined by what capabilities they are granted. There is no hierarchy.*

—Justin Tadlock

Admins vs. Super Admins

There are two administrator roles within WordPress: Administrator and Super Admin. The Super Admin appears only on multisite installs of WordPress, whereas usually there is only the Administrator role on a single site that has all the capabilities available.

However, working with multisite not only introduces the Super Admin role but also reduces the capabilities of the single site Administrator role (by default). In multisite, the Super Admin is the only one with all the capabilities for the entire network—including some capabilities introduced specifically for multisite. The ability to install themes and plugins, update the WordPress core, and add users are all now given only to Super Admins and removed from the multisite Administrator role.

Capabilities

Now let's look at the actual power behind the WordPress user system: capabilities. You can think of capabilities as permissions that users are given to do certain things in WordPress. For example, edit_posts is a capability that allows users to edit their own posts.

Capabilities are assigned to each role, and roles are assigned to users, which gives them their level of abilities in the system. The edit_posts capability is the one allowing you to edit your own posts, which is what is assigned to a contributor role. However, the contributor role does not have the publish_posts capability, meaning that another user with that capability must publish the posts written by a contributor.

In total, there are more than 60 different capabilities (and a few more with a multisite install). To see the full list and a table of how they relate to the default roles, see the Codex page: http://wp-themes-book.com/08001.

As a theme (or plugin) developer, you can modify these roles and grant different capabilities to different roles, but I suggest that you maintain the capabilities of each of the default roles as much as possible and build in other roles as and when they are needed.

One Special Capability

There is one very special capability in WordPress that needs to be enabled specifically: unfiltered_upload. This capability allows users to upload files of any type (normally uploads are filtered through a list of accepted file types before they are allowed).

To enable this capability, you need to define a constant in the wp-config.php file. Add the following line of code anywhere above the line where /* That's all, stop editing! Happy blogging. */ appears:

```
define( 'ALLOW_UNFILTERED_UPLOADS', true );
```

In a single site install, this code enables the capability for all user roles, but in multisite it is available only to Super Admins. This is clearly not a capability that should be enabled lightly; the filter on uploads is in place for security reasons, but if you are creating a site that requires the upload of certain files not accepted by the filter, this is how to activate that ability.

Customizing Roles and Capabilities

Now you can start to see how to use roles and capabilities to your advantage and manipulate them for your site. Customizing the roles and capabilities in WordPress enables you to give more specific permissions to your users and extend the default roles if you need to.

How Roles and Capabilities Are Stored

First, let's look at how WordPress stores roles and capabilities so you can understand exactly what's happening in the database when you're modifying anything. I think it's important to understand them in detail so it's easier to conceptualize and understand the methods you're working with.

In fact, it's amazing how easily user roles are stored in the database: as a single option in the `wp_options` table. The `wp_user_roles` option is where you'll find a serialized array of all the roles and capabilities used in WordPress; it looks similar to this:

```
a:5:{s:13:"administrator";a:2:{s:4:"name";s:13:"Administrator";s:12:"capabilities";a:62:
{s:13:"switch_themes";b:1;s:11:"edit_themes";b:1;s:16:"activate_plugins";b:1;s:12:"edit_
plugins";b:1;s:10:"edit_users";b:1;s:10:"edit_files";b:1;s:14:"manage_options";b:1;s:17:"moderate_
comments";b:1;s:17:"manage_categories";b:1;s:12:"manage_links";b:1;s:12:"upload_files";b:1;s:6:"impo
rt";b:1;s:15:"unfiltered_html";b:1;s:10:"edit_posts";b:1;s:17:"edit_others_posts"; [...]
```

That's not actually all of it, of course; if I included it all, it would take up the rest of this page! If you unserialize it, though, and take a look at the expanded array, you'll see segments like this:

```
[author] => Array
(
        [name] => Author
        [capabilities] => Array
        (
                [upload_files] => 1
                [edit_posts] => 1
                [edit_published_posts] => 1
                [publish_posts] => 1
                [read] => 1
                [level_2] => 1
                [level_1] => 1
                [level_0] => 1
                [delete_posts] => 1
                [delete_published_posts] => 1
        )

)
```

This code shows the Author role, but the other four are formatted in exactly the same way. Each role has its own array in which is stored the full name of the role and an array of the capabilities, with each one set to 1 (true). As you can see, capabilities are stored purely as strings in the keys of these arrays; there's not really much more to it than that. However, when you're creating new roles and capabilities, you'll start to understand just what's going on in the database.

You might also notice that in the array is a series of "level" entries:

```
[level_2] => 1
[level_1] => 1
[level_0] => 1
```

They date back to the old user system in WordPress, which was a series of "levels" for each user. The current roles and capabilities system was introduced way back in version 2, and the old levels system has since been deprecated from version 3 onward. However, there are some plugins that over time have not been updated and still use the very outdated levels system. So for their sake, the levels markers have been left in for each role. This is definitely not something you should be coding for in your themes/plugins, so ensure that you stick to the current capabilities system.

The WP_Roles Class

The WordPress WP_Roles class actually controls the user roles; it contains all the functions you'll be using to manipulate user roles and capabilities in your themes/plugins. You don't need to access the class directly because WordPress does it for you. When you call a function such as get_role, WordPress checks to see whether there is already an instance of the WP_Roles class; if not, it creates one and then runs the WP_Roles->get_role method.

Almost any time you work with roles and capabilities in WordPress you'll use methods of the WP_Roles class. These are the main ones you'll see in this section:

- add_role

- remove_role

- get_role

- add_cap

- remove_cap

There are several more, but you'll look at ways to use them later in the chapter.

Creating a Role

Creating a new role in WordPress is a simple case of using the add_role function and specifying the new role with a unique slug, a name, and some capabilities. The capabilities you specify can include some of those already set up in WordPress or custom capabilities.

To add a custom capability, you just need to specify a name for it in the array and set it to true (the value 1 in this case). There is no special function for creating a custom capability because everything is stored as part of the array in the options table of the database. When creating custom roles and assigning capabilities, be careful to spell everything correctly when you assign WordPress default capabilities.

Here's an example of adding a new role for your users. The role will enable them to create and publish their own posts, edit and publish others' posts, but not access the site's pages.

```
function prowordpress_add_moderator_role () {
        $result = add_role('moderator', 'Moderator', array(
                'read' => 1,
                'edit_posts' => 1,
                'delete_posts' => 1,
                'edit_others_posts' => 1,
                'edit_published_posts' => 1,
                'publish_posts' => 1,
```

```
            'delete_others_posts' => 1,
            'delete_published_posts' => 1,
            'moderate_comments' => 1,
            'manage_categories' => 1,
            'upload_files' => 1,
            'edit_pages' => false, // explicitly deny capability
    ));

    if (null !== $result) {
            echo "Role created";
    } else {
            echo "Role already exists!";
    }
}

add_action('after_switch_theme', 'prowordpress_add_moderator_role');
```

The add_role function shown here takes the first two parameters of a slug and name, followed by the array of capabilities for that role. Here you have all the capabilities for the moderator to be able to edit all the posts and comments. Notice that the last item in the array is 'edit_pages'. It is set to false, which means this capability is explicitly denied to the user role.

The result of the add_role function is then stored in the variable $result. The function will return null if the role type already exists and a WP_Role object if the role is created successfully. To illustrate this, the end of the function checked the result returned and just echoed out a message depending on the status of the result.

Because this function adds to the option in the database, there's no need to run it multiple times, so here I added it using the after_switch_theme action. It will be run as soon as your theme has been activated and only once, so as soon as someone installs and activates your theme, the new user role will be available (see Figure 8-1). It's not necessarily a theme activation hook, but you can be sure it will run only on the active theme because after the theme has been switched, only one theme's code will be available to be run.

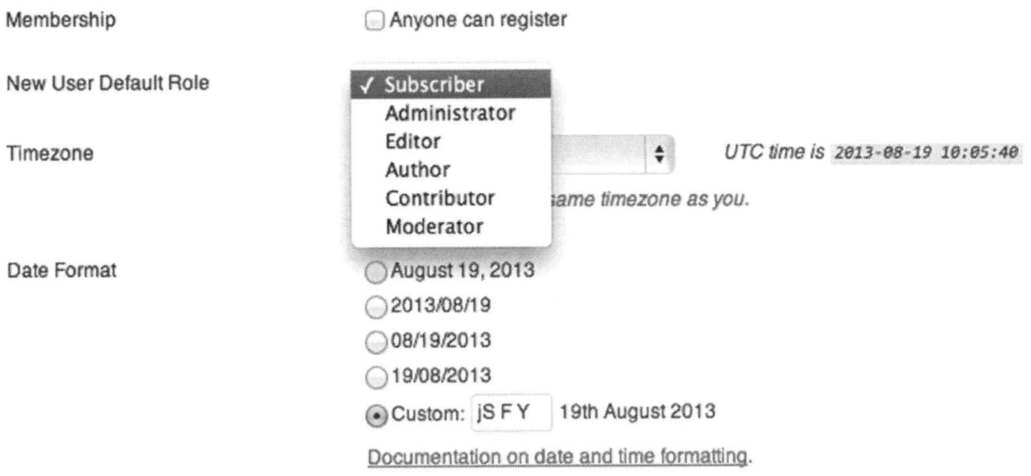

Membership	☐ Anyone can register
New User Default Role	✓ Subscriber
	Administrator
	Editor
Timezone	Author
	Contributor
	Moderator
Date Format	○ August 19, 2013
	○ 2013/08/19
	○ 08/19/2013
	○ 19/08/2013
	◉ Custom: jS F Y 19th August 2013

UTC time is 2013-08-19 10:05:40

same timezone as you.

Documentation on date and time formatting.

Figure 8-1. *The list of roles in Settings ➤ General with your new role*

Removing a Role

Besides creating a role when the theme is installed, you also need to make sure you clean up the WordPress site when the theme is deactivated. Although there's no deactivation hook for themes as there is for plugins, you can use a similar trick using the `after_switch_theme` action, which is run only on the theme that is being disabled at the time:

```
function prowordpress_remove_moderator_role () {
        remove_role( 'moderator' );
}

add_action('switch_theme', 'prowordpress_remove_moderator_role');
```

The code for this one is ridiculously simple; you just call the `remove_role` function with the slug of the role you want to remove.

Adding Capabilities

To add capabilities for existing roles, you can either add existing capabilities in WordPress to the default roles or you can create new capabilities entirely.

You need to run two functions to be able to add capabilities to a user role: get the user role you're going to add to by using the `get_role` function and then add the capabilities with the `add_cap` method of that role.

When you get the role with the `get_role()` function, you're creating a `WP_Role` object in the variable you assign. The `WP_Role` class is slightly different from the `WP_Roles` class discussed earlier in that it deals only with a single role at a time, which is why you're using it to edit a role and add capabilities. It still interfaces with the `WP_Roles` class eventually, but the object you're creating is defined through the `WP_Role` class, which is an important distinction to make.

As an example, you'll be editing the Author default role in WordPress; as I already mentioned, this is probably not the most ideal solution. People who use your theme might either know a little about WordPress or look to find out about WordPress when they're using it, and if you're editing the default roles, it might come as a surprise to them that the default roles don't do what they're supposed to. So this is for demonstration purposes only:

```
function prowordpress_setup_roles () {
        $author = get_role('author');

        $author->add_cap('edit_pages');
        $author->add_cap('publish_pages');
        $author->add_cap('delete_pages', false);
}

add_action('after_switch_theme', 'prowordpress_setup_roles');
```

The function shows how you can add new capabilities to the Author role: first you get the role and store it in the $author variable using the `get_role` function; then with that object you use the `add_cap` method to add the capabilities you need for the role. There are two things to note here. First, the method deals with only one capability at a time, so to add multiple capabilities, you need to call the method multiple times. Second, it's possible to add a second argument to the `add_cap` function, which is a Boolean, as to whether the capability is to be granted or denied. The default is true, but to deny a capability you can pass false as the second argument.

Because of the way the roles are stored in the database, you should be calling this function when the theme is activated so it is run only once.

Removing Capabilities

If you're setting up your theme and modifying roles and capabilities, you need to make sure you're resetting all your changes when your theme is deactivated. Or if you want to make a change to a user role by removing some of its default capabilities, you can do it this way (once again, this is not recommended unless absolutely necessary):

```
function prowordpress_reset_roles () {
        $author = get_role('author');

        $author->remove_cap('edit_pages');
        $author->remove_cap('publish_pages');
        $author->remove_cap('delete_pages');
}

add_action('switch_theme', 'prowordpress_reset_roles');
```

The remove_cap method works in the same way as add_cap requiring a WP_Role object to work from and only allowing you to remove one capability at a time.

WP_User Class

The WP_User class allows you to manipulate a user's roles and capabilities on a per-user basis, which means you can do things like assigning multiple roles to a single user or manually managing the capabilities of single users.

All the available functions act as methods of the WP_User class, so you need to get a user object before you can manipulate its roles and capabilities. To get a user object, use the new operator with the WP_User class and pass it either a user ID or the user's login name, or use the wp_get_current_user function if you want to manipulate the current logged-in user.

```
// Get the admin by user ID (admin user is always user ID 1)
$user = new WP_User( 1 );

// Get a user by their login name
$user = new WP_User( null, 'adamonishi' );

// Get the current user
$user = wp_get_current_user();
```

Once you have a user object, you can use any of the six available methods to modify the user's roles or capabilities:

- add_role()
- set_role()
- remove_role()
- add_cap()
- remove_cap()
- remove_all_caps()

Most of these methods should be fairly self-explanatory; the add_cap() and remove_cap() functions work exactly the same way as in the WP_Roles class, but per-user instead.

The add_role() function can be used to add a entire role to a specific user, which could possibly save you from having to add a bunch of separate new capabilities to a certain role when you're creating a series of new capabilities. For instance, if you add the moderator role and also want to add the same capabilities to your main admin user, you could just add the role to the admin instead of adding each new capability individually.

```
function prowordpress_add_moderator_role () {
        $result = add_role('moderator', 'Moderator', array(
                'read' => 1,
                'edit_posts' => 1,
                'delete_posts' => 1,
                'edit_others_posts' => 1,
                'edit_published_posts' => 1,
                'publish_posts' => 1,
                'delete_others_posts' => 1,
                'delete_published_posts' => 1,
                'moderate_comments' => 1,
                'manage_categories' => 1,
                'upload_files' => 1,
                'edit_pages' => false,
        ));

        if (null !== $result) {
                $admin = new WP_User( 1 );
                $admin->add_role('moderator');
        }
}
```

The example shows that after you create your new moderator role, you can also add this role directly to the site administrator. Of course, if you want all administrator users to also have these capabilities, it might be best to go through the process of adding the capabilities to the role so that new administrator users have these capabilities without having to check when each new user is created.

The other two role functions do what their names infer: the set_role() function changes the role of a current user to the one passed into the function, and the remove_role() function removes the role passed.

The final function, remove_all_caps(),can be used to remove every capability from a user. For instance, it could be used if a user is being blocked from accessing the site. Instead of deleting the user and allowing them to sign up again by freeing their e-mail address, you could remove all their capabilities. This would mean that they couldn't access anything in the site; and because they're still technically signed up, they wouldn't be able to sign up again.

Custom User Capabilities

So far, you've dealt with the default capabilities used within WordPress. But it's also incredibly easy to add custom user capabilities to WordPress because all they consist of is adding a unique capability name to a role via either the create role or add_cap functionality.

However, when you create a custom capability, you also need to be able to test the capability to make sure it means something within the site. There are a few ways to do this: you can assign custom capabilities to custom post types when registering them, you can assign custom capabilities to WordPress menu pages, and you can check custom capabilities manually.

First let's look at setting up custom capabilities for your users and then look at how you can apply them to various situations. To add a custom capability to a user role, you can just use the add_cap function as you did before and pass it a custom capability that you create:

```
function prowordpress_add_reviewer_role () {
        $result = add_role(reviewer', 'Movie Reviewer, array(
                'read' => 1,
                'edit_movies' => 1,
                'publish_movies' => 1,
                'delete_movies' => 1,
                'upload_files' => 1,
        ));
}

add_action('after_switch_theme', 'prowordpress_add_reviewer_role');
```

It then creates the user role with only custom capabilities to allow them to update and create movies of their own. You can then add to this function the following lines to allow your moderator role to also access movies and to access every author's movie posts:

```
$mod = get_role('moderator');

$caps = array (
                'edit_movies',
                'publish_movies',
                'delete_movies',
                'edit_others_movies',
                'delete_others_movies',
                'read_private_movies',
        );

foreach( $caps as $cap ) {
        $mod->add_cap( $cap );
}
```

In these few lines, I'm getting the moderator role, as with the Author role, and then instead of listing out lines and lines of $mod->add_cap() for each capability, I just put them in an array and looped through it to make it a bit easier to read.

Custom Post Type Capabilities

In Chapter 4, I discussed custom post types, but there was one bit I glossed over because it required quite a bit of explaining that related more to the subject of this chapter. So here you'll take a look at the two arguments I covered only slightly: capability_type and capabilities.

In the capability_type argument of the register_post_type function, you have two choices when creating a post type: post or page. Depending on which one you choose, different capabilities will apply (i.e., if post is selected, users with the edit_posts capability can access that post type). When customizing the capabilities needed to access a custom post type, however, you can create a custom capability_type, which needs to go hand in hand with a set of custom capabilities in the capabilities argument.

The following code shows how a version of the register_post_type function would look if you added custom capabilities for managing the post type, based on the ones you assigned to your custom roles:

```
register_post_type(
        'ptd_movie',
        array(
                'public' => true,
                'capability_type' => 'movie',
                'capabilities' => array(
                        'publish_posts' => 'publish_movies',
                        'edit_posts' => 'edit_movies',
                        'edit_others_posts' => 'edit_others_movies',
                        'delete_posts' => 'delete_movies',
                        'delete_others_posts' => 'delete_others_movies',
                        'read_private_posts' => 'read_private_movies',
                        'edit_post' => 'edit_movie',
                        'delete_post' => 'delete_movie',
                        'read_post' => 'read_movie',
                ),
        )
);
```

Adding a custom value to the capability_type argument results in capabilities being set automatically by WordPress, but you can have very granular control over capabilities if you want to by passing an array of custom capabilities to the capabilities argument.

Unfortunately, it isn't quite as simple to get a custom set of capabilities up and running for your custom post type: you have to set up the meta capabilities mapping. Meta capabilities refer to the last three capabilities listed in the previous example: edit_post, delete_post, and read_post. Notice that they are all in singular form; it's because they refer to a capability in context at their time of use. For example, is the user the author of this post?

The following function is courtesy of Justin Tadlock's brilliant post on this subject (http://wp-themes-book.com/08002), which shows you how to map the meta capabilities and filter it into the map_meta_cap function:

```
add_filter( 'map_meta_cap', 'my_map_meta_cap', 10, 4 );

function my_map_meta_cap( $caps, $cap, $user_id, $args ) {

        /* If editing, deleting, or reading a movie, get the post and post type object. */
        if ( 'edit_movie' == $cap || 'delete_movie' == $cap || 'read_movie' == $cap ) {
                $post = get_post( $args[0] );
                $post_type = get_post_type_object( $post->post_type );

                /* Set an empty array for the caps. */
                $caps = array();
        }

        /* If editing a movie, assign the required capability. */
        if ( 'edit_movie' == $cap ) {
                if ( $user_id == $post->post_author ) {
                        $caps[] = $post_type->cap->edit_posts;
                } else {
                        $caps[] = $post_type->cap->edit_others_posts;
                }
        }
```

```
        /* If deleting a movie, assign the required capability. */
        elseif ( 'delete_movie' == $cap ) {
                if ( $user_id == $post->post_author ) {
                        $caps[] = $post_type->cap->delete_posts;
                } else {
                        $caps[] = $post_type->cap->delete_others_posts;
                }
        }

        /* If reading a private movie, assign the required capability. */
        elseif ( 'read_movie' == $cap ) {

                if ( 'private' != $post->post_status ) {
                        $caps[] = 'read';
                } elseif ( $user_id == $post->post_author ) {
                        $caps[] = 'read';
                } else {
                        $caps[] = $post_type->cap->read_private_posts;
                }
        }

        /* Return the capabilities required by the user. */
        return $caps;
}
```

This function is a filter for the `map_meta_cap` and will run every time WordPress requires it to. It works like the WordPress default function that takes in the meta capability being tested as `$cap` and the capabilities of the user as `$caps`, along with the `$user_id` and some additional `$args`, such as the post ID.

In the function, you're testing what capability is being accessed and then returning the primitive capability required to access these functions. For instance, if the meta capability passed in is `edit_movie`, you set the capability required to `edit_posts` if the user is the author or to `edit_others_posts` if the user is not the post's author. With the primitive capability returned, WordPress then tests this against the current user's capabilities and decides whether they can perform the action they're attempting.

Being able to map meta capabilities like this is very powerful and allows you to customize what users can do with their capabilities. However, I suggest not customizing much beyond the example of Justin's function. Otherwise, you're beginning to manipulate the roles and capabilities system beyond what you can expect in WordPress, which could trip you up later in development.

Capabilities for Admin Menus

In the WordPress admin, by default each user role is allowed access to a different set of menus (see Figures 8-2 and 8-3).

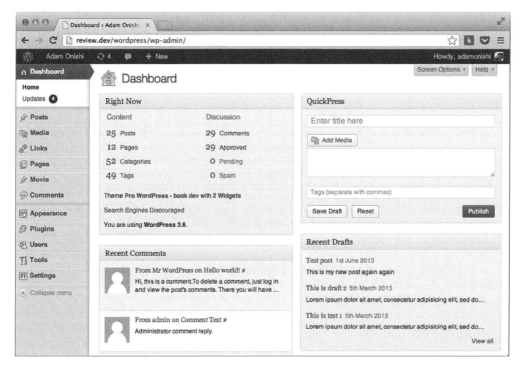

Figure 8-2. *WordPress admin when signed in as Administrator*

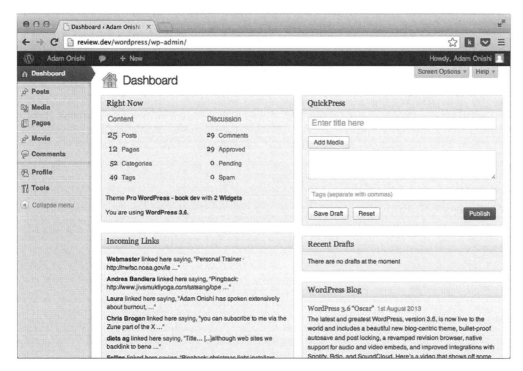

Figure 8-3. *WordPress admin when signed in as Author*

Being able to show and hide different menus in the admin is also controlled by the capabilities of users. For an Administrator, they have capabilities such as 'manage_options', which gives them access to the Settings menu and all the subpages associated with it. All the menu pages in WordPress are controlled this way, as you can see by the different menu options available in Figure 8-3 for a user with the Author role. They don't have capabilities for managing the options of the site or for any of the theme options such as the 'edit_theme_options' and 'switch_themes' capabilities.

You'll learn more about setting up administration menus in Chapter 13 when I cover WordPress plugin development, but here you see how to give access to different users when creating these menus. There are many functions available in WordPress to set up administration menus, but they all follow a similar format to the general functions add_menu_page() and add_submenu_page() shown here:

```
add_menu_page( $page_title, $menu_title, $capability, $menu_slug, $function, $icon_url, $position );

add_submenu_page( $parent_slug, $page_title, $menu_title, $capability, $menu_slug, $function );
```

Both functions are called with a number of standard function parameters, each relating to settings like the menu's name and location in the admin. The main parameter to focus on here is the $capability parameter, which is used to set the capability required for the menu to be shown to the user. Again, this is simply one of the many capabilities available in WordPress (depending on which roles you want to have access to the admin menu), or it can be a custom capability that you can then add to specific roles.

For example, suppose that you required the moderator role you created earlier to be able to see a custom page that held a summary of the details of the latest movie reviews submitted to the site and maybe some other analytical information. You could create a new menu page with a custom capability and then add it to the moderator role's capabilities:

```
function prowordpress_add_moderator_page() {
        add_menu_page( 'Moderation stats', 'Moderation Stats', 'moderator_view_stats',
'moderator-admin-menu', 'prowordpress_build_moderator_stats' );

        $mod = get_role('moderator');
        $mod->add_cap('moderator_view_stats');

        $admin = get_role('administrator');
        $admin->add_cap('moderator_view_stats');
}

if( is_admin() ) {
        add_action( 'admin_menu', 'prowordpress_add_moderator_page' );
}
```

This function would add a menu page to the WordPress admin with a custom capability called 'moderator_view_stats'. For now, don't worry about the rest of the parameters because they are discussed later in the book.

After you add the menu page, you need to add the capability to the moderator user and the admin user. (In general, it is always good practice for the site admin to be able to see all the available functionality in the admin.) The function is added with a hook in the last few lines of code. In this instance, you want to run this hook only when you're viewing the admin page, so wrap the hook inside a check for is_admin().

Testing User Capabilities

The final task to look at is how to test user capabilities manually in your own custom code. There are a few reasons why you may want to do this, such as checking whether to display a custom metabox depending on the user's capabilities. Three functions are available that allow you to test the user's capabilities:

- current_user_can()

- user_can()

- author_can()

The one you'll use most often is current_user_can() because it gives you a quick way to check whether the current logged-in user has a certain capability. All you need to do is pass the capability name into the function to get a true/false result; you can see the function used here in the WordPress core update.php file:

```php
if ( current_user_can( 'update_plugins' ) ) {
        $update_plugins = get_site_transient( 'update_plugins' );
        if ( ! empty( $update_plugins->response ) )
                $counts['plugins'] = count( $update_plugins->response );
}

if ( current_user_can( 'update_themes' ) ) {
        $update_themes = get_site_transient( 'update_themes' );
        if ( ! empty( $update_themes->response ) )
                $counts['themes'] = count( $update_themes->response );
}

if ( function_exists( 'get_core_updates' ) && current_user_can( 'update_core' ) ) {
        $update_wordpress = get_core_updates( array('dismissed' => false) );
        if ( ! empty( $update_wordpress ) && ! in_array( $update_wordpress[0]->response,
array('development', 'latest') ) && current_user_can('update_core') )
                $counts['wordpress'] = 1;
}
```

The series of checks see whether the current user has access to update certain parts of the WordPress site, such as plugins, theme, and core. Based on this, you can set up a similar check in your functions when you're setting up a custom metabox for certain posts based on the user's capabilities. Here is the metabox function from Chapter 5:

```php
function prowordpress_movies_meta_box () {
        global $post;

        if( current_user_can('publish_movies') ) {
                add_meta_box (
                                'ptd_movies_meta',
                                __('Movie details', 'prowordpress'),
                                'prowordpress_movie_meta_fields',
                                'ptd_movie',
                                'side',
                                'core'
                        );
        }
}

add_action ('add_meta_boxes', 'prowordpress_movies_meta_box');
```

To display it only for users who can publish the movie post type, wrap the entire add_meta_box() function in a condition with the current_user_can() function. By displaying the metabox only when a user has the capability to publish the posts means you can have specific post editors who enter the main content, but a moderator is needed to enter the more specific and maybe factual data before the post is published.

Of course, when doing this for metaboxes, it's also good practice to test whether the user has the correct capabilities in the function used to save the metadata as well. By adding this snippet of code before you save any of the data, you ensure that the data has been submitted by a user with the correct capabilities, just in case:

```
// Check if the current user has permission to edit the post.
if ( ! current_user_can( 'publish_movies', $post_id ) ) {
        return $post_id;
}
```

The snippet also shows a second parameter of the current_user_can() function because it can be passed the post ID for any post to check the specific information relating to that post.

The other two functions, user_can() and author_can(), work in much the same way. The user_can() function takes a user's ID and the capability to be checked; and author_can() takes either a post ID or post object as the first parameter, followed by the capability as the second. Both functions are less commonly used however (only three times in core between them), and you'll find that most of your capability checking will (and possibly should) be done with the current_user_can() function.

Customizing User Login

Now that you understand how the user system works in WordPress, you can take a look at some user features to add to your WordPress sites. First, you'll see some ways to customize how users log in to the web site, whether by simply modifying the default WordPress login page with custom branding or by creating a completely bespoke login page outside of the WordPress system. Later in the chapter, you'll look at some other user features, including how to manage users programmatically and even how to create a full user registration system.

Customizing the Login Page

This is definitely one of the easiest things to do with WordPress, and if you're building web sites for clients, this is a really quick way to make the site a little bit more tailored toward the company's brand.

Starting with the standard WordPress login page shown in Figure 8-4, you can customize everything from the logo and link, through to the styles for the entire form.

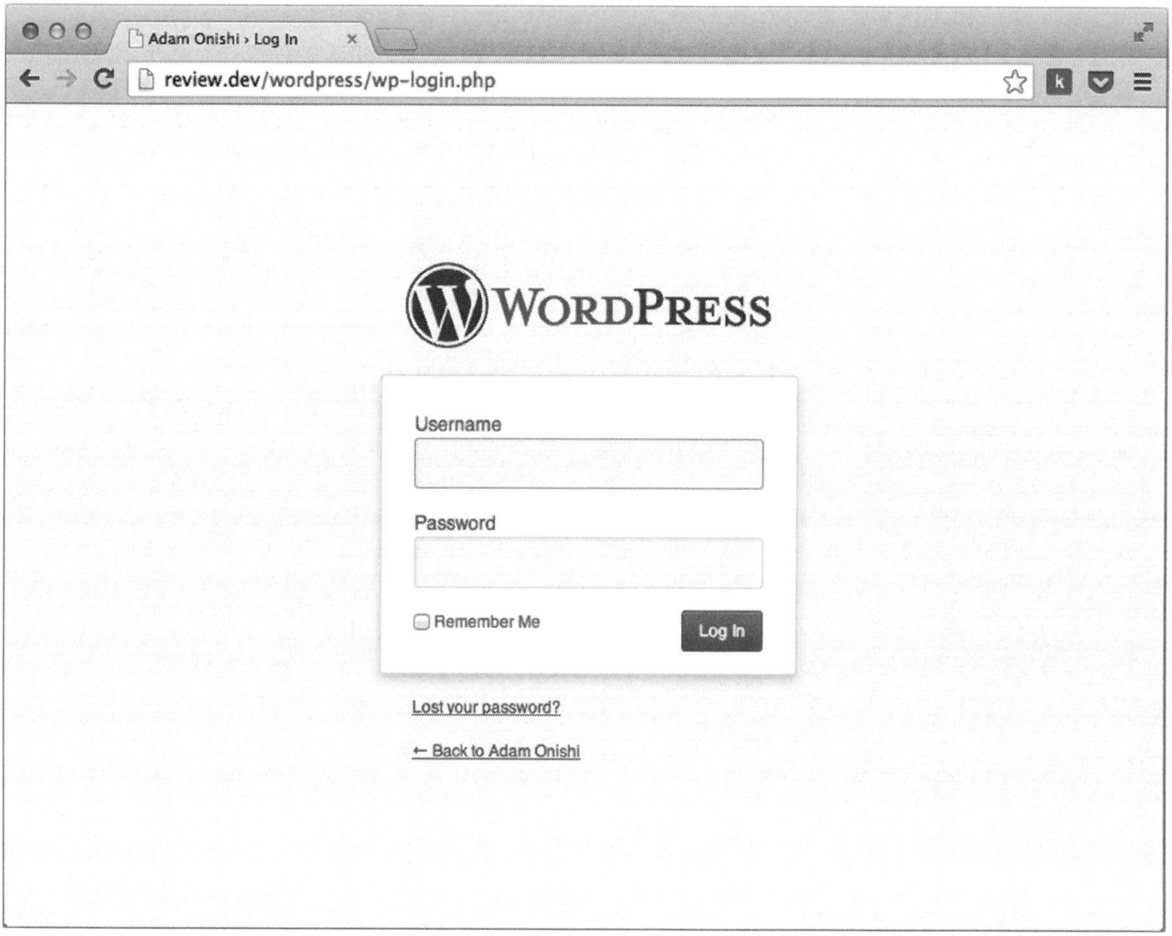

Figure 8-4. *Default WordPress login page*

Adding a Custom Logo

A custom logo is probably the easiest way to make the login page look a bit more familiar to a brand. The logo is displayed by default using CSS and is linked to the following HTML markup. (Notice that in the header, the title has a link to the wordpress.org site, so you'll probably want to change it.)

```
<h1><a href="http://wordpress.org/" title="Powered by WordPress">Your Site Name</a></h1>
```

The default CSS is quite verbose and sets a lot of styles on the link:

```
.login h1 a {
        background-image: url('../images/wordpress-logo.png?ver=20120216');
        background-size: 274px 63px;
        background-position: top center;
        background-repeat: no-repeat;
        width: 326px;
        height: 67px;
```

```
        text-indent: -9999px;
        outline: 0;
        overflow: hidden;
        padding-bottom: 15px;
        display: block;
}
```

To get around this, WordPress has a hook called 'login_enqueue_scripts' that allows you to add your own custom styles to the page after the inclusion of the standard style sheets in the head on the login page only. Depending on the level of styling you want to do, you could create a separate style sheet to be included here, but for now you'll just use inline styles to override the WordPress defaults. The following function creates a block of inline style that is hooked onto the login page using the previously mentioned hook:

```php
function twelvedevs_login_logo() { ?>
        <style type="text/css">
                .login #login {
                        padding-top:50px;
                }

                .login h1 a {
                        width:100%;
                        height:220px;
                        padding-bottom: 30px;
                        background-image: url(<?php
echo get_bloginfo( 'template_directory' ) ?>/images/12devslogo.png);
                        background-size:221px 220px;
                }
        </style>
<?php }
add_action( 'login_enqueue_scripts', 'twelvedevs_login_logo' );
```

The WordPress Codex mentions that you should use more-specific selectors in your CSS to ensure that you overwrite the default WordPress styles. However, because the inline style is included by the hook after the default style sheets are included, they will be overwritten as long as you use the same level of specificity. Because of the way WordPress defines the default background image, I had to be a bit more specific here and define styles such as the background size and size of the <a> tag itself.

The following code shows how the <head> of the login page now looks with the included inline styles. You can see the results of the new styles in Figure 8-5.

```html
<link rel='stylesheet' id='buttons-css'  href='http://12devs.dev/wordpress/wp-includes/css/buttons
.min.css?ver=3.5.2' type='text/css' media='all' />
<link rel='stylesheet' id='colors-fresh-css'  href='http://12devs.dev/wordpress/wp-admin/css/colors-
fresh.min.css?ver=3.5.2' type='text/css' media='all' />
<style type="text/css">
        .login #login {
                padding-top:50px;
        }

        .login h1 a {
                width:100%;
                height:220px;
                padding-bottom: 30px;
```

```
                background-image: url(http://12devs.dev/wordpress/wp-
content/themes/12devs/images/12devslogo.png);
                background-position:top center;
                background-size:221px 220px;
        }
</style>
```

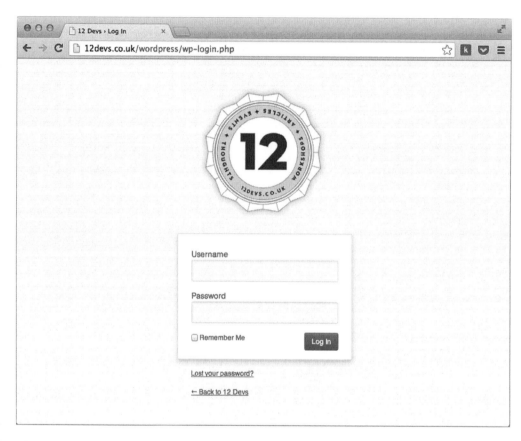

Figure 8-5. *Styled WordPress login with the 12 Devs logo*

The last part to do was the default link in the header of the login page that linked to wordpress.org and had a title "Powered by WordPress". This time, WordPress provides two very specific hooks to overwrite these two parts of the login header:

```
function twelvedevs_login_logo_url() {
        return get_bloginfo( 'url' );
}
add_filter( 'login_headerurl', 'twelvedevs_login_logo_url' );

function twelvedevs_login_logo_url_title() {
        return '12 Devs';
}
add_filter( 'login_headertitle', 'twelvedevs_login_logo_url_title' );
```

These two functions and hooks allow you to overwrite the link and title text in the login page header and results in the following markup being generated:

```
<h1><a href="http://12devs.dev" title="12 Devs">12 Devs</a></h1>
```

Adding Custom Styles to the Rest of the Login Page

Besides styling the header of the login page with the previous hook and knowing a few more CSS selectors, you can also customize the entire look of login page. Again, the WordPress Codex does provide a list of bespoke selectors to use, which are shown in the following code. However, because of the way the `wp_enqueue_scripts` hook works, your script should always be included after the default scripts. So as long as you use the same specificity in your styles, the defaults should be overwritten.

```
body.login {}
body.login div#login {}
body.login div#login h1 {}
body.login div#login h1 a {}
body.login div#login form#loginform {}
body.login div#login form#loginform p {}
body.login div#login form#loginform p label {}
body.login div#login form#loginform input {}
body.login div#login form#loginform input#user_login {}
body.login div#login form#loginform input#user_pass {}
body.login div#login form#loginform p.forgetmenot {}
body.login div#login form#loginform p.forgetmenot input#rememberme {}
body.login div#login form#loginform p.submit {}
body.login div#login form#loginform p.submit input#wp-submit {}
body.login div#login p#nav {}
body.login div#login p#nav a {}
body.login div#login p#backtoblog {}
body.login div#login p#backtoblog a {}
```

Most of these styles have been made more specific by adding the element as part of the selector, but this can be easily removed and the styles will still overwrite those of the defaults.

Although you could add these styles to an inline `<style>` block (as you did when customizing the header logo), because of the amount of styling you have to do here, it might be better to include the styles as a separate style sheet. To do this you can use the same action hook as before, but just include a link tag to your custom style sheet.

```
function twelvedevs_login_style() { ?>
        <link rel="stylesheet" id="custom_wp_login_css"  href="<?php echo
get_bloginfo( 'stylesheet_directory' ) . '/css/login.css'; ?>" type="text/css" media="all" />
<?php
}
add_action( 'login_enqueue_scripts', 'twelvedevs_login_style' );
```

When including styles in WordPress, the `wp_enqueue_style()` function is normally used. However, because of how late the function is called in the WordPress runtime, using it would result in the link tag not appearing until the footer of the document.

Adding Custom Content to the Login Page

Besides adding custom styles to the login page, WordPress provides some hooks that are called throughout the login page. You can use any of these hooks to add in custom content from your function.php file or a plugin. For example, custom messages or a custom footer could be added to the page, allowing for more customizations beyond that of just styling.

You've seen some of the hooks already when using them to customize the link and title of the login page header and when including your custom login CSS. The full list of available actions and filters is shown here:

- login_enqueue_scripts (action)
- login_head (action)
- login_form (action)
- login_footer (action)
- login_headerurl (filter)
- login_headertitle (filter)
- login_message (filter)
- login_errors (filter)

Creating a Custom User Login Page

Instead of just customizing the default login page, you can create an entirely separate login page of your own, enabling you to prevent people from going to the standard login page or even getting in to the WordPress admin entirely, for example.

WordPress provides a single function that allows you to create your own login form for the front end of your sites: wp_login_form. However, this function deals only with the form, so you have to take some additional steps if you want a truly custom page for users to log in to your site. Although the form is covered by WordPress, there are still things such as lost password links and handling login errors that need to be dealt with by you when creating your custom login page.

To start, you need to create a custom page template where the login form will go. Where you do this on the site is completely up to you; for now, you'll create this page as a custom page template that can be applied to any page. In the examples, you'll be using /login as the custom site URL, so ensure that if you are using a different URL, you substitute it in the examples.

```php
<?php
/**
 * Template Name: Login template
 */
get_header();
?>

        <div class="content">

                <h2><?php the_title(); ?></h2>

        </div>

<?php get_footer(); ?>
```

The code includes the site's default header and footer and a page title, but you can use any of the site's content to build a custom login page.

Now you need to look at the main function that will create your custom login form: `wp_login_form`. The function takes an array of arguments as its only parameter. These arguments allow you to customize almost every aspect of the login form—from the text used in the form to the redirect links and IDs used in the form for styling hooks.

```php
<?php
$args = array(
                'echo'            => true,
                'redirect'        => site_url( $_SERVER['REQUEST_URI'] ),
                'form_id'         => 'loginform',
                'label_username'  => __( 'Username' ),
                'label_password'  => __( 'Password' ),
                'label_remember'  => __( 'Remember Me' ),
                'label_log_in'    => __( 'Log In' ),
                'id_username'     => 'user_login',
                'id_password'     => 'user_pass',
                'id_remember'     => 'rememberme',
                'id_submit'       => 'wp-submit',
                'remember'        => true,
                'value_username'  => NULL,
                'value_remember'  => false
        );
?>
```

The code shows all the arguments and their defaults. The defaults are pretty good, so there's rarely much need to change them unless you want some more-specific labels or to change some IDs. For the login form, you'll keep most of the defaults, but change the `redirect` URL to be to the home page and add some different IDs to prevent any of the default WordPress login form styles from applying:

```php
<?php
$args = array(
                'redirect' => home_url(),
                'form_id'      => 'loginform-custom',
                'id_username'  => 'user-login-custom',
                'id_password'  => 'user-pass-custom',
                'id_remember'  => 'rememberme-custom',
                'id_submit'    => 'wp-submit-custom',
        );
wp_login_form( $args ); ?>
```

The login form is now on the page and ready to go (see Figure 8-6).

Login

Username [   ]

Password [   ]

☐ Remember Me

[Log In]

Figure 8-6. *The login form generated by the code*

However, if you look at the form generated in comparison with the ones in Figure 8-4 or 8-5, you'll see one handy link missing: the "Forgotten your password?" link. This is because you need to create this one outside of the login form using the wp_lostpassword_url() function. This function simply prints a link to the default WordPress password reset page, and you can pass it a redirect URL as well. So to complete your initial login form, you can add in a link to the "Forgotten your password?" page.

```
<p><a class="forgot-pass-link" href="<?php echo wp_lostpassword_url(); ?>" title="<?php
_e('Forgotten your password?', 'prowordpress'); ?>"><?php _e('Forgotten your password?',
'prowordpress'); ?></a></p>
```

At the moment, it links only to the default WordPress password reset page. It would, of course, be preferable if you were creating a fully custom login and registration system (which I'll cover later in the chapter) to have a custom page for the password reset as well. Unfortunately, WordPress doesn't provide any functions to create one of them easily, so it would require programming a custom form and coding the password reset. For now, leave the password reset page to WordPress to deal with; remember that any custom styling you added to the login page is also present on the password reset page as well, so it's not all bad news.

Handling Login Errors

The login form function deals only with handling the output of the form. If logins are successful, the user sees only the login page you created and is successfully redirected to the home page (or whichever redirect link you've chosen). When an error occurs, though, the user is directed to the default login page and given an error message. Obviously, if you're creating a custom login page, you'll prefer that errors be handled by the same page if and when they occur. So there are several functions you need to set up.

There are two conditions you need to catch when handling login form errors because WordPress handles them in slightly different ways. The first is when there has been a failed login attempt (i.e., the wrong username and password combination has been entered); the second is when no values are entered into either the username or password inputs. The reason for the difference is based on the point at which the redirect occurs in the WordPress core. When no data has been entered for either password or username, WordPress knows this will be a failed login attempt and immediately redirects back to the login page with an error. When values are entered, WordPress needs need to check the database for the user data before it can do a redirect.

To catch these two login errors, you need two functions. Both are pretty similar; for example, they both check the referrer to see where the login attempt originated so the user is redirected to the correct page. Because you're not actually disabling the default login page, users might be coming from that page, so it's best to redirect them to your custom login page only if they are using it.

```
function prowordpress_failed_login( $user ) {
        // save the referrer to a local var
        if( isset($_SERVER['HTTP_REFERER']) ) {
                $referrer = $_SERVER['HTTP_REFERER'];
        }

        // Check the referrer to make sure we're not coming from the default login page and there is
no user set
        if ( ! empty($referrer) && ! strstr($referrer,'wp-login') && ! strstr($referrer,'wp-admin')
&& $user !== null ) {
                // Make sure the current referrer doesn't already have the login failed query string
                if ( ! strstr($referrer, '?login=failed' ) ) {
                        // Redirect to the login page and append a querystring of login failed
                        wp_redirect( $referrer . '?login=failed');
                } else {
```

```
                    wp_redirect( $referrer );
            }

            exit;
        }
}
add_action( 'wp_login_failed', 'prowordpress_failed_login' );
```

Each step of the function is commented along the way, but I'll explain in more detail. The first condition checks where the referrer is coming from to ensure that you're redirecting to the correct place. The second condition makes sure that if you came from a page having an error that you don't add another query string to the end of the URL again. The function is then hooked into WordPress using the wp_login_failed hook that fires when there have been values entered into the form but no user records with those values.

Your second function uses most of the code from the first, but it also needs to check the values entered:

```
function prowordpress_blank_login( $username ){
        // save the referrer to a local var
        if( isset($_SERVER['HTTP_REFERER']) ) {
                $referrer = $_SERVER['HTTP_REFERER'];
        }

        $error = false;
        // Check if either the username value or POST password value is empty
        if( empty($username) || empty($_POST['pwd']) ) {
                $error = true;
        }

        // check that were not on the default login page
        if ( ! empty($referrer) && ! strstr($referrer,'wp-login') &&
! strstr($referrer,'wp-admin') && $error ) {

                // Make sure the current referrer doesn't already have the login failed query string
                if ( ! strstr($referrer, '?login=failed' ) ) {
                        // Redirect to the login page and append a querystring of login failed
                        wp_redirect( $referrer . '?login=failed');
                } else {
                        wp_redirect( $referrer );
                }

        exit;

        }
}

add_action( 'wp_authenticate', 'prowordpress_blank_login');
```

The main difference in the functions is that the first conditional checks whether there was a username or password value sent. If neither of these exists, you can conclude that there is an error and then perform the redirect. The function is then added on the wp_authenticate action hook, which fires before the default WordPress authentication of a user.

With those two functions set up in `functions.php`, you can now go back to your login template and make sure that you alert the user about an error with the login. Both the functions added a `login=failed` querystring to the URL if there was an error, so you can just check for that value and display a message if it is present.

```php
<?php
if( isset($_GET['login']) && 'failed' === $_GET['login']) :
?>
        <div class="message error-message">
                <p><?php _e('Login failed. Please check your details and try again.',
'prowordpress'); ?></p>
        </div>
<?php
endif;
?>
```

Now users have some feedback for when something goes wrong with their login, and they know to try again.

One last thing to do with your login page is to make sure that you display only the form when no user is logged in. It would be confusing to encounter a login form on the site when you are already logged in. To check whether a user is logged in, you can use a WordPress function called `is_user_logged_in()`, which returns true or false if there is a current user logged in to the site.

```php
<?php if ( ! is_user_logged_in() ): ?>
        <!-- Login form code -->
<?php else: ?>
        <p><?php wp_loginout( home_url() ); ?></p>
<?php endif; ?>
```

You can just wrap your login form in this if statement using the `is_user_logged_in()` function. If there is a user present, your form doesn't display and you can instead show a logout link using the `wp_loginout()` function. This function displays a login or logout link, depending on whether there is a user logged in or not. In this case, it always show a logout link.

Creating User-Only Content Areas

You can combine the `wp_login_form` and `is_user_logged_in()` functions to easily create user-only content areas of your site. By wrapping your page content in a check to see whether the current user is logged in, you can then display a message and login form on any content page in which you want a user to be logged in to view the content.

The following example uses the single page template of a site. By using the `is_user_logged_in()` function, you can check whether to display the content of the page. If there isn't a user logged in, you can display just the excerpt of the post's content, followed by a message and the login form:

```php
<?php
if( is_user_logged_in() ):
        the_content();
else:
        the_excerpt(); ?>

        <p>Please login to view the rest of the content:</p>

        <?php
        if( isset($_GET['login']) && 'failed' === $_GET['login']) :
        ?>
```

```php
            <div class="alert alert-error">
                    <p><?php _e('Login failed. Please check your details and try again.',
'prowordpress'); ?></p>
            </div>
        <?php
        endif;
        ?>

        <?php
        $args = array(
                    'form_id'          => 'loginform-custom',
                    'id_username'      => 'user-login-custom',
                    'id_password'      => 'user-pass-custom',
                    'id_remember'      => 'rememberme-custom',
                    'id_submit'        => 'wp-submit-custom',
            );
        wp_login_form( $args ); ?>
<?php endif; ?>
```

The only difference between the arguments you used in the login form on your custom page and the one here is that a custom argument for the redirect URL is taken out because it is preferable to leave it to the default argument, which is a redirect back to the current page. So once users are signed in, they are redirected back to the page they were viewing (because there is nothing more frustrating than logging in to a web site and being directed away from the content you are about to read). Because of the work you did earlier when handling potential login errors on the site, the user is always redirected back to the same page, so you can leave in your error handling messages as well.

Testing for Certain Types of Users

Besides being able to test whether a user is logged in to the web site, you can also take a look at the user's level of privileges and allow different levels of access for different levels of user. For instance, if you had a web site with three tiers of membership, you could create them as custom roles in WordPress and assign each user a custom capability based on their level of membership. Using the current_user_can() function you can then check for those capabilities if the user is logged in and display a message to the user if the level of access isn't high enough:

```php
if( is_user_logged_in() ):

        if( current_user_can('manage_gold_membership') ):
                the_content();
        else: ?>
                <p>Sorry that content is only available to Gold members, <a href="/membership">find
out more</a>.</p>
        <?php endif;
else:
        // Previous example continues...
```

This opens up endless possibilities for a members' site based on WordPress and is easily tailored to different use cases. If you're creating a membership system of this type, I suggest making sure to create member roles using custom roles and capabilities (covered earlier in the chapter) instead of modifying the default roles in WordPress.

Managing Users and User Data

The last thing to look at is how you can manage users on your WordPress sites them and the data you store for them programmatically. You've seen how to set up custom login pages. but you can also go as far as a full user section on the front end of the site. WordPress provides a lot of functions for you to be able to do all this from right inside your themes (or from a plugin), so making a members-only section with custom signup is relatively easy.

Creating Users

There are two ways to create users programmatically in WordPress: use either the wp_create_user() function or the wp_insert_user() function. The wp_create_user() function takes three arguments: the username, password, and e-mail of the user to be created; the wp_insert_user() function can take an array of all the values associated with a user in one go.

If you want to create a really quick signup form for your site users, you can use the wp_create_user() function to just get the username and e-mail of potential users and allow them to fill out further details when they have access to their profile in WordPress. If you prefer your signup process to take a lot of the users' information in one go, however, you can use the wp_insert_user() function to set up all the details at once, removing the need for users to access the WordPress admin to modify their profile.

Creating a User with wp_create_user()

First you'll take a look at the wp_create_user() function and set up a quick form on the front end of your site, which asks users to enter just their e-mail address. On submission, you'll create the user and e-mail them a generated password, using their e-mail address as the username. While asking a user to enter a username and password on registration is usually the norm and most people's preference (as surveyed on Twitter), I'll cover this method to show you some of the WordPress functions available. You'll look at how you can also deal with a user entering a username and password in the next example.

Let's look at how the wp_create_user() function works regarding parameters and their order. Remember that there are three separate parameters for this function:

```
wp_create_user( $username, $password, $email );
```

As you can see, just the three parameters are required for the function. The username and e-mail must be unique to WordPress, and the password can be passed as plain text because WordPress deals with the hashing and secure storage of the password for you. Notice that in the function you can't set a role for your user. The wp_create_user() function sets the user up with the default role from the WordPress settings, so make sure it is set to the user role you want your new users to have when using this function.

The next step is to set up your form for the user to sign up. You'll need only the e-mail address, so I'm using a single input field. (If you want to have an e-mail confirmation field, that's fine, too).

```
<form action="<?php the_permalink(); ?>" method="post">
        <label for="email-address">Enter your email address to register</label>
        <input type="email" name="email_address" id="email-address" placeholder="name@example.com"
required>

        <input type="submit" name="simple_registration" value="Register">
</form>
```

I'll quickly run through the way I set up the form. First, the action is to the current page, using the the_permalink() function inside the loop of the current page, with a POST method. Next is the your e-mail address field which is just a simple field, but the name I used uses an underline (_) as a separator. (This is generally personal preference, but it means that when I'm using PHP to process the form, the POST variables are already in a PHP style naming convention for me.) Finally, the submit button also has a name, so when I'm processing the form, I can see that I'm processing the correct one based on the presence of a unique name on the submit button.

With the form set up and on your page, you can now set up form processing. In this case, you'll do this from inside the functions.php file. (I've seen some people use the template file in which the page was accessed, but keeping everything in the functions file makes for much neater code.) Of course, this means you'll need to use a hook to get at the data before the page is generated again after the form submission. Here you use the 'template_redirect' hook because it's the last hook that gets called before the template is loaded. You can safely perform a page redirect from here when your form is processed because a PHP page redirect is possible as long as no HTML is output at the time.

```php
function prowordpress_process_simple_registration() {
        // Check that a POST request has been made
        // and that there is POST data
        // and the POST data contains the simple_registration field
        if( $_SERVER['REQUEST_METHOD'] === 'POST' && isset($_POST) && isset($_POST['simple_
registration']) ) {
                // Save the POST email value to a local variable
                $email = $_POST['email_address'];

                // Check if there is already a user with the email address or username already set up
                if( email_exists( $email ) || username_exists( $email ) ) {
                        // redirect to the same page with an error
                        wp_redirect( $_SERVER['REQUEST_URI'] . '?error=1' );
                        exit();
                } else {
                        // Generate a password for the user
                        $password = wp_generate_password( 8 );
                        // Create the user, returns either the User ID or error
                        $user = wp_create_user( $email, $password, $email );

                        // Test if there was an error when the user was created
                        if( is_wp_error($user) ) {
                                // redirect to the same page with an error
                                wp_redirect( $_SERVER['REQUEST_URI'] . '?error=1');
                                exit();
                        } else {
                                // Notify the new user and send them their password
                                wp_new_user_notification( $user, $password );
                        }
                }
        }
}

add_action('template_redirect', 'prowordpress_process_simple_registration');
```

Most of the function's actions can be described in the comments within the function but I'll describe the main process of what happens when you process the form data and create a new user. The first step is to check that you are actually getting a submission from your form. You first check the request method from the server (in this case, it is POST); then you check for the presence of the submit button named earlier in the form. When you know you have data coming from the correct form, you can start to process the new user.

WordPress has two functions available to check whether you can create a new user: `username_exists()` and `email_exists()`. They tell you whether there's already a user in the database with the same e-mail or username. Because you're using the e-mail address for both of these, you could test just one, but you should test both just in case. If either function returns true, you can then redirect back to your page, but add an `"error=1"` query string to the URL so you can show an error on the page for the user.

If the e-mail is unique for the user, you can safely create a new user account. The information needed for `wp_create_user` is e-mail, username, and password. So far, you have the username and e-mail because you're using the e-mail for both of them, so now you just need to create a password. Fortunately, WordPress has a function to do this, `wp_generate_password()`, which creates a random password to the number of characters specified and with a couple of optional settings such as `"use special characters"`. In the function, I specified an eight-character password with the default settings that get saved in a variable because you'll need to use it in the next couple of lines as well.

Finally, you can use the `wp_create_user()` function to create the new user account. The function either returns the ID of the user created or a `WP_Error` object if an error occurred, so the next step is to check the status of the return value using the `wp_is_error()` function. If there is an error, redirect back to the page you came from with the error in the query string; if the user creation was successful, all that's left is to send them a copy of the password they created. You can use the `wp_new_user_notification()` function, which takes the newly created user ID and their password.

This might not be the most popular way of setting up a new user; you didn't take much user information and didn't let users set up their own password (which, according to people on Twitter, is very much their preference). The `wp_create_user()` function is great when you need only a simple registration from your users, but for a more detailed registration process, use the `wp_insert_user()` function instead.

Creating a User with wp_insert_user()

The `wp_insert_user()` function allows you to set up much more than the standard data for the user, including everything from the first and last name, the user's WordPress "nickname," and even their "AIM" account details (if anyone actually uses that anymore). By default, anything you see in the WordPress user profile page can be set up using the `wp_insert_user()` function. Here's the full list:

- User ID: `ID`
- Password: `user_pass`
- Username: `user_login`
- Nicename: `user_nicename`
- Website: `user_url`
- Email: `user_email`
- Display name: `display_name`
- Nickname: `nickname`
- First name: `first_name`
- Last name: `last_name`
- Description: `description`
- Visual Editor: `rich_editing`

- Registered date: user_registered

- User role: role

- Jabber account: jabber

- AOL IM account: aim

- Yahoo IM account: yim

Included in this list is the user ID because wp_insert_user() can also be used to update a user if a there is a user ID passed in the array. I recommend that you use the wp_update_user() function for that purpose instead, for obvious reasons. I included all the keys for the values because you'll need to use them later in the array for the function.

When using the wp_insert_user() function, the process for setting up the user is similar to the wp_create_user() function, so you'll need a similar form setup and you'll do the processing in the functions.php file again. I won't show you the full form setup, I suggest that when creating the form you use the names of the values are needed for the array keys in the wp_insert_user() function to make processing the form a little easier. Here's an example:

```
<label for="email-address">Email address</label>
<input type="email" name="user_email" id="email-address" placeholder="name@example.com" required>

<label for="username">Username</label>
<input type="text" name="user_login" id="username" required>

<label for="firstname">First name</label>
<input type="text" name="first_name" id="firstname" required>
```

Set up as many or as few of the possible user settings as you like and then you can use the same function to process the user, no matter the number of fields you want to set.

You'll use a function similar to the one you used before with the wp_create_user() function. This time, you just need to set up the $userdata array for use in the function and notify the user as usual. Here's a look at the new function:

```
function prowordpress_process_full_registration() {

        if( $_SERVER['REQUEST_METHOD'] === 'POST' && isset($_POST) && isset($_POST['full_
registration']) ) {
                // Unset the submit button value from the postdata
                unset($_POST['full_registration']);

                $userdata = array();

                // Loop through the $_POST variable to create our $userdata array
                foreach($_POST as $key => $value) {
                        $userdata[ $key ] = $value;
                }

                if( email_exists( $userdata['user_email'] ) ) {
                        wp_redirect( $_SERVER['REQUEST_URI'] . '?error=1' );
                        exit();
                } elseif( username_exists( $userdata['user_login'] )) {
                        wp_redirect( $_SERVER['REQUEST_URI'] . '?error=2' );
                        exit();
                }
```

```
            else {
                    $user = wp_insert_user( $userdata );

                    if( is_wp_error($user) ) {
                            wp_redirect( $_SERVER['REQUEST_URI'] . '?error=3');
                            exit();
                    } else {
                            wp_new_user_notification( $user );
                    }
            }
        }
    }
}
add_action('template_redirect', 'prowordpress_process_full_registration');
```

Most of this process is very similar to the function you used before; there are just a few little changes to process the information into an array to use in the function instead. First, when you get into the function, you need to create the $userdata array from the POST values, which is really easy to do when you've named the inputs the same as the keys required for the $userdata array. The only thing to remember to do first is unset the POST variable for the submit input because it isn't needed in the array.

You still need to check whether a user with the same username or e-mail already exists on the site, but if you will allow the user to create their own username, it might be worth checking them separately. If either of the values exists, you redirect back to the form page again, but this time I set a different error code based on the error that occurred, so you can show different, more relevant error messages to the user.

Before you create your user, there's one point to note: in earlier versions of WordPress, the wp_insert_user() function didn't hash the user's password when setting up or updating a user. Since version 3.4.1, however, the function deals with the hashing of the user's password, so you don't have to worry about it in your user creation functions.

After the data is checked, you can create the user by passing your $userdata array to the wp_insert_user() function. If it returns an error, you can redirect to the registration page and show an error to your user. If it's successful, you can notify the user without passing the user's password to the wp_new_user_notification() function because the user set that password and doesn't need to have it sent.

With that, you now know both methods to create a user. The examples I used are just rough scenarios in which you could use either of the two functions to set up a new user. The function that you use will depend on how you want your site's user system to work and how much you need to know about your users, but there should be enough information for you to be able to set up any kind of system you require.

Updating and Deleting Users

Now you've seen how to create users, you can look at how to update or delete them once they're set up on the site. Not only does this include looking into the wp_update_user() and wp_delete_user() functions, but to also allow your users to update their details, you'll need to set up a profile page with a form where users can see all their information and make changes.

Setting Up a User Profile Page

The first step in allowing users to update their information is to create a profile page for them to view the information stored in WordPress. When you set this page up, you should show the form only to registered users. So when you set up your page template, check whether there is a current user logged in; if not, display the login form and a link to the registration page if they need to sign up to the site.

Here's the basic page template for the profile page:

```php
<?php
/**
 * Template Name: Profile page
 */
get_header(); ?>

        <div class="content">

        <h2>Your profile</h2>

        <?php if( is_user_logged_in() ): ?>

                <!-- User details form goes here -->

        <?php else: ?>
                <p>You need to be a registered member of the site to view your profile,
please either login below or <a href="/register">register here</a> to view your profile.</p>

                <?php
                $args = array(
                                'redirect' => home_url(),
                                'form_id'        => 'loginform-custom',
                                'id_username'    => 'user-login-custom',
                                'id_password'    => 'user-pass-custom',
                                'id_remember'    => 'rememberme-custom',
                                'id_submit'      => 'wp-submit-custom',
                        );
                wp_login_form( $args ); ?>

                <p><a class="forgot-pass-link" href="<?php echo wp_lostpassword_url(); ?>"
title="<?php _e('Forgotten your password?', 'prowordpress'); ?>"><?php _e('Forgotten your
password?', 'prowordpress'); ?></a></p>

        <?php endif; ?>
        </div>

<?php get_footer(); ?>
```

The form on this page is basically the same as the user registration form; depending on whether you limit the available fields upon registration and then open up new fields for users to set from their profile page.

Besides setting up the form, you need to get the current information you have for that user to display in the form. You can do with the wp_get_current_user() function, which returns a user object with all the details of the current user (every field available in the $userdata array discussed in the last section). With that user data, you can then populate the values of your inputs ready for the user to edit:

```php
<?php $userdata = wp_get_current_user(); ?>

<form action="<?php the_permalink(); ?>" method="post">
```

```
        <label for="email-address">Email address</label>
        <input type="email" name="user_email" id="email-address" value="<?php echo $userdata->user_
email; ?>" required>

        <label for="firstname">First name</label>
        <input type="text" name="first_name" id="firstname" value="<?php echo $userdata->first_name;
?>" required>

        <label for="lastname">Last name</label>
        <input type="text" name="last_name" id="lastnam" value="<?php echo $userdata->last_name; ?>"
required>

        <label for="website">Website</label>
        <input type="url" name="user_url" id="website" value="<?php echo $userdata->user_url; ?>">

        <input type="submit" name="update_user_profile" value="Update">
</form>
```

That's just a small example of a form with a few of the fields; you can set up the rest in a similar fashion. Again I just changed the name of the submit button, so you can look out for this in your processing function.

Processing the User Update with wp_update_user

Processing user updates is fairly similar to setting up a user with the wp_insert_user function. The only thing you need to do is to make sure that there is a user ID as part of the $userdata array you pass to the function so that the correct user is updated. You can set the user ID up as a hidden field in the form using the value from the $userdata object as before; or when processing the data for the update function, you can use the get_current_user_id() to return just the user ID, which is the method used here:

```
function prowordpress_process_update_user() {

        if( $_SERVER['REQUEST_METHOD'] === 'POST' && isset($_POST) && isset($_POST['update_user_
profile']) ) {
                // Unset the submit button value from the postdata
                unset($_POST['update_user_profile']);

                $user_id = get_current_user_id();

                $userdata = array(
                                'user_id' => $user_id,
                        );

                // Loop through the $_POST variable to create our $userdata array
                foreach($_POST as $key => $value) {
                        $userdata[ $key ] = $value;
                }

                wp_update_user( $userdata );
```

```
                    wp_redirect( $_SERVER['REQUEST_URI'] . '?update=1');
                    exit();
            }
    }
    add_action('template_redirect', 'prowordpress_process_update_user');
```

The function is pretty similar to the wp_insert_user() function from before, but a lot of the checks and redirects for errors have been removed. Before you build the $userdata array using the $_POST array, initialize the array with the user ID value that you got with the get_current_user_id() function and then run the function. The wp_update_user() function returns the user ID when it's complete; you can be fairly sure that unless something has gone drastically wrong with the get_current_user_id() function, the function should be successful because the only error it returns is when an invalid user ID is passed.

Updating the User Password

While the wp_update_user() function can be used to update the user's password as well, it might be the case that you want to set up a separate form to perform that action for usability or any other reason. Instead of creating a separate form and using the wp_update_user() function again, WordPress provides a separate function that can be used to update a user's password: wp_set_password().

You can set up a simple form that takes three inputs (the user's current password and then two fields for the new password) to be able to be sure that the user has set the correct password. Then you'll process the update with the wp_set_password() function. Here's the simple form:

```
<h3>Update your password</h3>

<form action="<?php the_permalink(); ?>" method="post">

        <label for="current">Current password</label>
        <input type="password" name="old_passwd" id="current" required>

        <label for="new-passwd">New password</label>
        <input type="password" name="new_passwd" id="new-passwd" required>

        <label for="confirm-passwd">Repeat password</label>
        <input type="password" name="new_passwd_confirm" id="confirm-passwd" required>

        <input type="submit" name="update_user_password" value="Update password">
</form>
```

Nothing much more to be said about the form—just the three password inputs for the current and new password along with a uniquely named submit button so you can process the correct form. The function to update the users password looks like this:

```
function prowordpress_update_user_pass() {

        if( $_SERVER['REQUEST_METHOD'] === 'POST' && isset($_POST) && isset($_POST['update_user_
password']) ) {
                $user = get_current_user();
```

```
                    if( $user && ! wp_check_password( $_POST['old_passwd'], $user->user_pass, $user->ID) ) {
                            wp_redirect( $_SERVER['REQUEST_URI'] . '?error=1');
                            exit();
                    } else {
                            if( $_POST['new_passwd'] && $_POST['new_passwd_confirm'] &&
$_POST['new_passwd'] === $_POST['new_passwd_confirm'] ) {
                                    wp_set_password( $_POST['new_passwd'], $user->ID );

                                    wp_redirect( $_SERVER['REQUEST_URI'] . '?update=1');
                                    exit();
                            } else {
                                    wp_redirect( $_SERVER['REQUEST_URI'] . '?error=2');
                                    exit();
                            }
                    }
            }
}
add_action('template_redirect', 'prowordpress_update_user_pass');
```

There are quite a few checks here just to make sure the data being submitted is correct. You could replace the check of the new password with some client-side validation, but I recommend always doing server-side validation as well (just in case), especially with something as important as the user's password.

There's a nice WordPress function to help here, too—the wp_check_password() function, which checks the current user password against the one stored in the database. The last check is to make sure there has been a new password entered and that both the new password and password confirm fields match. If any of these checks fails, do a redirect back to the page with an error as before.

If all the checks pass, you can safely update the user's password with the wp_set_password() function, which takes the new password and the user's ID for the user you want to update. The password is then hashed by the function before being stored in the database again.

Deleting a User with wp_delete_user

Besides creating and updating users, you can also delete users programmatically by using the wp_delete_user() function. This function takes the ID of the user you want to delete and an optional second parameter of a user ID to reassign any posts to that the user has created. If you don't pass the second parameter, the posts will be deleted along with the user.

To delete a user, you probably want to offer this as a button on the profile page, or you could create a small form with just a submit button so that you could handle the form as done with the others. That's the method I'll be using here; the form looks like this:

```
<h3>Close account</h3>
<form action="<?php the_permalink(); ?>" method="post">
        <label>To delete your account permanently please click the button below.</label>
        <input type="submit" name="delete_user" value="Delete account">
</form>
```

It's probably worth adding a JavaScript confirm dialog when this form submits, just in case the user clicked the button accidentally. But to process the form, you can use a function like this:

```
function prowordpress_delete_user() {
```

```
        if( $_SERVER['REQUEST_METHOD'] === 'POST' && isset($_POST) &&
isset($_POST['delete_user']) ) {
                $user_id = get_current_user_id();

                wp_delete_user( $user_id );

                wp_redirect( home_url( '/user-deleted') );
                exit();
        }
}
add_action('template_redirect', 'prowordpress_delete_user');
```

Probably the simplest of all the functions so far: you get the current user's ID and pass it to the `wp_delete_user()` function. In this case, you don't pass a second parameter to the function, so all posts by the user will be deleted; otherwise, you can add the user ID "1" to reassign all the deleted users' posts to the admin user.

Creating Custom User Data

The last part of managing WordPress user data I'll discuss is how to add custom metadata to your users. For instance, by default the user profile has fields for the user's Yammer, AOL, and Yahoo accounts, but nothing for either Facebook or Twitter. To manage custom metadata for users, WordPress provides you with a few functions that act similarly to the post meta functions you used in Chapter 5:

- `add_user_meta()`
- `update_user_meta()`
- `get_user_meta()`
- `delete_user_meta()`

Each function works with the user ID and a custom key that are similar to the post ID and key used by the post meta functions.

Adding Custom Meta

Although you can add new custom meta at any time, a good example of when to add it is when you create a new user from the register page you set earlier in the chapter. You could add some custom fields to the form and add this data to the user upon creation fairly easily with the `add_user_meta()` function. I won't go through updating the form because it should be fairly straightforward; instead, you'll go straight to the function used to add a user and update it to deal with the new user meta.

I'll just show you the updates because most of the function stays the same and it's quite long. First, update the processing of the $userdata array from the $_POST array:

```
$userdata = array();
$usermeta = array();

// Loop through the $_POST variable to create our $userdata array
foreach($_POST as $key => $value) {
        if( 'ptd_twitter_username' === $key || 'ptd_facebook_username' === $key ) {
                $usermeta[ $key ] = $value;
        } else {
                $userdata[ $key ] = $value;
        }
}
```

Here you just created a new array called $usermeta. In the foreach loop, check the key of the current array item; if it is one of the new two fields, add it to the $usermeta array instead of the $userdata array. If you had a longer list of meta fields to add to the user, you could create an array of keys and test the current key with the array_key_exists() PHP function to keep the if statement from getting too long.

Once you have two arrays of user data, you can create the user as usual with wp_insert_user and then add this code after the user has been created to add the user meta:

```
foreach( $usermeta as $meta_key => $meta_value ) {
        add_user_meta( $user, $meta_key, $meta_value, true );
}
```

This loop takes each of the custom meta values stored earlier in the $usermeta array and the $user variable, which stores the new user ID returned from the wp_insert_user() function. You can then pass all these values into the add_user_meta() function along with the final parameter true to add the meta field as a unique field for the user (as the add_post_meta() function does).

Retrieving and Updating Custom Meta

Now that you can add custom metadata to your users, you need to get the data back out to display it on their user profile pages and then update the data when users update their profile. You can display the data on your user's profile page by using the get_user_meta() function. This function requires the user ID, metadata key, and an optional Boolean parameter of whether to get a single record or retrieve all records (similar to the way the get_post_meta() function works):

```
<label for="facebook">Facebook</label>
<input type="text" name="ptd_facebook_username" id="facebook" value="<?php echo
get_user_meta( $userdata->ID, 'ptd_facebook_username', true ); ?>">

<label for="twitter">Twitter</label>
<input type="text" name="ptd_twitter_username" id="twitter" value="<?php echo
get_user_meta( $userdata->ID, 'ptd_twitter_username', true ); ?>">
```

Once the information displays on the user's profile page, make sure you update the information in the profile update function. Again, because the function is quite large, here are the bits you need to change to accommodate the new custom meta:

```
$usermeta = array();
$current_usermeta = array();

// Loop through the $_POST variable to create our $userdata array
foreach($_POST as $key => $value) {
        if( 'ptd_twitter_username' === $key || 'ptd_facebook_username' === $key ) {
                $usermeta[ $key ] = $value;
                $current_usermeta[ $key ] = get_user_meta( $user_id, $key, true );
        } else {
                $userdata[ $key ] = $value;
        }
}
```

First, get the metadata and store it in a separate array, as you did with the function when you first added the user meta. However, this time get the current user meta value as well by using get_user_meta(). After you have the data, you can perform the update function (this code is very similar to the code you used in Chapter 5 to update the post meta):

```
$user = wp_update_user( $userdata );

foreach( $usermeta as $meta_key => $meta_value ) {
        if ( $meta_value && '' == $current_usermeta[$key] ) {
                add_user_meta( $user_id, $meta_key, $meta_value, true );
        } elseif ( $meta_value && $meta_value != $current_usermeta[$key] ) {
                update_user_meta( $user_id, $meta_key, $meta_value, $current_usermeta[$key]);
        } elseif ( '' == $meta_value && $current_value ) {
                delete_user_meta( $user_id, $meta_key, $current_usermeta[$key] );
        }
}
```

After the user has been updated, you then go through the process of updating the user metadata. Here you're looping through each value, checking it against the previous value to see whether you need to create a new meta entry with the add_user_meta() function if no value was previously set. Or you can update the value if the new value is different from the current value in the database. Or if the value is empty, you can delete the meta field from the database entirely by using the delete_user_meta() function.

Finally a quick note on the delete_user_meta() function, during the update function is possibly the only place you'll need to use this function to delete the user metadata. You might think it would also be needed during the process of deleting a user to make sure any user metadata isn't left in the database for deleted users, but WordPress takes care of that in the wp_delete_user function for you—handy!

Displaying Custom User Meta in the WordPress Admin

Now that you have a good idea of how the user meta system works and can be used in your custom templates, you can add it in one more place: the WordPress admin. Unfortunately, when you create a new piece of user metadata, WordPress doesn't automatically add the information to the user profile screens in the admin, so a couple of functions have to be created to do this. It's probably best whenever you're using custom metadata to add the fields so they can be viewed in the WordPress admin system as well as on the site because it allows admin users and those with edit users' capabilities to view the data added-as well as the user if you're giving them access to the default WordPress admin.

To add the custom data to the WordPress user profile page takes one function; then you need to set up a second function to update the data if anything is changed through the admin page. First up is displaying the user data on the profile page.

When displaying the user data in WordPress, you'll hook into the function that displays the user's profile and add in your data with custom HTML. At the moment, this is the only way to add the user information to the page, although maybe there will be a method written into WordPress to do this in the future. For now, take a look at the source code of the user profile page and find the form in which the user information is displayed to see what HTML you'll be generating. This is a snippet of the HTML that displays the contact inputs in the user profile shown in Figure 8-7:

```
<h3>Contact Info</h3>

<table class="form-table">
<tr>
        <th><label for="email">E-mail <span class="description">(required)</span></label></th>
        <td><input type="text" name="email" id="email" value="onishiweb@gmail.com"
class="regular-text" /></td>
</tr>
```

```
<tr>
        <th><label for="url">Website</label></th>
        <td><input type="text" name="url" id="url" value="" class="regular-text code" /></td>
</tr>
```

Contact Info

E-mail *(required)*

Website

AIM

Yahoo IM

Jabber / Google Talk

About Yourself

Figure 8-7. *Contact info section of the user profile*

It is all in a table with a <h3> header at the top of the section; below is the function you'll use to add your data so that it looks the same as the default fields in WordPress do:

```
function prowordpress_show_user_meta_in_admin( $user ) {
?>

        <h3>User social media</h3>

        <table class="form-table">

                <tr>
                        <th><label for="facebook">Facebook</label></th>

                        <td>
                                <input type="text" name="ptd_facebook_username" id="facebook"
value="<?php echo esc_attr( get_user_meta( $user->ID, 'ptd_facebook_username', true ) ); ?>"
class="regular-text"><br />
                                <span class="description">Please enter your Facebook username.</span>
                        </td>
                </tr>
                <tr>
                        <th><label for="twitter">Twitter username</label></th>

                        <td>
                                <input type="text" name="ptd_twitter_username" id="twitter"
value="<?php echo esc_attr( get_user_meta( $user->ID, 'ptd_twitter_username', true ); ?>"
class="regular-text"><br />
```

```
                                    <span class="description">Please enter your Twitter username.</span>
                    </td>
                </tr>

        </table>
<?php
}

add_action( 'show_user_profile', 'prowordpress_show_user_meta_in_admin' );
add_action( 'edit_user_profile', 'prowordpress_show_user_meta_in_admin' );
```

The markup looks just like the default table markup in WordPress and includes custom fields using the get_ user_meta() function. You also run the output of your metadata through another function before it is entered into the values of the page, which is used to escape the various HTML entities.

Notice that the function needs to be called on two hooks for it to work correctly. The first hook, 'show_user_ profile', is run near the end of the user profile fields for the signed-in users when viewing their own profile page. The second 'edit_user_profile' hook is run in the same place, but when viewing a profile not of the signed-in user's. You can see the result of your function in Figure 8-8.

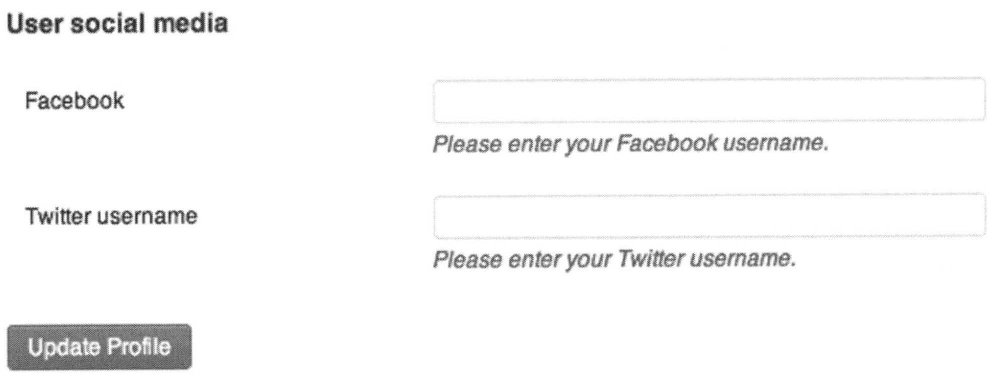

User social media

Facebook

Please enter your Facebook username.

Twitter username

Please enter your Twitter username.

Update Profile

Figure 8-8. *User profile page with two custom meta fields*

Next, you need to write a function to save the user information when you update any of the meta from the WordPress page. Again, this function works in pretty much the same way as when you code the form processing function from the theme templates, but you need to run this on a couple of hooks for the user profile once again:

```
function prowordpress_save_user_meta_in_admin( $user_id ) {

        if ( !current_user_can( 'edit_user', $user_id ) )
                return false;

        // Store all the custom user meta in an array
        $usermeta = array(
                        'ptd_facebook_username' => $_POST['ptd_facebook_username'],
                        'ptd_twitter_username'  => $_POST['ptd_twitter_username'],
                );
```

```
        // Loop through and process the updated meta values
        foreach( $usermeta as $meta_key => $meta_value ) {
                $current_value = get_user_meta( $user_id, $meta_key, true );

                if ( $meta_value && '' == $current_value ) {
                        add_user_meta( $user_id, $meta_key, $meta_value, true );
                } elseif ( $meta_value && $meta_value != $current_value ) {
                        update_user_meta( $user_id, $meta_key, $meta_value, $current_value);
                } elseif ( '' == $meta_value && $current_value ) {
                        delete_post_meta( $user_id, $meta_key, $current_value );
                }
        }
}

add_action( 'personal_options_update', 'prowordpress_save_user_meta_in_admin' );
add_action( 'edit_user_profile_update', 'prowordpress_save_user_meta_in_admin' );
```

This is very similar code to what you've seen, but instead of building up an array of current values with the POST data, you just query for it inside the foreach loop. Make sure to check the current user's capabilities before you update anything, so test for the 'edit_user' capability. If the user doesn't have the capability, simply return false. Note that you need to call this function on two different hooks: one for when users are updating their own profile and when they're updating another profile.

Displaying Custom Metadata for Post Author's

The final topic of custom user metadata is how to display the information you store for users when displaying their author information on a post page. Along with functions such as the_author() and the_author_link() to display information about the author of a current post, there's also a function called the_author_meta() as well as the return equivalent, called get_the_author_meta(). This function allows you to display any of the user meta stored in WordPress for the author of the current post, including custom meta you may have added.

To display any of the custom post meta you added to user author profiles for their posts, you can use this:

```
<?php the_author_meta('ptd_twitter_username'); ?>
```

To show the user metadata you stored for the custom field, use 'ptd_twitter_username'.

Building Your Theme, Part 7

In this chapter, you learned a lot about how the user system works and you saw some great ways to add a custom user interface for site members. Because this is the last part of the building your theme sections in the book, instead of taking you through features to add to your restaurant theme and showing you how to code them, I'll give you a list of features to create. Based on what you've learned so far in this chapter, you should be able to set up these pages without much help.

The main feature you'll add to the site is a member's area for the restaurant staff. The features needed for the member's area should be as follows:

- A custom role for staff members that allows them to
  - View their profile
  - Update their profile

- Access members-only areas of the site

- Edit posts and post to the site blog

- A custom login page for staff members

- A custom profile page for each staff member

- Custom metadata for each staff member for their Twitter and Facebook accounts

- Make the blog on the site a staff members-only area requiring them to log in to view the blog

All the code is available in the accompanying code for the book but give it a try before looking at the code used. You can use the part-7 SCSS file to style the pages and forms for you so, you don't have to worry about that.

Summary

This chapter discussed the user system in WordPress. I've covered everything from how the WordPress roles and capabilities system works through to how to create custom functions for users. By now, you should understand the following:

- How user roles work and how to create custom roles

- How capabilities control everything a user can do in WordPress and how to set up your own

- How to customize the WordPress login screen and create a completely custom login page of your own

- How to create, edit, and delete users; and extend the amount of data you can store about each user

You should now be able to put together a fairly comprehensive member system for any web site.

CHAPTER 9

Plugins: When the Time Is Right

If you've ever used WordPress before (and probably even if you haven't), you should be aware of WordPress plugins. Plugins are tools that allow users to extend the functionality of WordPress in a variety of ways, from adding SEO management features to managing spam commenters, and even turning WordPress into a fully capable e-commerce store. The plugin API was introduced way back in version 1.2 (Mingus), just 1 year into the development of WordPress in 2004. Since then, more than 25,000 plugins have been uploaded to the plugin directory at `http://wordpress.org/plugins/` (see Figure 9-1) with more than 450 million downloads.

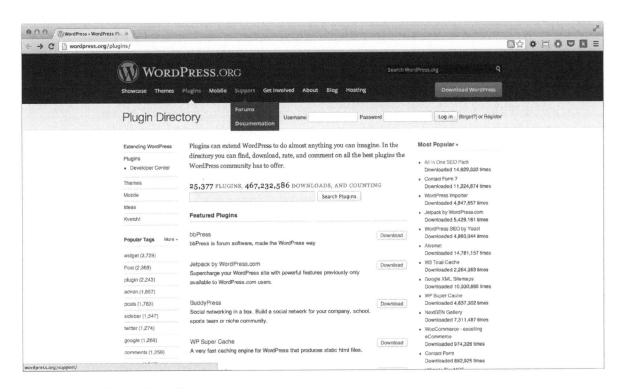

Figure 9-1. *WordPress plugin directory*

Plugins can be both a good thing and a bad thing; I've had some good experiences with plugins and I've had some bad ones. And sometimes I've even used a plugin when it's entirely unnecessary. I'll cover plugins in detail through this chapter, and in Chapter 13 you'll see how to develop your own plugins, looking at the key concepts and how to go about implementing them. However, before you get to that bit, in this chapter I'll discuss why and when you should consider using plugins, and give you some reasons why sometimes it's a solution you should definitely avoid.

Later on in this chapter, you'll take a look at some of the most useful plugins out there for both the sites that you manage and those that you can suggest to your users when setting up a premium theme.

Plugins Bring Power, but Can Also Facilitate Evil

Biggest lesson learnt from this current project: WordPress plugins are largely evil, and should not be relied on for core functionality

—Alex Jegtnes, from Twitter

I'll grant you that the preceding title and quote are a bit of an exaggeration about plugins in general, but they're a good example of how plugins can make you feel at times. Plugins can be extremely powerful and can bring great functionality to your WordPress site, and at the same time save you a ton of time not having to develop it yourself. However, sometimes when using plugins you can end up feeling exactly like Alex, frustrated and feeling like you've wasted a heck of a lot of time trying to get a plugin to work the way you expected it to.

Now before the many thousands of plugin developers out there lynch me, I should probably clarify a few things. The fact that a lot of the time WordPress is often used as self-hosted software where the configuration of everyone's servers can be vastly different, and your plugin is still supposed to work on each and every one of them. Then it's also deemed that it should be compatible in any number of combinations with any of the other 25,000+ plugins, not to mention the thousands of different themes out there, too! It's a heck of a task and one that plugin developers take on knowingly and with plenty of determination, so they deserve sack loads of credit for doing so.

Keeping that in mind, when I'm talking about the issues I've had with plugins and any bad experiences I may reference throughout the course of this chapter, I'm not targeting plugin developers specifically. I'm talking about bad experiences that can always happen when you allow control of code and functionality to go to a third party. In these circumstances, you need to be very cautious, and I'll talk about how to go about ensuring that you do as much as possible to avoid any horror moments when working with plugins and to keep plugins in mind when developing your themes.

WordPress plugins can be amazing; they can bring excellent functionality to your WordPress site with relative ease from the users'/developers' point of view. You're going to look at some examples of plugins like this later in the chapter, but first I'll list some reasons why you should always think first before installing the first plugin you see with a good title, or even before you even consider looking for a plugin in the first place. In the first half of this chapter, you'll learn when it's the right time to use plugins.

Is a Plugin the Right Option?

There are some simple things to keep in mind when considering whether to use a plugin. They aren't strict rules by any means; if there's a situation where you feel a plugin will do the job best, go for it; and likewise if you think it would be better coded by yourself or into the theme, that's fine, too. The aim is to make you stop and think for a moment before you download 20 plugins to do really simple things on your site that you could do yourself or make distributing your theme harder than it should be.

Create a Plugin or Use the Theme Functions File?

Should you add code to your theme functions file or should you create a plugin for the functionality instead? The things to consider are these:

- Is the functionality core to the theme your building only?
- Is the functionality reusable across many sites or themes?
- Will the functionality be needed across a site and not just for a theme?
- Are you planning to distribute your theme or use it for a site only you will manage?

The main goal of these questions is to get you to focus on the locality of the functionality you're writing. If you'll write something that could work in general across a multitude of sites and is not completely reliant on the functionality you're writing into your theme, it's worth building a plugin. If the functionality will work only with your theme specifically, put it in the theme functions file because it will invariably be useless if activated on any other site.

If you're writing a bit of functionality that is completely stand alone and could possibly work across a number of web sites with a little bit of coding into the theme (i.e., running a function to output the functionality), write it into a plugin. You can then reuse it across many sites you build (if needed) and even add it to the plugin repository to give the functionality to other users.

When writing some functionality, consider whether the feature you're writing will be used across the site you're working on constantly, even if you change the theme. Something like adding Google analytics to your site should be added with a plugin so that functionality is always there, no matter which theme you're using.

Likewise with custom post types, taxonomies, and custom fields—if you'll always have the same content types in your site, but potentially use a different theme when redesigning, you should keep them in a plugin. However, if you're going to retain the same theme throughout the life of the site and not use the content types anywhere else, there's no need to extract that functionality into a plugin.

You also need to consider how you'll distribute your theme. If you're planning on putting a theme you create into the themes repository or selling it as a premium theme (more on that in Chapter 11), you'll need to think about how the functionality you'll write will be distributed with it. If the functionality is fit for a plugin in almost every other way, think about making your theme function without the functionality so you can ship the two things separately. Or consider that the theme will need to be shipped with the functionality if that is one of the core selling points.

Obviously, it may not be as cut and dried as the scenarios mentioned previously; sometimes it will really be a coin flip as to the best method for creating the functionality. Hopefully, the preceding questions will make it a lot clearer and you'll be able to make the right choice.

Avoid Rewriting WordPress Core Functionality

There are a few plugins that I've seen recommended and at times have even used myself that seem relatively unnecessary because they simply reproduce core WordPress functionality. These examples are for functionality that as a theme developer you should be able to use without the aid of a plugin. Plugins, or even code you're writing for the theme specifically, should never need to replicate the functionality already provided in WordPress. Adding a plugin for something you can quickly and easily reproduce in your own code is a waste of time and adds something else to the site that either you or the user has to manage.

Two examples of this are a picture gallery and pagination (or specifically displaying page numbering).

Search the WordPress plugin repository; you'll find a whole host of plugins based around image galleries and slide shows. This functionality is actually easily built in to WordPress with the use of the Gallery shortcode (http://wp-themes-book.com/09001). I won't go into how to use the shortcode here, but knowing that one is built in to the WordPress core files should be enough to prompt you to think a little before installing one of the image gallery plugins.

The second example is pagination. Again, take a look at the repository and simply with a search for **"pagination"** you will find more than 61 pages of plugins dedicated to adding pagination to your WordPress themes (see Figure 9-2). When you consider that pagination in WordPress is a built in feature of WordPress and requires only a single function call to display page numbers, it is quite frankly ridiculous!

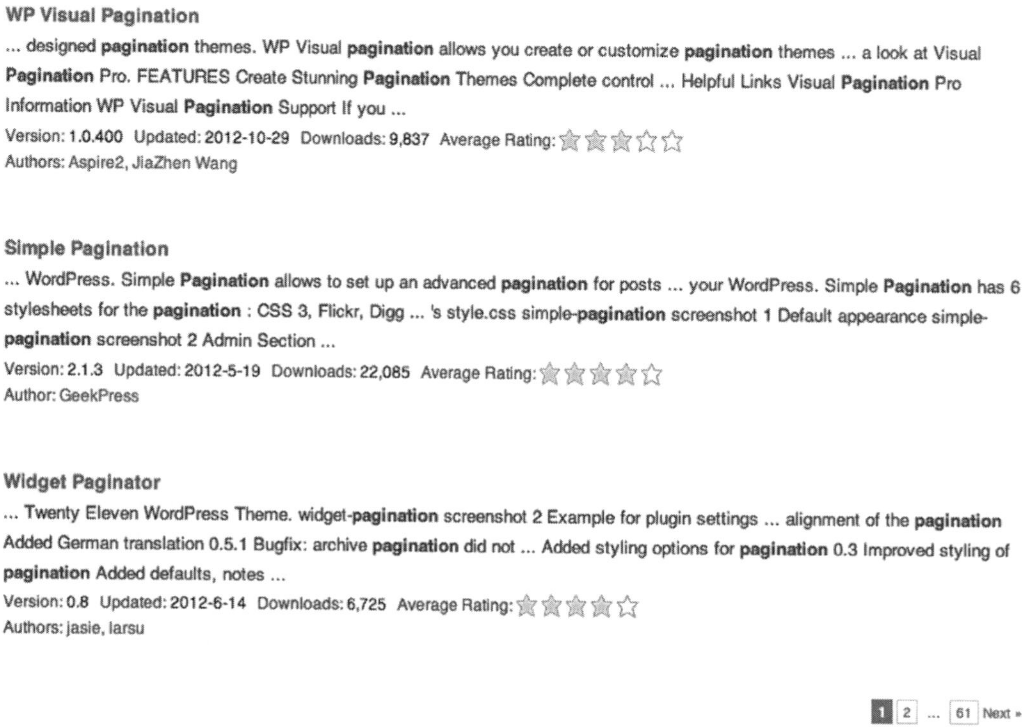

WP Visual Pagination

... designed **pagination** themes. WP Visual **pagination** allows you create or customize **pagination** themes ... a look at Visual **Pagination** Pro. FEATURES Create Stunning **Pagination** Themes Complete control ... Helpful Links Visual **Pagination** Pro Information WP Visual **Pagination** Support If you ...

Version: 1.0.400 Updated: 2012-10-29 Downloads: 9,837 Average Rating: ☆☆☆☆☆
Authors: Aspire2, JiaZhen Wang

Simple Pagination

... WordPress. Simple **Pagination** allows to set up an advanced **pagination** for posts ... your WordPress. Simple **Pagination** has 6 stylesheets for the **pagination** : CSS 3, Flickr, Digg ... 's style.css simple-**pagination** screenshot 1 Default appearance simple-**pagination** screenshot 2 Admin Section ...

Version: 2.1.3 Updated: 2012-5-19 Downloads: 22,085 Average Rating: ☆☆☆☆☆
Author: GeekPress

Widget Paginator

... Twenty Eleven WordPress Theme. widget-**pagination** screenshot 2 Example for plugin settings ... alignment of the **pagination** Added German translation 0.5.1 Bugfix: archive **pagination** did not ... Added styling options for **pagination** 0.3 Improved styling of **pagination** Added defaults, notes ...

Version: 0.8 Updated: 2012-6-14 Downloads: 6,725 Average Rating: ☆☆☆☆☆
Authors: jasie, larsu

1 2 ... 61 Next »

Figure 9-2. A search for "pagination" plugins returns 61 pages of results

In my early days of theme development, I used the plugin WP Pagenavi on a number of sites, but I realized this was a waste of effort considering that I could set it up in a matter of seconds using the paginate_links() function. (You'll take a quick look at this function and how to set it up shortly because there are a couple of options you need to set.) I will say that WP Pagenavi is a very good plugin; it allows you to set up all the different text options (see Figure 9-3) for page navigation links and comes with some default styles for you to apply. However, as a theme developer, you should easily be able to set things up, and unless you want to allow access to how the pagination is displayed and formatted in your theme, there's no need to ask users to download a plugin to manage such a simple bit of functionality.

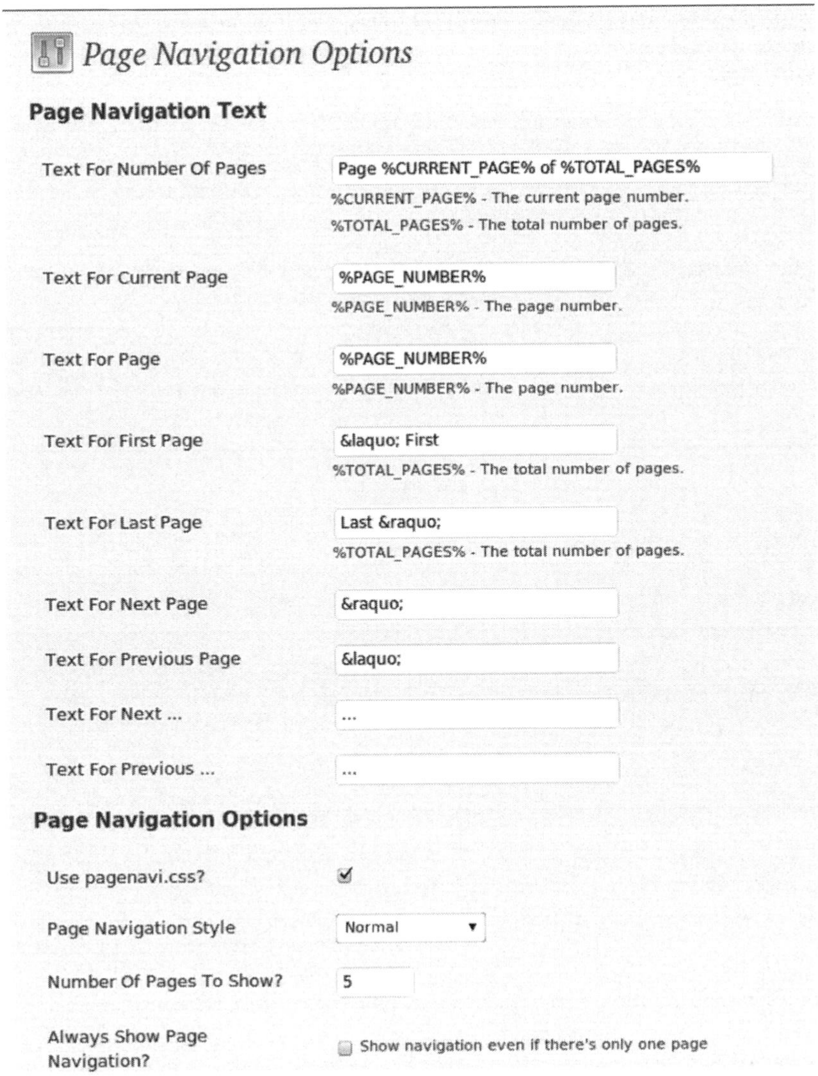

⟦⟧ Page Navigation Options

Page Navigation Text

Text For Number Of Pages	`Page %CURRENT_PAGE% of %TOTAL_PAGES%`
	%CURRENT_PAGE% - The current page number.
	%TOTAL_PAGES% - The total number of pages.
Text For Current Page	`%PAGE_NUMBER%`
	%PAGE_NUMBER% - The page number.
Text For Page	`%PAGE_NUMBER%`
	%PAGE_NUMBER% - The page number.
Text For First Page	`&laquo; First`
	%TOTAL_PAGES% - The total number of pages.
Text For Last Page	`Last &raquo;`
	%TOTAL_PAGES% - The total number of pages.
Text For Next Page	`&raquo;`
Text For Previous Page	`&laquo;`
Text For Next …	`…`
Text For Previous …	`…`

Page Navigation Options

Use pagenavi.css?	☑
Page Navigation Style	Normal ▼
Number Of Pages To Show?	5
Always Show Page Navigation?	☐ Show navigation even if there's only one page

Figure 9-3. *The WP Pagenavi options page*

Now take a quick look at just how easy it is to set up page navigation using built-in WordPress functionality. Here's the main function that deals with page numbers, `paginate_links`:

```
global $wp_query;

$big = 999999999; // need an unlikely integer

echo paginate_links( array(
        'base' => str_replace( $big, '%#%', esc_url( get_pagenum_link( $big ) ) ),
        'format' => '/page/%#%',
        'current' => max( 1, get_query_var('paged') ),
        'total' => $wp_query->max_num_pages,
```

```
        'prev_next'     => True,
        'prev_text'     => __('« Newer posts'),
        'next_text'     => __('Older posts »'),
) );
```

This short amount of code is all you need to create a simple list of pages as well as a next and previous link on either side of the page numbers (see Figure 9-4). A couple of options in there might turn your head, however, so let's have a quick look at them individually.

This post has far too many categories.

Read more »

« Newer posts 1 2 3 Older posts »

Blogroll

Figure 9-4. *Pagination links displayed using with the paginate_links function*

```
'base' => str_replace( $big, '%#%', esc_url( get_pagenum_link( $big ) ) ),
```

The base options looks a little complicated, but it's simply a way of setting up a base URL to be used to create the pagination links. The reason for the $big variable is to create a page URL containing a ridiculous and unlikely page number and then replace it with the formatting string. So if you were creating the pagination links on the posts page, the base URL would look like this:

```
http://website.com/posts/page/%#%/
```

The next option is the format of the page number URL you'll be creating. The end of the preceding URL looks exactly like the format option in the function.

Finally, this function gets the current page number to go into the current option of the function:

```
'current' => max( 1, get_query_var('paged') ),
```

This function uses the PHP max function to return the larger number of either 1 or the result of the get_query_var function that is getting the current 'paged' value. The reason for the max function is that when you're on the first page of anything in WordPress, the 'paged' var returns 0, and you need to pass in a 1 if you're on the first page of the pagination.

There are also a few other options you can set, such as 'show_all', 'end_size', and 'mid_size', which allow you to customize the way page numbers are displayed. (Find out more about them in the Codex (http://wp-themes-book.com/09002).

When it comes to styling the pagination, WordPress gives you some good, clean HTML and some useful classes to work with, so adding custom styles shouldn't be a problem:

```
<p class="post-page-navigation">
      <a class="prev page-numbers" href="http://prowordpress.dev/posts/page/1/">« Newer posts</a>
      <a class='page-numbers' href='http://prowordpress.dev/posts/page/1/'>1</a>
      <span class='page-numbers current'>2</span>
      <a class='page-numbers' href='http://prowordpress.dev/posts/page/3/'>3</a>
      <a class="next page-numbers" href="http://prowordpress.dev/posts/page/3/">Older posts »</a>
</p>
```

The point of taking a look at this pagination example is to show you that it really is that easy to add functionality instead of instantly reaching for plugins to do it. If you reduce the number of plugins that are installed needlessly for WordPress sites, you're making it easier to manage your site and for your users if they are in control of the site admin.

I'm not saying all plugins are unnecessary, however, or that you should code everything by hand. Obviously, it's quite possible that some plugins have more options and more functionality than the simple WordPress gallery shortcode or the pagination function. That's perfectly fine and a good reason to opt for a plugin ahead of coding the functionality yourself.

The aim of this chapter and these examples is to prevent you from having plugins be the first solution you look for. You should realize that sometimes it is easier to spend 5 minutes coding the functionality instead of spending 10 or 20 minutes searching the plugin repository for a plugin, working out how it works, customizing the settings, and then adding it to your theme.

Try to Avoid Plugins Forming the Core Functionality of Your Theme

This will be a bit of a controversial topic once again (I find that most conversations about WordPress plugins are), but I want to give you my thoughts nonetheless. Although plugins can be brilliant and can extend WordPress beyond its core functionality, keep in mind that using a plugin (especially one written by another developer) can be a risk. If you then use that plugin to form the core functionality of your site, that risk becomes even greater.

A good example of a situation where this applies is when you attempt to use WordPress as an e-commerce CMS. In this case, there is no built-in functionality to do it, so you'll need a plugin. There are a lot of options out there (47 pages in the repository, to be exact), including some plugins by extremely reputable companies (see Figure 9-5). However, in my opinion, using a plugin to provide the core functionality of the site you're building can be risky.

Figure 9-5. WooCommerce, an e-commerce plugin from WooThemes

As you saw in Alex's tweet earlier in the chapter, it can be quite frustrating working with a plugin to do something core to your web site. More specifically, when you work with a plugin, you rely on the plugin developer to do the following:

- Ensure the security of the code/functionality

- Provide clean and well-structured HTML

- Provide support

- Provide good documentation

- Keep regular updates to coincide with core WordPress updates

- Work with your theme

For me, these are big enough reasons not to want to rely on a plugin to form a core part of the functionality for the web site I'm building. Going back to the example of an e-commerce store, although plenty of options exist for plugins that can do this with your WordPress theme, I would consider not using WordPress at all for that type of site and look for another system entirely. An application such as Open Cart, Shopify, Big Cartel, or Tictail are better set up to provide you with a dedicated solution for e-commerce than adding a plugin to your WordPress site.

Managing Your Theme or Selling/Distributing?

I touched on this a little earlier when talking about whether to add functionality to the theme functions file or use a plugin. It's important to consider whether to use a plugin when writing your own functionality, but when considering using a third-party plugin you also need to consider how your theme will be used.

The majority of WordPress sites I've worked on so far have been for clients or for myself; I rarely spend time building a theme to be added to the themes directory or sold as a premium theme for others. So I've spent a lot of time managing my clients' sites and often being the only administrator for a web site. This means that there are moments when it makes a lot more sense for me to use a plugin to provide me as the site administrator with much easier management options. Things like creating custom fields for the user to add new content to the site can actually be made a lot easier when using a plugin (mostly because I can do all the admin for the custom fields and then set up the theme templates to work with them).

You don't often have this choice when distributing your themes. In that situation, a plugin used to manage custom fields for the site would require the user to edit a template file to specify where they're displayed (unless, of course, the plugin has a shortcode to allow them to be added to the main content). When distributing your themes, think about what your users might do or want to do with that theme. It's important to ensure when you're coding your theme to make it as compatible as possible with the way plugins usually work (which is discussed in detail next).

When choosing whether to use a plugin, think about the circumstances in which the theme will be used and how a plugin can fit in with that scenario. Plugins can be extremely useful and provide fantastic functionality to extend your WordPress site, but just be sure that when you're using them you've taken into account all the options first to ensure that using them won't come back to haunt you.

Making Your Theme Compatible with Plugins

When developing your theme and thinking about plugins, it's also important to ensure that your theme is set up so it's more likely to be compatible with as many plugins as possible. It's always likely that there's one plugin out there that breaks when used with your theme, but what you want to aim for is making sure it is the plugin's fault, not that of your theme. You've seen these techniques many times in the book so far, so as long as you're following along and coding your themes thoughtfully, you should have no problem when it comes to plugin compatibility.

Here are the main things you should be aware of when building your themes for solid plugin compatibility:

- **Naming conventions:** I talked about these conventions throughout the book when discussing writing custom functions and content types. Plugins are no different and should always stick to strict naming conventions, but if you're not coding them you have no control over whether they do. The best route to take is to make sure your functions and content types are always prefixed and namespaced correctly within your theme.

- **Hooks:** As mentioned in Chapter 6, four main hooks need to appear in your templates. The `wp_head` and `wp_footer` hooks are well known; `comment_form` is another hook that WordPress states should be in your themes, but in fairness this comes down to whether you have comments functionality in your theme. The last hook is `wp_meta`, an often-forgotten hook that for plugin compatibility should always be in your themes. The usual place it is expected to appear is at the bottom of sidebar templates.

- **Dynamic sidebars:** When building your themes, especially those for distribution or sale, remember to set your themes up to work with dynamic sidebars and widgets. Plugins can provide content in a variety of ways, and if one of them is through a widget, you need to ensure that users have access to that functionality when needed.

These are pretty sensible and common-sense actions to consider when you think about what has been covered in the book so far. If you write good themes, you'll have no problems with your theme being compatible with the majority of WordPress plugins.

How to Select a Plugin

If you're still certain that you'll require a plugin for your site, you should know how to choose the right one. With more than 25,000 plugins to choose from and sometimes tens of pages of search results based on a single feature, it's worth having a series of steps to take to choose the right plugin for the job.

A Note on Testing

I want to mention how to test a plugin after you choose it. If it can be helped, *never install a plugin on a live site before you have tested it.*

In this relatively modern era of web development, most people are working with development sites of all the production sites they maintain, so testing shouldn't be a problem. You can install the plugin on your development version of the site and test that it works and is compatible with all the other plugins you're already using on the site.

Plugins are notorious for being incompatible with each other because although there are coding standards in WordPress, every developer has his or her style and ways of working that inevitably lead to conflicts from time to time. To avoid catastrophe, always make sure you test everything where possible before adding a plugin to a site. With that word of warning out of the way, now you can look at how to choose the right plugin.

WordPress Plugin Directory

The best place to start looking for plugins is to go directly to the plugin directory. All plugins hosted in the WordPress plugin directory have gone through a manual testing process performed by a trusted member of the WordPress community, ensuring that they work correctly and adhere to certain standards.

One exception to the rule, however, is premium plugins. Premium plugins can't be hosted in the plugin directory, so if a premium plugin looks like the best option for the functionality you require, make sure that you go through the following steps to make sure you're not throwing away your money. You can also see whether they have a trial or lite version available in the plugin repository, which could be a good sign that at least some of the plugin has been tested by the community.

Another positive that comes from using the plugin directory is that all plugins in the directory are hosted by WordPress, meaning that you can easily search and install the plugin straight from your site's admin interface.

Check the Details

On the right side of the details page (see Figure 9-6) for all plugins in the directory is a list of information relating to the plugin. Using this information is a great way to check out useful details about the plugin. In Figure 9-6, you see the directory page for the Jetpack plugin. Down the right side there's a ton of information about its current status.

Figure 9-6. *Jetpack plugin by Automattic plugin page*

Always check the details of the plugin stored in that sidebar. Listed at the top is information on things like the minimum requirement for your WordPress version, as well as the highest version of WordPress the plugin is compatible with. There's also information on when the plugin was last updated, so you can tell whether the plugin has been kept up to date with any regularity. The number of downloads comes in useful because generally the more people downloading and using the plugin hopefully directly correspond to how well the plugin works.

Ratings

The rating system below the plugin info is also a great place to find out more about the plugin you're thinking of using. Pay attention to the number of reviews submitted as well as the overall rating; sometimes a low number of reviews might skew the results slightly. And always check out the reviews yourself; don't just take the star ratings as gospel. Sometimes people will rate a plugin extremely low based on something small because critical reviews are hard to give without some form of experiential bias. One of the one-star reviews I read recently stated that it was a great plugin and worked brilliantly until they installed another plugin, so they rated it one star. In that case, it's quite likely it was the fault of the other plugin that caused the poor performance of the rated plugin, therefore possibly an unjustified one-star rating.

Authors

At the bottom of Figure 9-6 you can see the top of the author section in the sidebar. A good idea is to look into the author's current plugin work and see how regularly they participate in the community, read the profile updates, and see what other contributions they make to the plugins directory. If an author is regularly active, it should give you some confidence that your questions will get answered and any bugs will be found and dealt with quickly and with little fuss.

Compatibility

Last in the sidebar for each plugin is a compatibility chart. It can be a bit hit-and-miss at times because it relies on user submissions about the plugin. There are a lot of different combinations to compare, especially with plugins that regularly get updated. Take the Jetpack plugin for example. It updates pretty regularly; at the time of writing it was updated just over a month ago.

In Figure 9-7 you can see that the status of the compatibility chart is Not Enough Data, which is based on nearly 40 submissions. This can at times be a great place to check and see which versions the plugin is compatible with, but again you need to take a lot more into consideration because the data might not be quite enough to give you a correct reading.

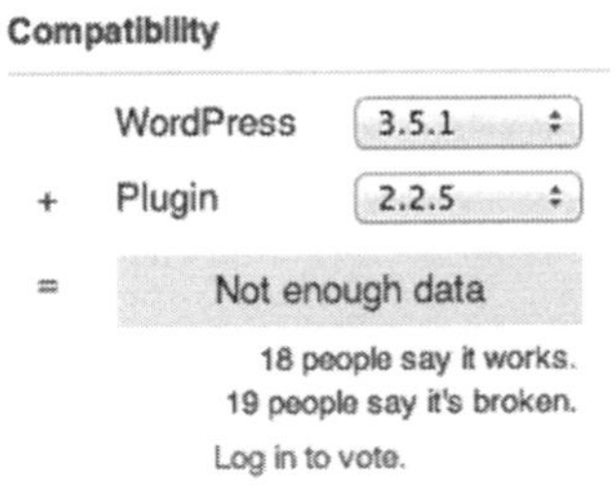

Compatibility

	WordPress	3.5.1 ⬍
+	Plugin	2.2.5 ⬍
=	Not enough data	

18 people say it works.
19 people say it's broken.

Log in to vote.

Figure 9-7. Jetpack plugin compatibility display

Read Everything

The sidebar is a treasure trove of information, including a variety of sources about the plugin, author-submitted requirements, information about the last update of the plugin, user-submitted reviews, and compatibility stats. But the plugin pages in the directory also come with a whole series of pages written by the developers about the plugin.

You can see the different pages in a series of tabs at the top of the page in Figure 9-6. There's everything from the changelog of updates to FAQs and screenshots of the plugin's functionality or output. It's worth reading everything to ensure that you know what the plugin will do and what the latest changes were. You can also check what's regularly asked about the plugin so you know ahead of time before those questions arise for your situation.

Be aware that not all plugins have these areas in the directory. It might be worth checking either a plugin's web site or, if there's hardly any information on the page or no web site to find, you might be better off looking for another plugin.

Support and Documentation

Another way to check the plugin you're thinking of using is to access the support forum and also look for some documentation that should help you find out more about using the plugin.

The support forum (see Figure 9-8) is another part of the WordPress.org site that hosts an area for people to submit support requests for plugins hosted in the directory. You can see how many support requests for the plugin have been submitted and how many have been dealt with, either by the community or by the plugin developers.

| Description | Installation | FAQ | Screenshots | Changelog | Stats | Support | Reviews | Developers |

Topic	Posts	Last Poster	Freshness
Official Jetpack Support Resources	1	Ryan Markel	
Jetpack comments - Error: your Twitter login has expired	4	manadeprived	28 minutes
Jetpack showing error upon activation	1	jasjotbains	30 minutes
Jetpack "like button" issue	5	sricejr	1 hour
Carousel broken in my theme	1	purestblue	2 hours
include link but NOT content in notifications	1	richokun	3 hours
Twitter comments 'Login expired'	1	houseofstrauss	6 hours
Useless tags before and after gallery	3	siebje	7 hours
How to restore Edit CSS if Jetpack plugin was deleted?	1	7billionbuddhas	10 hours
[resolved] How to style comments h3	31	JamesDoylePhoto	15 hours
Thumbnails are acting weird.	18	esmi	18 hours
Jetpack Stats	1	burnettsboards	19 hours
[resolved] Exlude pages from Top Posts Widget and change the thumbnails	6	Richard Archambault	20 hours

Figure 9-8. Plugin support forum

You can also find details of the current support stats on the plugin page (see Figure 9-9). With those stats, it's easy to see whether a plugin has good support from the community or developers. But it's also useful to check out the support requests individually to see who's responding to the requests and how they're dealing with the issues.

Support

276 of 484 support threads in the
last two months have been
resolved.

Got something to say? Need help?

Figure 9-9. *Support stats on the plugin page*

Documentation is another good thing to check when searching for a plugin. Sometimes this can be found on the plugin's directory page; other times it's best to look for a web site for the plugin where the developer might have a section for developer documentation. Depending on the plugin's functionality, for me documentation can be a make-or-break feature when I choose a plugin. If it's a complex plugin providing a lot of functionality, I will generally look for a plugin with the best documentation to ensure that if I get stuck I know exactly where to look.

As an example, the Advanced Custom Fields (ACF) plugin has a large section of its site dedicated to developer docs (see Figure 9-10) and is a great help for developers looking to use the plugin. Developer documentation also shows the amount of commitment an author has for the plugin—if he or she has taken the time to write a whole series of documentation, you can be relatively sure that a lot of effort was put into crafting the plugin.

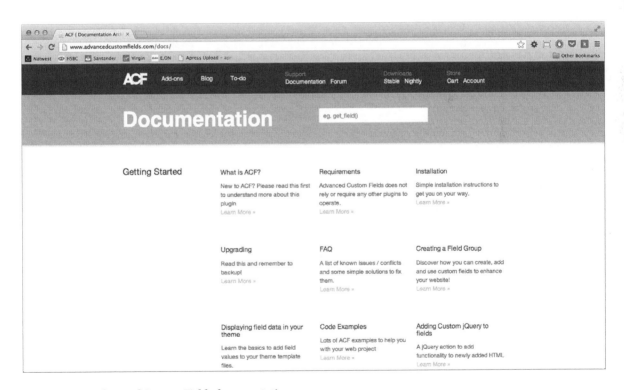

Figure 9-10. *Advanced Custom Fields documentation page*

Compatibility with Other Plugins

When you think you're close to choosing the plugin you want to use, make sure to test it alongside all the other plugins on your site. Add the new plugin and activate it with the rest of your plugins; then make sure you go through your site checking that everything is still working as it should be.

It's really worth doing this on a development site so you can activate the debug settings and give your theme a thorough test. If something does end up breaking, double-check the debug settings and then try deactivating all your other plugins and reactivating them one at a time. Doing this should help identify which plugins are conflicting, and then you can either fix it yourself or submit a support request to the developer.

Look at the Competition

Finally, if you find a plugin that you think will do the job, check out its competition. Search the forums and discussion boards to see what people are saying about that plugin and whether there are any alternative recommendations you see appearing often.

If you do find an alternative plugin, try both by installing them on your site and activating them one at a time. You'll see which one has the better admin interface and which outputs the nicest HTML; after all, the standard of the plugin code should be the best you can find. Also work out whether you can override any default styling the plugin adds to the elements it outputs. If you struggle to do this with one, try the other and see if it works better.

Another thing to try when you have two similar plugins is a site load test. Activate each one individually and test your site performance with each one and neither one activated. See what the performance times are like and choose the one that doesn't affect your site as much.

After considering these different factors, you should have enough information to choose the right plugin for your site. Just remember to keep checking often for updates and the latest discussions about the plugins you chose to be aware of latest developments or new features coming up—as well as any possible development issue with the latest releases of WordPress or other plugins you use.

Useful Plugins

To complete this chapter, you'll take a look at some of the more useful plugins with features that you are likely not to want to code into your theme or those that will help you manage your site if you're doing so for a client. By no means is this a list of plugins you should instantly go out and download for every site; each site is different and should be treated as such. They are merely a series of plugins I've either found useful myself or that have come highly recommended and provide great functionality.

As with all plugins, you sometimes have to weigh the good with the bad. Some of the plugins I list in the following sections will have some drawbacks, but I'll cover them also and tell you how you can get around them.

Site Management Plugins

The first few plugins you'll look at help with site management, allowing you to set things up for your clients or the site's content authors so they can have a few nice features that you don't have to worry about coding.

Advanced Custom Fields (ACF)

The ACF plugin is one I've been using for years. It always comes in handy when you set up sites for your clients. As you can guess from the name, ACF is used to manage your custom fields, but it also offers a huge amount of options for customization.

Besides allowing you to set up custom fields for posts and pages, you can go into minute detail about where your custom fields will appear, from the assignment of a certain taxonomy term all the way down to a custom page template. The customization doesn't just stop at field placement, though. ACF allows you to choose from more than 20 custom field types, including file or image fields and even jQuery fields such as a date or color picker.

Adding ACF to a web site you manage means you can extend the functionality of the site to hold any number of different content options without having to worry about coding them. For me, this is a real time saver because some of the field types that the plugin offers would be complex to code and would take more time than is justifiable when there is a plugin offering a solution.

ACF also comes with a host of simple functions to output the field data attached to each post. ACF still stores the data in the postmeta table in the database like standard custom fields, but instead of just using the normal `get_post_meta` function, it gives you its own set of functions (such as `the_field` and `get_field`) that work exactly as you would expect similarly named WordPress functions to do. It also works inside the loop so you have to pass only the name of the custom field you want to return.

ACF is also very well documented. As shown in Figure 9-10, the author, Elliot Condon, has gone to great lengths to make not only the plugin great to use but also easy for people to read about how best to use it.

When looking for a plugin for your theme, be on the lookout for efforts like these. People who put in this kind of effort are sure to be creating a superb plugin that will make managing your site much easier.

Akismet

This plugin should need no introduction, but I'll talk about it briefly. If you've ever installed WordPress and taken a look at the plugins screen, there are two plugins already installed by default whenever you set up a new WordPress site; one of them is Akismet (see Figure 9-11). Akismet is a plugin that helps save you from all the spam commenters on the Web (if you run a blog or a site with comments turned on, you know how prevalent they are).

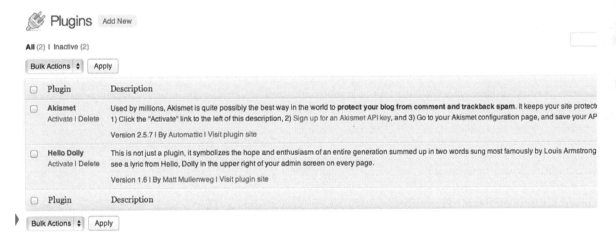

Figure 9-11. *Plugins page of a fresh WordPress install*

Akismet takes a lot of the pain out of managing your comments, and if you have a site with lots of traffic and commenters, you should be using it. Akismet uses the combined power of all the blogs it monitors to help detect spam commenters. By running every comment posted to your site through a series of tests on its servers, Akismet determines whether the comments are genuine or spam.

Akismet is now run by Automattic, the development team behind WordPress.com, which means you'll need a WordPress.com account to access the Akismet site. To use Akismet, you need an API key. For personal blogs, the key is available for free; there is monthly subscription fee of $5 per single site license and $50 for multiple low traffic site access for commercial clients. Anything higher, you need to speak to the Akismet team to work out a fee.

Once you have your API key, setting up Akismet is simply a case of plugging the API key in the Akismet settings; then you're free to go into your WordPress discussion settings (see Figure 9-12) and turn off the settings that hold a comment for moderation because you can be confident that Akismet won't let any spam comments through.

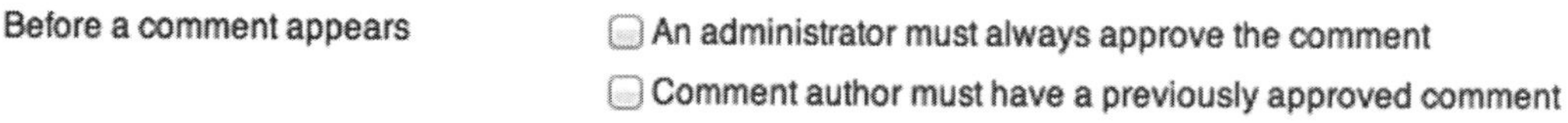

Before a comment appears

☐ An administrator must always approve the comment

☐ Comment author must have a previously approved comment

Figure 9-12. *With Akismet you can safely uncheck the discussion settings for holding back comments for moderation*

WordPress Multilingual (WPML)

If you want to create a multilingual web site, I highly recommend the WPML plugin (see Figure 9-13). Although it is a premium plugin (costing either $29 for limited features or $79 for the fully featured plugin), it is worth every penny because the plugin offers ways of seamlessly handling site translations.

Figure 9-13. *WordPress multilingual plugin web site*

I can attest that building a multilingual site can be quite challenging because I have dealt with a few in the past year or so. The latest project I've been working on has had the WPML plugin integrated from the start and it's been a revelation. In the past, I used WordPress multisite to manage different translations of the same site, but it is quite cumbersome to manage and requires content added to one site to be added to all sites separately. With WPML, the translations are all handled within the one installation of WordPress.

WPML handles not only the translations of core WordPress text but also text added in your theme or plugins as long as they use the correct WordPress translation functions:

```
__('This text can be translated by WPML', 'prowordpress');
```

Besides managing different menus for different languages on the site using the WordPress menus functionality, WPML enables you to set up the way your theme allows access to different language versions of the site—using the same domain, subdomains, or a different domain altogether. As with any good plugin, the site also offers detailed documentation to help you get your site set up and running with the functionality the plugin offers.

Form Management Plugins

I find plugins to add forms to a site to be a mix of extremely useful and extremely frustrating. Forms in HTML can be quite complex, and there are always debates about how they should be marked up and styled. It's a tricky subject. Creating a form that handles e-mail and data storage is another problem to tackle. So getting a form plugin to do the work for you can be both incredibly useful and sometimes frustrating. In this section, I'll discuss two of the better plugins I've used over time, showing you their strengths and some of their weaknesses to look out for.

Contact Form 7

Contact Form 7 is *the* most downloaded plugin in the WordPress plugin directory with more than 11 million downloads (see Figure 9-14). With those credentials, you can imagine that it might be a good choice for a form plugin.

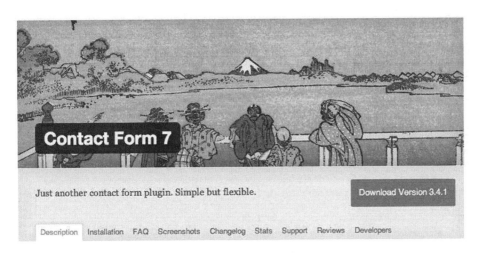

Figure 9-14. Contact Form 7 plugin page

One of the main reasons I like Contact Form 7 is that it allows me to mark up the forms I create the way I want them (see Figure 9-15). With this functionality, you can easily set out your forms and customize the styling for the way you want them to appear. The form fields generated by the plugin are well built, including a set of useful classes for styling purposes as well as aria roles for accessibility.

Figure 9-15. Contact Form 7 configuration page

Contact Form 7 also enables you to add forms straight to pages via a shortcode. Unfortunately, this is the only method to add forms to your site's pages, but you can still do so programmatically in your theme templates via the do_shortcode function if you need to.

The plugin is also kept pretty well up to date, although at present the details page shows that the minimum version nearly matches the current version of WordPress. This could either mean that Contact Form 7 added in new functionality to go with a recent update to WordPress or is offering full support of the plugin only for the current version of WordPress.

There are a couple of drawbacks I've found with this plugin, however. The form always submits via Ajax, with no ability to switch it off. Although most probably don't find it an issue, but I like to have the option. Although there is documentation for the plugin, it's relatively limiting. There are many FAQs, but the answers are very specific and don't give much wider detail. Also looking at the support for the plugin, there are currently only 178 out of 524 support threads resolved, which in some cases might be quite a concern.

Overall, though, for a simple form plugin that gives you the level of control over the code output to your theme, Contact Form 7 is a good solution.

The next plugin offers a lot more detailed functionality, but with a little expense.

Gravity Forms

Gravity Forms is a complete and complex form management plugin (see Figure 9-16). I include it because it really does bundle a whole lot of functionality into quite a nice little package. There's a variety of pricing tiers that start at $39, so you can choose the best solution for the site you're building. Even the base package is a good place to start.

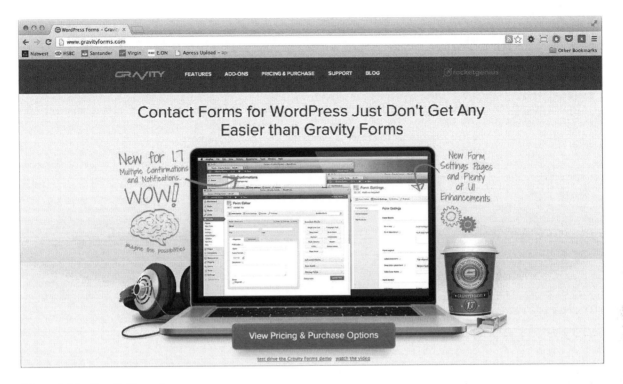

Figure 9-16. *Gravity Forms home page*

I've used Gravity Forms on a number of sites. It has allowed me to create a variety of different functionality, from a simple contact form through to creating user-generated content on the site using the feature that allows me to save submissions to a selected post type. There is also support for a myriad of field types, including the latest HTML5 form fields, and makes it easy to build forms with a nice drag-and-drop interface. There is support for paged forms and limiting entries; and it includes a whole host of predefined content for standard drop-down lists such as age, country, or state.

However, there are a couple of negatives to be aware of. Although the forms that Gravity Forms creates can be very advanced, the generated HTML is far from pretty. With an abundance of div and span elements cluttering the markup, it's not the best choice if you're really concerned about how good the site looks when you view source. Add the mess of CSS you have to create when styling the forms, the plugin can become quite a pain.

Overall the plugin is very good and can bring a heck of a lot of advanced functionality to your site in its use of forms. It's worth considering if you need such functionality.

The last thing to mention is the Gravity Forms documentation. You expect a premium plugin to have relatively good documentation; it's something that should definitely help sell the product and allow developers to work with the plugin more easily. Gravity Forms is relatively good for this, even if the docs can be a little hard to navigate at times. The documentation shows a load of plugin hooks for you to use that allow you to customize the plugin even more and add custom functionality. I used them a couple of times and it's great to have these capabilities at your fingertips.

SEO Plugins

The best reason to use a plugin is for help with your site's SEO. It's definitely not something you want to be spending time coding into your theme files, and it is functionality that should be kept on a site when changing themes. This is why you'll get more than a thousand results when you search the plugin directory for "SEO", and why the three plugins discussed here all appear in the top 10 most popular plugins across the plugin directory.

All in One SEO Pack

The third most popular plugin in the plugin directory, the All in One SEO pack, is probably one of the first choices for an SEO plugin to help manage a site. With all the usual functionality for the site in general, such as setting keywords and custom page title layouts, it comes with single page/post optimization as well. The plugin supports Google Analytics and Webmaster tools, which is very handy because you won't need to get a specific plugin for them.

The All in One SEO pack also comes with fantastic help text integrated into the plugin (see the large question mark next to each setting in Figure 9-17). This is a great little extra because even if you are managing the site, you'll probably not deal with the content on a day-to-day basis, good help text can really aid authors when creating their content.

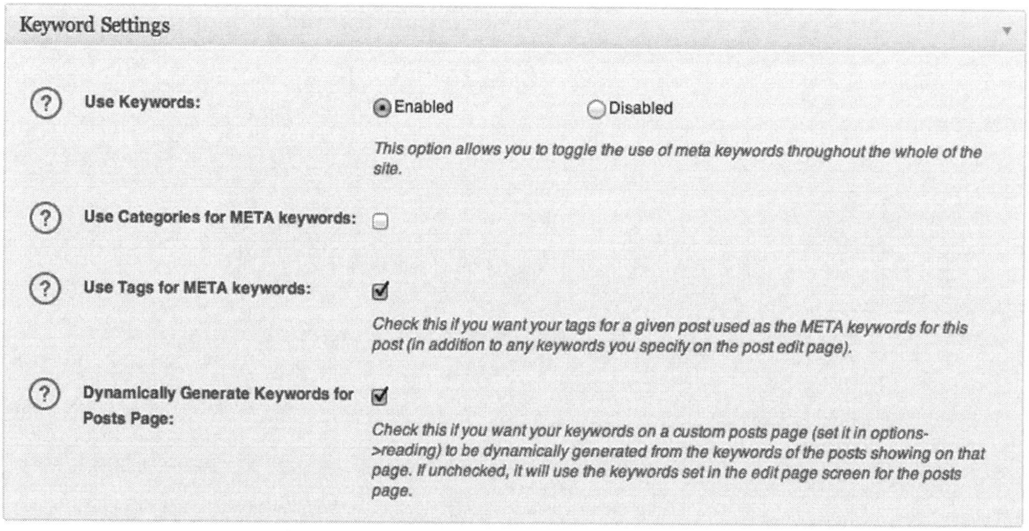

Figure 9-17. *All in One SEO settings with help text*

There's also a premium version of the plugin if you require the extra functionality. The plugin developer, Michael Torbert, is a very active WordPress developer who often writes about the latest WordPress developments on his web site. It's a good sign to see plugin or theme developers publishing often on their sites because they're keeping up to date with the state of the service and are likely to be around if and when any of their plugins require support.

WordPress SEO by Yoast

Another SEO plugin, WordPress SEO by Yoast (see Figure 9-18) also makes it into the top 10 most downloaded plugins. However, the difference with the Yoast plugin is that it hosts a lot more functionality relating to SEO than a more straightforward plugin like the one previously discussed.

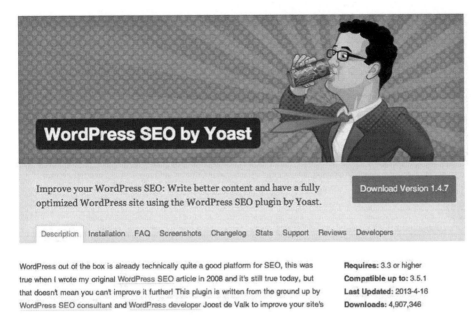

Figure 9-18. *WordPress SEO plugin by Yoast in the plugin directory*

The Yoast plugin includes settings not just for standard title and metadata across the site but also for specific post types, taxonomies, and even author page settings. This enables you to fully customize the SEO of your site. There are also settings for how your site integrates with social media, such as adding Facebook open graph data and settings for Twitter cards.

Along with the plethora of available options, you can also see from the plugin directory page that the Yoast developer (Joost de Valk) currently has 39 plugins to his name already, and the Yoast web site (http://yoast.com) is known for plenty of articles and tutorials on WordPress and SEO, so there's a good reason for the plugin's popularity.

However, notice the number of unresolved support requests for the plugin; currently only 30 of a whopping 442 support threads have been resolved. There could be many reasons for this, but it's always worth looking into just to put your mind at ease. The positive thing is that there's enough data based on the current version of the plugin and version of WordPress to give a positive compatibility rating for the plugin, another area you should be aware of.

Google XML Sitemaps

The last of the SEO plugins is the Google XML sitemaps plugin, which is a simple plugin used to generate the XML sitemap for your site to help Google index your web site. The Yoast SEO plugin has the functionality for doing this already built in, but the All in One SEO plugin is still waiting to add that feature, so it would be good when used in conjunction with a plugin that lacks the functionality.

There are loads of options included on the plugin's single settings page, so you can customize what gets included in the sitemap that's generated, and also the plugin submits any changes when you generate a new sitemap to Google for you.

Be aware that this is a function that's good for a single piece of functionality. Unlike the Yoast SEO plugin, it's possible that a plugin like this is more focused on the single task that it's looking to fulfill and will be better set to perform that functionality than a plugin that is trying too hard to do too much. Some plugins try to solve all the problems related to running a site, whereas others are more focused, such as the Google XML sitemaps plugin. By using plugins with small areas of functionality, you reduce the risk of using a plugin to do a lot of things. If it fails at any point, you could lose a whole load of work and functionality because you trusted one plugin too much.

Extra Feature Plugins

The last two plugins I'll cover add a little extra functionality to your sites. The first is the fantastic Jetpack by Automattic that brings a lot of the powerful add-ons for `WordPress.com` sites to hosted WordPress sites. The second is a plugin a lot of developers might find useful: the Markdown on Save Improved plugin that allows authors to write content in the Markdown syntax, which is popular with many developers.

Jetpack by `WordPress.com`

This plugin brings a lot of the functionality found in `WordPress.com` sites over to self-hosted sites on WordPress. Everything from adding simple contact forms, embedded content shortcodes, a complete mobile theme, infinite scroll, and even a JSON API for your site can be done using the Jetpack plugin (see Figure 9-19).

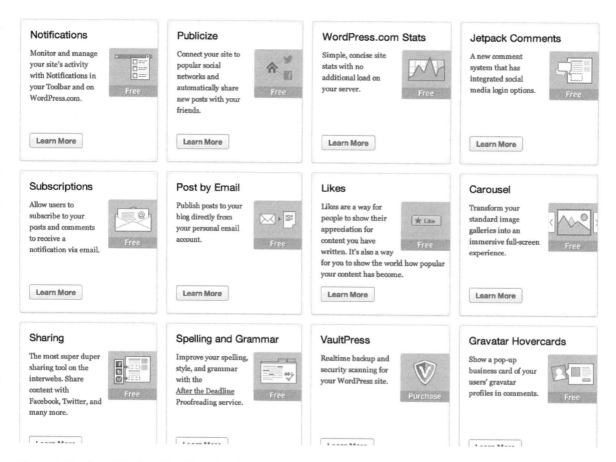

Figure 9-19. *Part of the long list of functionality provided by Jetpack*

Although I talked about using a single plugin for multiple functionalities possibly being the wrong choice, there's always one exception to the rule. In this case, the plugin is a culmination of a lot of features available on WordPress.com that are used a lot there already. And the plugin was written by a reputable set of developers, so there are a couple of good reasons to trust this plugin. I suggest, however, that if you use Jetpack, ensure that you're using it for more than one of the included features. Even with a very well-written plugin by trusted developers, installing a plugin with 25 features only to use one or two is not worth it for the amount you'll end up bloating your site.

Markdown on Save Improved

This is a little bonus plugin recommendation for all developers who are reading this book, who also write a little themselves. The Markdown on Save Improved plugin allows you to write your content in the markdown format and converts it to HTML when outputting it to the front end of the site.

I use Markdown a lot when writing and find it a lot easier to write than worrying about HTML all the time. It's especially a lot better than using the WordPress WYSIWYG editor to format content. The plugin even allows you to switch between using Markdown on specific posts and even to convert your content from HTML to Markdown.

Summary

This chapter discussed WordPress plugins—why they can be both a good and a bad part of WordPress web sites. You learned what you should consider first when thinking about using a plugin and then what to do when selecting a plugin.

You put that information into practice by looking at several useful plugins that fit the necessary criteria, learning what they're useful for, and understanding why some of them are among the most-downloaded plugins in the WordPress plugin directory.

Later on in Chapter 13 you will also be taking a look at how to develop your own plugin.

CHAPTER 10

■ ■ ■

Security and Performance

It's time to take a short break from learning about all the cool features and fancy functionality you can add to your WordPress themes and actually look at some important things you should know when developing sites with WordPress. Although WordPress has been built with performance in mind and takes security very seriously, there's still the need for theme developers to make sure that they take care in the themes they develop for the platform.

In this chapter, you'll learn how to make sure that the themes you develop are as secure as possible and that you take the necessary precautions when writing custom features and functionality. As a WordPress themes developer, you'll probably be installing WordPress sites, so I'll also cover security tips for WordPress as a contact management system (CMS) and how best to manage your WordPress installations.

Another big factor when building any web site is performance. Later in the chapter, you'll take a look at the best ways to increase performance in both WordPress and your themes, from practices like caching and serving images from a static domain, to techniques you might not necessarily think of, such as database and plugin maintenance.

Security

You'll start by taking a look at security in themes and in WordPress in general. Although WordPress is a very secure system, you need to be aware of certain things when writing custom functionality and features for your themes, as well as things you should be aware of when setting up a WordPress site of any kind.

Security is something to take seriously, no matter what site you're building or maintaining, but along with the upsides of the popularity of WordPress comes one major downside: it is now an even bigger target for hackers. Earlier this year, in fact, there was a major Botnet attack focusing on WordPress sites that gained a lot of interest from the WordPress community. Fortunately, though, because of the popularity of WordPress, the community identified the threat quickly, and there were numerous posts written with advice on how to stay secure.

Backing Up WordPress

Before you dive in to learning about methods to improve security on your sites, remember to keep a solid backup of your WordPress site, including core files, asset files, and the database. It is said that "an ounce of prevention is worth a pound of cure," but it's always good to have the peace of mind of having something to fall back on in an emergency. If your site is hacked or things go wrong, having an up-to-date backup ensures that you can get the site back up and running in no time—without losing too much data.

When backing up your site, keep regular backups of a couple of core elements; other parts of your WordPress install require only keeping a note of. The core elements you should always keep a regular backup of are these:

- Database
- Theme(s)
- Uploads directory

Although you can also keep a regular backup of the plugins directory to make sure that you have a copy of all the plugins your site has been using, it is not as important because plugins are easily downloaded again from the repository. As long as you have a list of the plugins you use on the site, restoring plugins is fairly simple. If you want to include the plugins directory in your backup, the easiest way to back up your files is to keep a regular backup of the entire wp-content directory.

■ **Note** Although you can keep a manual list of plugins you use on each site, remember that the WordPress database for each site has a list of all activated plugins. As long as you keep the database backed up safely, you'll always have a list of the activated plugins for each site; the database entry storing this information is in the wp_options table called active_plugins. The data is stored as a serialized array, but you should be able to pick out the plugin names quite easily or use an "unserialize" web site to see the full array of information.

Besides what you keep backed up, there are also multiple ways to perform backups of your site. I'll discuss three methods here; the method you use on your sites is up to you.

Using Manual Backups

The first method you'll look at is backing up your site manually without the aid of any systems or software. Backing up your site manually is simply a case of keeping regular copies of your main site files and then regularly downloading a backup of your database.

How you host and work on your site will determine how you back up your site files. A lot of my sites are set up and developed using Git, so the site files are mostly all backed up for me in the main Git repository and in any location that has a copy of the repo. Keeping your site in some kind of version control is good practice, not only for development of the site in general but also for easily keeping backups. I recommend that you keep your remote repository stored on a separate server from your production code. Many services allow you to do this, including Github (Git); BitBucket (Git, Mercurial); and Codebase (Git, Mercurial, and Subversion). Although some are premium services requiring a subscription, for your peace of mind it's worth the cost.

If you aren't using source control to look after your site files, you should keep regular copies of your site downloaded from your server as a backup. Keeping them on your local computer would be fine, but for even more peace of mind you can keep them stored in a cloud service such as Dropbox, iCloud, or SkyDrive.

Now that your files are all backed up, make sure that you keep your database backed up as well. The access you have to your database will depend on how you keep your database backed up. if you have a web control panel for your server/hosting there should be options in there to make a backup of your database.

Many hosting packages give you access to a control panel for your databases: PHPMyAdmin (see Figure 10-1).

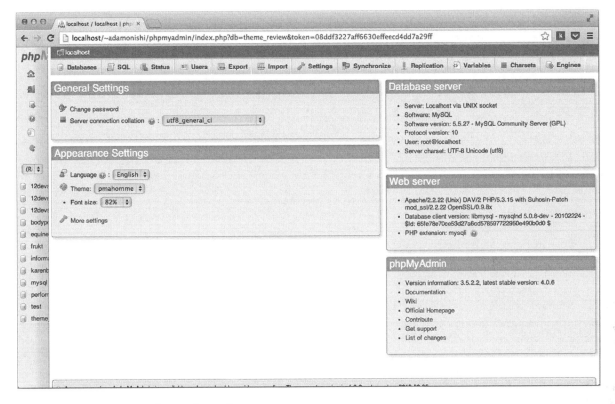

Figure 10-1. *The PHPMyAdmin web interface*

If you have access to PHPMyAdmin, making a backup is relatively straightforward. Once you're in the database you want to back up, you need to select the Export option from the menu across the top of the database page, which will bring you to a page like the one shown in Figure 10-2. In version 3.5.5 (as shown in Figure 10-2), there's a choice of Quick and Custom options. For the type of backup you need, the Quick option is sufficient; it enables you to download an SQL file containing all the database information needed for your site.

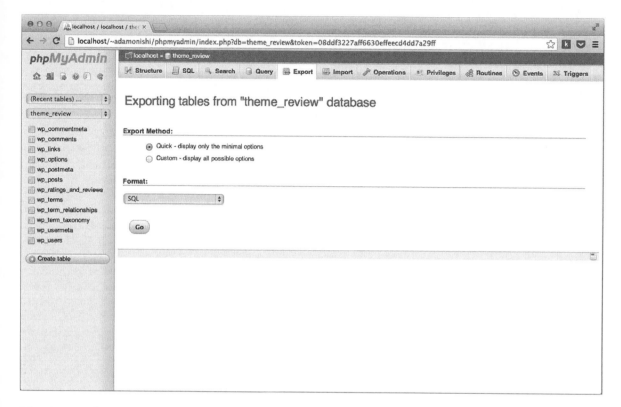

Figure 10-2. *The export page in PHPMyAdmin version 3.5.5*

BackupBuddy Plugin

If you prefer not to look after the backup process of your site manually, there are many plugins that can help you keep regular backups and even scheduled backups of your site, giving you the peace of mind that your site will be taken care of. There are many backup plugins, but the one I've been using on most of my sites recently is BackupBuddy (see Figure 10-3).

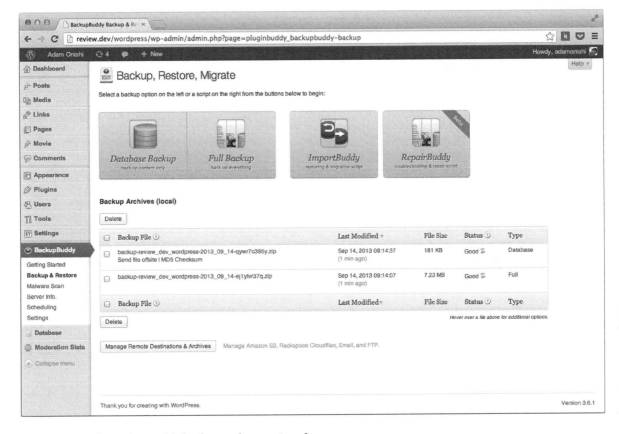

Figure 10-3. *The BackupBuddy backup and restore interface*

Although BackupBuddy has a premium plugin price ($80 for two sites and $150 for unlimited sites), I think it is a very worthwhile cost because sites are always backed up and are easily restored should something go wrong.

BackupBuddy also comes with the added bonus that its import function also works as a migration tool that enables you to easily transfer databases from a development environment to production. BackupBuddy makes this as simple as a few clicks; anyone who's worked with WordPress before knows that this is a major advantage.

Some backup plugins are freely available from the plugin repository, such as WP-DBManager (http://wp-themes-book.com/10001), as recommended by Chris Coyier and Jeff Starr in Digging into WordPress (http://digwp.com/).

InfiniteWP Site Manager

The last option for backup management I'll discuss is an offsite solution called InfiniteWP (see Figure 10-4).

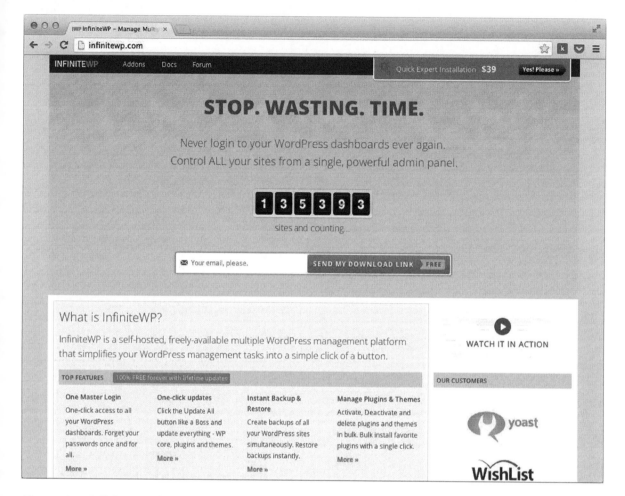

Figure 10-4. *InfiniteWP web site*

InfiniteWP is a free service (if you set it up on your own) that allows you to manage multiple WordPress sites from a single location. The site manager can do almost everything you need to maintain your WordPress sites, including these tasks:

- Database and file backups
- WordPress updates
- Plugin updates
- Instant access to the WordPress admin for all connected sites

So if you host or maintain a number of WordPress sites, InfiniteWP can make handling security, backups, and site updates really easy from a single location. The system also allows you to schedule your updates and keeps you updated with regular e-mail about the status of the managed sites if you request it.

Theme Security

Now that you've seen how to get back up and running if things go wrong, it's time to focus on prevention. Here you will learn what you can do to enhance security on your WordPress sites, starting with theme security.

A lot of what theme security boils down to is making sure that you're handling permissions, actions, and data correctly. There are two main topics I'll cover: when writing your theme, ensure that no one can perform any actions they shouldn't be allowed to and that no one can enter malicious data into your site in an attempt to break or hack into your site.

Actions, Permissions, and Intent

Chapter 8 looked at user permissions via the roles and capabilities system in WordPress; ensuring that a user has the correct abilities to perform an action in WordPress is important and something you should be doing whenever you perform an action in WordPress that requires a user to be present. However, that's only half the problem. When it comes to ensuring that actions are performed securely in any system, not only should you be ensuring that the user is allowed to perform these actions but also that the user intends to perform them.

Testing for intent is just as important as checking to see whether your user has permission to perform an action. For instance, without testing for intent, suppose that a user signed in to WordPress on one tab in the browser and then navigated to another site that contained a link to perform a function on the WordPress admin, such as Delete All Posts. Because the user in this instance is signed in to WordPress already, the user permissions would check out and all the user's posts would be deleted.

One way to get around this issue used to be by checking what page the user was on previously with the `HTTP_REFERER` value (which WordPress used to use). However, this value is not 100 percent reliable; it can be susceptible to hacking via JavaScript (in some browsers), and in some cases, it is not set at all. Because of this, a security update was added to introduce nonces in WordPress version 2.0.3.

■ **Note**   *Nonce* stands for *number used once*, which is similar to what's used in cryptography for securing communications.

Nonces in Forms

WordPress uses nonces throughout the core, and there are useful functions to help you easily use nonces throughout your themes. In fact, you have already seen nonces in action in Chapter 5 (although they were not discussed in detail). In that chapter, you used nonces in the forms when updating the custom fields you were creating, ensuring that updates were performed only if the nonce was verified.

```
// Setting the none at the start of the meta field function
function prowordpress_movie_meta_fields ( $post ) {
        // Use nonce for verification
        wp_nonce_field( basename( __FILE__ ), 'ptd_movie_meta_noncename' );

        // Code skipped for example purposes
        [...]
}

// Testing the nonce in the save function
function prowordpress_movie_meta_save ( $post_id ) {
[...]
        if ( !isset( $_POST['ptd_movie_meta_noncename'] ) || !wp_verify_nonce( $_POST['ptd_movie_
meta_noncename'], basename( __FILE__ ) ) ) {
                return $post_id;
        }
[...]
}
```

The `wp_nonce_field()` function outputs a hidden form field containing the nonce data based on the information you passed to the function. Although the parameters of `wp_nonce_field()` are optional, the first two, `action` and `name`, are commonly recommended, as the defaults used by WordPress will be known by hackers. The last two parameters are Boolean values that can be left as their defaults. The third parameter, `$referrer`, is true by default, meaning that a referrer hidden field will be created as well. The last parameter is `$echo` and is true by default, meaning that the fields will be echoed out to HTML. The `wp_nonce_field()` call shown in the preceding example will generate these two form fields in the form:

```
<input type="hidden" id="ptd_movie_meta_noncename" name="ptd_movie_meta_noncename"
value="d1e6fc97e6">
<input type="hidden" name="_wp_http_referer" value="/wordpress/wp-admin/post-new.php?post_type=ptd_
movie">
```

Now that the nonce field is generated in your form, you can simply check it when you process the form. As shown in the example, you need to use a function called `wp_verify_nonce()`. This function takes the nonce value and the action it was created with, so the previous function takes the POST value that was named `'ptd_movie_meta_noncename'` and the action `"basename( __FILE__ )"` that was used in the `wp_nonce_field()` function. This function tests the nonce passed through and returns `false` if they do not match, and either `"1"` or `"2"`, based on how long ago the nonce was created. Nonces in WordPress have a lifespan of 24 hours; if that period has expired, the verification will fail. The difference in return values between `"1"` and `"2"` is based on how old the nonce is. This means you can choose to process the action only if the nonce is less than 12 hours old, in which case you would check that the return value from the `wp_verify_nonce()` function is `"1"`.

Nonces in Links

Besides their common use in forms, a nonce can be generated to be part of a link as well. For instance, if you want to create a "delete post" link, make sure that you not only verify the user's permissions to be able to perform a deletion but also ensure that the intent to delete is there.

To do this, WordPress gives you another handy nonce function: `wp_nonce_url()`. The function takes two parameters, the original URL of the link and a name for the nonce, and then it returns a completely new link with the nonce as part of the query string. For instance, based on the "delete post" link I mentioned, you can create your links like so:

```php
<?php
$base_url = "http://website.com/admin/delete.php?post_id=7";
$nonce_url = wp_nonce_url( $base_url, 'delete_post_noncename' );
?>
<a href="<?php echo $nonce_url; ?>">Delete post</a>
```

The generated link from the function would look something like this:

```
http://website.com/admin/delete.php?post_id=7&_wpnonce=9631d79152
```

When you process the "delete post" function, you need to test for this nonce using the `wp_verify_nonce()` function. The nonce is in the GET value `_wpnonce` (as shown in the previous link), and the second parameter to add is the name of the nonce you created in the `wp_nonce_url` function:

```
wp_verify_nonce( $_GET['_wpnonce'], 'delete_post_noncename' );
```

Nonces should always be used in conjunction with testing the capabilities of the user to ensure that they not only have the permissions to perform an action in the admin but also that they intended to perform that action in the first place.

Handling Data Securely

When writing functionality in your WordPress theme, you always need to take precautions when handling data, including any data inserted into the database or output to the admin or page templates by your code. This process, called *data sanitization*, ensures that data going into the database or being displayed is prevented from being interpreted as code. The very popular XKCD web comic has one strip on this exact topic called "Exploits of a Mom" (http://xkcd.com/327/).

Sometimes the term *data validation* can get confused with data sanitization. The former is the practice of making sure that you have the correct data entered into a form (such as testing an e-mail field to make sure that it looks like an e-mail address). Data sanitization is used to make the data safe, ensuring that it's formatted correctly for where it will be used, which is why sanitization is more closely associated with security. Validation and sanitization can be used together to make security more robust (i.e., if you're expecting an e-mail address to be input, validation can ensure that it is the kind of data you receive), but ensuring that you correctly sanitize your data before using it is most important when it comes to security.

In Chapter 13 on plugin development, you'll be looking at working with the WordPress database in full, including performing your own custom queries. At that point, I'll fully cover how to deal with data sanitization when working with the database, so for now this section will focus more on data sanitization within a theme, mostly looking at how to sanitize data when it's output in templates or the WordPress admin.

Output Sanitization

WordPress deals with a lot of data sanitization for you when you use any of its output functions. For example, the `get_search_query()` function will ensure that the data is sanitized before it outputs it to the page. There are also different contexts for which you might want to output the same data but have it formatted a certain way.

The best example is when outputting a post title. The post title may not just be used in a header in one of your page templates; you might also want to use it as a title attribute in a link or output it to your RSS feed. In each of these contexts, there can be different ways to sanitize the title so it works as expected. Fortunately, WordPress has functions to do these:

- `the_title()`: Outputs the title for use in standard HTML tags.

- `the_title_attribute()`: Outputs the title, ensuring that HTML is escaped so it can be used in HTML attributes such as the `title` attribute in a link.

- `the_title_rss()`: Outputs the title again, escaping HTML characters, but bearing in mind the XML rules that require certain specific characters to be used.

You can clearly see that WordPress is set up to take good care of you and help out with your data. There are times when you'll have to perform the sanitization, but once again WordPress has a lot of functions to help you do so.

■ **Note** Although many PHP functions perform data sanitization, WordPress functions not only utilize them but also do a lot more and also cater for different contexts. Whenever possible, I recommend that you always prefer the WordPress function to using standard PHP functions.

A selection of the sanitization functions available in WordPress is listed here; you can find a full list at http://wp-themes-book.com/10002. These functions have different contexts and should be used where appropriate:

- `esc_html()`: Encodes HTML characters < >, & , ", and ' for use when outputting text to HTML.

- `esc_html__()`, `esc_html_e()`, and `esc_html_x()`: Each function encodes HTML characters as previously, but also translates the text. The `esc_html_e()` function echoes the result, and `esc_html_x()` translates with a given context.

- `esc_attr()`: Encodes characters in the context of an HTML attribute. Also has `__()`, `_e()`, and `_x()` variants like the `esc_html()` function.

- `sanitize_html_class()`: Ensures that a value can be used as an HTML class by returning only alphanumerics, hyphens, and underscores. However, it does not ensure that the class name is valid (i.e., that it cannot start with a number).

- `esc_url()`: Encodes and sanitizes all URLs to be safely used in links. WordPress has a secure whitelist of allowed protocols and also ensures that encoding is done with numeric entity references for use in a URL.

- `esc_url_raw()`: Works in a similar way, but is used when inserting a URL into the database. It doesn't encode ampersands and single quotes.

- `esc_js()`: In the rare instance when you need to output inline JS to a page template, it ensures that characters are encoded correctly.

- `esc_textarea()`: For use with text that will be displayed in a textarea. It does a similar job to `esc_html()`, but actually double-encodes entities; for example, encoding the & of a > encoded character.

These are most of the sanitization functions you'll need when you work with themes. (Others are covered when you look at database interactions in Chapter 13.) Again, you should be aware of the context and the need for using these functions in your theme. For example, if you take a look at the the_title_attribute() function, you can see that the esc_attr() function is being used in there, so you don't have to sanitize the output of that function:

```
function the_title_attribute( $args = '' ) {
        $defaults = array('before' => '', 'after' => '', 'echo' => true, 'post' => get_post() );
        $r = wp_parse_args($args, $defaults);
        extract( $r, EXTR_SKIP );

        $title = get_the_title( $post );

        if ( strlen($title) == 0 )
                return;

        $title = $before . $title . $after;
        $title = esc_attr(strip_tags($title));

        if ( $echo )
                echo $title;
        else
                return $title;
}
```

However, if you were to trace back the get_post_meta() function through to where it gets the data from the database, you'll see no sanitization functions applied to the output data. This is where you need to use the sanitization functions on the data, ensuring that the correct function is used based on the context of the data.

URL Query Strings

Besides the esc_url function, WordPress also provides a function for sanitizing query strings in URLs with the add_query_arg() function. This function takes an associative array of your query parameters (stored parameter => value) and outputs them onto the end of the current page URL, safely formatted:

```
$query_params = array(
                'post_type' => 'movies',
                'paged' => 2,
        );

$url = add_query_arg( $query_params );
```

Assuming that you're on the page 'http://website.com', the resulting $url will be http://website.com/?post_type=movies&paged=2.

Antispambot

Another handy function you can use when outputting data in your theme isn't necessarily a sanitization function, but it can be extremely handy when handling e-mail address data. The antispambot() function takes an e-mail address and encodes random characters to obfuscate and prevent spambots from scraping your site for e-mail addresses:

```
<a href="mailto:<?php echo antispambot($email, 1); ?>">Contact me</a>
```

The second parameter in the function is true or false (1 or 0) for whether the e-mail is for use in a mailto link. In this case, the e-mail will be randomly encoded using numeric entities.

Securing the WordPress Login

There are few less obvious ways to secure your WordPress site than protecting your login page. This is usually one of the first lines of attack for many WordPress sites, so knowing how to secure the login page and ensuring that people can't gain access to your site's admin area is extremely important. Here, you'll look at a few different techniques you can employ to secure the login page of your WordPress sites specifically.

Never Use "Admin"

Prior to version 3.0, whenever you set up WordPress, your default administrator account would be called "admin". This made attempting login hacks on a WordPress site easier because most people would either not change the default account (it's not possible to just simply change the username of an account, so most people just didn't bother), or they would not know that there was a need to in the first place. This meant that almost anyone trying to hack a WordPress site prior to version 3.0's release usually always knew the username of the main account, which makes hacking the login at least 50 percent easier.

Since version 3.0, upon installation WordPress gives you the option to choose a username for the main administrator account. My advice is to most certainly not set it up with the username "admin" (or "administrator" or any other variants). In fact, for added security I would ensure that the main site admin is not named anything related to the site or be set up with the intention of it being used to create posts on the site. Basically if the username or even a hint of the username set is displayed on the site anywhere, this offers a potential for a hacker to gain access to the site. The main admin account should be left for just the administration and maintenance of the site, and any posting should be left to user accounts with limited access to the majority of admin features.

Limiting Login Attempts

One common method used by hackers who attempt to access a site is to bombard the site with multiple login attempts, trying a combination of account names and passwords. It is harder for them now that most WordPress users aren't using the "admin" account username (you aren't, of course), but it is a common method of attack that needs to be prevented.

Fortunately, the community surrounding WordPress comes to its aid. Having seen many articles and read a few books covering WordPress security, I advise using a plugin against this type of threat. The current most recommended plugin I have found is Limit Login Attempts by Johan Eenfeldt (http://wp-themes-book.com/10003). This plugin does exactly what it says on the tin; it allows you to set various options for how to limit the number of times someone can try to log in to your site.

In the settings page shown in Figure 10-5, you can choose a variety of different configurations to protect the login page. The plugin will do things like collect a list of the IPs the login attempts have come from, allowing you to perhaps place more blocks on the IPs at a server level.

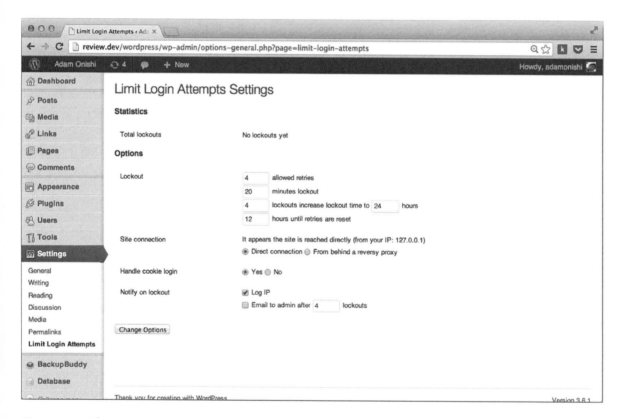

Figure 10-5. *The Limit Login Attempts Settings page*

Preventing the Default Error Message

Another potential issue with the WordPress login page is the error message that displays failed login attempts. If you enter an existing username on the site, you are asked whether you've forgotten the password for the username (see Figure 10-6). Initially you may not see this as such a big deal, but hackers who see this message knows that the username they have attempted to login with exists, so they can keep on trying to crack the password for that account.

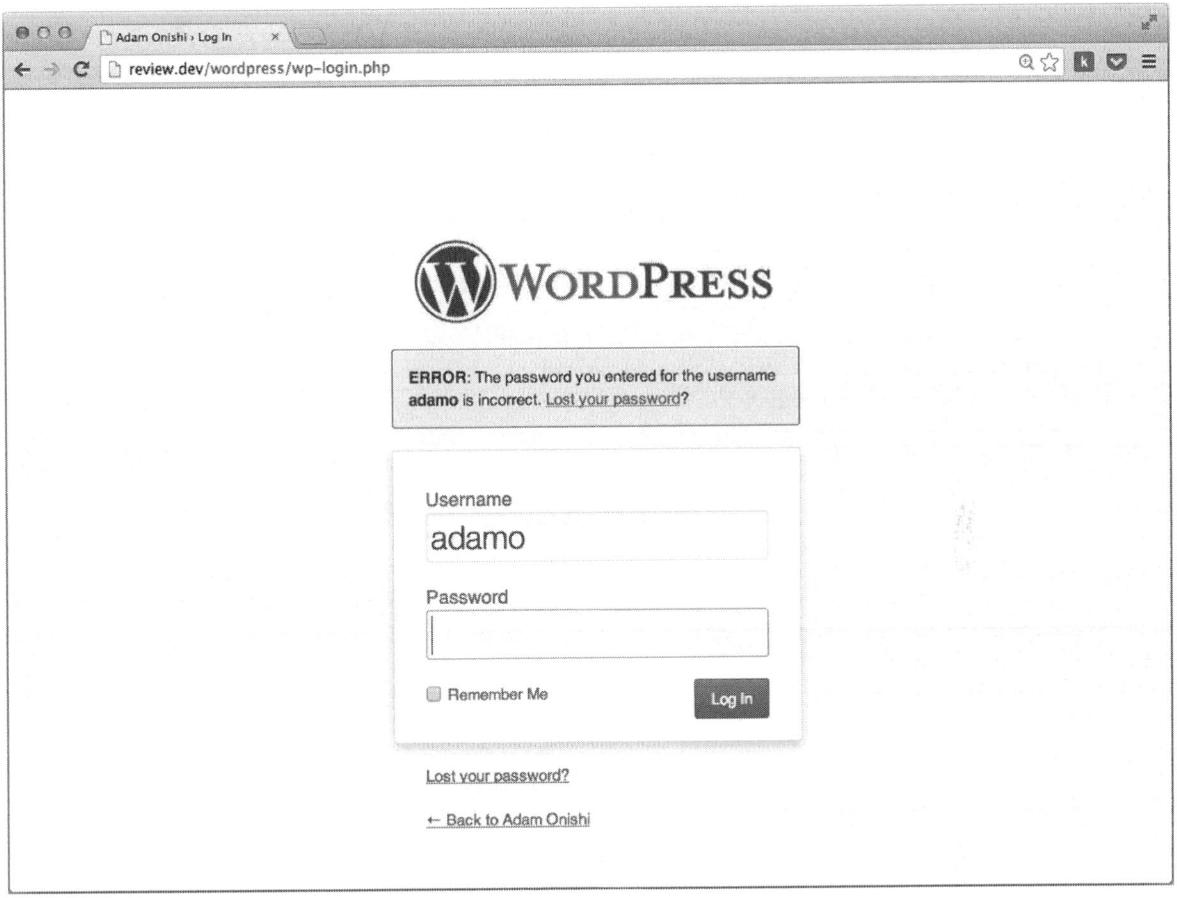

Figure 10-6. *The failed login page, showing the default error message*

Although the default error message is good for user experience (users now know they've entered the wrong password and have a nice link to reset it if they need to), it's very bad for security. The way to get around this is to change the error message displayed by WordPress, making it a bit more general. You can do this with the WordPress 'login_errors' filter:

```php
function plain_error_message($message) {
        $message = "<strong>Error</strong>: Incorrect username or password.";
        return $message;
}

add_filter('login_errors', 'plain_error_message' );
```

The plain_error_message() function is fired only when there is a failed login attempt. The function then takes the default message and replaces it with a much more general message about the login attempt.

■ **Note**   The Limit Login Attempts plugin also deals with the default error message as an added bonus and comes with multiple language translations.

Securing your Login Page with Secure Socket Layer (SSL)

WordPress makes it extremely easy to add Secure Socket Layer (SSL) security to the login and admin pages of your sites. You have to obtain and set up an SSL certificate for your domain, but it's worth checking with your hosting to see whether it provides the certificate and can get it set up for you. I host most of my sites with Media Temple, which offers SSL certificates from $75 per year per domain—and that includes setting it up for me, so that's pretty good.

Once you have your SSL certificate in place, you can add a couple of lines to your `wp-config.php` file to enable SSL usage on your site's login or on all admin sessions:

```
// Require SSL for all Admin sessions
define('FORCE_SSL_ADMIN', true);

// Require SSL for login page
define('FORCE_SSL_LOGIN', true);
```

Using SSL means that all your usernames, passwords, and access cookies will be encrypted, so your sessions will be a lot more secure. However, because the site pages are running through an encryption/decryption process, things might slow down a little, but for the added security it's more than worth it. And remember that it's being used only on the admin pages, so the speed on the front end of your site won't be affected.

General WordPress Security

Besides keeping your theme secure, it's also good to ensure that whenever you install a WordPress web site (whether for yourself or your clients), you do so as securely as possible and take into account all the possible risks. In this section, I'll go through a series of quick security tips to ensure that you reduce the risks of being hacked as best you can each time you install WordPress.

Some of these tips can be implemented at the theme level, so I suggest that you use them in all your themes. Others are to do with the server and database setup, which you should always be aware of if you provide hosting or at least an installation service for the sites you build.

Staying Up to Date

WordPress is continually being worked on, and with each major and minor version comes not only a host of new features but also a large number of security fixes. At the time of writing, version 3.6.1 has not long been released (just a few weeks after the major version 3.6). This version included fixes for three security issues, so it shows just how important it is to have the latest version of WordPress running.

It applies to plugins and any themes you may have installed as well, so having the latest version of a plugin or a theme ensures that you have all the latest security updates.

Updating in WordPress 3.7

During the writing of this chapter, WordPress 3.7 was released, which comes with the handy feature of automatic updates. From now on, your WordPress install automatically updates to the latest minor version releases of the core, so you are instantly up to date with every new release.

There are some caveats to automatic updates, however. I mentioned already that only minor versions are automatically updated; for instance, from 3.7 to 3.7.1 will be automatic but 3.7 to 3.8 will have to be a manual process. This probably helps because minor versions are more likely to be security updates and bug fixes, whereas major versions usually include feature updates and so on. It enables you to thoroughly test the major version updates in case any functionality breaks because a new version of jQuery is included or a plugin hasn't quite been updated to the new version for instance.

Another potential issue with automatic updates comes with the way you manage your WordPress install. If you have WordPress in version control with a deployment strategy, for instance, you probably don't want your production version of WordPress to be updated automatically; otherwise, it will break your version control. You can get around this, though, by disabling automatic updates in certain cases. For a longer post on this topic, see what Andrew Nacin wrote on the Make WordPress blog: `http://wp-themes-book.com/10004`.

Hiding Unnecessary Data

As discussed earlier in the chapter, always do as much as you can to not give potential hackers any information that can make it easy to hack your site. WordPress, by default, adds a few extra bits of meta information in the <head> of your site:

```
<link rel="alternate" type="application/rss+xml" title="Adam Onishi &raquo; Feed"
href="http://review.dev/feed/" />
<link rel="alternate" type="application/rss+xml" title="Adam Onishi &raquo; Comments Feed"
href="http://review.dev/comments/feed/" />
<link rel="alternate" type="application/rss+xml" title="Adam Onishi &raquo; Home Comments Feed"
href="http://review.dev/home/feed/" />
<link rel="EditURI" type="application/rsd+xml" title="RSD"
href="http://review.dev/wordpress/xmlrpc.php?rsd" />
<link rel="wlwmanifest" type="application/wlwmanifest+xml"
href="http://review.dev/wordpress/wp-includes/wlwmanifest.xml" />
<link rel='prev' title='Clearing Floats' href='http://review.dev/clearing-floats/' />
<link rel='next' title='Posts' href='http://review.dev/posts/' />
<meta name="generator" content="WordPress 3.6.1" />
<link rel='canonical' href='http://review.dev/' />
```

As you can see, a lot of this information is certainly not essential for your site to display, especially the generator tag showing the latest version of WordPress. Each of these meta and link tags is added from the WordPress core using the wp_head() action, meaning that they can be easily removed with the remove_action() function.

In most of my sites, by default I add in this list of remove_action() functions to clean up the <head> section of my sites:

```
remove_action('wp_head', 'rsd_link');
remove_action('wp_head', 'wp_generator');
remove_action('wp_head', 'wlwmanifest_link');
```

This just leaves a couple of generated tags in the <head>, such as the canonical link, RSS feed, and next/previous links. The meta tags you're removing are these:

- 'rsd_link' removes a meta with the edit page link.

- 'wp_generator' keeps the WordPress version number from being displayed.

- 'wlwmanifest_link' removes a link to an XML file containing a lot of information about your WordPress site setup.

A few other tags can be used to exclude more meta from the document head, but these three tags should always be removed for added security on your WordPress blog. Removing this information means that you're not handing over extra information about your site when you don't need to.

Security Keys

WordPress security keys, also known as secret keys, are eight variables set to large random strings to help improve the security of passwords and cookies on your site. Security keys came into existence in version 2.5, in which one key was defined, but over time they have increased to the eight you see now in version 3.7. Within the keys are four main keys and four salts. The four keys should always be defined, but the salts are optional because WordPress generates salts for you if they do not exist.

You can find the security keys in your `wp-config.php` file. At first, before installation in the `wp-config-sample.php` file, they look like this:

```
define('AUTH_KEY',         'put your unique phrase here');
define('SECURE_AUTH_KEY',  'put your unique phrase here');
define('LOGGED_IN_KEY',    'put your unique phrase here');
define('NONCE_KEY',        'put your unique phrase here');
define('AUTH_SALT',        'put your unique phrase here');
define('SECURE_AUTH_SALT', 'put your unique phrase here');
define('LOGGED_IN_SALT',   'put your unique phrase here');
define('NONCE_SALT',       'put your unique phrase here');
```

If you use the web interface to run through the initial setup of your site (see Figure 10-7), the `wp-config.php` file is created for you, and the security keys are populated automatically. If, however, you create your `wp-config.php` file manually, you have to also set up the keys yourself. To do this, you can create the keys, but WordPress already has a fantastic generator for you to use. You can generate the full eight keys at `http://wp-themes-book.com/10005`; or if you prefer to have only the keys without the salts, you can delete "salt" from the end of the URL and just use `http://wp-themes-book.com/10006`.

The result of the generator (shown here) should be pasted straight into your `wp-config.php` file in place of the initial key declarations:

```
define('AUTH_KEY',         'Wb5~jPIg7B,a2nO=dX|m3isl?fdtNYfzJ]#GD|d7eS Rr9j;4>Qi+>]mWTdXeF:C');
define('SECURE_AUTH_KEY',  'JyI!yx%+F 1@6^|h,xbp,]lodujgsmkT)%G&=5I`d+V<c#m|U(=VV#x@=*F7r] a');
define('LOGGED_IN_KEY',    'Fo,;o3%Bc7+80nn9CA~v#LgJgNUEI_K+vO5+GB3KFOlFZ3q.-4C` |V1HY93WpcD');
define('NONCE_KEY',        ':l8p-Lv7}!qpsIBv+o]s^S<)Owh6wOgS/Z4KY|xZi]p|NuOAWs~eMtYKIC{X6qs8');
define('AUTH_SALT',        '>^XMIB*125ghly/~[>fO]o*bBr$5 oawgbQt$;8nspE4*@rwjQx|McC6cz#Y5RRs');
define('SECURE_AUTH_SALT', 'C;r+t:hOSf`REd}fY`%^-R2Ah9+$Z[E,$kwv%vrt%KO,Gx|y=>{wH}/[Z11;:&CR');
define('LOGGED_IN_SALT',   'ouoz*]&D>Y@_&~;q!Oe|v_E9Vcb-b8ajT!_yAt-bDI|C+cy?IodH6^M+:{&9{oo4');
define('NONCE_SALT',       'd,Xc)M;2DX-WtV>46re]>2mk~.}FfsFt3sAs?w5a`l;r!=ma~QA5y%=+]X[}%7KS');
```

File Security

When you work with WordPress, it's important to ensure that the main files of your WordPress install are also secure. Many files include important information about your server (such as the `wp-config.php` file, which should not be accessed from outside the confines of your server administrators). There are a lot of ways to ensure that your files are secure; they can range from simply moving the file directories around to going as far as working with the `.htaccess` file on your server to provide even more file-specific security.

File Permissions

When installing WordPress, make sure that your files are owned by the correct user and modifiable only by the users who need access to them. Most servers do this for you, but if you're given access to the files, it's worth looking into the permissions as well. I run a UNIX-based server with Apache as my web server, so a lot of the information from here on in will be based around this setup (the process is similar across IIS and Nginx servers).

With your server setup, you should aim for all files being owned by your user account and in a group that contains the Apache user account. With the file ownership set up correctly, you need to ensure that your file permissions are correct for the WordPress files and directories. For files, the permissions should be 0644, which means that files are writable only by the user and readable by everyone else. Directories should then be set up as 0755, which means read, write, and execute permissions for the owner and read and execute permissions for the group.

When I install WordPress, this is one of the first steps I perform before opening WordPress in the browser. For a few years now, as soon as I've downloaded and unzipped the WordPress install, I change the ownership and group of all files and directories and then the permissions using the following two lines in the shell, from inside the root directory of the new install (it may require sudo or root user to run):

```
find . -type d -exec chmod 755 {} \;
```

```
find . -type f -exec chmod 644 {} \;
```

These two functions go through every directory from the top directory you're in, finding every directory or file, and then run the chmod function with the given parameter (755 and 644). For full information on file permissions in WordPress, as well as more in-depth guides into handling different server setups, refer to this very useful page in the Codex: http://wp-themes-book.com/10007.

One issue with setting up file permissions like this is that WordPress likes to update the .htaccess file when you make changes to your permalink settings (as well as plugins like WP Super Cache, which modifies the .htaccess file to add caching directives). WordPress suggests slightly looser permissions for the .htaccess file, but in both cases, the changes that have to be made to the .htaccess file will be displayed in WordPress (see Figure 10-7). So you can copy them into your .htaccess file manually and still retain the secure permissions on the .htaccess file.

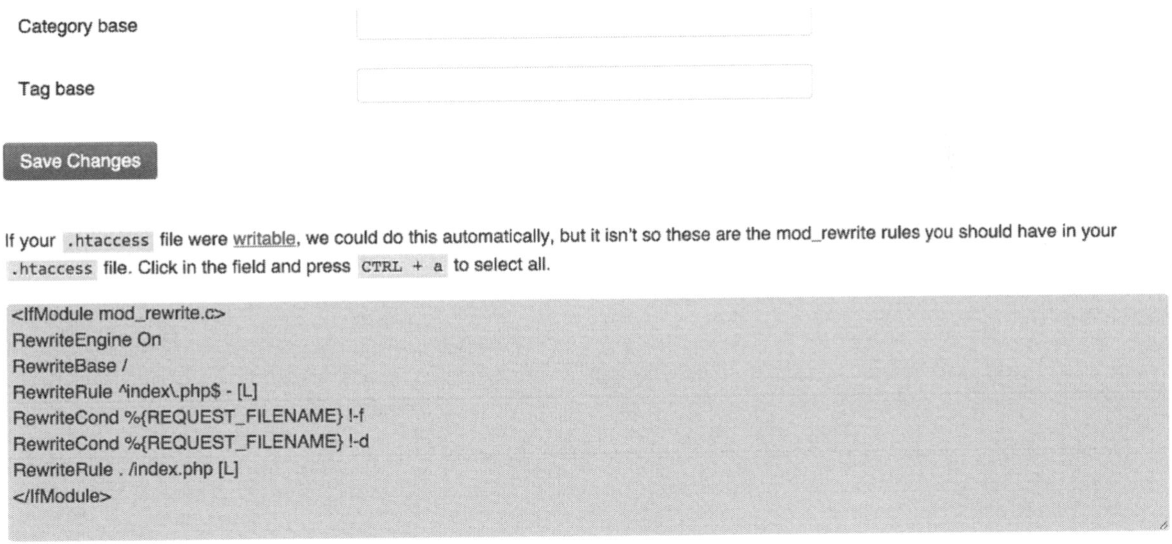

Category base [   ]

Tag base [   ]

Save Changes

If your `.htaccess` file were writable, we could do this automatically, but it isn't so these are the mod_rewrite rules you should have in your `.htaccess` file. Click in the field and press `CTRL + a` to select all.

```
<IfModule mod_rewrite.c>
RewriteEngine On
RewriteBase /
RewriteRule ^index\.php$ - [L]
RewriteCond %{REQUEST_FILENAME} !-f
RewriteCond %{REQUEST_FILENAME} !-d
RewriteRule . /index.php [L]
</IfModule>
```

Figure 10-7. *The .htaccess update prompt from changing permalinks*

Blocking File Access

Besides ensuring that your files are protected by the correct permissions, a couple of files could use some more specific protection: the .htaccess and wp-config.php files. The wp-config.php file contains important information about your WordPress install, and the .htaccess file contains control information for your server, so it is a target for hackers wanting to attack your site.

Fortunately, the .htaccess file comes in handy to help protect both of these files—by adding a simple few lines of code, you can block any attempts to access either file from the web:

```
<Files wp-config.php>
order allow,deny
deny from all
</Files>

<Files .htaccess>
order allow,deny
deny from all
</Files>
```

Another tip to help protect your .htaccess file is to do away with it entirely—well, not quite entirely. If you run your own server on which you have WordPress installed, it is recommended that instead of having an .htaccess file in the root directory of the site, you add the directives that should go in the .htaccess file to the site configuration file instead. This way, there is no .htaccess file for you to protect because it's protected at a much higher level on your server.

Protecting Directory Access

Along with protecting file access, you'll also want to protect your site from directories being displayed on the web (where all files and directories in that folder are listed on the page when navigating to it). There are two easy ways to protect your directories from being viewed: through the .htaccess file or with blank index files (HTML or PHP) that simply show a blank page if the directory is viewed in a browser.

You'll often see the latter in use by WordPress (see Figure 10-8), with each index.php file often containing the following simple PHP comment:

```
<?php
// Silence is golden.
?>
```

Figure 10-8. *The wp-content directory with its blank index.php file*

The first method is rather easy to set up as well: inside your .htaccess file, you can simply add a one-line directive anywhere in the file to prevent directories from being displayed.

```
Options -Indexes
```

The install.php File

Another file to be aware of is the install.php file, which shows the database configuration page when you're installing WordPress using the web interface. When the install is over, the file is almost redundant, but in some rare cases it could show up (i.e., if your database goes down entirely), which isn't exactly fantastic once you have your site fully set up.

There are a couple of easy ways to prevent this from happening: the first is to completely delete the file after installation, which is a bit crude, but it ensures that the page won't ever be displayed. The second is to protect the file using the .htaccess file, as you did with the wp-config.php file: copy the same section of code used for the wp-config.php file and change the file name to install.php.

A third option, which is slightly more involved but a lot more useful, replaces the entire file with a new custom page that will be displayed instead. The best way to find out more about this is to read Jeff Starr's post on the vulnerability of the install.php file and read more about the "Fix #3" at http://wp-themes-book.com/10008.

Relocating Files and Directories

Finally, it's time to take a look at the different methods you can use to add further protection to your WordPress install by completely relocating certain files or the entire WordPress system. By moving directories or specific files into different locations, you're removing the predictability of your WordPress install, thus reducing the chance that hackers can find the file they need to exploit. Even the slightest change to something that is usually predictable adds inconvenience to a hacker, and if your site is just one of hundreds or thousands being targeted, it might just be enough discouragement for the hacker to just ignore yours and move on.

There are three things that can be easily moved in your WordPress install:

- wp-config.php file
- Entire WordPress system
- wp-content directory

Moving the wp-config.php File

If you're hosting WordPress on a server that has a directory for the site with another directory inside for the public files (such as public_html or www), you could move the wp-config.php file up outside of your public directory, and without any modification WordPress will still work fine. The reason for this is the way WordPress loads the wp-config.php file. Take a look at the top of the wp-load.php file (the third file to be loaded as part of the WordPress init sequence); you'll see that there's a conditional for where to load the wp-config.php file:

```
if ( file_exists( ABSPATH . 'wp-config.php') ) {

        /** The config file resides in ABSPATH */
        require_once( ABSPATH . 'wp-config.php' );

} elseif ( file_exists( dirname(ABSPATH) . '/wp-config.php' ) && ! file_exists( dirname(ABSPATH) .
'/wp-settings.php' ) ) {

        /** The config file resides one level above ABSPATH but is not part of another install */
        require_once( dirname(ABSPATH) . '/wp-config.php' );

}
```

As you can see from the comments in the code, at first WordPress tries to load the wp-config.php file from the main WordPress directory: the ABSPATH. If there is no file found in that path, it will look one directory above using the dirname() PHP function, but only if there are no other WordPress core files in that directory (in this case, the code is checking for the wp-setting.php file).

Based on this block of code, it means that you can safely move the wp-config.php file up one directory from your core files; if you're running a server with a public directory, that's extremely useful.

Relocating the WordPress Core Files

Another method of creating obscurity in your WordPress install is to move the entire WordPress core files' structure around. This is the route I always take when working with WordPress, so much so that now that it is part of my routine install process. I keep WordPress in its own separate directory, which not only allows for a tidier site setup but also adds to the security of the site.

My install process looks a little like this (all commands are run from the command line):

```
~ mkdir newsite.dev
~ cd newsite.dev
~ wget http://wordpress.org/latest.zip
~ unzip latest.zip
~ mv wordpress wp
~ mv wp/index.php .
```

After the index.php file is moved into the root directory of the site, there's one little edit to make before you can get up and running. The index.php file is responsible for loading the rest of the WordPress system with the following line:

```
/** Loads the WordPress Environment and Template */
require('./wp-blog-header.php');
```

Instead of the line reading './wp-blog-header.php' with the new location of the core files, you just need to add the new folder location to the require statement:

```
/** Loads the WordPress Environment and Template */
require('./wp/wp-blog-header.php');
```

This way, the wp-blog-header.php file will be run as normal, and because all the PHP constants aren't set until later in the wp-load.php and wp-config.php files, the directory structures will be correct.

One last thing to do with this structural change is to tell the WordPress install that the site should be served from the root directory as normal, not from the new directory structure. To do this, once WordPress is installed, you need to go to the general settings page and update the site address URL to be the root of the site URL instead of the new WordPress core files directory (see Figure 10-9).

Tagline	Just another WordPress site
	In a few words, explain what this site is about.
WordPress Address (URL)	http://newsite.dev/wp
Site Address (URL)	http://newsite.dev
	Enter the address here if you want your site homepage to be different from the directory you installed WordPress.

Figure 10-9. *The address settings in Settings ➤ General with the new directory structure*

▓ **Note**　If you move your entire WordPress install into a subdirectory, you can no longer move the wp-config.php file outside of the public directory for your site (if you have one). The wp-config.php file can only ever be moved up a single directory, whereas in the case of the restructure of the core files, moving wp-config.php outside of the public directory would be a jump of two directories.

Moving the wp-content Directory

The final restructuring you can do to your WordPress site is to move and/or rename the wp-content directory. This directory is not crucial to WordPress in that it contains no core files that would need updating, just the themes, plugins, and uploads related to the site specifically.

When changing the wp-content directory, you just need to make sure that the rest of WordPress is aware of it by changing a few constants. The constants should be added to your wp-config.php file above the line with the "stop editing here" comment:

```
// Relocating the wp-content folder
define('WP_CONTENT_DIR', $_SERVER['DOCUMENT_ROOT'] . '/content');
define('WP_CONTENT_URL', 'http://review.dev/content');
define('WP_PLUGIN_DIR', $_SERVER['DOCUMENT_ROOT'] . '/content/plugins');
define('WP_PLUGIN_URL', 'http://review.dev/content/plugins');
define('PLUGINDIR', $_SERVER['DOCUMENT_ROOT'] . '/content/plugins');

/* That's all, stop editing! Happy blogging. */
```

With those constants defined everything should be working fine, in previous versions of WordPress you used to also have to update a URL in the Media settings page, however since version 3.5 this has been removed.

Database Security

As with any database-driven CMS, the database is another point of potential attack for hackers. You already learned how important it is to keep your database backed up should the worst happen, so now you'll see some preventive actions you can take to help stop people from getting in in the first place.

Changing the Default Table Prefix

Something that should be done immediately when you first install your WordPress site is to change the table prefix. This is an option when you first install WordPress using the "famous 5-minute install" and is also easy to locate in the wp-config.php file as the $table_prefix variable:

```
$table_prefix = 'wp_';
```

Again, this method of security is about changing what you can to make your system as unpredictable as possible. If you already installed WordPress and left the default table prefix in place, I recommend changing it as soon as possible (i.e., when you finish reading how to do it in this section).

To change the table prefix on a site that's already up and running, you have to edit your database tables. The easiest way to do so by far is through a database manager such as PHPMyAdmin (see Figure 10-10). First ensure that you backed up your database recently before you make any edits; the last thing you want to do is break your database by accident and not have any way to recover it. When you have a backup, select the table you want to change, select operations from the top menu, and then edit the table name in the rename table box on the left.

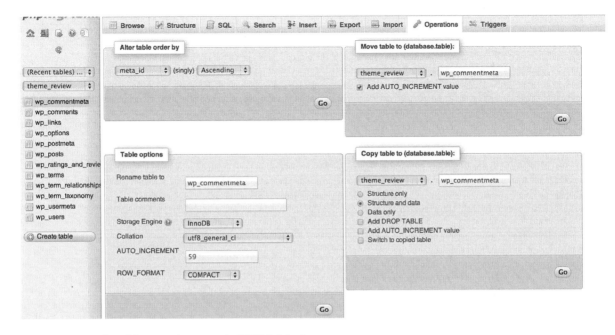

Figure 10-10. *The table operations page in PHPMyAdmin*

Alternatively, if you have only shell access to your database, or have access via the shell and a control panel but don't want to spend your time clicking through each table of your database to rename them, you can just use the RENAME TABLE command in MySQL:

```
RENAME TABLE wp_links TO new_links,
             wp_commentmeta TO new_commentmeta,
             wp_comments TO new_comments,
             wp_options TO new_options,
             wp_postmeta TO new_postmeta,
             wp_posts TO new_posts,
             wp_ratings_and_reviews TO new_ratings_and_reviews,
             wp_terms TO new_terms,
             wp_term_relationships TO new_term_relationships,
             wp_term_taxonomy TO new_term_taxonomy,
             wp_usermeta TO new_usermeta,
             wp_users TO new_users;
```

With that command run or when you finish manually changing all your tables in PHPMyAdmin (or the like), you just need to edit the $table_prefix variable in the wp-config.php file.

Never Use Root User

Whenever you install a new WordPress site on your server, you must never use the root user for your WordPress database. If your sites were ever hacked and the database compromised, having your WordPress system use the root user would give the hacker free rein over your entire database.

The method that I stick to when creating a new site (and I even do this on my local setup as well) is to create a new database user for each web site along with a stand-alone database that only that user has permissions for. This is easily done with PHPMyAdmin: you just need to create a new user and select the "Create database with same name and grant all privileges" option. Alternatively, if you only have or prefer to use the shell to work with MySQL, you can use the following two lines to create a new database and new user for that database:

```
// Create a new database (UTF-8)
CREATE DATABASE mydb DEFAULT CHARACTER SET utf8 DEFAULT COLLATE utf8_unicode_ci;

// Add a user with all privileges
GRANT ALL PRIVILEGES ON table_name.* To 'user_name'@'localhost' IDENTIFIED BY 'password'
```

Remember to replace user_name, password, and mydb with your own settings.

General Security

The final two tips cover more general security elements, but they can still be relevant to WordPress, so I include them as well. Although they may not relate directly to WordPress, they are still relevant for your sites and can be used elsewhere outside of WordPress.

Preventing Script Injections

Script injections happen when an attacker attempts to hijack or modify the data on your site by injecting malicious data or scripts into anything it can possibly access. Although PHP GET and POST requests are usually handled securely by most systems (including WordPress), others may attempt to be hacked (for example, the PHP GLOBALS and _REQUEST variables).

Preventing this is pretty simple with another modification to your .htaccess file. The following directives test the current request to see whether it contains a <script> or has made an attempt to modify the GLOBALS or _REQUEST variables.

```
Options +FollowSymLinks
RewriteEngine On
RewriteCond %{QUERY_STRING} (\<|%3C).*script.*(\>|%3E) [NC,OR]
RewriteCond %{QUERY_STRING} GLOBALS(=|\[|\%[0-9A-Z]{0,2}) [OR]
RewriteCond %{QUERY_STRING} _REQUEST(=|\[|\%[0-9A-Z]{0,2})
RewriteRule ^(.*)$ index.php [F,L]
```

If the request looks like it's doing any of that, it returns a 403 error to the browser.

Preventing Hot-linking

Although it is not necessarily a security concern, it will still affect your web site if someone is scraping content from it and displaying it elsewhere—otherwise known as hot-linking. To prevent hot-linking, there is simple set of rules that you can add to your .htaccess file:

```
RewriteEngine On
#Replace ?website\.com/ with your site url
RewriteCond %{HTTP_REFERRER} !^http://(.+\.)?website\.com/ [NC]
RewriteCond %{HTTP_REFERRER} !^$
#Replace image with your "stealing is bad" image url
RewriteRule .*\.(jpe?g|gif|bmp|png)$ /images/stealingisbad.gif [L]
```

These lines see whether the referrer is your own site; if not, and the referrer is trying to access a `.jpg`, `.gif`, `.bmp`, or `.png` image, this code will serve the `'stealingisbad.gif'` instead of serving the image.

Monitoring Security

As much as you can do to protect your site against attackers, there's always a chance that someone can break through and harm your site. The best way to keep on top of your security (apart from doing all the things up to now that I've talked about) is to monitor your sites to make sure that everything is as it should be.

There are a variety of ways to monitor your site and server. You can keep an eye on the logs created by your server (most servers do this automatically) if you have shell access, or through your server admin panel because a method to monitor your server activity should always be provided by your hosting company.

There is also a vast array of security plugins such as Acunetix WP Security (http://wp-themes-book.com/10009) and Better WP Security (http://wp-themes-book.com/10010). OSSEC (http://wp-themes-book.com/10011) comes recommended from the WordPress Codex for monitoring your server logs; a handy setup guide can also be found here: http://wp-themes-book.com/10012.

Performance

Performance is a big topic of late in the web industry. With the advent of Responsive Web Design in the last couple of years and mobile traffic souring, it's time to take a serious look at how your web site performs. In the last year or so, Grolsch, Oakley, and even Apple have been criticized for the size and slow loading of their web sites; the industry is taking performance seriously, and so should you when it comes to your web sites.

Fortunately, you're off to a good start if you use WordPress, which is built with performance optimization in mind and is carefully crafted to ensure that it does the best possible job to serve its content. However, there are plenty of things you still need to be aware of when building any web site as well as a WordPress site. This section discusses a range of performance optimizations, including those that you should be doing on every site you build as well as looking at some specific WordPress techniques you can utilize.

I don't want to just give you a list of plugins to install; there are plenty of blog posts and articles out there that do just that. However, some plugins stand out it comes to performance, so I'll show you two of the most popular performance plugins for WordPress toward the end of the chapter.

Testing Performance

Before looking at how to tackle performance improvement on your web site, you need to understand how to test your site's performance in the first place. There's no point in making performance optimizations if you don't have a benchmark to test against; otherwise, you don't know whether your improvements are making any difference.

There are two main tools you'll look at when it comes to performance: Google Page Speed and Google Analytics. Google has a team dedicated to web performance, the "Make the web faster" team, which takes performance very seriously, so the services it creates are guaranteed to help you improve your site performance. There's even a fantastic talk on web site performance from one of the team, Ilya Grigorik from WordCamp 2012, which is definitely worth watching: http://wp-themes-book.com/10013.

Google Page Speed not only tests your site against a series of different criteria (see Figure 10-11) but it also gives you advice to help improve your site to reach a higher score. Also divided into desktop and mobile performance, it helps you easily see where your site can be faster and what improvements need to be made.

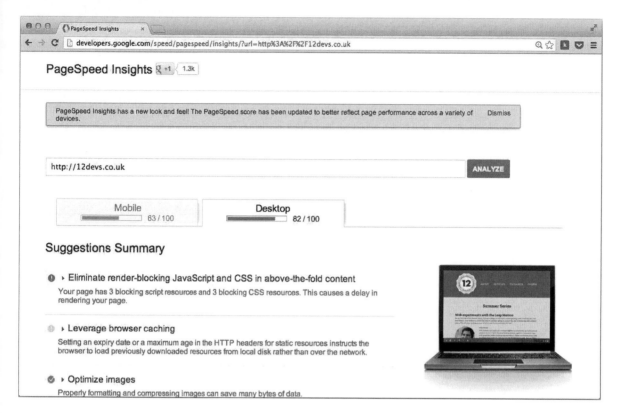

Figure 10-11. *Google Page Speed results page*

The other fantastic tool is Google Analytics, which is on all my sites by default. It's not only good for tracking traffic to your site but it can also be used to view your site's performance as well. As good as testing site load times from your own browser is, there's nothing like real-life user data. Google Analytics gives you all this information in the content menu under site speed (see Figure 10-12).

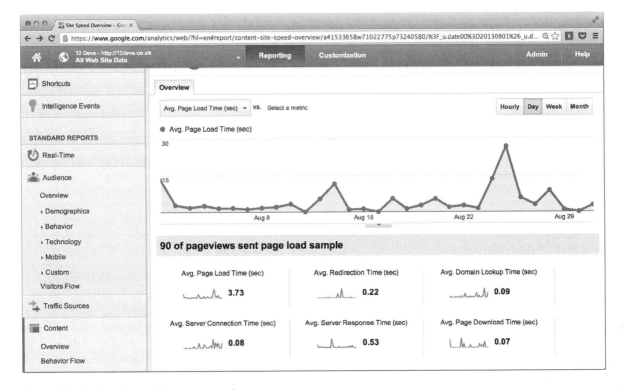

Figure 10-12. *Google Analytics page speed view*

Not only does Analytics allow you to get real user data, you can also see exactly where your site is performing well or not so well. For instance in Figure 10-13, you can see the performance based on each different browser, which can tell you that all your fancy CSS3 transitions and animations are actually slowing down your site load time if IE doesn't have them.

	Browser	Avg. Page Load Time (sec) ⬇ ⓘ	Pageviews ⓘ	Page Load Sample ⓘ
		3.73 Site Avg: 3.73 (0.00%)	**7,378** % of Total: 100.00% (7,378)	**90** % of Total: 100.00% (90)
☐	1. Android Browser	**4.88**	138	1
☐	2. Firefox	**4.62**	1,079	11
☐	3. Chrome	**3.69**	4,873	75
☐	4. Safari	**1.40**	696	1
☐	5. Internet Explorer	**0.92**	189	2

Figure 10-13. *Google Analytics average page load by browser*

Equipped with tools like this, you can see exactly how well your site is performing and where you need to make improvements.

How Much Do You Need to Optimize?

There are hundreds of ways to optimize your site, from simple asset compression to complex load balancing servers. However, the best way to optimize your site isn't to do everything under the sun; you should be basing your optimizations around your site and your audience.

If you have only have a small blog with few images and mostly small text pages, for example, you probably don't need to do much to make sure that the pages load quickly. Likewise, if you have only a small number of visitors to your site, the likelihood is that your server can handle a few hundred requests per day. Optimization is not only about going through a checklist of things that should help improve performance; it's also about making the improvements in the right places and with the right goals in mind.

WordPress performs well if you're just a simple blog on some shared hosting without many optimization techniques. But it can also cope with hosting more than 72 million sites (as seen on WordPress.com), with a number of optimizations on every single piece of hardware and software that WordPress uses. So it's a more than capable piece of software.

In this section, it's a little out of scope to cover the processes used by WordPress.com to be able to successfully host those 72 million blogs. Instead, I'll show you some simple and straightforward optimizations that you can use on your site and with WordPress to serve your sites quickly and effectively. The optimizations are aimed at things you should be considering when building your themes through to things you can do when you set up your server because performance comes from everywhere.

KISS: Do the Simple Things that Make the Most Difference

Now that you're all set up with how to benchmark your site and starting to think about how best to improve performance on your site(s), it's time to look at some actual techniques to do so. I'll take you through some simple but effective things that you need to consider that will help improve the performance of your site, They won't take much time to implement and may not seem that complicated, but they will definitely help when it comes to site performance.

Hosting

The best starting point for performance is to make sure that you have good hosting. There are hundreds of different hosts out there that range from cheap and cheerful shared hosting to fully dedicated servers that only you will use. For starters, I always avoid the cheap and cheerful option because it usually entails shared hosting in which you have no control, and the hosting provider looks after the servers. With hosting like that, you can't control anything when it comes to performance. Of course, you can optimize your WordPress install, your theme, and everything else, but if the servers are slow, you can't help speed them up.

The best method is to spend a little bit of money on your hosting; it doesn't have to be much (maybe $30–$40 per month for a virtual server that you control). I host my sites through a virtual server with Media Temple without a problem. I have a dedicated virtual box in which I control everything that's installed on the box and all the configurations as well.

It might feel a little daunting at first to run your own web server, but there are some other options. For example, you might like a managed box in which all the setup is done for you, but it's still your own dedicated virtual machine. However, picking up some systems administration skills is worth the effort; the documentation is usually easy to follow, and you'll be set up in no time. I can't stress enough how important good hosting is for your sites to perform well, so make sure that you spend a bit of money to have a good solid host at the foundation of your sites.

Building Your Themes Responsibly

When it comes to creating your themes, there a lot of little things you can do to make a big performance difference, as discussed in the following sections.

Concatenating and Compressing CSS and JavaScript

Reducing the size and number of requests is important for performance. You want as few files going down the wire as possible and you also want them to be as small as possible to make downloading faster. For production, I usually concatenate all the JavaScript into a single file (including all jQuery plugins and my own code), along with using the jQuery source from the Google API. (As discussed before, this is worth doing because many users have it cached on their machines already.) I also use a CSS preprocessor when generating my CSS files, which is great for optimizing CSS because it can compress everything into the smallest file possible.

Optimizing Images and Using Sprites

When serving images as part of your theme, ensure that they are optimized as much as possible. Apps such as ImageOptim (http://imageoptim.com/) or CodeKit (http://incident57.com/codekit/) can do image optimization for you on your machine (see Figure 10-14). Smushit (http://smushit.com) is a service from Yahoo! that optimizes images for you in the browser; it even has a WordPress plugin that can do this from inside WordPress. You can also use sprites when you have a series of small images, like icons, to serve. This will help reduce requests and speed up your site.

Figure 10-14. *The CodeKit app showing image optimization in the sidebar*

Removing Unnecessary Dynamic Content

Although earlier you looked at ways to make WordPress as dynamic as possible using a range of functions to get information from the settings and such, sometimes these functions are just not necessary. For example, the style sheet, script paths, and the meta charset tag can lead to unnecessary function calls that could be replaced with static text. Note this meta charset definition:

```
<meta charset="<?php bloginfo( 'charset' ); ?>" />
```

It would probably best be served as static content like this, saving a function call and a request to the database:

```
<meta charset="UTF-8" />
```

Likewise with style sheet and script includes: in production, you're probably better off replacing the dynamic includes set up in your functions file with static links in your header and footer files.

Compressing and Browser Caching

The next optimization is setting up Gzipping (compression) and browser caching with expires headers in your .htaccess file. Setting up file compression on your server through the .htaccess file means that all text files served are compressed on the server before being sent for each request. Doing this really helps to speed up the transfer.

Besides compression, the .htaccess file is the place to set up browser caching as well, by implementing expires headers for certain file types. This means that when a browser receives an image or JavaScript file, for instance, it keeps a cached version of the asset for as long as the expires time sets out. With an asset cached in the browser, the next time an asset is requested by the same user, it will already be there and ready to serve without needing to make another request to the server.

When it comes to setting up compression and browser caching, the great HTML5 Boilerplate (http://html5boilerplate.com/) has all you need. The code is much too long to include here; the .htaccess file can be found at http://wp-themes-book.com/10014 (look for the part that starts with the 'Compression' comment). Remember to always keep checking back because it's always being updated with the latest techniques.

Creating a Static Domain for Content

A browser can download multiple assets from a single domain in parallel (a very large simplification, I assure you), but there is a limit to the number of files that can be accessed simultaneously. To improve parallelization in the browser, you can serve your assets from a separate domain from your main site. You'll look at content delivery networks shortly, which allow for something similar, but for now there's something you can do within WordPress.

As you saw in the security tips, it's possible to set a different content domain from inside the WordPress configuration file by defining this constant:

```
define('WP_CONTENT_URL', 'http://review.dev/content');
```

Instead of simply changing the content URL to a different folder within your site, you can actually set up a completely separate subdomain of your site from which you serve your assets:

```
define('WP_CONTENT_URL', 'http://assets.website.com');
```

By using this new URL, you improve parallelization in the browser and increase the speed at which your assets are downloaded. To do this, you need access to your server config files to be able to point the new subdomain to your content directory. When you then use the bloginfo('template_directory') function when displaying assets (or hard-coding the content URL yourself), you are serving the assets from the new subdomain.

When it comes to setting up an asset domain, one more thing has to be set up because WordPress sends cookies to any domain it's loaded on that will reduce the effectiveness of having a static domain from which to serve your assets. To prevent this, add this WordPress constant to the `wp-config.php` file:

```
define( 'COOKIE_DOMAIN', 'www.website.com' );
```

It should be set to the domain that you *want* cookies to be passed to; the static asset domain you've set up will then be free from cookies and perform a bit better.

Using a Content Delivery Network (CDN)

Using a content delivery network (CDN) is quite similar to setting up a static domain for your assets, except that the CDN is a network of optimized servers storing your content around the world to serve your content as fast as possible. When you set up a static assets domain on your server, the assets would still be requested from your server, but with a CDN the content is hosted on a range of different servers, reducing the load on your own server.

Many large sites make use of CDNs and, depending on what your site is for, you might use one to increase performance on your site and reduce load on your servers. If you have a photo-blog, for instance, or a site with a large number of heavy images, you might find a CDN worthwhile to increase performance.

CDNs do come at a cost, however, but it depends on how much content you put through them and how often the site is accessed. The most popular asset CDNs include these:

- Amazon CloudFront (http://wp-themes-book.com/10015)

- MaxCDN (http://wp-themes-book.com/10016)

- Akamai (http://wp-themes-book.com/10017)

For some of my sites, I use the Cloudflare free service (http://wp-themes-book.com/10018), which is less an asset CDN and more a full site CDN in which the domain is set up to go through the Cloudflare servers. There are also some premium packages with Cloudflare that allow for increased security (including SSL) and other services to help optimize performance and protect against problems such as DDOS attacks.

Maintaining WordPress for a Smoother Site

Besides all the performance optimization gains you can make from using some of the previous techniques when developing and hosting your WordPress site, there's also a lot to be said for ensuring that your site is well maintained. Making sure that your WordPress site is well looked after is a simple way to make sure that it is performing at its best.

Plugin Maintenance

Making sure that plugins you no longer use are deactivated is often overlooked, but can greatly help with performance. If you have tens of plugins loading and not doing anything on your site, it's bound to run a lot slower. Also ensuring that you carefully select plugins and test them against the performance of your site both before and after they are installed is important. If your site suddenly drops in performance once a plugin gets installed, it might be time to look for an alternative solution.

It's also important, not only for security but also for performance, that you keep your plugins up to date and keep testing your site once a plugin has been updated to see whether there are any performance effects.

Finally, if you do have a plugin disabled that you are sure that you will never use again, remove it from WordPress entirely along with any files it may have created. You want to ensure that you keep the leanest possible setup of WordPress you can, which means that there's no room for discarded plugins lingering about.

Database Maintenance

Database maintenance is important; because the database is the main store of all the information and content on your site, you need it to be performing at its best. Keeping a regular eye on your database, optimizing it, and keeping it backed up often is a great way to keep performance up. You can optimize your database from PHPMyAdmin or via MySQL with the `'OPTIMIZE TABLE'` command, but you probably need a plugin for more WordPress-specific optimization. Here are two good options:

- **WP Clean Up** (http://wp-themes-book.com/10019) gives you a lot of controls to keep your database in check, allowing you to delete revisions, drafts, and trashed comments from the WordPress admin. You can use the controls to optimize the database as you would in PHPMyAdmin, and so on.

- **WP-DBManager** (http://wp-themes-book.com/10020) is a very comprehensive plugin, allowing you to not only optimize the database but also perform scheduled backups and other tasks easily.

More Performance Resources

You have learned about some of the simple performance optimizations that can be made quickly and easily on any site you make. I recommend that if you want to get a lot deeper into performance, you should take a look at some of these resources:

- Harry Roberts' (@csswizardy) post on frontend performance: http://wp-themes-book.com/10021

- Ilya Grigorik's (@igrigorik) web site; there are lots of great performance articles there: http://wp-themes-book.com/10022

- The WordPress Codex, especially if you want to read more on high traffic performance: http://wp-themes-book.com/10023

Caching

One of the biggest performance improvements to have on your site is caching, which in this case is the process of storing a static version of something that is dynamically generated in WordPress. With most things being dynamically generated in WordPress, caching provides a massive improvement in performance. Caching can be quite complex, however, which is why when you look for information on caching in WordPress, you usually find discussions of plugins. Two plugins in particular are usually discussed: W3 Total Cache and WP Super Cache.

These two plugins are by far *the* go-to plugins for anyone looking to speed up a web site, and rightfully so. Each boasts several million downloads from the plugin repository. Figure 10-15 shows the results of a poll on plugins at the Digging into WordPress site (http://digwp.com), in which the two are far and away the most popular.

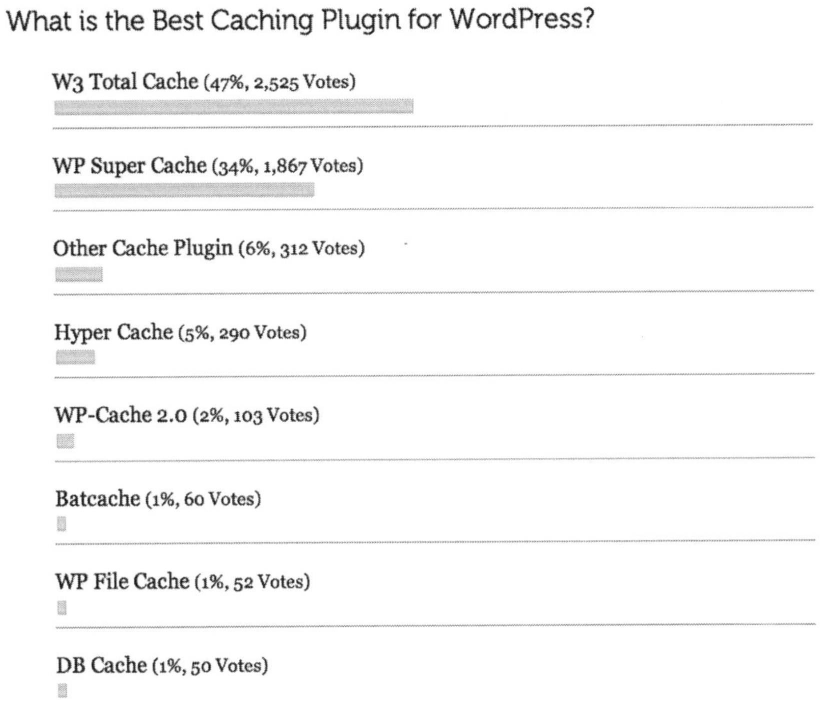

What is the Best Caching Plugin for WordPress?

W3 Total Cache (47%, 2,525 Votes)

WP Super Cache (34%, 1,867 Votes)

Other Cache Plugin (6%, 312 Votes)

Hyper Cache (5%, 290 Votes)

WP-Cache 2.0 (2%, 103 Votes)

Batcache (1%, 60 Votes)

WP File Cache (1%, 52 Votes)

DB Cache (1%, 50 Votes)

Figure 10-15. *The top results from the Digging into WordPress poll*

Neither plugin completely removes the complexity of setting up caching, and they both take plenty of time to set up and require some level server access for you to set up and configure files and directories for the plugin. But they do make caching a lot more user friendly.

Of the two, W3 Total Cache is the more complex and feature-packed option. It comes with the capability to implement browser-caching, page-caching, object-caching, database-caching, file-minification, CDN support, Varnish caching, and much more. So a lot of the techniques you've looked at in this chapter can be taken care of by one single plugin. This improvement comes at the cost of complexity, however: W3 Total Cache is a behemoth to set up and will definitely take you the best part of a morning. But once you're all set up and running, the caching is taken care of and happily sits working in the background (see Figure 10-16).

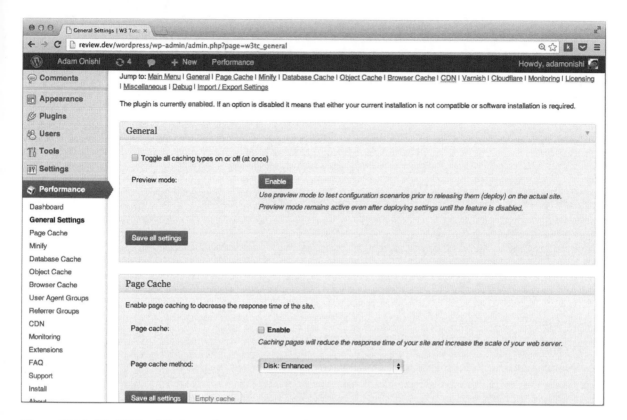

Figure 10-16. *The W3 Total Cache configuration page and sidebar menu*

In contrast, WP Super Cache is quite a minimal plugin, at least when compared with W3 Total Cache: it offers only page caching and CDN support (see Figure 10-17). However, although it lacks the features of W3 Total Cache, it makes up for it in ease of setup and still delivers major performance enhancements for your site. With WP Super Cache, you can still implement all the regular performance techniques covered in this chapter to help speed up your web site.

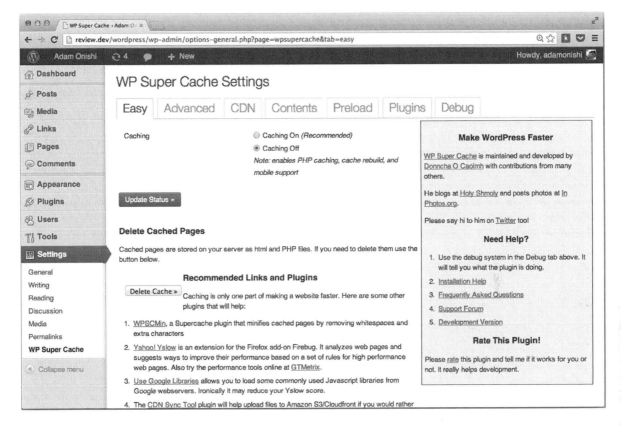

Figure 10-17. *The WP Super Cache plugin setup screen*

Again, I put the choice of which one you use down to the complexity and needs of the site you're using it for. If you just want simple page caching for a blog and not much else, you can't go wrong with WP Super Cache. Its minimal feature set and relatively quick setup should be perfectly suited. But if you have a large blog serving thousands of requests per day and hosting some quite complex pages, it's worth the extra time and work to get W3 Total Cache set up and running on your site.

You can find both plugins in the plugin repository; here are some links to a couple of handy setup guides for each plugin by John Saddington:

- W3 Total Cache (`http://wp-themes-book.com/10024`)

- Setting up and optimizing W3 Total Cache (`http://wp-themes-book.com/10025`)

- WP Super Cache (`http://wp-themes-book.com/10026`)

- Setting up and optimizing WP Super Cache (`http://wp-themes-book.com/10027`)

Summary

Although WordPress is a very secure and optimized system, there is still a lot you can do to ensure that you keep your sites safe and performing to the best of their capability. You now know that although WordPress's popularity gives it a lot of strength, it also comes with some downsides that make it a prime target for hackers. So security has to be considered outside of the system you just downloaded. Ensuring that WordPress is secure should be your number one priority.

You learned how to ensure that your theme is secure and that you protect it from being the source of any problems for your web site. Using nonces correctly and sanitizing data where appropriate means that your theme will stand up against a lot of malicious attacks.

The second half of the chapter covered performance, looking at how to improve and optimize WordPress in general to serve faster web sites, and at improvements you can make when developing your themes.

CHAPTER 11

■ ■ ■

Distributing Your Theme

You've learned a lot about how to build great themes using the full power of WordPress. Now it's time to see how to distribute your themes, whether for free or for profit.

The themes ecosystem is a huge overcrowded place from both sides of the coin; many developers are creating themes as well as a mass market of consumers looking for themes for their own sites. With a market so crowded, you might think it might be too full of competition already for anyone to be able to successfully distribute their themes, either for free or at a price. However, many people are still joining the theme development business each day, and many are successful and making money from it.

In this chapter, I'll talk about the reasons why people can still get into the theme development business by not only showing you how to get your themes on to a web site for sale but also how it's possible to make a name for yourself as a great theme developer.

One of the first things to consider is how much you want to put into this venture as a developer and business. If you're looking for something short-term to make a few dollars, you might have a hard time getting your themes in front of many consumers. Whereas if you take a long-term approach and set yourself up for a future as a theme developer, even if it's only part-time, you'll definitely see the results of your hard work.

There's a lot more to theme development when your goal is to eventually distribute and potentially sell your themes. This chapter covers everything from what you should be considering at the very start of your project before writing a single line of code, a marketing plan for your themes, and how to support the customers using your themes once they're out in the wild. As you might expect, this chapter involves a lot less coding than usual. So if you're serious about making some money with your themes, get comfy, shut down your text editor, grab a cup of tea, and settle in for a bit of a read.

Before You Begin

So, you've decided that you want to create a WordPress theme to sell or release for free to other WordPress users. Where do you start? Before you download the latest WordPress and create a new theme folder, you have to decide several things, including who your theme will be aimed at, what features will be included, and how it will be coded.

Before you start coding, you need to start planning; and to start planning, you need to do some research. Even if you have a great idea and design in mind for the end result, it's still good to start off by researching every element you can think of and probably a few more you haven't—that's why you're reading this book, I hope. In this section of the chapter, I'll discuss the main areas you should be looking into before you start to build your theme, show you how to plan what features to include, and even give you a few ideas on how to start the build.

Target Audience

Before you start, think about what sort of audience you're expecting for your theme. If your answer is "everyone," you'll likely have a rough time trying to get your theme in front of people who want to use it. There are currently more than 2,000 themes in the WordPress Themes Directory, and nearly 3,500 are available on ThemeForest. Those are just two web sites; there are tens of thousands of WordPress themes available. How can your theme stand out from the rest?

The answer is to target a more specific audience. If you target your theme at bloggers, that's a start; if you target your theme at food bloggers, you've narrowed down your audience even more. Making your theme target such a specific niche may sound like your cutting yourself off from a lot of potential customers, but when you look at how many themes are bought or downloaded (80,835,212 at last count on the WordPress Themes Directory alone), you'll realize that this is far from the case.

By narrowing down your audience and targeting your theme more specifically, it also helps you in more ways than just sales. Having a specific niche to aim for means you can be more targeted with your development: a food bloggers web site may need to allow for easy uploading of videos for recipes, whereas a music blogger is more likely to need integration with audio and sites like Sound Cloud. The niche also transfers to the style of the design, so you give yourself even tighter rules on how to design and build your theme.

Marketing to a niche is much easier because you know exactly whom to market to. I'll talk more specifically about marketing in the next section, but for now it's enough to know that aiming your marketing at a specific set of people is easier than trying to be heard by everyone. It might also reduce the amount of marketing you need to do in the first place.

For example, the Wedding category on ThemeForest (shown in Figure 11-1) currently has nine themes in total. If you target such a specific niche, your competition for customers has just been cut by several thousand.

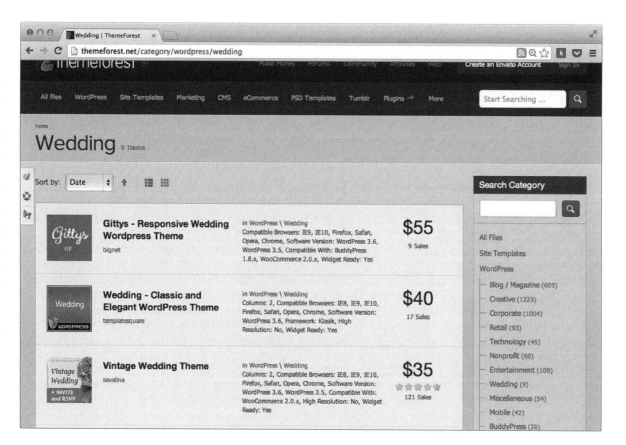

Figure 11-1. *The wedding category on ThemeForest, currently boasting only nine themes to choose from*

Competition

Next, consider the competition your theme will have in the marketplace. I touched on this a little bit when talking about competition for your target audience, but it's worth researching for many other reasons as well. Throughout this chapter, you'll see many examples of the advantages of seeing what others are doing. Doing so will help guide you with what you could or should be doing with your theme, whether it's doing enough to compete or going one step farther to beat your competition.

When you find your audience/niche, start to look at the competition: the styles of each theme, its features, and the sales for each one. You should also look at posts like "top 10 WordPress themes of October"-style posts (see Figure 11-2). Although I'm not a huge fan of posts like these, they're a great source of research because you can see what other people are doing with their themes. What made these 10 themes stand out above the others? As bad as following the next hot trend can be for various reasons, if enough people like this current trend for X, Y, or Z, you can capitalize on it and bump up the potential sales for your theme.

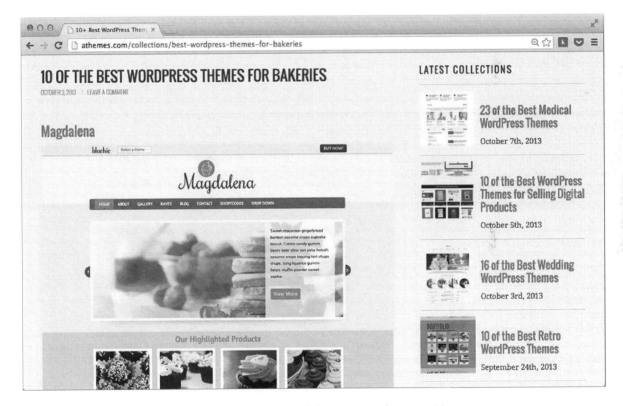

Figure 11-2. *"X best WordPress themes" posts can be helpful to scope out the competition*

What Features to Add

Although you may think that the features you choose for your theme depend entirely on how you want your theme designed and how you want to build it, there is a certain amount of expectation (certainly when creating a premium theme) that some features should always be there. Ultimately, the decision does rest with you when you create your theme, but be aware that if certain "core" features are missing when you release it, you will be hard-pressed to compete with the other themes available.

In this section, I'll show you lots of potential features for your theme, splitting them into two rough categories. *Must-have* features are often found in a lot of premium themes and your users will likely expect them. *Could-have* features are those that you might want to consider including because a lot of premium themes have them. In order to compete, no matter what you might think, users often choose a theme based on its features.

"Must-have" Features

The must-have features I'll talk about here are key features your theme should almost certainly be shipping with.

Standard WordPress Functionality

Always make sure that your theme supports as many of the standard WordPress features as possible. Features such as custom headers, custom menus, post formats, and widgets should be supported without fail. Almost all WordPress users will be familiar with the features; if your theme doesn't support them, potential customers might look elsewhere, no matter how good your theme is. Fortunately, these features are covered throughout this book, so there's no excuse because you're well equipped to add them to your theme.

Internationalization

Ensuring that your theme is easily translated is another important feature your theme should have. There are millions of people using WordPress all around the world; cutting off thousands of potential customers because they can't use your theme easily in their native language is definitely something you want to avoid. Be aware that some languages are displayed right-to-left, so it's important that you include an RTL style sheet with your theme, too.

In the next chapter, I'll cover how to go about internationalizing your themes, so be sure to read up on how to avoid missing out on potential customers.

WordPress Coding Standards

This feature is so important that it was discussed in Chapter 1. Ensuring that your theme sticks to the WordPress coding standards is not only good for working on the theme but it's also positive when you're in a position to distribute or sell your themes. There's the possibility that some of your customers will be able to code to some degree, whether they're part-time developers or users trying to learn how to code. Ensuring that your themes are well coded and stick to the WordPress coding standards allow people to easily modify your themes if they want to. I'll get to the reasons why this might occur later in the chapter when I talk about licensing.

Although I'm a competent WordPress developer, when working for various agencies I've sometimes had to work with a premium theme or two. Unfortunately, most of them have been terribly coded and have completely ignored the coding standards. Don't put another one of those terrible themes out there; you may think that your customers won't need to work with your code, and although sometimes that may be the case, there's still no excuse for writing poor code. Think of it as good karma.

When coding, it's important to remember to comment your code well to make it easier for people to find certain parts they're looking for and understand what the code does at certain points. I'll cover more about code documentation later in the chapter in the section on support.

SEO

I must admit that whether SEO is a "must-have" feature might be a topic for debate, but hear me out for a moment. I'm not talking about ensuring that your theme adds all the features of an SEO plugin; that's a plugin's job, as you would expect. The level of SEO I'm talking about here is to ensure that your theme is well coded so that it's good for SEO in the first place. It should ensure that your images have alt text, your links have title tags, and your main title tag outputs the correct information based on each page as standard. Just these little touches should be easy enough to achieve and enable you to add a much-sought-after "SEO" keyword to your feature list, which will gain some traction with potential customers.

"Should-have" Features

Should-have features are features that you should definitely at least consider adding to your theme. Some of them are broader in relation to how your theme will be designed; others are specific features that a lot of themes have and your potential customers might be looking for. Once again, researching your competitors to see what they're including is important.

Responsive Design

Responsive design is another feature that might have to go in the "must-haves," based on the current state of play in web design. If you take a look at the top WordPress themes on ThemeForest, you'll be hard-pressed to find a single theme listed that isn't responsive—a lot of them even include the word "responsive" in the theme title (see Figure 11-3). Clearly there is a huge market in responsive themes now; the Web in general is moving toward responsive design as standard, including major brands such as Starbucks, *The Guardian*, Barak Obama's campaign web site, and Virgin (which just launched its new responsively designed web site at the time of writing this book).

Figure 11-3. *Popular WordPress themes on ThemeForest*

Ensuring that your theme is built with a responsive design enables you to compete in the WordPress themes market as it stands at the moment. Because design is out of scope for this book, you can find some great resources from the *A Book Apart* series (http://www.abookapart.com/), including *Responsive Web Design* by Ethan Marcotte (http://wp-themes-book.com/11001) and *Mobile First* by Luke Wroblewski (http://wp-themes-book.com/11002).

Retina Ready

This is something else you will see cropping up more and more with WordPress themes (a theme shows "retina" in its title in Figure 11-3). Lots of phones now boast screens with high-pixel density as well as the "retina" screen in Apple products (including some MacBook Pro's), so providing this feature in your theme is becoming almost as important as a responsive design.

At the company I work for now, all web sites are built responsive by default and with high-resolution graphics ready for all devices. It's become a standard that our clients are expecting, and I can see it being the same case for consumers in the theme market as well.

Multiple Page Layouts

Besides providing theme templates to cover most of the standard page types you will likely encounter (page, single post, post archives, 404 page, and so on), note that customers might want to customize pages on an individual basis. Furnishing your theme with some custom page templates to add some simple layout adjustments, such as a full-width page or single/double sidebar options (depending on your default options), will give your end users the freedom to lay out a page as they like. You don't have to go overboard here; just adding a simple full-width page is usually enough, but choosing which extra layouts would be worthwhile to your customers depends on your theme and your design.

Custom Widgets and/or Shortcodes

This is a highly debated subject because some people think that a theme should come with various amounts of custom shortcodes or widgets for the user to add functionality through the theme. On the other hand, some people believe that widgets and shortcodes should be left to plugins to add, thus removing the need for users to change all their settings/content every time they change their theme.

Again, I think this entirely depends on your theme. If there is functionality that works explicitly with your theme and would be best achieved with a shortcode or widget, you should be adding it. However, if your theme doesn't require it, maybe it's best to leave it to plugins to add the functionality instead.

You also need to consider your competition. Going back to the ThemeForest's most popular themes, a few of them (but certainly not all) boast shortcodes as a feature (in some cases, "tons of shortcodes"). So you should consider whether this is a popular selling point for themes; if including some shortcodes or widgets makes your theme more attractive to potential customers, you may have to bite the bullet and add them.

Sliders and Galleries

Another contentious subject is whether to add a slider (rotating banners, carousel, and so on) and gallery features to your theme. Once again, I think this one comes down to how suitable it is for your design and how much you think the feature will give you an advantage over the competition.

A quick note on galleries: WordPress has a standard feature for users to easily add a gallery to the content of their pages and posts content, so supporting this is a must. However, supporting other gallery plugins or adding your own system to WordPress is the optional aspect I'm talking about here.

Social Media Integration

This one depends a bit on the content your theme is aimed at and also whether you want to bake this functionality into your theme by default or allow the user to add it with a plugin. The latter option depends more on how you feel about the design of your theme because social media plugins can dish out some pretty ugly-looking widgets. If your theme is for a blog, for instance, you can be fairly certain that some form of social sharing will be sought after.

Don't think only about integrating content with social media; you might also find that users want to share their own social network details on their site for others to link to. Another standard WordPress feature enables all users to have social media details in their profiles, so you may want to utilize this (see Figure 11-4). You could also add some more up-to-date social networks to the defaults or add a custom options page for the theme that allows users to add their social links to the main site.

Contact Info

E-mail *(required)*

Website

AIM

Yahoo IM

Jabber / Google Talk

Figure 11-4. *Social media details in the user profile page*

Advertising Space

Building your theme with potential advertising spots coded in that allows users to add their advertising through the WordPress admin could make your theme more appealing to potential customers as well. Many web site owners create their sites with the aim of monetizing them to a certain extent, so allowing them to easily include advertisements on their site and have their placement designed by the theme creator can be a major selling point.

Considering Features

You've just seen a large number of features that you can add to your theme. It may seem like quite a bit of work to do so, but (as I talked about previously) lots of these features, although not being core to the way your theme is designed, are actually core to customer expectations and can greatly affect the success of your theme in a marketplace. Once again, it all comes down to research. When you consider creating your theme, its' important to look into the competition and your target audience and see what features other themes in that area have and what you'll have to compete against.

Theme Options and Customizations

Although this is another feature technically, I think it's important enough to demand its own section. In fact, I deem it so important that you've already read an entire chapter on theme options and the theme customizer back in Chapter 7. With this in mind, I'll talk only about theme options very briefly because I discussed a lot of the theory around adding theme options back in that chapter. I do think it's important to reiterate a couple of things, though:

- Your theme should definitely include options and customizations (through the theme customizer).

- Don't go overboard with the amount of options the user can change.

- Be smart about the options you offer—think color scheme over single color change options.

As long as you give users enough options to customize their themes to feel unique, you'll be fine. Doing so also saves you time in the long run by avoiding a lot of support requests asking for help with customizing certain parts.

Building Your Theme

Here I just want to talk through a few considerations to think about before starting to build your theme. The main consideration is defining your short and long-term goals for getting into theme distribution because they can really affect how you'll build your theme(s) in the first place. For instance, if you're building only a single theme and want to do so quickly and effectively, finding a theme framework to build on top of (or even creating a child theme of a popular theme already in existence) might be an option. However, if you're thinking about starting a theme distribution business and have a more long-term plan, you might want to consider building your own framework from the ground up so that you know what you're working with throughout the life of your business.

Framework Your Theme(s)

A framework is a base set of files and code from which you can start building your theme. Many general theme frameworks are in existence already, and a lot of people who go into the theme distribution business tend to build their own. Even though I haven't worked on creating themes for distribution so far, I created a framework to use when I was building a lot of themes back in my first job—which still exists today, in fact.

When you start creating your own themes for distribution, you have a couple of options: either create your own framework on which to base your themes or choose one of the many existing frameworks. The decision will again depend on short and long-term plans for your theme(s) and how much time you have/want to invest in your theme(s). Noting all the features you've read about so far, you know there are many features to code into your theme. Many theme frameworks out there already include lots of them.

If you have the time, I recommend that you start your own framework from scratch. Obviously, looking at and learning from other frameworks in the process is good practice, but ensuring that at the end of the day you've compiled the framework yourself will be better for it in the long term.

There's a great talk on this kind of process by Stu Robson, called *Make your code delicious* (http://12devs.co.uk/summer-videos/) from the 12 Devs events (shameless plug), which covers how to learn from others while still making your code your own.

If, however, you are pressed for time, there are some great frameworks that you can use as a base. Some are more general theme frameworks, such as Starkers by Viewport Industries; or you can find more fully functional frameworks built with child theming and distribution in mind, such as the Hybrid framework. Here's a full list with links to some of the more popular frameworks:

- Hybrid: http://wp-themes-book.com/11003

- Thematic: http://wp-themes-book.com/11004

- Starkers: http://wp-themes-book.com/11005

- Underscores: http://wp-themes-book.com/11006

- Genesis: http://wp-themes-book.com/11007

- Elemental: http://wp-themes-book.com/11008

Beware of Reliance on Third-Party Code

Although this statement applies to frameworks, I'm talking about relying on plugins for theme functionality, too. When working with anyone else's code, whether it's a framework or a plugin, you are relinquishing control over that aspect of your own theme. If the original author opts to change how something works, you need to be aware of it, and you may end up having to rewrite code in your own theme to compensate.

Of course, everything associated with WordPress is GPL licensed (more on that later in the chapter), meaning that you are free to edit other people's code as you want. However, by editing third-party frameworks or plugins, you then lose the ability to update the code further down the line if the original author makes any changes. This might sound all right if you've modified some code and are happy with what the framework does from the point at which you started using it. But updates are generally good because they include bug fixes, code optimizations, and new features; so cutting yourself off from those benefits can be a major disadvantage.

Those are the downsides of using a third-party theme framework. If you also rely on many plugins for your theme features, you might end up with the same problems, as well as a few others. If your theme is using certain plugins to set up features and functionality, how will users make sure that they have these plugins? Do you add in the documentation a list of required plugins for users to install before they use your theme? This would only frustrate users and make them take more time to set your theme up over others that just work out of the box as soon as they've activated the theme. You could get around this by adding a list of various plugins that your theme is designed to support, but again it would be a hassle if it were relied on for key features.

This section was not intended to put you off from using any third-party code ever, because sometimes it is worth doing for the time-saving nature of using code that someone has spent days, months, or even years developing for a certain feature. Although there are still benefits to using others' code in your projects, I think it's important to know the downsides as well so you are aware of what could potentially happen and you can plan for it should you need to.

Marketing

Now that you've decided what your theme will do and how you will build it, you need to start thinking about how to market your theme. You may think marketing is something that should be considered only after your theme is ready to go and available to download or buy, but it should start a lot earlier—you might even start marketing yourself and your theme before you start building anything.

In this section, you'll look at how to gain a user base from the very beginning before you release your theme, how to promote yourself through various avenues, and how to price and demo your theme. It all entails more research: looking at your competitors, looking for people who might be interested in your theme, and finding ways of communicating with them to get your themes in front of them.

In this section, I'll mostly talk about theme distribution from a position of selling themes; although the advice is still useful for people looking to distribute themes for free.

Building a Customer-Base

Without customers, your theme will not sell. That's a very matter-of-fact statement, but it's hard to say it any other way. For your themes to sell, or even if you're giving them away for free, you need people to know about your theme in order to buy it. If you plan to just create your theme and upload it to a marketplace and expect to get sales, you won't. You could be coding the best themes in the world, but if no one knows about them how can you expect people to buy them?

For instance, if you refer to Figure 11-4 and Figure 11-5, you'll see that all the information the users of ThemeForest gets is a very small preview of the theme and list of a few features, at first glance at least. How will your theme stand out from the rest of these?

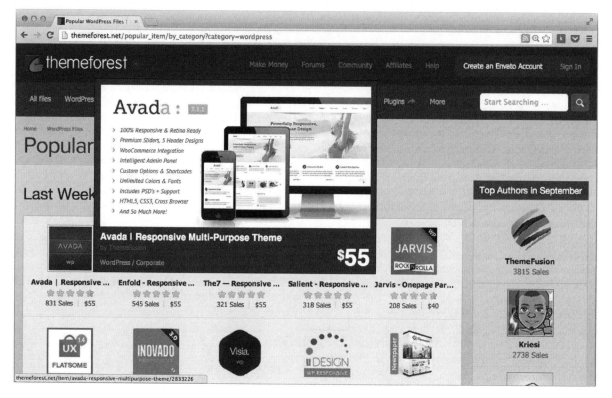

Figure 11-5. *The theme preview (hover) on ThemeForest*

The answer is not to rely on your theme to just automatically stand out from among the thousands of others on a marketplace site, but to have users going to the marketplace looking for your themes.

Create a "Light" Version of Your Theme

Before looking to sell your theme, it's worth releasing a free or light version of the theme want to sell. A light version of your theme can have a few reduced features that would make creating a premium version worthwhile for you and for prospective users. By creating a light theme and offering it for free, you're giving potential customers the opportunity to try out your theme ahead of them making a purchase because no one likes to just blindly throw their money at something without knowing what they'll get with their hard-earned cash.

Of course, some people won't want a premium version of your theme, and some will just use the light theme forever, but that's not a bad thing, either. It means that people are using what you've built and can act as great promoters for you. And because it's a free version of a theme, you can always leave a little "theme by" text in the footer with a link back to your site.

> *The free theme was unique and easy to use, and people liked it so much that they began requesting a premium version.*
>
> —Sawyer Hollenshead

The real outcome you want is for users to have Sawyer's experience: to try out your light theme and like it so much they actually come to you asking for a premium version.

Creating a Presence on the Web

When I say "have a presence on the Web," I mean to ensure that people know about you, where to find you, what you're good at, and why they should come to you for their themes. It's likely you will already have a web site; if not, create one because it gives people a place to find you online. If you have a Twitter account and use it regularly, ensure that it is linked to as well. Just be careful that if you're using it in a more professional capacity, ensure that what you're talking about reflects that.

All this is about ensuring that you have a "brand." I hate to call it that, but it's the best description of what you should be aiming for. It means that when people read something by you or see something with your name on it, they instantly associate it with your work. If you've done it right, branding should be a good thing.

If you can and want to, writing is another way to bolster your brand. It doesn't have to be a book or anything too overwhelming; just writing blog posts on your site about what you're doing and probably some things about WordPress is good. Even writing tutorials or guest posts on your site and others' can help you to reach a wider audience. The more people that see your work, read about you, and generally make a connection between you and good output in whatever form, the more it will help your theme sell.

Set Up a Mailing List

When you've built this audience, you want to keep it—or at least find a way to keep in touch with everyone in it—and there's no easier way of doing this than to create a quick mailing list. The aim of the mailing list isn't to mail people that often; by creating a contact list, you'll be able to send out information about your latest project or product, so you instantly have an audience ahead of a new theme release.

You can e-mail the list on a more regular basis to keep people up to date with happenings on the Web in general or with the work you're doing. Providing a free or helpful service alongside a premium service such as your themes business can be a great way to gain new potential customers.

Utilizing Your Audience

Once you have an audience, it's important to use it to good effect. You want to be able to not only promote your themes and your work but also to research your future themes and get feedback on your ideas. You could invite some people to be beta testers—they can get your themes early in exchange for giving you feedback and flagging bugs in the theme.

All this helps to build your audience because the more you can engage with audience members, the more likely they are to recommend you to friends and other contacts.

Taking a Helpful vs. Promotional Attitude

Success is a lot about the attitude you adopt when engaging with your audience. Having a helpful attitude toward your marketing shows that you're not there just to get people to buy things from you; you're actually part of the wider community and looking to help people where you can.

Contrast this with a purely promotional attitude in which the only communications you make are promoting yourself or your products. This can put people off and your audience might dwindle. People are more receptive to someone willing to offer them a solution to a problem or help with something than by someone who writes about how amazing their products are and how great they are at what they do.

Bear in mind your target audience; think about who they look to and what publications they might read. Then offer your themes or services to those blogs or people. Getting your name in front of the blogs or industry professionals who have a large following of your target audience helps you get your name in front of more potential customers.

Getting Case Studies

Finally, don't forget that when you have an audience and have worked with different people who like your work and/or your themes, make sure that you collect case studies and positive quotes to add to your marketing site. Having good case studies means people can see that your work has been verified by others, and it gives people more confidence in you.

To collect case studies or quotes, you can reach out to your mailing list or to past customers and ask for feedback. That way, you can add any positive feedback to your site (always ask permission first), and if you get some constructive feedback about improvements your customers want, you have something to work on. Speak to people who have worked with you before, even if it's not with your themes; positive feedback is always good to have and it's great for other users to see when they visit your site.

Creating a Marketing Web Site

When you have an audience and when your theme is nearly ready to release is the time you should start thinking about making a promotional site for your theme (or eventually your theme business). Before release, you can use the site as a teaser site, showing off the design and explaining the features, as well as collecting more e-mail for your mailing list. When you release your theme, you want it to be either the place customers can download your theme from or easily direct them to where they it can be bought. You can even use the site to demo the theme. Once your theme has been released for a while, you can then use the tracking data to see what worked well and what didn't, and also use the site to keep promoting more of your themes or products.

To create a marketing site, you need to ensure that you get the best features of the site in front of the user while also being sharp and to the point. People want to know exactly what your theme looks like, what it does, how much it will cost, and where they can get it. Some good tips for a great marketing site include these:

- Include screenshots of how your theme will look on various pages and on various devices (if responsive). Don't forget to include screenshots of the admin/settings pages.

- Write good sales copy—not too long or wordy, clear and to the point—to ensure that your users know exactly what they're getting.

- Include a demo of the theme.

  - Ensure that your demo has appropriate content for the target audience for the theme.

  - Use good related photography; don't use *lorem ipsum* for text.

  - Allow users to see customizations; for example, changing skins/color palettes if the option is available.

- Add strong calls to action: where the theme can be bought, how to get in contact, and price.

- If possible, include a short demo video of your theme, especially the theme admin.

Keeping these few points in mind will make sure that your site is promoting your theme as best it can and getting the right information to users.

Marketing Through Pricing

You'll look at pricing in detail later in the chapter when I talk more about distribution and selling your themes. From a marketing point of view, however, there are a few things you can do that might increase your sales and help improve your customer base in general.

Pricing sensibly when you first start out is, of course, a good idea. Look at the competitors of your theme idea; don't undercut them, but try to price at least at a comparable level. Undercutting other theme developers leads only to devaluing the market in general, which helps no one. But pricing higher than established theme shops won't help sales, either. Theme marketplaces such as ThemeForest actually decide the price of your theme for you (you'll read more about that later in the chapter).

Once they have a series of themes, some theme shops also offer subscription or one-off membership–style pricing as an option (see Figure 11-6). A customer can sign up for a monthly fee or a larger one-off payment and receive access to all the shop's themes and future releases. This option can be a bit of a trade-off, depending on what you hope to achieve and who you're marketing to: you can obviously make more money selling the themes individually, but you can make a lot more money up front and have a regular income by getting monthly or yearly subscribers. A lot of shops that offer this pricing scheme often still sell themes separately as a sort of hybrid approach; they're catering for a variety of customers and maximizing their options when it comes to potential selling points. Theme shops such as Elegant Themes (`https://www.elegantthemes.com/`) offer three subscription options ranging from $39-$89 per year to an unlimited membership of $249 for life. Theme Foundry (`http://thethemefoundry.com/`) offers a yearly subscription to all their themes for $199.

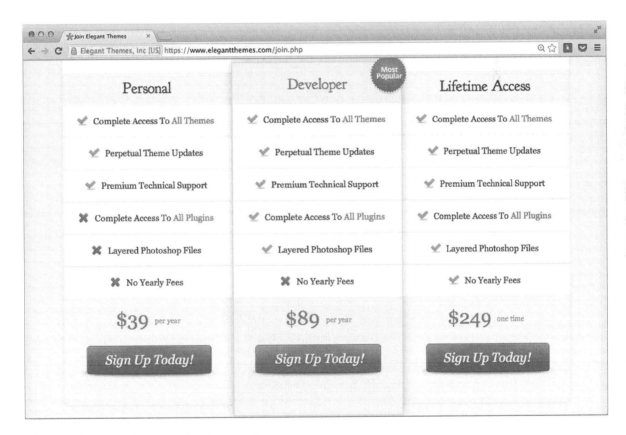

Figure 11-6. *Elegant Themes' subscription options*

To generate more talk about your themes, you might offer sale prices at various points in the year (such as a Black Friday sale) or run competitions to give away a free theme. Again, you don't want to devalue yourself, your themes, or other theme distributors by holding these promotions so often that they're almost like DFS sales, but having them every now and then can give you a quick boost in sales. Using contests every now and then can also be good to promoted a new theme or keep more regular interest in your themes business.

Tracking Metrics

So far, you've seen all the options available to you to from before you start coding your theme right through to the launch and pricing of your theme. However, your marketing isn't over once you make a few sales. To keep improving sales over time, it's important to keep track of as many metrics and as much data as possible. Knowing what has worked well and what your customers are thinking will help you over time to increase your sales and get out in front of the right audience to do so.

Any data you can get your hands on can be analyzed and used to find out how well your site, your e-mail marketing, and your sales are going. Ensuring that you have some sort of web site tracking on your site (such as Google Analytics) allows you to see how people are finding your site, what they're looking at when they're on your site, and what page they're on when they leave.

If you send out an e-mail to your mailing list, most services have reports and add tracking data to the contents of the e-mail so you can see how many people opened the e-mail, how many followed a link to something you added, and so on. Many e-mail services also allow you to do some form of A/B testing, so trying this with various marketing e-mails can also help you explore what works and what doesn't for your future e-mail.

If you sell your themes on a marketplace or distribute them via the Themes Directory, you should be able to see stats on how many people have viewed your theme, check downloads, and so on, It's all worth keeping track of and ensuring that you use that information to help improve your marketing over time.

Theme Testing

The final stage of theme development before you release the theme into the wild should be testing your theme. Testing can cover a lot of areas, including appearance, functionality, and code quality. Although each place you choose to distribute your theme might have different levels with which you will be required to test your theme, the most thorough theme testing I can think of probably comes from the WordPress team and the community.

To start, here's the checklist of items the WordPress Codex has when it comes to testing:

- Fix PHP and WordPress errors.

- Check template files against Template File Checklist (`http://wp-themes-book.com/11009`).

- Do a run-through using the Theme Unit Test.

- Validate HTML and CSS.

- Check for JavaScript errors.

- Test in all your target browsers.

- Clean up any extraneous comments, debug settings, or to-do items.

This is a thorough list of things you should be covering when testing your theme, no matter where it will be distributed. In this section, I want to go through all the testing processes necessary for you to get your theme into the Themes Directory. If your theme can pass the Theme Review team checks, you're in a good place to be able to distribute your theme anywhere you choose.

Theme Review Process

When each theme is submitted to the Themes Directory, before it can be made available for download it must first go through the WordPress theme review team, which will test it and ensure that it's of a high enough quality that it can go into the directory. The review team consists of some staff of Automattic, but are mostly members of the WordPress community. Anyone can join the review team and help review themes, and the team is always looking for people to do so. For more information, take a look at this post by Justin Tadlock: `http://wp-themes-book.com/11010` and at the WordPress blog post on joining the theme review team: `http://wp-themes-book.com/11011`.

The review team goes through each and every theme, reviewing them in the same manner by following the process outlined in the Codex: http://wp-themes-book.com/11012. This process ensures that all themes are coded to the same standard as WordPress, are up to date with current releases, and don't contain any obvious errors. To appreciate the amount of detail theme reviewers go into over each and every theme, I highly recommend reading up on the process written by Chip Bennett (http://wp-themes-book.com/11013) and also check out the guidelines on the WordPress web site (http://wp-themes-book.com/11014). The guidelines are being added to all the time, so it's worth checking back on them regularly, especially when you're about to test a new theme. Only recently, in fact, the guidelines were updated with a new set of accessibility guidelines for themes going through the theme review process (http://wp-themes-book.com/11015).

When you have seen the amount of detail that goes into the review process, you can understand how important it is that your themes are coded well. If you can pass the scrutiny of the theme review team, you've done a good job. In the rest of this section, I'll take you through the process of testing your theme with some of the tools provided by the WordPress theme review team to ensure that you're ready for the review and so you can test all your themes to meet the high standard set by the team.

Testing Your Theme

Now it's time to actually start testing your theme. You know that there's a lot to test, but here I'll cover only the main parts that will get you most of the way to a completely sound theme. If you'll be submitting your theme to the Themes Directory, I recommend that you read as much of the testing guidelines as possible, making sure that you know the full degree to which your theme will be scrutinized.

When testing your themes, it's important to set up a completely separate install of WordPress—one that you can use only for testing. The testing process I'll describe will involve a lot of imported content and use of plugins, which can update and potentially break your WordPress install. So the safest option is to use a completely separate install of the content management system (CMS) entirely and copy your theme over to that install to test while keeping it separate from your main development environment.

Testing Content and Theme Unit Tests

When you test your theme, the best place to start is with the content. Fortunately, WordPress has been very nice and provided some quite comprehensive test content for you to use: http://wp-themes-book.com/11016 (this link will take you directly to the XML download).

The test content consists of everything from posts and pages through to a load of categories, tags, and even users to test everything in your theme. There are posts with content that represent different conditions such as image placement that have far too many tags and categories (see Figure 11-7), and some menus have varying degrees of unexpected situations. Your blog should be able to handle this content gracefully, whether it means hiding tags when there are too many or just displaying them neatly, as the Twenty Thirteen theme does in Figure 11-7.

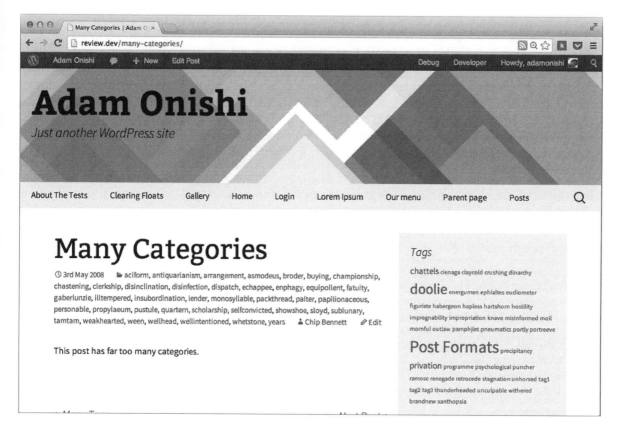

Figure 11-7. *The Twenty Thirteen theme with the WordPress test content*

For an example of an even more thorough set of test data, take a look at WP Test (http://wptest.io/), which has taken the core WordPress test data and added in a load more edge cases to the tests to further push your theme to its limits.

Once you have your content in and have made sure that everything seems to be working well, check out the Theme Unit Test page from the WordPress Codex: http://wp-themes-book.com/11017. This page gives you a thorough checklist of what your site should be doing, how it should display the main types of content, and everything a user can possibly do with content in your theme. Doing this will ensure that you not only test your theme thoroughly before it goes through the theme review process but you should also know exactly what to look out for when coding your themes after going through it a few times.

Testing with Plugins

After you've tested your site with a load of content from whichever source you choose, there's a lot of code testing you should be doing. Thankfully, to save you from doing a lot of it manually, the Automattic team and various people from the WordPress community have set up a series of plugins that test every single part of your theme, from the main PHP code to validating the HTML and Cascading Style Sheets (CSS), and everything in between.

You can find the list of suggested test plugins on the How to Join the Theme Review team page (http://wp-themes-book.com/11011). However, to make life easier, Automattic set up another plugin that allows you to set them up all at once: the Developer plugin (http://wp-themes-book.com/11018), shown in Figure 11-8. The only suggested plugin not found in the Developer plugin is the DeBogger plugin by Simon Prosser (http://wp-themes-book.com/11019).

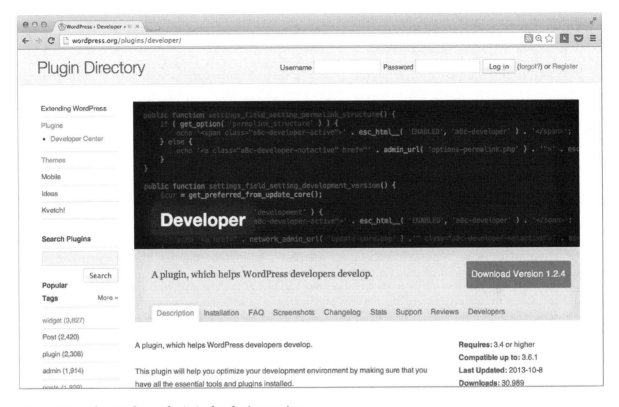

Figure 11-8. *The Developer plugin in the plugin repository*

With all the suggested plugins installed, you're ready to start testing. Go through Chip Bennett's post on how to review themes and ensure that your theme passes all the tests and things to look out for in the list. The first plugin to use that will give you a lot of hints about your theme is the Theme Check plugin. If there are any *Warning* or *Required* notices returned from the Theme Check plugin, your theme will be instantly rejected from the Themes Directory; make sure to fix these errors immediately. Any remaining notices, such as *Recommended* or *Info*, should be checked to ensure that you're not missing some default functionality or doing something you could avoid but otherwise can be left for a theme reviewer to comment on (if you're submitting to the Themes Directory).

WordPress Beta Tester

Another suggested plugin is the WordPress Beta Tester plugin (`http://wp-themes-book.com/11020`), which allows you to test the very latest beta releases of WordPress. Although it is normally used for testing WordPress core updates, you can test your themes against it to ensure that you are up to date with the latest developments and get a head start on any new features you need to add to your theme.

Just to reiterate, you should use a completely separate install of WordPress to perform your testing. Even more importantly, when it comes to the WordPress Beta Tester plugin, the theme completely updates your WordPress version to the latest beta. Depending on how brave you are, you can even set it to update to the "bleeding edge nightlies" instead of just the point release nightlies if you want to really see the cutting edge of WordPress core development.

Testing with a Fresh Perspective

No matter how much you test your theme, there's always the possibility that you will miss something. When you're so familiar with the code you're writing, even simple errors can be missed. This is where the various testing plugins come into play, of course, but an automated plugin test is no substitute for a human eye. That's why the theme review process is so worthwhile. It gives you an opportunity to have your theme seen by someone else, and a fresh pair of eyes can always help to catch last-minute bugs and tiny little errors.

If you won't be adding your themes to the Themes Directory (if you're going to sell your themes for instance), it's always worth asking a friend or another theme developer to cast their eye over your work. You can always offer to do the same if they're in the same business or even offer them free access to your theme if it helps add that extra bit of reassurance to your theme's quality.

Distributing Your Theme

Finally it's time to talk about the actual process of getting your theme online somewhere for people to download and use, whether it's for free or as a premium theme. There's a lot to consider about distributing your theme, which depends a lot on what your overall goal is for the theme: whether you want to distribute it for free or at a cost; and if at a cost, what your long and short-term goals are for your themes business.

If you'll distribute your themes for free, the best option is to get it into the Themes Directory. Not only will it go through the rigorous themes review process but it also goes in front of the most potential customers. Although there might be more than 2,000 themes already in the Themes Directory, the number of downloads is staggering at more than 80 million. Combine this with the additional marketing you'll do to get your theme in front of as many people as possible, and you have the potential to reach quite a substantial audience. Not only that; the themes that go into the WordPress.com theme selection are sometimes sourced from the Themes Directory. So if your theme stands out, you might be approached by WordPress to use your theme in the WordPress.com site.

If you're hoping to sell your theme and make some money, you have a plethora of options on hand to do so. You'll look through these options a bit later in the chapter, but once again it comes down to the goals of selling your theme and whether you're trying to start a business or just want to make a few quick dollars.

Licensing Your Theme

Before you get to the how of getting your themes online, there's one last thing to cover: your theme's license. In the past, there has been a lot of contentious debate over how WordPress themes should be licensed. Some people were unsure whether the GNU General Public License (GPL) held by WordPress should also apply to themes, but Matt Mullenweg cleared it up with a blog post in July 2009 titled "Themes are GPL Too" (http://wp-themes-book.com/11021).

The GPL license says that any work holding the license allows any user to modify or redistribute the source code under certain conditions. This is the contentious part: people didn't like the idea that a theme they created could be modified and/or redistributed for free without reparations. However, the license is about allowing users the freedom to modify and redistribute the source code, which does not in turn mean it has to be for no cost.

The difference is often referred to as "free as in speech vs. free as in beer." The GPL license means *free as in speech*. Although people are allowed to modify your theme, you can still charge them to get access to it in the first place.

The other contentious point came from whether themes were considered "derivative works," therefore requiring the use of the license in the first place. This is what Matt cleared up in his post, which contains a letter from the Software Freedom Law Center referring to the licensing of WordPress themes. It was deemed that any PHP in a theme must be considered a derivative work because it's so tightly linked to the WordPress system (one can't work without the other). However any CSS, JavaScript, or image assets could potentially be open to a separate license, depending on their initial origins.

I prefer to look at it in a similar light to that of Matt Mullenweg when he says in his post:

> *Even though graphics and CSS aren't required to be GPL legally, the lack thereof is pretty limiting. Can you imagine WordPress without any CSS or JavaScript?*

—Matt Mullenweg

Therefore, I think it's important to ensure that your theme is licensed under GPL; you should also keep the spirit of WordPress as intended within your theme. To this point also, if you are submitting your theme to WordPress, the entire theme must be 100% covered by the GPL with no exceptions; otherwise, you will have to find another place to host your theme.

Adding Your Theme to the Themes Directory

If you decide to distribute your theme for free, there's no better place to do so than in the WordPress Themes Directory. I've already talked in great depth about the review process in place for themes that go into the directory as well as a few other benefits that add to the reasons for hosting your theme there.

When compared with the process of getting a plugin into the plugin repository (which you'll find out more about in Chapter 13), the theme upload process is relatively simple. The directory is still controlled with Subversion (SVN), but because of the review process in place for themes, theme developers get no access to their own theme repository. Instead, everything is handled via a simple ZIP file upload through the WordPress.org site and uses your WordPress login (http://wordpress.org/themes/upload/), as shown in Figure 11-9.

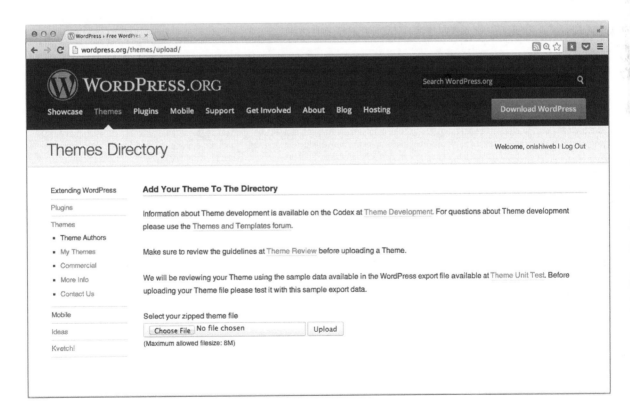

Figure 11-9. *The theme upload page*

When you upload your theme, it is instantly run through a series of automated tests such as the Theme Check plugin and deprecated functions test, with the upload process finally creating a ticket on the Themes-Trac system, ready to be assigned to a reviewer. At this point, the results of the automated tests are passed over to a reviewer for a detailed human review of your theme. The reviewer will make comments and note any issues found in the review in the Trac ticket. If your theme has any *REQUIRED* actions from the review, it is set as "not-approved" and will be sent back to you for fixes and resubmission. If the theme comes back with no issues or only *RECOMMENDED* issues, it is set to "approved," and the ticket is closed. Once your theme is approved, it will be set up in the WordPress Extend SVN repository, which will then be synced manually by a member of the review team, usually on a daily basis.

Once your theme has been uploaded and synced with the Extend repository, it will be available in the Themes Directory. With plugins, the pages that appear in the repository are generated from the contents of the readme.txt file (more on that in Chapter 13). However, with themes all the information for the directory pages comes from the style.css and screenshot.png files, covered back in Chapter 2 (see Figure 11-10).

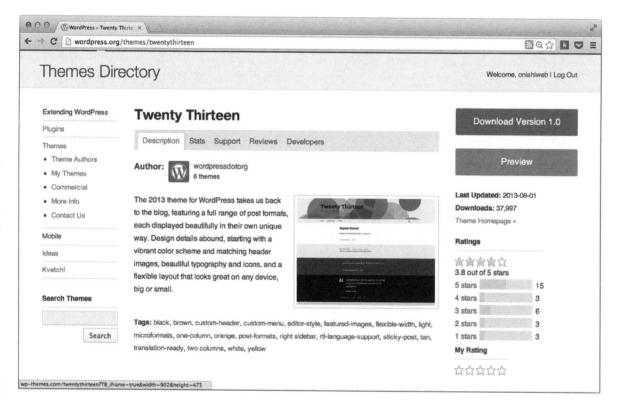

Figure 11-10. *The Twenty Thirteen Themes Directory page*

The only page the style sheet header and screenshot are used to generate is the main page with the name, description, screenshot, and author details. The rest of the theme page is generated by WordPress, including the stats, ratings, and support tab. When it comes to tagging your theme, you must use only tags that are allowed by the Themes Directory, which allows WordPress to keep standard control over the classification of themes and ensure that all themes are searchable based on similar tags. (A list of all the available tags can be found at http://wp-themes-book.com/11022.) Make sure that you use all the tags that apply to your theme specifically; don't just add all tags in the hope that your theme will appear in more searches because it will be checked by the theme review team.

After this process, your theme will appear in the Themes Directory as well as the theme search from inside the WordPress admin, making it available to all to download and add to their site.

Selling Your Theme

When it comes to selling your themes, you have three main options to choose from: whether you decide to sell on your own site, use one of the many marketplaces available, or use a combination of the two. What you choose depends on your situation, what your long-term goals are for selling your theme, and what amount of effort you're willing to put into your theme business. Once you've answered these questions, it's a lot easier to make a choice, but to help you with the decision, let's look at the options in a bit more detail.

Choosing any of the approaches results in a trade-off between different positives and negatives. If you go with a marketplace, for example, your theme will be in front of a lot more potential customers, but you must be prepared to compromise on the overall profit you will receive from sales. The reverse is generally true for selling on your own site; you will sacrifice the reach and potential audience in favor of taking more profit from the sales.

Selling on Your Own Site

Selling your themes through your own web site comes with a lot of advantages: being able to control the price of your themes, take a lot more money from the sale of your themes, and have complete control over the process. However, to be able to sell your themes successfully, you have to be able to reach a wide and varied audience, which can be difficult on your own. There's also the issue of trust; if you're new to theme selling and people aren't aware of your work, it's possible that not many people will be instantly willing to trust your expertise.

However, setting up alone can be worth it if you have a long-term goal with a good marketing plan and a business strategy to go with it. If you have an audience already or plan to build up an audience around your business, making sure that you have your own site where people can see your work and find your themes is crucial. You have seen in the marketing section of this chapter that there are ways to can build yourself as a brand and go on to be a successful theme developer.

The Theme Foundry took this approach with its theme business (http://thethemefoundry.com/), in order to build itself into a brand as a premium shop for WordPress themes. It did so with a site of its own. By focusing on the product it was creating and interacting with the WordPress community (blogging, writing tutorials, contributing to the core, and so on), the Theme Foundry built a reputation as a supplier of a premium product. You can do this with your own work if you take the time and make the effort to build yourself and your brand as a point of expertise on WordPress.

When thinking about how to price your themes on your own site, consider the competition and the level at which you are entering into business as a theme developer. Themes can range in price from free to $200+, so there's a broad range for your themes. Themes in a theme marketplace such as ThemeForest go for $12 for more simple themes through to $60 for more complex and high-end themes, with most averaging around the $40–$50 mark. Themes from The Theme Foundry are priced a bit higher at $68 ($51 for returning customers) because it built a brand first and made itself a name as a high–quality premium theme shop.

Take these prices, the level of complexity of your themes, and how you're positioned in the market into account first, before making your decision. Consider setting up a subscription structure, which I talked about earlier in the marketing section of the chapter.

When it comes to setting up a site to sell your themes, remember that you need a way to take payments from customers and allow them to download your theme. Although this is possible via a WordPress site with a few plugins, you'll have to add this process to the work you do before you can sell your themes. Of course, once you've created it, you have the system set up and ready for the rest of your themes.

Selling Through a Marketplace

The other option is to get your themes on one of the many theme marketplaces available. These marketplaces come with a ready-made audience for your theme and can provide that level of security for a user, not only for online payment transactions but also for the quality of the theme as well.

Marketplaces are also good for you if you don't want to sell themes as a long-term business investment and just want to make a few extra dollars on top of your regular work. Marketplaces already have the infrastructure to get you up and running selling your theme; adding your theme to their directories is as easy as setting up an account and uploading your theme (although it may have to go through a review process). There are no extra costs or time implications for selling your theme; you leave that to someone else and can get on with building your themes.

However all these positives do come at a cost; to make money, marketplaces only pay out only a certain percentage of every sale to theme developers. The marketplace you choose will affect how much you get from sales. Two of the top marketplaces, ThemeForest (`http://themeforest.net/`) and Mojo Themes (`http://www.mojo-themes.com/`), offer developers between 50–70% per theme depending on sales, and this is only for themes sold exclusively on their sites. If you were to sell themes on more than one marketplace or through your own site as well, you would have to put up with a meager 33% of the sale from ThemeForest and a lowly 25% from Mojo.

Pricing your themes on a theme marketplace is almost always taken care of for you, with themes going through a review process to decide not only on the quality of your theme and whether the marketplace wants to host it but also the price it will be sold for. This is something you should factor in to your decision making because not having control over the price of your theme can really impact how and where you want to sell your work. Before offering your theme to a marketplace, be sure to check out the themes already hosted there; see which themes demand higher prices and which are going cheap. This research will give you some insight into what the theme you're creating could potentially be sold for.

Each marketplace is different, as mentioned. For ThemeForest, you need to set up an account and go through its simple multiple-choice authoring quiz (visible for users with an account at `http://wp-themes-book.com/11023`) to ensure that you understand how selling on the ThemeForest site works. After you're set up as an author on the site, you can upload your theme, which will then go through a review process. If it is accepted, the theme will be available in the marketplace for the price set by ThemeForest.

Making the Most of All Your Options

Each of these options has its own positives and negatives; by combining both, however, you can attempt to alleviate some of the negatives and come away with the positives from both. This is a nice idea, but it does require you to be in a certain situation with your themes business before you decide to take on both routes.

To get the most from a marketplace, it is best to offer an exclusive theme for sale; otherwise, you risk your profit from the sales being extremely low. You could say this low profit would be negated through selling your theme on your site, though. You should see which theme will likely sell better, and you might be better off choosing one option over the other.

If you have multiple themes you want to sell, putting some exclusively in a marketplace and others on your own site can allow you to maximize your presence around the Web. In time, your site will start to build its brand and you can offer more premium themes for a higher price on your site while keeping some sales going through the marketplace.

Whichever way you choose to sell your theme(s), be sure to do your research in all possible avenues; make the most of the possibilities available to you, and you will be able to make something from selling your themes.

Supporting Your Theme

The job of being a theme developer isn't over as soon as the theme is in the hands of its users. Supporting your theme is just as important as the process of building it and marketing it in the first place. When customers experience good support and service from you, they are more likely to return and even recommend you to others. When it comes to selling your themes, there is a certain level of customer expectation that you will provide some kind of support. Free themes from the WordPress directory can sometimes get away with minimal support, but if you're trying to develop a brand or keep a good reputation, ensuring that you provide good customer support is a surefire way to do so.

If you want to go into the theme-selling business for the long term, you must take customer support seriously. This approach is taken by both WooThemes (http://www.woothemes.com/) and The Theme Foundry, which take supporting their themes very seriously. WooThemes also releases its themes licensed fully under the GPL, so customers could technically distribute the themes after purchasing them. However, WooThemes relies on the high standard of its customer service and support to keep customers coming to it directly, and it seems to be working well so far.

When providing support, it's important to be prompt and get back to a customer as soon as the request comes in. Even if you don't know the answer right away, the customer is reassured and knows there is someone looking into the issue. You will sometimes get difficult customers or customers asking you things completely unrelated to your themes. Always be courteous to your customers and try to help them find a solution. Saying that it's not your problem because it's not related to your theme is not an option. Even if you don't know the answer to a question, be honest and try to help customers find a solution. Giving no answer the right way is better than giving the wrong answer.

Ways of Providing Support

Customer support requests are a reality, so it is important to find a good method of dealing with them (this is all about ensuring that your themes have a location where they can be found on the Web. The Themes Directory provides a handy support page for each theme (see Figure 11-11).

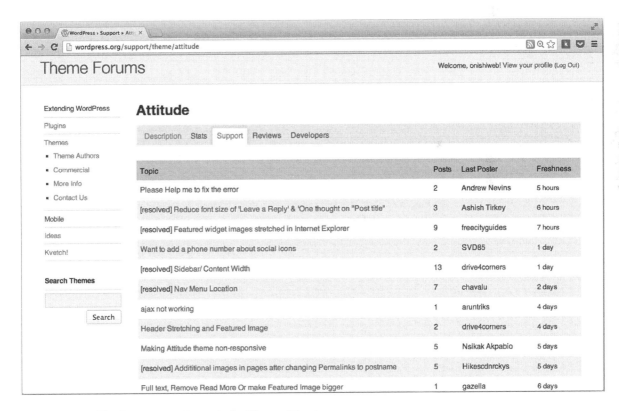

Figure 11-11. *The theme support page in the Themes Directory*

For every theme you upload to the directory, the support page is added as standard, and you should monitor it to make sure that you're replying to support requests from your customers. Having a support page as the Themes Directory does is great because your customers know exactly where to go to look for support and get your help.

Another positive of the Themes Directory support forums is that anyone can get involved with a thread, so if you do get bogged down with requests, sometimes the WordPress community will take care of some of the requests for you. However, I would not rely on this support; make sure that you are always keeping an eye on the support requests coming through and to answer as many as possible.

With your theme in a marketplace, you can get a very similar system to the Themes Directory. Mojo Themes offers a similar support request forum, whereas ThemeForest offers the option to theme developers to choose how they deal with support. Some theme shops have their own support systems and forums; others opt to support the theme through comments on the marketplace.

If you'll be selling themes on your own site, you have to offer your customers an easy way to submit support requests for your themes—whether you just allow customers to contact you via e-mail with requests or whether you set up a forum for them. At first, using e-mail might be sufficient, but as you grow and your sales and customer base increase, you will be dealing with large numbers of support requests. At this point, you might find setting up a support forum on your own site to be much more effective because it allows users to see previous requests that can answer their questions or allow you to point them to the answer you've provided in a previous thread.

Preventing Support Requests

Besides finding a good way to deal with requests, you can take some preventive measures to reduce the number of requests you get in the first place. Measures such as good documentation, a series of frequently asked questions, or tutorials enable users to find the information they need without having to e-mail you or set up a new support thread.

Ensuring that you provide good documentation for your theme can mean anything from a thorough setup guide to ensuring that your code is well commented. Remember that your users will have varying degrees of skill when it comes to WordPress and themes—from complete beginners all the way to professional developers. Ensuring that your theme has a decent step-by-step setup guide and well-commented code for all the custom functionality, and even within the CSS to some degree, allows you to cater for all levels of skill.

The Theme Foundry takes pride in its customer support and also provides its users with bespoke support for each of its themes. This support can even include a video walkthrough of the theme (see Figure 11-12). Besides specific theme guides, the Theme Foundry also provides general WordPress help and tutorials so its customers know that it is a resource for expert knowledge. This sort of service can really set you apart from your competition when it comes to your theme business, and ensuring that your customers feel they are getting a great service is clearly just as important as the products you create for them.

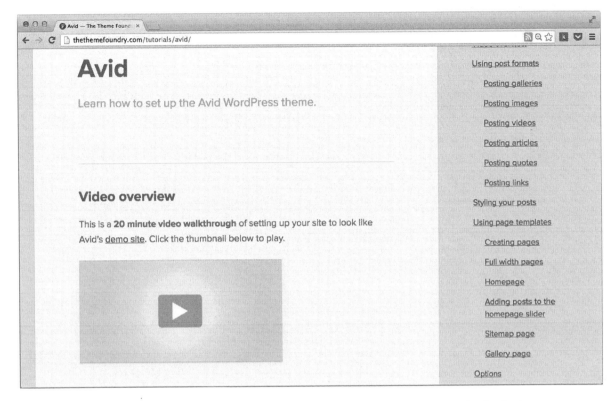

Figure 11-12. The Avid theme tutorials page on The Theme Foundry, including an intro video for the theme

Summary

This chapter has been all about setting you up to distribute your WordPress themes. Whether you want to create themes to give away in the Themes Directory or to eventually sell to make a profit, there's a lot more to consider than which marketplace to throw your theme up on. Hopefully, this chapter has equipped you with all the knowledge you need to set up a good marketing plan and business strategy to be a successful theme distributor.

You started by looking at how complicated it could really get when you're building themes for other people because there's a certain level of expectation that comes with a theme, especially when it has a price tag. WordPress users expect lots of features, and you may need to cater to as many as possible to ensure that you have the best chance of selling your theme.

Along the way, you learned that it's not all just about the theme you create but also about the way you market yourself and your business. If you want a long-term business in theme development, you need to set yourself up as a brand, making sure that people know your name and relate to it positively and with WordPress and your themes.

You should now also know what it takes to get your theme online, whether it goes into the Themes Directory or onto a marketplace. You know how to test it, what to expect from the theme review team as well as other marketplaces, and the best options when it comes to selling your theme.

Finally you saw how important customer service is when you start a theme business; it's not just about creating great products but also providing your customers with great support and service along the way to ensure that they keep coming back and hopefully recommend you to others.

CHAPTER 12

■ ■ ■

Extending Your Theme

As you near the end of this book and before you take a look at two things not directly related to WordPress theme development (but still extremely important and really useful), I want to discuss a few subjects that I think are important to know for theme development but don't necessarily work in a chapter on their own. So welcome to the chapter that is an amalgamation of handy little extras that are good to know and can help you out in your life as a theme developer.

Three topics will be covered in this chapter, beginning with child themes. Child themes are a way in WordPress to extend an existing theme, make modifications, and add functionality that the main theme doesn't have. Although the goal of this book is teaching you how to create your own themes from scratch (which is my overriding preference), sometimes it's worthwhile to create a child theme instead. I'll look at the reasons why that might be a good idea and show you how to create a child theme.

WordPress, at its roots, is a blogging platform, with the content management system (CMS) part happening more recently in its history. It would therefore be remiss to leave out one of the major parts of a blog: the comments. In this chapter, you'll look at how to add comments to your theme, how to customize the way they're displayed, and how to create the forms for users to add them.

The third and final topic of this chapter is internationalization (or i18n for short). As mentioned in the previous chapter, if you'll be distributing your theme, it's important that your users be able to use the theme in their native language. Even if you're not distributing your themes and just making them directly for clients, there might also be the need to ensure that the themes you create can be localized if your client has a global audience. I know this to be the case, having worked with a series of global brands over the last couple of years, and when your theme is not set up well to be localized, it can be horrendous to maintain.

Admittedly, there are probably even more topics I could cover in this chapter, but I want to keep it down to the techniques I think will help you most and really improve your theme development skills.

Child Themes

A child theme is one that takes all the functionality, templates, and (in some cases) styles from another theme called the parent theme. The purpose of child themes was to allow WordPress users to easily modify themes without having to edit the theme directly. This comes with many advantages, including allowing the parent theme to continue being updated without affecting the modifications made by the child theme.

Child themes are fairly ubiquitous in WordPress; many are available through the Themes Directory for popular parent themes (see Figure 12-1). Developers also choose child theming as a way to speed up their development process for their client service business. A child theme looks and behaves almost exactly like a regular WordPress theme: it lives in the Themes Directory with all the other themes and can contain style sheets, JavaScript files, images, and template files. The difference comes with the template files; the child theme will use all the parent theme template files unless there is a more specific template file available in the child theme.

Figure 12-1. *Child themes of the Twenty Eleven theme are some of the more popular parent themes in use*

Before you start looking at how to build a child theme however, I want to take a more detailed look at why child theming exists, what it's being used for in the WordPress ecosystem, and what some of the positives and negatives can be.

Why Work with Child Themes?

Now you know roughly what a child theme is, it's worth looking at why they're useful and also quite popular among the WordPress community. From web site owners to theme development agencies, lots of people are making good use of child themes.

Advantages

The first benefit of using child themes is that you can leave the code from the parent theme completely alone, so it can still be updated and you won't lose your changes. Retaining the ability to update a theme is important because you can keep getting all the new features developers might add as well as any bug or security fixes they may need to release for the theme. If you edited the original theme, it would be hard to update without losing all your changes.

You might wonder why anyone would want to modify a theme in the first place. A lot of web site owners use child themes because they find a theme they like that offers them the functionality they're looking for, but they want to make some changes to how it looks or add in a couple of extras. Instead of hacking away at the main theme, they can create a child theme to inherit all the functionality they desire and then modify the look from within the parent theme.

Developers also use child themes for a similar reason, but usually the parent theme they use has been designed specifically for this purpose—created with a lot of functionality and probably very little styling. It means developers can use the parent theme as a base for a lot of the other themes they build. By doing this, they speed up their development process because they have a base to start with each time, and they need to add only the custom styling and layout for each new theme.

So there are many advantages to using child themes. Modifications are kept separate from the parent, allowing it to be updated when necessary. A lot of the heavy lifting is already done for you, speeding up development and having a secure fallback for anything you might miss if you were developing a theme yourself. You can be almost certain that the parent theme has taken into account almost all possible outcomes and has coded for them, such as 404 pages and the search template. Although this may not apply to you personally, it's also a great way for people to learn WordPress themes. Instead of delving straight into creating a custom theme, they can work with an established theme and learn through using the parent theme while still working with their own.

Disadvantages

There are a few disadvantages to working with child themes as well. There can be performance issues. For example, by using a child theme, you are adding a second place for WordPress to look for template files, so it has to do almost twice the work. It's a relatively small performance hit, but it's worth mentioning. The other performance issue can come with the recommended way styles work if you want to retain the styles from the parent theme. You'll look into this in more detail shortly, but essentially it requires the use of the @import directive in your CSS, which can potentially have a significant effect on front-end performance. However, if you are particularly concerned about this, you can use a CSS preprocessor or look at clever ways of working with two CSS files.

Another disadvantage comes from working with the parent theme. If it's something you haven't developed, there will be a learning curve to get up to speed with how it works. This is often mitigated after the first few times you build with the parent theme, so it's really much more of a short-term disadvantage. Of course, if you're working with someone else's code, it often means that you are subject to their way of doing things—not only good code but also bad code. With WordPress, this should be less of a problem thanks to the very thorough coding standards. However, people have their own nuances when coding, so be aware of the code quality of the parent theme you choose to work with.

When it comes to using a theme as a parent that's developed by someone else, support and updates for the theme might not continue. This disadvantage depends on what theme you decide to use as a parent; popular parent themes are unlikely to have their development discontinued because of their popularity. Also it is likely that even if the main developer were to stop developing the theme, the community around it would be big enough to continue to work on updates, anyway. Yet another great thing about the WordPress community.

When to Use a Child Theme

It's important to know when to use a child theme and when you're better off creating a standalone theme. For starters, if you're working with anyone else's theme as a web site owner and just want to make some minor modifications, you're always best served by making a child theme. Although this might not pertain to you, the next time you are asked for advice on where to start with a WordPress-based site, you'll know how to answer.

When working with child themes for development purposes in your own workflow, however, you'll need to consider what the end result will be compared with the parent theme you plan to work with. The first point is making sure that you have a good parent theme to work with. Ensuring that you have a powerful, functionality-packed (but not bloated) theme at the base of your development will mean you can almost always create child themes from it for your theming work.

Assess each theme you plan to develop on a case-by-case basis; there is never a one-solution-fits-all approach. If you're building a simple blog, for instance, and your parent theme is set up with all the bells and whistles of a full web site, you probably won't use a lot of it in your blog theme, so you're probably better off creating a separate custom theme. Likewise, if you have a large custom site to build with a lot of unique requirements (you're overriding a lot of the default templates from the parent theme), you should probably create a new custom theme instead of wasting a lot of effort trying to get two themes to work together.

Theme Frameworks or Parent Themes?

I've been very careful not to refer to parent themes as *frameworks*. The terms *framework* and *parent theme* are often referred to as the same thing. This is a problem because there is definitely a fundamental difference between the two. The WordPress Codex refers to the two as a "drop-in code library" and a "stand-alone base/starter theme," respectively (http://wp-themes-book.com/12001).

A parent theme can refer to almost any theme except a child theme (because it can't be used as a parent). However, as I've discussed in this chapter, themes can be developed to specifically be parent themes—offering functionality but perhaps a lack of styling/layout.

A theme framework mostly contains a set of coded features, usually used within a theme or as the basis of a theme, ultimately being used to create a theme that can then be used as a parent theme. Frameworks can often be just a set of files that set up some functionality for a theme to use; or, in the case of themes such as Underscores (http://underscores.me/) and Starkers (http://wp-themes-book.com/12002), the frameworks are a set of base files on which to build.

The language issue can cause a lot of confusion when people are working with frameworks and parent themes, so it's important to know the difference so you can work with them to the best effect.

Some good parent themes include these:

- Genesis (premium): http://wp-themes-book.com/12003

- Thematic (free): http://wp-themes-book.com/12004

- Thesis (premium): http://wp-themes-book.com/12005

And good theme frameworks include these:

- Carrington JAM (free): http://wp-themes-book.com/12006

- Hybrid Core (free): http://wp-themes-book.com/12007

Creating a Child Theme

As mentioned earlier, a child theme looks and behaves exactly like a regular theme. It can have all the same things a parent theme has, including CSS, JavaScript, images, and more. The main difference with a child theme is what it requires. In Chapter 2, you learned that all WordPress themes are required to have a `style.css` file and an `index.php` file. However, all a child theme requires is a `style.css` file.

The `style.css` file in a child theme is used to tell WordPress that it is a child theme, for this to be possible you have to go back to the style sheet header comments:

```
/*
Theme Name: Adam's Twenty Thirteen Child
Theme URI: http://wp-themes-book.com/twentythirteen-child
Author: Adam Onishi
Author URI: http://adamonishi.com
Template: twentythirteen
Text Domain: twentythirteen-child
*/
```

The header comment shown here looks almost like a regular `style.css` header: it has the theme name, theme URI, and author details; the part that makes the theme act as a child theme is the "Template" declaration. The child theme template attribute points to the directory in which the parent theme is stored. Figure 12-2 shows the directories for the Twenty Thirteen theme and child theme I just created.

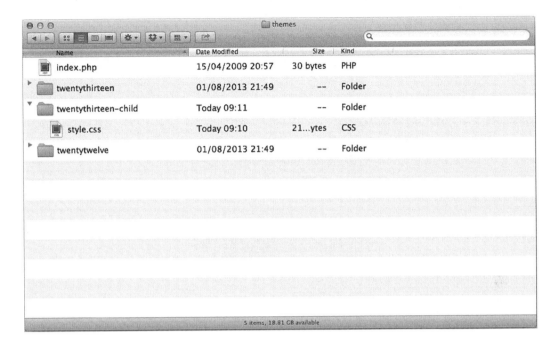

Figure 12-2. *The themes directory including the new child theme*

You can name your child theme whatever you prefer, although it has become a convention to add "-child" in the theme directory. This convention is probably more suited to those who want to modify a theme they want to use for their web site, but if you're developing with custom themes for clients, you'll probably want to put together your own naming convention. As for the rest of the statements in the style sheet header, they're all left up to you. You can include any of the available settings for your theme, and as always it's recommended that you also include the GPL license for your theme.

Once your child theme is created and in the themes directory, it will be available in the WordPress admin to be activated (see Figure 12-3).

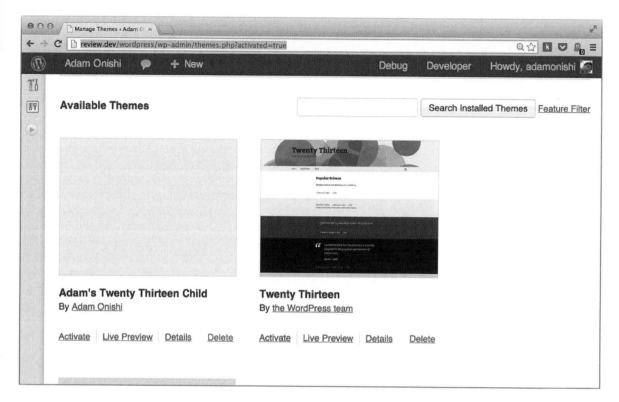

Figure 12-3. The child theme apparing in the themes admin menu

When you activate the theme, you'll see a message alongside the activated theme at the top of the themes admin screen noting that "This child theme requires its parent theme, Twenty Thirteen." This message is shown in Figure 12-4.

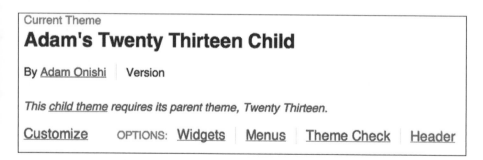

Figure 12-4. The activated child theme

Child Theme Styling

Before you finish with the `style.css` file for your child theme, there is one last thing to do. Due to the way child theme files override the corresponding files from their parent file, the child theme will now have no styling because the child theme style sheet is empty except for the comments. This is all well and good if you want to write completely new CSS for your child theme, but you'll often want to modify the existing styles from the parent theme. To do this, you need to include the parent theme's `style.css` file.

Use a CSS @import directive, calling the style sheet from the parent theme:

```
/* Import styles from the parent theme
-------------------------------------------------------------- */
@import url('../twentythirteen/style.css');
```

This code includes the Twenty Thirteen styles, so your theme is now a complete clone of the Twenty Thirteen theme. I mentioned already that this does cause a slight performance hit; for example, if you looked at a network diagram of your child theme loading now, you would see that the parent theme style sheet causes a network request as well as the child theme CSS file. This occurs because of the way the @import directive works in CSS: it tells the browser to go fetch that CSS separately, and the parent theme CSS doesn't start loading until the child theme's file has finished. This can be a performance hit, but you can plan for it and overcome its disadvantage.

To modify styles from the parent theme, you can now include any CSS of your own beneath the import of the parent theme style sheet. It will override the styles from the parent theme, provided that you're using the same or higher specificity of selectors. (I won't go into detail about writing CSS for child theming because I think most readers have a good enough understanding of CSS to get by.)

Remember to use the cascade to your advantage. You don't need to write extremely complex selectors to override the parent theme's CSS; just as long as you use the same specificity, it will work fine. For best results, I tend to use the element inspector in Chrome to view the element and see what CSS is being applied; to change anything, I can just copy the CSS selector used for the element to my style sheet and it will override the parent styles.

Theme Template Files

If you need to modify anything more than just some styles in the parent theme, you can do so easily by creating a template file in the child theme to override the one from the parent theme. Any template file you add to the child theme will override the equivalent template file from the parent theme, and you can also add other files to your child theme that do not appear in the parent theme. Study the WordPress template hierarchy (`http://wp-themes-book.com/12008`) because any file that is more specific for the content being requested found in your child theme will be included before any other files in the parent theme.

This means that a specific page template for your about page (`page-about.php`) will be used ahead of the standard template for pages (`page.php`) found in the parent theme. Likewise, if the parent theme has a template file more specific to the content than the child theme, you have to ensure that you create a template to the same specificity or higher for the child theme template to be loaded.

An example is the archive page for categories. If you were to create an `archive.php` file in the child theme, it would be used for all archive pages except for the categories page because the Twenty Thirteen theme has a `category.php` template file. To override it in your child theme, you would have to create a `category.php` template file or a more specific `category-{category-name}.php` file to force the override. Having the template hierarchy around for reference is very useful in these situations, and after you make a few child themes, you'll probably be able to navigate it by memory.

Modifying a theme template file from the parent theme requires copying the original template file from the parent theme and making your modifications in the child theme version of the file. This procedure can lead to a bit of hassle when it comes to updates to the parent theme: if you modify something that is subsequently updated, your child theme will not receive those new updates. Ensure that you know the parent theme well enough so that you can easily spot these upgrades to the parent theme files and transfer them over to your own template files in the child theme if necessary.

Functions File

There is one exception to the overriding templates rule in child themes: the `functions.php` file. If you include a functions file in your child theme, it will not override the functions file from the parent theme because that would remove all the functionality created by the parent theme (which is probably why you're using it as a parent theme in the first place). Instead, the child functions file and the parent theme's functions file are included.

Allowing the child theme to have its own functions file means that you can easily add your own features and functionality to the child theme. For example, you can add another taxonomy to the already existing post types in the parent theme or just add some more general functions to the child theme. You can easily do this through the child theme's own `functions.php` file. There is absolutely no need to copy the functions file from the parent theme because everything is included for you, which also means that any updates to the theme's functionality will also be transferred to your theme.

For theme development, note that the child theme's functions file is included *before* the functions file of the parent. This is an important feature that allows the child theme to override functions from the parent if it needs to and if the functions in the parent theme have been written to allow for it. This is done with a method called pluggable functions; by creating pluggable functions in your themes, anyone can write a function in their child theme to overwrite specific functions to achieve their own custom functionality. To achieve pluggable functions, use the `function_exists()` function to check whether there is already a function with that name declared in the system; if so, the function will simply not be created.

You have seen this used throughout the book when declaring a setup function in the functions file:

```
if ( ! function_exists( 'prowordpress_setup' ) ) :
    function prowordpress_setup() {
        [...]
    }
}
```

This code allows the child theme developer to create a function called `prowordpress_setup()` that will then override this function from the parent theme. The Twenty Thirteen theme has a mix of pluggable functions and normal functions declared. Most of the pluggable functions control the output of content in the theme so that child theme developers can override them to create their own content display.

■ **Note** In your functions file, you can define support for things like post formats and post thumbnails by using the `add_theme_support()` function. If you include these definitions in your child theme, you will override those made in the parent theme. So if you want to include additional post formats, for example, you have to include all the post formats you want to use in your theme, not just the extra ones not defined by the parent theme.

Referencing Locations in Your Theme

In theme development, you'll usually use the `get_template_directory()` function to output the location of your theme. It is usually used for images, and JavaScript files, and so on. However, to reference anything in your child theme, you need to use the `get_stylesheet_directory()` function instead.

The difference stems from the locations of the main files for each theme. By creating a child theme, you have changed the location of the main style sheet—hence the use of the `get_stylesheet_directory()` function. The template directory remains to be that of the parent theme because that's where the main template files still exist. This allows for a parent to still refer to itself with the `get_template_directory()` and similar functions, and the child theme has a reference with the `get_stylesheet_directory()` function.

As a theme developer, you should always reference locations in your theme with the `get_template_directory()` or subsequent functions. The only file you should be referring to with the `get_stylesheet_directory()` function is the main style sheet.

Hooks in Child Themes

Hooks are a great way of adding functionality to your themes. You learned about hooks in Chapter 6, and they are no different in child themes. However, there is an issue that goes back to how the functions files are included in the parent and child themes: because the files are included in the child theme first, any hooks you set up in the child theme can be overridden by the hooks in the parent theme, which is a problem for the child theme developer.

To get around this problem, you can use an action hook in your theme to unhook any of the undesired hooks from the parent themes functions file. Use the `'after_setup_theme'` action, which is performed after both functions files have been loaded, to unset any action or filter the hooks made in the parent theme.

For example, if you wanted to remove the Twenty Thirteen hook on the `body_class` filter and replace it with your own, you could do the following:

```
function remove_parent_hooks() {
    remove_filter( 'body_class', 'twentythirteen_body_class' );
}

add_action('after_setup_theme', 'remove_parent_hooks');
```

Likewise, you can remove any other action the parent theme adds with the `remove_action()` function.

Child Themes Summary

That's now pretty much it when it comes to working with child themes in WordPress. You should now know how to create a child theme and some of the considerations you need to use when thinking about doing so. There are a lot of positives that can come from working with child themes, and they can speed up your development incredibly if you're working with a parent theme you know inside and out.

Be aware of how child themes work for theme development in general, especially if you plan to release your themes at some point (as discussed in Chapter 11). By knowing how child themes can be used and how they get their functionality from the parent theme, you can improve your theme development to allow others to easily create child themes of your themes. People will able to customize your work further, which can be a great benefit to your more tech-savvy customers.

WordPress Comments

With its roots as a blogging platform, WordPress has always had a built-in functionality for comments. Comments enable you to interact with the audience on your site, promoting discussion and further exploration of the topics you talk about through your site. Although comments in recent years have been dropped by some bloggers because of the overwhelming moderation task they face or finding discussion happening elsewhere such as Twitter or in forums, some major blogs and magazine sites are thriving with comment systems. Two that come to my mind are Smashing Magazine and Chris Coyier's CSS Tricks site, both of which have a thriving comments section for most of their posts, with the community involved in discussions around the topics posed by the articles.

So commenting is still a successful arena for discussion and interaction with your site's readership. In this section of the chapter, I want to take a deeper look at the commenting system in WordPress, how to make it work best for you and your site, and how to add some nice customizations to improve the level of interaction you can get from your readers. For some great thoughts on the nature of commenting, do check out Matt Browne's talk from WordCamp San Diego in 2011 called "Comments are King: Make Sure that You Rule Over the Right Platform" (http://wp-themes-book.com/12009).

Comments: An Overview

WordPress has three different types of comments that your site can receive: comments, pingbacks, and trackbacks. You know how regular comments work: users want to add an opinion or discussion point relating to a post on your site. They usually complete a form on your site, and the comment is then output along with that post for everyone else to read and discuss further. It is what we all recognize as a "comment" system.

Pingbacks and trackbacks are related to how your post is being discussed on someone else's site (in Figure 12-5, you can see them in action on one of the posts on my site). They show where your article is being discussed in other parts of the Web. The difference between the two comes from the way people link to your post from their sites.

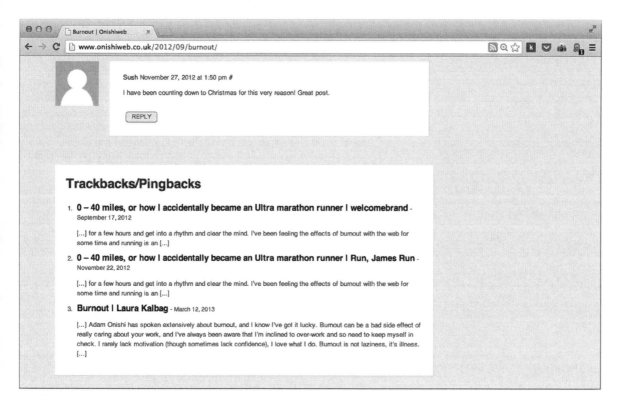

Figure 12-5. *Trackbacks and pingbacks on my onishiweb.co.uk blog*

A *pingback* occurs when another blogger has explicitly added a link to your posts on their site. WordPress detects this link and creates the pingback on your site automatically. A *trackback* occurs when someone may have written about your site, but did not include a direct link to your article. In WordPress, you can then set this up as a trackback via the Send Trackbacks To function in the post edit screen (see Figure 12-6).

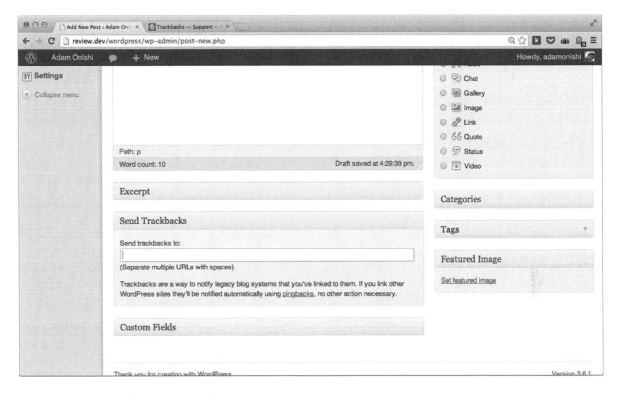

Figure 12-6. *The trackbacks section of the post editor*

The difference comes down to the way the other site has referenced your content. Nowadays, I would say that pingbacks are usually the standard for this type of interaction; with trackbacks are used only on rare occasions. It is unusual for someone to talk about a post you've written but not link back to it in their content.

Comment Spam

One disadvantage of the popularity of WordPress is that it is a prime target for spam; if you've ever run a WordPress blog with comments, you'll know you can be subject to a lot of it. The popularity of WordPress means that there are many systems already set up on the Web to specifically seek out WordPress blogs and target any comment forms they can find. These spammers attempt to post comments using the default fields you would expect in a WordPress comment form (name, e-mail, URL, and comment) to get a link back to their own site posted on your web site. This site could be a phishing site or one of the many fake medication sites, for example.

Besides automated spammers like these, manual attempts at spam are made by people trying to get links back to their web sites posted on your site. Although a lot of automated spam is more random, the manual spammers actually go to your site and leave comments through the comment form, saying things like "great post" or "your should check out my solution here," again with the aim of getting links back to their own sites posted on yours.

The best solution I've found to deal with comment spam is to use the well-known and highly praised plugin (so much so it's bundled with WordPress by default): Akismet. Akismet takes a lot of the hassle out of running a site with comments. (I discussed the service back in Chapter 9 as one of my recommended plugins—it's that good.) Although extremely efficient at catching all the automated spam your site might receive, Akismet sometimes finds it difficult to keep up with some of the manual spam. You'll probably have to keep a little bit of an eye on your comments, just in case. However, if you start getting too many comments to be able to manually moderate them all, there is a simple solution Paul Und discussed in his post on the subject of WordPress comments (http://wp-themes-book.com/12010).

The solution is to simply remove the URL field from the comment form, so spammers can no longer link back to their site from their name in the comments. Instead, they have to do so in the comment text, which can be automatically moderated by WordPress for you. This approach simply requires a filter set on one the comment form hooks:

```
function remove_comment_url_fields($fields) {
    if(isset($fields['url']))
    {
        unset($fields['url']);
    }
    return $fields;
}
add_filter('comment_form_default_fields','remove_comment_url_fields');
```

This code removes the URL field from the array of default fields that appear in the comment form before returning the array back to the function to continue generating the form. With this field removed, you can then use the moderation setting in the WordPress discussion settings to force comments with a certain number of links in them to be held for moderation by default (see Figure 12-7).

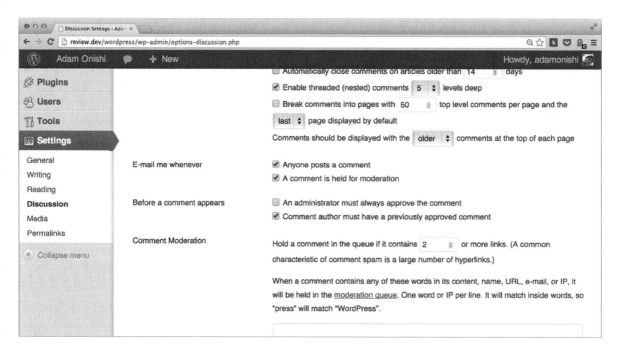

Figure 12-7. *The discussion settings with comment moderation in the center*

Commenting Options (Non-WordPress)

Finally, I want to briefly look at some of the options you have for adding comments to your site in addition to the WordPress default system. Of course, I'll cover the WordPress system in detail during this section, but there are other methods of adding comments to your site that might be more tempting, depending on how you envision your readers interacting with you and your content.

These external commenting systems are usually used to take the onus away from WordPress to manage the comments you're getting or to allow people to use their social media accounts to post comments on your site. The former reason can stem from the spam issue with WordPress comments. And some people don't like having their comments linked to their site; they'd rather it be more open with social networks and such. This adds some ease for your users: they don't have to sign up or sign in to anything; they just add their comments from one of their social media accounts.

There are a fair number of commenting options available, but I'll cover just three of the more popular solutions, some of which you may have seen already in operation on the Web:

- **Disqus** is a third-party commenting system that can be run from its WordPress plugin (http://wp-themes-book.com/12011). This system allows your users to comment via any of their social networks or a Disqus-specific account. They don't have to authenticate with your blog at all; it can all be left up to Disqus. Disqus comments via the plugin also handily sync up with the WordPress comments system, so you can choose to remove the plugin at any time and retain the comments on your site.

- **Facebook** comments can be added to your site, again with a simple plugin (http://wp-themes-book.com/12012). The plugin syncs up comments with users' Facebook accounts and actually posts their comments to their Facebook timeline if they allow it to. So the article they're commenting on can be shared throughout that network as well.

- **Jetpack**, which is a plugin I recommended in Chapter 9, is by Automattic (the company behind WordPress) and comes with a whole host of features for your self-hosted WordPress site that are usually available by default on WordPress.com sites. The comments system that Jetpack offers ties in with the WordPress comments system, but allows users to sign in with their various social media accounts or their WordPress.com account to leave a comment. This is useful if you want users to have an account somewhere in order to post comments.

Working with Comments

Now it's time to work with comments in your theme. There are three parts to adding comments to WordPress: the comments template, the form, and the list of comments. The template is the PHP file that holds the markup for your comments and the other two are output via functions in that template.

By default, comments are available to all default post types and can be added to your custom post types by adding 'comments' to the supports argument in the register_post_type() function. Of course, you must include the comments template on the page to enable people to leave comments on your post.

Comments also come with a hefty number of settings (in Settings > Discussion). The discussion settings cover everything, including how the site admin is notified about new comments on the site, rules governing who is allowed to post comments, and settings covering how comments will be moderated. There is also a theme support setting to automatically add RSS feed links to the head of a page, specifically for post comments.

For a full list of comment settings and what they do, check out the page in the Codex: http://wp-themes-book.com/12013.

Comments Template

To include comments in your theme, start with the comments template: `comments.php`. Prior to version 3.0, WordPress had a default comments template that would output everything for you. However, in version 3.0, it was deprecated in favor of theme developers creating their own template files. Currently, there is still a default comments template residing in `wp-includes/theme-compat/comments.php`, which will be used if you do not have a `comments.php` (or specify an alternate template name), but because this has been deprecated for more than six major versions, it should not be relied on for your themes.

Comments are included in your theme via the `comments_template()` function that can reside either inside or outside of the WordPress loop. By default, the function requires no parameters, but can accept two: a template file name if you want to use a template other than the default `comments.php` (to display multiple styles of comments, for instance); and a Boolean `separate_comments` parameter used to set whether to display the different comment types separately from each other or together in the same timeline.

The construction of a comments template can vary in complexity, depending on how your theme will use certain features. For example, a template I've used in the past consisted of not much more than including the comments form and list of comments:

```php
<?php if ( have_comments() ) : ?>
        <section class="comments">
                <h2>Comments</h2>

                <ul>
                        <?php wp_list_comments(); ?>
                </ul>
        </section>
<? endif; ?>

<section id="comment-form">
        <h2>Leave a comment</h2>
        <?php comment_form($args); ?>
</section>
```

This code was all I needed for some of the sites I built to output the standard formatting of the comments and the basic comments list. Even this basic template would be enough to pass the theme review if you were uploading your theme to the Themes Directory.

The Twenty Thirteen comments template has a lot more going on:

```php
if ( post_password_required() )
        return;
?>

<div id="comments" class="comments-area">

        <?php if ( have_comments() ) : ?>
                <h2 class="comments-title">
                        <?php
                                printf( _nx( 'One thought on &ldquo;%2$s&rdquo;', '%1$s
thoughts on &ldquo;%2$s&rdquo;', get_comments_number(), 'comments title', 'twentythirteen' ),
                                        number_format_i18n( get_comments_number() ),
'<span>' . get_the_title() . '</span>' );
                        ?>
                </h2>
```

```
            <ol class="comment-list">
                    <?php
                            wp_list_comments( array(
                                    'style'       => 'ol',
                                    'short_ping'  => true,
                                    'avatar_size' => 74,
                            ) );
                    ?>
            </ol><!-- .comment-list -->

            <?php
                    // Are there comments to navigate through?
                    if ( get_comment_pages_count() > 1 && get_option( 'page_comments' ) ) :
            ?>
            <nav class="navigation comment-navigation" role="navigation">
                    <h1 class="screen-reader-text section-heading"><?php _e( 'Comment navigation',
'twentythirteen' ); ?></h1>
                    <div class="nav-previous"><?php previous_comments_link( __( '&larr;
Older Comments', 'twentythirteen' ) ); ?></div>
                    <div class="nav-next"><?php next_comments_link( __( 'Newer Comments &rarr;',
'twentythirteen' ) ); ?></div>
            </nav><!-- .comment-navigation -->
            <?php endif; // Check for comment navigation ?>

            <?php if ( ! comments_open() && get_comments_number() ) : ?>
            <p class="no-comments"><?php _e( 'Comments are closed.' , 'twentythirteen' ); ?></p>
            <?php endif; ?>

    <?php endif; // have_comments() ?>

    <?php comment_form(); ?>

</div><!-- #comments -->
```

In the default themes comments, there are a lot of different functions making use of all the features available for your comments template. Let's have a closer look at some of them.

post_password_required()

Because the comments template doesn't need to be included inside the Loop, you can use this function to test whether the current post is password protected. If not, you can continue in the template; otherwise, as used in the Twenty Thirteen template, you can use the return; statement to stop rendering the remainder of the template file.

get_comments_number()

This function can be used to display the number of comments for the current post in a title of the comments section, for instance. The Twenty Thirteen theme does exactly that with a nice combination of functions that incorporate internationalization of the title as well (more on that later in the chapter).

get_comment_pages_count()

If you have allowed comments to be paginated via the discussion settings, you can use this function to output the number of pages of comments for the post. You can also test whether there are any extra pages to decide if you need to output the pagination section of your comments area.

previous_comments_link() and next_comments_link()

Relatively self-explanatory; these functions output the pagination links for your comments section.

comments_open()

A conditional tag used to test whether comments are allowed for the current post. Comments can be turned off for individual posts through the post editor screen (see Figure 12-8), so it's useful to test whether comments are allowed for the post and maybe output an alert message to the current user if comments are closed for a post.

Figure 12-8. *The individual post discussion settings*

Configuring your comments template to include all these features allows the site administrator and post editors to have full control over the comments section. In this single template, you can ensure that many discussion settings are handled gracefully in your template and that the users will get the output they expect on their site.

Comments Form

The comments form is included in your comments template via the `comment_form()` function. By default, the comment form output contains fields for the commenter's name, e-mail address, web site URL, and comment (see Figure 12-9).

Figure 12-9. *The default comments form*

The comment_form() function takes two parameters. First is an array of arguments you can use to customize the default output of the form. The second parameter is a post ID that allows you to add a comment form to another part of a theme and post comments for a specific post instead of the current post. Neither of these parameters is required, but they can be used to alter the form output.

The default arguments array comprises a lot of options to customize the form and can be broken down into four main types:

- Form fields: fields and comment_field

- Instructions/information: must_log_in, logged_in_as, comment_notes_before, and comment_notes_after

- HTML attributes: id_form and id_submit

- Title & link text: title_reply, title_reply_to, cancel_reply_link, and label_submit

The form field's arguments allow you to set up the way the default fields will appear in the form: `'author'`, `'email'`, and `'url'`. The `'fields'` argument is an array including the field name (array key) and markup of each input element (array value). The defaults for the `'fields'` argument looks like this:

```
$fields = array(

        'author' =>
                '<p class="comment-form-author"><label for="author">' . __( 'Name',
'domainreference' ) . '</label> ' .
                ( $req ? '<span class="required">*</span>' : '' ) .
                '<input id="author" name="author" type="text" value="' .
esc_attr( $commenter['comment_author'] ) .
                '" size="30"' . $aria_req . ' /></p>',

        'email' =>
                '<p class="comment-form-email"><label for="email">' . __( 'Email', 'domainreference' )
. '</label> ' .
                ( $req ? '<span class="required">*</span>' : '' ) .
                '<input id="email" name="email" type="text" value="' .
esc_attr(  $commenter['comment_author_email'] ) .
                '" size="30"' . $aria_req . ' /></p>',

        'url' =>
                '<p class="comment-form-url"><label for="url">' . __( 'Website',
'domainreference' ) . '</label>' .
                '<input id="url" name="url" type="text" value="' .
esc_attr( $commenter['comment_author_url'] ) .
                '" size="30" /></p>',
);
```

The comment_field argument and the instruction/information type fields work in a similar way except they are on a single level in the arguments array where the value is the markup of the main comment field or the information/instruction you want to output in a certain place. For example, the default for the comment_notes_after argument is the following, which you can see output beneath the comment textarea in Figure 12-9:

```
'<p class="form-allowed-tags">' . sprintf( __( 'You may use these <abbr title="HyperText Markup
Language">HTML</abbr> tags and attributes: %s' ), ' <code>' . allowed_tags() . '</code>' ) . '</p>'
```

The remaining types of arguments for the comment_form() function are fairly standard: the HTML attribute fields take in single strings, and the title & link text fields should be set as translatable strings.

Modifying the Default Form

The main way to modify the comments form is to edit the arguments passed to the comment_form() function. If you look at the defaults in the fields argument, however, you see that there are a few functions besides just the markup for the field included. Make sure to always retain the use of these functions, first to ensure that your form labels are translated (the __() function) and (as discussed in Chapter 10) to make sure that the form is secure (the esc_attr() function).

Another way to manipulate the default fields in the comment form is to use a filter, as you saw earlier in the chapter. As a security feature, you could use the comment fields' filter to remove the URL field. Probably one of the main reasons for using a filter to modify the comments form is because you have no direct access to the templates or do not want to alter them. This could mean that you're working from a plugin or maybe from a child theme, where just removing or altering the comment fields from the functions file is cleaner than copying the entire comments template.

When modifying the form fields using either of these two methods, note that if you want to use any of the current commenter information or output HTML based on the $req variable, you need to set them up in your code before you modify the fields. This can be done using these three lines:

```
$commenter = wp_get_current_commenter();
$req = get_option( 'require_name_email' );
$aria_req = ( $req ? " aria-required='true'" : '' );
```

The first line sets the current commenter if a user is logged in. The second gets the value of the required setting that will allow you to output the required text if you want to. The final line then checks the value of the $req variable to set a string, including the aria-required attribute that should be added to the input fields of the form.

Adding Custom Fields to the Comment Form

Besides modifying the default fields in the comment form, it's also possible to add your own if you want to capture more details from the commenter. Custom fields for comments are manipulated in a similar way to custom fields in a post: by using a series of familiar-looking functions: add_comment_meta(), update_comment_meta(), get_comment_meta(), and delete_comment_meta(). Before you start storing and updating comment meta, however, you must add the custom fields to the form.

There are three methods you can use to add custom fields to the comments form: via the fields array in the comment_form() function; the comment fields hook; or a pair of actions that can be used to add content into the form after the default fields: comment_form_logged_in_after and comment_form_after_fields. The reason for the variety of methods is because it depends on what data you want to capture and when that data should be captured. The first two methods, manipulating or adding to the default fields, are best for when you want to capture data only once for each commenter. The default fields will be visible on the form only when the commenter is not logged in; if WordPress detects the user is logged in, the default fields are hidden (see Figure 12-10).

Figure 12-10. *The default fields are hidden in the comment form when the user is logged in*

If you want to add fields that users should complete each time they leave a comment (for instance, a rating of the post they're commenting on), you want those fields to be visible whether the user is logged in or not. That's where the final method—using the two action hooks—comes in. These two hooks are fired directly before the comments field is output, whether the user is logged in or not.

■ **Note**   There are many action hooks available for the comments form that allow you to output content at many different points and under different circumstances in which the form is being displayed. For instance, the `comments_form_top` action is used to output directly after the title of the form, and the `comment_form_comments_closed` action is used to output content when the comments form is closed. For a full list of actions, take a look at the Codex page: `http://wp-themes-book.com/12014`.

You've already seen how to manipulate the default fields, so now look at how to add a persistent field to the form that the user will always complete:

```
function comments_rating_field () {
        echo '<p><label>' . __('Rating', 'prowordpress') . '<span class="required">*</span></label>' .
            '<select name="ptd_comment_rating">' .
                    '<option value="">Please choose</option>' .
                    '<option value="rubbish">Rubbish</option>' .
                    '<option value="ok">Ok</option>' .
                    '<option value="excellent">Excellent</option>' .
            '</select></p>';
}

add_action( 'comment_form_logged_in_after', 'comments_rating_field' );
add_action( 'comment_form_after_fields', 'comments_rating_field' );
```

This function is hooked into the two actions talked about previously. When called, it prints out the `rating` field just above the comments field, whether the user is logged in or not. With the field added, you now need a way of processing the field and saving it with the `add_comment_meta()` function. To do this, you need two more hooks, a filter, and an action.

To check that the `rating` field has been set when the form is submitted, you need to use a filter to get at the comment form data: the `preprocess_comment` filter.

```
function process_comment_rating_field( $commentdata ) {
        $ratings = array('rubbish', 'ok', 'excellent' );

        if ( ! isset( $_POST['ptd_comment_rating'] ) ) {
                wp_die( __( 'Error: You did not add a rating. Use the Back button on your Web browser
to revisit the post and resubmit your comment.' ) );
        } elseif ( ! in_array($_POST['ptd_comment_rating'], $ratings) ) {
                wp_die( __( 'Error: You did not set a rating correctly. Use the Back button on your
Web browser to revisit the post and resubmit your comment.' ) );
        }

        return $commentdata;
}

add_filter( 'preprocess_comment', 'process_comment_rating_field' );
```

The contents of the function check to see whether the `rating` field has been set and if the rating is one of the expected values (a good piece of validation if you know what values your function can expect). If not, it forces an error with the `wp_die()` function. If all is okay, the filter simply returns the comment data, and WordPress continues to process the comment normally.

■ **Note** Using the `wp_die()` function is not the best method of creating an error for the user, as you can tell by the error message used in the comments processing function. To prevent the user from getting this error, you could perform some client-side validation with JavaScript instead. This method would be used as a fallback in case there is a JavaScript error or the user has JavaScript turned off.

Once you validate the comment submission for the required field, you need to use an action to save the comment meta to the database. The action for doing this is `comment_post`:

```
function prowordpress_save_comment_meta( $comment_id ) {
    if ( ( isset( $_POST['ptd_comment_rating'] ) ) && ( $_POST['ptd_comment_rating'] != '' ) ) {
        $rating = wp_filter_nohtml_kses($_POST['ptd_comment_rating']);
        add_comment_meta( $comment_id, 'ptd_comment_rating', $rating );
    }
}

add_action( 'comment_post', 'prowordpress_save_comment_meta' );
```

The function to save the `rating` field just needs to check that the field exists (because it's a required field, you should know that already, but it's still good to check). It then saves the field using the `add_comment_meta()` function. There's also a quick filter run on the value of the form data using the `wp_filter_nohtml_kses()` function, which ensures that all HTML is stripped from the string. Again this might be a bit over the top, but it's always better to check things too much than not enough.

So far, the process of adding custom comment fields has been fairly familiar with the use of the `add_comment_meta()` function. Once you have the data stored for a comment, you'll also want to output it to the WordPress admin comments section, which is similar to adding custom meta fields to posts: through the `add_meta_box()` function. To add a custom meta box to comments, you can follow the same process as you would with a post meta box: substituting the post type for `'comment'`, the `get_post_meta()` and other functions for `get_comment_meta()`, and so on. The two actions you'll need to use are `add_meta_boxes_comment` to add the meta box and `edit_comment` to save the comment meta values.

Comments List

Now you're on to the final piece of the comment jigsaw: listing the comments. To output comments to your theme, use the `wp_list_comments()` function. It again takes two parameters: the first is an array of arguments, and the second is an array of comments to output. Neither parameter is required for the function to work, but they do allow you to customize the comments that are displayed.

To add an array of comments to the function as the second parameter, you need to use the `get_comments()` function. It allows you to specify through a whole range of arguments what comments are returned that can then be passed to the `wp_list_comments()` function to be output normally. For example, you can return only comments by a specific author if you want to list only the post author's comments in a sidebar or refine comments by meta data (based on the previous example—when you added the rating meta to the comments, you could specify a list of comments that gave an `'excellent'` rating). As you can see, this would be great for adding a filter to comments for users to show a specific subset of the current post's comments.

The first parameter contains an array of arguments similar to a lot of functions in WordPress. The arguments you can pass are these:

- `$avatar_size`: Choose the size of the avatar returned (size is in pixels, but requires only a single number; i.e., 50 = 50px square avatar). Default is 32.

- `$style`: Whether the list will be inside a `<div>`, `<ul>`, or `<ol>` tag (the default is `<ul>`). You still need to specify the container that will set whether to output the comments within `<li>` or `<div>` tags.

- `$type`: Type of comment to return, comments, trackbacks, pingbacks, pings (both trackbacks and pingbacks), and all. Default is `all`.

- `$page`: Current page of comments to display (if paginated).

- `$reply_text`: Text for the reply link. Default is `'reply'`.

- `$login_text`: Text to display if the commenter must log in before commenting. Default is `'Log in to reply'`.

- `$callback`: Name of the function used to display the comments (more on this shortly). Default is `null`.

- `$end-callback`: Name of the function used to close each comment; replaces the default functionality that will close each comment based on the `'style'` setting. Default is `null`.

- `$reverse_top_level`: Boolean; set to `true` will display most recent comments first. Default is `false`.

- `$reverse_children`: Boolean; set to `true` will display threaded comments with the most recent first. Default is `false`.

- `$format`: Can be used to set the comment markup to HMTL5 using the value `'html5'`. Default is `null`.

- `$short_ping`: Boolean; whether to display a `'short'` ping style (i.e., just the link). Default is `false`.

The default output of the `wp_list_comments()` function will contain comments with the commenter's name, avatar (via Gravatar), date of the comment, comment text, and a reply link (see Figure 12-11).

Figure 12-11. *The default comments list output*

Depending on your settings, in the function arguments the default HTML generated will mostly use the `<div>` tags to break up the content with a series of classes explaining each section; or when the format is set to HTML5, it will use more detailed markup, including HTML5 tags. You can also set this across your theme for a lot of functionality where WordPress outputs HTML using the new HTML5 theme feature, included via the add_theme_support('html5') function. The default output of the comments with HTML5 turned on is shown here:

```
<li id="comment-12" class="comment odd alt thread-odd thread-alt depth-1">
        <article id="div-comment-12" class="comment-body">
                <footer class="comment-meta">
                        <div class="comment-author vcard">
                                <img alt='' src='...' class='avatar avatar-32 photo' height='32' width='32' />
                                <b class="fn"><a href='...' rel='external nofollow' class='url'>Matt</a></b>
                                <span class="says">says:</span>
                        </div><!-- .comment-author -->

                        <div class="comment-metadata">
                                <a href="...">
                                        <time datetime="2007-09-04T10:15:32+00:00">
                                                4th September 2007 at 10:15 am
                                        </time>
                                </a>
                                <span class="edit-link">
                                        <a class="comment-edit-link" href="..." title="Edit
comment">Edit</a>
                                </span>
                        </div><!-- .comment-metadata -->

                </footer><!-- .comment-meta -->

                <div class="comment-content">
                        <p>Anonymous person pretending to be Matt.</p>
                </div><!-- .comment-content -->

                <div class="reply">
                        <a class='comment-reply-link' href='...' onclick='return addComment.
moveForm("div-comment-12", "12", "respond", "149")'>Reply</a>
                </div><!-- .reply -->
        </article><!-- .comment-body -->
</li><!-- #comment-## -->
```

This entire HTML is output via the default Walker_Comment class. Walker classes are used throughout WordPress to output any tree-like structures that may occur in themes, including multilevel menus and category lists (and the comments list in this instance). The walker is fairly complex in nature, or at least complex enough for it to be beyond the scope of explanation here. However, there is a much easier way to customize the output of comments that doesn't require creating a custom walker class. Among the arguments for the wp_list_comments() function is the callback argument that allows you to specify a function name that will be called when outputting the comments from within the Walker_Comment class.

Customizing Comments with the Callback Function

In the custom callback for displaying comments in your theme, you have a range of functions at your disposal to print out any and all information stored for each comment. You can use as many or as few of these as you like to create the simplest or most comprehensive comments display. You can also add in your own markup to style your comments the way you want.

The full list of functions available in your comments callback is listed here; in most cases these functions also have a `'get_'` modifier to return the output as PHP. If the function is list as a `'get_'` function, there is no standard echo equivalent (without the `'get_'` prefix).

- `comment_author()` outputs the name of the commenter.

- `comment_author_email()` outputs the e-mail of the commenter.

- `comment_author_email_link()` outputs an HTML link for the commenter's e-mail; can be customized with passed parameters.

- `comment_author_link()` outputs a link to the comment author using the URL submitted from the comment form; link text is commenter name.

- `comment_author_IP()` outputs the IP address of the commenter (probably shouldn't be output in your theme templates).

- `comment_author_url()` outputs the URL the commenter submitted with the comment form.

- `comment_author_url_link()` outputs a link to the URL submitted by the commenter; output can be customized.

- `comment_class()` outputs a class attribute for use in comment elements; very useful for styling.

- `comment_date()` outputs the date the comment was submitted.

- `comment_excerpt()` outputs an excerpt of the comment text.

- `comment_ID()` outputs the ID of the comment.

- `get_comment_link()` returns the link of the current comment.

- `comment_text()` outputs the full comment text.

- `comment_time()` outputs the time the comment was submitted.

- `comment_type()` outputs the type of the comment (comment, trackback, pingback).

- `comment_reply_link()` outputs the reply link for the current comment.

- `cancel_comment_reply_link()` outputs a cancel link for a comment reply.

The most basic information you should be outputting for each comment is probably the name of the commenter, the date of the comment, and the comment text. However, if you have threaded comments turned on, you'll also want the comment reply link to add to those basic elements. A simple comments callback function can be seen in the Starkers starter theme by Viewport Industries (`http://wp-themes-book.com/12015`), which simply contains the most basic information within some simple markup:

```php
function starkers_comment( $comment, $args, $depth ) {
    $GLOBALS['comment'] = $comment;
    ?>
    <?php if ( $comment->comment_approved == '1' ): ?>
    <li>
            <article id="comment-<?php comment_ID() ?>">
                    <?php echo get_avatar( $comment ); ?>
                    <h4><?php comment_author_link() ?></h4>
```

```
                       <time><a href="#comment-<?php comment_ID() ?>" pubdate><?php comment_date() ?>
at <?php comment_time() ?></a></time>
                       <?php comment_text() ?>
              </article>
          <?php endif;
}
```

Notice that at the beginning of the comment markup there is an opening `<li>` tag, but at the end of the comment there is no closing tag. This is due to the `Walker_Comment` class; as mentioned earlier, it will walk through the comments and output the different hierarchies of the potential tree of comments. Therefore, it's important to leave the closing tag of the comments to the walker class.

An example of a more complex callback function is used in the Underscores starter theme from Automattic. It is a little too big to include here, but it makes use of many of the functions available for outputting comments, so it's good to check out if you're looking for inspiration for your comments callback. The comment function can be found in the template tags file of the Underscores Github repository at `http://wp-themes-book.com/12016`.

Some of the parts I will pick out of the Underscores function that are nice little additions to your comments include these:

```
<?php if ( '0' == $comment->comment_approved ) : ?>
        <p class="comment-awaiting-moderation"><?php _e( 'Your comment is awaiting moderation.', '_s' ); ?></p>
<?php endif; ?>
```

This shows a user a message when their comment is awaiting moderation. A signed-in user can see their comment appear on the site automatically before it is moderated and visible to the rest of the site's visitors:

```
<?php if ( 'pingback' == $comment->comment_type || 'trackback' == $comment->comment_type ) : ?>

<li id="comment-<?php comment_ID(); ?>" <?php comment_class(); ?>>
        <div class="comment-body">
                <?php _e( 'Pingback:', '_s' ); ?> <?php comment_author_link(); ?>
<?php edit_comment_link( __( 'Edit', '_s' ), '<span class="edit-link">', '</span>' ); ?>
        </div>

<?php else : ?>
```

The section at the beginning of the function is used to display pingbacks and trackbacks differently from the rest of the comments.

Styling Comments with comment_class()

You saw the `comment_class()` function earlier in the list of functions available for use when outputting comments. Like the `body_class()` and `post_class()` functions, it outputs a `class` attribute with a list of useful classes for styling purposes. The classes' output have a number of uses, including odd and even classes if you want to add some Zebra-style effects to your comments style, an author class for styling comments made by the author slightly differently, and even specific classes for each author if you want to style them individually.

```
<li id="comment-30" class="comment byuser comment-author-adamonishi even thread-even depth-1">
```

Here you can see a typical class output in the `<li>` tag of the comment. It shows that the comment was posted by a user of the site, gives the author name, and furnishes information on the position of the comment (even, thread-even, and depth-1).

```
<li id="comment-33" class="comment byuser comment-author-adamonishi bypostauthor odd alt depth-2">
```

If the author of the post commented, you would see the class "bypostauthor", which is really useful for picking out the comments posted by the author of the current post and highlighting them separately from the rest. You can see this used to great effect in the *Smashing Magazine* comments section (see Figure 12-12).

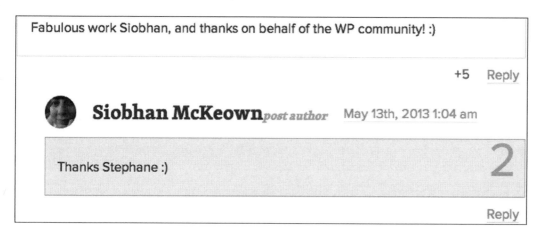

Figure 12-12. Smashing Magazine author comments

Adding Custom Meta to Comments Output

Finally, it's time to look at how you can add the custom meta you added to the comments form earlier in the chapter. You will use the `get_comment_meta()` function (similar to the `get_post_meta()` function, which you learned about in the earlier custom fields discussion).

All you need is to get the current comment ID using the `get_comment_ID()` function to be able to output the custom meta using the meta key you entered when saving the data:

```
<p class="comment-rating">
        Rating: <?php echo get_comment_meta( get_comment_ID(), 'ptd_comment_rating', true ); ?>
</p>
```

Because you made this field a requirement when you stored the data, you can be sure that it is there to be output. So there's no need to test whether the field is set. The data was sanitized safely when input into the database, so outputting again will be safe as well.

Comments Summary

This fairly lengthy section of the chapter covered all you need to know to get up and running with comments in your theme. You saw how to fully customize the information you receive in your comments and to customize the output to appear the way you want it to.

Comments are an important part of WordPress' role as a blogging platform. Although WordPress is now being used more as a CMS, it will always still be used for blogging. And with comments being so pivotal for bloggers to engage with their audience, as a theme developer you should know how to help engage that audience through the comments section of your theme.

Internationalization

Lastly, I want to talk about an important topic that is sometimes overlooked in WordPress discussions: *internationalization* (or i18n, for short). Internationalization is the process of enabling your theme or plugin to be translated into another language.

Why is internationalization important? Statistics in 2011 (http://wp-themes-book.com/12020) showed that only 27% of Internet users used English as their first language. And a study in 2012 by the UN Broadband Commission found that Chinese-speaking users will overtake English speakers on the Web by 2015. Proof enough?

As mentioned, internationalization is the process of making your theme translatable (not to be confused with actually translating your theme, which is known as *localization*, or l10n). I don't suggest that you find and translate every string in your WordPress themes and plugins—that would be unrealistic. However, as a developer you should make sure that your theme can be easily translated if the user wants to do so. Without your theme being internationalized, there is no way to localize it.

If you want to distribute or sell your theme and you don't translate it, you cut off a large number of potential customers. Because WordPress is such a popular system for creating web sites around the world, a large percentage of these sites will be in languages other than English.

How i18n Works in WordPress

WordPress uses the GNU gettext package and libraries to support internationalization in its themes and plugins. This software is created by GNU, the same company behind the license WordPress uses and the GNU Translation Project, which is a large project for translating software.

GNU gettext utilizes three types of files: portable object template (POT) files, portable object (PO) files, and machine object (MO) files.

The POT file is used as a template for translators and is generated through parsing the source code of your theme or plugin. Note that your themes are parsed only to generate the POT files, not executed first—more on that shortly.

The PO file consists of the output from the translators and contains the original and translated strings.

The MO file is generated from the PO file, which is a machine-readable format of the translations.

As a theme developer, the main file you should be concerned about is the POT file, which enables people to translate your themes. However, if you are running a WordPress site that needs translating, you can easily generate the MO files from the translated PO files by using the msgfmt tool, which is part of the gettext tools you need to install on your machine. For more information on using and installing gettext, visit the GNU site: http://wp-themes-book.com/12017.

Text Domain

You came across the text domain in Chapter 2 because it is part of the style sheet header of your theme:

```
/**
 * Theme Name: Pro WordPress Theme Development
 * Author: Adam Onishi
 * Text Domain: prowordpress
 */
```

This text domain is used throughout your theme or plugin as a unique identifier (it has been used in code throughout this book). To set the text domain for internationalization in your theme or plugin, you also need to load it within your functions file with the load_theme_textdomain() function:

```
function prowordpress_setup() {

        load_theme_textdomain('prowordpress', get_template_directory() . '/lang');
}
add_action( 'after_setup_theme', 'prowordpress_setup' );
```

There is some discussion about which action is best for loading the text domain: the init or after_setup_theme action. They are similar in execution, but I use the after_setup_theme action because it is loaded slightly before the init action and I can include the function from within my regular theme setup function.

For plugins, use the load_plugin_textdomain() function on the plugins_loaded action:

```
function prowordpress_plugin_init() {
        $plugin_dir = basename(dirname(__FILE__));
        load_plugin_textdomain( 'prowordpress', false, $plugin_dir );
}

add_action('plugins_loaded', 'prowordpress_plugin_init');
```

For child themes, load a separate text domain from the parent theme and use the load_child_theme_textdomain() function as well:

```
function prowordpress_child_theme_setup() {
        load_child_theme_textdomain( 'prowordpress-child', get_stylesheet_directory() . '/lang' );
}
add_action( 'after_setup_theme', 'prowordpress_child_theme_setup' );
```

What these functions are doing is loading your text domain, which will be used when looking for the translation files and setting up a location where the language files will be found. You don't have to name your MO files with the text domain; it is done automatically through the gettext functions.

Readying Text for Translation

Without exception, all hardcoded text in your themes or plugins should be made ready for translation. To make your text translatable, WordPress has a series of functions that allows you to translate text in many forms and with the context in which the text is being used.

There are three main text-related functions to use when adding translations to your themes:

```
$hello = __('Hello, World', 'prowordpress');
```

The __() (double underscore) function is for returning text in PHP, the first argument is the string to be translated, and the second is the theme text domain.

```
<h1><?php _e('Hello, World', 'prowordpress'); ?></h1>
```

Where you would normally echo a string, you can use the _e() function. However, some text is not as straightforward to translate as others; in English, for example, words can mean different things based on their context. Fortunately WordPress has a contextual function to take care of that:

```
$instruction = _x('Add comment', 'verb', 'prowordpress');

$title = _x('Comments', 'noun', 'prowordpress');
```

The _x() function takes three parameters: the string to be translated, the context in which it is being used, and the text domain. There is also an echo equivalent of the _x() function, the _ex() function:

```
<a href="#"><?php _ex('Add comment', 'verb', 'prowordpress'); ?></a>

<h2><?php _ex('Comments', 'noun', 'prowordpress'); ?></h2>
```

There is a whole series of internationalization versions of escaping functions in WordPress, including esc_attr__(), esc_html__(), and esc_attr_x(), as well as many other versions and varieties.

Dealing with Variables in Strings

Because the translation functions require the entire string to be added to the translation files, it is critical that no variables be used in the strings. For example, the format of the string in the following function should never be used:

```
<h2><?php _e("There are $count comments for this post.", 'prowordpress'); ?></h2>
```

Instead, use placeholders via the printf() and sprintf() PHP functions. These functions format text with PHP variables entered into placeholders of the string. To use these functions within your themes, do something along the lines of the following code:

```
<h2><?php printf( __( 'There are %d comments for this post.', 'prowordpress' ), $count ); ?> </h2>
```

The printf() function uses a placeholder, in this case %d for decimal number, in the string you want to output. The following argument(s) contain the values to substitute into the string. There can be multiple placeholders in each string as long as there's an argument with which to replace it passed to the printf() function.

If you want to return the string, you can use the sprintf() function with the same __() function inside.

Dealing with Plurals

For text that can change depending on a number (for example, '1 comment' or '2 comments'), you can use the _n() function:

```
<h2><?php printf( _n( 'There is %d comment for this post.', 'There are %d comments for this post.', $count, 'prowordpress' ), $count ); ?></h2>
```

The _n() function takes four arguments: the singular text, the pluralized text, the count/number variable on which to base the output, and the text domain.

Important Rules

Finally, I want to cover some important ground rules for using the translation functions in WordPress. Be aware that these are rules, not just recommendations. If you don't follow these rules when internationalizing your themes, people won't be able to translate your themes—and all your work will have been for nothing.

First, never use variables for either the string or the text domain in the translation functions. You've already seen how to work with variables in your strings using the printf() and sprintf() functions, but some people like to take a shortcut and set their text domain as a variable as well. *This does not work.* As I mentioned earlier, to create the POT files for translators, your theme is parsed but not executed, which means that variables are not translated to the strings needed for the POT files. There is also an automated process that happens with plugins through the plugin repository, which again only parses the files and doesn't execute them.

Second, do not mix double and single quotes in your internationalization functions. Stick to one convention throughout your theme or plugin. I recommend single quotes, although WordPress isn't picky about choosing either. Just pick one and stick to it.

Finally, always ensure that you internationalize entire phrases, not just single words. Don't break up phrases so that you don't have to use printf(), for instance. The reason for this is that languages are complicated; if you can't see the entire phrase being output, you can't understand the meaning and the context. Some languages have the subject in a different place than is found in English, so it's important that you allow the translator to see how the words are being used. Also remember that in printf() and sprintf() the %d is just a placeholder, meaning that the translator is free to move it around to output the phrase in the correct order.

Generating Translation Files

Once your theme has been set up for internationalization, you need to generate the POT file to enable translators to localize your theme or plugin. From this file, the translator can create the PO files; then the MO files can be generated to translate the theme.

I'll discuss a couple of ways of translating your theme. First, you can use the WordPress internationalization tools to translate your theme by using a command-line function. Then I will show you one of the more popular and straightforward of applications to generate the files for you: POEdit.

The WordPress internationalization functions may seem to be the optimal solution—after all, you can use a WordPress-created solution by running a single command in the command line. The only tricky part comes from the need to use Subversion (SVN) to download the tools. To read more on using SVN, see the WordPress docs (http://wp-themes-book.com/12018) and download the internationalization tools from here: http://wp-themes-book.com/12019. (Note that it is an SVN link for which you will need to use SVN to download.)

With the internationalization tools downloaded, you can now run the makepot.php file from the command line for your theme using the following command:

```
php makepot.php wp-theme your-theme-directory
```

You can also use the same file to generate the POT file for your plugin, too; you just need to swap wp-theme for wp-plugin and point the command to your plugin directory:

```
php makepot.php wp-plugin your-plugin-directory
```

If you are generating a POT file for your plugin that is in the WordPress plugin repository, there is a function you can run from your repository admin page that will generate the POT file for you.

Using POEdit

POEdit is one of the more popular applications used to work with translation files. It was released under the MIT license as well and can be downloaded from the POEdit web site for Mac, Linux, or Windows: http://www.poedit.net/.

To create your POT file, open POEdit and create a new catalog from File > New Catalog. The Catalog settings menu will display (see Figure 12-13). Add in your details and then go to the sources paths settings.

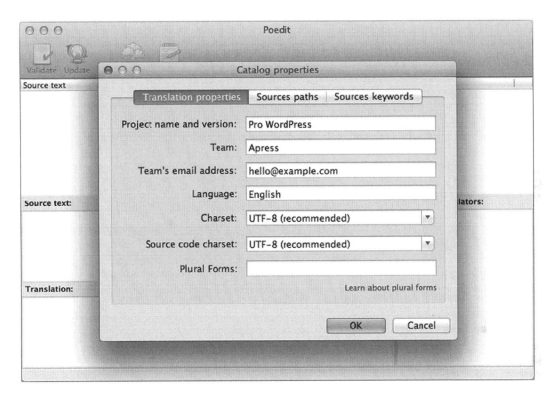

Figure 12-13. *The POEdit new Catalog properties screen*

In the sources paths settings, you need to set the base path; in this case, it is where the translation files are stored: the lang folder. Set the sources paths for where the translation-ready files are; in this case, it is the directory up and any other folders you may have added templates to (the inc folder, as shown earlier in the book). See Figure 12-14.

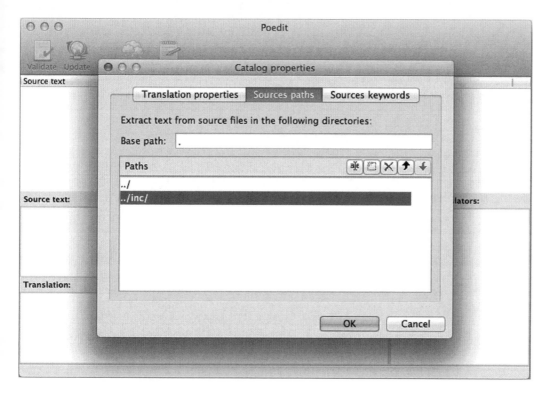

Figure 12-14. *The source paths screen in POEdit*

In the keywords settings, add the functions that POEdit needs to search for in order to generate the translations. Although this depends on what you have coded into your theme, most of the time you need at least the four main translation functions and maybe some of the attribute escape functions.

Add the following keywords to the settings without any brackets (see Figure 12-15):

- __
- _e
- _n
- _x
- _ex
- esc_attr__
- esc_att_e

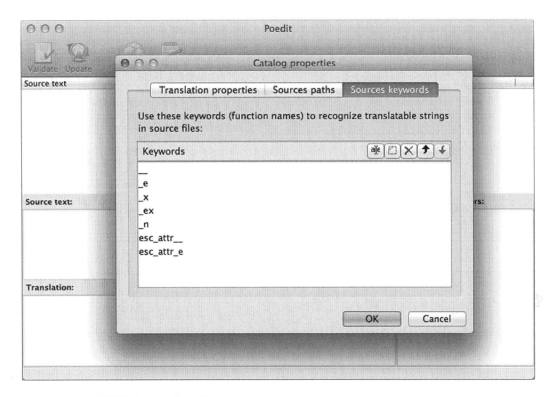

Figure 12-15. *POEdit keywords settings*

After you press OK, you will be asked to locate the folder you want the files to be generated to (the themes 'lang' folder, in this case). POEdit will scan the theme and produce the POT file. You can now either package the POT file with the theme for distribution or hand the POT file to translators to make the translations. POEdit also has the functionality to create the MO files from a completed PO file if you need to.

Internationalization Summary

You should now know not only how important it is to ensure that your themes are fully internationalized but also have the knowledge to make it possible for each of the themes or plugins you create. Internationalization is so important that it should never be overlooked. Whether you're creating themes for distribution or for clients, internationalize your themes from the start to avoid hours of pain in the end.

Once you've gotten into the habit of internationalizing a couple of themes or files as you develop them, it will become second nature and part of your workflow. This is exactly what you are aiming for. As I mentioned at the start of the section, with the actual low percentage of people on the Internet speaking English as their first language, and that number set to decrease in the future, there is no reason not to prepare your themes for localization.

Summary

This chapter has been a bit of a cluster bomb of information. You looked at three important topics related to WordPress: child themes, comments, and internationalization. These are all subjects core to the WordPress platform, so as a theme developer you should be aware of when and how to use them properly.

You saw how child themes can be a great way to increase productivity or customization, allowing you to create a top-level theme to provide all the complex functionality allowing you to add customizations through the child theme. Being aware of child themes ensures that you are developing your themes carefully and allowing users to create child themes to add their own customizations.

A blogging system isn't complete without comments. Although WordPress is now being used more as a CMS, it is still very much a blog at heart. You've seen the importance of comments in your theme and how to fully customize them to make them fit into your theme exactly the way you want.

Most importantly, the chapter discussed internationalization and how important it is to ensure that everything you work on with WordPress is internationalized and ready to be used in any language around the world. Getting internationalization into your workflow as a standard is important and will help improve your potential customer base and your work with clients who have a global audience.

All these concepts are core to the WordPress system and won't be going away any time soon, so it's important to be aware of them and make the best use of them in your themes.

CHAPTER 13

■ ■ ■

Plugin Development

In chapter 9 you looked at when to use plugins and furnished some useful plugins already in existence that can come in handy when running a WordPress site. This chapter will show you what to do when you can't find a plugin that already handles the functionality you're looking for: learn how to create your own. Plugin development in WordPress is a topic that can certainly take up a whole book on its own. However, based on what you've learned about WordPress development so far, you can apply it to the subject of plugin development, enabling you to create some pretty robust plugins (as you'll see as the chapter progresses).

This chapter will cover all the important things you need to know about creating your plugins, not only from how to develop the functionality and interact with WordPress but also how to distribute your plugin via the plugin directory. You'll learn everything you need to know about giving users and developers access to the functionality you create, and also how to choose the best way to store the data your plugin will use.

Writing Your First Plugin

If you've found some functionality you want WordPress to have, or if you have some functionality you wrote into your theme but think that maybe it should really be in a plugin, here's the place to start. I'll run through everything you need to create your first plugin; later in the chapter, you'll learn about more-advanced functionality such as adding custom tables to the WordPress database. For now, I'll show you how to get up and running with your first WordPress plugin.

Plugin Names

Before I go any further, I need to do what I've done many times before in the book: discuss names. Because WordPress is a massively open community in which anyone can develop for the platform, you need to be aware of what to name your plugin so it doesn't clash with any of the 25,000 + other plugins. Therefore it is not only a good idea, but also a requirement that WordPress plugins have unique names, especially for (but not limited to) those that are stored in the plugin directory. This not only prevents confusion when differentiating plugins during selecting one to add to your WordPress site but also stops any collisions in functionality when installing them on your site.

Although trying to come up with a unique name compared with 25,000 others may seem rather daunting, it's actually a lot more straightforward than it sounds. For starters, basing the name around the feature you're writing the plugin for is a good idea because the name gives a clear indication of what the plugin will do, to potential users. You've seen examples of this many times already in chapter 9: plugins such as All in One SEO Pack, Contact Form 7, and Google XML Sitemaps are all pretty indicative names based around what the plugin does. The name can be made up of multiple words if needed; just keep it simple and make sure the intended functionality of the plugin is clear.

Naming your plugin is also important when it comes to naming functions within your plugin. Similar to writing custom functions in your WordPress theme, it's important to ensure that your functions are prefixed to prevent clashes with other plugins and themes. You'll look at another way of ensuring this later in the chapter.

Plugin Location and File Structure

Now that you've dealt with the naming part of your plugin, it's time to decide where to put it. If you are familiar with WordPress, you know where plugins are stored in the WordPress application directories. If you have installed plugins only from the admin interface, plugins get stored in the `wp-content/plugins` directory.

You can add a plugin in one of two ways: as a single PHP file with the same name as your plugin; or as a directory containing a set of files, which must contain at least one PHP file with the same name as your plugin. You can see both these methods in use in the plugins directory of a brand new WordPress install. As shown in Figure 13-1, the two default plugins, Akismet and Hello Dolly, are examples of each method.

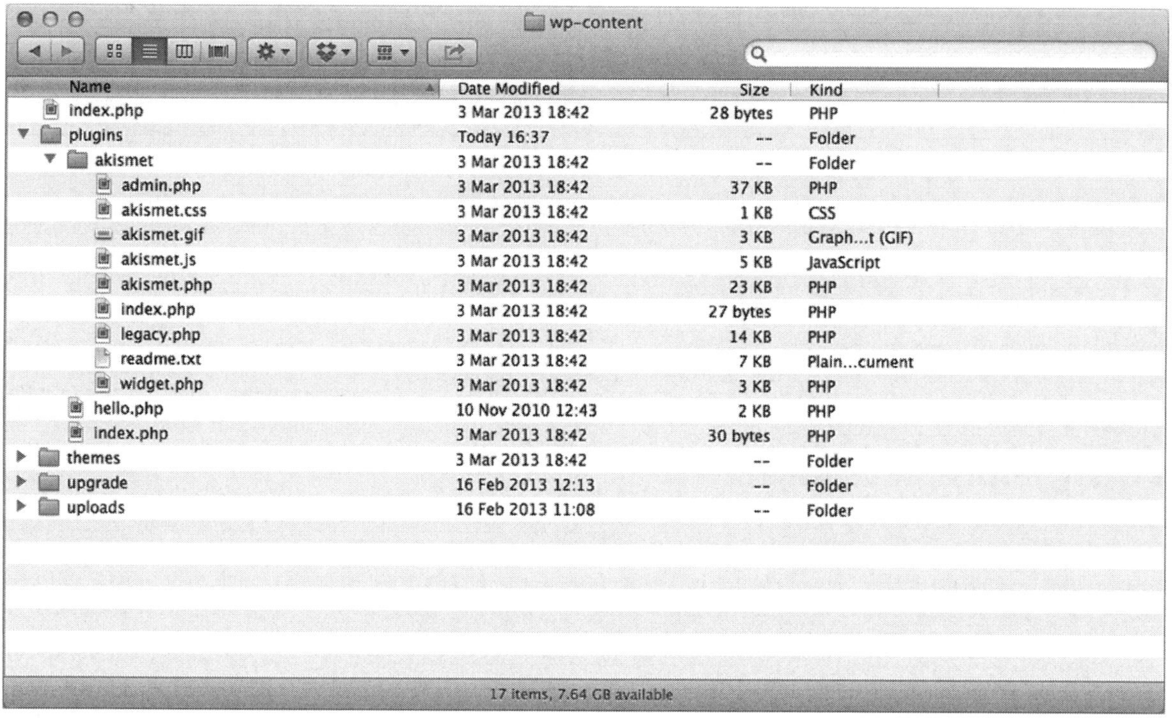

Figure 13-1. *Default plugins directory of a new WordPress install*

You structure your plugin depending on both the plugin you're creating and whether you intend to upload it to the WordPress plugin directory. If you have some small functionality you want to add as a custom plugin to one of your sites, you can use a single PHP file. However, if you want to add more complicated functionality or upload the plugin to the plugin repository, you have to use the directory method.

Take a look at the Akismet plugin in Figure 13-1. There's no deeper structure to the plugin files; they're all kept in the root directory. However, a lot of plugins use a structure similar to a theme directory when creating more complex functionality and storing CSS, images, and JavaScript in their own folders. For example, look at the Advanced Custom Fields plugin discussed in chapter 9 (see Figure 13-2); you'll see that the directory structure looks incredibly similar to that of any theme you might develop.

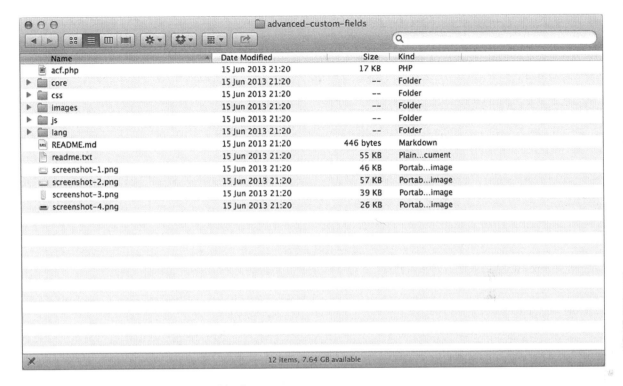

Figure 13-2. *The Advanced Custom Fields plugin structure*

For me, this structure feels the most sensible choice because it's consistent and easy to follow. I recommend sticking to this structure when you write your plugins.

Referencing the Plugin Directory

If you're building a complex plugin with a number of files, you have to reference the location of these files when loading scripts or styles, or when including other PHP files in your main plugin file (if you separate functionality into multiple files). Note that the `wp-content/plugins` directory can be relocated when setting up WordPress, so remember to reference the plugin directory correctly to prevent errors. The best way to do this is to use the `plugin_dir_path()` and `plugins_url()` functions, which return the absolute path of the plugin directory and plugins URL, respectively. Using these functions in your plugin when referencing its location prevents any errors if a plugin directory is moved from the standard `wp-content/plugins` location.

Plugin File Header

Now you can start actually building the plugin. First, set up the main PHP file, the one with the same name as your plugin name. Although it may not be the file where you put all the main functionality in the end, it is the file that WordPress will look for to load your plugin from. It is also the file from which WordPress takes all the information about the plugin from, all of which is contained in the plugin header.

The plugin file header works similarly to the way in which the style sheet header works in your WordPress themes. This is where WordPress gets all the information about your plugin; without it, the plugin can't be recognized and activated in the WordPress admin.

Following is an example of a full plugin header with all the information you can set for your plugin. The bare minimum is just the plugin name, but it's good to include as much information as possible so that WordPress can display the information to the user.

```php
<?php
/*
Plugin Name: Name Of The Plugin
Plugin URI: http://URI_Of_Page_Describing_Plugin_and_Updates
Description: A brief description of the Plugin.
Version: The Plugin's Version Number, e.g.: 1.0
Author: Name Of The Plugin Author
Author URI: http://URI_Of_The_Plugin_Author
License: A "Slug" license name e.g. GPL2
*/
?>
```

Most of the details are fairly self-explanatory and work in the same way as the theme style sheet header information. The two parts to pay special attention to are the version and license information.

The version of your plugin relates to how the plugin is updated and is especially important when using the plugin directory. It is necessary to stick to a consistent format for use throughout the development of your plugin so WordPress can tell when your plugin has been updated. For example, you can choose from *x.x*, *x.x.x*, or *xx.xx.xx*.

The plugin license is important if you'll be uploading the plugin to the plugin directory. The general rule for anything being hosted in the WordPress repositories is that it must be compatible with the GNU General Public License v2 or a later version. Using the tag GPL2 as the preceding license information is fine, but you should also indicate the license of the plugin using the following comment in your plugin header following the plugin information (replacing your plugin details where necessary):

```php
<?php
/*  Copyright YEAR  PLUGIN_AUTHOR_NAME  (email : PLUGIN AUTHOR EMAIL)

    This program is free software; you can redistribute it and/or modify
    it under the terms of the GNU General Public License, version 2, as
    published by the Free Software Foundation.

    This program is distributed in the hope that it will be useful,
    but WITHOUT ANY WARRANTY; without even the implied warranty of
    MERCHANTABILITY or FITNESS FOR A PARTICULAR PURPOSE.  See the
    GNU General Public License for more details.

    You should have received a copy of the GNU General Public License
    along with this program; if not, write to the Free Software
    Foundation, Inc., 51 Franklin St, Fifth Floor, Boston, MA  02110-1301  USA
*/
?>
```

With the plugin header set up and your file saved in the plugins folder in WordPress, look at the plugins page in the WordPress admin where the plugin will now be visible and can be activated (see Figure 13-3).

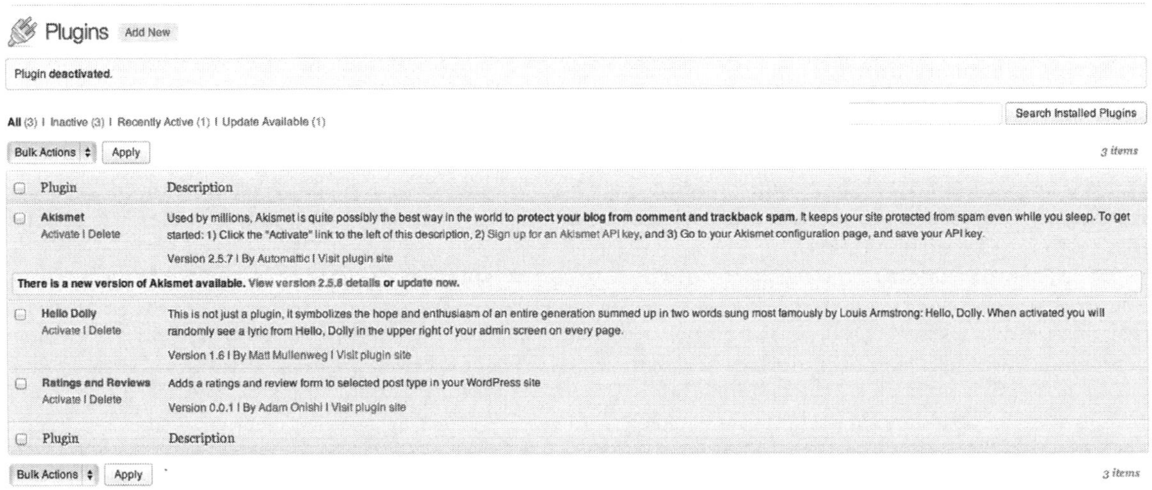

Figure 13-3. *The plugin is now available in the Plugins admin page*

Of course, the plugin doesn't do anything yet; you need to start writing some functionality.

How to Add Functionality

The plugin is set up and recognized by WordPress, so now you have to get your plugin to actually do something. At this stage, you'll look at plugins that work with a theme that returns content or provides extra functionality for use in a theme. There are plugins that have the sole purpose of working in the WordPress admin and provide extra functionality to the content editors. You'll take a brief look at those later in the chapter, but for now you'll concentrate on plugins that enable functionality or content for a theme.

For these plugins, you have four ways of adding functionality at your disposal. You can choose from the following:

- Hooks
- Shortcodes
- Widgets
- Custom template tags

The first three were discussed in Chapter 6, so I'll talk about them only briefly and then focus a bit more on how to create custom template tags.

Hooks

Hooks were covered earlier in the book; I talked about using them specifically to add custom functionality to your themes. Working with them in your plugin is done in much the same way. Any functionality you want to create can be hooked into an action at a particular time during the WordPress execution or onto a filter so you can modify content from inside the plugin.

When hooking into actions, plugins and their functionality are loaded and run very early in WordPress. If you take a look at the action reference (http://wp-themes-book.com/13001), you see that the action 'plugins_loaded' is fourth on the list. That means that it is almost always safe to run functionality from your plugin on most of the other actions in WordPress because your functionality is loaded early enough to catch these actions. Note that plugins are loaded even earlier than the themes are, with the `setup_theme` and `after_setup_theme` actions not being triggered until a little later. This just means that any functionality you write in your plugins will be accessible to the themes being used.

Remember that specific hooks are available to plugin developers that should be available in any theme being used. I mentioned this in chapter 9 when talking about setting up your theme to be compatible with plugins. The main two hooks, `wp_head` and `wp_footer`, enable you to inject code into the <head> and at the end of the web pages generated by the theme. For example, you can add custom meta information or extra functionality to the theme. Examples include SEO plugins, which add meta descriptions to the head or the WordPress admin bar, which is added to the page using the `wp_footer` hook.

The other two rarely used theme hooks are `wp_meta` and `comment_form`. The `wp_meta` hook should be found at the end of the `sidebar.php` content according to the Codex, usually within the `<li>Meta</li>` section. However, as I discussed in Chapter 6, this is sometimes seen as a relatively outdated convention in WordPress themes. So I recommend being cautious when using this hook—document it fully so theme developers and users are aware of the functionality you're providing. The `comment_form` action can usually be found at the end of the `comments.php` file and can be used to add custom content alongside the comments form. An example of using it is to display a preview of the comment being added.

Shortcodes

Shortcodes are a great way of enabling web site owners/authors to add custom content created by a plugin by just adding them to post content. You looked at how to do this from within your themes in Chapter 6, and it is no different creating them in plugins—once again by using the `add_shortcode()` function.

Just remember that when using a shortcode, the options you set can be anything you like, so it's a good idea to ensure that you document the functionality well so users know how to get the best out of the options you set up. I'll talk about this more later on in the chapter.

Widgets

Another subject covered in Chapter 6 was how to add custom functionality via WordPress widgets. Again the coding is exactly the same as what was already discussed: you can just take the code you would have created in your theme and add it to your plugin. This is another method that better suits site authors ahead of developers; you add functionality in a nontechnical method that users can add to their site with ease.

Custom Template Tags

The final way to give custom functionality to your plugin users is through custom template tags. This method is used particularly when your plugin will be aimed at theme developers, giving them a method of using your plugin's functionality from within their templates.

Put simply, a custom template tag is just a PHP function made available by the plugin that provides some content that can be used in theme templates. Most of the template tags you already use are functions created by WordPress to output data/content for you. You looked at a lot of them in Chapter 3 when getting content into templates was discussed. You took a look at what template tags were available; now you'll look in a bit more detail at the template tag.

Taking the `the_title()` function as an example, the template tag is a function regularly used to get the title of your post in your templates. For example, you'll often see this:

```
<h1><?php the_title(); ?></h1>
```

Let's take a look at what's going on in the WordPress core when you call that function. The function declaration for the the_title function can be found in the wp-includes/post-template.php file:

```php
function the_title($before = '', $after = '', $echo = true) {
        $title = get_the_title();

        if ( strlen($title) == 0 )
                return;

        $title = $before . $title . $after;

        if ( $echo )
                echo $title;
        else
                return $title;
}
```

It's not a very complicated function; it actually starts by calling the get_the_title function that returns just the title of the post. It does a quick check to see whether a title exists, builds up a title with a before/after value, and outputs or returns it based on the parameters set.

To make a template tag in your plugin, you could do something as simple as create a function and place it in the body of your plugin. When the plugin is loaded, the function will be available to the theme templates. To create a plugin to get the word count of the post content, your plugin would look similar to this:

```php
<?php
/*
Plugin Name: Content word counter
Description: Returns the word count of the content of a post
Version: 1.0
Author: Adam Onishi
Author URI: http://adamonishi.com
License: GPL2
*/
?>
<?php
/* Copyright 2013  Adam Onishi  (email :)
        [...]
*/
?>

<?php
function ptd_get_the_content_word_count($post_id = false) {

        if( ! $post_id ) {
                $post_id = get_the_ID();
        }

        $content = get_the_content($post_id);

        $word_count = str_word_count($content);

        return $word_count;
}

?>
```

The previous code shows you a fairly simple plugin, with a shortened header containing all the plugin details, the copyright (I removed the full license information that would normally be there), and your word count template tag. The function takes a parameter of the post ID, similar to the get_the_content function; checks to see whether one was passed; if not, it uses the get_the_ID() function to get the post ID. Use the get_the_content function to return the post content, and use the PHP function str_word_count to get the word count for the content, which is then returned at the end of the function.

For users to use this function in their theme templates, they can simply do this:

```
<?php echo ptd_get_the_content_word_count(); ?>
```

Or they could even set the return value to a PHP variable and perform any operations they want using the data returned.

Dealing with Parameters

In the example function, I added a parameter to the function so users can pass in a post ID if they want to use the template tag outside of the Loop. Many template tags in WordPress take parameters to enable users to customize the content output or returned. Just to make things more complicated, there are functions that take parameters in different ways: some are in the standard method of a comma-separated list of parameters, others take an array, and some can take a single string parameter containing multiple options.

I won't go into detail about how to set up a function with standard parameters because you should be used to this already, but I will discuss the way WordPress deals with the other two methods.

When you're dealing with taking an array of parameters, you need to be able to set some defaults for the circumstance in which a user chooses not to set anything. Of course, some options can be made mandatory, but it is likely that at least a few of the options will have some default setting that produces a standard output. Also, the functions that allow for a string of options to be passed to the function then need to be able to parse that string and return the options in a manageable format to use in the function. For both these situations, WordPress has a handy function for you to use: the wp_parse_args function.

The wp_parse_args function is an example of why a function can take a string of options or an array, depending on user preference. For example, the wp_list_categories function, which has a lot of potential options, can accept both an array and a string of options, but also has a lot of default settings that the user may not always want to change.

Let's take a quick look at the first few lines of the function to see what's going on:

```
function wp_list_categories( $args = '' ) {
        $defaults = array(
                'show_option_all'    => '', 'show_option_none' => __('No categories'),
                'orderby'            => 'name', 'order'         => 'ASC',
                'style'              => 'list',
                'show_count'         => 0, 'hide_empty'         => 1,
                'use_desc_for_title' => 1, 'child_of'           => 0,
                'feed'               => '', 'feed_type'          => '',
                'feed_image'         => '', 'exclude'            => '',
                'exclude_tree'       => '', 'current_category'   => 0,
                'hierarchical'       => true, 'title_li'          => __( 'Categories' ),
                'echo'               => 1, 'depth' => 0,
                'taxonomy'           => 'category'
        );

        $r = wp_parse_args( $args, $defaults );

        [...]
}
```

The part of the function I included is just the very start, which deals with the options the rest of the function requires. As you can see, the very first part is an array declaration of all the defaults used in the function. Then the `wp_parse_args()` function is used, taking the $args variable, which could be either a string of URL-style options or an array, as the first argument and the array of defaults as the second argument. The function then returns an array of the full set of options from the combined defaults and passed options, with the passed options overwriting the defaults, as you would expect.

It's not necessarily what you need for every function you write; for example, the earlier word count function doesn't need to be set up to take an array of arguments. There will be really only one (maybe two if you added an option to echo or return the value) parameter and it can be dealt with using the standard PHP method of passing arguments. However, when creating a template tag with a lot of options, it can be much easier to set up the function to take an array or string of options ahead of creating a very long function call.

Encapsulating a Plugin in a Class

So far, I've covered the basics of how to create a plugin. For the rest of the chapter, you'll look into some more advanced functionality—for example, how to deal with data storage in your plugin, create options pages in the WordPress admin, and recognize the best methods for dealing with the WordPress plugin repository.

However, first you'll learn how to write a more complex plugin using PHP classes to better organize your plugin code. This process is probably the most sensible way to construct your plugin, especially if you are creating a plugin with complex functionality. Encapsulating your plugin code within a class means that you get to stop worrying so much about function prefixing for a start; once your functions become methods of your class (which is prefixed), you can start to use more straightforward names for your functions and not worry about them colliding with functions from other plugins or from WordPress. Of course, you still need to make template tag functions that you create prefixed because they will be accessible to the rest of the WordPress execution code.

However, before I show you any code examples, I should point out that what I'll be covering isn't exactly full-on object-oriented coding. I don't cover inheritance and variable scope, for instance. The subject is far too large to include here, so I'll just discuss ways to use a class to set up your plugin with the aim of creating more readable and reusable code. The base you create here enables you to expand on your plugin using full object-oriented programming (OOP) techniques in the future.

To start encapsulating your plugin code, you need to create a class. Although you can do this in your main plugin file, to stick with WordPress conventions, classes should be contained within their own file (see Figure 13-4). This means that you need to create a second file in your plugin folder and then include and call your class from inside the main plugin file.

Figure 13-4. *The Snoopy class file and a view of the class files in the wp-includes directory*

Once you set up your main two files, you can set up the basic code for your plugin:

```php
<?php
/**
 * Ratings and reviews plugin class file.
 *
 * @package    RatingsAndReviews
 * @author     Adam Onishi < >
 * @license    GPL2
 * @copyright 2013 Adam Onishi
 */
class RatingsAndReviews {

        protected static $version = '0.0.1';

        protected static $plugin_slug = 'ratings-and-reviews';

        protected static $instance = null;

        private function __construct() {

                // Where we set up our plugin's functionality

        }
```

```
    public static function get_instance() {

            // If the single instance hasn't been set, set it now.
            if ( null == self::$instance ) {
                    self::$instance = new self;
            }

            return self::$instance;
    }
}
```

The absolute basic class file you need to set up is shown here. It contains a couple of properties and a couple of methods for your plugin (variables and functions for "non-OOP" folk). The first property simply keeps the plugin version number as a property you can use in enqueuing style sheets and script files, for example. The second is the plugin name or "slug" that is used as the text domain for the plugin when using it for processes such as internationalization, exactly as you would in your themes (as discussed earlier in the book). The final property will hold an instance of your class. This is an example of the Singleton pattern in OOP.

Along with the second method of the get_instance class, the $instance variable allows you to make sure that one and only one instance of your class is created. The get_instance() method handles how you access the instance of the class, either by returning the one already created and stored in the $instance property, or by creating a new instance and setting it to the $instance property before returning it. By ensuring that there is only one instance of the class created, you can prevent any hooks you add to your constructor function being called multiple times. And if you access the WordPress database from your plugin class, having only one instance means that the same database connection will be used each time, and multiple connections will not be made to the database from your plugin.

Going back to the first method in your class, the __construct() method is the constructor function that gets called every time a new instance of the class is created. This is where you would put all your WordPress hooks, allowing for your plugin methods to be hooked into the site. You'll take a look shortly at how to add hooks and template tags to your plugin using the class method, but for now let's quickly go back to the main plugin file and look at how you can access your plugin class.

After the plugin header and license information, you can add the following few lines of code:

```
<?php

// If this file is called directly, abort.
if ( ! defined( 'WPINC' ) ) {
        die;
}

require_once( plugin_dir_path( __FILE__ ) . 'class-ratings-and-reviews.php' );

RatingsAndReviews::get_instance();

?>
```

The first part of your plugin file is a bit of security; a little check to make sure that the plugin is indeed being called from within WordPress. If it is, the WPINC constant will be defined, and you can carry on; otherwise, you kill the execution. Next you need to get the plugin class file using the require_once function, coupled with the plugin_dir_path function to get the current path to your plugin directory; then add on the name of your class PHP file. Finally, the last line makes a static function call to the plugin class you created, which creates an instance of your plugin class and in turn fires the constructor function setting up your plugin.

Actions and Filters from Within a Class

As I mentioned briefly, when an instance of the class is created, the constructor function is called, and this is where you want to declare all the hooks that your plugin needs to use. In Chapter 6, in which hooks were covered, I talked about how to declare a function when it's a member of a class, so to enqueue your style sheets and scripts you can create the following constructor function:

```
private function __construct() {

        // Load stylesheets and scripts
        add_action( 'wp_enqueue_scripts', array( $this, 'enqueue_styles' ) );
        add_action( 'wp_enqueue_scripts', array( $this, 'enqueue_scripts' ) );

}
```

Here you're using the same add_action function you used before, but the second argument, which would normally be a single function name, becomes an array. In the previous examples, the first element of the array was a string to represent the class name; however, because you're inside your class, you pass the $this pseudo-variable, which returns a reference to the current class you are within.

The functions that you're calling can be seen here. They are standard enqueue style and script functions, but with a couple of tweaks you can include the plugin slug and version number programmatically so you're not tied down to manually changing files if you need to change your plugin name or (more likely) when the version number changes further along in development.

```
public function enqueue_styles() {
        wp_enqueue_style( $this->plugin_slug . '-styles', plugins_url( 'css/style.css', __FILE__ ),
array(), $this->version );
}

public function enqueue_scripts() {
        wp_enqueue_script( $this->plugin_slug . '-scripts', plugins_url( 'js/scripts.js', __FILE__ ),
array('jquery'), $this->version, true );
}
```

▨ **Note**   Notice that these methods do not use the static keyword when being declared because they shouldn't be able to be called without an instance of the class being created. In the previous example of a class method, the get_instance function required the static keyword so that it could be called before an instance of the class is created using the scope resolution operator ('::') because that function is being used to set up an instance of the class in the first place.

With your initial actions set up and ready to go, your class-based plugin is now actually adding some functionality to your site. Next you'll look at how to create a template tag using the functions from within your class.

Template Tags from Within a Class

You've already seen that creating template tags for your plugin is a good way to get plugin functionality into the hands of theme developers. When working with a class, you need to consider how these functions will be made available to developers without them having to worry about knowing OOP techniques because you want to make it as simple as possible to work with your plugins.

The way you'll do this for your class is with wrapper functions to your class stored in your main plugin file. You can write all your logic into the class and abstract that as much as you need, but by creating a wrapper function you can create simple template tags, making your plugin functionality accessible to developers. Take a look at the following code: the first is an example of a method declaration in your class; the second is an example of the wrapper function you can put in your main plugin file:

```
// The method of our class
public function get_rating() {

        // do stuff

        return $rating;
}

// The function for our template tag in our main plugin file
function rar_the_rating($echo = true) {

        $ratings = RatingsAndReviews::get_instance();

        if( $echo ) {
                echo $ratings->get_rating();
        } else {
                return $ratings->get_rating();
        }

}
```

In the example above there is a method as part of your class that does all the logic and returns a value. The wrapper function in your main plugin file is where I'll point out a few things. First, the function has a prefix. You're back to prefixing your functions again out in the main plugin file because it's no longer contained within the class, so it might collide with other functions.

Next there's a parameter in your template tag function, but not in your class method. The parameter is an 'echo' parameter that defaults to true. It is a parameter you see a lot in WordPress—for instance, the the_title function you looked at earlier does the same thing. With a parameter like this there's no need to pass it on to the class method; you can simply check the variable inside your template tag and either echo or return the result of your class method based on the result.

This is a good example of how you need to be aware of the functions your main class method is doing and the function of your template tag. The main logic for the function should be processed in the class method; however, a simple check for whether to echo or return the data can be done within your template tag function. It comes down to a separation of concerns. Suppose that you had a set of arguments being passed in. These arguments, along with the parsing of the arguments with defaults, would be passed along to the class method because that should be processed from within the class. Any defaults should be decided in there in case you decide to add defaults as properties of the class.

Finally I'll mention how to actually access the class and method. First, you create a variable to reference the instance of the class:

```
$ratings = RatingsAndReviews::get_instance();
```

You can still use the static method get_instance because it now returns the same instance of the class that was created when the plugin function was first run. If, for instance, you used the 'new' operator without the call to the get_instance function, you would be working with a second instance of your plugin class, and it would negate the work you've done previously to set up the singleton pattern within your class. The method is then called using the instance variable you set up, as you normally would with any other class method.

Now that you've seen how to set up a class to contain your plugin functionality, let's look at doing something a bit more complex with your function and work with some data.

Dealing with Data

Most of the time when creating a WordPress plugin, the aim will be to work with or create content stored in the WordPress database. Sometimes this will be working with data that's already stored; other times, it will consist of adding more data to be stored alongside the content natively created by WordPress.

There are three main options you have to set up a plugin to store data on a site:

- Custom post types and taxonomies
- Custom meta data (meta boxes)
- Custom tables in the database

The first two options you should be fairly familiar with. You can set up custom post types from within your plugin using the regular hooks as you would do in a theme functions file, and the same goes for custom taxonomies and custom fields. So let's look at the third option: how to add new tables to the database in WordPress to store custom data.

There is a lot to consider before going ahead and creating custom tables in the WordPress database. Using this method means you lose a lot of the functionality of WordPress entirely; the CMS and a lot of its plugins aren't expecting your tables to be there, so you'll lose all their functionality. The adding, removing, querying, and updating database functions will need to be performed by the plugin, taking into account the need for all this to be done securely and efficiently as well.

However, there are some cases that better suit a custom table in the database: when the data structure you want to create doesn't fit into the schema of the WordPress tables or when there's a need for more complex queries that the WordPress database does not lend itself to. Or possibly in when adding more content to the posts table by creating new post types would bloat it so much that it would essentially cause major performance issues for the entire site.

I recommend that before you start adding things to the database, consider the pros and cons of the choice you're making. Ensure that you are aware of how the decision will affect the end users of your site and if the effect will be worth it in the long run.

Creating a Table

There's an awful lot to consider when creating a database table: table schema, naming conventions, data types, and many more. Unfortunately, I don't have the space here to go into so much detail about the best options for planning your database. I'll show you some examples for setting up a database in WordPress and the things you need to consider when working with the WordPress database and built-in functions.

When working with the database in WordPress, you should be aware of the wpdb class and the dbDelta function. The wpdb class is used by WordPress for all database interactions throughout the system and is instantiated early on in the WordPress execution process as the $wpdb global variable. The dbDelta function is used when you want to create or update a table in WordPress. Although it isn't an official WordPress function, it is the most-used method for creating or updating WordPress database tables.

■ **Note**   For more information on how to plan and build your database, see these references: MySQL Data types: http://wp-themes-book.com/13002 and Best practices for database schema design: http://wp-themes-book.com/13013§

The dbDelta function is used a lot because it has some fantastic features that WordPress plugin developers find really useful. It has the capability to examine the current table structure, compare it with the one you intend to create, and then either add or modify the structure as necessary. This functionality is a lot more useful when updating your plugin, but it is still useful nonetheless. There are, however, some small caveats to using the dbDelta function, especially that it is very fussy about how you format SQL.

For the dbDelta function to work properly, these are the constraints you need to work with:

- Each field must be on its own line in your SQL statement.

- There must be two spaces between the words PRIMARY KEY and the definition of your primary key.

- The key word KEY must be used rather than its synonym INDEX, and there must be at least one KEY.

- There can't be any apostrophes or back ticks around field names.

With these requirements taken care of, you can start to look at building the query to construct your table. First, you need to know what table you're building (in this example, I continue with the ratings and reviews plugin example). This is something that can be stored as a custom post type with custom fields, but for purpose of this example, you'll create it into a custom table.

First you need to name your table. Tables in WordPress are named using a prefix; usually this prefix is 'wp_', but you can't rely on that being the case all the time because it is easily changed (this was covered in the security part of Chapter 10). Fortunately you have easy access to get the current prefix thanks to the $wpdb global because it is stored as a property of the class.

Next you need to define a data structure for the table. Your ratings and reviews plugin should store the user ID of the reviewer (because all reviewers will already be a member of the site), a subject/title for the review, the review content, the rating, the date it was posted, and the movie the review is for.

With this information, you can now set up your function to create the table in the database:

```php
function rar_create_table() {
        global $wpdb;

        $table_name = $wpdb->prefix . "ratings_and_reviews";

        $sql = "CREATE TABLE $table_name (
                id mediumint(9) NOT NULL AUTO_INCREMENT,
                user_id bigint(20) unsigned NOT NULL default '0',
                post_id bigint(20) unsigned NOT NULL default '0',
                posted datetime DEFAULT '0000-00-00 00:00:00' NOT NULL,
                review_title VARCHAR(255) DEFAULT '' NOT NULL,
                review_content text NOT NULL,
                rating tinyint(10) unsigned NOT NULL default '1',
                PRIMARY KEY  (id)
                );";

        require_once( ABSPATH . 'wp-admin/includes/upgrade.php' );
        dbDelta( $sql );
}
```

Take a look at this function and pay attention to a few key points. First, you get the $wpdb global and create your table name with the prefix property. You're sticking with the established convention of using an all lowercase (and spaced with underscores) table name as with the WordPress tables.

The next part is setting up your SQL statement, paying close attention to stick to the format I spoke about regarding how the dbDelta function needs to have the SQL set up.

Because the dbDelta function is not a standard part of WordPress, toward the end you need to include a file from the WordPress core in which the function resides: the upgrade.php file (in wp-admin/includes).

Finally, you can call the function with your SQL variable, which when run, results in your table being created in the database (see Figure 13-5).

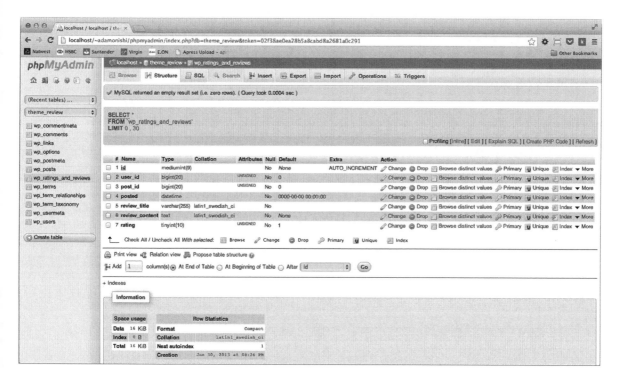

Figure 13-5. *The database table for the ratings and reviews plugin*

Adding, Moving, and Updating Data

With your database table created, you can now learn how to interact with it in the form of adding, removing, and updating data. With the ratings and reviews plugin, you'll be adding new reviews a lot. You also want to give authors the opportunity to edit or remove their reviews whenever they want to.

All the functions discussed here use the wpdb class, which comes with a lot of the functions necessary to do all the previous operations on the database, as well as some extra ones to help with preparing and formatting your data. For the following operations, you'll work with the global $wpdb, the main instance of the wpdb class.

Remember that when working with the database, you need to take security measures to prevent potential SQL injection attacks. An entire article in the WordPress Codex is dedicated to data validation, and it should be read by any plugin or theme developer, especially the section on database validation: http://wp-themes-book.com/13003. You'll take a brief look at how to prepare your database queries in this section as well, but for a better overview make sure you read the section mentioned here.

Adding to the Database

Adding to the WordPress database is relatively simple thanks to the wpdb class and the insert function. To insert a new row to your database, simply call $wpdb->insert with the name of the table you're adding to and the data being added. The wpdb::insert function takes care of everything related to preparing the query and sanitizing your data.

Here's a function that sets up your data and passes it to the wpdb::insert function:

```
function rar_add_review( $data ) {
        global $wpdb;

        $table_name = $wpdb->prefix . "ratings_and_reviews";

        $column_formats = array(
                        'post_id'        => '%d',
                        'user_id'        => '%d',
                        'posted'         => '%s',
                        'review_title'   => '%s',
                        'review_content' => '%s',
                        'rating'         => '%d',
                );

        $defaults = array(
                        'user_id' => get_current_user_id(),
                        'posted'  => current_time('mysql')
                );

        $data = wp_parse_args( $data, $defaults );

        // Remove any unneeded data from the first array where
        // a column does not exist (based on the column_formats array)
        $data = array_intersect_key($data, $column_formats);

        // Reorder $column_formats array to match the order of columns in the data array
        $data_keys = array_keys($data);
        $column_formats = array_merge(array_flip($data_keys), $column_formats);

        $wpdb->insert($table_name, $data, $column_formats);

        return $wpdb->insert_id;
}
```

Even with a function that does a lot of the work for you, you still have to prepare the data for the function. I'll take you step by step through each part of the code so you'll understand what's going on in the function. Be aware, however, that this function assumes it's being passed a final set of data that has been checked and validated before being added to the database.

The first four bits of the function are declarations for the information and objects you'll need further on down. I set up the global variable for the $wpdb object, the table name using the database prefix as you've seen before, an array for the format of each column, and some defaults to be added to your data. Once you have your variables set up, you can start to work with them to prepare your data for the insert function.

With your data being passed in to the function, and your defaults defined you can use the wp_parse_args function to create a complete data set in the $data array. You add the current user and date here because you can find them programmatically, and they don't need to be set in the form creating the data. After you create your full data set, you use the `array_intersect_keys` PHP function, which returns only the entries from the first array (`$data`) that are present in the rest of the arguments (in this case, the `$column_formats` array). Doing this allows you to remove any extra data from the array that can't be added to the database because the `$column_formats` array holds the full list of your columns.

With your data set up and ready to go, you need to ensure that the two arrays you'll pass to the `insert` function are in the same order. Get the keys from the `$data` array and store them in a separate array; the following line then takes a flipped version of that array and merges it with the `$column_formats` array. The reason for the flip is that the keys of the `$data` array are returned as values to the `$data_key` array, but you need them to be the keys so that the merge will work. By doing this, you now have both arrays in the correct order.

Finally, you can call the `insert` function with your `$table_name`, `$data`, and `$column_formats` variables and then return the ID of the inserted row that gets stored in the `insert_id` property of the `$wpdb` instance.

Removing Data from the Database

Now you've inserted some data, let's look at how to remove it. The `delete` function of the `wpdb` class, which was added in version 3.4, ensures that deleting from the database is just as easy as inserting. When deleting from the database, you need to create a specific `WHERE` clause, ensuring that it will delete only the record you are looking for. Of course, there might be times when you want to delete multiple rows using a single delete command, so be sure that the `WHERE` clause isn't too general.

For the following example, I assume that you're only deleting only a single record from the database and will have the ID of the record passed into the function:

```
function rar_delete_review( $review_id ) {
        global $wpdb;

        $table_name = $wpdb->prefix . "ratings_and_reviews";

        // Final check to ensure the ID is a positive integer
        $review_id = absint($review_id);
        if( empty($review_id) ) {
                return false;
        }

        // Set up arrays for the delete function
        $where = array( 'post_id' => $review_id );
        $where_format = array( '%d' );

        return $wpdb->delete( $table_name, $where, $where_format );
}
```

A much simpler function this time around because you create the arrays for the function and with only one value being passed in the `$where` array, there's no need to match them up.

As with the `insert` function, you globalize the `$wpdb` instance and set up the table name variable, followed by one final check on the ID that was passed into the function. You're just making sure that the ID you have is a positive integer using the WP function `absint`, which is a wrapper for two PHP functions: `abs` and `intval`. If you don't have a positive integer, the function quits and returns `false`.

The last part of the function is where you set up the array of the `WHERE` clause, once again using the column name and value as the key-value pair, and a format array containing the format of your `post_id` value. Along with the `$table_name` variable, they get passed into the `delete` function, which becomes your `return` value because the return value is the number of rows affected by the deletion.

Updating a Record

Finally, the update operation contains a combination of actions from the previous two functions. You'll be sending data to the database and specifying which record should be updated by using a WHERE clause. Take a look at the following function and see if you can recognize elements taken from each function before you see what the function is doing afterward:

```
function rar_update_review( $review_id, $data ) {
        global $wpdb;

        $table_name = $wpdb->prefix . "ratings_and_reviews";

        $column_formats = array(
                'post_id'        => '%d',
                'user_id'        => '%d',
                'posted'         => '%s',
                'review_title'   => '%s',
                'review_content' => '%s',
                'rating'         => '%d',
        );

        // Final check to ensure the ID is a positive integer
        $review_id = absint($review_id);
        if( empty($review_id) ) {
                return false;
        }

        // Remove any unneeded data from the first array where
        // a column does not exist (based on the column_formats array)
        $data = array_intersect_key($data, $column_formats);

        // Reorder $column_formats array to match the order of columns in the data array
        $data_keys = array_keys($data);
        $column_formats = array_merge(array_flip($data_keys), $column_formats);

        // Set up arrays for the delete function
        $where = array( 'post_id' => $review_id );
        $where_format = array( '%d' );

        return $wpdb->update( $table_name, $data, $where, $column_formats, $where_format );
}
```

As you can see, the function is almost a complete amalgam of the two previous functions. Set up the $wpdb instance, the table name, and the column formats data first; then check to ensure that you have a valid ID for your WHERE clause. With your ID checked, set up the data and column formats array as before. Notice that because you take the array keys from the $data array and then merge them with the $column_formats array, you'll get only the formats for the relevant columns that have been passed to you in the data.

Set up the $where array and $where_format array before passing all the data through the update function, which will return false if nothing was updated or the number of rows if the update was successful.

Now that you have functions for adding, removing, and updating data stored in your custom table, you can look at how to query the data to display the stored data on your site.

Querying the Data

The next and probably most important part of using a custom database table for your plugin is to query the data so you can display it on the site. Querying data is a little more complicated because you have to build the entire query, but thanks to WordPress helper functions, you have help along the way.

I could get quite detailed in this example and build a full API-like system that allows you to query the database in a variety of ways and return an unlimited variety of results. However, because of the expected functionality of your ratings and reviews plugin, I'll show you only a limited form of querying. But with the methods shown here it won't take much for you to expand on them to create a fully blown API to give you unlimited access to the data.

First you'll determine how to allow your data to be queried. Under the circumstances in which the plugin is likely to be used, you can limit your queries to be able to do the following:

- Return all entries attached to a specific post

- Return all entries attached to a specific user

- Return a single entry

- Limit the number of entries returned

- Order the entries by date (latest or oldest first)

- Return results based on an offset (for pagination)

Even though I mentioned that this would be a limited function to return results only as you can see them being used in the plugin, it's still quite a hefty list.

Take a look at the code to do this; again, I'll take you through the code so you can understand what's going on. You should recognize a lot of the code from previous sections, which gives you a good start.

```php
function rar_get_reviews( $query = array() ) {
        global $wpdb;

        // Set table name
        $table_name = $wpdb->prefix . "ratings_and_reviews";

        // Setup array of default arguments
        $defaults = array (
                        'id'       => false,
                        'post_id' => false,
                        'user_id' => false,
                        'order'    => 'ASC',
                        'number'  => 10,
                        'offset'  => 0
            );

        // wp_parse_args to set full arguments
        $args = wp_parse_args( $query, $defaults );

        // Create variables of the array keys
        extract($args);

        // Start SQL
        $sql_start = "SELECT * FROM {$table_name}";
```

```php
// Check if the ID is set first, if so we're just doing a query for a single result
if( $id ) {

        // Prepare the WHERE clause
        $sql_where = $wpdb->prepare('WHERE id = %d', $id);

        // Join all SQL parts
        $sql = "$sql_start $sql_where";

        // Return the single result
        return $wpdb->get_row($sql, ARRAY_A);

} else {

        // Initialise the WHERE clause with an automatic true condition
        $sql_where = "WHERE 1=1";

        // Create a post__in query
        if( $post_id ) {

                // Force $post_id to be an array
                if( ! is_array( $post_id ) ) {
                        $post_id = array( $post_id );
                }

                $post_id = array_map('absint',$post_id); // Cast as positive integers
                $post_id__in = implode(',',$post_id);
                $sql_where .=  " AND post_id IN($post_id__in)";

        }

        // Create a user__in query
        if( $user_id ) {

                // Force $user_id to be an array
                if( ! is_array( $user_id ) ) {
                        $user_id = array( $user_id );
                }

                $user_id = array_map('absint',$user_id); // Cast as positive integers
                $user_id__in = implode(',',$user_id);
                $sql_where .=  " AND user_id IN($user_id__in)";

        }

        // Create order part of query
        $order = strtoupper($order);
        $order = ( 'ASC' == $order ? 'ASC' : 'DESC' );

        $sql_order = "ORDER BY posted $order";
```

```
                   // Create limit part of query
                   $offset = absint($offset);              // Ensure positive integer
                   if( $number == -1 ){
                           $sql_limit = "";
                   } else {
                           $number = absint($number); // Ensure positive integer
                           $sql_limit = "LIMIT $offset, $number";
                   }

                   // Build full SQL statement
                   $sql = "$sql_start $sql_where $sql_order $sql_limit";

                   // return results using the $wpdb->get_results function
                   return $wpdb->get_results($sql, ARRAY_A);
           }
}
```

A page and a half of function there, let's go through it one bit at a time. You should recognize the first 17 lines: getting the $wpdb global, setting the table name, creating some defaults for query arguments, and parsing them to get the final arguments in the $args array.

You should also recognize the next line as well; the extract function takes your array and outputs a series of key variables. So instead of accessing $args['id'], you can use the $id variable. The next line is the start of the SQL query; you say that you want to return all columns ("SELECT *") from your table:

```
$sql_start = "SELECT * FROM {$table_name}";
```

After you have the start of your query, you need to decide what the rest of your query will look like. Check to see if you're looking for a specific record via its ID. If so, you need to create your query a little differently, as you know you're only looking for one result because you're querying for a specific ID, so you can separate it from the rest of the query building:

```
// Prepare the WHERE clause
$sql_where = $wpdb->prepare('WHERE id = %d', $id);

// Join all SQL parts
$sql = "$sql_start $sql_where";

// Return the single result
return $wpdb->get_row($sql, ARRAY_A);
```

In these three lines, you build and run your query and return the results from the function. The first line introduces a new function: the $wpdb->prepare function. It works in a similar way to a sprintf function because you pass in a string with placeholders followed by the variables that will be substituted into the placeholders. The available placeholders are these:

- %d: decimal
- %s: string
- %f: float

The function requires a minimum of two arguments that were introduced in version 3.5 with the intention of stopping developers from passing the variable directly into the string. It defeats the point of the function, so you must remember to pass in your arguments separately using the placeholders.

When the WHERE clause is built, you string together the full SQL query and pass it to the $wpdb->get-row function. This automatically limits your query to one result and can take an offset as the third argument, but that isn't required in this case. The second argument is the return type in which the data is given, which can be OBJECT, ARRAY_A (associative array), or ARRAY_N (indexed array).

Now you can build your query for a number of results. The first line looks a little odd:

```
$sql_where = "WHERE 1=1";
```

Granted, it's not exactly a regular beginning of a WHERE clause, but it does give you one advantage. Because you'll go through a series of different possible arguments to add to the query, you don't know whether you'll have to chain the clauses at any one time. By initializing the WHERE query with an automatic true condition (1=1) for the rest of the clauses you build, you can always prefix your clauses with "AND" to make sure you're chaining them correctly.

The next snippet covers both the $post_id and $user_id arguments. The way you'll build them enables you to do a query similar to the $post__in query WordPress allows natively. It will still return results if only one post or user ID is asked for, but it gives you that flexibility.

```
if( $post_id ) {

        // Force $post_id to be an array
        if( ! is_array( $post_id ) ) {
                $post_id = array( $post_id );
        }

        $post_id = array_map('absint',$post_id); // Cast as positive integers
        $post_id__in = implode(',',$post_id);
        $sql_where .=  " AND post_id IN($post_id__in)";
}
```

First check whether you've had that argument passed. Force the variable to be an array if it's not already one by creating a new array and adding the current value. The next line ensures that the values passed are all positive integers that you already saw; then you build your $post__in style query by using the implode function, which chains the IDs in the array into a comma-separated string. Finally, add this to your WHERE clause with the AND added to the beginning of the string.

Once you've done the same with your $user_id argument, you can start to build the final parts of your query. The next part is the ORDER clause; you can allow your reviews to only be ordered by date, so it's a fairly simple string to build. Just make sure that the $order variable being passed in is one of the two possible options, ASC or DESC, and that it's uppercase.

```
$order = strtoupper($order);
$order = ( 'ASC' == $order ? 'ASC' : 'DESC' );
$sql_order = "ORDER BY posted $order";
```

Before you build your full query using the method from before, you need to build the limit part of the query by using the same method as WordPress (if "-1" is passed in, there is no limit). If you do need to limit the query in the else part of the condition, make sure that the $offset and $number arguments are both positive integers and then create the limit part.

```
$number = absint($number); // Ensure positive integer
$offset = absint($offset); // Ensure positive integer
$sql_limit = "LIMIT $offset, $number";
```

With all the parts created, you can join them all together in a string and pass it to the `$wpdb->get_results` function that is similar to the `get_row` function and has a second argument for the type in which the results should be returned:

```
// Build full SQL statement
$sql = "$sql_start $sql_where $sql_order $sql_limit";

// return results using the $wpdb->get_results function
return $wpdb->get_results($sql, ARRAY_A);
```

That was a heck of a function, but the parts are pretty easy to comprehend when broken down, so you should be able to use that as a basis for building more-complicated querying APIs in the future.

Next you'll look at how to take all the functions you just created and integrate them with the plugin code you built so far and then how to initialize and deactivate your function.

Initializing and Cleaning Up

In the last section, you looked at working with the database from within your plugin, but only the standalone functions to make these things happen. In reality, when creating a plugin, you want to do these things at certain moments in the plugin's life: when it's activated, deactivated, and removed. For these circumstances, WordPress again has three functions to help you out:

- register_activation_hook

- register_deactivation_hook

- register_uninstall_hook

These three functions are used like regular hooks because they set up a function to be called upon a particular action. In this case, WordPress creates actions for `activate_PLUGINNAME`, `deactivate_PLUGINNAME`, and `uninstall_PLUGINNAME` (where `PLUGINNAME` will be replaced with the name of the plugin, including its subdirectory; in the case of the ratings and reviews plugin, it is `activate_ratings-and-reviews/ratings-and-reviews.php`). These functions are used as a nice convenience wrapper for you to make use of.

Let's put these functions into action. Sticking with the ratings and reviews plugin from the previous examples, do a little initialization of the plugin when it's first activated: namely, setting up the custom database table. This means adding the `create_table` function to the plugin class and calling it from the main plugin file using the `register_activation_hook` function.

```
register_activation_hook( __FILE__, array( 'RatingsAndReviews','create_table' ) );
```

This function call must happen outside of any other hooks, which is why it's usually placed inside the main plugin file, not within any other functions or classes (although it can be added to the `__construct` function of the plugin's class).

Now that the plugin is activated and the database table is set up, the plugin is ready to be used. However, from time to time users will either deactivate or completely remove your plugin, which is where two other hook functions come in.

First I'll discuss what actions you do need to take when your plugin is deactivated and removed, and what it might mean for users. For example, suppose that a user deactivates your plugin. If you remove the database table and all the data within it, it could cause an issue if a week later the user decides it was actually the best solution and wants to reactivate it. Unfortunately, they will discover that all their data is gone.

I think there are certainly a lot of reasons for cleaning up the databases and removing any data your plugin may have added to WordPress, but always be aware of what your plugin is doing and what the potential impact might be on your users. If, for instance, the plugin adds information to the standard WordPress database only in the form of a few settings for the plugin, it is perfectly okay to remove them on deactivation because they can be easily put back if/when the plugin is reactivated. However, if you're adding custom database tables and custom data (as in in the ratings and reviews example), perhaps you should remove this data only if the plugin is deleted. You should ensure that your user is aware that it will happen with an alert message or warning in your plugin settings.

With that caveat in mind, let's take a look at a function that removes the database table and data from the WordPress database when your plugin is deleted/uninstalled. There are actually two ways to run an uninstall function from your plugin: via the register_uninstall_hook (already mentioned) and through an uninstall.php file in the plugin directory. Because you are already familiar with the first method, let's take a brief look at the second option. The code for both instances is technically the same (except the code has to be inside a function when the hook is used).

```php
<?php
/**
 * Called when the plugin is uninstalled.
 */

// If uninstall, not called from WordPress, then exit
if ( ! defined( 'WP_UNINSTALL_PLUGIN' ) ) {
        exit;
}

global $wpdb;

// Set table name
$table_name = $wpdb->prefix . "ratings_and_reviews";

// Remove the table (if it exists)
$wpdb->query("DROP TABLE IF EXISTS $table_name");

// Remove any other options the plugin installed
```

That's the entire uninstall.php file in one go. The main function sets up the table name as before and then runs a DROP TABLE query on the database using the $wpdb global object. The first step your function needs to take, though, is to check that it is being called via WordPress by testing for the WP_UNINSTALL_PLUGIN constant. It is set only when a plugin is being uninstalled, which prevents any malicious attempts by someone to run your uninstall script from outside of WordPress.

There's also some space at the end of the file to tidy up any settings or data you may have stored in the WordPress options table. Adding options to your plugin is a great way to allow users to customize the way your plugin works with very little effort. To do so, you can create your own custom settings pages (you'll do that next).

Admin Settings Pages

To allow users to get the most from your plugin, WordPress enables you to add pages to the admin interface to create settings pages for your plugin. Settings can be great for allowing users to customize how the plugin works or what it outputs to the front end, for example. However, remember not to add too many options for the sake of it because sometimes giving users more choices leads to a worse experience. They might be forced to make decisions that could easily be taken care of by the developer in the first place.

With that in mind, you'll look at the ratings and reviews plugin you've been creating and add a couple of options for users to customize the default output. A small number of options help the user control the functionality from one central location and just replace your currently hard-coded defaults. Users can still customize from the function call.

Adding Menu Pages

The first part of creating a settings page for your plugin is to set up the page. There are a few ways to do this, which depend on the complexity of the settings pages you want to create. For these examples, you'll look at them as plain functions, which will work well in your plugin file. Moving them to work in the plugin class should be relatively straightforward now that you know the basics.

The first method of setting up an admin page is to set one up as a subpage of the main settings tab in the WordPress admin. This is probably the best method if you have a small number of settings that require only one page. This way, you again stick to the WordPress UI style, enabling your settings to be easily found and adding no surprises for a user who is familiar with the interface.

Following is an example of the code to do this. You're running this code only if you're on an admin page and using the is_admin function to check. As you normally do, set up a hook to call your function that sets up the admin page. To do this, use the add_options_page function, which works similarly to add_submenu_page (which you'll look at shortly), but doesn't require you to tell it what the parent page will be. WordPress has a series of these functions that allow you to add submenu pages to all the WordPress default admin menus, including add_posts_page, add_pages_page, add_comments_page, and so on—one for every default menu page. All these functions take five parameters, which are required parameters because each has a specific role to set up the page. (Technically, the last parameter isn't required, but without it there would be no content on the page.)

The parameters are these:

- page_title: Title for your menu page, which is displayed in the title tags when the page is selected

- menu_title: Title to appear in the menu

- capability: Capability the user role must have to be able to access the page (more on that in Chapter 9)

- menu_slug: Slug name to refer to the menu by; in most cases, it must be unique (you'll see when it doesn't have to be unique later in the section)

- function:–Function to be called that outputs the content of the page

Look at the code in action to see how you set up your menu page:

```php
if( is_admin() ) {
    add_action( 'admin_menu', 'rar_add_plugin_options_page' );
}

function rar_add_plugin_options_page(){
        add_options_page('Ratings & Reviews settings', 'Ratings & Reviews', 'manage_options',
'rar-settings-admin', 'rar_create_admin_page' );
}

function rar_create_admin_page(){
?>
<div class="wrap">
    <?php screen_icon(); ?>
    <h2>Ratings &amp; Reviews Settings</h2>

</div>
<?php
}
```

The action hook you need to use to register your settings page is admin_menu because it is the point when the basic structure of the admin menus is set up and you can start adding any extra pages. The function used to set up the page comes with the very basic but still important page structuring.

For your admin page to look like the rest of WordPress, you should use the div with a class of 'wrap'. Add the screen_icon function to add an icon like those at the top of each WordPress admin page, followed by the title of the page as an <h2>. You'll learn how add the rest of your settings content to the page in a minute; first look at the other way to add a menu page to your WordPress admin.

If you have a rather complex plugin (such as the Yoast SEO plugin), you'll sometimes have lots of settings for the user to configure. The best way to do this is with a separate main menu item and subpages to allow for all the options to be separated out in a clear and easy-to-use way. Figure 13-6 shows the structure of the admin pages for the Yoast SEO plugin.

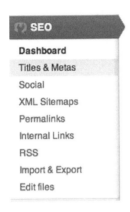

Figure 13-6. *Admin pages for the Yoast SEO plugin*

There are two functions to create a menu like this: add_menu_page is used to add a top-level menu page; add_submenu_page adds the submenu pages. Both functions work similarly to the add_options_page example you looked at before; they all have the main five core parameters that set up the name, permissions, content, and slug of the menu page.

The add_menu_page function has two extra optional parameters:

- icon_url: Takes the URL of an icon to use in the main menu (like the menu_icon parameter when setting up custom post types).

- position: The position in the menu in which the page should appear. By default, it appears at the bottom of the menu, which is probably the best case, but you can specify it to be higher up. This position parameter is different from the custom post type parameter, however, because any menu pages with the same setting could overwrite the other; one suggested way to avoid this is by using decimals (if doing so, it needs to be passed in quotes: '50.5' for example).

The add_submenu_page adds just one extra parameter to the add_options_page function, which goes at the start of the list:

- parent_slug: The slug (or file name for standard WordPress admin pages) of the menu page under which it should appear.

Following is an example of the functions used to create a menu similar to the one created by the Yoast SEO plugin in Figure 13-6.

```php
if( is_admin() ) {
    add_action( 'admin_menu', 'rar_add_plugin_menu' );
}

function rar_add_plugin_menu() {
        // Add the top level menu page
        add_menu_page( 'Ratings & Reviews settings', 'Ratings & Reviews', 'manage_options',
'rar-admin-menu' );
        // Add the first sub-page - overwrite default
        add_submenu_page( 'rar-admin-menu', 'Ratings & Reviews - Dashboard', 'Dashboard',
'manage_options', 'rar-admin-menu', 'rar_create_admin_dashboard' );
        // Add more sub-pages
        add_submenu_page( 'rar-admin-menu', 'Ratings & Reviews - View posts', 'View posts',
'manage_options', 'rar-admin-view-posts', 'rar_create_admin_view_posts' );
}

function rar_create_admin_dashboard() {
?>
<div class="wrap">
    <?php screen_icon(); ?>
    <h2>Dashboard</h2>

</div>
<?php
}

function rar_create_admin_view_posts() {
?>
<div class="wrap">
    <?php screen_icon(); ?>
    <h2>View Posts</h2>

</div>
<?php
}
```

This set of functions creates the menu shown in Figure 13-7.

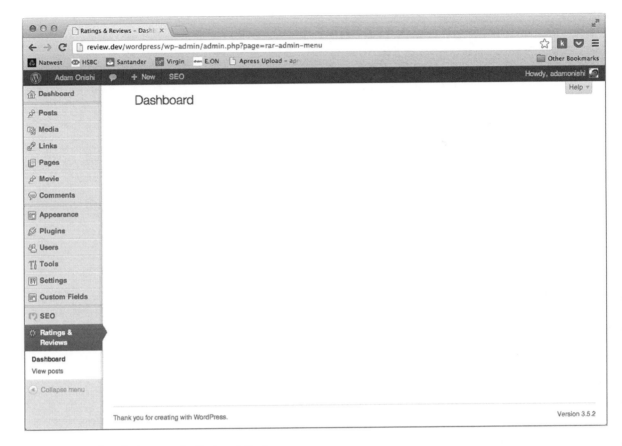

Figure 13-7. *The admin menu for Ratings & Reviews*

Notice the first function: `rar_add_plugin_menu`. Three function calls are being set up by using the `add_menu_page` and `add_submenu_page` functions. The `add_menu_page` is used to create the top-level page within the WordPress admin. It also generates a default subpage of the same name, but you want to replace it with a Dashboard page. To do this, set up the Dashboard page in your first `add_submenu_page`; when it comes to the "unique" `menu_slug` parameter, you simply use the same slug as the one in the `add_menu_page` function. This tells WordPress to overwrite the default page and use your Dashboard page instead. Finally, add an extra subpage and go back to using a unique menu slug. Your last two functions are the page creation functions that build the pages content.

There are two final functions that you can use to set up your admin menu pages: `add_object_page` and `add_utility_page`. They work in a similar way to the `add_menu_page` function, but don't take a position parameter because each places the menu page in a defined position for you. The `add_object_page` adds a menu page to the group of menu items next to Posts, Pages, Media, and so on; and the `add_utility_page` adds to the group with Appearance, Plugins, and Tools. They can work with the `add_submenu_page` in exactly the same way as well; they are just different functions to help with the positioning of your menu page.

Settings API

Now you have menu pages, so you can put something into them. The settings API (introduced in version 2.7) is an extremely powerful and helpful way of creating your settings pages by taking out a lot of the hassle for you. You can add settings pages, sections, and fields, all through the API, and it handles most of the complex parts for you. There is still some effort required for processes like validation, however (you'll look at that shortly).

■ **Note** When using the settings API, users need to have the `manage_options` capability (admins and super-admins in multisite (which you've been using so far in the chapter) to enable the settings form to work. To create settings forms for nonadmins, you'll need to do a lot of the work manually.

To add the settings form to your page, go back to the first settings menu example and add to the `rar_create_admin_page` function, which looked like this:

```
function rar_create_admin_page(){
?>
<div class="wrap">
    <?php screen_icon(); ?>
    <h2>Ratings &amp; Reviews Settings</h2>

</div>
<?php
}
```

At the moment, you have only the screen icon and the header, so you'll add a form to take care of the viewing and updating of the plugin options. The form must submit to the `options.php` page and use the `"post"` method to work correctly. You also have to add a standard submit button using the WordPress `submit_button` function; you can customize it with some parameters if you like, but for now just use the defaults:

```
function rar_create_admin_page(){
?>
<div class="wrap">
        <?php screen_icon(); ?>
        <h2>Ratings &amp; Reviews Settings</h2>

        <form action="options.php" method="post">

                <?php submit_button(); ?>
        </form>
</div>
<?php
}
```

To populate the form with fields, you'll use the API functions `settings_fields` and `do_settings_sections` settings (you'll see examples in a second), but first you need to create the options you want for your plugin. Registering fields for your options is done using two main functions, and you can use a third function to set up groups of fields for better formatting. Here you'll look at all three functions.

To get started, register some options with the `add_settings_field` function. This function can be used not only to generate fields for your custom plugin settings page but also for the default WordPress settings pages. There are four required parameters and two optional ones to use when setting up a field. Here's an example:

```
add_settings_field( 'display-count', 'Display count', 'rar_field_display_count',
'rar-settings-admin', 'rar-defaults' );
```

This code sets up an option to choose the number of reviews to display by default. The first parameter is the field ID that will be used in the ID attributes of tags and then the field title for the label in your form. Next is the callback function that will generate the field input for the option. Next is the ID of the page the setting is to appear on; in this case, the same ID as the options page you already set up. The final parameter is the ID for the section the field will belong to.

You'll set the section up in a moment, but first you still need to create the callback function to set up the input field of your option:

```
function rar_field_display_count() {
        $options = get_option('rar-options');

        if( isset( $options['display-count']) ) {
                $display_count = $options['display-count'];
        } else {
                $display_count = '';
        }

        echo '<input name="rar-options[display-count]" id="rar-display-count" type="text"
value="' . $display_count . '" />';
}
```

The callback function gets the options by using the get_option function, checks that the option you're looking for exists in the array, and then outputs an HTML input that will appear on the settings page. You must always output the current value of the option along with the input, and the HTML must always be echoed to the screen.

The name attribute used in the input is also important because you have to use the same name as the name used in the register_setting function (you'll see it in a moment). You use the name attribute "rar-options[display-count]" because WordPress can store options as both a single value and a serialized array. So instead of registering a different setting for each field, you can use the one option name and add each field to it as part of the array.

The next part to set up is the section for the settings page, which can be a nice way to separate out different groups of options and is especially handy if you're thinking of adding custom settings to the default WordPress admin pages. The function takes four required parameters: the first is for the ID of the section, the second takes a page title, the third is the callback to display the section information, and the fourth is for the page ID on which the section should appear:

```
add_settings_section( 'rar-defaults', 'Defaults', 'rar_section_info', 'rar-settings-admin' );
```

As before, you set up a unique ID and added a title, followed by the callback function name and the ID slug for the settings page. The callback function for the section is used just to output a single line of text about the section:

```
function rar_section_info() {
        echo '<p>Set the default outputs of the plugin</p>';
}
```

Now that the section and field are defined, you need to register them so that WordPress knows they are there and will do all the saving and returning of your option for you. The register_setting function takes just three parameters; the first two, option group and option name are required, the third "sanitize_callback" is optional but really you should always be doing some form of validation on your option fields so you'll be including it here.

```
register_setting( 'rar_options', 'rar-options', 'rar_options_validate' );
```

423

Here you'll notice that the option name (second parameter) is the one you're using for the rest of your settings in their name attribute. The callback function is going to do a quick validation test on your option; a simple is_numeric check is all you need here.

```php
function rar_options_validate ( $input ) {

        if( is_numeric($input['display-count']) ){
                $newinput['display-count'] = $input['display-count'];
        } else {
                $newinput['display-count'] = '';
        }

        return $newinput;
}
```

If the input is numeric, you can simply return it; if not, you just want to return a blank string. You can validate options however you like in this function; you just need to return a value in the same format (you have an array of inputs coming in, so an array must be returned).

Going back to the register_setting function, there's one parameter I haven't mentioned: the option group parameter. The value for this parameter comes from when the settings page is originally created. It's important that the option group is already defined by the time the register_setting function is called, which is the reason why all these functions need to be called on the admin_init action that runs after the admin_menu function used to set up the options page.

The final part of putting this all together is to finish the settings page. You know that you need to have the option group defined before you can run the register_setting function; you do this with the settings_fields function. This function sets up all the hidden fields and values you need, including a security nonce, for your settings page. It just takes the name of the option group that you then use later on when registering settings.

The second function to use is either the do_settings_sections or do_settings_fields function, depending on what you have set up. Both functions take the page ID slug that you created earlier as their only parameter.

Here's the final code to set up and output all the fields for the options page (the result is shown in the admin in Figure 13-8):

```php
function rar_create_admin_page(){
?>
<div class="wrap">
        <?php screen_icon(); ?>
        <h2>Ratings &amp; Reviews Settings</h2>

        <form action="options.php" method="post">
                <?php
                // This prints out all hidden setting fields
                settings_fields('rar_options');
                do_settings_sections('rar-settings-admin');

                submit_button(); ?>
        </form>
</div>
<?php
}
```

```php
if( is_admin() ) {
        add_action( 'admin_init', 'rar_register_options' );
}

function rar_register_options() {
        register_setting( 'rar_options', 'rar-options', 'rar_options_validate' );

        add_settings_section( 'rar-defaults', 'Defaults', 'rar_section_info', 'rar-settings-admin' );

        add_settings_field( 'display-count', 'Display count', 'rar_field_display_count',
'rar-settings-admin', 'rar-defaults' );
}
```

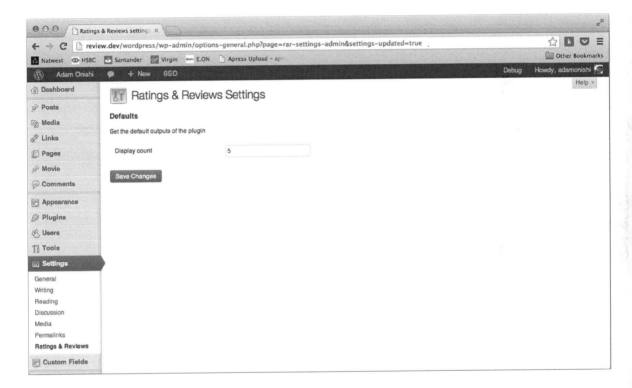

Figure 13-8. *The settings page including the display count option*

You can extend the options page to allow your users to customize any of the defaults for the plugin and any other details you want.

Using Options

The last part of the options discussion is how to get the options out of the database and use them in a plugin. To get at the options you created, you use a function from the WordPress Options API: get_option.

When you get the function, remember to use the option name you created in the register_setting function. If you created an array as in the previous examples, it will give you all your options back at once via an associative array.

To show how it works, here's a snippet from the previous function that output data from the database:

```
[...]
$options = get_option('rar-options');

// Setup array of default arguments
$defaults = array (
                'id'      => false,
                'post_id' => false,
                'user_id' => false,
                'order'   => 'ASC',
                'number'  => $options['display-count'],
                'offset'  => 0
        );
[...]
```

Where you previously set up the defaults for your query parameters, now you use the get_option function to retrieve your settings and use them in place of hard-coded defaults. Doing so allows the option defaults to be overwritten by the function call, but gives the user the option of setting a custom default from the WordPress admin, avoiding overwriting the defaults each time.

Settings Link in the Plugins Management Page

The last little thing I'll show you when it comes to setting up options pages is how to add a link to the settings page in the action links for your plugin on the plugins screen. This is a handy little function that enables you to give users quick access to your settings page as soon as they activate the plugin (or indeed whenever they visit the plugins page):

```
function rar_settings_link($actions, $file) {

        if(false !== strpos($file, 'ratings-and-reviews')) {
                $actions['settings'] = '<a href="options-general.php?page=rar-settings-
admin">Settings</a>';
        }

        return $actions;
}

add_filter('plugin_action_links', 'rar_settings_link', 2, 2);
```

You hook the function in to the plugin_action_links action and then check which plugin is currently being displayed using the $file parameter and the slug of your plugin. If you're on your plugin, you just add a link to your settings page to the actions array. If you're not sure what the URL for your settings page is, go to it and check the address bar.

Adding to the Plugin Repository

The more important topics of creating a WordPress plugin have now been covered. In this last section, you'll see how to take your finished plugin and add it to the WordPress plugin repository.

As you saw in chapter 9, the plugin repository is home to more than 25,000 plugins with more than 450 million downloads. It is a great resource for not only WordPress site owners/developers but also for plugin developers to get their plugin in front of potential users.

In the next few pages you'll learn how best to prepare your plugin for submitting to the repository, how to submit the plugin, and how to keep it updated over time.

Before you learn how to set up your plugin and get it into the repository, there are a few requirements your plugin must adhere to so that WordPress will allow it in the repository. Although the requirements are pretty reasonable, there are some that you need to make sure you pay attention to (the full list of detailed guidelines can be found here: http://wp-themes-book.com/13004):

- Your plugin must be compatible with the GNU General Public License v2 or above, and it must be clearly stated in your readme.txt (more on that shortly). If no license is stated, WordPress will consider your submission to be GPLv2 anyway, which is in line with everything WordPress hosts.

- Your plugin can't be offensive or do anything illegal.

- Your plugin can't post any external links or "powered by" links on the web site on which it's installed without asking permission from the site admin.

- To submit your plugin to the repository you must use Subversion (I'll cover this in more detail later on).

Preparing a Plugin

When I say "preparing your plugin," I mean what you need to do besides just coding the plugin to get it ready for submitting to the repository. As you saw in chapter 9, when you look at a plugin in the repository, you see loads of information about what it does and how to use it, as well as information on the update history of the plugin (see Figure 13-9). You need to create all this information (well, apart from the update history, of course) before you submit your plugin to the repository.

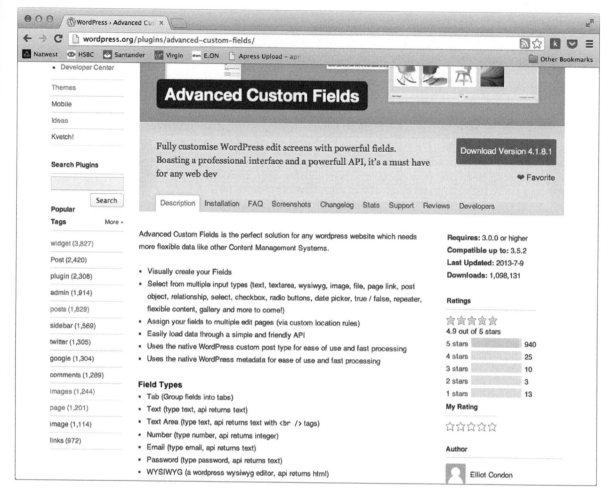

Figure 13-9. *The Advanced Custom Fields plugin page*

This section discusses the options you have when it comes to writing about and documenting your plugin. The mandatory requirement from WordPress for submitting a plugin is that it must have a readme.txt that the plugin repository will use to generate the informational tabs for the plugin page. It can also be useful to create a page on your own web site to promote, document, and give further information about your plugin that might be too much for the repository pages.

Readme File

The readme.txt file for your plugin is probably the most important part of your plugin after the plugin code itself. This file is where all the information for your page in the WordPress plugin repository comes from. It's important because having good, clear, and concise information about your plugin can make the difference between someone using your plugin instead of someone else's. The readme file is saved as a .txt file in the root folder of your plugin and uses a "Quasi-Markdown" style of formatting. As a developer, you should hopefully be familiar with Markdown, however as you'll see in the examples later on, there are just a few slight differences when you write your readme.txt.

Readme Header

The readme file contains a ton of information that's used to build up all the sections on your plugin repository page. Let's start by looking at the readme header:

```
=== Plugin Name ===
Contributors: (this should be a list of wordpress.org userid's)
Donate link: http://example.com/
Tags: comments, spam
Requires at least: 3.0.1
Tested up to: 3.4
Stable tag: 4.3
License: GPLv2 or later
License URI: http://www.gnu.org/licenses/gpl-2.0.html
```

Here is a short description of the plugin. This should be no more than 150 characters. No markup here.

This is from the example plugin readme file on wordpress.org (http://wp-themes-book.com/13005); here you can see a list of information similar to what you find in the main plugin file and in the main style.css of a theme. The only difference here is that the name of the plugin is included as a header (at the top wrapped with === on either side), which is one of the few differences between Markdown and this version.

Most of the settings are pretty self-explanatory, although a couple are missing from the WordPress example "Plugin URI" and "Author URI", which should definitely be included to ensure that users get links to both the plugin web site and your web site as the author. It ensures much better promotion of yourself and the plugin.

I'll quickly go through some of the settings that need to go in your readme.txt because it's really important that you fill these out as accurately as possible to give potential users the best information possible:

- Contributors: As shown in the preceding example, it is important to list contributors with their WordPress.org user IDs. It allows their profiles to show up in the repository page and link to them and their other work.

- Tags: It's important that you tag your plugin with an accurate representation of what your plugin does. Because it's possible to search the repository by tag, you want yours to show up only where appropriate. Otherwise, it might appear in the wrong places and could potentially gain a bad reputation.

- Requires at least: This setting is the minimum WordPress version number your plugin needs to work with. Some people don't upgrade WordPress for several reasons, so it's good to know what the minimum requirements are for your plugin.

- Tested up to: This setting lets people know whether the plugin has been tested with the more recent versions of WordPress. As a plugin developer, you should test with all new WordPress releases and keep it up to date with the latest release. However, if you discontinue support, this setting gives users a heads up of when it was last tested.

- Stable tag: This setting is for WordPress to tell users which plugin version should be the main download from your Subversion repo (more on that later). It should almost always be the version number; the only time you should specify anything other than a number is when you use the trunk of the subversion repository.

The rest should be fairly self-explanatory, and you can always check out other plugins for more detailed examples.

The last line of the plugin header section, the plugin's short description, stands alone from any setting tag. It is a 150-character-max description of your plugin that will appear in the plugin banner in the repository and in the plugin listings, both in the plugins repository (see Figure 13-10) and in the WordPress admin. It's important to keep this description short, clear, and to the point. There's no need to include any code or technical descriptions because this short description is there to grab potential users so they become interested enough to read more about your plugin.

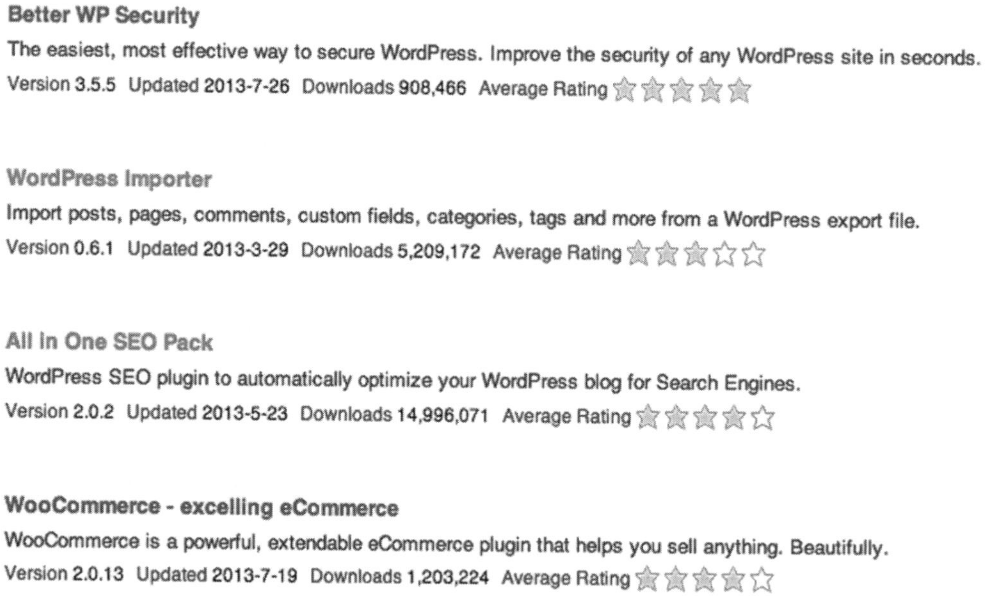

Better WP Security

The easiest, most effective way to secure WordPress. Improve the security of any WordPress site in seconds.

Version 3.5.5 Updated 2013-7-26 Downloads 908,466 Average Rating ☆☆☆☆☆

WordPress Importer

Import posts, pages, comments, custom fields, categories, tags and more from a WordPress export file.

Version 0.6.1 Updated 2013-3-29 Downloads 5,209,172 Average Rating ☆☆☆☆☆

All In One SEO Pack

WordPress SEO plugin to automatically optimize your WordPress blog for Search Engines.

Version 2.0.2 Updated 2013-5-23 Downloads 14,996,071 Average Rating ☆☆☆☆☆

WooCommerce - excelling eCommerce

WooCommerce is a powerful, extendable eCommerce plugin that helps you sell anything. Beautifully.

Version 2.0.13 Updated 2013-7-19 Downloads 1,203,224 Average Rating ☆☆☆☆☆

Figure 13-10. The most popular plugin's listing with short descriptions

Remaining Readme Sections

After your plugin header, the rest of the readme file should be split into sections that will make up the tabs of your plugin page (see Figure 13-11). Each section is defined by a header that is defined by the header being within double equal signs (== Header ==). And there are some standard tabs that you would normally include—Description, Installation, FAQ, and so on—and you can also make additional tabs by adding extra headers if needed.

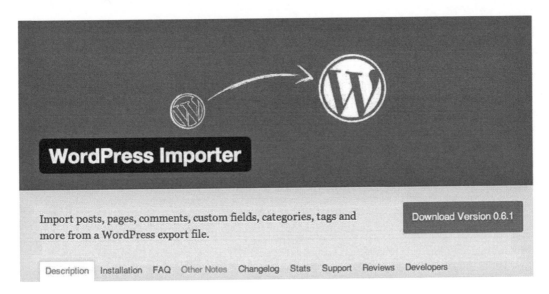

WordPress Importer

Import posts, pages, comments, custom fields, categories, tags and more from a WordPress export file.

Download Version 0.6.1

Description Installation FAQ Other Notes Changelog Stats Support Reviews Developers

Figure 13-11. *The WordPress importer plugin page with the tabs along the bottom of the header*

The remaining sections of your readme file give you an opportunity to not only promote your plugin to possible users but also give them more detailed instructions and documentation on how to use it. As discussed in chapter 9, people will be looking into the information and documentation for each plugin, so it's important that when writing your own, you ensure that the information is readily available and as helpful as possible. Let's look at the sections you should be thinking about getting into your plugin page and see why they're important:

- **Description**: This section contains the full description of your plugin—what it can do and why it's so good at doing it. This is really where you sell your plugin's features and detail why people should be using it. You can use this long description for options such as features, requirements, upcoming improvements, and basic usage. You can also use standard markdown here to format the description, making it clear and easy to read.

- **Installation**: This section lets users know exactly how to install and set up your plugin. The usual instructions for downloading the plugin and uploading it to your plugins directory is fine, but you also need to let users know about any activation and initial setup your plugin needs. Tag descriptions and functionality can be saved for other sections, however.

- **FAQ**: An FAQ is important for your users because it is the place in which you can answer some really simple troubleshooting problems. And if people come to you for support, you can point them to this section and save yourself a lot of time. FAQs are structured in headings and standard text; a question should be enclosed in single equal signs (= *Question goes here* =), and the answer should follow directly after.

- **Screenshots**: Granted, you might not think your plugin that appears only in the back end of WordPress to add some simple functionality is that pretty, but it's worth showing an example of what your plugin will look like when installed. If your plugin outputs things to the front end, though, make sure that you have screenshots of that functionality. Screenshots should be titled screenshot-1.jpg, screenshot-2.jpg, and so on, and can be captioned under the Screenshots section using a numbered list corresponding to the screenshot numbering. Screenshots should be stored in the assets directory at the root of your main SVN folder (I'll discuss that shortly).

- **Changelog**: The changelog section contains the list of all the updates your plugin has gone through for each version. It is important to show users the previous history of the plugin and how it's being maintained. It can also be useful to show users why they should be updating the plugin if you've made a recent change.

- **Upgrade notice**: This section doesn't show up in the plugin repository page, but it is useful when updating your plugin because it will be shown on the Installed plugins page of the user's WordPress site. It gives you the opportunity to highlight why the plugin should be updated and what updates there are. This is a short piece of text and should be kept to fewer than 300 characters. However, like the others, you can write a short description and provide a link to further upgrade information in the repository.

- **Other notes and arbitrary sections**: This section is often titled Other notes, but you can add extra tabs with whichever title you prefer. You can use extra tabs in your plugin page to give users more information about setup and installation, for credits to the developers behind the plugin, localization instructions, or anything that doesn't really fit into the other tabs.

The more information you furnish in your plugin page, the more likely it is that users can decide whether your plugin is best suited to the functionality they're looking for. Remember to be concise and clear with all the information you add—don't just ramble and add sections just for the sake of doing so.

If it is your first plugin, consider talking to friends about the plugin and have them ask you questions about its usage and how they do certain things. These conversations can give you a good basis for your initial description and FAQ page, which can then be updated over time as more people start to use your plugin.

Readme Validator

The last thing to mention about creating your plugin readme files is that WordPress also has a readme validator, which can be found at http://wp-themes-book.com/13006. It's a handy resource allowing you to check your readme file before you upload your plugin so you know it's going to work and generate the information correctly.

Banner Image

Along with your readme file you can create a banner image to appear across the top of your plugin page. A lot of plugins have them, as you saw in examples from this chapter and the previous one. To add a banner for your plugin page, add an image to the assets folder in the root of your plugin's SVN directory root (more on that shortly). The image can be a PNG or JPG file only, and must be sized 772px x 250px with the file names banner-772x250.png or banner-772x250.jpg. The plugin repository also allows you to support retina/high-DPI screens with a second image sized at 1544px x 500px with the file names banner-1544x500.png or banner-1544x500.jpg.

Creating a Plugin Web Site

To go along with a plugin, sometimes people create a web site or page on their own site with further information and documentation for the plugin. This is a good idea when you have a relatively complex plugin that requires a lot of documentation or to use as extra promotion for your plugin.

Plugins such as Advanced Custom Fields (http://wp-themes-book.com/13007) have a complete web site to go along with the plugin, with full documentation and their own support forum. Although you don't necessarily need to go to those sorts of lengths with your plugin, it might be useful for you to provide more complete documentation on a web site of your own or use it for road mapping and suggestions, for example.

Another benefit of having a custom web site is that you can update it more easily and quickly over the plugin repository page, which requires you to use a Subversion (SVN) repository as you'll see shortly. Directing people to your web site enables you to promote yourself and other plugins or themes you may have created.

Submitting to the Repository

Now that you've prepared your plugin and created your readme, screenshots, banner image, and maybe a web site, you have to actually get your plugin in the repository for people to download. To do this, you use a source control program called Subversion (SVN). All the plugins in the repository are hosted and updated via SVN, so here you'll take a brief look at how to use SVN and get your plugin uploaded to the repository.

The first step is to sign up and get a WordPress account at http://wp-themes-book.com/13008. Anything WordPress-related nowadays goes through WordPress.com accounts (including using plugins such as Akismet), so if you will work with WordPress a lot (you have this book, after all), it's probably worth signing up to get an account.

Once you're all set up with a WordPress account, you can go to the Add Your Plugin page (http://wp-themes-book.com/13009) shown in Figure 13-12. You'll be prompted for some initial information. Remember that the name you submit will be the final name for your plugin; you won't be able to change it without creating a new plugin page, so make sure that you're happy with the name you chose. You also need to provide a description of the plugin and a link to a zip file on the web of your full plugin code. This allows WordPress to check your plugin and set up the initial SVN repository for you. After you've submitted your plugin, you can expect a wait of about 24–48 hours for a response that will include a link to the SVN repository of your plugin.

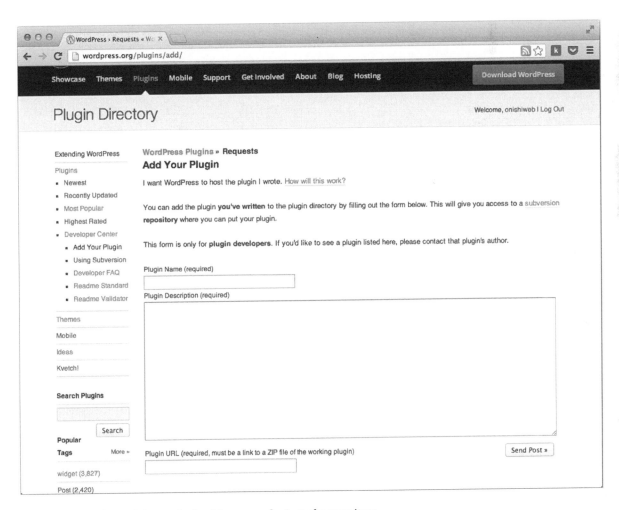

Figure 13-12. *The initial step of submitting your plugin to the repository*

■ **Note**   You will need SVN installed on your computer for the next section. Most Macs have it already, but to double-check, go to http://wp-themes-book.com/13010 and download and install the latest version.

Using the SVN Repository

Now you have the SVN repository link for your plugin, you need to get the files onto your local working environment so that you can make further changes and update your plugin. If you've used a source control system before, you should be familiar with terms such as "check out," "check in," "revisions," and "repository," but here you'll take a quick crash course in SVN to get you up and running. For more detailed documentation, see the docs on the Subversion web site (http://wp-themes-book.com/13011) or take a look at the SVN book (http://wp-themes-book.com/13012).

My experience with source control is with Git, which is a distributed version control system (everyone working on the project has their own copy of the repository and they all update to one main repository). SVN, on the other hand, is a nondistributed version control system. meaning that you are always working from the remote repository; any changes you make have to be "committed" back to the remote repository. So when working with SVN, the main thing you'll do, especially when it comes to working on WordPress plugins, is to check out and check in changes to the repository.

I'll make this clearer with an example of what to do when you first receive your plugin repository URL. Open your command line or terminal and go to the directory in which you'll be working with your plugin. There you'll create a new directory for the plugin and check out your plugin repository:

```
~ mkdir your-plugin-name
~ svn co http://plugins.svn.wordpress.org/your-plugin-name your-plugin-name
```

This code downloads the repository to your local directory and creates three new folders: trunk, branches, and tags. The trunk directory is the main directory for your core files; tags is for previous revisions of the main files; and branches is used for major development from a copy of the trunk in which the development will be kept in version control, but not put live right away.

Now that you have the repository on your local environment, you can add your plugin files to the repository. The repository you get from WordPress will be blank (or filled with the files you submitted via the web site), if blank, you should copy your main plugin files into the trunk folder of your SVN repo. This is where your main development files will be kept. In a moment, you'll see how to tag and release a stable version of your plugin, but for now you'll add the files to the repository and check in the additions.

Copy or move your files from their current location to the trunk directory and then run the add command:

```
~your-plugin-name/$ svn add trunk/*
```

This command adds all the files in the trunk folder to the repository; you can also add individual files by using the full path of the file after the add command.

Now you need to check in the changes to the main repository:

```
~your-plugin-name/$ svn ci -m 'Adding initial pluging files to repo'
```

The preceding command should then list a couple of lines that tell you which files have been added, followed by two lines similar to these:

```
Transmitting file data .
Committed revision xxxxx.
```

The ci command stands for "check in," and the -m flag followed by a string in single or double quotes is used to add a message to the check in. If you run the ci command without the -m flag, you will be prompted to add a check-in message in the text editor your command line is set up to use.

Once a file has been added to the repository, it will be tracked for life inside the repository. So when you edit a file that's already been added, all you have to do is another check in. However, for new files you have to go through the same process of adding files to the repository followed by a check in.

Tagging and Releasing a Plugin

Once you have a complete and fully functional version of your plugin ready to release, you need to tag it to create a formal release of your plugin. This will be the version that is downloaded automatically as the "latest" version of your plugin from the repository and from the WordPress admin area.

Before you create your tagged version of the plugin, ensure that you know what the version number will be and then update your plugin header and readme.txt with the correct stable tag.

Next, you need to copy the trunk folder into a new directory in the tags folder. The new directory should use the name of the current version you are creating, for instance 1.0 or 1.0.1, not Latest.

```
~your-plugin-name/$ svn cp trunk tags/1.0
```

This code creates the new directory and adds it to the SVN repository. The last thing to do is check in the new tagged version and wait for it to be updated in the plugin repository:

```
~your-plugin-name/$ svn ci -m 'Tagging first major release'
```

When SVN has finished updating the repo, your latest version will have been submitted to the repository. After about 20–30 minutes, your plugin repository page on the web site should be up to date and ready for people to download your plugin.

Updating a Plugin

As with any type of software, releasing the first version of your plugin doesn't signal the end of development. If only. There will be features you'll always want to add, bugs you'll need to iron out, and the possibility of requests from users for updates/changes.

Upgrading plugins from the user's perspective (when the plugin is in the repository) is extremely easy; from a developer's viewpoint, it isn't that much more difficult either.

There are, however, a couple of things to consider before updating your plugin:

- Does the new version offer any extra features that require new options, database tables, and so on?

- Will the new version potentially break some of the previous settings from an older version?

- Have you added any features the user will need to set up to the new version?

- Will the plugin require the latest prior version to have been installed? How will you manage your plugin if a user is jumping a couple of versions?

These are all valid concerns when thinking about how your plugin will handle upgrades. Fortunately, they can all be solved by taking one simple action in the very beginning (or in the second version if you've already gotten that far).

▓ **Important** Store the current version of the plugin in the WordPress database.

When you first run the activation script of your plugin, you can add an option to the WordPress options table that records the current version of your plugin. As part of the upgrade process, your plugin is reinstalled and activated again, which means the register_activation_hook gets called again and your activation function can be used to run a check against the previous version number. You can then make any database or functionality upgrades necessary.

Admin Notices

If the new version of your plugin has added any new settings or anything that users need to configure to get their web site working again, it's important to let the users know. You can obviously do this in the version notes and the upgrade notice, but you can't be sure that users will pay attention to them all the time. One solution to this is to create a notice in the WordPress admin that appears after your plugin has been updated.

Going back to the ratings and reviews plugin, I added a function that checks the current version of the plugin against the plugin version that is currently active in WordPress. If the versions are different, an upgrade notice is shown to the user with a link to the settings page of the plugin:

```
public function plugin_upgrade_notice() {

        if( self::$version != get_option( 'ratings_and_reviews_version' ) ) {
                update_option( 'ratings_and_reviews_version', self::$version );

                $html = '<div class="updated"><p>';

                $html .= __( 'Ratings and reviews has been updated. Please <a href="options-general.
php?page=rar-settings-admin">check your settings now</a>.', 'ratings-and-reviews' );

                $html .= '</p></div><!-- /.updated -->';

                echo $html;
        }
}
```

The only thing to note about the HTML you're outputting is the use of the updated class, which is used in WordPress to make sure that the notice has the correct styles and feels like part of the admin interface.

This function needs to be called on the admin_notices hook to output the HTML in the correct place and should be hooked in via the constructor function of your plugin class. The reason for not including it through the register_activation_hook is that after the activation hook has run, the page is reloaded, so any hooks you run there would be lost before they could be displayed.

So you need to add the following to the constructor function:

```
add_action( 'admin_notices', array( $this, 'plugin_upgrade_notice' ) );
```

The end result is that every time your plugin is updated and the version numbers differ, you'll see the notice shown in Figure 13-13 at the top of the plugins page.

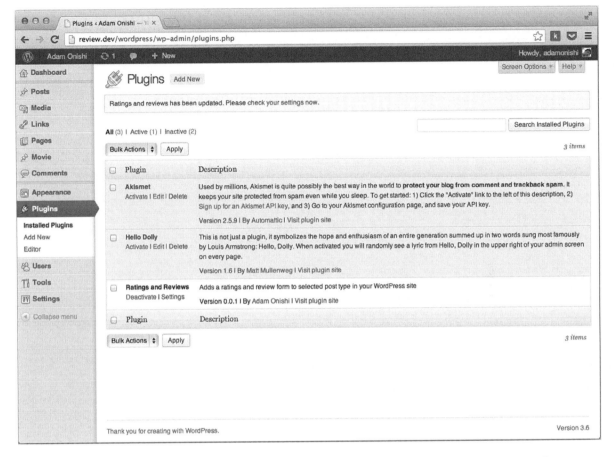

Figure 13-13. *The upgrade notice at the top of the screen when a new version of the plugin has been detected*

Summary

Congratulations on making it to the end of another huge chapter! A lot was covered, and hopefully you're now feeling confident enough to get to work on that incredible bit of functionality you think deserves to be a plugin.

The chapter covered everything you need to get started with plugin development, from writing your very first basic plugin to looking at the various ways you can add functionality to WordPress. You learned how to make your plugin code smarter by encapsulating it in its own class and how to work with the WordPress database to store data for your plugin. You also looked at how to work with the WordPress Settings API and administration pages to allow users to customize settings within your plugin.

Finally, I took you through all the steps necessary to get your new plugin into the WordPress plugin repository, making it available to other WordPress users, and how to use a bit of SVN to update your plugin safely.

The next chapter takes a quick look at WordPress multisite, discussing how to install and configure multiple sites, and how the theming and plugin systems work in a multisite environment.

CHAPTER 14

▪ ▪ ▪

WordPress Multisite

In this final chapter of the book, I want to talk about a topic that is not directly related to WordPress themes, but is certainly something that you'll come across when working with WordPress: *WordPress Multisite*. Multisite is a feature of WordPress that allows you to set up multiple sites, managed and maintained from a single install of WordPress. Perhaps it sounds slightly crazy, but before you dismiss it, you should be aware that Multisite is a very powerful tool when used in the right circumstances. The best example of a well-known instance of WordPress Multisite is WordPress.com itself. This network of sites is run and maintained via a single install of WordPress running Multisite-of course this does entail a complex set up of servers and databases in order to run the network.

In fact, there are many sites using WordPress Multisite for a network of blogs. WordPress.com is the largest, of course, with more than 71 million blogs being hosted via a single instance of WordPress Multisite (see Figure 14-1). Another site, Edublogs, hosts more than 2 million blogs via its install of Multisite, and there are many more, including New York Times blogs, Reuters blogs, and Harvard Law School blogs.

Figure 14-1. The current number of WordPress blogs on WordPress.com

WordPress Multisite began as a separate entity from the main WordPress platform known as WordPress MU (Multi User), but it merged into the WordPress core in version 3.0. Multisite is not active by default in a WordPress install; it needs to be activated in the configuration file for the site before you can set up a *network* (the term for an instance of Multisite) via the WordPress admin.

When to Use Multisite

WordPress Multisite allows you to create a network of sites and manage everything to do with those sites in one central place. Although it sounds as if Multisite could be applied to anything, there are certain circumstances in which it's a good idea to use Multisite, and others in which it's certainly best to avoid using it. Some of the scenarios in which WordPress Multisite might be a good solution are these:

- An events site needing multiple sites for different events

- A conference using a different web site for each year

- Academic sites needing a site for each faculty or school in the institution

- A theme demo site, showing off each theme on each site—as used by the Theme Foundry for its demo site

- Different localized web sites for a brand or product

These examples show that Multisite is great when you want to create a series of sites related to a single purpose. Each example here would have benefits in having the network of sites managed centrally by a single team, for instance.

Another potential scenario, as mentioned in the introduction, is a site that acts as a platform for its users to run their own web site. You can see this in sites such as WordPress.com, Edublogs, and Reuters. Reuters uses Multisite to build a separate microsite/blog for each of its columnists or for specific topics, allowing each one to have an individual section with categories, tags, and more specific related content. Multisite is great for this type of scenario because it enables users to quickly create a new site on the network whenever they need it, while the network admin is still in control of the general look and functionality of each site on the network.

Some people have used Multisite to host and maintain multiple client sites from the same install. This does have its benefits, but I argue that some of the downsides of combining your client sites into a single Multisite far outweigh its ease of maintenance. To understand why Multisite might not always be the best solution, it's best to look at the many pros and cons of running Multisite.

Advantages

So far, you've seen some good reasons to use Multisite for certain purposes. Why are these scenarios so well-suited to running a Multisite network? Here are some of the advantages WordPress Multisite has to offer:

- **Central control**: Multisite allows you to control all sites on the network via one admin. You control what themes and plugins are available, so you have control over what gets added and how to ensure the best fit for the sites on the network.

- **Expansion**: New sites can be created easily. You can enable users to create their own sites or control what sites are created. Either option means that there is an opportunity to easily expand the network of sites whenever needed.

- **Network wide updates**: With everything controlled by a central admin, plugins and themes are installed once, so any updates to a theme apply to the rest of the network instantly.

- **Single site customization**: Users can still customize their own sites with widgets, menus, and the theme customizer.

- **Multisite content**: You can share content across multiple sites on the network (although this should be done sensibly). For example, the front page of the Reuters blog shows content from all the web sites on the network, but links through to the single site to display the full content.

Disadvantages

There are some disadvantages of using Multisite as well. Here are some reasons why you should keep web sites separate:

- **Compatibility**: Some themes and plugins may not work well with Multisite (although most should if they are coded correctly).

- **Architecture**: To run Multisite well, you need a good architecture behind your network (you probably shouldn't try to run Multisite on shared hosting). You also need access to the server in order to manually configure files. So there are systems administration skills required, and hosting may cost slightly more than average if you intend to build a large network.

- **Single point of failure**: If one site on the network is hacked, chances are that all sites will be vulnerable as well. The same can be said about broken code in a plugin or theme—probably all sites on the network will be affected.

- **Admin bottleneck**: An advantage and a disadvantage is that single-site admins can't install their own themes or plugins—they must go through the network admin. Depending on the size of the network, this might cause a lot of work for the network admin.

- **Performance**: All sites are run from the same database (unless you use a plugin) and from the same server, which might cause low performance. Also the fact that a single install is serving multiple sites might affect server performance.

- **Users**: With Multisite, your users can tell they're on a network. This may not sound like a big deal, but if the information on the site has privacy issues or should not be accessed by anyone outside of the site, it may be a problem for users to know that multiple sites are connected to theirs.

When Not to Use Multisite

Multisite can be a great solution, but sometimes it isn't the best answer to a problem you're trying to solve. If any of the preceding disadvantages seem completely insurmountable, you probably don't need Multisite.

Don't use Multisite if you're looking for a way to categorize content. Categories and tags are core to WordPress, and you can configure the URL structure of your site to appear however you like (sometimes with the help of plugins), which doesn't require a Multisite install. Likewise, when a custom post type might be more suitable for different content types on your site, you don't need to set up a new site for each type of content.

If your single-site users need any sort of control over their site, Multisite is not the answer. This is probably the biggest reason why you should not use Multisite for client web sites. If you're hosting radically different client sites across your network that require different functionality and different themes, and your users want control of their sites, you're better off keeping them as separate installs.

There are many ways to set up management for multiple single WordPress sites, including the one I discussed earlier in the book: InfiniteWP. If you're just looking for a way to maintain multiple sites more easily, you're probably better off using a management system instead of installing Multisite.

Installing and Configuring Multisite

Since version 3.0, WordPress has come packaged with Multisite features built in, although by default these features are hidden unless you enable Multisite from the configuration file. There are a few prerequisites you need to be aware of before you install it.

I'll discuss installing Multisite on your local machine so you can set up a development version first. This is something you should always do anyway before you set up a version on your server. The general principles will apply to any Multisite setup, but you may need to be aware of a few things specific to your own setup. Although the development version I will create will be set up on a Mac running the built-in server, the same theory applies if you are running MAMP or WAMP on your machines.

When setting up your Multisite on any server or local install, I recommend that you not only read the rest of this chapter but also read these articles in the WordPress Codex:

- *Before you create a network* (http://wp-themes-book.com/14001)

- *Create a network* (http://wp-themes-book.com/14002)

- *Multisite network administration* (http://wp-themes-book.com/14003)

Prerequisites

To enable Multisite, you'll have to be an admin of the site you are turning into a network and have access to the files either through FTP or SSH. Because I'll be showing you how to do this on your local machine first, it shouldn't be an issue, but it's important to know that you'll need that access once you set it up on a production server.

There are also differences in requirements based on the type of Multisite network you intend to run. The two types available are *subdomain-based* and *path-based*.

Subdomain-Based Multisite

This type of setup means that the sites on your network will be visited via a separate subdomain on your main top-level domain (for example, *site1.example.com*). WordPress.com uses this method of Multisite: adamonishi. wordpress.com.

Domain-based Multisite requires you to have access to the configuration of your DNS settings, controlling how certain domains will be directed to your server. There are a few ways to do this, including setting up a wildcard domain. (If you're creating a network that can have new sites added quickly, this is probably the best option.) You can also set up virtual hosts in your Apache (or other) configuration, specifying the same document root for each subdomain.

With a subdomain-based setup, you can't set up WordPress in its own directory; the WordPress install must be located in the root of your web folder on your server.

Path-Based Multisite

This type of Multisite install adds sites reachable via subfolders on your main domain (for example, *example.com/site1*). You can see this method being used on the Reuters blog (i.e., http://blogs.reuters.com/talesfromthetrail/.

For path-based Multisite, as long as you have the WordPress "pretty-permalinks" working, a path-based install will work fine.

If you are up to date with WordPress (which you should be), you can set up an initial WordPress install and retain the ability to run WordPress from its own folder (as mentioned in Chapter 10). Prior to version 3.5, doing so wasn't possible.

One caveat with path-based Multisite installs is that the main site (the initial site you set up in Multisite reachable at http://example.com) allows posts (and custom post types) to be accessed only from a URL with the pattern *example.com/blog/*. At the moment, it can't remove */blog/* from the URL. Here's why: when the subdirectory style of Multisite is used, it is hard to ensure that the posts or post types you add don't conflict in some way with one of the site names in your network.

There is a potential workaround for this issue when it comes to the standard "posts" post type, although it depends on your taste for the use of "blog" on your site. Pages are not affected by this setup, so you can create a page titled "blog" and set it as the main page for posts—with a static home page, set Home as the home page, for example, and "blog" as the posts page. With this setup, your site will list posts at /blog/, and all posts will appear under /blog/post, which doesn't look quite as out of place. Remember, though, that this workaround doesn't affect subsites of your network; just the main site from which the network was set up.

Enabling Multisite

To get started setting up Multisite, you need to have a fresh install of WordPress. (Although you can set up Multisite on an existing site, there are some caveats to doing so that you can find out about in the WordPress Codex.) With WordPress set up, enable the Multisite feature from the wp-config.php file. Add the following line to the file above the line that says /* That's all, stop editing! Happy blogging. */:

```
define( 'WP_ALLOW_MULTISITE', true );
```

This code doesn't change anything right away, but it enables the network setup page inside the WordPress admin (see Figure 14-2). The setup page allows you to choose from either a subdomain-based network or a path-based (subdirectories) network, and offers you a few more settings for the network name and admin e-mail address.

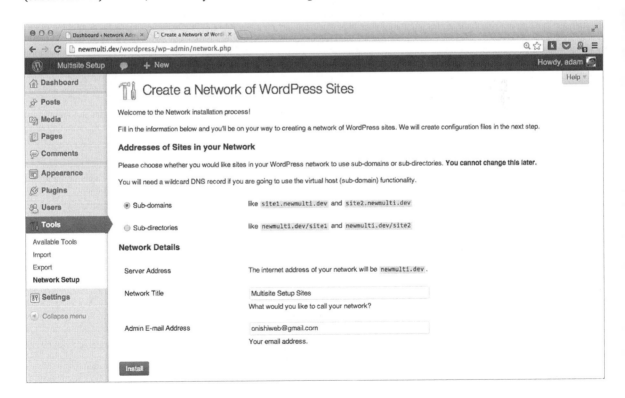

Figure 14-2. Network setup page

Enabling Multisite

With your settings entered, press Install, and WordPress will set up your WordPress site as a network. The second page of the install (see Figure 14-3) guides you through the remaining setup of the configuration file and .htaccess file. Unlike the pretty-permalinks settings, WordPress doesn't auto-complete these settings for you whether it has permission to edit files on your server or not; it is very much a manual process.

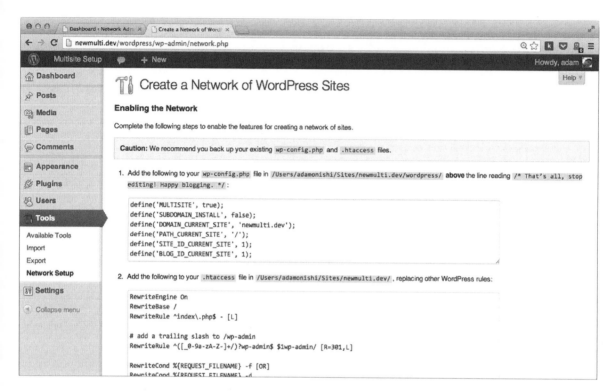

Figure 14-3. *Settings for wp-config.php and .htaccess files for your network*

You should add the new settings to the wp-config.php file directly after the define() statement for enabling Multisite, which keeps all the settings for Multisite together in one place. Your wp-config.php file should now have some settings that look like this:

```
define('WP_ALLOW_MULTISITE', true);
define('MULTISITE', true);
define('SUBDOMAIN_INSTALL', false);
define('DOMAIN_CURRENT_SITE', 'newmulti.dev');
define('PATH_CURRENT_SITE', '/');
define('SITE_ID_CURRENT_SITE', 1);
define('BLOG_ID_CURRENT_SITE', 1);
```

The .htaccess updates are next, and they should completely replace the existing WordPress rules already in the file. The existing rules should look something like this:

```
<IfModule mod_rewrite.c>
RewriteEngine On
RewriteBase /
RewriteRule ^index\.php$ - [L]
RewriteCond %{REQUEST_FILENAME} !-f
RewriteCond %{REQUEST_FILENAME} !-d
RewriteRule . /index.php [L]
</IfModule>
```

Retain the <IfModule> blocks and just replace the rules inside. Each set of rules for the .htaccess file depends on your chosen type of WordPress install and the version of WordPress you're using. In my running of the path-based network with version 3.6.1, the .htaccess rules now look like this:

```
<IfModule mod_rewrite.c>
RewriteEngine On
RewriteBase /
RewriteRule ^index\.php$ - [L]

# add a trailing slash to /wp-admin
RewriteRule ^([_0-9a-zA-Z-]+/)?wp-admin$ $1wp-admin/ [R=301,L]

RewriteCond %{REQUEST_FILENAME} -f [OR]
RewriteCond %{REQUEST_FILENAME} -d
RewriteRule ^ - [L]
RewriteRule ^([_0-9a-zA-Z-]+/)?(wp-(content|admin|includes).*) wordpress/$2 [L]
RewriteRule ^([_0-9a-zA-Z-]+/)?(.*\.php)$ wordpress/$2 [L]
RewriteRule . index.php [L]
</IfModule>
```

After you have updated your files with the new settings, log in again to your site, which will return you to the admin of the main site. It will look familiar except for the addition of the new My Sites drop-down list in the admin bar at the top of the page (see Figure 14-4).

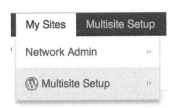

Figure 14-4. *The My Sites menu in the admin bar*

You now have access as the main administrator to the Network Admin section (see Figure 14-5). In this location, you can manage all the sites and users on your network; as well as add plugins, themes, and perform updates to WordPress and any installed themes and plugins from one central location.

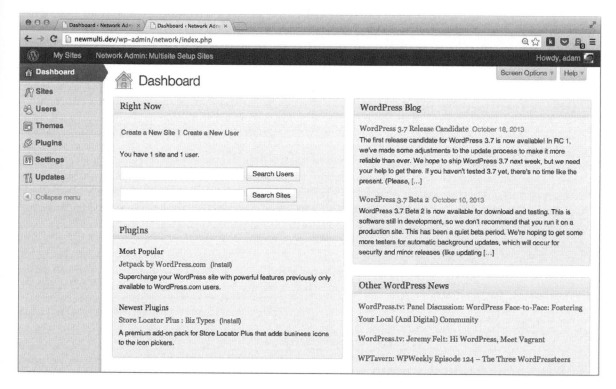

Figure 14-5. *Network Admin dashboard*

As a network administrator, you can use settings that control the way users interact with the sites on the network, and configure how new sites are set up and what default content they have:

- **Operational settings**: Network name and admin e-mail.

- **Registration settings**: How new sites and users can be set up on the network. By default, this setting is switched off so that only the network administrator can create new sites and new users. The other settings allow for either users or sites to be set up by site users or both. There are also settings here for banned site names and banned e-mails that are prevented from being created as sites or users. (You'll look at users and user settings in Multisite in more detail later in the chapter.)

- **New site settings**: Contain a series of options for how a new site will be created, including how a user is notified through to the initial posts and comments of the new site.

- **Upload settings**: Allow you to set upload limits for files and sites on the network as well as file type restrictions.

- **Menu settings**: Allow you to enable or disable the plugins menu on single sites for site admins.

Creating a New Site

The first thing you probably want to do when Multisite is set up is to create a new site. With path-based Multisite set up, go to the Sites > Add New Site menu (see Figure 14-6) and provide the settings for a new site to be created:

- **Site Address**: Path for the new site (must consist of only lowercase letters and numbers)

- **Site Title**: Title of the new site

- **Admin Email**: E-mail address of the new site admin; can be the same address as the network admin if you want to manage both

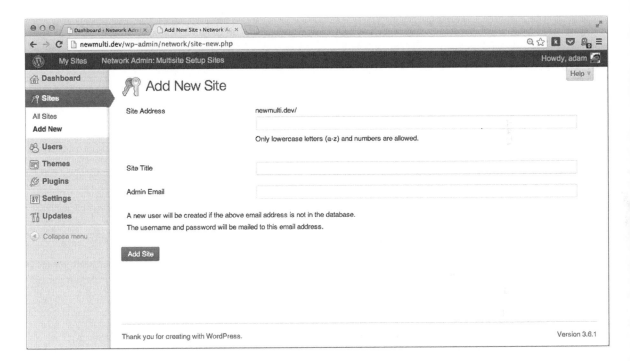

Figure 14-6. *The Add New Site page*

The site is now set up and ready to go; it really is that simple. Your new admin will get an e-mail with the username and password for the new site, and an e-mail will be sent to the network admin to notify them of the new site as well.

How the Database Works in Multisite

For every new site in your network, a new set of tables will be added to the main database (see Figure 14-7). Each site has its own set of tables used to store the site content, site-specific options, and metadata such as terms and taxonomies. The users and user metadata, as well as network-specific settings, are stored in separate table from the rest of the single sites data (i.e., no single site has a users table).

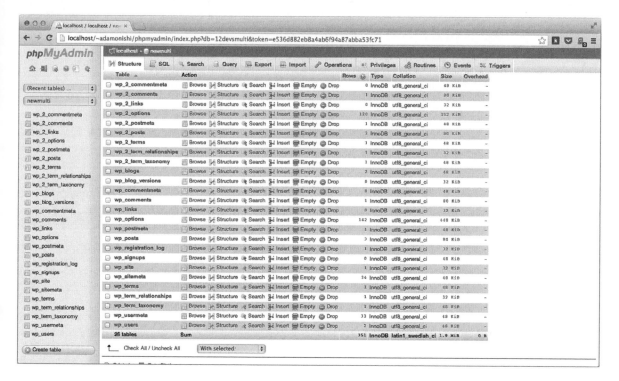

Figure 14-7. *Multisite database setup*

One reason for potential performance problems in WordPress Multisite is that because new sites are adding new tables to the database all the time, you'd start running into database performance issues and eventually run out of space if you had enough subsites. So how can sites such as WordPress.com and Edublogs host blogs in the millions or even tens of millions?

This is possible thanks to a plugin developed by WPMU DEV: Multi-DB (http://wp-themes-book.com/14004). It is the plugin being used by Edublogs to run its Multisite install and is similar to what WordPress.com uses. Multi-DB allows you to distribute your Multisite databases across 16, 256, or 4096 separate databases. Combined with good server architecture, as James Farmer of Edublogs describes here, Multi-DB should enable you to scale easily into the hundreds of thousands (and millions), as seen on Edublogs.

> *The database architecture wasn't the real problem—we cracked that fairly on with Multi DB—but the servers, the configs, and finding the staff to get that right was an utter nightmare.*

James Farmer, Edublogs

Unfortunately, the topic of server architecture for large-scale Multisite installs is a bit out of scope for this book and beyond my knowledge at the moment. However, as always with the WordPress community, you can find some great resources online:

- *Scaling WP blog* (http://wp-themes-book.com/14005)
- *WPMU Multisite blog* (http://wp-themes-book.com/14006)

- *Scaling WordPress like Edublogs* (post by James Farmer on WPMU)
  (http://wp-themes-book.com/14007)

- *Scaling WordPress and MySQL on multiple servers for performance*
  (http://wp-themes-book.com/14008)

Domain Mapping

When you create new sites with Multisite, instead of using a subdomain or subdirectory style URL for your site, you may want to have an entirely different domain for the sites on your network. When creating my sites 12 Devs and 12 Devs of Xmas, I wanted to set them up as a Multisite install, but with separate domains: 12devs.co.uk and 12devsofxmas.co.uk. I did this through WordPress Multisite with the help of a plugin: WordPress MU Domain Mapping (http://wp-themes-book.com/14009).

   This plugin allows you to set up your WordPress Multisite normally and then map custom domains to each site. The plugin is still in active development, and even the team at Automattic is involved in updating it.

   To get started with domain mapping, you'll need access to your server configuration and your WordPress files. The MU Domain Mapping plugin needs to be installed manually in this instance and should not be installed from the plugins menu in the WordPress admin. Download the plugin and extract the files from the downloaded zip file. After the download is complete, add/upload the main plugin folder to the wp-content/plugins folder and then move the sunrise.php file out to the wp-content folder (see Figure 14-8).

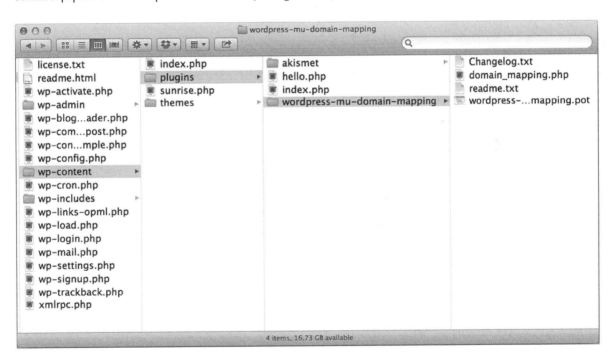

Figure 14-8. *WordPress MU Domain mapping files in place*

   With the files in place, add another line to the wp-config.php file to enable the plugin. Add the following line to the config file, along with the rest of the Multisite configuration settings you added earlier:

```
define( 'SUNRISE', 'on' );
```

With the plugin files and configuration now set up, you can visit the Settings > Domain mapping page in the Network Admin section (see Figure 14-9). Visiting the page sets up the database for the domain mapping plugin and then you can enter your settings.

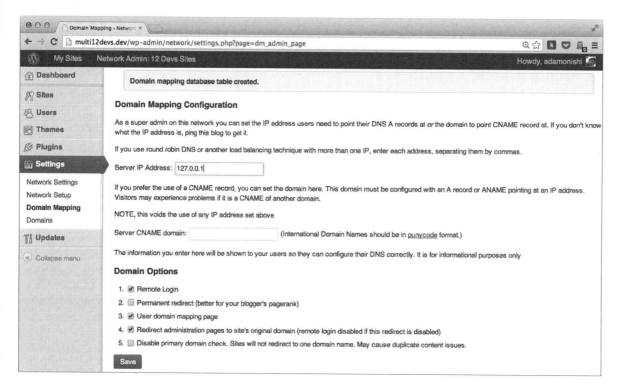

Figure 14-9. *Domain mapping setup page*

You can set up domain mapping with either your IP address (if you have a static IP address with your hosting—or in this case on your local machine) or via CNAME (if your CNAME settings are pointing at an IP address). Following the instructions on the page will help guide you to enter the correct settings. The remaining settings on the page configure how redirection among your domains will work for the network.

- **Remote Login:** Redirects users to log in to the main network site, so they are logged in to all sites at once. Uncheck if you plan to have your sites set up as individual entities as much as possible.

- **Permanent redirect**: Forces the domains you initially set up to redirect to the new mapped domains. Leave this checked because it's best for search engine optimization (SEO).

- **User domain mapping page**: Allows single-site users to have their own page to set up domain mapping.

- **Redirect administration pages to site's original domain**: Check this to redirect users back to their own site when logging in via the remote login system.

- **Disable primary domain check**: Removes the ability to set up a primary domain for your subsites, allowing people to access the site from either address. Best left unchecked to prevent issues with duplicate content on multiple domains.

Once you configure the main settings, you can set up some domains for each of your subsites. I've done this on my local machine using some development addresses. To first configure the domains, point all the domains at the same server. On your local machine, you can do this by editing the hosts file (on Mac and Windows) so that your domains point to your local IP address. With the domains configured, set up your virtual hosts file on your server or your local machine. In this case, I set up two virtual addresses pointing to the same document root in my Apache virtual hosts file:

```
<VirtualHost *:80>
        DocumentRoot "/Users/adamonishi/Sites/multi-12devs.dev"
        ServerName multi12devs.dev
</VirtualHost>

<VirtualHost *:80>
        DocumentRoot "/Users/adamonishi/Sites/multi-12devs.dev"
        ServerName multiofxmas.dev
</VirtualHost>
```

You can now set up domains for your second site because the first site is already pointing to the main domain. Go to the network admin again to the menu Settings ➤ Domains, which will display a short form to complete to add a new domain (see Figure 14-10). You can find the ID of the site through the database. Or if you edit the site in the site's settings page, the ID will be in the URL: `http://multi12devs.dev/wp-admin/network/site-info.php?id=2`. Ensure that the Primary option is selected so the domain you enter will be used as the main location for the site. Otherwise, when you visit the site domain you will be redirected to the subdirectory path you set up for the site initially.

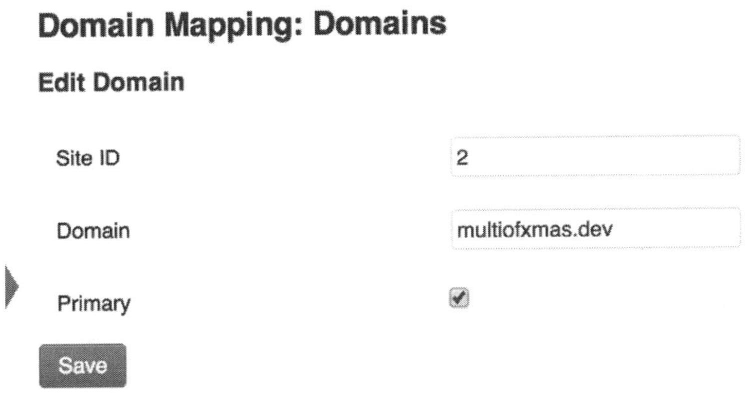

Domain Mapping: Domains

Edit Domain

Site ID	2
Domain	multiofxmas.dev
▶ Primary	☑

Save

Figure 14-10. *Domain mapping settings*

You can also set up domains from the single site admin panel in Tools ➤ Domain Mapping, which displays the screen shown in Figure 14-11. It gives you a much more informative view of the domains available for the site and allows you to change the primary domain with ease. However, this is available only if you've enabled the option in the Network Admin domain mapping settings.

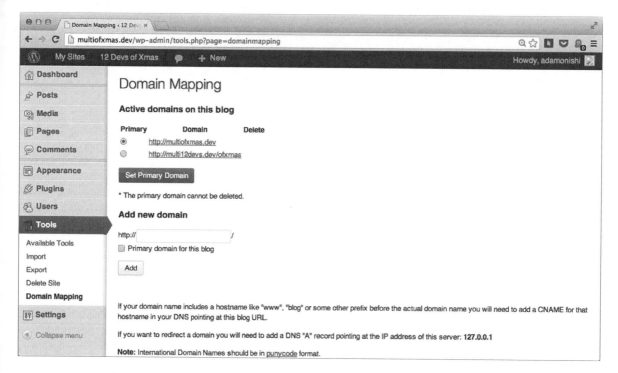

Figure 14-11. *Single site domain mapping settings page*

■ **Note** If your new primary domain isn't pointed to your server when you set up domain mapping, you won't be able to access the site at all because even the admin section uses the mapped domain. You have to disable mapping from the network admin section.

Uninstalling Multisite

Besides understanding how to install Multisite, you should also know how to uninstall it if you need to (it's always a good idea to know how to undo something, just in case). Unfortunately, there is no "Undo Multisite" feature; undoing it requires a bit of work to manually update the configuration files and edit the database.

Before you start doing anything, however, it's important that you take a full backup of the database and site files, just in case something goes wrong. You'll manually edit the database, so it's important to ensure that you have full backups. From here, I assume that all the sites in your network have been either moved away and set up elsewhere or are safe to delete.

Once everything is backed up, deactivate all plugins before starting the uninstall process. Go to the wp-config. php file and remove all the lines added for the Multisite install except the WP_ALLOW_MULTISITE definition, which should be the ones listed here (if you activated the Domain Mapping plugin, you have to remove the SUNRISE setting as well):

```
define('MULTISITE', true);
define('SUBDOMAIN_INSTALL', false);
define('DOMAIN_CURRENT_SITE', 'multi12devs.dev');
```

```
define('PATH_CURRENT_SITE', '/');
define('SITE_ID_CURRENT_SITE', 1);
define('BLOG_ID_CURRENT_SITE', 1);
```

After they have been removed, change the `WP_ALLOW_MULTISITE` setting to `false`:

```
define( 'WP_ALLOW_MULTISITE', false );
```

You then need to edit the `.htaccess` file, returning it to its former settings (the code for it is a few pages back).

Finally, you need to edit the database and "drop" any tables related to the subsites of your network (those with a number in the table names) and remove the global tables for the network as well:

```
wp_blogs
wp_blog_versions
wp_registration_log
wp_signups
wp_site
wp_sitemeta
```

That should leave you with the 11 initial tables for a standard WordPress install and you should be back up and running with a single site instance of WordPress.

Users in Multisite

In a Multisite network, users work a little differently than they do in a regular WordPress single site. When talking about the database setup in WordPress, I mentioned that new sites have tables created for all the different content types, but the users and user meta tables are kept general because every user on a Multisite network is a member of the entire network, not just a specific site.

I've been referring to a special user in the Multisite as a network admin, which is a new level of user introduced by Multisite. The network admin is referred to in the WordPress Codex as the *super admin*, but I prefer *network admin* because it better describes the role of the user. The super admin (network admin) has the capabilities (in the WordPress sense) to manage the entire network of sites.

This super admin is the user you set up when you first install Multisite. This section will cover how to manage users across a network, how the super admin and single site admin users work and a little about the implications of network users in Multisite.

Super Admins and Site Admins

To start with let's look at the role of the super admin (network admin) and site admin in Multisite. Super admins are the user roles with the highest level of access throughout a network; they are the ones that control everything, including theme and plugins installation, and updates. In some cases, they are the only ones allowed to add users.

The site admins, on the other hand, have most of the control over the sites for which they are the administrator. In comparison with an administrator of a single site install, their permissions are very limited: they can't install themes or plugins for their site unless they're already active on the network and can add users to the network only if the super admin has granted them permission.

Capabilities

In terms of capabilities, the super admin is given all capabilities available to the admin user from a single site install of WordPress, as well as a few more Multisite-specific capabilities:

- manage_network
- manage_sites
- manage_network_users
- manage_network_themes
- manage_network_options

A single site admin on a network has capabilities similar to the regular site admin from a normal site, but has quite a few taken away as well:

- create_users (can be allowed via the Network Settings)
- delete_themes
- edit_plugins
- edit_themes
- edit_users
- install_plugins
- install_themes
- update_core
- update_plugins
- update_themes

Removing these capabilities means that the site admins are very limited in what they can do on their own site. To get plugins or themes installed, they must go to the super admin user and request their addition. Although this can be a pain, as discussed earlier in the chapter, it is probably the most secure way to manage a network of sites when it can have a single point of failure. You want to be able to protect what is installed on the network.

The create_users capability is the only exception to the rules of removed capabilities because it can be granted back to site admins through the network settings page in the network admin area. If the Allow Site Administrators to Add New Users to Their Site via the "Users → Add New" Page option is checked, site admins get back the ability to add brand-new users to their site. Otherwise, they can add only users who are already members of the network. Figure 14-12 shows both of these options available to the site admin.

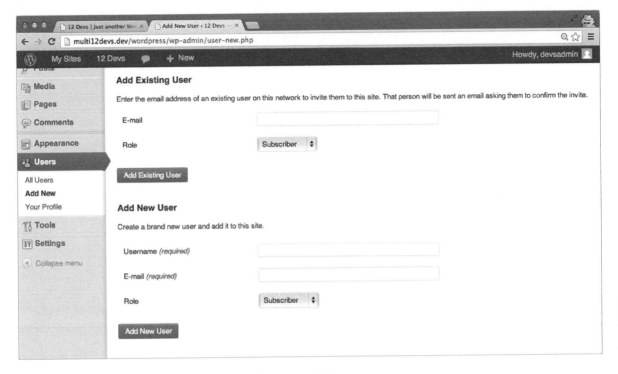

Figure 14-12. *Add user screen for a single site admin in Multisite*

Managing Users in Multisite

As mentioned before, every user in a Multisite install becomes a member of the network, so they can be recognized as a user of every site on the network at a subscriber level. By default, only the super admin can add members to the site, but a couple of options can be set so that users can register to the site—and even so that users can register and create their own subsites of the network. As a super admin, you can give permissions to your site admins to create users for their own site via the option in the Network Settings page.

During the Multisite setup, you can set the way registration can work on the network with the registration settings (see Figure 14-13). Depending on the setting, different levels of user and site management on the site are enabled.

Figure 14-13. *Registration settings in the Network Settings page*

- **Registration is disabled**: Only the super admin can create new users and new sites on the network (unless they allow access to the site admins).

- **User accounts may be registered**: Users can sign up to the network using /wp-signup.php. To display the link to the registration page, use the wp_register() function, which outputs the link to register for the site if the user is not logged in.

- **Logged in users may register new sites**: Only users with an account can create a new site, but the site admins must create the user first.

- **Both sites and user accounts can be registered**: A user can sign up via the registration page and create a site at the same time (see Figure 14-14).

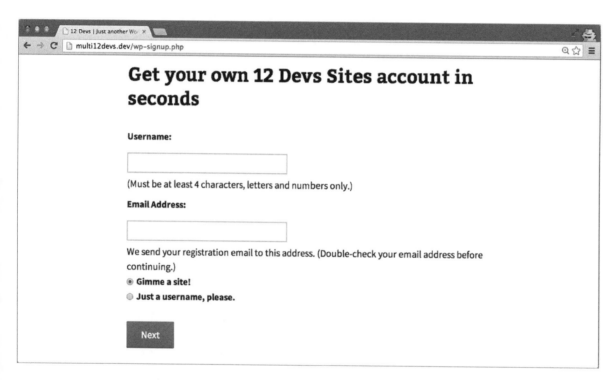

Figure 14-14. *User signup with site creation*

Creating Additional Super Admins

Even if you are a super admin and add a user from the Network Admin section of your Multisite, you won't find the super admin role to add to a user in the user roles drop-down list. You must create the user first (of any role), edit the user, and select the Grant This User Super Admin Privileges for the Network setting in their profile.

General Implications of Multisite Users

Under "general implications," I just want to cover a few things that you should be aware of when you work with Multisite and manage a number of users. The main implication of running Multisite is that there are no site-specific users at all. There are users who have capabilities to do things on specific sites, but they are active as users on other sites at only a subscriber level.

This might not sound too bad—users can't log in to a site for which they don't have explicit membership—but they can definitely tell they're on a network of sites. For instance, if they are logged in and visit another site on the network, the admin bar appears, inside of which is the My Sites drop-down list. Granted, it shows only the site(s) they are registered for, but they know the network they're part of. And if they try to log on to another site in the network, instead of getting the usual WordPress error, they will see an error screen with a message telling them that they do not yet have access to that site; they have to contact the network administrator to ask for it (see Figure 14-15).

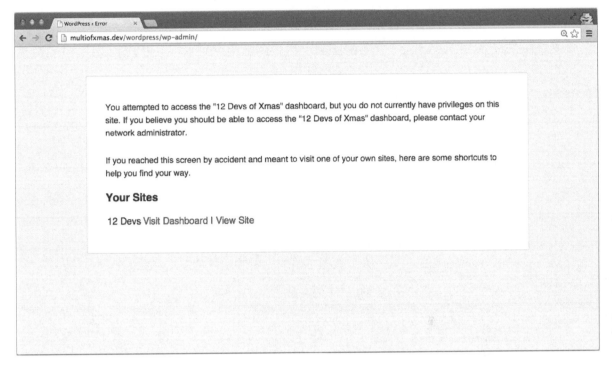

Figure 14-15. *Error seen by user trying to log on to another site on the network*

The way the user accounts work across networks might actually have some benefits however. WordPress.com makes great use of it for interacting with sites on the WordPress.com network, with your user account allowing you to comment and access many different sites on the overall WordPress.com network (Gravatar, for instance).

Remember that users will be aware of the network, however. Fortunately, there are ways around this with some plugins if you require your users to have more privacy or be locked down to a single site:

- Multisite Privacy (premium): http://wp-themes-book.com/14010

- More Privacy Options (free): http://wp-themes-book.com/14011

Theme Development for Multisite

Theme development in Multisite is not really all that different from regular theme development. Because sites still act as separate entities, you can still develop themes as you would with standard WordPress to work with any site in a Multisite network. However, there are some added functions and techniques you can use when you have a Multisite network available to you, including looking at stats for the network, and even the potential to share content across the network of sites.

Suppose that you work with a Multisite network that is using the network to enable different groups of the community: a university or college or an events company. The sites on the network have the same basic site with shared functionality, but with the potential to need customization across different sites. There is no better situation to use parent and child themes across your network. By having a single parent theme present once in your network, you use it as the base for multiple different child themes for each of the subsites of your theme, making developing for subsites as simple as creating a new child theme with a few style or layout alterations. That way, the management of the site becomes even more central, with an update to your parent theme affecting all the child themes on the network.

Multisite comes with its own series of functions that can be found in the WordPress Codex Function Reference: http://wp-themes-book.com/14012. In the next section, I'll discuss a few of the more interesting ones that can provide useful functionality for your sites.

Multisite Stats and Information

The Edublogs home page shown in Figure 14-16 is the central site in its network. I show this image because in the top left there is a stat with the number of blogs currently hosted on Edublogs. In Multisite, it's really easy to find out the number of active sites on your network by using the get_sitestats() function. The function outputs an array with two values: the number of active "blogs" and the number of active users. The count in each case is a cached number updated twice per day.

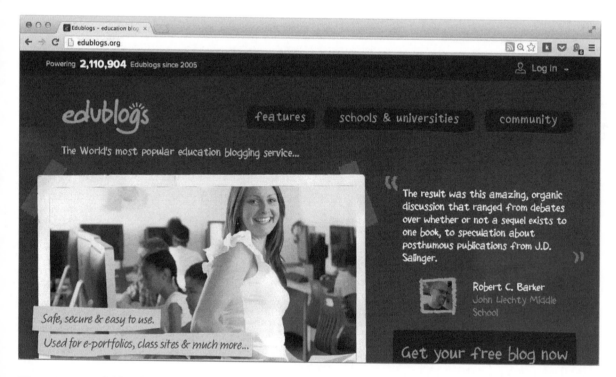

Figure 14-16. Edublogs home page

The `wp_get_sites()` function, introduced in WordPress 3.7, returns an array of all the sites in the network according to the parameters you set. There might be a performance issue with this function if you have a network of many thousands of sites. Another function, `wp_is_large_network()` returns `true` when your network has more than 10,000 sites. If `true`, it means that an empty array is returned from the `wp_get_sites()` function.

For more general information about a particular site, use the `get_blog_details()` function, which outputs the full details for the current site. Or you can pass in an ID, slug, or query parameters to the first parameter of the function to search for a site from which you can get details. The array of fields can contain the site domain name, site ID, or site path. The returned fields contain information such as site name, site ID, and post count, among others.

The `get_last_updated()` function returns an array of the most recently updated sites on your network.

These types of functions are great if you're creating a network home page for people to see information about your network of sites. For instance, a university can use the main site of the network to display information about the status of the blogs on the site and list the most frequently updated sites. In fact, combined with the next technique you'll learn about, you could output a list of the most recent posts on your network's main site home page (similar to the way Reuters does it on its blogs home page).

Accessing Content Across the Network

This next technique is useful if you want to show off the content from around your network from your main web site or, for instance, how I will be using it on the 12 Devs sites to promote content from each site on the other. However, be aware that this is done through using the blog IDs, so you need to be certain of the correct IDs you'll use with these functions. The functions in question are `switch_to_blog()` and `restore_current_blog()`.

These functions allow you to switch to another blog on the network, run queries, and output content related to that blog; then switch back to the previous blog to continue processing the site as normal, like this:

```
switch_to_blog( 2 );
// Do stuff
restore_current_blog();
```

Be cautious: the `restore_current_blog()` function switches you back only to the *previous* blog. If you do multiple switches (loop through a number of sites on the network, for example), save the current blog ID. After you finish switching, call `switch_to_blog()` a final time with the saved ID of the starting site:

```
$current_blog = get_current_blog_id();

$updated = get_last_updated();
foreach ( $updated as $blog ) :

        switch_to_blog( $blog['blog_id'] );

        // Do stuff

endforeach;

switch_to_blog( $current_blog );
```

There is no need to call `restore_current_blog()` after each switch because it just adds to the switch stack global variable. Instead, do all your switches in a row and then call `switch_to_blog()` with the original blog ID when you're finished.

If you want to be more specific and retrieve the content of a single post from a site on your network, you can use the get_blog_post() function, which requires you to know the ID of the blog and of the post you are looking for:

```
$about = get_blog_post( 1, 64 );
```

This function returns the entire post object of the queried post, so to output the content with WordPress functions, either run setup_postdata() with the returned post object or use a filter to format the content. Here's an example:

```
echo apply_filters( 'the_content', $about->post_content );
```

This can be useful if you have an about page on the main site of your network and want to list this information somewhere on all the sites in your network.

Extending Your Themes for Multisite

Many other functions work specifically for Multisite, including enough for you to set up and run a complete front end for adding blogs to your network from templates you create. However, that is a little beyond the scope of the book, and I want to concentrate on functions that are useful for a theme developer working with Multisite.

To take a look at some of the other functions available to you in Multisite, view the Function Reference in the Codex or take a look in the WordPress core file, wp-includes/ms-functions.php.

Plugins with Multisite

As mentioned when talking about theme development in Multisite, plugin development isn't much different. If a plugin is well written, it should work on single sites on a Multisite network perfectly well. However, not all plugins are made equal, so it's very important that you test your plugins thoroughly on a development version of WordPress Multisite if you intend to use them on a full-blown production site.

Just like anything with WordPress, some plugins specialize, and quite a number of plugins have been made specifically for WordPress. The WPMU DEV team makes a whole host of plugins specifically for WordPress Multisite (http://wp-themes-book.com/14013), some of which were previously discussed in this chapter.

Plugins are installed and maintained by the network admins (super admins) who can install, activate, and deactivate plugins across the network. In fact, there are three ways in which this can be achieved:

- **Site controlled plugins**: If the network admin decides to enable the Plugins menu in the network settings, single site admins can enable and disable plugins on a site-by-site basis.

- **Network controlled plugins**: The network admin has the power to "network activate" a plugin, meaning that it will be active for all sites on the network. Network active plugins will also be removed from the single site Plugins pages so the site admins can't see them to deactivate them.

- **Must-use plugins**: These plugins are installed in a specific folder in the wp-content directory: mu-plugins. Once installed, these plugins are activated across all sites all the time and don't appear in the single site plugin pages.

Must-Use Plugins

Must-use plugins are quite unique so they're worth their own section in the chapter. As you've just learned, must-use plugins are installed slightly differently from regular plugins; they exist in their own folder (mu-plugins) inside the wp-content directory. You can't upload plugins in subdirectories as you can with regular plugins; must-use plugins must appear as single PHP files only in the folder, but can have additional plugin files in a subdirectory if needed.

Must-use plugins are not enabled or disabled in the network or site settings; once they're uploaded to the mu-plugins folder, they become active, and the only way to deactivate them is to remove them from the folder entirely. Although they do appear in the Plugins page of the network admin, they cannot be updated from there. You must update must-use plugins manually, so it's important if you are using one or more that you keep up to date with their development and updates.

Must-use plugins can't run activation hooks as other plugins do because of the way they're activated. This is important for you as a plugin developer (as well as from a network admin point of view) because you can technically add any plugin to the mu-plugins folder. However, if the plugins rely on the activation hooks, they probably won't function correctly. If a plugin hasn't specifically been developed as a must-use plugin, I would be cautious and use it as a network-activated plugin instead to ensure that you reduce the risk of running into these problems.

Useful Plugins for Multisite

Throughout the chapter, I've mentioned and used some plugins to get WordPress Multisite up and running. The first is the WordPress MU Domain Mapping plugin (http://wp-themes-book.com/14009), which helps to map custom domains to the sites on your network. I also mentioned a couple by the WPMU DEV team. For managing scalability, use the Multi-DB plugin (http://wp-themes-book.com/14004); and for better single site privacy across the network, use Multisite Privacy (http://wp-themes-book.com/14010).

Here are a few more plugins to take a look at if you'll be using WordPress Multisite:

- **Network Shared Media** (http://wp-themes-book.com/14014): Enables shared media across the network by adding a tab to the media library to enable you to select files from another site on the network. It's useful if you're running a network of similar sites that might want to use the same imagery in posts, for example.

- **Multisite language switcher** (http://wp-themes-book.com/14015): If you're using Multisite to control multiple language versions of the same site, this plugin can help manage the relationships between posts, allowing for easier switching between languages on the site's front end.

- **Multisite user management** (http://wp-themes-book.com/14016): Allows you to add users automatically to the entire network of sites with a custom default role.

- **Anti-splog** (http://wp-themes-book.com/14017): If you want to allow site creation from outside of your network admins, there is huge potential for automated spambots to make attempts at creating spam sites on your network without your knowledge. This plugin from the WPMU DEV team helps protect your site against unwanted spam blogs.

- **InfiniteWP and InfiniteWP Client** (http://wp-themes-book.com/14018): I talked about InfiniteWP back in Chapter 10 when discussing site updates and backups. The client also works for WordPress Multisite, allowing you to manage your network and make backups of your entire network database easily.

That's just a short list of plugins you might find useful for your WordPress Multisite networks. To search for more, I recommend visiting the WordPress plugin repository and looking under the Multisite tag: http://wp-themes-book.com/14019. Visit the WPMU DEV site to see its range of plugins as well: http://wp-themes-book.com/14020.

Summary

This chapter has been whistle-stop tour of WordPress Multisite, from looking at when and why you might want to use Multisite to some tips on theme development and understanding how users work in the network. You should now be fully equipped to know when Multisite will be your best friend and help you manage a series of sites under one roof, and when to avoid it as much as possible and stick with a single site setup.

You now know exactly how to install and configure Multisite, how to create your first site network, and how to set up domain mapping so that your sites can have their own unique domains instead of using the standard subdomain or subdirectory setup.

With Multisite installed, you know how the user system works across a network of sites and the difference between a super admin and a standard admin, apart from the adjective.

Finally, you took a quick look at themes and plugins in Multisite. You learned how you can develop your themes with some Multisite functions, enabling you to promote content from across the network of sites, and show off statistics about the network and understand the features of plugins in Multisite and how they work across the network.

Index

■ Q

■ R

■ U, V

■ W, X, Y, Z

Get the eBook for only $10!

Now you can take the weightless companion with you anywhere, anytime. Your purchase of this book entitles you to 3 electronic versions for only $10.

This Apress title will prove so indispensible that you'll want to carry it with you everywhere, which is why we are offering the eBook in 3 formats for only $10 if you have already purchased the print book.

Convenient and fully searchable, the PDF version enables you to easily find and copy code—or perform examples by quickly toggling between instructions and applications. The MOBI format is ideal for your Kindle, while the ePUB can be utilized on a variety of mobile devices.

Go to www.apress.com/promo/tendollars to purchase your companion eBook.